16.60.

FINANCIAL ACCOUNTING THEORY I:
Issues and Controversies

McGraw-Hill Accounting Series

Robert K. Jaedicke
Consulting Editor

ANTON AND BOUTELL—Fortran and Business Data Processing
ARKIN—Handbook of Sampling and Accounting
BACKER AND JACOBSEN—Cost Accounting: A Managerial Approach
BRUNS AND DECOSTER—Accounting and its Behavioral Implications
BURNS AND HENDRICKSON—The Accounting Primer: An Introduction to Financial Accounting
BURNS AND HENDRICKSON—The Accounting Sampler
DAVIS—An Introduction to Electronic Computers
DAVIS—Computer Data Processing
EASTON AND NEWTON—Accounting and Analysis of Financial Data
EDWARDS AND RUSWINCKEL—The Professional CPA Examination: *Volume 1*, Text and Problems, *Volume 2*, Solutions
FOULKE—Practical Financial Statement Analysis
GRANT AND BELL—Basic Accounting and Cost Accounting
GRAY AND JOHNSTON—Accounting for Management Action
GRAWOIG—Decision Mathematics
HENRICI—Standard Costs for Manufacturing
KELLER AND FERRARA—Management Accounting for Profit Control
KELLER AND ZEFF—Financial Accounting Theory II: Issues and Controversies
KERRIGAN—Fund Accounting
LI—Accounting/Computers/Management Information Systems
LIVINGSTONE—Management Planning and Control: Mathematical Models
LYNCH—Accounting for Management: Planning and Control
NICKERSON—Managerial Cost Accounting and Analysis
SANDERS—Computers in Business: An Introduction
TEICHROEW, SMITH, AND SNELL—Computerized Practice Set
VANASSE—Statistical Sampling for Auditing and Accounting Decisions: A Simulation
WENTWORTH, MONTGOMERY, GOWEN, AND HARRELL—The Accounting Process: A Program for Self-instruction
WILLINGHAM AND CARMICHAEL—Auditing Concepts and Methods
ZEFF AND KELLER—Financial Accounting Theory I: Issues and Controversies

FINANCIAL ACCOUNTING THEORY I:
Issues and Controversies

SECOND EDITION

Edited by

STEPHEN A. ZEFF, Ph.D.
Professor of Accounting
Graduate School of Business Administration
Tulane University

THOMAS F. KELLER, Ph.D., CPA
Professor of Accounting
Graduate School of Business Administration
Duke University

McGRAW-HILL BOOK COMPANY

New York   St. Louis   San Francisco   Düsseldorf   Johannesburg
Kuala Lumpur   London   Mexico   Montreal   New Delhi
Panama   Rio de Janeiro   Singapore   Sydney   Toronto

FINANCIAL ACCOUNTING THEORY I:
Issues and Controversies

Copyright © 1964, 1973 by McGraw-Hill, Inc. All rights reserved.
Printed in the United States of America. No part of this publication may be reproduced, stored in a retrieval system, or transmitted, in any form or by any means, electronic, mechanical, photocopying, recording, or otherwise, without the prior written permission of the publisher.

3 4 5 6 7 8 9 0 K P K P 7 9 8 7 6

This book was set in Caledonia by Monotype Composition Company, Inc.
The editors were Jack R. Crutchfield and Annette Hall; the cover was designed by Rafael Hernandez; and the production supervisor was Joan M. Oppenheimer.
The drawings were done by John Cordes, J & R Technical Services, Inc.
The printer and binder was Kingsport Press, Inc.

Library of Congress Cataloging in Publication Data

Zeff, Stephen A   comp.
  Financial accounting theory I: issues and controversies.

  (McGraw-Hill accounting series)
  Bibliography: p.
  1. Accounting—Addresses, essays, lectures.
I. Keller, Thomas F., joint comp.   II. Title.
HF5635.Z332   657   73-3314
ISBN 0-07-072778-3 (pbk.)
ISBN 0-07-072779-1

CONTENTS

	Preface	ix
1	**INTRODUCTION**	**1**
	Stephen A. Zeff: A First Guide to the Accounting Literature	2
2	**PROBLEMS CONFRONTING THE ACCOUNTING PROFESSION: Introductory Considerations and Background**	**15**

A. The Clamor for Better Financial Reporting
Accountants Turn Tougher — 19
Why Accountants Need to Tell a Fuller Story — 25
Accounting: A Crisis over Fuller Disclosure — 29
Stephen A. Zeff: 1926 to 1972 Chronology of Significant Developments in the Establishment of Accounting Principles in the United States — 39
Samuel R. Hepworth: Smoothing Periodic Income — 51
Martin J. Whitman and Martin Shubik: Corporate Reality and Accounting for Investors—Part I and Part II — 62

B. Financial Reporting Objectives and Strategy
Homer Kripke: The Objective of Financial Accounting Should Be to Provide Information for the Serious Investor — 80
Alfred Rappaport: Establishing Objectives for Published Accounting Reports — 93
John K. Shank: Case of the Disclosure Debate — 108

C. Relationship between Economics and Accounting
Kenneth E. Boulding: Economics and Accounting: The Uncongenial Twins — 122

D. Conflict between Accounting Principles and Taxation
Arthur M. Cannon: Tax Pressures on Accounting Principles and on Accountants' Independence — 131
Related Readings — 141

3 **INCOME DETERMINATION: Generally** — **147**

A. Nature of the "Accrual" Approach: Why We "Match" the Way We Do
Reed K. Storey: Cash Movements and Periodic Income Determination — 150

B. Criteria for Revenue "Recognition"
John H. Myers: The Critical Event and Recognition of Net Profit — 158

C. Interrelation between Asset Valuation and Income Determination
Robert T. Sprouse: The Balance Sheet—Embodiment of the Most Fundamental Elements of Accounting Theory 164
Alfred Rappaport: Discussion of "The Balance Sheet—Embodiment of the Most Fundamental Elements of Accounting Theory" 175

D. The Rôle of "Different Circumstances" in Achieving Comparability
Thomas F. Keller: Uniformity versus Flexibility: A Review of the Rhetoric 184
A. M. C. Morison: The Rôle of the Reporting Accountant Today,
Part I 198
Part II 209
Gary M. Cadenhead: "Differences in Circumstances": Fact or Fantasy? 229
Related Readings 238

4 VALUATION OF SHORT-LIVED "TANGIBLE" COST FACTORS 241

A. The Valuation Problem: Generally
Charles E. Johnson: Inventory Valuation: The Accountant's Achilles Heel 244
F. K. Wright: A Theory of Inventory Measurement 257

B. LIFO against the Field
Maurice Moonitz: The Case against LIFO as an Inventory-pricing Formula 263
H. T. McAnly: The Case for LIFO: It Realistically States Income and Is Applicable to Any Industry 275

C. Direct Costing
John R. E. Parker: Give Consideration to Direct Costing for External Reporting 287
Howard Clark Greer: Alternatives to Direct Costing 295
Related Readings 305

5 VALUATION OF LONG-LIVED "TANGIBLE" COST FACTORS 307

A. Depreciation
D R Scott: Defining and Accounting for Depreciation 310

B. Impact of Changing Prices
Edgar O. Edwards: Depreciation Policy under Changing Price Levels 319
Philip W. Bell: On Current Replacement Costs and Business Income 335

	Herbert E. Miller: Quasi-reorganizations in Reverse	346
	Sheraton Corporation of America: Annual Report 1961	351
	Sheraton Corporation of America: Annual Report 1967	363
	Related Readings	376

6 GOODWILL, OTHER "INTANGIBLES" — 379

A. The Valuation Problem
George O. May: The Valuation of Goodwill — 383
William A. Paton: Valuation of the Business Enterprise — 390

B. The Disposition Problem
Robert H. Nelson: The Momentum Theory of Goodwill — 398
George T. Walker: Why Purchased Goodwill Should Be Amortized on a Systematic Basis — 409
Related Readings — 420

7 NATURE OF LIABILITIES — 423

A. Problem of Definition
Maurice Moonitz: The Changing Concept of Liabilities — 426

B. Long-term Leases
Gordon Shillinglaw: Leasing and Financial Statements — 435
Alvin Zises: Disclosure of Long-term Leases — 448
Kenneth S. Axelson: Needed: A Generally Accepted Method for Measuring Lease Commitments — 465

C. Income Tax Allocation
Sidney Davidson: Accelerated Depreciation and the Allocation of Income Taxes — 476
Thomas F. Keller: The Annual Income Tax Accrual — 486
Related Readings — 496

8 PROBLEMS CONFRONTING THE ACCOUNTING PROFESSION: Proposed Needs — 499

A. Need for a Cohesive Theory
Henry Rand Hatfield: What Is the Matter with Accounting? — 503

B. Need for Reexamination of Doctrine
George H. Sorter: An "Events" Approach to Basic Accounting Theory — 512
Robert Sterling: Conservatism: The Fundamental Principle of Valuation — 520
John E. Kane: Structural Changes and General Changes in the Price Level in Relation to Financial Reporting — 543
Edward Stamp: Income and Value Determination and Changing Price-levels: An Essay towards a Theory — 552
Indiana Telephone Corporation: Annual Report 1971 — 580

C. Need for a Reevaluation of Accounting "Authority"

W. T. Baxter: Recommendations on Accounting Theory   596

Edward Stamp: The Public Accountant and the Public
  Interest   607

Related Readings   621

PREFACE

In 1963, when we were compiling the first edition of this volume of edited readings, it was not usual in most universities to complement textbooks with articles drawn from the periodical literature. One of our objectives was to enable students and teachers to interweave critical and argumentative articles with standard textbook presentations in undergraduate and graduate courses. A second volume was added in 1969. These two volumes, together with readings books edited by others, have, we believe, encouraged many instructors to broaden their approaches to the subject and to make more extensive use of controversial writings.

As we reviewed the literature since 1963, we noted several shifts of emphasis. We have attempted to incorporate these shifts in this revised edition. First, we discerned considerably more interest among accounting educators in the process by which accounting principles are determined. Perhaps the criticism in the 1960s of the Accounting Principles Board, culminating in the "Wheat Report" of 1972, has alerted academics to the dynamic and pressurized environment in which decisions about accounting principles are made. Accounting is today the subject of frequent reports in the financial press, in contrast to the stony silence on the subject in the 1950s. Lawyers, security analysts, corporate executives, and stock exchange officials are actively concerned with accounting matters, and students who expect to enter either the accounting profession or one of the above-mentioned fields should acquire an understanding of the decision-making process by which accounting principles are determined.

A second trend is the shift from the age-old debate between historical costers and current costers to arguments over which notion of current value is superior to the others. Accounting academics and a growing number of practitioners seem to be queueing up behind current value, and writers are choosing between entry and exit prices.

Another trend is toward the establishment and clarification of accounting objectives. The paramountcy of users' needs is widely accepted, and many writers believe that progress will be made by deriving accounting objectives and concepts from a knowledge of users' decision models and their resulting informational needs. Some academics believe that accounting might best serve these needs by not imposing an articulation requirement on the financial statements.

A final trend, which mirrors a recent redirection in the concerns of society as a whole, is a sensitivity to the broader purposes of accounting. Researchers are interested in devising measurement systems for gauging the effectiveness of social and economic redevelopment programs in the areas of poverty, urban decay, pollution, and racial unrest. These studies are but in their infancy, and no definitive findings have yet appeared.

In selecting the articles for this second edition, we have endeavored to reflect these trends, while at the same time preserving the balance of coverage we believe is essential. The articles have been chosen primarily for their capacity to arouse the reader's critical faculties and to alert him to the pivotal issues which confront the accounting profession. He should be convinced after reading these selections, if not before, that the field of accounting is not free from controversy, debate, and disagreement. Our first attempt to provide students with collected readings of this nature convinced us, as teachers, that such volumes can be effective vehicles for pinpointing current problems and placing the issues in institutional and historical perspective. To this end, we have prepared contextual notes which appear at the outset of Parts 2 through 8.

The distinctive features of each accounting curriculum will determine where this book might be used with profit. In our experience, the articles may be used as early as the second year of undergraduate accounting study and as late as the fourth-year honors seminar or the theory colloquium at the graduate level. We have deliberately chosen articles that challenge the reader without, at the same time, being abstruse or excessively mathematical.

An introductory article written especially for the volume explores for students the general shape of the accounting literature. It has been the editors' experience that students do not appreciate at first the gradations of importance that accountants attach to Opinions of the Accounting Principles Board, SEC Accounting Series Releases, reports by committees of the American Accounting Association, pronouncements by accountancy bodies in other countries, and articles in the several journals. What is meant, they ask, by "authoritative"? Why do the SEC and the American Institute separately issue "authoritative" statements? It is the editors' hope that an explanation of the role of authority in the literature, together with some guidance on how to use the literature in general, will aid the novice in deriving the most benefit from published writings on accounting.

Each part closes with one or more lists of Related Readings that contain selections of writing published since 1968. A great many of the items are annotated and cross-referenced in order to facilitate entry into the literature.

The authors' biographies are offered as more than a curiosity, since writings by many of the individuals included in this collection will be studied by accountants for years to come. As explained in the introductory article, the reader's perspective and insight into a writer's philosophy can sometimes be enhanced by a familiarity with his background. In reading D R Scott, for example, one is aided measurably by an awareness of Scott's intellectual link with Veblen. In reading George O. May and William A. Paton, one can assess their contrasting views in light of May's lifelong orientation to the practicing profession and Paton's lifelong dedication to accounting research and education. The writings of Maurice Moonitz and H. T. McAnly, who disagree on the pedigree of LIFO, can be more fully appreciated when the academic credentials of the former are contrasted with the long practical experience and involvement with LIFO of the latter. Since lawyers, economists, security analysts, and corporate executives are represented in this collection, together with accounting practitioners and academics, it would be instructive to know something of the backgrounds of which these articles are, to some extent, the product.

We wish to thank the authors and publishers for allowing us to reprint the articles contained in this volume.

Stephen A. Zeff
Thomas F. Keller

FINANCIAL ACCOUNTING THEORY I:
Issues and Controversies

PART 1

INTRODUCTION

STEPHEN A. ZEFF

STEPHEN A. ZEFF (1933–   ), B.S. 55, M.S. 57 Colorado; M.B.A. 60, Ph.D. 62, Michigan. Currently professor of accounting, Tulane University. Major publications: *Uses of Accounting for Small Business* (1962); *The American Accounting Association: Its First Fifty Years* (1966); *Public Reporting by Conglomerates* (editor, with Rappaport and Firmin, 1968); *Business Schools and the Challenge of International Business* (editor, 1968); *Forging Accounting Principles in Five Countries: A History and an Analysis of Trends* (1972). Book review editor, *The Accounting Review*, 1962–66. Founder and editor (1968–71), *Boletín Interamericano de Contabilidad*. Contributor to various journals.

Has visited the University of California (Berkeley), 1964–65, University of Chicago, 1966; Instituto Tecnológico y de Estudios Superiores de Monterrey (Mexico), 1969; and Monash University (Australia), 1972. Served as director of education, American Accounting Association, 1969–71.

Principal research interests: contemporary history of accounting practices, institutions, and thought; and comparative accounting.

A FIRST GUIDE TO THE ACCOUNTING LITERATURE

STEPHEN A. ZEFF

In accounting, as in many other fields, new knowledge is accumulating at an incredible rate. The need to keep informed of new developments and current modes of thought has never been so important—or more difficult to fulfill. Formal accountancy study is only a springboard. As a student, one learns a framework for thinking about accounting problems and, it is to be hoped, acquires a critical attitude toward accounting ideas and practices, whether conventional or novel. Textbooks, however, are only an introduction to the subject. They must soon be complemented by forays into the "open literature" in order to appreciate the breadth and depth of the ideas that buffet current practice. It is the aim of this article to provide the novice with some insight into the makeup and organization of the accounting literature.

As the accounting literature is written both by professionals and by academics, a certain schizophrenia is evident. The portion attributable to professionals consists of "authoritative writings" and the expression of personal views. In a professional field like accounting, the authoritative literature is an essential guide to accepted practice. Its importance in the overall scheme of writings on accounting cannot be gainsaid; and, in the next section, the sources of authority are described and discussed. In the final section of this introductory article, we will discuss the other branches of the literature, including those that are traceable to the research of academics.

AUTHORITY IN THE ACCOUNTING LITERATURE

Society expects independent auditors to give an opinion on the accounting content of companies' financial statements. The opinion is to disclose whether or not the financial statements have been prepared in accordance with prescribed accounting standards. The laws or regulations that impose this duty provide only the briefest sketch of the standards to which the auditors must adhere. In Great Britain and Ireland, Australia, and New Zealand, company law requires that the financial statements "give a true and fair view of the company's state of affairs." In the United States and Canada, auditors are required to determine whether the financial statements "present fairly" the company's position and results of operations "in accordance with generally accepted accounting principles applied on a consistent basis." In other countries, the auditor's opinion usually contains representations similar to one of these two formats.

The identity of these accounting principles (also known as standards or practices), as well as the criteria for revealing their identity, is very much an open question; however, boundaries do exist. Not all practices are regarded as acceptable. To a significant degree, pronouncements issued by professional accountancy bodies have narrowed the range of acceptable practices, but much is yet to be done. Among the countries in which professional bodies have issued such pronouncements are the United States, Great Britain, Ireland, Canada, Australia, South Africa, Mexico, Argentina, and New Zealand. In these countries, accounting practitioners and company accountants are well advised to study this literature, for the practices recommended in the pronouncements carry the "authority" of the highest councils of the profession.

Recent studies suggest that accounting practices first developed in the United States are soon "exported" to other countries.[1] Accounting influence follows economic influence, and the growth of investment abroad by United States corporations has widened the sphere of American accounting influence. Since American subsidiaries abroad are usually required to use accounting practices accepted in the United States, auditors of those subsidiaries are obliged to become familiar with American practice. This in turn has led to formal links between American accounting firms and those in other countries, further accentuating American influence abroad. Other factors are also at play, but one cannot ignore the influence of the U.S. Securities and Exchange Commission (SEC), which controls the access of foreign companies to the United States capital market. Foreign companies seeking such access may be required by the SEC to use American accounting practices in their periodic reports to United States security holders.

Whether or not United States accounting practices are appropriate for other countries is itself an interesting question. Yet it is a fact that the accountancy bodies in such countries as Canada, Mexico, England, and Australia pay considerable attention to, and sometimes adopt, United States accounting solutions. Because of this pervasive influence, the writer believes that an understanding of the composition and structure of the "authoritative" literature in the United States

---

[1] Lee J. Seidler, *The Function of Accounting in Economic Development* (New York: Frederick A. Praeger, 1967), chap. 9, and Stephen A. Zeff, *Forging Accounting Principles in Five Countries: A History and an Analysis of Trends* (Champaign, Ill.: Stipes Publishing Co., 1972), pp. 310–314. Much of the historical material that follows is drawn from the second of these two books.

would serve the interests of not only American students but also those in other countries.

Accounting Role of the Securities and Exchange Commission

Unlike the countries of the British Commonwealth, the United States does not have a companies act. Limited-liability companies are formed under state corporation acts which are effectively silent on the accounting and disclosure standards of corporations' periodic financial reports to shareholders. Prior to 1933, the financial reports of the largest United States corporations were not subject to the effective constraints of any federal or state law.[2] Owing to efforts of the New York Stock Exchange, the accounts of most listed industrial companies were audited by independent accountants. But companies could choose from a wide range of accounting practices, for no "authoritative" pronouncements on the subject had yet been issued by a United States professional accountancy body.

In 1933–1934, during the depths of the Great Depression, Congress passed two major securities acts. One of their chief objectives was to regulate the financial disclosures of corporations that sell significant amounts of securities in interstate markets or whose shares are listed on national securities exchanges. Complete authority to determine the accounting practices used by such corporations in their financial reports was vested in the newly created Securities and Exchange Commission (SEC). In its early years, the SEC moved steadily but not aggressively into the accounting sphere. An accounting staff was appointed, and, in late 1935, Carman G. Blough was named Chief Accountant. The Commission relied to a considerable extent on agreements worked out in 1932–1934 between a committee of the American Institute of Accountants (now the American Institute of Certified Public Accountants) and a committee of the New York Stock Exchange. One of those agreements was for a standard wording of the independent auditors' opinion, the essence of which remains in use today. Another agreement was on a brace of five "accepted principles of accounting" to which all listed companies were asked to subscribe. These "principles," which in 1936 became known as "generally accepted accounting principles," were to be broad statements of accounting policy rather than detailed rules. It was the hope of George O. May, chairman of the Institute's committee, that all listed companies would be required to make a public record of their adopted "principles," but neither the New York Stock Exchange nor the SEC imposed this requirement. Only today, as a result of pronouncements issued by United Kingdom and United States accountancy bodies in 1971–1972, are companies' principal accounting policies required to be disclosed in their annual reports to stockholders.

The term, *generally accepted accounting principles,* caught on. It was used by the SEC Chief Accountant in his speeches and by other influential accountants. But accounting practices continued to be as diverse as in the 1920s. Finally, in 1937, the SEC began to issue *Accounting Series Releases,* setting forth its views on accounting and auditing matters. In the landmark *Release No. 4,* issued in early 1938, the Commission said, in effect, that it would expect accounting practices used in reports filed by corporations under its jurisdiction to have "substan-

---

[2] For a discussion of the state of accounting practice prior to 1933, see David F. Hawkins, "The Development of Modern Financial Reporting Practices among American Manufacturing Corporations," *The Business History Review,* Autumn 1963, pp. 135–168.

tial authoritative support," a term which to this day has not been officially defined. It became evident to the United States accounting profession that, unless it acted to provide the Commission with such support, the future determination of "generally accepted accounting principles" would devolve in the first instance on a federal regulatory agency. To provide the SEC with the guidance it sought, the American Institute of Accountants created a twenty-one-member Committee on Accounting Procedure with authority to issue pronouncements (*Accounting Research Bulletins*). Since 1938, when the committee was established, the SEC has largely followed a policy of relying on the Institute committee's pronouncements. At times, the SEC has prodded the Institute's committee into action when the latter was reluctant to enter a controversial field. At other times, the SEC itself has retreated from controversial decisions when the Institute's committee was eager to seize the initiative.

The SEC has had five Chief Accountants:

Carman G. Blough 1935–1938
William W. Werntz 1938–1947
Earle C. King 1947–1956
Andrew Barr 1956–1972
John C. Burton 1972–

The first four men to become Chief Accountant joined the Commission's staff in the 1930s when the SEC's opposition to departures from traditional historical cost was hardening. It seems likely that the appointment of thirty-nine-year-old John C. Burton in 1972, until then an academic, could mark the beginning of a new era at the Commission, one in which the SEC's traditional attitudes toward accounting may be reexamined from a fresh perspective.

The names of the SEC Chief Accountants are important to a reader of United States accounting literature. Over the years, the Chief Accountants have given many speeches, most of which were later published, on their accounting views. While these speeches have always borne the *caveat* that the views expressed are not necessarily those of the Commission, they are nonetheless regarded as indications of current thinking within the SEC's influential accounting staff. For this reason, the Chief Accountants' speeches, together with the occasional speeches of the Commissioners themselves, form part of the "authoritative" literature in the United States.

Only a small minority of the more than 125 *Accounting Series Releases* issued by the Commission since 1937 have had an important impact on "generally accepted accounting principles." Instead, the Commission guides the development of accounting practice by more subtle means: through regular consultation with committees of the Institute, by confidential meetings with the executives of companies whose accounting practices have been questioned by the Commission, by selective disclosures of its activities in the Commission's annual report to the Congress, and (as noted earlier) through the speeches of the Chief Accountant and the Commissioners.

The Commission's historic 1938 decision to cooperate with the accounting profession in the development of accounting principles has been repeatedly endorsed by Commissioners in later years. Although it has sometimes seemed that the Commission had lost patience with the profession's slow pace of progress, the SEC continues to base its accounting policy on an active liaison with the profession.

American Institute of Certified Public Accountants

Unlike the principal professional accountancy bodies in Canada, Great Britain and Ireland, Australia, New Zealand, and some other countries, the American Institute of Certified Public Accountants is not a licensing body. In the United States, one becomes a certified public accountant (CPA) by complying with the law of one of the fifty states, the District of Columbia, Puerto Rico, the Virgin Islands, or Guam. All fifty-four jurisdictions have consented to use the American Institute's examination and advisory grading service, but each jurisdiction confers its own certificates. Once one becomes a CPA, he may elect to become a member of the American Institute as well as a member of the professional society in his state. Of the more than 135,000 American CPAs in 1972, about 85,000 were members of the Institute. If a CPA were expelled from membership in the American Institute or a state society, he would not *ipso facto* lose his right to practice as a CPA. That right can be withdrawn only by the jurisdiction that granted it. As a legal matter, therefore, the American Institute possesses less authority over the professional behavior of its members than do the professional bodies in many other countries. Notwithstanding this legal distinction, it has long been a custom in the United States for partners in the large public accounting firms to be Institute members. Much of the Institute's leadership, in fact, is supplied by partners of large firms. Nonetheless, since the Institute cannot compel all CPAs to conform to the technical recommendations of its committees, formal endorsement of those recommendations by the SEC, which has the legislative authority to prescribe the accounting practices for some 10,000 of the largest United States corporations, is of no small import.

Between 1939 and 1959, the Institute's Committee on Accounting Procedure issued fifty-one *Accounting Research Bulletins* (*ARBs*), of which eight dealt solely with terminology. *Accounting Research Bulletin No. 43* and *Accounting Terminology Bulletin* (*ATB*) *No. 1*, both issued in 1953, superseded the first forty-two *ARBs*. They were followed by eight *ARBs* and three *ATBs* in the 1950s. In 1959, following a study by a special committee, the Institute replaced the Committee on Accounting Procedure with the Accounting Principles Board, similarly constituted as its predecessor but complemented by a full-time accounting research staff. It had been a criticism of the old committee that its pronouncements on diverse subjects did not produce either a coordinated set of objectives of financial statements or an integrated body of accounting principles. It was argued by some that progress in accounting could not be achieved without reaching agreement on objectives and basic principles. Such agreement, in turn, could not be expected without the kind of research that only a full-time staff could undertake. Thus, the cornerstone of the Institute's new program, initiated in 1959, was a new accounting research staff which was charged with developing research studies on the "postulates" and "broad principles" that underlie accounting.

Maurice Moonitz became the first Director of Accounting Research, and wrote the first accounting research study, *The Basic Postulates of Accounting*, in 1961. After publication of Study No. 2, *"Cash Flow" Analysis and the Funds Statement* (1961), by Perry Mason, Moonitz joined Robert T. Sprouse to write *A Tentative Set of Broad Accounting Principles for Business Enterprises* (1962). The research studies on postulates and broad principles drew sharp criticism from a number of leading practitioners, including some members of the Accounting Principles Board. The Sprouse-Moonitz study recommendation to shift from historical costs to current values provoked the Accounting Principles Board to disclaim both studies as "too radically different from generally accepted accounting principles for acceptance at this time." The Board has never reconsidered the two studies, although it eventually implemented some of the authors' specific proposals.[3]

Between 1962 and 1972, the Institute published nine additional research studies. All but Study No. 7 have dealt with specific controversial areas, such as leases, price-level accounting, pensions, goodwill, and the problems of extractive industries. Study No. 7, written by Paul Grady, was entitled *Inventory of Generally Accepted Accounting Principles for Business Enterprises*. It undertook to generalize basic concepts and principles from extant practice. While it has been used extensively as a reference work and has been translated into two foreign languages, the study has played scant role in the Board's series of pronouncements.

The Accounting Principles Board issued twenty-seven Opinions and four Statements through 1972. In 1964, the Institute's Council decided that material departures from the Board's Opinions should be disclosed either in the auditors' report or in the footnotes to the financial statements. (In 1968-1971, the major accountancy bodies in Canada, Great Britain, and Ireland took similar action with respect to their pronouncements.)

Although the Opinions of the Accounting Principles Board are the most important single source of "generally accepted accounting principles" in the United States, they owe their standing to the tacit support of the SEC. Only in rare instances has such support not been forthcoming, but the Board is careful to consult with the SEC prior to taking positions. The Board's Statements are intended to encourage voluntary experimentation with novel disclosure or accounting practices. They do not have the force of Opinions. The research studies do not carry the imprimatur of the Board. They are authorized for publication by the Director of Accounting Research and represent the views of their respective authors.

In 1972, responding to criticisms of the Accounting Principles Board, the Institute's Board of Directors and Council accepted the recommendations of a blue-ribbon inquiry into the process by which accounting principles are established.[4] The new plan provides that the Accounting Principles Board, now composed of eighteen part-time members, be replaced in 1973 by a full-time, seven-member Financial Accounting Standards Board to be created under the aegis of a new Financial Accounting Foundation. Research is to be emphasized even more strongly than before. The chief aim of the new program is to establish the accounting principles function as a separate activity apart from the Institute and the public accounting firms. As the first products of the new program are published, the makeup of the United States "authoritative" literature will undergo yet another significant change.

Other United States Accountancy Bodies

Since 1936, committees of the American Accounting Association, an organization of academics, have produced concise statements of accounting concepts and standards. Those issued in 1936, 1941, and 1948 probably were used by the

---

[3] See George A. Gustafson, "Status of Accounting Research Study Nos. 1 and 3," *The Journal of Accountancy*, March 1970, pp. 56-60.

[4] Known as the Wheat Report, the document is entitled *Establishing Financial Accounting Standards* (New York: American Institute of Certified Public Accountants, 1972).

SEC as "substantial authoritative support," for their conclusions did not depart significantly from accepted practice. The 1957 statement, however, contained a number of innovations and thus would have been relied upon less by the Commission.

In 1966, an AAA committee issued a monograph, *A Statement of Basic Accounting Theory*, which has been widely quoted and discussed in the scholarly literature. Owing to its espousal of current values in conjunction with historical costs, the monograph has attracted greater interest among academics than among practitioners and, in particular, the SEC.

Between 1937 and 1965, the AAA published a series of seven monographs on a variety of accounting subjects. Foremost among these was *An Introduction to Corporate Accounting Standards*, by W. A. Paton and A. C. Littleton, published in 1940. In strong demand for more than three decades, the Paton-Littleton monograph has been one of the most influential statements in the accounting literature. It is at once intelligible to the academician and to the practitioner, and is a progressive document.

Since 1968, the AAA has published a new series of accounting research studies. These, like the monograph series terminated in 1965, have been primarily of interest to academics.

Two other influential bodies, the National Association of Accountants (NAA) and the Financial Executives Institute (FEI), began to take a serious interest in financial accounting research in the 1960s. NAA research studies have concerned the accounting and reporting problems of conglomerate companies, the informational needs of users of financial statements, and interim reporting, among other subjects. *Financial Reporting by Diversified Companies*, published in 1968 by the Financial Executives Research Foundation (the research arm of the FEI), evidently influenced the SEC when it subsequently formulated regulations on the subject.

Since 1967, a newly created Management Accounting Practices Committee of the NAA has been developing, through subcommittees, pronouncements on accounting principles. Several exposure drafts have appeared, and in 1972 the first pronouncement was issued.

Accounting Authority in Other Countries

It may be useful to discuss the role of authority in the literatures of three countries in which the accountancy bodies have been particularly active: Great Britain, Canada, and Australia.

In Great Britain, The Institute of Chartered Accountants in England and Wales began to issue *Recommendations on Accounting Principles* in 1942. These pronouncements were intended as general guidance to Institute members and were seldom unambiguous and definitive on controversial subjects, such as inventory valuation. By 1969, the English Institute had issued twenty-nine Recommendations on a broad assortment of subjects. Criticism in the financial press that the Institute's pronouncements allowed for too many interpretations and diverse practices prompted the Institute to reform its entire program of providing members with guidance. It inaugurated a series of *Statements of Standard Accounting Practice*, which are intended to reflect a more forthright and less equivocal position on controversial issues. Because of the new program's important implications for the whole of accounting practice in the British Isles, four other accountancy bodies joined with the English Institute in the new effort:

The Institute of Chartered Accountants of Scotland
The Institute of Chartered Accountants in Ireland
The Association of Certified Accountants
The Institute of Cost and Management Accountants

An Accounting Standards Steering Committee, consisting of representatives from all five accountancy bodies, has been established to formulate drafts of proposed Statements which would eventually be submitted to the five councils for decisive action. So far, several Statements have been issued under the new program. In June 1972, the London Stock Exchange made it known that its listed companies would be required to disclose, in their annual reports, any material departures from accounting practices recommended in *Statements of Standard Accounting Practice*. Current developments in this program of pronouncements are regularly reported in the weekly accountancy journal, *The Accountant*, the weekly newspaper, *Accountancy Age*, and in the monthly or bimonthly journals published by each of the participating accountancy bodies.

In Canada, the Canadian Institute of Chartered Accountants commenced a series of bulletins on accounting and auditing practices in 1946. Most of the bulletins on accounting practices, like the majority of the Recommendations of the English Institute, tended not to take definitive positions on contentious matters. In the 1960s, the Canadian Institute launched a series of research studies on such subjects as inventory valuation, pensions, current values, basic accounting principles, and the accounting problems in particular industries. In 1968, the bulletins were superseded by an integrated handbook. In recent years, the Canadian Institute has sought to issue pronouncements in rather less flexible terms than before, reflecting to some extent the activities of the American Institute. While the Canadian Institute's program is an independent and energetic undertaking, it must be recognized that the enormous economic influence of the United States in Canada necessarily carries over into the accounting sphere. Current developments in the Canadian program are regularly reported in the *Canadian Chartered Accountant* and in *Dialogue*, the bimonthly membership newsletter of the Canadian Institute.

The Institute of Chartered Accountants in Australia began to issue *Recommendations on Accounting Principles* in 1946. As the title of the series suggests, the Australian Institute's Recommendations were closely patterned after the Recommendations previously issued in England. In the late 1960s, the Australian Institute modified its program and started a series of *Statements on Accounting Practice*, which dealt more forcefully with such controversial matters as income tax allocation and depreciation on buildings. In 1971, the Institute advised its members that they should endeavor to follow the Statements and that any departures from recommended practices should preferably be disclosed in the published accounts. Also in 1971, the Institute entered into an agreement with the Australian Society of Accountants, which is primarily an organization of accountants employed in industry and commerce, so that, wherever possible, future accounting pronouncements would be issued on a collaborative basis by both bodies. Some years before, the Institute and the Society had formed the Accountancy Research Foundation, which has since published several research studies on accountancy subjects. Current developments in these programs are reported in the two bodies' monthly journals.

THE LITERATURE AT LARGE

In the 1950s, it would have sufficed to mention a few journals and a "short list" of books and monographs, and the canvass of the accounting literature would have been complete. But in the last dozen years, practitioners and academics alike have swelled the literature with articles and books on a broader array of subjects than ever before. Plainly, one cannot read everything. But neither should we feel overwhelmed by the challenge.

At an early stage, students should be encouraged to explore the literature—not only to become acquainted with the credos, arguments, and methodologies of different authors, but also to facilitate their effective use of the literature as a resource base in future years. One learns of the opportunities and adventures in accounting only by sampling the provocative writings of scholars and practitioners. This experience should form part of every program of instruction in university-grade institutions.

The march of knowledge continues apace following graduation from the halls of académe, and the professional quickly falls behind if he neglects the current writings in his field. A program of regular reading and the development of a facility for finding what one seeks in the literature are necessary ingredients in a professional career. It is the aim of this guide to suggest some avenues of approach to the literature in order to render it more serviceable to the reader.

Probably the most effective means of keeping abreast of writings in the periodical literature is to scan the contents of several accountancy journals on a regular basis. Some articles can be marked for immediate reading, others can be put off until time allows, and still others can be noted for future reference. It is especially important to include in the selection a diversity of both domestic and foreign journals, so that the reader will be aware of developments over a broad spectrum.

For purposes of discussion, accounting journals can be divided into "applied research" and "basic research." Those principally concerned with applied research contain articles on both the theoretical and the practical aspects of problems facing practitioners. Among the leading journals that regularly carry several articles on applied themes are the following:

The Journal of Accountancy, published monthly by the American Institute of Certified Public Accountants

The Accountant's Magazine, published monthly by The Institute of Chartered Accountants of Scotland

Canadian Chartered Accountant, published monthly by the Canadian Institute of Chartered Accountants

The CPA Journal (formerly *The New York CPA*), published monthly by the New York State Society of Certified Public Accountants

The Australian Accountant, published eleven times a year by the Australian Society of Accountants

Accountants' Journal, published eleven times a year by the New Zealand Society of Accountants

The Chartered Accountant in Australia, published monthly by The Institute of Chartered Accountants in Australia

Journal UEC, published quarterly by the Union Européenne des Experts Comptables, Economiques et Financiers, with editorial offices in Düsseldorf

Accountancy, published monthly by The Institute of Chartered Accountants in England and Wales

The Accountant, published weekly by Gee & Co. (Publishers), Ltd., London

Articles on financial accounting frequently appear in the *Financial Analysts Journal* and the *Financial Executive*, both published in the United States.

Journals catering more to the "basic research" interests of accounting academics are the following:

The Accounting Review, published quarterly by the American Accounting Association

Journal of Accounting Research, published semiannually by the Institute of Professional Accounting at the University of Chicago, and the London School of Economics

Abacus, published semiannually by the Sydney University Press

Accounting and Business Research, published quarterly by The Institute of Chartered Accountants in England and Wales

The International Journal of Accounting Education and Research, published semiannually by the Center for International Education and Research in Accounting at the University of Illinois

Articles on financial accounting theory sometimes appear in *The Journal of Business*, the *Journal of Business Finance*, and *Decision Sciences*.

By examining the contents of these journals for six or eight issues, readers will soon gain an impression of the kinds of articles that can usually be found in each. Journals have distinctive personalities which change only infrequently as major editorial policies are revised. Once the informed reader has identified these personalities, he will be better able to find articles written on particular subjects, which appeal to a particular audience, and which reflect a particular mode of research and writing style.

Several journals regularly provide synopses of articles published elsewhere. Such departments may be found in *The Journal of Accountancy, The Chartered Accountant in Australia, The Australian Accountant*, and the *Accountants' Journal*.

Abstracts of new books and articles, cross-referenced to their authors and subjects, are contained in *Accounting Articles*, a loose-leaf service published by Commerce Clearing House, Inc. *The Accountants' Index*, published by the American Institute of Certified Public Accountants, carries the most comprehensive catalog of accounting works in the English language, indexed by subject, author, and title.

A large collection of annotated references to journals and books by major subject areas is available in Rosemary Demarest's *Accounting: Information Sources* (Gale Research Company, 1970). This work is valuable for academics, practitioners, and general readers.

Often overlooked as a source of references to published writings are authors' footnotes and bibliographies. Some academics and practitioners are especially helpful in referring readers to worthwhile writings that are germane to the topic. Such footnotes commonly appear at the outset of an article or a book, when the author undertakes to outline the problem and to draw attention to the attempts of other writers to find a solution.

Book reviews are potentially one of the richest sources of insight into the evolving literature. Only one journal, *The Accounting Review*, regularly reviews all significant accounting books. *Abacus, The Australian Accountant, The Accountant's Magazine*, the *Accountants' Journal, The Chartered Accountant in Australia, The Journal of Accountancy*, and the *Journal of Business Finance* frequently contain book reviews in some depth. The *Journal of Accounting Research* and *Abacus* occasionally run full-length review articles on major treatises. *The Accountants Digest*, a quarterly journal consisting of references to recent articles and books, confines its commentaries to a summary of contents.

The literature is sometimes better understood when one is able to link the ideas of particular writers with their backgrounds and institutional affiliations. If one knows something of the philosophies and policies of the large United States public accounting firms, he should not be surprised to find the partners of a particular firm expressing opinions that reflect their firm's views. It is hardly a coincidence, for example, that the thoughts contained in the many writings of the late George O. May are also to be found, to a greater or lesser degree, in the writings of his partners in Price Waterhouse & Co. The published speeches of Leonard Spacek, long a prominent partner in Arthur Andersen & Co., reflect a point of view that is found also in the writing of his partners. Although most of the large firms have not had partners with the dominant personalities of May or Spacek, the policies of their firms nonetheless find a degree of expression in the speeches and articles of their leading spokesmen. Once the student has come to associate firms with recurrent themes that appear in the writings of their partners, it becomes somewhat easier to order the literature into schools of thought.

Writers in the academic literature may sometimes be identified with schools of thought, when one knows something of the academic background and current university affiliation of the writers. Such generalizations must always be carefully qualified, as a range of views may be found in any academic department. Nonetheless, it was commonplace for many years to juxtapose the University of Illinois and the University of Michigan with respect to the controversy over traditional historical cost versus one or more types of price-level adjustments. The associates and disciples of A. C. Littleton have often tended to defend the former, while those of W. A. Paton have usually been sympathetic to the latter. In recent years, the emphasis on empirical research and a concern with the predictive ability of reported earnings have come to be linked, more often than not, with the University of Chicago. The influence of R. J. Chambers, whose persistent advocacy of "continuously contemporary accounting" has been etched in the literature during the last half-dozen years, is sometimes to be found in the writings of other faculty members at the University of Sydney. Over the years, the accounting philosophy of William J. Vatter, who is probably best known for the "fund theory" of accounting, has had a profound impact on the writings of quite a number of scholars. Some of them were Vatter's students in the 1940s and 1950s at the University of Chicago. The perceptive reader will soon discover that the literature, however formidable it may appear at first, is permeated by themes that may be traced, in many instances, to groups of thinkers who share common understandings on objectives, arguments, or methodologies. Once these patterns are uncovered, the literature seems less intractable, less forbidding.

Articles that synthesize a segment of the literature are especially useful. At conferences and seminars for academics, an innocent soul is frequently invited to summarize and analyze the papers, drawing out the issues and points that divide the authors. Examples of this handiwork are the articles by Anthony,[5] Anton,[6] and Vatter.[7] Occasionally, the synthesis is written by a reviewer of the conference proceedings volume.[8] Unfortunately, the periodical literature in accounting is undersupplied with articles that provide comprehensive analyses of recent developments in accounting thought or practice.

Encyclopedic handbooks are available for readers seeking intensive coverage of special subjects. Practitioners will find the *Handbook of Modern Accounting* (McGraw-Hill, 1970), and the fifth edition of the *Accountants' Handbook* (Ronald Press, 1970) of especial value. Academics may prefer *Modern Accounting Theory* (Prentice-Hall, 1966) or the revised edition of Hendriksen's *Accounting Theory* (Irwin, 1970).

Another useful guide to meanings in the literature, frequently overlooked by academics and practitioners alike, is Kohler's *A Dictionary for Accountants* (Prentice-Hall, 1970). Now in its fourth edition, it is much more than a traditional dictionary. In a great many of its entries, it endeavors to instruct the reader on the concepts embodied in the terms.

CONCLUDING OBSERVATION

There are no effective avenues to the literature that do not require a fair investment of time and systematic effort. The serious student will notice that progress, though slow at first, begins to accelerate at almost a geometric rate. He will discover that the literature is not only an excellent resource base, but also that it enables a great many intellectual excursions that are not possible through textbook reading alone.

[5] Robert N. Anthony, "Research in Accounting Measurement," in Robert K. Jaedicke, Yuji Ijiri, and Oswald Nielsen (eds.), *Research in Accounting Measurement* (American Accounting Association, 1966), pp. 257–267.

[6] Hector R. Anton, "Critical Synthesis of Conference Papers," *Empirical Research in Accounting: Selected Studies 1968*, a supplement to volume 6 of the *Journal of Accounting Research*, pp. 166–176.

[7] William J. Vatter, "Current Issues about Current Costs," in Robert R. Sterling (ed.), *Asset Valuation and Income Determination: A Consideration of the Alternatives* (Lawrence, Kan.: Scholars Book Co., 1971), pp. 114–130.

[8] Robert T. Sprouse, "Diversified Views about Diversified Companies," *Journal of Accounting Research*, Spring 1969, pp. 137–159.

PART 2

PROBLEMS CONFRONTING THE ACCOUNTING PROFESSION: INTRODUCTORY CONSIDERATIONS AND BACKGROUND

In recent years, corporate financial reporting has come under continuing scrutiny in the financial press, in academic journals, and in meetings of investment analysts. As the securities market becomes a more integral part of the economic fabric of the nation, the quality of financial information that reaches investors and their advisers becomes a policy concern of national importance.

Accounting, in particular, has been "found out." Long believed to be a collection of fixed rules requiring little judgment, accounting has been discovered to be a controversial and, indeed, a major variable in discussions of the quality of financial reporting. This discovery has come as no surprise to accountants. They have known it right along.

The securities market is attuned to accounting today as never before. A New York investment house circulates a "quality of earnings" newsletter which censures companies for financial reports that are less than candid. Attempts by companies to "play" with accounting practices are especially highlighted. The New York Society of Security Analysts publishes an *Accounting Newsletter* to inform the financial community of trends in accounting thought and practice. The financial press, for its part, covers accounting in a manner that would have been inconceivable even a dozen years ago. Controversies within the accounting profession which would have been shunned by the press in the 1950s are eagerly reported in *The Wall Street Journal, The New York Times, Forbes, Business Week, Dun's Review, Barron's,* and *Fortune*. In England, *The Economist, The Financial Times,* and *The Times* are alert to accounting developments, while in Canada both *The Financial Post* and *The Globe and Mail* cover the accounting beat. Thanks to one reporter, *The Australian Financial Review* may be the best of the lot.

As the outside world has begun to stare incredulously at the world of accounting, leaders of the profession have become more self-critical. In 1938–1939, when the American Institute of Certified Public Accountants was prodded by the Securities and Exchange Commission into clarifying the meaning and application of "generally accepted accounting principles," the accounting profession hardly relished the assignment. But in 1958–1959, when the American Institute substantially redesigned its accounting principles program, it began to warm to the task. The view was encouraged that the Institute's new Accounting Principles Board would, with the assistance of a well-staffed research division, finally unravel some of the most perplexing accounting controversies. When the new program failed to produce the expected results, professional leaders again modified the structure. In the end, the profession itself set in motion a comprehensive review of the program, which led to the replacement of the Accounting Principles Board and the accounting research division after a life of only thirteen years.

But in the 1960s, the private world of the accounting profession became intensely public. The federal government became deeply involved in decisions on how to account for the investment credit and business combinations. Corporations came under increasing pressure for better profit performance. Scores of companies changed from accelerated to straight-line depreciation in order to improve their profit reports. Other reasons were given, but one financial executive admitted that accounting had become a "competitive tool." Companies have opposed the introduction of accounting practices that would lower their profits or endanger their debt-equity ratios. The view is often advanced in corporate boardrooms that the accounting profession has no right to tell industry how it should report to investors. Companies have made their views known emphatically and often, through letters to Congressmen, discussions with the SEC, and in communications with the Accounting Principles Board. The accounting profession has had to learn to live with constant political pressures coming from both government and industry.

Participation by outside agencies in the development of accounting principles has hardly been confined to the United States. At the outset of the 1970s, the accountancy bodies in the United Kingdom were keen to issue a pronouncement on inflation-adjusted accounting. But the political climate in a nation where the rate of inflation has approached 10 percent in recent years made it necessary for the United Kingdom accounting profession to "sell" the proposed pronouncement to such powerful bodies as the Bank of England, the Board of Inland Revenue, the Government Department of Trade and Industry, and the Confederation of British Industry. Government and industry are alive to the ramifications of such a decision, and it has become *politically* necessary for the accounting profession to try to change attitudes on this emotionally charged subject.

The pressurized environment in which the United States accounting profession has been called upon to resolve its controversies is well portrayed in a series of three articles from *Business Week,* which open this part. "Accountants Turn Tougher" reviews the trials and tribulations of the Accounting Principles Board during the 1960s. In "Why Accountants Need to Tell a Fuller Story," *Business Week* draws attention to the tendency of companies to take advantage of the flexibility in "generally accepted accounting principles" in order to tell their own stories in a better light. "Accounting: A Crisis over Fuller Disclosure" examines the problems confronting the profession shortly after the publication of the

"Wheat Report" on the establishment of accounting standards. The recommendations contained in the report were quickly endorsed by the Board of Directors and Council of the American Institute.

The attempts by the American accounting profession to contribute to the improvement of accounting practice are succinctly reviewed in the "1926 to 1972 Chronology of Significant Developments in the Establishment of Accounting Principles in the United States."[1] The chronology gives an indication of the range of problems and forces with which the profession has had to deal. In 1973, the United States accounting profession embarked on a wholly new approach to influencing the future course of accounting practice, in the form of a full-time Financial Accounting Standards Board. Whether or not the new Board can surmount the many obstacles encountered by its predecessor is one of the intriguing questions of the decade.

Samuel R. Hepworth deals with a subject that has captivated accounting researchers: the extent to which companies seek to "smooth" earnings trends. Hepworth was among the first to discuss the "smoothing" phenomenon. After mentioning a number of reasons why company directors might prefer stability to volatility in earnings trends, he explores the controversial areas of asset valuation and income determination which seem particularly vulnerable to "smoothing" influences. In 1964, Myron J. Gordon argued that managers *can be expected* to choose accounting practices that have the effect of "smoothing" earnings trends.[2] In the last several years, academic investigators have conducted empirical tests to the "smoothing hypothesis," seeking to establish the motives of company directors. (The Related Readings at the conclusion of this part contains references to several of these studies.)

Martin J. Whitman and Martin Shubik, a financial analyst and an economist, question the emphasis placed by accountants on net income. "Reported earnings are important on Wall Street," they write, "not because they are really so vital in valuing a business, but rather because everyone on Wall Street thinks that everyone else thinks that reported earnings are vital." But net income, they argue, is a stereotype. Entirely different kinds of information are needed in order to understand the dynamics of an enterprise. In Part II of their article, the authors train their sights on the credo of the SEC (and perhaps securities commissioners generally) that its role is to protect the "average investor." Whitman and Shubik contend that the SEC should more properly be concerned with the needs of the *serious* investor. In view of the current emphasis on users' needs, accountants must be aware of the decision models used by investors and the kinds of information required to make them operative. This article presents an uncommon insight into those needs.

Homer Kripke, a lawyer who has written extensively on accounting, strongly endorses the belief of Whitman and Shubik that accounting should pay more attention to the creation of values, whether realized or not. Accountants, writes Kripke, cannot "assert that their priesthood of accounting principles entitles them

---

[1] For a more complete discussion, including coverage of developments in Canada, England, Scotland, and Mexico, see Stephen A. Zeff, *Forging Accounting Principles in Five Countries: A History and an Analysis of Trends* (Champaign, Ill.: Stipes Publishing Co., 1972).

[2] Myron J. Gordon, "Postulates, Principles, and Research in Accounting," *The Accounting Review*, April 1964, p. 262.

exclusively to determine the principles to be prescribed, to the exclusion of the desires and felt needs of the consumers." He agrees with Whitman and Shubik that accounting reports should be addressed to the serious investor, not to the uninformed layman.

In "Establishing Objectives for Published Corporate Accounting Reports," Alfred Rappaport argues that clues to accounting objectives may be found in the basic values of society. If corporations publish reports in order to discharge their social obligations, he reasons, the nature and scope of those reports can be determined only by reference to values that create these obligations. The burden of Rappaport's message is that accountants cannot themselves resolve this question. They will need to collaborate with social scientists who are capable of perceiving the identifying societal norms and values. As Kripke suggests that accountants must broaden their team to include consumers of financial information, Rappaport warns that accountants need to consult, in the first instance, social philosophers.

In the "Case of the Disclosure Debate," a playlet written by John K. Shank, attention is focused on the factors that shape a corporation's disclosure strategy. Who are the readers of the company's financial statements, and how much do inquisitive competitors already know about the company's operations? The subject at issue is a possible breakdown of sales and profit by product line. Of particular interest are the intangibles that may result from a company's decision to become a leader in financial reporting. One may be interested to compare the considerations discussed in this fictional boardroom setting with the issues raised by Kripke and Rappaport.

Contrary to the expansive views of Whitman and Shubik, Kripke, and Rappaport, Kenneth E. Boulding suggests that accountants, faced with an impossible task, would be wise to take the low road. "What the accountant tells us may not be true, but if we know what he has done, we have a fair idea of what it means." Boulding seems to echo the voice of George O. May, who said in the 1930s that "within quite wide limits" it does not much matter which accounting methods are used so long as they are disclosed and consistently maintained. Are accountants building castles in the air, or is the potential of accounting reports greater than Boulding suggests?

In the final selection, Arthur M. Cannon, a late insurance executive who once patrolled the halls of académe, awakens us to the silent, but powerful impact on accounting of income tax legislation. It cannot be gainsaid that many of today's accounting practices became established well before the separation of ownership from management in corporate enterprise. In those earlier days, income tax laws were one of the chief *raisons d'être* of careful accounting, and the persistence of the realization concept is, at least in part, one product of the era. It is known that not a few corporations neglected to account for depreciation on a systematic basis until it qualified as a tax deduction. Even today, taxation exerts a strong pull on accounting. Were the amortization of goodwill deductible for tax purposes, its appearance in income statements would be opposed in fewer quarters. The very notion of tax allocation presupposes a parallel relationship between accounting income and taxable income. The view will emerge from these readings that unless clear and emphatic objectives are established for accounting, future trends may be in the direction of least resistance—toward the convenient quantity known as taxable income.

A. THE CLAMOR FOR BETTER FINANCIAL REPORTING

ACCOUNTANTS TURN TOUGHER

In the popular mind, accountants are precise, logical people—flinty-eyed men wearing green eyeshades who toil over dusty ledgers searching for errant numbers. But far from being models of precision, accountants have gotten into hot water in recent years because they have failed to be precise enough.

More and more, they have found themselves differing over what constitutes "generally accepted accounting principles"—the yardstick that each accountant uses in passing judgment on a corporation's financial records. In theory, the American Institute of Certified Public Accountants keeps its 65,000 members marching in step, eliminating conflicts and changing standards when necessary. But AICPA debates tend to drag on for years. As the discussions continue, ambiguities multiply, and the rules accountants live by fall out of date.

Suddenly, in the face of a crescendo of complaint that has rocked the accounting profession right down to its toes, all that is changing. For one thing, there are more investors—and more sophisticated ones, at that—poking into corporate financial statements. For another, the nature of corporate financing has changed dramatically. The rise of the conglomerate, and of conglomerate-style accounting, has brought cries for new standards from both the Securities & Exchange Commission and harried Wall Street analysts. A rash of lawsuits aimed at some of the biggest and most prestigious accounting firms has forced the profession to grapple not only with accounting standards but also with such thorny issues as the potential conflict of interest that exists because an accountant's fees are paid by the same management whose books he audits.

NEW DAY

Nothing shows the change more clearly than a proposal made a few weeks ago by the rule-making Accounting Principles Board of the AICPA to outlaw the "pooling of interest" method in merger accounting. Using that approach, the acquiring company can show "instant growth" by adding the acquired company's earnings and assets to its own, as though the two had never been apart. The alternative to pooling of interest is "purchase" accounting, in which the acquired company's earnings and assets are counted only from the date of merger.

Conglomerates have grown huge almost overnight by using the pooling-of-interest method. If the SEC and much of Wall Street question the technique, it obviously has powerful advocates. In tackling the pooling-of-interest concept, the APB has launched what promises to be the bitterest fight in the board's 10-year history.

Beyond that, the APB in just a few months has:

SOURCE: From *Business Week* (Oct. 18, 1969), pp. 124–130. Reprinted by permission of *Business Week*.

- Laid groundwork to require that goodwill (the difference between a property's book value and the price paid for it) be written off the balance sheet over a period of time by deducting a portion of it each year.
- Required companies to start reporting an earnings-per-share figure that includes the potential dilution from all outstanding convertible securities.
- Helped federal bank regulators devise a new method of computing bank earnings. Instead of showing net operating earnings, banks now must report a net income figure that includes operating earnings, loan losses, and results from sales of securities.

Occasionally, when the APB fails to move, others step in. When the accountants dragged their feet on an SEC request that they propose standards of reporting divisional sales and earnings of diversified corporations, the agency asked the Financial Executives Institute to do the job. Rules based on the FEI study went into effect two months ago. They apply only to SEC registration statements.

The aim of the APB is to hush some of the controversy by narrowing the bookkeeping alternatives open to companies. While the APB has changed many standards in the past, it never before has delved into so many highly controversial areas in so short a time—a clear indication of the pressures the profession is under.

But even if the APB does come up with a clear set of standards that accountants can follow, it still would not silence all of the critics. The touchy issue of the dual role that accountants play would remain, and here the going is very slow.

CONFLICT

In theory, the basic job of an accountant is to audit a corporation's books for the enlightenment and protection of shareholders and the investing public. In that sense, an accountant is looked upon as an independent seeker of truth. But in fact, accountants are hired by management, and while shareholders must then pass judgment on management's choice, they seldom, if ever, balk.

There have been few cases of fraud involving accountants. But given the nature of the role, there always is a question as to how much scope an accountant has for outright independence, particularly when he serves not merely as an auditor but also as a management consultant to the client. It is common for an accounting firm to play both roles—meaning that the accountant often is asked to pass judgment on the results of his own recommendations.

"Some firms," says the senior partner of a big New York accounting firm, "say they draw the line against consulting that involves them in management decision-making. But don't let anybody fool you. We take on any job."

STANDARDS

Foremost among accounting notions is the tradition, borrowed from the British, that the client—not the auditor—knows best how to present his own financial statements and which accounting principles should be used in drawing up a balance sheet. The corporation prepares the financial statement; the auditor checks to see if acceptable accounting principles and procedures have been used.

No less a tradition—indeed, it is part of the AICPA's code of ethics—is the confidential relationship that is supposed to exist between the auditor and his client. This sometimes brings on agonizing decisions. The New York accounting firm of Peat, Marwick, Mitchell & Co. faced such an experience several years ago when it learned that annual reports it had certified for Yale Express Co. were false and misleading. Peat, Marwick, when sued by Yale stockholders, maintained it had no ethical duty to disclose the facts publicly. Then the SEC jumped in saying prompt public disclosure was called for.

Recently, the AICPA moved to clear up the issue by ruling that accountants are obliged to flag the SEC and appropriate stock exchanges when they determine that certified statements are false and management will not publicize the fact. While that clears up one issue, it hardly comes to grips with the conflict-of-interest question.

OVER THE SHOULDER

Worrying accountants today is the threat of federal rule-making, a hazard the profession thought it had buried after the 1929 market collapse. At that time, accountants were unable to stop Congress from handing the SEC powers to make accounting rules, but they did wangle an important concession. Public financial statements filed with the SEC would be audited by independent accountants and not, as Congress had considered, by federal employees.

In the years since, the relationship between SEC and accountants has blown hot and cold, and on some occasions the SEC has felt accountants were not holding up their end of the bargain.

Finally, in 1959, the Accounting Principles Board was established. Basically, its mandate was the same as that of a predecessor, the Committee on Accounting Procedure, which in 20 years made little progress in imposing more uniformity on business accounting practices. The APB, though, was to have moved faster.

But now, after 10 years, the APB has come under the same pressure for accounting reforms as did the CAP. Whether it can stand the pressure or be toppled, as was its predecessor, is an open question. "The foremost obstacle," the AICPA's executive director Leonard Savoie said earlier this year, "is the complexity of the problems the board is facing."

ROLE

On the APB falls the responsibility of establishing accounting principles that American business follows. While the board has no legal authority, its decisions are binding on CPAs, and they must take exception in a company's certificate if it fails to follow the board's principles.

The board's members, 15 practicing CPAs, two businessmen, and one university professor, are among the elite of the profession. They also represent the views and desires of their accounting firms, which include the Big Eight that audit most companies listed on stock exchanges. Price Waterhouse & Co. is the biggest, followed by Arthur Andersen & Co.; Peat, Marwick, Mitchell & Co., Lybrand, Ross Bros. & Montgomery, Haskins & Sells, Ernst & Ernst, Arthur Young & Co., and Touche, Ross, Bailey & Smart.

Despite the fact that these firms and the AICPA have spent millions on the board and its work, the APB has a spotty record in trying to formulate accounting principles. One of the problems, says John Queenan, senior partner of Haskins & Sells who recently finished a six-year term on the board, is that the board "always ended up fighting brush fires."

On its first major issue in 1961, accounting for investment tax credit, the board split badly. The APB wanted companies to take the credit into income over a period of years; most companies, however, wanted to take it all in one year and give earnings a boost. Business put intense pressure on the accounting firms, and three of the Big Eight—Price Waterhouse; Haskins & Sells, and Ernst & Ernst—decided to ignore the APB ruling. Then the SEC showed no interest in backing the board. Finally, the APB backed down and said that both ways of figuring the credit would be acceptable.

FULL LOAD

Since then, the board has handled a host of issues. Opinions have gone out on accounting for pension costs, and on reporting of leases by both lessors and lessees. The board has tackled the question of resolving differences that arise in using one form of depreciation on tax returns and another on annual reports, and it has made companies separate earnings from other activities, such as gains in the sale of a plant, in the reports.

But some of these and other opinions left unanswered many questions, and on several occasions the board had to go back and make revisions. In 1967, a ruling on convertible bonds created a furor. The APB held that since investors were willing to buy convertibles at rates lower than those for conventional bonds, the discount represented the value of conversion to investors. The board wanted companies to capitalize this value and amortize it over the bond's life.

The opinion created a storm. Investment bankers said it was impossible to fix the value of the conversion feature. Businesses worried about the impact on earnings, especially because the amortization charges were not deductible. Finally, a few months ago, the ruling was killed except where bonds are issued with warrants, which have market value.

LISTENING FIRST

These days, the board seeks advice from businessmen before issuing an opinion. It works closely with the Financial Executives Institute, whose members are largely company treasurers and controllers, and with other groups such as the National Assn. of Accountants, the Financial Analysts Federation, and the American Assn. of Accountants.

These groups do not always see eye-to-eye with the board and sometimes oppose its opinions. In July, the NAA organized its own Management Accounting Practices Committee. However, I. Wayne Keller, chairman of the group and Armstrong Cork's general manager of international operations, said the committee would work to reconcile differences with the APB before taking a stand.

One reason outsiders want a bigger say in the board's decision-making is that it appears to deal with issues that directly affect corporate earnings reports. For management, earnings per share are sacred, and often go far to determine market value of stock. But in recent years, accountants have worried that investors were relying too much on the per-share figures and failing to take into account the potential for dilution represented by convertible securities issued in mergers.

In 1967, accountants required companies to report two per-share earnings figures: the conventional amount, based on the average number of common shares outstanding, and another to show potential dilution. But business claimed the rule posed too complex a formula, and they got around it by issuing warrants and stock options in mergers, both of which were exempt from the rule. But this year, accountants came back with a new opinion, and this time warrants and options were included as convertible securities.

The latest ruling also banned the use of traditional earnings-per-share figures altogether, and that angered companies. "There is considerable investor confusion over just what an earnings-per-share figure means," says John Hangen, chairman of the FEI's Corporate Reporting Practices Committee. But while accountants still may be forced to reopen the question of earnings dilution, another hassle appears settled for good.

BATTLE

For years, banks resisted the contention that they should include loan losses and results of portfolio transactions in earnings figures. Instead, they reported results of these operations separately. At first, accountants did not press the issue hard because banks, like other regulated businesses, follow accounting rules laid down by federal and state agencies. But when banks began listing their shares on stock exchanges, a fight began.

The APB made ready to rule on the question, but banks resisted. The American Bankers Assn. went so far as to advise banks to ignore the accountants, even if it meant having their auditors take exception to their financial statements. Finally, banks capitulated, but only after a heavy bargaining session in Washington that involved the ABA, SEC, AICPA, the Federal Reserve, and other bank regulatory agencies. The banks, however, were allowed to report a five-year average of annual provisions for loan losses, rather than the actual provision each year.

Even with aid from federal agencies, the bank earnings question was rough enough. But in the pooling-of-interest hassle, the APB may stand alone. The issues may be too hot for even the SEC.

The pooling idea—simply adding together companies' assets and liabilities in a merger—was practically unknown before the great merger movement of the 1960s. But the practice suited conglomerates perfectly, and they quickly made it the most controversial of all accounting procedures.

With pooling, last-minute mergers could be made, and the earnings of the acquired company added retroactively to those of the conglomerate. But the accounting mechanics in pooling left no clue as to how well, or poorly, the companies had performed separately. Poolings also avoided an unpleasant alternative: the transaction which resulted in a large amount of goodwill popping up on the balance sheet. Not only do creditors deduct goodwill from a company's net worth in determining how much money to lend, but the possibility has existed that accountants might require it be written off.

Accountants debated long and hard on whether poolings were a legitimate bookkeeping practice, even though they continued to approve it. Meanwhile, protests were mounting from investors and others that poolings were being abused. At one point, trustees of Westec Corp. sued Ernst & Ernst, the company's auditors, accusing them, among other things, of allowing Westec to report dramatic earnings increases that, for technical reasons it was claimed, should not have been approved.

STAND

When APB finally looked hard at the pooling concept, which wasn't until this fall, the majority could see no justification at all for allowing the practice. Next week the APB will have an opportunity to defend that position. Starting Oct. 22, [1969] the board begins a four-day session in New York at which it hopes to reach a final decision. The session opens with an all-day symposium on the pooling question, with the SEC and business and professional organizations.

No matter what the outcome, says LeRoy Layton, the APB's chairman and partner at Main Lafrentz & Co., board members feel APB will survive. Even though it has quarreled with business, it remains the major bulwark against a government takeover of accounting rule-making. Further, organizations such as the Financial Executives Institute and National Assn. of Accountants are not trying to take the APB's place. Both want the board to keep the rule-making role.

The accountants still face potentially controversial issues in the next year. Questions include how companies should handle research and development costs and the reporting of equity and earnings in unconsolidated subsidiaries.

While the SEC's stand on poolings is not known, the board has the agency's strong backing in what Savoie calls the board's "integral part of the regulatory process."

"The SEC," says Andrew Barr, the agency's chief accountant, "still looks to the accountants to deal with the problems of principles and procedures."

WHY ACCOUNTANTS NEED TO TELL A FULLER STORY

All over the U.S. this month, auditors are combing through the financial records of the great corporations—verifying, questioning, cross-checking. For this is annual audit time, when all publicly held companies must open up their books to inspection by independent accountants. Later this year, when the companies issue their 1970 operating reports, each will carry the traditional certificate, signed by a certified public accountant, testifying that it has been prepared "in accordance with generally accepted accounting principles." On the basis of these statements, stock analysts and investors will decide which companies are growth situations and which are dogs; banks will decide who gets a loan and who is a bad risk; and managements will be judged smart or dumb by their stockholders.

The accountant occupies a crucial spot in the U.S. business and financial system. Essentially, his job is to keep the game honest. Yet the boom-bust cycle of the past few years exposed some glaring cases of dishonesty, and the accounting profession inevitably has found itself under fire.

In a growing list of cases—Westec, Yale Express, and Bar-Chris, for instance—angry stockholders or creditors have sued the accountants as well as the management when a company went under. And the courts have shown what the accounting firms consider an alarming tendency to push the law into new ground and take a tough view of the auditor's liability.

All this explains why the senior partners of the big firms have begun to do some intensive worrying about the status of the accountant and the state of the accounting art. At the root of their troubles, they see three major problems:

- The principles that the accountants apply in setting up or reviewing a corporation's financial statements are not clearly defined. There are too many different ways to handle the same item, ways that produce dramatically different results in the reported profits or losses.
- The relationship between the client and the auditor puts the accountant at a disadvantage. The auditor is supposed to make an impartial report to stockholders, potential investors, and the public. But it is not the public that hires him and fires him; it is the client.
- Although accounting is considered a profession, it has not yet established itself as a profession in the sense that it stands completely independent of its customers. The Fourteenth Edition of the Encylopaedia Britannica, published in 1929, remarked patronizingly: "Accountancy in the United States is among the newer professions. In the short time of its existence it has not acquired the traditions which characterize such of the older professions as law, medicine, and theology." There was more than a trace of British snobbery in that dig. But 40 years later, accountants are still not quite a self-governing profession in the way that doctors, lawyers, and parsons are.

The uneasiness of accountants over their vulnerability in these three areas has

SOURCE: From *Business Week* (Feb. 6, 1971), pp. 86–87. Reprinted by permission of *Business Week*.

been reflected by a rising tempo of activity in the American Institute of Certified Public Accountants, the somewhat loose-jointed organization that provides accountants with an apparatus for collective action.

Whipped along by its energetic executive vice-president, Leonard Savoie, the AICPA has begun to bring a tougher discipline into the rather disorderly ranks of the profession. In the past two years, the AICPA's Accounting Principles Board, which makes the rules on disputed points of accounting theory, has tackled such thorny subjects as merger accounting and proper statement of per-share earnings. Meanwhile, a committee headed by Wallace E. Olson, of Alexander Grant & Co., has been working on a restatement of the code of professional ethics. Significantly, one of the changes it is proposing would require a member to comply with the technical standards set up by the institute. Under the present code, an auditor can decide for himself whether or not he will go along with a ruling of the APB.

Strengthening the authority of the APB is essential if the accountants expect the public to trust them. Much of the trouble in the past few years has come from the fact that the present system leaves too much latitude. If the individual accountant is to force a client to stick to the rules, accountants collectively must agree on what the rules are. Given a free hand with such things as valuation of assets, depreciation, and deferred charges, a fair-sized company can show just about any profit or loss that it likes. And its auditor, whatever his doubts, can certify that it is in accordance with generally accepted principles.

The AICPA itself has just given its members an inadvertent example of how much difference a switch in methods can make. In the fiscal year ending Aug. 31, 1970, it changed from partial accrual to full accrual in handling some of its own cost items. This improved its showing of income against costs by $233,220, and boosted the general fund by $483,851. The institute also decided to capitalize its fixed assets instead of treating them as a current expense in year of purchase. That added $437,463 to the general fund, and $22,189 to the excess of income over costs.

AUDITORS ARE ONLY EMPLOYEES

The AICPA directors made the change because they thought it was better accounting. Corporate managers often change accounting methods for less salutary reasons—to bolster flagging earnings, for instance. The auditor may not like the change but the relationship between accountant and client puts him in a weak position when he wants to do one thing and they want to do something else.

This is where the crucial question comes up: Does the accountant work for the stockholders, the creditors, the public—or the management that hires him and pays his fee?

Theoretically, the answer is cut and dried. Any accountant will tell you that his first responsibility is to the stockholders and that he would resign an account rather than certify a deceptive statement.

So it was in the 19th Century, when many U.S. companies were audited by bright young Englishmen sent over by British investors to check the inventories, count the cash, and report back as to whether those wild American cowboys were cheating them. A number of the young Englishmen liked life on the New

York range, and several old American accounting houses trace their ancestry to British auditors who never went home.

In December, 1886, when Edwin Guthrie, FCA of Manchester, England, arrived in New York on his firm's business, there was no question in his mind as to where his allegiance lay. He was working for the Manchester money men who had hired him to check on their American investments.

The modern accountant, American or British, faces a far more complex situation when he takes on a job. Although theoretically he is hired by the stockholders, this usually amounts to no more than rubber-stamping a management decision. For most practical purposes, the management is the client, and the client has the leverage in the relationship. He can always get another auditor, while the auditor may not be able to get another client.

The structure of the accounting profession complicates the situation. Competition is fierce, not only among the Big Eight firms that lead the profession but also among the dozens of smaller ones fighting to get into the big time. This competitive pressure is concentrated on the partner in charge of the account. While most firms have accounting principles committees to make decisions on tough points, the man in charge of the job is the one who feels the heat, and the bigger the client the more heat he can turn on.

The AICPA has been chewing on this problem. But it has not moved fast enough to satisfy some accountants.

Within the past year, something like a revolutionary movement has begun to take shape within the profession. Late in 1970, representatives of three of the biggest and most respected firms—Touche Ross & Co., Arthur Andersen & Co., and Arthur Young & Co.—pushed the president of the AICPA, Marshall S. Armstrong, to call a special meeting. For two days in early January, representatives of 21 firms met in Washington. Before they adjourned, they decided to set up two special groups—one to study ways to strengthen the Accounting Principles Board, the other to restate the objectives of financial reporting.

If the revolutionaries have their way, these study groups will waste no time thumb-sucking. They will hammer out plans for restructuring the accounting profession.

One proposal that the study group on APB will consider is making membership on the board a full-time salaried job. Members would sever all ties with the accounting firms or clients. The idea is to make the APB a sort of supreme court of accounting.

Says Robert M. Trueblood, of Touche Ross, one of the leading revolutionaries: "The cohabitation of an accountant with the board and with his firm, company, or industry is an incestuous relationship."

MORE INDEPENDENCE IS NEEDED

The study group on financial statements will also be dealing with problems of cohabitation by grappling with the question of client-auditor relationships.

One obvious move would be to insist on a closer relationship between the auditor and the stockholders. In England, accountants have the right to appear at company meetings, and if they are replaced they can make a statement to the stockholders defending themselves and challenging the management's decision.

In the U.S., where stock ownership is far more diffuse, this probably would not do much good. Stockholders are inclined to sleep it out until the company gets into trouble and someone starts a proxy fight.

A more effective approach would be to work through the board of directors. The same court decisions that have shaken up the accountants have expanded the definition of directors' liability. The best hope of establishing the accountant as a completely independent operator probably is to ally his interests with those of the outside directors.

A program for reforming the client relationship would include at least these major points:

- Each client company would be required to form an audit committee consisting of directors who were not members of management. The audit committee would hire the accountant, give him instructions, and receive his report. If the management objected to something, it would have to take its fight to the audit committee, not to the accountants.
- Any time a company changed accountants, it would be required to make a public statement of its reasons. The outgoing accountant would be free to make a public reply.
- If a company made a major change in its accounting methods it would have to say so at the start of the year and explain why. This would stop the practice of shopping for accountants and procedures that will put the brightest face on a year's operations after they are over.

To make these or any other rules stick, the accountants will need some real backing from the Securities & Exchange Commission, the official watchdog of the investor's interests. If the SEC throws its power on the side of restructuring the profession, things could move fast.

It may also be necessary for Congress to give accountants additional immunity from antitrust prosecution, and to relieve them of liability to management for statements made about a company.

In a showdown, however, management itself will have to back any move to increase the independence of the auditor—for the simple reason that management must have ways of convincing stockholders and investors that its financial reports are true and accurate. "The functioning and, indeed, the perpetuation of our private enterprise system," says Leonard Savoie of the AICPA, "depends on the continuing confidence of investors and creditors in the reliability of financial statements. To provide this confidence is precisely the role that the auditor assumes."

ACCOUNTING: A CRISIS OVER FULLER DISCLOSURE

The first law for accountants was not compliance with generally accepted accounting principles but, rather, full and fair disclosure, fair presentation and, if principles did not produce this brand of disclosure, accountants could not hide behind the principles but had to go behind them and make whatever disclosures were necessary for full disclosure. In a word, "present fairly" was a concept separate from "generally accepted accounting principles," and the latter did not necessarily result in the former.

When U.S. Court of Appeals Judge Henry J. Friendly wrote those words in his landmark Continental Vending decision in 1969, he set off shock waves that are still shaking the accounting profession. All the ramifications of that statement are yet to be fully tested in the courts, but its message comes through loud and clear: Merely sticking to the rules will not keep an accountant—or his client—out of trouble.

Judge Friendly's interpretation of what it means when a certified public accountant puts his signature to a company's financial statement goes to the heart of the public accountant's problem: He makes his report to the management of the corporate client that hires him, but the statement that he attests to is relied on by others whose interests may be directly opposed to the corporate management—creditors, investors, government policymakers. What management considers fair presentation may be outright deceit from the standpoint of a potential lender or a disgruntled stockholder.

From the accountant's standpoint, he cannot win. Some stockholders, too, particularly the short-term traders, would like the auditor to put the best face on company reports to enhance the market price of the stock. This inherent conflict on disclosure is prompting some frustrated CPAs to insist that financial reports be prepared not just for stockholders, but for prospective investors as well.

The problem is complicated by the enormous complexity of modern business. Companies can operate in a dozen different countries and two dozen different industries. To reduce such complex operations to a simple balance sheet and consolidated income statement—even with supporting tables and pages of detailed footnotes—calls for sweeping simplification. It also calls for a high degree of faith in the company's own system of financial reporting and controls. No accounting firm can hope to count the last carton of rivets in the inventory of the Tanzanian subsidiary, and an accounting firm will be careful to put language in its attestation that says it did not. But who pays attention?

SOURCE: From *Business Week* (Apr. 22, 1972), pp. 55–60. Reprinted by permission of *Business Week*.

THERE ARE NO PRECISE RULES

This is why the fair disclosure doctrine has thrown the accounting profession into a state of confusion, confrontation, and crisis. Accounting is not a precise body of rules covering every case that comes up. It is a set of general principles—some of them going back to the Middle Ages and the invention of double-entry bookkeeping—applied in the manner that the accountant on a particular job thinks appropriate. Inevitably, it contains a large component of personal judgment. Should a securities firm, for instance, value the securities on its shelves at the price it paid for them or the going market price? Or at liquidation value? A simple question, but the answer may determine whether or not the securities firm goes into default on New York Stock Exchange capital requirements. Naturally, the management will want to value at market when the price has gone up and at cost when the bottom has fallen out. Conservative accounting calls for carrying securities at the lower cost or market, but many CPAs contend that some estimate of long-term value should be made.

The rapid growth of the accounting business has put a new twist on this problem: It is harder and harder to find enough top-level, trained men who can make judgments of the sort that modern accounting demands. The steadily increasing number of corporations listed on one of the stock exchanges (which require an audit by outside accountants), plus the expansion of the accounting firms into new fields, has brought a bonanza in revenues. But it has put a severe strain on auditing manpower. Inevitably, this means a dilution of the total of real accounting talent a firm can command.

Public accounting has become a big business—and a growth business. Recent estimates put total domestic revenues of U.S. accounting firms at $2.5-billion a year. It also is a concentrated business. Eight big firms at the top—known as the Big Eight—together generate at least $1-billion of those revenues. These firms and their dozen or so nearest competitors have seen net billings double in the past five years—fed by a rapid expansion of management services that range from the design of information systems and data processing controls to pension planning and executive recruiting.

At the same time, CPA firms have been aggressively offering their audit, tax, and consulting services to sectors outside the industrial corporate milieu: to federal, state, and local governments, and to banks, insurance companies, hospital and health care agencies, labor unions, trade associations, churches, and universities. Growth has also been rapid in the international arena, with the larger U.S. accounting firms establishing offices of their own in major trading cities overseas, or entering into joint working ventures with large and prestigious British and Canadian CPA firms.

Such rapid growth has set up new potential conflicts. When a firm expands into a new area such as auditing big banks, as Peat, Marwick, Mitchell, Ernst & Ernst, and Price Waterhouse have done, is there a conflict of interest created because the accountant audits both the bank and some of its corporate borrowers? Since the auditor has to offer an opinion as to the quality of loans in the bank's portfolio, will he reveal inside information obtained by examining the borrower's books?

PUBLIC DISILLUSIONMENT

In this fast-paced, emotionally charged atmosphere of mergers and acquisitions, increasingly complex tax laws, and brand-new financing devices, accountants are caught more keenly than ever before between the pressures of serving their clients and their traditional public role as independent, objective auditors. Recent efforts within the profession to end some of the major accounting abuses, and to narrow accounting alternatives so that "like things look alike and unlike things look different," have been met with inter-firm squabbling among the Big Eight, intense industry opposition, and political pressure from government.

Last autumn, when the CPAs' rule-making Accounting Principles Board finally agreed after 10 years of debate that the investment tax credits could not be flowed through immediately to income, but would have to be spread out over the life of the new assets, corporate executives howled so loudly that Congress, with the Treasury Dept.'s backing, legislated an accounting rule to allow the immediate flow-through. And as more and more questions have arisen about the ability of present accounting principles to deliver full and fair disclosure in financial statements, the public has become disillusioned.

James J. Mahon, a top partner at the Big Eight firm of Lybrand, Ross Bros. & Montgomery, explains the roots of that disillusionment this way: "First, we failed to perceive the growing cleavage between independent ownership and professional management; second, we were slow to recognize the emerging power of the institutional investor in the financial community; third, and perhaps the most important, we did not anticipate the public clamor for exactitude in financial reporting."

As a result, the accounting profession now has a brand of consumerism growing in its own backyard. A barrage of lawsuits by shareholders, creditors, and trustees, and complaints by the SEC have emerged from the drama of the past few years following the spectacular stock price dips, corporate bankruptcies, brokerage house failures, and other misfortunes. Suits against management have become commonplace, but these newer cases have an added dimension: They also include the company's outside accountant.

The complexity of modern business has produced devious and complicated new sets of shenanigans that have sometimes escaped the auditor: complex circular relationships in which a company sells off, at inflated prices, stock or real estate that is doing badly to a friend or officer just before the audit is performed and then later buys it back at the real market value, paying the "buyer" a fee for his service. Or selling a small piece of a large real estate holding at a high price to raise the value of the entire parcel. Or manipulating dividends in subsidiaries to make up for losses in operating income. Or issuing a bewildering variety of debentures with convertible features, warrants, or other "funny money" financing devices.

The 18-man, part-time Accounting Principles Board has been unable to move fast enough to cope with such complexities. Repeatedly, it has not tackled problems until 10 years after they started showing up on corporate books. And then, their sometimes rather harsh, arbitrary response has earned them the angry fire of the Financial Executives Institute—the spokesman for top corporate financial men.

THE SEARCH FOR STANDARDS

For example, the APB did not face up to requiring a corporation to consider the potential impact of convertible debentures on earnings per share until 1969, years after James J. Ling, an imaginative pioneer in financial strategy, started using them at Ling-Temco-Vought to acquire companies. And only late last year did it start probing the off-the-balance sheet financing of jet aircraft and other kinds of leasing devices.

There are signs, however, that accountants are at last moving together to put their own ledger into better balance. Last week, directors of the American Institute of Certified Public Accountants, the CPAs' professional association, urged immediate implementation of a new broad-based structure for setting accounting standards.

That plan, the work of a blue-ribbon study group headed by former SEC commissioner Francis M. Wheat, would replace the much criticized Accounting Principles Board, the profession's present part-time rule-making body, with a seven-member Financial Accounting Standards Board that would move faster. Each member of the new body would serve full-time at an annual salary of $75,000 to $100,000 and would be independent of CPA firm or organizational ties.

The Wheat scheme also calls for a nine-member upper level foundation of accountants, financial executives, security analysts, and educators to select and fund the Standards Board, as well as a 20-member advisory council that is to include some users of financial statements: shareholders, businessmen, analysts, economists, and government. Finally, the report asks that a greatly expanded accounting research program be launched. The total bill for the new structure is pegged at $2.5-million to $3-million annually.

Since the Wheat study was released on Mar. 29, [1972] it has gained widespread endorsement within the profession. Even the powerful Financial Executives Institute, which one accountant describes as having been "against every piece of rule-making that's ever been proposed," has endorsed the plan in concept. But the FEI has reservations about financing the program and the qualifications for board appointments.

The Wheat recommendations go up for what many CPAs hope is final approval at next week's meeting of the AICPA's governing council in Boca Raton. If adopted, the new Standards Board could be ready to go to work by fall. "We can't afford to lose momentum," says John C. Biegler, senior partner of Price Waterhouse and a member of the Wheat group.

But even with a more responsive full-time board with a wider base of support, a more serious problem remains. When loopholes are closed and detailed rules are drawn up on an issue-by-issue basis, the result often is illogical, arbitrary, and inconsistent.

One source of discontent is APB opinion 17, on accounting for intangible assets or goodwill, issued in 1970. The board could never decide whether to let goodwill pile up as an asset on the balance sheet indefinitely or to insist that it be written off immediately against shareholders' equity. The result was a compromise no one was happy with. Now, the difference between what one company pays for acquiring another business and the net value of those assets—goodwill—must be written off over an arbitrary period of not more than 40 years. But conglomerates and others who piled up huge amounts of goodwill in the 1960s can still carry it unamortized on their books.

What constitutes fair presentation is still largely a matter of professional judgment. No rule can cover every contingency. What has been missing is an over-all, logical accounting framework—a broad set of goals or objectives. A second AICPA-appointed study group, headed by Robert M. Trueblood of Touche Ross, has been named to delve into just what the objectives of financial statements should be, and has scheduled public hearings for mid-May.

Key to that group's deliberations will be the accountant's basic dilemma: What is full and fair disclosure—and for whom? Trueblood says that his committee is discussing whether CPAs should furnish different statements to different users, disclose the impact of social costs and benefits in financial statements, or include forecasts and budgets in the basic financial report.

Leonard Spacek, former head of the Big Eight firm of Arthur Andersen and long an outspoken accounting critic, envisions the Trueblood report as a constitution for the new Standards Board. "It's not a court, but a legislature," he says. "And it's got to have a constitution. Otherwise, it's a dictatorship."

Nowhere are the implications of what is happening being studied more closely than behind the traditional wood-paneled doors or the modern sparkling glass partitions in the home offices of the Big Eight firms: Arthur Andersen; Ernst & Ernst; Haskins & Sells; Lybrand, Ross Bros. & Montgomery; Peat, Marwick, Mitchell; Price Waterhouse; Touche Ross; and Arthur Young. Together, they audit more than 80% of the companies listed on the New York and American stock exchanges.

Just below the Big Eight in size is another group of 15 to 20 well-known national CPA firms, including Alexander Grant; Hurdman & Cranstoun, Penney; J. K. Lasser; Laventhol, Krekstein, Horwath & Horwath; Main Lafrentz; S. D. Leidesdorf; and Seidman & Seidman. Of an estimated 125,000 CPAs in the U.S., AICPA counts about 84,000 as members, 65,000 of whom are in actual professional practice. Of that number, approximately one-third are from the 25 largest CPA firms. After that, the firm size drops off rapidly; of the AICPA's 14,500 member firms, 9,500 have only one member.

THE BIG EIGHT DRAWS FIRE

Because the Big Eight firms audit the books of so many publicly held companies, they have been hit with the major lawsuits and with the publicity when something goes wrong. Arthur Andersen has had to defend its accounting practices in Four Seasons Nursing Homes, King Resources, and Black Watch Farms. Ernst & Ernst is named in the long and messy Westec suit. Haskins & Sells has been sued along with American Express in the wake of the "salad oil scandal" and after the brokerage house failure at Orvis Bros. Lybrand was named in Mill Factors, R. Hoe, and Continental Vending. Peat, Marwick has had a score of complaints arising from Penn Central, National Student Marketing, and the recently settled Yale Express fiasco. Price Waterhouse is a defendant in Performance Systems actions. Touche Ross caught fallout from Revenue Properties. And Arthur Young is involved in suits following troubles at Commonwealth United.

And it has been the Big Eight, too, that have moved the most aggressively into such tangential fields as consulting, often through mergers with smaller, specialized regional and local accounting firms. Like drummers with wagon loads of new wares, most of the big CPA firms are stocking a full line of management advisory services these days. Peat, Marwick will help clients find a new president or top financial officer, or tell top executives they should switch part of their pay into tax shelters. Lybrand will help a company set up a new pension plan; Touche Ross and Ernst & Ernst will undertake detailed marketing plan strategy. Arthur Young will help a corporation defend itself against a takeover.

But accountants are divided over where to draw the line on consulting to avoid conflicts—either in fact or in appearance—with their audit work.

Many Big Eight firms contend that they have provided management advice for clients since they were founded around the turn of the century. But consulting began to emerge as a separate area for CPAs in the mid-1950s and it mushroomed with the rise of the computer and its impact on accounting and records systems. Most firms moved quickly into the design, planning, and control of EDP and management information systems. But they also have picked up more and more of the old-line management consultant's offerings: executive search, pension planning, job evaluation and manpower planning, executive compensation, marketing analysis, organizational studies, and merger and acquisition work.

Most top partners quickly defend this array of services as "meeting client needs." Says Richard T. Baker, managing partner of Ernst & Ernst, a Big Eight firm that has been one of the most active in consulting: "Our attitude has always been that we really weren't giving clients service unless we helped them with their problems."

But for some CPAs, management service is fraught with potential hazards and conflicts. "The profession is going the route of conglomerates," growls Harvey E. Kapnick, Jr., chairman of Arthur Andersen. "They hate for me to say that, but they are." Kapnick is especially critical of executive recruiting, tax shelter, and actuarial activities by CPAs. "There is absolutely no reason why we should grow just for the sake of growth," he insists.

Although there have been no major lawsuits involving consulting and auditing conflicts, Kapnick says flatly that "some day this is going to come right down around the neck of the profession." If that happens, accountants might lose all their consulting work, including their biggest, most lucrative non-audit, non-tax service: financial planning and computer control systems. "Somebody's going to say you've got to give up all those extra services," Kapnick warns. "That's the risk involved."

In the recruiting area, that risk turns on answering questions like these: Can an auditor be critical of the abilities of a financial executive it recruited for the client? Does the CPA have the credentials to make such a critical appraisal in the first place? Is the financial executive, hired through the offices of the auditor serving as an executive recruiter, likely to fire the firm if it does not perform adequately?

Others argue that the accountant's independence can be maintained through elaborate quality control procedures for both auditing and consulting, and by focusing on consulting's quantitative aspects. Accountants should develop the numbers and present the alternatives, they say, but must insist that the clients make the final decision. Touche Ross, the youngest of the Big Eight firms, has heavily emphasized consulting since it was founded in 1947. Its managing partner, Robert Beyer, says: "If you, in effect, make the decision for management, you've lost your independence."

Most Big Eight partners recognize the inherent dangers in mergers and acquisition work, and they claim that their firms stop short of recommending actual takeovers or setting an appropriate offering price. "Things do go wrong," explains Ralph E. Kent, managing partner of Arthur Young. "What if a company should buy another company at our urging and it turns out to be a dog? Then there certainly would be the appearance of an unwillingness on our part to be able to say at the next audit: 'By the way, that was a lousy acquisition you made, and now we want to write it off.'"

THE QUESTION OF FORECASTING

In the merger and acquisition game, some CPAs maintain a double standard. When the accountant accepts a client's consulting assignment to evaluate the quality of earnings reported by a would-be acquisition, he can be very tough and very specific about the real value of receivables and inventories and their discounting effect on reported profits. But wearing his auditing hat in signing his name to the same client's balance sheet and operating statement, the CPA will stick to his familiar "in compliance with generally accepted accounting principles" for inventories and receivables in the report the client makes public.

Another controversy that more nearly splits the profession is the question of what role public accountants should play in financial forecasting. The SEC, particularly its chairman, William J. Casey, wants to include forecasts in at least some financial reports to give investors a better notion of a company's future prospects. Arthur Andersen's Kapnick already has registered his disapproval to the SEC on the ground that it is not a proper role for auditors to play. And Biegler of Price Waterhouse terms forecasting a "treacherous area" for CPAs.

But from the SEC's public statements, says Michael N. Chetkovich, managing partner of Haskins & Sells, "It's probably not a question of if, but when." Chetkovich confesses that he is bothered by the possibility that such forecasts might mislead investors and by the auditors' potential liability should they affirm the forecasts.

Walter E. Hanson, senior partner at Peat, Marwick, Mitchell, believes that the profession should move into forecasting, provided the proper guidelines can be worked out. There is a question of independence if the accountant who vouches for the forecasts comes back to do the audit. But Hanson believes the answer to that problem is simple: Have one CPA firm do the forecast and another make the audit.

MORE ACTION FROM THE SEC

There is ample evidence to suggest that the SEC will be taking a more active role in other accounting areas as well. Under the Securities Act of 1934, the SEC is empowered to establish and enforce accounting rules. In practice, however, it has allowed the accounting profession to come up with appropriate standards. The SEC retains the ultimate enforcement power, and most accountants assert that the commission is the only body that can effectively enforce the rules.

That basic relationship will not change under the new Wheat plan or under the regime of the SEC's new chief accountant, John C. Burton, who takes office this summer. But already the SEC seems to be clamping down on the way it interprets accounting standards.

As one Big Eight managing partner notes: "For a while, they were giving everything away, but now they're coming back, particularly in real estate accounting and other areas, and tightening up." But critics charge that in this process of running to the commission for clearance, the SEC, companies, and their accounting firms are playing out their own kind of Gresham's Law, in which bad accounting drives out good accounting.

Take the "pooling-of-interests" method of accounting for mergers. Before the era of the big conglomerates, it was generally accepted that the accounting method called "pooling" was to be used when two corporations of relatively equal size merged by exchanging stock. The assets and liabilities of each would be combined—pooled—without revaluation, since both businesses were being continued. (Otherwise, the merger was to be counted as a "purchase," the merged company's assets revalued, and any difference between net assets and the purchase price carried as goodwill on the balance sheet.)

But some saw pooling as a way to create instant earnings, with the true acquisition cost buried in the shareholders equity section, or hidden away off the balance sheet if warrants or other fancy financing devices were used for purchase. In the 1960s, the scenario went something like this:

First XYZ Co. would ask for and secure from the SEC approval for pooling a slightly smaller company—say 40% as large. Then, PDQ Inc. and their public accountants, so as not to be at a competitive disadvantage, would march down to the SEC and get an okay for a smaller pooling than XYZ got, perhaps using "funny money" securities rather than common stock. And then IJK Corp., sensing a leak in the dike, would appear on the SEC's doorstep. "At the end," says Thornton O'glove, who writes an accounting newsletter for Coenen & Co., a Manhattan brokerage firm, "you had elephants swallowing mosquitos," and the birth of the part-pooling, part-purchase monstrosity.

The Wheat report was particularly critical of such secret reviews, and urged that they be made public. The SEC is said to be looking favorably on that suggestion, with the idea that public scrutiny might cut down on requests for favorable treatment.

'BLESSING THE QUARTERLIES'

There also has been talk of requiring interim financial statements—a particularly sticky area for both company managements and CPA firms. The unaudited quarterly statements now issued by management frequently require extensive year-end adjustments when accountants make the annual audit. But if securities are issued or acquisitions made between audits, and company fortunes take a downturn, investors or the SEC sometimes take both management and accountants to court, charging that the public was misled. That is what happened in the recent National Student Marketing complaint filed in early February by the SEC.

"I personally think we are going to have to move toward year-round audits in order to satisfy the investing public on the financial data they get," says Peat, Marwick's Hanson. "There's no way we can do anything in the way of blessing the quarterlies unless we're in there right around the year."

In addition to keeping its eye on accounting standards, the SEC will also be pushing the AICPA to speed up its work on reviewing and strengthening auditing standards. Many feel that in the great debate over broad accounting standards, the more technical and detailed auditing procedures have been neglected. Referring to the major lawsuits, Dick Baker of Ernst & Ernst contends that when accountants get into trouble it is usually on the "meat and potatoes" of their business—their audits. "Most of these cases involve two things—inventories and receivables," he says.

One approach for improving both accounting and auditing would be for the profession to undertake a simultaneous review of both, industry by industry, particularly in some of the currently controversial sectors, such as leasing, brokerage, land development, franchising, and real estate. As Price Waterhouse noted in its recent paper to the Trueblood study group: "The manner in which the most successful real estate investments regularly report a loss is an accounting scandal."

Such an industry approach would present obvious problems in the accounting of companies that are in two or more widely diversified industries, but it would cut down on the number of alternative accounting methods open to similar companies and make intraindustry financial statements more comparable. As things stand now, as long as the accounting devices are generally accepted, public accountants allow their clients to pick and choose—or, frequently, to switch, if another method will put a better face on things.

"The client can make that choice," says Baker. "Anyone that tells you different isn't leveling with you." Adds one Big Eight partner rather ruefully: "We try to keep away from the low end of the totem pole in acceptability. We're not trying to get by with the lowest compliance, but we have a couple of real tough guys as clients."

Lack of clear-cut rules in real estate accounting and a tough guy management is behind the accounting mess at Realty Equities, Inc. With part of its business in real estate, one problem—as it often is in real estate—is when to take sales into income. Because of this and other complicating factors, the accountants and the company management have not been able to agree on just how the accounts should be reported. Realty Equities has switched accounting firms several times, causing delays in filing audited financial statements with the SEC.

Lee J. Seidler, professor of accounting at New York University's Graduate School of Business Administration, sees the reason behind an industry-by-industry review this way: Nobody, he says, has "an inalienable right to mess with his own accounting." Other critics would take that principle further.

In his forthcoming book, *Unaccountable Accounting*, Abraham J. Briloff, professor of accounting at Baruch College of the City University of New York, and a long-time accounting gadfly, suggests that the individual accounting rules for larger public corporations be set by a consortium representing management, its legal counsel, independent auditors, and outside directors acting on behalf of shareholders. Other critics, however, would place the entire responsibility for accounting rules with government.

Before such sweeping moves are widely demanded, the Wheat proposals give the accounting profession another chance to demonstrate that workable accounting and auditing procedures can be set in the private sector, with the broad-based cooperation of accountants, financial executives, security analysts, and educators. At the same time, the SEC has indicated that it may be willing to press for new legislation to limit the CPA's sweeping liability under the 1933 Securities Act.

In the final analysis, despite all of the detailed rules and no matter how carefully an accountant's legal and social responsibilities and liabilities are defined, the ultimate quality of the financial statements, the fairness of their presentation, and their usefulness to the investor turns on the competence and independence of the individual professional auditor.

One thoughtful CPA looks at the role of the independent certified public accountant this way: "Accountants are too worried about service to the client. Most times they're too friendly with the client. I think there's simply got to be a mild adversary relationship there." And in that kind of critical relationship lies the public's best guarantee of full and fair disclosure.

1926 TO 1972
CHRONOLOGY OF SIGNIFICANT DEVELOPMENTS IN THE ESTABLISHMENT OF ACCOUNTING PRINCIPLES IN THE UNITED STATES

STEPHEN A. ZEFF

Biography appears on page 2.

1926	New York Stock Exchange (NYSE), recognizing the need for more effective surveillance of financial reporting by listed companies, names J. M. B. Hoxsey to the new, full-time position of Executive Assistant to the Committee on Stock List.
1926–27	In three articles in *The Atlantic Monthly* and a book, *Main Street and Wall Street*, Harvard Economist William Z. Ripley accuses large corporations of, *inter alia*, deceptive and misleading financial reporting practices.
1927	Price Waterhouse & Co. becomes accounting adviser to the NYSE, being represented by George O. May.
1930	Hoxsey proposes that the American Institute of Accountants (AIA) and NYSE cooperate on improving corporate financial reporting.
1931	AIA Committee on Accounting Terminology compiles a 126-page book of definitions, *Accounting Terminology*, which is published as a preliminary report by the Institute.
1932–34	AIA Committee chaired by May and NYSE Committee on Stock List exchange proposals on unsettled accounting and auditing matters. AIA Committee proposes that within quite wide limits it does not matter which accounting methods are used by corporations, so long as they are used consistently and that full disclosure is made of the choices. AIA Committee suggests five accounting "principles or rules," which are accepted by the NYSE, communicated to NYSE-listed companies, and are approved (1934), together with a sixth, by the AIA membership. AIA Committee also recommends a standard form of the auditor's short-form report, which rapidly achieves wide acceptance, and introduces the term, "accepted principles of accounting."

SOURCE: From *Corporate Financial Reporting: The Issues, the Objectives and Some New Proposals*, edited by Alfred Rappaport and Lawrence Revsine (Chicago: Commerce Clearing House, Inc., 1972) pp. 219–233. Reproduced by permission from *Corporate Financial Reporting*, published and copyrighted 1972 by Commerce Clearing House, Inc., Chicago, Ill., 60646.

1933	NYSE, for the first time, threatens a listed company (Allied Chemical) with delisting unless it improves its financial disclosures.
1933	NYSE announces that, henceforth, it will require independent audits of companies seeking a listing. By this time, more than 90 percent of industrial companies already listed have independent audits.
1933	Enactment of the Securities Act, providing for "full and fair disclosure" in registration statements (prospectuses) accompanying large, interstate flotations of securities. Act is administered by the Federal Trade Commission.
1934	Enactment of the Securities Exchange Act, which requires the filing of periodic reports by companies whose securities are listed on national securities exchanges. (Amended in 1964 to include over-the-counter companies having more than $1 million of assets and 500 or more stockholders.) 1934 Act also establishes the Securities and Exchange Commision (SEC), which will administer the 1933 and 1934 Securities Acts.
1935	Carman G. Blough becomes first SEC Chief Accountant and urges (1935–38) the accounting profession to narrow the range of diversity in accounting practices. (Blough is succeeded by William W. Werntz in 1938, Earle C. King in 1947, and Andrew Barr in 1956.)
1936	AIA Committee issues *Examination of Financial Statements*, a document principally oriented to auditing procedures, but which also discusses accounting, and for the first time adds the term, "generally" to "accepted principles of accounting."
1936	American Accounting Association (AAA), formerly the American Association of University Instructors in Accounting, issues a pamphlet entitled "A Tentative Statement of Accounting Principles Underlying Corporate Financial Statements," which employs the deductive approach to developing accounting principles. (Revisions are published in 1941, 1948, and 1957.)
1937	SEC Chief Accountant issues first Accounting Series Release (ASR).
1937–38	Deadlock occurs among SEC Commissioners regarding the Commission's posture on accounting, which leads to the issuance by Blough of ASR No. 4, stating that accounting methods will be presumed to be misleading unless they have "substantial authoritative support" and the Commission has not previously issued a rule opposing such methods.
1938	AIA publishes *A Statement of Accounting Principles*, by Thomas H. Sanders, Henry Rand Hatfield, and Underhill Moore.
1938	AIA Council approves an enlargement of the Committee on Accounting Procedure (CAP) to 21 members.

1939	At the suggestion of the CAP, the AIA Council authorizes the CAP to issue pronouncements on accounting, and establishes a research department. Thomas H. Sanders of Harvard University is appointed Director of Research, and is succeeded in 1941 by James L. Dohr of Columbia University. The research directorship is a part-time position. Also in 1939, a Committee on Auditing Procedure is established within the Institute, with authority to promulgate Statements on Auditing Procedure.
1939	CAP issues first four Accounting Research Bulletins (ARBs).
1940	AAA publishes *An Introduction to Corporate Accounting Standards,* by W. A. Paton and A. C. Littleton. Monograph elaborates upon the AAA's "Tentative Statement."
1940	AIA Committee on Terminology issues a report in the form of an ARB. Seven other Committee reports are issued later in the 1940s.
1941	CAP issues ARB No. 11 in which it recommends that stock dividends be recorded at fair value by the issuer. In 1943, the NYSE publicly supports the CAP position.
1944	AIA recognizes the need for more effective research and appoints Carman G. Blough as the first full-time Director of Research. Shortly after the appointment, the AIA research department begins to circulate exposure drafts of proposed ARBs to various interested groups.
1944–45	CAP issues ARB Nos. 23 and 24 on income-tax allocation and goodwill, respectively, which are followed by ASR Nos. 53 and 50 in which the SEC takes issue with portions of the two bulletins.
1947	Blough begins to edit a new department, "Comments on Accounting Procedures" (later "Accounting and Auditing Problems") in *The Journal of Accountancy,* which he relinquishes in 1963.
1947	CAP issues ARB No. 32 in which it favors the "current-operating-performance" concept of the income statement, which the SEC Chief Accountant replies will not be enforced if it results in misleading financial statements.
1947–48	CAP hastily issues ARB No. 33, which recommends against the use of price-level depreciation. It is opposed by several large companies and some leaders of the accounting profession. As a result, the CAP's role in influencing the course of accounting practice is formally questioned, and sustained, within the Institute.
1947–52	A Study Group on Business Income, largely guided by George O. May, issues several monographs and a final report (*Changing Concepts of Business Income*) on the nature and measurement

42   PROBLEMS CONFRONTING THE ACCOUNTING PROFESSION

	of accounting net income in inflationary conditions. Study is jointly financed by the AIA and the Rockefeller Foundation.
1949	CAP proposes to compile a comprehensive statement of "generally accepted accounting principles," but later abandons the effort as infeasible.
1949–50	SEC proposes to incorporate Accounting Series Releases on accounting subjects into its Regulation S-X on disclosures, also to require the "all-inclusive" income statement of registrants. In response to adverse comments by the AIA and AAA, the SEC decides to incorporate the ASRs in Regulation S-X only by a single, general reference and agrees to a compromise on the matter of the all-inclusive v. current-operating-performance concepts of the income statement.
1952	CAP issues ARB No. 11 (Revised) on stock dividends, which is publicly supported in 1953 by the NYSE.
1953	CAP issues ARB No. 43, a restatement and revision of the 34 ARBs on accounting, and the Committee on Terminology issues Accounting Terminology Bulletin (ATB) No. 1, which is a review and résumé of the eight ARBs on terminology. Three more ATBs are issued in the 1950s.
1956	Leonard Spacek, managing partner of Arthur Andersen & Co., begins to criticize the pace and direction of the accounting profession in establishing accounting principles.
1956	AIA Executive Committee proposes that the CAP prepare a comprehensive statement of basic accounting principles.
1957	Spacek charges that the CAP and the Institute's Committee on Relations with the Interstate Commerce Commission yielded to industry pressures on matters of accounting principle and auditing procedure. The AIA refers the charges to a special investigating committee which reports that they are groundless.
1957–58	Alvin R. Jennings, incoming AICPA (formerly AIA) President, recommends creation of a research foundation and appoints a Special Committee on Research Program, of which Weldon Powell is Chairman, to formulate a specific recommendation. The Committee's principal concern is the lack of research, understanding and agreement on the basic postulates and principles underlying accounting practice.
1959	Council accepts the comprehensive recommendations of the Special Committee on Research Program, replaces the research department by an accounting research division having an expanded role and replaces the CAP and the Committee on Terminology by the Accounting Principles Board (APB), of which Weldon Powell is to be Chairman. AICPA Executive Committee insists that the Big Eight firms be represented on the Board by their managing partners. The CAP issues ARB No. 51, on consolidations, its last bulletin.

1926 TO 1972 CHRONOLOGY 43

1959–60   Two large subsidiaries of a public utility holding company seek to enjoin the CAP from issuing a clarifying letter to its ARB No. 44 (Revised) on income-tax allocation. The Federal District Court and Second Circuit Court of Appeals hold for the AICPA, and *certiorari* is denied by the U.S. Supreme Court. The letter is issued. In early 1960, the SEC issues Accounting Series Release No. 85, which forbids the designation of "deferred tax credit" as part of stockholder's equity.

1959–60   Perry Mason is named Acting Director of Accounting Research in November, 1959. On July 1, 1960, Maurice Moonitz becomes Director. (He is succeeded in 1963 by Paul Grady, as Acting Director, and in 1964 by Reed K. Storey, as Director.) During 1960, eight Accounting Research Studies are commissioned.

1960   Two-part article, "The Auditors Have Arrived," by Tom A. Wise, in the November and December issues of *Fortune,* does much to awaken interest in accounting and the accounting profession.

1961–62   AICPA publishes Accounting Research Studies 1 and 3, on postulates and principles, which are rejected by the APB as "too radically different . . . for acceptance at this time."

1962–64   By a bare two-thirds majority of 14 to 7, including a 4-4 split of Big Eight firms, the APB approves Opinion No. 2, which recommends that the "investment credit should be reflected in net income over the productive life of acquired property and not in the year in which it is placed in service." Prior to issuance, industry had vigorously objected to this treatment. Following issuance, three of the Big Eight firms make it known that they will not expect their clients to conform to the Opinion. In view of widespread opposition to the Opinion, both in Government and in the private sector, the SEC issues ASR No. 96, in which it allows both the deferral and the flow-through methods of accounting for the investment credit. In early 1964, by a vote of 15 to 5, the APB issues Opinion No. 4, which acknowledges the "events and developments occurring since the issuance of Opinion No. 2" and declares that both the deferral and the flow-through methods are "acceptable."

1962–present   Controversies over the investment credit (1962–63 and 1967), product-line reporting (1966–68), and pooling of interests (1969–70), together with criticisms by the SEC, the Financial Executives Institute (FEI), and members of the profession, excite an almost continual interest by the financial press in accounting principles and the accounting profession.

1963–64   APB issues Opinion No. 3, which recommends that funds statements "be presented as supplementary information in financial reports." Shortly afterwards, the NYSE sends copies of the

Opinion to the presidents of listed companies, strongly recommending that funds statements, preferably covered by the auditor's opinion and presented on a comparative basis, be included in annual reports to stockholders. In its first public endorsement of an Institute pronouncement, the Financial Analysts Federation (FAF) also urges companies to include funds statements in annual reports.

1963–64   APB, in a divided vote, asks Council to require that material departures from Board recommendations be disclosed in the financial statements or in the auditor's report. AICPA Executive Committee goes further, suggesting that Board Opinions be the only "generally accepted accounting principles." Council, in a compromise resolution following three days of intense debate, adopts the APB proposal in principle. Following a report by a special committee, Council in Fall, 1964 implements the compromise proposal.

1964   SEC amends proxy rule 14a-3 to require that any material differences in the application of accounting principles between reports filed with the Commission and reports sent to security holders must be reconciled or explained in the latter. As a result, the SEC asserts indirect surveillance over annual reports to stockholders issued by most companies under its jurisdiction.

1964   Clifford V. Heimbucher becomes APB Chairman, creates subcommittees to decentralize the Board's work, and supports establishment of an Administrative Division to provide staff support for the Board.

1964   Manuel F. Cohen, SEC Commissioner since 1961, becomes Commission Chairman, and begins to criticize the accounting profession for lack of progress in "narrowing areas of difference."

1964–66   Big Eight managing partners on the Board are gradually replaced by their senior technical partners.

1965   Publication of Paul Grady's *Inventory of Generally Accepted Accounting Principles for Business Enterprises*, as Accounting Research Study No. 7.

1965   SEC issues ASR No. 102 on the balance-sheet status of the deferred tax credit arising from installment sales—a controversial subject which had been included in an APB exposure draft but was later omitted from Opinion No. 6. This is one of the few instances in which the SEC has issued an ASR on accounting without exposing a draft or holding hearings.

1965   FAF establishes a Financial Accounting Policy Committee to liaise with the APB.

1965–70   Following by several months an inquiry from the U.S. Senate's Subcommittee on Antitrust and Monopoly, SEC Chairman

Cohen publicly calls for product-line reporting by conglomerates, APB issues Statement No. 2 encouraging voluntary disclosures, and the FEI and its research affiliate, the Financial Executives Research Foundation (FERF) take a strong interest in the subject. The FERF commissions R. K. Mautz to prepare a comprehensive research study, which appears in early 1968 under the title, *Financial Reporting by Diversified Companies*. The National Association of Accountants (NAA), also evincing its first serious research interest in financial accounting, commissions two studies: *External Reporting for Segments of a Business* (1968), by Morton Backer and Walter B. McFarland, and *A Framework for Financial Reporting by Diversified Companies* (1969), by Alfred Rappaport and Eugene M. Lerner. The SEC gives consideration to these studies in formulating its guidelines in 1968–70.

1966 — AICPA begins a series of financial writers' seminars designed to educate financial journalists about the accounting problems faced by the Board.

1966 — A committee of the AAA issues a monograph entitled *A Statement of Basic Accounting Theory*.

1966–67 — APB issues Opinion Nos. 8 (pensions), 9 (extraordinary items and earnings per share), and 10 (omnibus), which are endorsed by the NYSE. Numbers 9 and 10 are supported by the American Stock Exchange (ASE). SEC expresses pleasure with the Board's resolution of several difficult problems.

1966–67 — AICPA creates the full-time position of Executive Vice President to assume operating and policy supervision of Institute technical activities. Leonard M. Savoie, formerly a partner in Price Waterhouse & Co., is appointed and quickly becomes the Institute's spokesman on accounting and auditing matters.

1967 — APB issues an exposure draft on accounting for income taxes, including a reassertion of its position of 1962 on the investment credit. As a result of an open letter of objection from Stanley S. Surrey, Assistant Secretary of the Treasury (Tax Policy), an expression by the SEC that it cannot promise support, and other communications, the ensuing Opinion No. 11, on income-tax allocation, is published without any recommendations on the investment credit. In 1969, the AICPA publishes a 70-page guidebook containing unofficial interpretations of the Opinion.

1967–69 — Acting on the strong suggestion of the Investment Bankers Association of America that they are undesirable and unworkable, the APB temporarily suspends paragraphs 8 and 9 of Opinion No. 10, dealing with the imputation of debt discount to issues of convertible debt and debt issued with stock warrants. In Opinion No. 14, issued in 1969, the APB rescinds its recommendation as regards convertible debt, while reinstating the proposed treatment in the case of debt issued with detachable stock warrants.

1968   FEI's Corporate Reporting Committee becomes an active collaborator on exposure drafts with the APB, sets up subject-area subcommittees to liaise with counterpart subcommittees of the APB.

1968   AICPA, FAF, FEI, and Robert Morris Associates jointly sponsor the Seaview Symposium on Corporate Financial Reporting, bringing together accounting practitioners, accounting educators, financial executives, financial analysts, and bank loan officers in a dialogue on accounting principles. The papers and proceedings are published by the AICPA in 1969 under the title, *Corporate Financial Reporting: Conflicts and Challenges.*

1968–70 Controversy over pooling-of-interests accounting becomes intense as the conglomerate merger movement reaches its zenith, then collapses. Direct and indirect pressure from the SEC, Congress, Federal Trade Commission, the Administration, financial analysts and financial executives begins to bear down on the APB. Board issues an exposure draft, holds two symposia and numerous private meetings, agonizes during much of 1970 over various proposals and drafts, and finally issues Opinion Nos. 16 and 17 amid much dissent and criticism. Shortly after the Opinions' effective date of November 1, 1970, the NYSE and ASE send identical letters to the presidents of companies listed on their respective Exchanges, urging full support of both Opinions and giving notice that they will require letters from a company's independent auditor attesting to the company's compliance with Opinion No. 16 in connection with listing applications authorizing shares to be issued in poolings of interests.

1968–71 After considerable discussion between the banking industry and the Institute's APB and Committee on Bank Accounting and Auditing, the latter prepares and issues an audit guide, *Audits of Banks,* which, among other things, recommends that commercial banks provide for loan losses and securities gains and losses prior to arriving at net income, contrary to industry practice. Complaints by bankers precipitate further meetings, following which the APB, in 1969, issues Opinion No. 13 in which it rescinds its exemption, in Opinion No. 9, of commercial banks, obliging them to adhere to the two controversial recommendations in the audit guide. Shortly thereafter, the NYSE announces that banks (and insurance companies) will no longer be exempt from submitting audited financial statements in listing applications. Later in 1969, the recommendations contained in the audit guide are made mandatory by the bank regulatory agencies. Bankers' criticisms of the recommendations continue into

	1970. In ASR No. 121, issued in 1971, the SEC deletes the exemption from certification of the financial statements of banks.
1968–present	Abraham J. Briloff writes a series of articles for *Barron's*, calling into question the accounting and disclosure practices of numerous publicly held corporations. While placing primary emphasis on abuses of pooling-of-interest accounting, Briloff also deals with the particular practices of computer leasing companies, land development companies, franchisers and home builders. Briloff's articles generate increased stock-market sensitivity to the quality of financial reporting.
1969	APB begins to hold a series of symposia on preexposure drafts of proposed Opinions. Participation is by invitation only, the Board inviting several organizations to all symposia and various other bodies to particular symposia, depending on the subject. Memoranda and brief oral presentations are requested of participants. The object of the symposium idea, which was suggested by the belated reaction of investment bankers to Opinion No. 10, is to inform affected groups of the Board's current thinking on subjects under consideration so as to secure reactions and suggestions before the Board reaches its conclusions. The symposium approach leads to a formalization of the Board's liaison with other interested groups.
1969	AICPA announces a new Unofficial Accounting Interpretations service to clarify the APB's intent on specific questions arising from APB Opinions. Each interpretation requires the approval of the Executive Vice President and the APB Chairman.
1969	For the first time, a practicing certified public accountant, James J. Needham, is named to the SEC.
1969	APB issues 60-page Opinion No. 15 on earnings per share, modifying Opinion No. 9. Extensive detail in the Opinion provokes criticism that the Board is trying to impose a "cookbook" on the profession. Institute issues a 189-page guidebook of unofficial interpretations of the Opinion.
1969	APB issues Statement No. 3, proposing that the price-level adjustments explained and illustrated in Accounting Research Study No. 6 be presented as supplementary information to the basic financial statements.
1969	NAA forms a Management Accounting Practices Committee with authority to issue statements of opinion on accounting principles.
1969–71	Following a recommendation in its 1969 Disclosure Policy Study report, the SEC in 1970 amends its forms to require the presentation of audited funds statements in prospectuses and periodic filings. A week later, the NYSE announces that, effec-

	tive with 1973 annual reports, all listed companies will be required to present comparative, audited funds statements. In 1971, the APB issues Opinion No. 19 which recommends that a "Statement of Changes in Financial Position," embodying a broadened concept of the funds statement, be made part of the "basic financial statements."
1970	After five years of study and numerous drafts, the APB issues Statement No. 4, "Basic Concepts and Accounting Principles Underlying Financial Statements of Business Enterprises," the Board's first pronouncement on basic principles.
1970–71	In February, 1970, the APB issues an exposure draft on the subject of accounting changes, which proposes that prior years' financial statements be restated to reflect the new accounting principle or method of application. By mid-1970, support for that position deteriorates, and a second exposure draft on the same subject, issued in January, 1971, recommends against the restatement of prior years' financial statements and instead favors showing the cumulative effect of retroactive application of the new accounting principle or method immediately in the current period's income statement, together with the "pro forma" income of each period affected. Later in the year, the APB approves by a bare two-thirds majority, 12 to 6, including a 4-4 split of Big Eight firms, Opinion No. 20, which, with some exceptions, embodies the philosophy of the second exposure draft.
1970–71	On the heels of several recent Treasury decisions which permit taxpayers to change accounting methods for tax purposes if the taxpayer were to use the new method in all its reports for other purposes, the Treasury Department announces, in April 1971, a study "to set forth more specifically the circumstances under which a new tax accounting method may be used by a taxpayer only if [also] used for financial accounting and reporting." After considerable debate within the profession, the AICPA Board of Directors (formerly the Executive Committee) advises the Treasury that it opposes such enforced conformity of tax accounting to financial accounting.
1970–71	Arthur Andersen & Co. petitions the Federal Power Commission (FPC) to require natural gas companies to use full-cost accounting for exploration costs incurred in working oil and gas reserves. Comments invited by the Commission are almost equally divided for and against full-costing. Accounting Research Study No. 11, published in 1969, had counseled against full-costing. The APB Chairman requests the Commission to postpone a decision until the Board can act on the subject. In November, 1971, the FPC decides in favor of full-cost accounting, which is to be applied on a nation-wide basis.
1971	Responding to criticism both inside and outside the accounting profession, the AICPA commissions two major studies. One deals

with the process by which accounting principles should be established, and the second concerns the objectives of financial statements. The first is chaired by former SEC Commissioner Francis M. Wheat, the second by former Institute President Robert M. Trueblood. The AAA, in an action by its Executive Committee, also calls for a blue-ribbon commission to make a comprehensive study of the way in which accounting principles should be established. In view of the Institute's study on the subject, the AAA decides to hold its proposal in abeyance.

1971 APB replaces the series of symposia by public hearings at which all interested parties may present their views on subjects being considered by the Board for prospective Opinions. The hearings are intended to meet three criticisms of the symposia, to wit: (1) participation was by invitation only, (2) the Board had already reached its conclusions before the symposia were held, and (3) presentations by participating groups were dogmatic and uncompromising, thus frustrating attempts at developing a dialogue. Three hearings are held in 1971, on the valuation of marketable equity securities, accounting for long-term leases, and accounting practices in the oil and gas industry. The prepared papers and hearing transcripts are published by the Institute.

1971 Several weeks after President Nixon recommends that Congress revive the investment credit, AICPA representatives meet with Treasury officials to urge the Administration to refrain from expressing a view on the proper accounting treatment of the credit. The Institute receives a letter from the Treasury that it will remain neutral on the question. Following a meeting between AICPA representatives and the SEC Chairman, the APB prepares and issues an exposure draft again reasserting its 1962 preferred treatment of the investment credit. A letter of support is received from the SEC Chairman. Partly in response to industry pressures, the Treasury revises its neutrality stand and advises the Senate that it "strongly supports a continuation of the optional [accounting] treatment" of the credit and "will support a legislative resolution of this matter." Notwithstanding the eleventh-hour pleas of Institute leaders, Congress amends the tax bill, which later becomes law, to provide that taxpayers may freely choose which method of accounting for the credit they prefer. In the face of this Congressional dictum, the APB withdraws its exposure draft and issues a statement deploring Congressional involvement in the establishment of accounting principles.

1972 John C. Burton, a Columbia University accounting professor, is named SEC Chief Accountant. An era ends, as Andrew Barr, who is the last of four successive Chief Accountants who joined the Commission's staff in the 1930s, retires.

1972   The Wheat Study recommends that a seven-man, full-time Financial Accounting Standards Board be established under the auspices of a Financial Accounting Foundation, which is to be composed of representatives of the AICPA, FEI, NAA, FAF, and AAA. The Board's budget is proposed at between $2½ and $3 million. A Financial Accounting Standards Advisory Council, made up of "persons conversant with and involved in the problems of communicating financial information," is suggested to keep the Board in touch with current thinking in the business and professional world. The entire recommendation receives the support of an overwhelming majority of the AICPA's Board of Directors and Council, and several Big Eight firms promise donations of $1 million to the Foundation. The APB continues its activities during 1972, but is to be replaced in early 1973 by the program recommended by the Wheat Study. Marshall S. Armstrong, a former member of the APB and 1970–71 AICPA President, is named Chairman of the Financial Accounting Standards Board.

SAMUEL R. HEPWORTH

SAMUEL R. HEPWORTH (1920–1967), B.S. 41 Kansas; M.B.A. 45 University of California, Berkeley; Ph.D. 54 Michigan; CPA. Major publications: *Reporting Foreign Operations* (1956); *Standards of Education and Experience for Certified Public Accountants* (with Smith, 1956). Contributor to handbooks and accounting journals.

Was on the Ohio State University faculty, 1947–49, spent the following three years at the University of Michigan, and then joined the faculty of the University of California (Berkeley) in 1952. Two years later, he returned to the University of Michigan, where he remained until his death in 1967.

SMOOTHING PERIODIC INCOME

SAMUEL R. HEPWORTH

Fifty years ago the principal interest of those concerned with the financial data of business enterprises centered on the periodic display of assets and liabilities (balance sheet). Evidence of this situation may be readily obtained by an examination of what published financial reports existed during the first decade of the twentieth century. Typically the only financial statement presented in these reports was a balance sheet, with any information relating to the results of the operations of the business being presented principally as a means of explaining changes in financial position. Over the course of the last half century there is little question that a pronounced shift in the interest of the users of published corporate reports has occurred. Thus, at the present time the principal attention of investors, financial analysts, employees, and the general public is focused on the statement setting

SOURCE: From *The Accounting Review*, Vol. XXVIII, No. 1 (January, 1953), pp. 32–39. Reprinted by permission of the American Accounting Association.

forth the periodic net income or earnings of the business, with the balance sheet being viewed ". . . as the connecting link between successive income statements and as the vehicle for the distribution of charges and credits between them."[1]

This emphasis on the significance of the amount of periodic net income has resulted in a considerable amount of attention on the part of professional societies and regulatory bodies being directed toward the establishment of principles and procedures aimed at achieving a high degree of objectivity in the determination of periodic net income for the individual enterprise, with the resulting increased meaningfulness of the comparison of the operating results of two or more enterprises. The need for objectivity in the periodic income determination process has been emphasized by the not infrequently expressed lack of confidence in reported net income data on the part of the general public.

Unquestionably great progress has been made toward a more objective determination of net income. On the other hand, there seems little question that considerable latitude exists within the confines of "generally accepted accounting principles" in the determination of periodic earnings. It will be the purpose of this article to survey some of the accounting techniques which may be applied to affect the assignment of net income to successive accounting periods. As the title indicates, emphasis will be placed on the possibilities for smoothing or leveling the amplitude of periodic net income fluctuations.

CONCEPTS OF NET INCOME

In view of our experiences of the last two decades, probably the most fundamental point to be made in this connection is the distinction between monetary and real income. Current accounting practice is almost exclusively concerned with the measurement of the difference between dollar costs consumed or expired and dollar proceeds realized in connection therewith. This may be described as a purely monetary conception of income. If, on the other hand, we consider income to represent an increase in command over goods or services, an entirely different result may emerge. The latter position involves recognition of the changing value or purchasing power of the dollar. Consideration of income in the real sense embraces numerous problems typically identified with common-dollar or stabilized accounting, which the limitations of space do not permit considering in this article. Hence, in the pages which follow, income will be considered from a strictly monetary point of view, although little thought is necessary to visualize the shortcomings of such a position.

We may consider the term income to be indicative of the "normal earning power" of a business enterprise. This is the usual connotation of the term "operating income" or "operating profit," as employed by accountants, and is generally measured by the difference between gross revenue from the major activity of the

[1] Accounting Research Bulletin Number 1, *General Introduction and Rules Formerly Adopted,* Committee on Accounting Procedure, The American Institute of Accountants, September, 1939.

[Bulletin No. 1 was superseded (with no major change in substance) by the Introduction and Chapter 1 of Accounting Research Bulletin No. 43 (in 1953). The first of the two quoted coordinate clauses was retained in the Introduction; the second clause was not carried forward to Bulletin No. 43. Eds.]

enterprise and applicable costs of a regular or recurring nature, but exclusive of "abnormal" or non-recurring items. From this point of view, it is apparent that considerable "juggling" of income may be accomplished by management decision as to the normality or abnormality of an item of revenue or expense, and the resulting statement classification. More detailed attention will be given to this area in a later section of this article.

MOTIVATION FOR INCOME SMOOTHING

From a practical point of view, there is little doubt but what the most compelling motivation for income smoothing is the existence of tax levies, based upon income. Even with the existence of a non-progressive corporate income tax (except for the smallest concerns) and the availability of the carry-forward or carry-back provisions relating to operating losses, there may be distinct tax advantages to income shifting or smoothing. This is most apparent in the case of changes in tax rates or the addition or removal of types of income taxation. It would obviously have been advantageous taxwise to have maintained a relatively stable level of taxable income in the period 1944 to 1948, rather than to have had high income in 1944 and 1945, subject to the excess profits tax, offset by lower income in 1946, 1947, and 1948. In the case of proprietorships and partnerships, the steeply progressive personal income tax rates make direct tax saving possible by means of income smoothing, without tax structure or rate change.

A less tangible, but perhaps more fundamentally important type of advantage of a relatively stable level of periodic income lies in the area of management relations with investors and workers. Certainly the owners and creditors of an enterprise will feel more confident toward a corporate management which is able to report stable earnings than if considerable fluctuation of reported earnings exists. The stable dividend policy which level earnings facilitate does nothing to lessen satisfactory stockholder relations. The absence of peaks and valleys in the earnings record of an enterprise may do much to maintain continuing satisfactory industrial relations. A sharp increase in reported profits is very likely to produce the feeling in the minds of the members of the working force that they should participate to a greater extent in such profits, with resulting demands for wage increases, strikes and general industrial unrest. Finally, in the case where a considerable amount of the fluctuation in income may be attributed to changing price levels, the recognition of this cause may be vitally significant to corporate management as a guide to dividend policy, in order to assure preservation of corporate capital.[2]

The above factors are significant from the point of view of an individual firm. It seems essential to mention a further point incident to the smoothing of income fluctuations which may well be of considerable importance to an entire economy. It is reasonably well recognized by economists that psychological factors, particularly in the area of producers' expectations, are an important factor in the determination of economic activity. By the same token, changes in such psychological attitudes or expectations are significant in the explanation of cyclical upswings and downswings in business activity. Since, in the formulation of expectations, prediction of future events and conditions is an extremely hazardous process, current

[2] As illustrated by an analysis of the effect of price level changes on nine major steel companies. See "Effect of Inflation on Capital and Profits: The Record of Nine Steel Companies," Ralph C. Jones, *The Journal of Accountancy*, January, 1949, pp. 9–27.

conditions have a very important influence upon future expectations. Hence, a current condition of declining business income may cause expectation of further decline, bringing upon actions which make these expectations a reality, and a cumulative process is initiated resulting in substantial stagnation of business activity, employment, etc. The opposite process may occur in the other direction when rising income appears. It would seem that the maintenance of a relatively stable level of periodic income might do much to reduce the effect of "waves of optimism and pessimism" on the level of business activity. It should be emphasized that the author is not subscribing exclusively to a completely psychological theory of business cycles, but is merely indicating that psychological expectations, motivated by fluctuations in income, are of some significance in this connection.

In the preceding paragraphs, several reasons, both practical and theoretical, in favor of profit smoothing have been set forth. With these in mind, it is now appropriate to turn to an investigation of some of the accounting techniques by which such smoothing may be accomplished.

ACCOUNTING TECHNIQUES AIMED AT THE SMOOTHING OF PERIODIC INCOME

Gross Revenue Manipulation

A rather direct approach to the objective of income smoothing may be made through the process of inter-period shifting of gross revenue. Given actual knowledge of or expectations about the operating results of two accounting periods, speeding or delaying the shipment of and billing for product and hence the recognition of revenue, may accomplish some degree of leveling of the income of the two periods. The effect of shifting gross revenue may be particularly significant in service rendering enterprises where the amount of direct costs related to such revenue would be relatively much smaller than in a manufacturing or merchandising enterprise. In many concerns the magnitude of the effect upon periodic income from this source would be minor, since only transactions occurring relatively near the closing date would be susceptible to such shifting. However, in an enterprise which has a relatively small number of revenue transactions, each involving a sizable dollar amount, the effect of such inter-period shifting on periodic revenue could well be substantial. Similarly, the use of production as a criterion for revenue recognition by a concern engaged in a small number of large and extended construction or manufacturing contracts, would tend to produce a more stable level of periodic income than would strict application of the conventional accrual basis. However, it is hardly appropriate to consider this as a method of artificially smoothing income, but rather as the use of a realistic and logical method of gross revenue booking.

Deferred Charge and Intangible Asset Accounting

The accounting for so-called deferred charges and intangible assets represents an area in which "generally accepted accounting principles" seem to provide for substantial latitude in the matter of original recognition of such items as assets (as opposed to expense) as well as subsequent amortization thereof.

It is possible to discover, in the writings of a number of widely accepted authorities, a broad range of recommendations relative to the accounting for organization costs or expenses. These range from immediate recognition as expense of this type of cost to capitalization and permanent retention in an asset category. A middle ground involving capitalization and speedy write-off is probably most widely accepted. The following statement indicates this position and the resulting availability of this type of item for income smoothing:

> The best plan is to charge organization expense off as rapidly as possible, preferably in the first year of operations and certainly over a maximum period not to exceed five years.[3]

Similar flexibility as to amortization exists in connection with many other items of intangible assets, perhaps largely due to the difficulty of determining, with any degree of precision, the service life of such assets. In discussing recommended procedure relative to the accounting for intangibles for which no limited period of existence exists (such as goodwill, trade names, secret processes, etc.), the Committee on Accounting Procedure of The American Institute of Accountants states:

> . . . when the term of existence of such intangibles has become limited . . . the cost should be amortized by systematic charges in the income statement over the estimated remaining period of usefulness or, if such charges would result in distortion of the income statement, a partial write-down may be made by a charge to earned surplus, and the balance of the cost may be amortized over the remaining period of usefulness.[4]

Published corporate balance sheets contain innumerable examples of the carrying of all intangible assets at one dollar. It is apparent that the alternatives available both as to timing and manner of handling the charge created by the reduction from cost to nominal value may allow a considerable effect to be produced in the direction of smoothing income.

Of course, more direct action in the direction of income smoothing may be accomplished by arbitrarily accumulating current expense in deferred charge accounts during bad years, together with liberal amortization of such deferred costs during periods of high revenue. An element of respectability may even be attached to such techniques when the reason put forth therefor is that of future benefit from such expenditures in the form of enhanced revenue in future periods. The existence of subsequently increased revenue then becomes the signal for the proper recognition as expense of the previously deferred costs.

The above comments indicate that the very nature of intangible assets and deferred charges make such items readily available for the purpose of smoothing periodic net income.

Inventory Accounting

Alternative techniques of inventory valuation may provide a very significant method of income smoothing. This has become particularly true with the emer-

---

[3] *Auditing Principles and Procedure,* Third Edition, Arthur W. Holmes (Chicago: Richard D. Irwin, Inc., 1951), p. 380.

[4] Accounting Research Bulletin Number 24, *Accounting for Intangible Assets,* Committee on Accounting Procedure, The American Institute of Accountants, Dec., 1944. [Bulletin No. 24 was superseded (with certain changes in substance) by Chap. 5 of ARB No. 43 (1953). While the exact quotation from Bulletin No. 24 is not found in Chap. 5, its sense is included in para. 6. Chap. 5 of ARB No. 43 has been superseded by APB Opinion No. 17, "Intangible Assets" (Aug. 1970). The practice at the date of this Opinion is described in para. 12. The Opinion concludes that the cost of acquired intangible assets with indeterminate lives should be capitalized; however, the cost of developing or maintaining these assets should be deducted from income as incurred (para. 24). The Opinion also requires that the cost of each type of intangible asset be amortized over its estimated useful life preferably in accordance with the straight line method. The maximum amortization period is 40 years. Eds.]

gence and wide adoption of the last-in, first-out method of inventory pricing. The effect of the use of LIFO may be described, in summary form, as causing the matching of sales revenue expressed in terms of the current period price level with cost of merchandise or product expressed in similar terms. This is accomplished by valuing the inventory of unused material or unsold product substantially in terms of a fixed base price, the aggregate thereof being changed only to the extent of changes in physical inventory quantities. It is apparent that this matching of "current cost with current revenue" will have a decidedly stabilizing effect on income, as compared with the results of the more traditional first-in, first-out assumption. This will be particularly true in the case of an enterprise with a lengthy manufacturing process, using substantial quantities of raw materials subject to fluctuating supply prices and, in particular, during a period of rapid price level changes. It seems appropriate to remark that the recent extension of last-in, first-out to such concerns as department stores can be defended by few of the theoretical arguments which may be applied in the case of certain types of manufacturing enterprises. It would appear that smoothing of income, particularly due to the income tax effects thereof, represents the principal motivation for the use of LIFO in many (if not most) cases. Other pricing techniques, more recently suggested, which will produce the same general effect are next-in, first-out; highest-in, first-out; and, more-in than-out. Since no general use of these methods exists, it seems adequate to merely indicate their existence, without attempting detailed discussion thereof.

Less fundamental methods of income smoothing through the inventory valuation process are also available. These arise through the subjective decisions made by management relative to reduction of inventory value for unsalable, obsolete, or damaged material or merchandise. The timing of adjustments for these conditions may well produce a smoothing effect on periodic income.

The effect of provision for estimated future inventory losses through addition to reserves is discussed in a later section of this paper.

In summary, it can be seen that the process of inventory valuation offers considerable latitude to management, which may be employed to achieve or assist in a leveling of net income.

Property Accounting

The existence of long-lived depreciable or depletable assets presents one of the most potent (and in many cases most essential) opportunities for income smoothing. The importance of this area will obviously vary in direct proportion to the significance of physical plant in the operations of a particular enterprise. Although not mutually exclusive, the following three points present a convenient basis for discussion in this area:

1. Original acquisition of plant assets.
2. Determination of the base to which depreciation rates are applied.
3. Alternative methods of calculating periodic depreciation.

Original Acquisition of Plant Assets

The absence of a specific and consistently applied distinction between asset and expense charges may provide considerable possibility for income smoothing. Thus in a period of high revenue many items of major repair or replacement may be charged to current expense, which in a less prosperous period would be capitalized and become expense only over their estimated service lives. In the same manner alternative treatment of installation and related costs may permit the shifting of expense between accounting periods. There are often borderline cases of this type, and inconsistent treatment thereof may produce substantial effect on periodic operating results.

Another possibility in the same general area, which has found current acceptance in some of our prominent corporations, is that of considering a part of the cost of new facilities as being abnormal and charging this amount directly to current expense. The effects of this policy on income of the current and subsequent accounting periods are obvious.

Determination of the Base to Which Depreciation Rates Are Applied

Substantial alteration in the depreciation base may produce significant changes in net income during periods of rapid change in business activity or price level. Thus the recording of upward appraisals in plant value and the calculation of depreciation on these higher values may serve to offset a substantial increase in dollar revenue in a period of increased activity or higher prices. The same effect on income may be produced by basing depreciation charges on the higher replacement values without recording appraised value in the property accounts.[5] Similar results, in the opposite direction, were rather widely achieved in the thirties, by the write-down of plant values against capital, with subsequent depreciation based on the adjusted values. Many so-called quasi-reorganizations produce similar results, but in these cases the objective is not so much the stabilizing of income as the achieving of positive income in any amount.

Another situation, which has caused considerable current controversy, that may be classified in this area, is that of the restoration and re-depreciation of assets which are fully depreciated (or amortized) on the books, but still possess substantial service life. If the decision in this situation is based on the current revenue status (which should certainly not be the case except insofar as current revenue is a reflection of the value of such assets) an element of income stabilization may be introduced.

Perhaps a more arbitrary method of affecting primarily the income of a single accounting period through the medium of depreciation exists in connection with the determination of the date upon which depreciation begins to accrue on new plant items. This effect may be sizable where large construction projects are involved. A transfer from construction in progress to a depreciable asset classification near the end of an accounting period may well allow taking a full year's depreciation on the new item. If the timing of this transfer is affected by expectations as to the relative profitability of the two periods, the resulting effect on periodic income is apparent. Changes, actual or expected, in tax structure or rates may exercise considerable influence in this connection.

Alternative Methods of Calculating Periodic Depreciation

Doubtless the most extreme situation in this classification exists in connection with proposals to calculate depreciation as a function of gross revenue or of income not considering depreciation as a cost. In certain situations (notably utilities) gross revenue may be a reasonably accurate index of physical activity, and

[5] As was done by the United States Steel Company in its 1947 annual report.

the calculation of periodic depreciation as a percentage of gross revenue may cause the depreciation charge to vary with physical utilization of plant. However, in many situations, this acceptable result may not be present, and this sort of theory of depreciation calculation may well be purely the product of a desire for the smoothing of periodic income.

The use of percentage depletion, as allowed by the Internal Revenue Code, in wasting asset operations produces precisely the same result as that outlined above. It is probably true, however, that very few concerns employ percentage depletion for book accounting purposes, restricting the use thereof to the calculation to taxable income.

It should be noted that the use of "units of production" or comparable activity bases for depreciation calculation will normally tend to smooth income fluctuations, as compared to the results of the use of the conventional straightline depreciation method.

An important recent illustration of the timely adoption of a particular technique of calculating periodic depreciation is found in connection with so-called "accelerated depreciation." Briefly, this method involves the recognition as expense of a substantial part of the cost of fixed assets during the early years of use, with the periodic depreciation charge becoming progressively smaller as the end of the estimated service life approaches. As has been pointed out[6] this involves nothing more than the use of the traditional "constant percentage of diminishing balance" method, which has been discussed in every standard intermediate or advanced accounting textbook for many years. Without considering the theoretical advantages or disadvantages of such a method (and there are unquestionably a number of each), it is apparent that the use thereof will currently produce very substantial depreciation charges when applied to the large amount of recently acquired facilities, with progressively lower charges as these facilities become older. Given the high level of current revenue, together with the distinct possibility of decreasing revenue in future years, the effect of the use of this type of depreciation calculation on the level of periodic income is readily apparent.

Reserve Accounting

Historically, there have been extreme examples of the use of reserves as profit equalization devices, involving additions to or deductions from such reserves, offset by income statement accounts having the professed intention of income smoothing. Fortunately, such crude and arbitrary techniques are rare or even nonexistent at the present time, at least in concerns in which there is any sort of public interest. However, the war and postwar period have produced a tremendous increase in the use of reserves, particularly those established to provide for such intangible future events as "general contingencies" and "possible future inventory losses." This situation has produced considerable justifiable concern on the part of individual accountants and professional societies, as reflected by the following classification of possible improper use of reserves as a method of income smoothing:

1. When reserve provisions for future contingencies of one kind or another are charged to current income, largely at the whim of management.

[6] "Accelerated Depreciation: Criteria for Its Use," George D. Bailey, *The Journal of Accountancy*, November, 1949, pp. 372-377.

2. When reserves created by charges to income are used in later years to absorb losses (sometimes without adequate disclosure).

3. When items of income are credited directly to reserves which then are used to absorb later losses or are ultimately transferred to surplus.[7]

The above three classifications indicate adequately, without necessity for further technical discussion, the several ways in which reserves may be employed to achieve at least a degree of income smoothing. The following tabulation of the combined operating results of four large listed corporations for the years indicated illustrates the possible effect of such reserve provisions on periodic income:[8]

	1942	1941	1940	1939
Reported net income	$37,448	$37,337	$37,053	$36,235
Add back provisions for war contingencies and postwar adjustments	11,000	10,000	—	
Revised net income	$48,448	$47,337	$37,053	

The American Institute of Accountants has recommended that "general purpose contingency reserves" and/or "inventory reserves" be established directly from and restored to retained earnings, without effect upon the income statement.[9] Compliance with these recommendations would seem to substantially eliminate reserve accounting as a source of income smoothing.

Treatment of Non-recurring Charges or Credits

The possibility of alternative treatment of unusual or non-recurring charges or credits as between inclusion in the computation of net income or direct addition to or deduction from retained earnings, may well present an opportunity for the smoothing of periodic income. Fundamentally, these alternatives exist because of differing opinions as to the real nature of the income statements. On the one hand, many accountants subscribe to the point of view that the final figure on the income statement should be indicative of the "normal" earning power of an enterprise, exclusive of the effect of any unusual or non-recurring transactions occurring during the particular reporting period. Opposed to this concept, is the theory that the income statement should be "all-inclusive" in the sense that it reports the results of all "revenue and expense (including losses) given accounting recognition during that period. This practice assures that the income statements for a period of years will disclose completely the entire income history of that period."[10] The American Institute of Accountants has taken a position in

---

[7] "Weaknesses in Financial Reporting Caused by Improper Use of Reserves," Maurice H. Stans, *The Journal of Accountancy*, March, 1948, pp. 191-192.

[8] "Reserves for War Contingencies and Postwar Adjustments," Herbert E. Miller, *The Accounting Review*, July, 1944, p. 249.

[9] Accounting Research Bulletins Numbers 28, 31, and 35, Committee on Accounting Procedure, The American Institute of Accountants.

[Bulletins No. 28, 31, and 35 were superseded (with no major change in substance) by Chapters 6 and 8 of Accounting Research Bulletin No. 43 (in 1953). The validity of the footnoted statement is not affected by the supersession. Eds.]

[10] *Accounting Concepts and Standards Underlying Corporate Financial Statements*, American Accounting Association, 1948.

support of the first of these concepts of the income statement, and in connection therewith recommends the exclusion from the computation of net income of five broad classifications of "material" charges or credits "when their inclusion would impair the significance of net income so that misleading inferences might be drawn therefrom."[11]

It is sufficient for the purpose of this article to note that the rather broad area of management discretion in the determination of what is "material" and also what constitutes impairment of the significance of net income, would seem to open the door to a rather subjective meaning of the term income or net income. That this subjectivity *may* be employed to assist in the process of income smoothing goes without saying.

[11] Accounting Research Bulletin No. 32, Committee on Accounting Procedure, American Institute of Accountants, December, 1947. [Bulletin No. 32 was superseded (with no change in substance) by Chap. 8 of ARB No. 43 (in 1953). The quotation was retained in Chap. 8 and appears in para. 11. Chap. 8 of ARB No. 43 has been superseded by APB Opinion No. 9, "Reporting the Results of Operations" (Dec. 1966). The practices discussed here are described in paras. 9–16. The APB reversed the opinion of the Committee on Accounting Procedure with the following statement: "The Board has concluded that net income should reflect all items of profit and loss recognized during the period with the sole exception of the prior period adjustments described below. *Extraordinary items* should, however, be segregated from the results of ordinary operations and shown separately in the income statement. . . ." Eds.]

MARTIN J. WHITMAN

MARTIN J. WHITMAN (1925–   ), B.S. (hons.) 49 Syracuse; M.A. 56 New School for Social Research; C.F.A. Currently chairman of the board, The Alpha Group, Inc., New York. Author of several booklets on financial topics.

Since 1950, has held various positions with New York investment houses, including Shearson, Hammill & Co., 1950–56; Gerstley, Sunstein & Co., 1960–67; and Blair & Co., Inc., 1967–69. Became chairman of the board of The Alpha Group, Inc., in 1969. Has been a part-time lecturer on securities and valuations at Princeton University, University of Pennsylvania, and Yale University.

MARTIN SHUBIK

MARTIN SHUBIK (1926–   ), B.A. 47, M.A. 49 Toronto; A.M. 51, Ph.D. 53 Princeton. Currently professor of economics of organization, Yale University. Major publications: *Readings in Game Theory and Political Behavior* (editor, 1954), *Strategy and Market Structure* (1959), *Game Theory and Related Approaches to Social Behavior* (editor, 1964), *Essays in Mathematical Economics in Honor of Oskar Morgenstern* (editor, 1967). Frequent contributor to journals of economics and the management sciences.

Was a research consultant in management science at the General Electric Co., 1956–60, and a research scientist in mathematical economics at International Business Machines Corp., 1961–63. In 1963, he joined the Yale University economics faculty. He visited the faculties of the Universidad de Chile (1965), and the Institute for Advanced Studies, Vienna (1968 and 1970).

Principal research interests: computerization of gaming laboratories; gaming experiments and artificial intelligence; concept of threat as it appears in bargaining, game theory, and other literature; social implications of the computer and modern communications; simulation of socioeconomic systems; game theory as applied to microeconomics, welfare economics, and general equilibrium analysis; and the theory of money and financial institutions.

CORPORATE REALITY AND ACCOUNTING FOR INVESTORS

MARTIN J. WHITMAN
and MARTIN SHUBIK

PART I

Accounting is a tool—and frequently an essential one—for anyone who wishes to make seasoned judgments about corporate reality, be he investor, insider, supplier, customer, labor union representative, or government regulator. However, accounting for investors as it is visualized by much of the accounting profession and the regulatory authorities, especially the Securities and Exchange Commission, is frequently not very useful as a tool for determining anything other than what the authorities think other people think is important in the stock market. To the profession, for example, accounting for investors has two missions: first, figures should be stated "fairly" so that, second, there can be a proper determination of net income. The watchwords here are "fair" and "net income."

But the fact is that these two watchwords, whatever may be their value as an influence on short-run stock market fluctuations, are extremely limited as determinants of corporate reality; i.e., the results of the operation of a business for a period and the value of the business. The problem is that accounting is based on a relatively rigid set of limiting assumptions. Since the assumptions themselves are limited, accounting cannot be, and should not be, expected to be either realistic or to reflect fairly all the myriad situations that exist in the real world. But to the extent that accounting liberalizes the assumptions on which it is based in order to reflect reality more closely, the less useful it becomes as a system which establishes comparability among businesses and among the results within one business from one period to the next. Accounting cannot be both realistic and useful. At best, it can provide diligent and serious investors with an appropriate abstract model for the construction of objective benchmarks which they can use as *one tool* of analysis in determining their own view of corporate reality.

Concentration on the proper determination of net income also makes accounting less useful for investors because it results in either distorting or hiding important corporate disclosures. First is the fact that, contrary to the stock market view (what everyone thinks everyone else thinks about corporations), few, if any, corporate managements strive for net income when there are other methods of creating wealth which are not so heavily taxed. Second, emphasis on the proper determination of net income frequently hides more than it discloses. For example, Opinion No. 7 of the Accounting Principles Board, issued in May 1966, describes procedures to be followed in accounting for lessors so that lease accounting might "result in a fair measurement of the lessor's periodic income during the term of the lease." As a consequence of the company's attempt to measure periodic in-

SOURCE: From *Financial Executive*, Vol. XXXIX, No. 5 (May, 1971), pp. 52–56, 58, 60, 62, 64, 66, 68, 70, 72, and 81. Reprinted by permission of the Financial Executives Institute.

come fairly, which relegates other factors to some sort of limbo, no outside investor can have any good idea of what the cash income and the cash outgo is for the leasing corporation as a whole or by transaction for any period. Neither can any outside investor have any clear idea of the actual profitability of each lease as long as different numbers of leases are written each year.

Another example is Opinion No. 3 which is typical of the emphasis accountants now ascribe to net income. The Opinion states that "A statement of source and application of funds cannot supplant the income statement." Nowhere do the accountants state what is equally obvious—that an income statement cannot supplant the statement of source and application of funds, (or, for that matter, a balance sheet cannot replace an income account or a source and application of funds; a source and application cannot replace a balance sheet, and an income statement cannot replace a balance sheet). In corporate reality, everything in the accounting cycle (income account, balance sheet, surplus and cash reconciliations) not only is of various degrees of importance, but is also derived from, modified by, and related to every other component of the cycle.

(The overemphasis placed on net income in accounting for investors is not unique. In most spheres, people tend to focus on just one number. For example, in accounting for governments, the same overemphasis is usually placed on the source and application of funds; i.e., there tends to be overemphasis on balancing budgets and obtaining "favorable" balances of payments.)

It is important to understand why the accounting profession and the regulatory authorities place so much emphasis on making accounting fair and on making the goal of accounting the proper determination of net income. The basic misconceptions about accounting seem to stem from two sources:

1. A naive, simplistic view of who the investors (i.e., the users of accounting) are, what their needs are, and how these needs should be satisfied.
2. A stereotyped, old-fashioned view of how companies and their stocks should be analyzed.

NAIVE, SIMPLISTIC VIEW OF INVESTORS

Why have net income and its corollary, earnings per share, received such undue emphasis in analysis? There are several reasons:

1. They *are important*, even though their importance is overstated in corporate analysis.
2. They are related to other factors in wealth creation; i.e., reported accounting profits are frequently the basis for realized and unrealized appreciation.
3. There is confusion between economic profits and accounting profits.
4. There is a failure to distinguish between stock market analysis on the one hand and corporate analysis on the other.

Reported accounting results, and earnings per share in particular, are especially important in market analysis. What a company has to report may influence the price at which its stock will sell. As a matter of fact, two things seem most important in making a stock promotable (that is, making it susceptible to selling at a high price/earnings ratio): identification as a glamour industry and a favorable trend in earnings per share. However, making stock promotable is related to the stock market and is not necessarily an integral part of corporate analysis. *And, in market analysis, one is not interested in what is actually going on in a company, but rather in what one thinks others think.*

That part of the financial community involved with common stocks and their fluctuations over time periods of not more than, say, six months to a year, are not that much interested in the real corporate facts of life. Rather, they are interested primarily in trying to figure out what other people think; they are interested in what John Maynard Keynes called "the average opinion of the average opinion" and in the kind of thinking "Adam Smith" discussed in his book, *The Money Game*. Reported earnings are important on Wall Street not because they really are so vital in valuing a business, but rather because everyone on Wall Street thinks that everyone else thinks that reported earnings are vital. Correspondingly, although financial position is vital in appraising any business and its economic potential, most common stock investors give it little or no weight in security analysis because they think no one else thinks financial position is important.

What is the rationale for this Wall Street irrationality, this emphasis on figuring out (or influencing) investor psychology rather than on purchasing and selling securities based on abstract concepts of underlying value? There seem to be four general reasons why this is the way things are:

1. *There is a lack of knowledge.* The investor usually has little intimate knowledge about a company, its management, its direction, its opportunities, and its problems. And he usually has little opportunity to find out. Even the best securities documents—for example, SEC prospectuses and lengthy institutional studies—are sometimes superficial in terms of what is essential to understanding a company. Further, a typical investor rarely studies these documents, and, even if he did, he might not be in a position to judge them. The performance investor, on the other hand, could not care less about voluminous detail concerning a company; even if he did, he rarely has the time or training for careful study no matter how big the organization behind them.

2. *There is a lack of control of a company.* The investor is purely passive and is almost never in a position to alter the way a company's resources are used.

3. *There is limited exposure for the individual investor.* Because the investor deals in highly marketable securities, he is flexible and can move readily in and out of situations.

4. *The economics of stock market investing are directed toward the short run.* In the short run, psychology will have a much greater influence on market prices than underlying corporate facts, and almost everybody knows this. As a result, there are many pressures making people in the "Street" short-run conscious. First, there is the tendency for money managers to be judged by their peers and, more importantly, by their customers on how much appreciation they obtained for portfolios in recent periods—sort of a "what have you done for me lately" attitude. Second, there is a finance factor—those who borrow heavily to finance a portfolio need to have near-term upside market action because, if the value of the portfolio goes down, their losses as a percentage of equity can be horrendous, and, if the value of the portfolio does not go up,

the attrition inherent in interest costs can be unsettling. Finally, short-run considerations tend to govern investment decisions simply because many people don't realize that there are factors other than near-term price performance in judging investments or they are untrained in analyzing these other ways of investing.

The accounting rules and regulations seem designed largely to satisfy the needs of these average-opinion-of-average-opinion investors, who have two characteristics: they really don't care about what is going on in business, and they have a vital interest in near-term market fluctuations.

STEREOTYPED VIEW OF CORPORATE ANALYSIS

Security Analysis, by Graham, Dodd, and Cottle (the revised edition published in 1962), is a typical and in many ways superior book about so-called fundamental (as distinct from technical) security analysis. In that book, the authors observed (page 443):

"The basic components in a common stock valuation are fourfold, viz:
"1. The expected future earnings
"2. The expected future dividends
"3. The capitalization rates—or multipliers—of the dividends and earnings
"4. The asset values."

In typical fundamentalist fashion, the asset value factor is denigrated by Graham, Dodd, and Cottle, who state on page 445: "The balance sheet factors enter into the valuation in two different ways. First, the indexes of financial strength—supplied by the working capital ratio and the common stock ratio—exert an influence upon the capitalization rate of earnings and dividends. Second, the asset value per share of stock—in terms both of all tangible assets and of current assets alone—may, in somewhat exceptional cases, affect the final valuation."

The authors realize that using future earning power (of which dividend rates and capitalization rates are functions) as a valuation cornerstone has limits. As they say on page 437, "Public utility common stocks have qualities of stability and predictability which make them ideal for formal appraisal. In theory, the mere factor of variability in earnings would not be a bar to a worthwhile valuation, provided that we could be reasonably certain what the average earning power would prove to be. But in practice, we find that the more a company's results are subject to fluctuation, the less predictable becomes the future average. Thus the best industries for valuation are those which do not show large profit declines in periods of recession. Such industries would include, in addition to public utilities, the insurance companies, chain stores, chemical and pharmaceutical companies, can manufacturers, and others." It should be realized that, when the fundamentalists speak of future earnings, they mean reported accounting earnings.

The real limitations of a Graham, Dodd, and Cottle analysis go much farther than might be indicated by saying it is a good tool in the appraisal of public utility commons and a poorer tool for appraisal of commons of volatile companies. Indeed, it seems to us that this stereotyped analysis is of such limited usefulness that it should be viewed properly as a special-purpose analysis rather than as the standard.

Here's the rub! The accountants, the regulatory authorities, and the so-called fundamentalists have taken a limited tool of analysis which is useful for appraising large, stable public utilities which enjoy little, or no, tax shelter; which reinvest virtually all their retained earnings in their own industry; and whose common stockholders tend to be non-speculative and dividend-income conscious; and they have assumed that this is either the appropriate tool of analysis for almost all investor-owned companies or that everyone else thinks that it is an appropriate tool of analysis.

In various sections of *Security Analysis*, the authors point out that their tools of analysis are limited for the appraisal of natural resources companies, real estate companies, certain financial institutions, secondary (i.e., unpopular) common stocks selling at ultra-low prices, high growth rate companies, and high technology companies, among others. It is of crucial importance to examine systematically those factors which make analysis based on accounting earnings as reported so limited an appraisal tool. To accomplish this, six overlapping factors must be examined:

- The conventional fundamental tools of analysis become less useful as accounting for investors becomes further removed from actual corporate experience. Accounting for investors becomes increasingly removed from actual experience in companies with opportunities for tax-sheltered activities. For example, reported accounting results are an accurate gauge of the values and results of Consolidated Edison, but reported accounting results tell little or nothing about Tishman Realty & Construction because the company strives for tax shelter and tries to create wealth by methods other than net income, which is taxable, and the values in the business are determined by appraisals which have little relationship to accounting figures.
- The conventional fundamental tools of analysis which stress reported net income results are especially limited in the analysis of companies where management goals are to create values by having realized or unrealized appreciation rather than ordinary income. For example, earnings do not mean much for investment trusts. It is easy to recognize that earnings have little value for investment trusts because precise market prices for portfolio securities are available to outsiders, and they can readily measure unrealized appreciation. But just because other managements do not have precise daily market prices by which their asset values can be measured does not mean that, given a choice, many would not elect to strive for asset appreciation by means other than earnings; i.e., they act about their company's assets just the way investment trust managements act about theirs. Such investment trust-like behavior pervades management attitudes in real estate situations, natural resource discovery companies, and high technology enterprises, among others, including practically all companies which take advantage of opportunities for tax shelter.
- Insofar as conventional tools are useful, they are useful for the valuation of short-run price behavior of common stocks rather than for the valuation of companies. There are times, of course, when a company's best self-interest is identical with the common stockholder's short-run best interest, and a good case can be made for the thesis that a company's best interests are exactly the

same as its very long-term stockholders. Less obvious, though, is the fact that a company's interests may be far from identical with that of many common stockholders. This is especially true where common stockholders are not permanent investors i.e., where stock market fluctuations have an important effect on them.

For example, two areas of conflict between companies and stockholders are in reporting earnings and paying dividends. Stockholders tend to want companies to report earnings on as favorable a basis as possible even if doing so carries an income tax penalty, and they also want companies to maintain or increase dividends even though the companies may have highly productive uses for retained cash. Many stockholders want earnings and dividends, even at the expense of long-term corporate well-being, because they believe earnings and dividends affect the near-term price performance of common stocks.

The areas of conflict sometimes are more complicated than in this example because *the price at which a stock* sells can be a real, but non-accounting, corporate asset or liability. As a matter of fact, the most important asset a company has may be a market valuation for its stock far higher than would be dictated by corporate reality. When this is case, the corporate best self-interest tends to be identical with the best self-interest of the short-run stockholder. This situation usually occurs when companies are in the acquisition business and are continually trying to issue equity for earnings assets. The management focuses on what will get the stock price up, not what would be in the best self-interests of the company if it did not have opportunities to issue equity securities, the immediate market value of which will be of prime interest to the recipients. In any event, the focus on earnings (and dividends) is based essentially on stock market, rather than corporate, considerations.

Graham, Dodd, and Cottle are interested in where a stock will sell in periods (say up to one year) just ahead rather than in what a business is worth as a business. They, and other fundamentalists, never really seem to make the distinction that the variables one would use to appraise a business are usually quite different than the variables that one would use to estimate where a stock might sell today and in the foreseeable future. Graham, Dodd, and Cottle, for example, seem to restrict their discussion of this point to statements that book values are more important in valuing private corporations than investor-owned corporations.

The truth is that for analyzing many, if not most, companies, fundamental analysis is really not very fundamental. Insofar as analyzing a common stock is concerned, fundamental analysis focuses on the variables—reported earnings in particular—that are not necessarily vital for appraising a specific business, but which the fundamentalist thinks everybody else thinks is important. In this sense, the fundamentalist gets pretty close to the cousin he sometimes tends to abhor, the technician. Both tend to be psychological.

For all its limitations, the fundamentalist approach tends to approximate corporate reality in two situations and to be a good measure of corporate reality in these situations:

(a) Stable, predictable businesses where management has little choice other than to strive for taxable earnings and where reinvestment of retained earnings is in the same operation in which the company is already engaged.

Public utilities are the best example of such types of companies. To a lesser extent, giant manufacturing companies, such as Union Carbide and General Motors, can also use this type of analysis successfully.

(b) In a limited sense, too, the analysis is useful in understanding the *modus operandi* of managements which have tended to be acutely conscious of the short-run performance of their outstanding stock, such as Gulf & Western, Teledyne, and Occidental Petroleum. These managements have used favorable trends in reported earnings to obtain a relatively high stock price and then issued equity to buy earnings assets. Because the successful sale of the issue depends in part on its market value, an inflated stock price may be the most important asset these companies have. Peculiarly enough, the conventional tool of analysis—reported earnings—is useful in appraising management of companies like public utilities for their abilities as operators of businesses. Yet, in the case of the companies oriented to the stock market, the ability to report earnings reflects management abilities, not so much as operators, but as stock promoters and investors. The more they can inflate the price of their stock, the less stock their companies are likely to have to issue to buy a given amount of reported earnings. The fewer shares issued to obtain a given amount of earnings, the larger the per-share earnings will be and the better the growth trend will look.

• While everyone thinks that everyone else thinks that reported earnings are a principal determinant of stock market prices, there seems to have been very little research on the question. As a matter of fact, we believe investors (as distinct from short-run market traders), when given sufficient disclosure, tend to be corporate realists: they tend to strip away accounting veils to find underlying values.

• In economic reality, to say that values are determined by future earning power is to say nothing. First of all, future earning power means economic earnings, which may or may not be the same as accounting earnings. Second, in the market, it is just as true that values determine earning power as that earning power determines values. Something may be worth 100 because it earns 10; but the reverse is also true: if the market will pay 100, it may be possible to make it earn 10. Put simply, the old financial saw that assets have value only insofar as they can be used to create earnings is only a half-truth. It is equally true that earnings have value only insofar as they can be used to create assets.

Conventional security analysis is based in part on the thesis that the past earnings record is the best predictor of future earnings performance. However, past earnings may be no better a predictor than asset values. In any event, one is no substitute for the other. As a matter of fact, placing primary emphasis on the past earnings record as a predictor of future performance in companies other than public utilities is fraught with danger in part because there is little evidence that the past will serve as a predictor and in part because the competition from those who place heavy reliance on the past earnings record may be so great that companies with good earnings outlooks become so overpriced that their securities become distinctly unattractive.

• Both fundamental analysts and accountants tend to take one-sided and, therefore, unrealistic views of how financial data should be used. They assume that certain factors—e.g., net income and dividends—have positive values, and that other factors—e.g., lack of dividends and losses—have negative values. Nothing could be farther from the truth. Any factor can be negative or positive, depending on the position of the company and investor purposes.

This one-sided attitude toward corporate analysis on the part of accountants is seen not only in the opinions of the Accounting Principles Board which emphasize the determination of net income and earnings per share to the exclusion of other factors, but also in statements of leading industry figures. For example, in 1965, Herman W. Bevis, then a member of the APB, in the section on stockholders' needs in *Corporate Financial Reporting in a Competitive Economy* (Macmillan, New York; 1965), states (page 50): "If one were forced to choose from among the financial statements that which bears most directly upon the stockholder's primary interest, it would, of course, be the income statement. And, if one were forced to choose the most significant of all figures thereon, it would have to be net income for the year." However, be you an accountant, stockholder, or regulator, you are not forced to make the choice he describes. And Bevis does not explain whether he refers to all stockholders in all corporate situations when he describes the income statement as the "stockholder's primary interest." Such emphasis (assuming one were forced to do anything) on net income is appropriate only to corporate situations resembling public utilities or situations where stockholders are interested primarily in market reality rather than in corporate reality.

There are numerous examples of how financial data disclosed should be interpreted differently in varying corporate contexts and investor-interest contexts. Put simply, making up the type of general rule that Bevis put forth is a poor substitute for knowing your business.

Take dividends, for example. Fundamentalists tend to think high dividends are favorable for stockholders. Graham, Dodd, and Cottle (page 481) compare New Amsterdam Casualty Insurance Company with New Hampshire Fire Insurance Company for the 10 years, 1938–1947, saying, "The relationships of these figures are surprisingly pat. New Hampshire paid twice the dividend of New Amsterdam and sold twice as high, although its earnings were just half as great. Incidentally, the price of New Amsterdam averaged about one-third less than book value while that of New Hampshire was only 8 per cent less—although average earnings on book value were 12.5 per cent and 4.3 per cent, respectively."

As of the end of 1947, it was clear that it was better to have owned New Hampshire Fire for the previous 10 years.

But the meaningful question to ask as of the beginning of 1948 was which stock should the investor buy at that time, the low- or high-dividend payer. As it turned out, New Amsterdam was the far better buy for, as Graham, Dodd, and Cottle point out (page 482), "In 1948, after considerable prodding by stockholders, New Amsterdam Casualty began a gradual advance in its dividend from the $1.00 rate it had maintained for several years previously. In early 1950 the dividend rate had reached $1.40, and the price of the shares had risen to 42, within a few points of that of New Hampshire."

What caused the relatively good performance of New Amsterdam from 1948 to 1950? The fact that dividends were more liberal, or the fact that there was a trend to increased dividends (or something not related to dividends, such as stockholders being influenced by management's favorable responses to prodding)? If the primary cause of better market performance was a good trend of dividend payments rather than a high rate of dividend payments, the performance-oriented investor would rather have small dividend payments which are periodically increased than a constant high rate of payments.

The same performance investor might feel otherwise, though, if he invests in a security about which he is uncertain, but which he feels has reasonable upside potential. Then a high dividend rate may be a factor which limits downside risk. But even this is two-sided. A high dividend rate frequently can be counted on to provide something of a floor for stock prices, but reduction of a dividend frequently can be counted on to cause a stock's price to plummet as people who had invested for income, or to find a floor, dump their holdings. Thus, had New Hampshire been forced to reduce its more liberal dividends during the period 1938–1947, it could have well been a far poorer market performer than New Amsterdam. Furthermore, New Hampshire's management might have harmed the legitimate interests of the company itself, its creditors (in this case its policyholders), and its stockholders. Graham, Dodd, and Cottle think all this is provided for by a liberal dividend (except in the case of "high growth rate" stocks).

In truth, a New Amsterdam-New Hampshire comparison à la Graham, Dodd, and Cottle is not very meaningful. It happens that the Graham, Dodd, and Cottle analysis did not take into account a number of crucial factors which justify a considerably more conservative dividend policy by New Amsterdam. The factors they used in their analysis were (1) 10-year average dividend; (2) a 10-year average increase in liquidating value plus a 10-year average dividend payment; (3) average book value; and (4) average earnings on book value.

Factors they did not consider included (1) capital and surplus as a percentage of loss reserves; (2) capital and surplus as a percentage of annual premium income; (3) senior securities as a percentage of total assets; and (4) underwriting profit margins. The comparison of these factors for the two companies is shown in Table 1.

The figures in the table point out that New Amsterdam had greater need to retain cash and earnings to meet the requirements of its insurance operations than did New Hampshire. Its dividend policy should have been much more conservative than New Hampshire's, even though New Amsterdam's underwriting profit margins were better than New Hampshire's. New Amsterdam's capital and surplus had to support a larger insurance operation—with

Table 1

	New Amsterdam	New Hampshire
Capital and surplus as a percentage of loss reserves 1947	70.9%	250.5%
Capital and surplus as a percentage of net premiums written 1947	50.2%	61.1%
Senior securities as a percentage of total assets 1947	54.1%	31.8%
Underwriting profit margin; i.e., combined ratio 1943–1947	96.3% (estimate)	102.1%

greater liabilities and premium income—than did New Hampshire. The fact that New Amsterdam generated such a large return on book value when compared with New Hampshire (12.5 per cent vs. 4.3 per cent according to Graham, Dodd, and Cottle) reflected only that New Amsterdam had more assets employed on its equity base.

Besides the need for differences in dividend policy, New Amsterdam should have been different from New Hampshire in many other respects. Because its liabilities were so large, New Amsterdam's investment operations had to be less flexible than New Hampshire's. Both legal requirements and business common sense dictated that New Amsterdam limit its investment in common stocks and other equities. Notice, for example, the difference in investment policies: 54 per cent of New Amsterdam's total assets was in bonds, compared with 33 per cent for New Hampshire. And insurance income account figures do not take into account the fact that New Hampshire had far more hidden earnings on its investments than New Amsterdam. The investment income accounts for both New Amsterdam and New Hampshire reflect only the cash returns they receive on portfolio investments; i.e., rents, dividends, and interest. The net investment income figures do not reflect the fact that a holder of common stocks has an equity in the earnings of portfolio companies which are not paid out. Whether or not this fact is ever reflected in insurance company liquidating value where common stocks are valued at market is questionable.

As a highly leveraged insurance operation, New Amsterdam, in 1938 or 1948, probably had a far greater potential for capital appreciation than did New Hampshire, regardless of its dividend policy, provided its insurance operations could be made profitable. This would be true even if its investment policies were unimaginative; for example, if the company was merely buying bonds at a time when interest rates were continually increasing. (As a matter of fact, this is what happened in the life insurance industry and to life insurance stocks in the 20 years after World War II.)

Incidentally, almost all insurance companies are dollar averagers in their investment policies, or, at any event, their insurance departments generally generate cash to be invested either out of underwriting profits or out of increasing premium volume or both. Thus, investment income tends to increase most rapidly for those companies which have the poorest investment performance in terms of appreciation. Given securities with relatively constant payout rates, new money invested in falling markets will earn higher returns and new money invested in rising markets will earn lower returns.

Part of the reason the net investment income of life insurance companies increased so much faster than fire insurance companies during the 1950s was that life companies were investing in debt securities while interest rates were rising (i.e., bond prices were falling), while fire companies were investing in common stocks while dividend returns were falling (i.e., stock prices were going up at a faster rate than dividends were rising).

It is not that Graham, Dodd, and Cottle are wrong *per se* in using such a limited number of factors in comparing New Amsterdam with New Hampshire, or that Herman Bevis is not describing a real world when he directs emphasis toward net income for the year. Rather, they apply standards to all security analysis and to all accounting for investors that are most appropriate to analysis of public utilities or are designed to fill the needs of people who are interested in making investments which are based on what they think other people think rather than on an understanding of the dynamics of particular corporate situations. One cannot understand the dynamics of insurance industry operations merely by looking at a few stereotyped factors—dividends, earnings, book values. Rather, one has to understand the nature of the liabilities, the quality of the assets, and the profit and risk potential inherent in the insurance operations alone. In plain English, one has to understand how the business ticks. And the way the insurance business operates is not the way the public utility business operates or the way the department store business operates or the way the auto parts business operates, etc., though they all have common denominators.

In our view, the goal of accounting for investors should be to supply enough information, wherever possible, so that an intelligent, diligent investor who is willing to apply himself can get a good idea of how a business operates and is able to appraise it based on this view. Knowledge of how businesses operate cannot be obtained if one concentrates on a stereotyped view of what is important and not important. It is time for the accounting profession to graduate from the view that either all businesses are like public utilities or that the profession's mission is to see that investors who are naive and not really interested in corporate dynamics are not misled.

In the paragraphs above, we went through some of the diverse factors that go into a rational analysis of the several meanings of dividends to stockholders and of the several factors that ought to go into the analysis of any insurance operation. This is only part of the analysis of a security, even though it is the only part that appears to be discussed by the conventional literature on security analysis and accounting for investors. Another element of security analysis consists of a close look at securities, and the companies behind them, to determine the probability of takeover by outsiders. Further, managements can be appraised not only as operators (which is how we and Graham, Dodd, and Cottle approached the New Amsterdam and New Hampshire managements above), but as investors engaged in mergers and acquisitions. Looked at this way, many new elements enter the analysis, not the least of which is the price at which a company's common stock sells. That price can be either the corporation's most important asset or most important liability, depending on which viewpoint a particular person holds.

PART II

SEC AND CORPORATE DISCLOSURE

It seems to us as financial analysts that in recent years the Securities and Exchange Commission has taken the position that the primary purpose of disclosure regulations is to prevent manipulative trading practices from being perpetrated against people who are interested primarily in market reality. The Commission sometimes may be unmindful that disclosure is an essential tool for serious investors, who are interested primarily in determining corporate reality. Our position is that the basic standard for determining what should be disclosed and what should not be disclosed (as distinct from when something should be disclosed) should be based on the needs of the serious investors without placing undue burdens on issuers. But the present SEC standard, though not stated explicitly, may be based more on providing whatever information is necessary to prevent the "average investors" from being misled.

The principal disclosure acts are the Securities Acts of 1933 and 1934, as amended. The acts themselves are skeletal. Most of the meat of the acts comes out of administrative rules and regulations, presumably originated by the staff and approved by the commissioners. The acts, for practical purposes, really deal with three related areas of regulation—broker-dealers; trading (i.e., prevention of manipulative practices); and disclosure. For our purposes here, broker-dealer regulation is not germane.

In our view, there has been a tendency for the SEC more and more to view disclosure as merely a branch of trading regulation. Its efforts in this area have been to try to insure fairer markets at the expense of informing those investors who really want to know something about companies. The SEC has not been alone in this respect—the legal profession seems to have followed suit. For example, in 1967, the Practising Law Institute published a book, *Disclosure Requirements*, of which at least two-thirds was involved with unfair and manipulative trading practices rather than disclosure *per se*.

The SEC emphasis on insuring fair markets rather than on informing investors goes in three directions. First, there are 10-b-5 matters, which deal with the timing of the disclosure. It is the Commission's position in the Texas Gulf and Merrill Lynch cases, the most highly publicized 10-b-5 matters, that it is illegal for anyone who comes under a broad definition of "insider" to use, for trading purposes, information that influences the market price of a stock unless that information is available to all investors. So many insiders play it safe and withhold all sorts of information from all sorts of investors, including serious investors, who are not particularly attuned to ask for, or to take advantage of, trading information.

The second area of disclosure regulation, covered by 10-b-6 and related rules, concerns what issuers are prohibited from disclosing. There is not much question that this area is far more important than 10-b-5 from the points of view of both issuers and serious investors, even though it received not nearly as much attention as 10-b-5. By 10-b-6 type matters, we mean SEC rules and regulations which prohibit disclosures which "condition markets" during periods of "distribution." Such prohibitions on disclosures are principally before, during, and after an issue is in registration under the 1933 act (i.e., prospectus rules) or in connection with certain proxy solicitations under the 1934 act. If the basic standard is to be disclosure for serious investors interested in corporate reality without placing undue burdens on issuers, anyone would be free to disclose, at any time, any opinions they have, or any facts or projections they believe to be true, provided that required disclosures are also made.

The third area of disclosure regulation is the one that is most pertinent to this article—What Must Be Disclosed. The cornerstone of What Must Be Disclosed in the SEC scheme of things is the financial statements. In one respect, the SEC does an outstanding job in the financial statement area in terms of its requirements and standards for independent, certified audits. In two other respects, however, the Commission does less well in providing the conditions for the flow of information to those interested in determining corporate reality. The first is caused by their failure to realize how limited the role of accounting may be in the analysis of situations not like the public utilities. The second is caused by their failure to realize how serious investors use accounting data to make determinations of what are the meaningful corporate values. Both failures stem directly from the Commission's preoccupation with satisfying what the Commission thinks are the needs of average investors.

The 1968 Sunray matter is one of the best examples of how the SEC can give accounting such importance that key disclosures are denied to those who really want to know something about a company. Sunray was a nonpublic utility type of company insofar as the uses and limitations of accounting were concerned; estimates of oil reserves were crucial to understanding the company. Use of such estimates can easily mislead those who are naive and those who are more interested in thinking about what other people think than in corporate facts.

Sunray DX Oil Company, in 1968, issued a merger proxy statement asking its stockholders to approve the merger of Sunray into Sun Oil Company. A stockholder brought suit claiming the Sunray proxy statement was deficient because it did not go into sufficient detail about the value of certain probable oil reserves in the Santa Barbara Channel off California. There was no dispute that these reserves were extremely valuable, though there were differences as to just how valuable. The U.S. District Court agreed with the stockholder that the Sunray proxy material was deficient. Sunray appealed to the Circuit Court; the Securities and Exchange Commission, siding with Sunray, submitted an *amicus curiae* brief to the Circuit Court arguing that the Sunray proxy material "properly omitted estimates of probable oil reserves in an offshore California lease and anticipated earnings from it." The Commission went on to argue, "The district court's opinion could be construed as requiring the inclusion in proxy material of figures representing the estimated number of barrels of Sunray's 'probable' oil reserves and the anticipated future income from those reserves. If so construed, the opinion would be contrary to the Commission's traditional information to be included in proxy material." The Commission went on to say that it would not have such information included because investors "would attribute to any numerical estimates of probable reserves a degree of certainty which isn't warranted."

The Commission's position in Sunray is understandable if one grants in all situations that investors are supposed to place primary reliance on reported accounting results, and that the Commission's primary, or sole, mission in disclosure is to keep naive investors from being misled. This latter point is especially important when one looks at the way unscrupulous promoters work. Basically, they are tempted to seek out situations with which to fool the naive where accounting is least meaningful and undisciplined estimates most important. Such promotable entities besides natural resource situations (which Sunray was) include companies characterized by high technology, discovery, or tax shelter. If the Commission allows estimates in literature it reviews, it feels it is opening a Pandora's box, at least insofar as it dilutes investor attention by giving investors more information than the SEC deems material and that some of this information would be given irresponsibly.

From the point of view of any serious investor interested in trying to ascertain whether or not to vote for a Sunray-Sun merger based on comparative corporate values, the Commission's position was an absolute abortion. It is interesting to look at the reasons why the position was so ill-advised from this point of view.

First, it is obvious that estimates of probable reserves were important if one wanted to have any idea of what Sunray was really worth.

Second, even though the Commission properly assumes that there is a degree of certainty in accounting results not present in other types of results, especially estimates of probable oil reserves, this does not mean by any means that there is a degree of business reality involved in accounting results not present in other measures. Numerical estimates of probable reserves, as long as they are made with a modicum of responsibility, in a tax-sheltered, extractive industry happen to have a degree of reality, materiality, and meaningfulness that could not possibly be present in accounting figures. If anything, accounting figures are designed to mislead in tax-sheltered, extractive endeavors, since an extractive company may maximize its well-being through creating wealth in the ground without reporting it as accounting income or as an accounting asset. Furthermore, there is a strong tendency for average opinions of average-opinion investors to use accounting results with a degree of certainty not warranted by business reality.

Third, appraising management is extremely important to sophisticated investors. The quality and quantity of appraisals made, or used, by management give intelligent investors good clues as to managerial calibre and interests.

Fourth, one can ask also why excluding estimates of probable reserves from a Sunray proxy protects any Sunray stockholder whether intelligent or stupid or whether interested primarily in corporate reality or market trading. In a buy situation, investor protection would require presenting information with a conservative bias. But in a sell situation, stockholders should be given some idea of just how good things might be.

Sunray was, of course, a sell situation; the Sunray stockholders were being asked to give up their Sunray stock for something else, Sun Oil stock. However, to the SEC, financial statements are the cornerstone of disclosure, and financial statements are supposed to have a conservative bias. The SEC's attitude precluded the disclosure of the estimated value of Sunray's underground reserves.

The SEC is largely inactive in promulgating accounting rules. Rather, it has relied primarily on the accounting profession, which adheres to the concept of the fair presentation of net income on a conservative basis. Furthermore, the SEC's most rigorous statute is the Securities Act of 1933, which refers primarily to "Offers to Buy" rather than "Offers to Sell."

From a layman's point of view, there seems to be little in the 1933 and 1934 Securities Acts themselves to suggest that the SEC must adopt as its basic disclosure policy protection of an "average investor" with "average investor" really defined as someone who does not know and does not care to know much about the company in which he is investing and who has a vital interest in near-term fluctuations in the prices of stocks. It is this latter point that we think got the SEC into a position where it thinks of disclosures, not as something to inform investors, but rather as something to prohibit manipulative practices.

To us, the acts themselves seem to indicate that disclosures should be directed toward investors intelligent enough to use them. In our view, these investors are interested primarily in corporate, not market, reality. The acts seem to have visualized that two levels of investor protection are necessary: broker-dealer and trading is one level, disclosure for the investor is the other. In broker-dealer and trading spheres, absolute protections were deemed necessary because there really were no other ways investors could be protected. Disclosure is something else again. Here, self-protection should have been the rule: give an investor enough information and if he does not use it to protect himself, the loss is his. From a security analyst's point of view, the investor himself should be able to make up his mind whether estimates of Sunray's probable oil reserves are material, as long as such estimates are provided him in a manner that permits him to determine how much weight, if any, he ought to give to those estimates as compared with, say, Sunray's five-year earnings record.

Further indications to us that the 1933 and 1934 acts were not necessarily designed to give disclosures for average investors lies in the Investment Company Act of 1940, which seems to have been designed to protect average investors. In the 1940 act, Congress seemed to be saying, "If you are a naive investor, do not expect to get real protection from the 1933 and 1934 acts. Rather, invest in investment companies and you will receive not only professional management, but also far greater SEC protection under the 1940 act than the Commission can properly afford you under the 1933 and 1934 acts."

The present emphasis of the SEC and the accounting profession on average investors and what the SEC and the accounting profession think the average investor ought to be interested in would merely be silly if it weren't potentially dangerous. The potential danger becomes apparent when one looks at what the SEC prohibits issuers and insiders from disclosing, the so-called 10-b-6 limitations. Many 10-b-6 type strictures arise because, as in Sunray, the Commission seems to want primary emphasis placed on financial statements even where financial statements give few, if any, clues to business reality.

Briefly, our reasons for thinking the present emphasis is so misdirected are as follows:

- The average investor is not much interested in SEC disclosures and does not use them. The serious investor *is* interested. Why not set the disclosure standards best suited to those users who actually read prospectuses and merger proxies?
- The present system has not worked, judging by the number of speculative bubbles that quite apparently made up so much of 1967–1969 trading activity.
- Information that the SEC precludes from being disseminated publicly tends to be disseminated privately. In the real world every new issue market, and indeed, virtually every active market is, in our opinion, conditioned by word of mouth, which tends to magnify the damage caused by the SEC's strictures on what must not be done during distributions.
- The present system frequently prevents investors who are interested in corporate reality from obtaining publicly information that is valuable to them, such as management opinions, real estate appraisals, or news of new developments. The SEC indulges in many semantic fictions, one of which is that, during distributions, investors should be given only "material facts," with the definition of what is a material fact determined by the Commission. To most investors in most situations, management's thoughts and opinions about the future are material facts. The Commission disagrees.

- The present system places undue burdens on issuers not only in terms of limiting free speech, for example, while an issue is in registration, but also in barring actual corporate activities. For example, companies will terminate or indefinitely postpone acquisition negotiations while an issue is in registration.
- The present system, with all its artificialities in the disclosure area, creates disrespect for the SEC, which carries over into other areas where the Commission may be making important and positive contributions.
- The present system, which in part is directed toward providing disclosures to satisfy the presumed needs of short-run market speculators, gives these groups a degree of respectability they might not otherwise have. The SEC's disclosure attitudes seem to do little to encourage investors who are interested primarily in market reality to become more interested in corporate reality.
- The securities market has an economic function in channeling the nation's resources. If it is not based in great part on corporate reality, these resources are going to be misallocated. As a matter of fact, we think the market is so irrational in relation to corporate reality that it is fortunate that the securities market channels so much smaller a proportion of the nation's resources than was the case in the 1920s. Changes have come about because of the growth of governmental investing on federal, state, and local levels, the increasing amount of debt financing done through private placements, and the large amount of equity financing done through corporate retention of cash and retained earnings. However, if the market continued to channel resources as it did during the speculative trends during 1967 to 1969, the country might have ended up with an electronics or computer leasing conglomerate in the middle of each block serviced by a franchised hamburger stand on one corner and a nursing home on the other.

In taking a new approach, the Securities and Exchange Commission should give up many of its old semantic myths. The trouble with saying something, even if you know it is untrue, is that if you say it long enough, you start to believe it.

There are three myths which are particularly burdensome to us. We have already pointed out the first—that what the SEC thinks is a material fact is not necessarily what those involved in using facts consider either material or fact. Investors ought to be able to get more facts which the SEC does not now consider either material or fact. The second is that the SEC states its goal under the 1933 act is to provide "full disclosure." Nonsense. What can be provided is at best adequate disclosure. The third has to do with the SEC requirement that the cover page of every 1933 act prospectus carries the legend in bold face type that the Commission has not "passed upon the accuracy or adequacy of this prospectus. Any representation to the contrary is a criminal offense." But try to issue a prospectus which the Commission has not passed on! Indeed, new rules have been put into operation under which the Commission will review cursorily certain prospectuses which meet certain requirements. The purpose of the new rule is to relieve the staff workload in reviewing registration statements even though it is a criminal offense to state that such work is done by anybody at the SEC.

A FINAL WORD

Accounting is a set of conventions which provides a traditional and highly useful guidepost or benchmark for the sophisticated and intelligent investor who is primarily interested in what is really going on within companies. It also provides a surefire method for misleading all others by presenting them with irrelevant "facts." These others include the industrious but stupid and those who are more interested in ascertaining factors which they think will affect near-term stock market performance—for example, reported accounting earnings—than they are in ascertaining what is really going on in a company.

Both the stupid investor and the market players, whether stupid or brilliant, are perfectly capable of misleading themselves, but often they will be helped by promoters. Two excellent ways to mislead are to present information that the individual does not understand or to present information which is in accordance with generally accepted accounting principles, but which, instead of giving meaningful corporate information, gives market information which investors think other investors will think is important. Thus, in some instances, "full disclosure" arising out of generally accepted accounting principles may be one of the best ways to confuse.

Does this statement mean that we are opposed to current accounting, or that great revisions should be made in order to protect the "typical investor" (whoever he may be)? Not at all. If the typical investor is to be protected, the major revisions that need to be made are in his brain and psychological make up. There are overwhelming reasons which lead us to conclude that no single accounting system yet invented or to be invented will be sufficient for all industries, all purposes, and all people. A different stress is needed if accounting is to be used for internal control of an industry than if it is to be used for investment and over-all evaluation. The meaning of fixed assets may be extremely different when evaluating a railroad or an oil company.

If we are so convinced that different stress is needed for different industries and purposes, then why not invent thousands of accounting systems where each one fits a special industry and purpose? The answer to that is simple. If you are a serious professional, that is exactly what you do and that is exactly what we do. However, to coordinate the use of different special accounting systems, one needs a benchmark or central system with which to start; that is exactly the purpose that generally accepted accounting principles should serve. It is the same in any science or profession. The heart specialist, if he is any good, utilizes much specialized knowledge about how hearts function. Furthermore, he knows where the general descriptions of how the heart works are incorrect, but he still uses the general descriptions to establish a means of communicating with other doctors. In the same way, standard accounting procedures provide a common but highly limited language which enables professionals to begin to communicate with each other. As soon as they wish to become specific, however, they will start to speak different languages, such as Accounting for the Professional Investor for the Chemical Industry.

A professional investor must be a translator. He has to recognize the language being spoken and put it into his own words. Often the accounting information available will have been produced to satisfy governmental or organizational requirements. In this form, the information may not answer his questions.

Interestingly enough, an entire profession has grown up out of taking relatively rigid and precise accounting and legal concepts and interpreting economic events so that they either meet or fail to meet those relatively rigid definitions. The profession is Income Tax Regulation and Counsel. Federal income taxation is, in effect, an accounting system with a relatively fixed definition of income. However, everybody knows that economic net income and net income for tax purposes are frequently quite different things. The name of the game for law-abiding taxpayers is to have economic net income and to avoid having it called net income for tax purposes, such as, for example, depreciating a fixed asset much faster for tax purposes than the property actually depreciates for economic purposes.

The sophisticated investor should view accounting principles the way the sophisticated tax advisor looks at the Internal Revenue Code and related rules and regulations—for the tax advisor, the Code provides benchmarks to be used to minimize income taxes; for the investor, accounting principles provide benchmarks to be used to determine reality.

B. **FINANCIAL REPORTING OBJECTIVES AND STRATEGY**

HOMER KRIPKE

HOMER KRIPKE (1912–), A.B. 31, J.D. 33 Michigan; member of the New York, New Jersey, Illinois, Ohio, and Federal Bars. Currently professor of law, New York University. Major publications: *Consumer Credit: Text, Cases, Materials* (1970), *Accounting for Business Lawyers* (with Fiflis, 1971). Contributor to *The Business Lawyer, New York University Law Review,* and other journals.

Was assistant solicitor, Securities and Exchange Commission, 1939–44. Joined the New York University law faculty in 1966.

Since 1971, has been a member of the Council, Section on Banking, Corporation and Business Law, American Bar Association.

Principal research interest: the concept of meaningful disclosure in reports filed with the SEC.

THE OBJECTIVE OF FINANCIAL ACCOUNTING SHOULD BE TO PROVIDE INFORMATION FOR THE SERIOUS INVESTOR

HOMER KRIPKE

It is easy to contend that accounting is in deep trouble. Yet, if one contrasts accounting's position with that of the legal profession, one might conclude that the problems of accountants are not nearly as desperate as those of lawyers. In law we have almost a complete collapse of criminal administration. Little progress is being made toward the goal of rehabilitation as against punishment or mere confinement. We almost have a breakdown in some areas of the civil law,

SOURCE: From *Corporate Financial Reporting: The Issues, the Objectives and Some New Proposals,* edited by Alfred Rappaport and Lawrence Revsine (Chicago: Commerce Clearing House, Inc., 1972), pp. 95–111, as reprinted in *The CPA Journal,* Vol. XLII, No. 5 (May, 1972), pp. 389–397. Reproduced by permission from *Corporate Financial Reporting,* published and copyrighted 1972 by Commerce Clearing House, Inc., Chicago, Ill., 60646 and by permission of *The CPA Journal.*

where our procedures more nearly resemble those of Britain two and three centuries ago than they do the modern, efficient, restrained British system of justice. Only the absence of any theory that lawyers are supposed to be impartial or that they render judicious and impartial opinions to private clients prevents the law from being in even worse trouble than accounting on the question of independence.

With these as background comparisons, it is possible to approach accounting issues with some perspective, recognizing the problems as extremely serious, yet not incapable of solution. In contrast with the practice of law, which has a history of hundreds of years behind it, with the lawyer as an officer of the court, the public accounting profession is only two generations old. But to be realistic about the sources of current problems in the financial field, both the modern corporate lawyer and the modern public accountant go back only to the advent of mass production at the turn of the century, and to a lesser extent back to the development of finance capitalism in connection with the railroad.

Many of the current cries of anguish from the accounting profession are unfortunately not fully persuasive because they are so directly inspired by the involvement of the persons speaking. For instance, the most slashing attack on the position of those who are allegedly trying to subject the accountant to unreasonable risks of liability comes from the general counsel of one of the major firms.[1] The assertion of the Second Circuit that accounting reports must fairly present the situation, and not merely present the situation fairly in accordance with generally accepted accounting principles was opposed by the counsel for the American Institute of Certified Public Accountants whose views in an amicus brief filed in the case of United States v. Simon were rejected by the Court.[2] The Financial Executives Institute asserts that internal accountants are also entitled to implement their judgment and professional expertise and should not be directed by the auditing firms. The spokesman for this group (Herbert C. Knortz, Senior Vice President and Comptroller, International Telephone & Telegraph Corp.) vigorously resisted the opinion on pooling.[3] Without questioning the integrity and sincerity of those speaking from these vantage points, it is obvious that they are affected by the point of view represented. Other examples of this kind of interested viewpoint could be cited.

The writer's vantage point in trying to appraise the situation of modern financial accounting is that of one who has sought to follow its development closely but is not an accountant and not actively part of the contemporary involvement of accountants with their clients.

WHAT IS THE GOAL OF ACCOUNTANTS?

When we search for enlightenment, the first question ought to relate to the goal of accounting. For many years I was puzzled by the constant assertion, par-

[1] Remarks of Victor M. Earle, Esq., General Counsel of Peat, Marwick, Mitchell & Co., as reported in *New York Times*, May 1, 1971, p. 41, and in Metz, "Market Place," *New York Times*, May 4, 1971, p. 67.

[2] David B. Isbell, "The Continental Vending Case: Lessons for the Profession," *Journal of Accountancy* (August, 1970), pp. 33–40.

[3] Herbert C. Knortz, "The Credibility of Accounting Principles," *The Conference Board Record*, April 1971, pp. 33–38.

ticularly in the writings of the Arthur Andersen firm, that nothing could be accomplished in the choice of accounting principles until the goals of accounting were determined. Long ago George O. May argued that a single set of financial statements could not serve the needs of all users any more than a single utensil could serve all of one's needs for table silver.[4] Assuming that a single set of accounting statements cannot simultaneously serve the purposes of all parties, our question regarding goals can be narrowed. Thus, we may ask what should be the goals of published financial reports that are circulated to stockholders and contained in the official reports filed with the SEC.

Mr. Knortz concludes that if one adjusts for the facts that the modern financial report is based on historical cost figures, ignores values and preserves the present realization rules, its significance is that of a report of the stewardship of management to the stockholders of the business.[5] A modern financial report is a blend of many things and no simple generalization is possible (as Mr. Knortz recognized), but his assertion has a large element of truth.

The Stewardship Concept

However, to the extent that traditional historical cost accounting is a stewardship of the dollars invested in the business by its owners, it is stewardship by a grossly inadequate standard. We have passed the point where the fluctuating value of the dollar can be disregarded. If managers need only account for the number of dollars invested and not for the preservation of true economic capital in the face of inflation, there is no meaningful standard of stewardship. Recent proposals for price level accounting are one effort to solve this problem.[6] The anxious arguments that regulated rates of return on the historical cost basis are confiscatory[7] are other evidences of appropriate concern with the adequacy of reports of stewardship based on historical cost.

The Reflection of Legal Capital

Another question that may be briefly considered is whether accounting is designed to show the legal capital, the legality of dividends or of the purchase of treasury stock, etc. On the one hand, one opinion of the Accounting Principles Board is explicit to the effect that the accounting principle announced is subject to legal requirements.[8] On the other hand, there has been an unfortunate surplus of accounting statements to the effect that proper accounting has no reference to the legal situation.[9] Yet most accountants would never go as far as the last cited assertion would indicate. They always show in footnotes, for instance, the restrictions on the availability of retained earnings for dividend purposes arising from terms in loan agreements or otherwise.

---

[4] George O. May, "Eating Peas with Your Knife," *Journal of Accountancy* (Jan., 1937), pp. 15–22.

[5] Herbert C. Knortz, supra note 3.

[6] Accounting Principles Board Statement No. 3, Financial Statements Restated for General Price-Level Changes (1969).

[7] Leonard Spacek, "Utility Accounting Must Awaken to True Economics of Operations," (address before AGA-EEI Conference, Cincinnati, April 20, 1971).

[8] APB Opinion No. 6, paragraphs 12–13 (1965).

[9] See the view of an accountant reported in Homer Kripke, "Conglomerates and the Moment of Truth in Accounting," *St. John's Law Review* (Special Edition, 1970), pp. 791–797, at 792.

In the long run it must be admitted that disclosure of the legal situation (controlled as it is by a local law of a state of incorporation although financial reports are filed with the SEC and are read by investors everywhere) is of little importance as a basic goal of financial disclosure.

Conclusion as to the Goal of Accounting

My conclusion is that the goal of financial accounting should be to provide the most useful information for serious securities investors, financial analysts and money managers who serve investors, and for economists.

This type of goal fits in, of course, with the thought that for most enterprises accounting is (or could be) controlled by the Securities and Exchange Commission, whose legislative mission is to protect the investor. The ultimate sanction for the opinions of the Accounting Principles Board presently comes not from the Ethics Committee of the AICPA or from the APB itself, but from the fact that the SEC refuses to accept accounting statements that are not certified as being in accord with generally accepted accounting principles, and thus the SEC has made the Accounting Principles Board its unofficial legislative arm.[10] Not only that, the Commission in effect forces financial reports to stockholders, which are not technically filed with it, to conform to the reports that are in fact filed with it. The compulsion is not direct, but exists in the form of a requirement that if the filed reports and the financial reports to stockholders are different, the differences must be disclosed and reconciled.[11]

Since our goal is to provide information for the financial analyst and the economist, it is surprising that neither the literature of economics nor that of financial analysis has to any extent recently focused on the extent to which accounting information, and particularly the accounting concept of net income, conforms to the concepts of income which economists and financial analysts have in mind in their respective uses of the term.

DIFFERENCES BETWEEN ACCOUNTANTS AND ECONOMISTS

Efforts to compare economic concepts of income with accounting concepts founder because there is no agreed-upon economic definition. Efforts of an earlier

---

[10] See Homer Kripke, "Is Fair Value Accounting the Answer?", *The Business Lawyer* (November, 1970), pp. 289-295.

[11] See Rule 14a-3(b)(2), 17 C.F.R. §240 14a-3(b)(2). To reach the foregoing conclusion as to the goals of accounting does not mean, of course, that other special purpose reports may not be prepared. Management itself may want additional reports, or other reports directed in different areas for internal control purposes. But these may come from adaptations of the basic financial reports either by the internal accountants alone or with the cooperation of the auditors. Likewise there continue to be special regulated accounting for public utility purposes, etc., and bank and insurance accounting with heavy regulatory emphasis on liquidity and the protection of depositors and policyholders. But it is submitted that our basic public accounting system would be better served if financial reports were on a uniform basis oriented and controlled in the manner to be discussed below, and if any special purpose reports were designated as such and if they specifically disclosed their departure from the investor-oriented financial reports.

generation to probe the subject[12] have, with relatively few exceptions,[13] not been updated in this generation, and the economists have seemingly given up accounting as a "bad job"; indeed, a noted economist is explicit on the subject.[14] Possibly one reason for the discouragement is that the SEC, which ultimately has the decisive voice, fights a rear-guard action against any proposal to change basic accounting theory.[15]

In general, however, it may be said that one economic concept of income is increase of net worth between balance sheets. This concept would therefore recognize unrealized appreciation, and is founded on the concept of value, not historical cost.[16]

The financial analysts have in general appeared to give up on accounting, except as a lode from which they could derive information which they could fashion and use for their own purposes. Financial analysts have called for divisional reporting and for more and more information;[17] but in general they have not seriously addressed themselves to the question whether the net result of the accounting process does supply the key information which they can adapt to their analysis.

It is therefore encouraging to find a recent article by a financial analyst and an economist, focusing on the defects of accounting from the point of view of analysts and investors. The article by Martin J. Whitman and Martin Shubik, "Corporate Reality and Accounting for Investors," [included in this volume] in *Financial Executive*, May, 1971 is so important that I urge it on every reader of this article. It is earnestly to be hoped that the financial analyst group will produce further studies as to the relationship of accounting to the information needed by them.

Superficially the conclusion reached by Whitman and Shubik conforms to that of Professor George J. Benston, who says:

---

[12] John B. Canning, *The Economics of Accountancy* (Ronald Press, 1929); Stephen Gilman, *Accounting Concepts of Profit* (Ronald Press, 1939), Chapters 34 and 35; Roy A. Foulke, *A Study of the Theory of Corporate Net Profits* (Dun & Bradstreet, Inc., 1944); Study Group on Business Income, *Five Monographs on Business Income* (American Institute of Accountants, 1950); Study Group on Business Income, *Changing Concepts of Business Income*, (Macmillan, 1952).

[13] Palle Hansen, *The Accounting Concept of Profit* (North-Holland Publishing Co., Amsterdam, 1962); Robert R. Sterling, *Theory of the Measurement of Enterprise Income* (The University Press of Kansas, 1970). See also the reference in footnote 14.

[14] Kenneth E. Boulding, "Economics and Accounting: The Uncongenial Twins," in W. T. Baxter and S. Davidson, eds., *Studies in Accounting Theory* (Richard D. Irwin, Inc., 1962) p. 54: "What the accountant tells us may not be true but, if we know what he has done we have a fair idea of what it means. For this reason I am somewhat suspicious of many current efforts to reform accounting in the direction of making it more 'accurate.'" [Article is included in this volume. See p. 122.—Eds.]

[15] See the dissent of Earle C. King, then Chief Accountant of the SEC, to very mild proposals to recognize price level changes, in *Changing Concepts of Business Income*, supra note 12, at 122. See also the SEC reaction to a proposal to use market values for investment securities, infra, text at notes 20, 23 and 29.

[16] E.g., James C. Bonbright, *The Valuation of Property* (1937) at 906–907.

[17] E.g., C. Reed Parker, "A Professional's Thoughts—Needed Information," *The Business Lawyer* (November, 1968) 63–68.

The accounting information that the SEC requires is, on the whole, not relevant for investors. In part, this is due to the basic inability of accounting data to measure economic events effectively. But the insistence on traditional, historically-based accounting by the SEC contributes to the lack of usefulness of financial reports.[18]

But further study of Messrs. Whitman and Shubik's assertions, such as the one that a realty company "tries to create wealth by methods other than net income," need not leave us as disheartened as might be suggested by their statements that accounting is almost useless to financial analysis. Analysis indicates that they concentrate on those businesses which strive for appreciation in value of assets, which accounting ignores so long as it is unrealized; and they are seemingly unaware of the ferment in accounting circles toward reformation along the lines of a value basis with recognition of unrealized appreciation. Secondly, they are probably thinking (although they do not state the point explicitly) about the process of building values by expenditures which accounting permits to be "expensed" even though they leave substantial residual values. Here, too, accounting on a value basis would cure the point.

The Value Basis As a Link

Thus, if Messrs. Whitman and Shubik seriously entertained the possibility that accounting might shift to a value basis in which the creation of wealth was recognized even though not realized, they might find accounting a more useful tool than their present judgment suggests.

The Whitman and Shubik thesis is consistent with the views of many current writers. For example, in a recent article this writer strongly expressed a belief that accounting must switch to a value basis rather than a historical cost basis.[19] There is no need to expand on an argument that is already well known.

The writer finds it impossible to reconcile the SEC's position questioning the use of a market value basis for securities in the insurance field[20] with its requirements for recognition of unrealized gain or loss in the investment company field, especially since it is recognized by many that with insurance underwriting experience at little better than a break-even basis, many non-life insurance companies must be regarded for financial analysis purposes as little more than closed-end investment companies.

The fallacy of this position is acutely shown by the defense of historical cost by Mr. Earl Clark, President of Occidental Life Insurance Company of California, at the same hearings as follows: "I believe that adoption of your proposals could lead to such violent fluctuations in earnings as to be intolerable." This clearly would perpetuate the present situation by which a company with marketable securities can create income to suit itself by realizing selected capital gains and

---

[18] George J. Benston, "The Effectiveness and Effect of the SEC's Accounting Disclosure Requirements," in Henry G. Manne, ed., *Economic Policy and the Regulation of Corporate Securities* (George Washington University and American Enterprise Institute for Public Policy Research, 1968).

[19] Homer Kripke, "The SEC, The Accountants, Some Myths and Some Realities," *New York University Law Review* (December, 1970), pp. 1151–1205.

[20] Arthur Anderson & Co., "Cases in Public Accounting Practice," Volume 8, *APB Public Hearing on Accounting for Investments in Equity Securities Not Qualifying for the Equity Method* (Chicago, 1971), pp. 369–370.

ignoring unrealized market losses. If it be argued, as Mr. Clark implies, that earnings based on recognition of unrealized gain or loss would depend on market performance, the proper answer is that the ability of money managers to foresee shifts in the economy and the markets and to ride the waves with profit or a minimum of damage is an essential to the measurement of their performance.

COROLLARY ONE: ACCOUNTING NEEDS GREATER EMPHASIS ON QUALITY OF EARNINGS

Consistent with this emphasis on growth of values that is now concealed by cost basis accounting is Whitman and Shubik's emphasis on the quality of earnings, that is, the likelihood of their repetition. This is a point that has long been disregarded by the accounting profession and particularly by the SEC. The SEC fought a long battle to resist what it considered the attempts of the profession to "normalize" net income or to exclude anything from the final net income figure.[21] Yet the current solution[22] leaves corporate managements free to create ordinary income whenever they want to by realizing gains on a portfolio of securities (i.e., on a sale of an investment which is other than one "not acquired for resale"). It is all but incredible that the SEC should have resisted a proposal which would eliminate this possible manipulation by requiring insurance companies to carry their securities portfolios on a market value basis[23] even though it has in the past scolded investment companies for this purposive realization of gain.

There are other illustrations of the same type of point. The writer recalls his amazement when he learned about 10 years ago that the SEC and accountants would permit a securities issue of a franchising company to go out with almost its entire reported revenue coming from the sale of area franchises. It took years for the profession to realize the dangers of this presentation.[24]

Again, as early as 1964 the writer warned the credit industry about the dubious value of instalment notes received by land developers, including particularly the question of appropriate discount to present value;[25] but the accounting profession has only very recently begun to face the problem squarely in relation to its effect on reported income.[26]

---

[21] S.E.C. Accounting Release No. 53 (1945), 17 C.F.R. §211.53. In part this opposition was justified because of the skill of corporate managements in distorting any permissible classification of income elements so as to include favorable elements as normal and to exclude unfavorable elements.

[22] APB Opinion No. 9, paragraphs 17–22 (1966). Apart from the point mentioned in the text, this treatment contains some careless omissions, such as the failure to deal with the classification of debt discount written off in bulk in connection with a refunding, a point mentioned in the earlier treatment of the subject. ARB No. 43, Ch. 8, paragraph 11(e) (1953).

[23] *New York Times*, May 25, 1971, p. 53. See text at note 20, supra.

[24] Archibald E. MacKay, "Accounting for Initial Franchise Revenue," *Journal of Accountancy* (January, 1970), 66–72. Its emphasis is still on the question whether the income is earned, and not yet whether (even if earned) it should be designated as an "Extraordinary Item."

[25] Homer Kripke, "Some Valuation Aspects of Intangible Collateral," in *Proceedings of the Twentieth Anniversary Convention of the Commercial Financial Industry* (1964), 68–75 at 71–72.

[26] APB Opinion No. 21: Interest on Receivables and Payables.

So much does this defective disclosure of quality of earnings permeate current accounting that several investment houses publish monthly information letters on this subject for money managers.[27]

COROLLARY TWO: A SYSTEM OF ACCOUNTING POINTING TOWARD VALUES MUST MINIMIZE THE RISK OF LIABILITY BY CHANGING THE PROCESS BY WHICH ACCOUNTING PRINCIPLES ARE DETERMINED

To be feasible, any move toward accounting constructed on a value basis must consider a number of additional problems.

It should be recognized that the present emphasis on historical cost has a basis other than the view of the accounting profession and the SEC on the bare theoretical merits of the question. An important factor is the uncertainty of estimates of value based on forecasts of earnings and of capital appreciation. The accountants are afraid of liability and the SEC is afraid of criticism by aggrieved investors, if they switch to something which is less objectively ascertainable than historical cost. We are dealing with the phenomenon that the participants make important what they can measure and denigrate what they cannot measure.[28]

The accounting profession does have a crisis of liability causing caution on the matters under consideration, with numerous suits against its leading members. That crisis will not be solved except by restoring confidence in the accountant's opinion that financial statements are fairly presented in accordance with generally accepted accounting principles, and immunizing from liability the accountant who properly gives that opinion. To reach that result three things are necessary:

First, accounting principles must be determined on an interdisciplinary basis. Accountants who have recently watered down their certificates, who have ceased to call them certificates, and who have eliminated assertions about truth and correctness should be the first to recognize that income as reported by accountants is not a concept of nature which can be measured by physical tools; it is merely an agreed-upon definition. The persons who determine the agreed-on meanings control the manner in which most persons perceive reality. To leave these meanings to the APB as presently constituted is wrong. The spectacle of the SEC submitting position papers to the APB as to what accounting principles should be, in order that the APB can make a determination which the SEC will then enforce (presumably whether or not the Board has agreed with the SEC's submission) reverses the appropriate state of affairs. This reversal of role happened only recently on a question of cost and value intimately related to our present problem, as reported in the *New York Times*

---

[27] E.g. Quality of Earnings Report, ("A Continuing Assessment of Corporate Financial Accounting").

[28] I do not suggest that the SEC and the accountants are symbiotically engaged in a conscious downgrading of the most useful information for their own convenience. Rather the pressures are indirect. The difficulties of switching to value accounting provide easy reasons for reaching on logical or practical grounds a conclusion that may be otherwise unconsciously motivated. Yet, I must admit the same support for historical cost appears in matters where there is little difficulty of valuation, because it can be based on market quotations. Thus the SEC defended historical cost for marketable securities on historical and authoritative grounds in the APB's recent hearings on insurance company portfolio valuations. *New York Times*, May 25, 1971, p. 53.

of May 25, 1971, p. 53, when the APB held a hearing on the valuation of marketable securities by insurance companies. The SEC submitted that the continuing weight of authority for adherence to historical cost should not be disregarded.[29]

The proper allocation of responsibility. A more proper allocation of responsibility would have the Accounting Principles Board and other accountants submitting their views to the SEC before the SEC announced the rules governing accounting measurements that would be enforced on the public. While this writer has strongly argued[30] that the SEC should exert its accounting powers more forcefully, every theoretical position is subject to *ad hoc* considerations; thus it may be questioned whether, given the SEC's present attitudes, it would be wise to have it intervene more forcefully in accounting matters.

This does not mean that I therefore support continuation of the present dominant role of the APB as presently constituted. No one would contend that architects or engineers should construct buildings without regard to the necessities of the clients, or that computer programmers should program the machines without inquiring what information users want. Thus, it is unacceptable to me to have accountants assert that their priesthood of accounting principles entitles them exclusively to determine the principles to be prescribed, to the exclusion of the desires and felt needs of the consumers. The consumers of the information in financial reports are investors and the financial analysts and lawyers who serve the investors, and the statisticians and economists who aggregate the information of specific companies.[31]

A new interdisciplinary APB is needed. If the SEC is not the right institution to do the job, a new interdisciplinary APB should be organized. My principal interest is in reiterating that the determination of accounting principles must be an interdisciplinary effort. It is not enough to invite the opinions of the financial community either before or after a committee (the Accounting Principles Board) of a single organization of the accounting profession unilaterally drafts opinions, with only accountants represented. Not only should representatives of the financial community be heard in connection with the drafting but their *right* to be heard and participate in the decision should be clearly understood, and their standing to insist on goals should be as great as that of the accountants. I do not denigrate the role of accountants as experts any

---

[29] The Commission should have recognized the extent to which the current weight of authority is influenced by the Commission's adamant opposition to anything but historical cost. See the position of a former Chief Accountant of the SEC, Earle King, supra note 15. On the substance of the SEC's position on marketable securities, see text at note 20, supra.

[30] Homer Kripke, supra note 19.

[31] Whether the financial information for specific companies so prepared, when aggregated, is the proper figure for use in the statistics of corporate income which figure in the national income statistics is a subject to be carefully considered, and study might result in some form of modification of the aggregation of statistics of individual companies; but in the first instance our concern should be with investors and prospective investors of the individual companies.

more than I would that of architects and engineers in advising an owner as to the construction of the building; but I think that the analogy is exact, and in the long run the desires and needs of the client must prevail as to what accounting principle should be within the limits of technical possibility.

A perfect example of this is the long standing controversy about pooling and purchase accounting. I have several times argued[32] that the heart of the problem is the same cost or value question which is at the root of Messrs. Whitman and Shubik's rejection of the usefulness of accounting. A fundamental principle of accounting is stated to be that it accounts for entities and that the basis of accountability becomes discontinuous when there is a substantial change of ownership with new costs to the acquiring entity. Accounting does not seek to apply this when an ordinary minor shareholder of a corporation sells his stock, but it does apply this principle in purchase accounting on substantial changes of control resulting in mergers or the like.

Accountants presently report income after deducting depreciation based on historical costs, ignoring increased economic values consumed. Purchase accounting would require increased depreciation based on the purchase price of the acquirer (as well as amortization of goodwill) and consequently lower profits. But the corporations have made it clear that they will not willingly accept this discontinuity of earnings, after an acquisition or merger. That is, they object to the disappearance of potentially reportable earnings which may have in part prompted the acquisition. The result was a rapid whittling away of the principles of Accounting Research Bulletin No. 48 (1957), which unrealistically sought to distinguish between purchases and poolings by mechanical tests.

After years of controversy the Accounting Principles Board came up with Opinion No. 16 (1970) which again created mechanical tests in an unrealistic effort to distinguish purchases and poolings; and this time the Board made its intention unmistakably clear that these tests were to be applied with absolute rigidity. Yet corporate management was not to be denied in their insistence on the continuity of earnings despite changes of ownership. To achieve this continuity, they resort to the pooling concept. I am reliably informed that the listing applications at the New York Stock Exchange covering poolings subsequent to the effective date of Opinion No. 16 in a significant number of cases show material departures from the rigid standards of that Opinion, justified by the corporations and their accountants either on the grounds of immateriality or on the grounds that compliance with a substantial number (even though not all) of the standards of Opinion No. 16 is substantial compliance and entitles them to use the pooling method of accounting.

This experience tells us that there will be no permanent or satisfactory solution to this problem until the accountants grasp the nettle and in some way meet the desires of their customers. The only way to meet the desires of corporate management for continuity and at the same time be fair to securities investors, the consumers of the financial standards, is to go to accounting on a value basis, both before and after acquisitions.

---

[32] Homer Kripke, Comments in George R. Catlett and Norman O. Olson, "Accounting for Goodwill," *Accounting Research Study No. 10* (American Institute of Certified Public Accountants, 1968); Homer Kripke, supra notes 9 and 10.

Of course, the new capital structure which often follows such changes of ownership may also result in changed financial costs for interest, etc. Additionally, increased investment by the purchasers may result in a change in yield. But there is nothing unreasonable in the clients' insistence that a change of ownership should not result in discontinuity of operating results. Here it is the ingrown nature of the accounting process, with only accountants represented on the APB, that is responsible for the complete failure of the profession to appraise the difficulty realistically.

Second, in cases where opportunity for choice of accounting principles exists, the accountant and not the client must control the selection, and the accountant must be subject to effective disciplinary procedures of a self-regulatory organization. I have elsewhere argued[33] that accountants cannot be fully independent of those from whom their fees come. But the useful role of the certified financial statement and the accountant as ombudsman is so great that we must continue the present method and the key role of accountants, while trying to strengthen their independence. The fundamental principle must be that while the clients remain responsible for the raw data, the accountant must be the one who chooses the applicable accounting principles where there is room for choice.[34] (This point on selection between available accounting principles must be distinguished from the interdisciplinary formulation of principles discussed above). Only in this way can the accountant be required to take full moral responsibility for the statements. He must not be able to hide behind the assertion that all he can give the selection of principles is "the smell test" (to repeat one leading accountant's explanation to me of his process), because the clients pick the principles provided there is enough practice supporting them to give them authoritative support.

The next requirement is that there be some adequate policing of accountants' performance under these standards by an appropriate regulatory agency. The certification of financial statements by accountants is a vital part of the statutory disclosure process. The SEC is quite frankly delegating most control over accounting, including at present the selection of accounting principles, to the profession. Its Chief Accountant, Andrew Barr, and its accountant Commissioner, James J. Needham, have been explicit on the point. So long as this is so, the present informal and possibly illegal delegation of the power to make rules which the SEC enforces as law ought at least to be formalized in a manner similar to the legal position of other self-regulatory agencies in the securities business, namely the stock exchanges and the National Association of Securities Dealers, Inc.

Thus, new legislation ought to constitute the AICPA (or whatever body succeeds to its present role) as an official self-regulatory agency for the accounting profession, and give its pronouncements on accounting principles the force of law by statute as well as by courtesy of the SEC. Concomitant with this formalized status would be an acceptance of the consequences of the role of a self-regulatory agency. The first consequence is that it must perform its job of administration and discipline, and no longer act as a gentlemen's club. Another consequence is that it may be liable to injured members of the public

---

[33] Homer Kripke, supra note 19.
[34] These views are expanded in Homer Kripke, supra note 9.

if it does not enforce its own rules.³⁵ With all the suits against accountants that are presently pending and the total public uproar, it is inconceivable that there have not been some matters which should have required self-regulatory discipline, but any such discipline has not been in evidence under the present framework.

Third, after these reforms accountants should be entitled to have their work judged according to "generally accepted accounting principles" and no more amorphous standard. I have argued strongly that Judge Friendly's decision in United States v. Simon³⁶ was sound, and the readiness of other accountants to defend the non-disclosure in that case showed the extent to which accounting has been administered by a gentlemen's club. As I read it,³⁷ the decision holds that a lay jury may be permitted to find that financial statements did not fairly present the facts even though they did fairly present the facts in accordance with generally accepted accounting principles. This is indeed a dangerous posture of affairs for accountants, but a necessary one so long as accounting principles are exclusively made by accountants, and there is no effective professional disciplining of departures. If the changes in methods of formulating accounting principles here urged are made and a suitable self-regulatory mechanism devised, accounting principles would become a legislative judgment formulated by the financial community (and not merely by accountants) as to the best way to analyze facts when necessarily some degree of conventionality and arbitrariness is involved. Under these circumstances I believe that the law would change, and that it would be inappropriate to present to a jury any issue other than the factual elements of a dispute.

COROLLARY THREE: THE CLIENTELE TO WHICH ACCOUNTING MUST ADDRESS ITSELF MUST BE THE SERIOUS INVESTOR AND ANALYST

The SEC has long struggled to achieve prospectuses and proxy statements which could be read by the average lay investor, and one of its top officials has again recently reiterated this as its necessary goal.³⁸ I have argued that modern accounting is too complex for this to be a feasible goal³⁹ and I agree with Howard Ross:

> In studying the investment decision process, let us again dismiss from our minds the problems of the uninformed layman. He needs help, but it is no service to him to get him trying to value his investments by his own research. If he is uninformed, he should seek the advice of someone who is informed. Our problem is confined to providing information that will be intelligible to a serious analyst.⁴⁰

---

³⁵ Baird v. Franklin, 141 F.2d 238 (2d Cir., 1944), cert. den. 323 U.S. 737 (1944); Pettit v. American Stock Exchange, 217 F.Supp. 21 (S.D. N.Y. 1963).

³⁶ United States v. Simon, 425 F.2d 796 (2d Cir. 1969), cert. den. 397 U.S. 1006 (1970); see Homer Kripke, supra note 9.

³⁷ But compare David B. Isbell, supra note 2.

³⁸ Alan B. Levenson, "Appropriate Disclosure," *The Review of Securities Regulation* (March 4, 1971) 961–965.

³⁹ Homer Kripke, supra note 19.

⁴⁰ Howard Ross, *The Elusive Art of Accounting* (Ronald Press, 1966) at 177.

The Whitman and Shubik article referred to above is particularly strong on this point.

Expansion of Permissible Information

With our attention focused on the serious investor and analyst, there can be no justification for the failure of the SEC to permit all relevant information, such as the existence of probable mineral or oil reserves, to be presented and estimates of value made, or to permit projections of future earnings to be made. Any sophisticated view recognizes that there is no firm line between historical fact and projection. Any statement of past results is based on a deferral of certain costs in reliance on projections that, for example, deferred Research and Development will continue to be useful, that Closing Inventory will be salable, and even that the cost of fixed assets will be recovered through revenues that will cover depreciation.[41]

The SEC has made it clear that it is fearful that projections if authorized might turn out to be the wild ones made by speculative promoters, that the promoters would deceive the naive public and that the SEC would be criticized.[42] But the Commission would have no difficulty in blocking the use of unreasoned speculative projections any more than it does the other aspects of speculative securities promotions. The real question concerns the availability of such material to sophisticates, who are certainly able to apply appropriate *caveats* and discounts from their experience. Indeed, if the management accountants (who seem to function as industrial psychologists) are to be believed,[43] a safety margin of "slack" is always built into any budget forecast to allow ample room to achieve the goals. Whether or not this is true, it seems time for regulation of financial disclosure to be mature and to stop stultifying itself for fear that occasional naive investors might be misled. That approach reduces disclosure to its lowest common denominator and precludes its effectiveness.

The Role of Accounting in Projections and Value Estimates

The question then remains as to what role accounting should play in the presentation of projections and estimates of value. In the British procedure the accountants attest to the bases of the forecasts and the accuracy of the calculations.[44] I see no harm in this nor any undue burden on accountants; but neither do I see the participation of accountants in this kind of projection as necessary for proper working of a sophisticated system of disclosure. The matter can be left to development by the individual choices of particular accountants.

---

[41] See Kenneth E. Boulding, supra note 14.

[42] Philip Loomis (the Commission's General Counsel, now a Commissioner), "Corporate Disclosure and Inside Information" (Panel Interview at Fall Conference of the Financial Analysts Federation, October 7, 1968), p. 7, quoted in *New Trends and Special Problems under the Securities Act* (Practising Law Institute, 1970), p. 300.

[43] Michael Schiff and Arie Y. Lewin, "Where Traditional Budgeting Fails," *Financial Executive* (May, 1968), pp. 50–62; Michael Schiff and Arie Y. Lewin, "The Impact of People on Budgets," *The Accounting Review* (April, 1970) pp. 259–268.

[44] John J. Willingham, Charles H. Smith and Martin E. Taylor, "Should the CPA's Opinion Be Extended to Include Forecasts?", *Financial Executive* (September, 1970) pp. 80–89; Bertrand J. Belda, "Reporting on Forecasts of Future Developments," *Journal of Accountancy* (December, 1970) pp. 54–58.

ALFRED RAPPAPORT

ALFRED RAPPAPORT (1932–), B.B.A. 54 Case Western Reserve; M.S. 61, Ph.D. 63 Illinois; CPA. Currently professor of accounting and information systems, Northwestern University. Major publications: *Public Reporting by Conglomerates* (editor, with Firmin and Zeff, 1968); *A Framework for Financial Reporting by Diversified Companies* (with Lerner, 1969); *Information for Decision Making: Quantitative and Behavioral Dimensions* (edited readings, 1970); *Corporate Financial Reporting: The Issues, the Objectives and Some New Proposals* (editor, with Revsine, 1972); *Segment Reporting for Managers and Investors* (with Lerner, 1972). Contributor to *The Accounting Review* and other journals.

Prior to joining the Northwestern University accounting faculty in 1967, served for four years on the Tulane University faculty.

ESTABLISHING OBJECTIVES FOR PUBLISHED CORPORATE ACCOUNTING REPORTS[1]

ALFRED RAPPAPORT

In response to the increasing significance of corporate information in our economy, accountants have demonstrated an active interest in developing a cohesive and useful framework to guide the selection, measurement, and communication of information for published corporate accounting reports. Despite some notable contributions, especially over the past three decades, most qualified observers would undoubtedly agree that such a framework or theory has not been satisfactorily developed.

The emerging philosophy of accounting research characterized by a commitment to a scientific attitude has enhanced greatly the potential for accounting

SOURCE: From *The Accounting Review*, Vol. XXXIX, No. 4 (October, 1964), pp. 951–962. Reprinted by permission of the American Accounting Association.

[1] More specifically, this paper is concerned with business enterprises where "there is both a substantial separation of enterprise ownership from management and a wide public interest in the corporation's affairs." ("Accounting and Reporting Standards for Corporate Financial Statements—1957 Revision," *The Accounting Review*, October, 1957, p. 537.)

theory. Discussions and demonstrations of alternative research methodologies are making encouraging inroads into the plethora of *ad hoc*-based inquiries in accounting literature.[2] Each of these methodological studies shares the common goal of attempting to improve the basis for scientific inquiry in accounting. Although serious concern with the alternative patterns of inquiry suitable to accounting theory formation is of relatively recent origin, the methodologists have advanced certain ideas which merit careful consideration. The special interest of this paper concerns the methodological proposition advanced by Professor Devine that the development of objectives is the appropriate first step in formulating a system of theory for a service function such as accounting.[3]

The essential purposes of this paper may be outlined as follows:

1. To demonstrate that objectives for published corporate accounting reports should be an integral part of the development of corporate accounting theory formation.
2. To propose a methodology for the development of objectives for published corporate accounting reports.
3. To employ the proposed methodology in the logical development of basic objectives for published corporate accounting reports.

NEED FOR OBJECTIVES

Professor Devine's succinct advocacy of stated objectives in a system of accounting theory is compelling:

> Yet, this writer is committed to the doctrine that the *first* order of business in constructing a theoretical system for a service function is to establish the purpose and objectives of the function. The objectives and purposes may shift through time, but for any period they must be specified or specifiable. Once this first step is taken we have a framework that lets us investigate and conduct research in terms of carefully constructed objectives. When research is approached in this fashion, the objectives along with the usual logical apparatus become the deductive framework from which, by means of quantitative and behavioral relations, we may proceed to appraise the adequacy of the entire machinery of accounting and the consistency of its rules and procedures.[4]

---

[2] Among recent articles which characterize this movement are: Richard V. Mattessich, "Towards a General and Axiomatic Foundation of Accountancy, with an Introduction to Matrix Formulation of Accounting Systems," *Accounting Research*, October, 1957, pp. 328–355; Carl Thomas Devine, "Research Methodology and Accounting Theory Formation," *The Accounting Review*, July, 1960, pp. 387–399; R. J. Chambers, "The Conditions of Research in Accounting," *The Journal of Accountancy*, December, 1960, pp. 33–39; Norton M. Bedford and Nicholas Dopuch, "Research Methodology and Accounting Theory—Another Perspective." *The Accounting Review*, July, 1961, pp. 351–361; Norton M. Bedford and Vahe Baladouni, "A Communication Theory Approach to Accountancy," *The Accounting Review*, October, 1962, pp. 650–659.

[3] Devine, *op cit*. While Devine is not the first to advance this view, he is its most eloquent spokesman.

[4] *Ibid*., p. 399.

Surprisingly, even the utilitarian nature of accounting has not prompted serious research into the objectives of published corporate accounting reports. References to reporting objectives found in accounting and management literature suffer from two principal deficiencies: (1) they are presented in such vague terms that little or no direction is offered to the further development of a system of theory, or (2) they are presented in more specific terms, but the underlying criteria and rationale for the stated objectives are not apparent.[5] Nevertheless, it would be highly unrealistic to assume that accounting theorists disregard objectives in their work. A more realistic assumption is that in the absence of explicitly stated objectives the researcher's intended objectives do find their way implicitly into his theoretical structure. However, an intelligent appraisal of the structure cannot be initiated by the competent observer until the researcher's intended objectives are made explicit. Indeed, it seems proper to suggest that without a consensus regarding the essential premise of accounting objectives the current debate concerning basic accounting theory is likely to continue indefinitely with limited possibility for substantial progress.

The urgent need for authoritative statements about the objectives of published corporate accounting reports has been underscored by the recent research into accounting postulates and principles sponsored by the American Institute of Certified Public Accountants.[6] The absence of well developed and explicitly stated objectives even in these studies compels the individual reader to superimpose his own ideas of what the objectives should be. Consequently, judgments about the relevance of the postulates and the validity of the principles depend upon the varying conceptions of reporting objectives held by interested readers.

UNRESOLVED ISSUES

Although there appears to be a definite trend toward the assumption of greater reporting responsibility by corporations and their independent public accountants, the extent of this broadened responsibility is as yet uncertain. Recent accounting literature suggests the following as basic unresolved issues relating to reporting objectives:

1. What should be the scope of reporting responsibility to investors? Should it comprehend stewardship and/or investment guidance?[7]

---

[5] This conclusion is supported by this writer's research in *A Proposal for Deriving Objectives for Published Corporate Accounting Reports from Relevant Social Values*, Unpublished doctoral dissertation, University of Illinois, 1963.

[6] Maurice Moonitz, *The Basic Postulates of Accounting*, Accounting Research Study No. 1 (New York: American Institute of CPAs, 1961) and Robert T. Sprouse and Maurice Moonitz, *A Tentative Set of Broad Accounting Principles for Business Enterprises*, Accounting Research Study No. 3 (New York: American Institute of CPAs, 1962).

[7] George O. May differentiates between these two viewpoints as follows: "Whether the experience of a company in the recent past is likely to be repeated in the near future is practically immaterial if financial statements are to be considered as reports of stewardship or as guides to the profits that may be properly distributed. It is of paramount importance if they are to be used as a guide in determining whether to buy, hold, or sell securities." (*Financial Accounting: A Distillation of Experience*. New York: The Macmillan Company, 1943, p. 21).

2. What should be the scope of reporting responsibility to interested parties beyond the investor, e.g., employees, consumers, suppliers, local communities, and the public at large?

3. What should be the required technical comprehension level of the so-called "standard reader" of corporate reports?

4. What should be the proper limits of the field, e.g., measurement exclusively in financial terms versus measurement in any quantitative terms; *ex post* measurement versus *ex post* and *ex ante* measurements?[8]

An analysis of the four basic issues enumerated above suggests the following as a reasonable line of attack:

1. Determine to whom published corporate accounting reports *should be* directed.

2. Determine what types of information *should be* communicated to the selected audience.

3. Determine what part of such information *should be* examined by independent public accountants as part of their attest function.[9]

SOCIAL VALUES AND REPORTING OBJECTIVES

The third-party need for reliable and independently attested accounting reports of socially significant business corporations establishes important obligations for such corporations and their independent public accountants. *It is a fundamental proposition of this study that guidance in the proper discharge of these social obligations can be derived from a value structure which has at its foundation basic social values.*[10]

Some may question the direct concern of accountants with identifying social values, but can any profession whose work is endowed with a public interest not be irrevocably committed to the guidance offered by the basic ideals of that public? An examination of the relationship between the corporation and the fundamental ideals or values of society affords the accounting profession a framework for selecting both an "appropriate" audience and an improved concept of relevant

---

[8] Another dimension to "limits of the field problem" is suggested by Professor Norton M. Bedford's proposed "welfare concept" for accounting. "The welfare concept is broader than the wealth concept and would provide for effectiveness reports on both wealth and nonwealth objectives. Only under the welfare concept could accounting provide reports on all objectives of management in terms of effectiveness." "Management Motives and Accounting Measurements." (*The Quarterly Review of Economics & Business*, Autumn 1963, p. 37).

[9] The third consideration, the limits of the field dilemma, will not be undertaken in this article.

[10] The term "social value" as used here denotes a "conception, explicit or implicit, characteristic of a group, of the desirable which influences the selection from available modes, means, and ends of action." (Clyde Kluckhohn and others, "Values and Value Orientations in the Theory of Action," in *Toward a General Theory of Action*, edited by Talcott Parsons and Edward A. Shils, Cambridge: Harvard University Press, 1959, p. 395). Using this as a point of departure, a "value structure" may be defined as the organization of values into a logically integrated system which provides a basis for facilitating appropriate choice among alternative actions.

information. With respect to the selection of an "appropriate" audience, social values can serve as the basis for establishing the "right" to information. Relevant information, on the other hand, may be broadly described as (1) measurements of the extent to which values, or approximations thereof, have been satisfied, and (2) information which will influence a fuller satisfaction of values. In brief, social values are the criteria which will enable accountants to judge most efficiently the relative desirability of alternative objectives for published corporate accounting reports.

Before presenting the social values themselves two important questions must be resolved.

1. By what ethical criterion or standard shall social values be selected?
2. How can social values be organized into a value structure which provides a reasonable basis for recommending corporate reporting objectives?

A STANDARD FOR SOCIAL VALUES

J. M. Clark has suggested three broad classifications among value criteria. "First, there is the currently effective standard, expressed in the conditions society maintains or permits. This includes things approved as desirable, but it includes also many recognized abuses which society has merely not found effective ways of removing. . . . Secondly, there is the known and expressed community judgment of what is desirable—where such a judgment exists. It implies a consensus prevalent enough to be regarded as representative—complete unanimity would be an unreasonable requirement. By this standard, many existing practices and conditions may be judged unsatisfactory, as evidenced by efforts to improve them. . . . Third, there is the search for more ultimate ethical standards by which the prevailing judgment might be held right or wrong."[11]

Although we should fully recognize that the selection of any particular ethical standard is of itself a value judgment, let us demand that one major criterion, freedom from vagueness, be met by the selected standard. Based on this requirement, the "more ultimate ethical standards" are rejected as philosophical imponderables beyond even the broadest view of accounting responsibility.

Among the three value criteria, the social consensus concept which includes constructive attempts to remove recognized social abuses appears to be best suited to the professional (socially responsible) role of accountants. Consequently, this value criterion will be used as the guideline in selecting values. Devine, an advocate of such a "relativistic" approach to social values, offers some especially useful comments regarding its responsible implementation for accounting theory formation:

> If accounting is to be a profession, the accountant must look to the accepted social standard of the place and time and use existing social attitudes as they are expressed in the form of laws, customs, administrative decisions, religious edicts, and the like, as the basis for subjective decision. Members of the accounting profession should sense and appraise the relative desirability or unde-

---

[11] John Maurice Clark, "Aims of Economic Life as Seen by Economists," in *Goals of Economic Life,* edited by A. Dudley Ward (New York: Harper & Brothers, 1953) pp. 27–28.

sirability of certain demands by applying the customs and laws that guide the social group. Then with knowledge of the probable effects of certain lines of accounting action the profession can translate the general attitudes of society into accounting rules that will help accomplish socially desirable behavior and discourage undesirable behavior.[12]

LANGUAGE AND LOGIC

Now let us turn our attention to the language form of the values as a means of clarifying the logical basis for subsequently derived corporate reporting recommendations. Let us begin with the question of whether the values are normative or descriptive. The reader is urged to note that it is the values which are under consideration at this particular point, *not* the logical implications which are a consequence of the values. It is submitted that the values in themselves are descriptive ethical symbols rather than normative ethical symbols. The following passage from the noted contemporary British philosopher, Alfred Jules Ayer, serves to make the distinction:

> It is advisable here to make it plain that it is only normative ethical symbols, and not descriptive ethical symbols, that are held by us to be indefinable in factual terms. There is a danger of confusing these two types of symbols, because they are commonly constituted by signs of the same sensible form. Thus a complex sign of the form "x is wrong" may constitute a sentence which expresses a moral judgment concerning a certain type of conduct, *or it may constitute a sentence which states that a certain type of conduct is repugnant to the moral sense of a particular society. In the latter case, the symbol "wrong" is a descriptive ethical symbol, and the sentence in which it occurs expresses an ordinary sociological proposition;* in the former case, the symbol "wrong" is a normative ethical symbol, and the sentence in which it occurs does not, we maintain, express an empirical proposition at all.[13] [emphasis added].

While it is held that the values presented in this study are descriptive ethical symbols, the values themselves should be clearly distinguished from the implications for corporate reporting derived from such values. Insofar as these value-prescribed implications recommend action different from that presently existing in corporate reporting they may be appropriately termed "normative." But, as pointed out by Ayer, a statement which simply expresses the values of a par-

---

[12] Devine, *op. cit.*, p. 398.

[13] Alfred Jules Ayer, *Language, Truth and Logic*, (New York: Dover Publications, Inc., 1946) p. 105. Ayer's "emotive" theory of ethics suggests that many statements about moral matters are simply expressions of emotion on the part of the speaker or writer. "In saying that a certain type of action is right or wrong, I am not making any factual statement, not even a statement about my own state of mind. I am merely expressing certain moral sentiments. And the man who is ostensibly contradicting me is merely expressing his moral sentiments. So that there is plainly no sense in asking which of us is in the right. For neither of us is asserting a genuine proposition." (pp. 107–108). Thus, Ayer suggests that argument is possible on moral questions only if some system of values is presupposed.

ticular society is descriptive rather than normative in nature. Such a statement appropriately may be called a "sociological proposition."

The values to be presented here may then be characterized by three basic features. First, the selection of the values is guided by the particular "social consensus concept" developed earlier. Secondly, the values are presented as sociological propositions. Third, as sociological propositions the usefulness of the values may be judged by their ability to yield further propositions which can serve as recommendations for corporate reporting objectives and whose consequences are consistent with the values themselves.[14]

BASIC SOCIAL VALUES

The basic social values underlying the determination of an "appropriate" audience for corporate accounting reports and the broad categories of information which should be developed for this audience are presented below. The list of values is followed by a brief evaluation of each as an approximation of a fundamental belief of our society.

1. Certain restraints upon individual freedoms are necessary to preserve and enhance an orderly society based essentially on the principle of self-determination.
2. Governing power should be distributed among as many decision-making centers as possible, consistent with the effective functioning of society.
3. The power to govern is a recallable trust subject to the consent of the governed.
4. The conflict of diverse group interests should be resolved by peaceful compromise and not by violence.
5. Continuing economic progress is desirable as long as its pursuit does not invalidate other basic values.

Freedom via Judicious Restraint

Certain restraints upon individual freedoms are necessary to preserve and enhance an orderly society based essentially on the principle of self-determination.

Authority is sometimes thought of as the antithesis of freedom, but this is not necessarily valid in all cases. While individual self-determination is undoubtedly one of the most fundamental values of our society, it must be admitted that certain restraints on self-determination are necessary for the maintenance as well as enhancement of the social welfare. The exercise of one freedom may invalidate the exercise of one or more other freedoms. Conversely, the restraint of a particular individual freedom may be a prerequisite for individual freedom in other respects.

It is the business of society to choose which freedoms it particularly values. For example, we restrain the thief from taking property that does not belong to him. His lack of freedom in this respect gives meaning to the right to property. Some states have enacted anti-discrimination laws in housing. While such legisla-

---

[14] Every effort has been made to select social values which are "basic" to our society. To facilitate this, an independence requirement is desirable. Meeting this requirement calls for editing the list of values to determine whether the attainment of any one value is significant only because it is a means to the attainment of one or more of the remaining values.

tion restrains the landlord from choosing his tenants solely from racial and religious groups congenial to him, it also provides freedom for members of minority groups to live where they desire.[15] One could continue indefinitely with other illustrations: however, the purpose of this paper is not to enumerate, justify, or condemn the choice of particular freedoms over others, but simply to call attention to the existence of a continual process of choice among freedoms.

The desire for individual freedom serves as a point of departure or organizing principle for law and authority in our society. The influence of individual freedom on legal values can be noted in the following primary classifications of our legal values:

1. The legal rights of the individual (freedom of contract, association, labor, property rights, enterprise, and the person):
2. Equality before the law (as the only effective device for assuring justice):
3. Control of government by the people (representative government, minority rights, universal suffrage): and
4. The rule of law (administration of rules without distinction as to persons, and acceptance of the legal rule that everyone counts for one.)[16]

In summary, we are a society founded upon the principle of individual self-determination, but self-determination tempered by consideration for over-all social welfare—a condition which necessitates certain restraints upon individual freedoms.

Political Pluralism

Governing power should be distributed among as many decision-making centers as possible, consistent with the effective functioning of society.

The theory that a diffusion of power among many organizations can help prevent a concentration of power leading to a totalitarian society is widely known as "political pluralism." Pluralistic theory is often used by social commentators to encourage the maintenance of balance between the public and private governments in our society.[17]

There is an abundance of pluralistic manifestations in our society. Aside from the division of decision-making power between public and private governments, there is the further division of power within each of these two sectors. For example, in the public sector we find Federal, state, and local governments. In turn, each of these is further subdivided into functional decision-making bodies.

Within the private sector we have such major decision-making centers as corporations and labor unions. The enactment of certain anti-trust and management-labor relations legislation are but two of many examples of our concern over the potential breakdown of pluralism within the private sector.

[15] "The Power of the Democratic Idea," Report VI of The Rockefeller Panel Reports in *Prospect for America*, (New York: Doubleday & Company, Inc., 1961) p. 345.

[16] Wolfgang Friedmann, *Legal Theory* (London: Steven & Sons, 1953) pp. 477–510. Cited by Richard Eells and Clarence Walton in *Conceptual Foundations of Business* (Homewood, Ill.: Richard D. Irwin, Inc., 1961), p. 501.

[17] For example, see Clark Kerr, "An Effective and Democratic Organization of the Economy," in *Goals for Americans* (Englewood Cliffs, N. J.: Prentice-Hall, Inc., 1960), pp. 148–161.

Consent As a Source of Power

The power to govern is a recallable trust subject to the consent of the governed.

The first value establishes the idea that certain restraints upon individual freedom are necessary to obtain the advantages of living in community with others. The responsibility for formulating and administering these restraints is delegated to representatives of the people. These representatives not only are accountable to the governed, but they must also gain consent for the continuation of their right to govern.

Evidence of the "consent of the governed" idea in our society is best highlighted by citing the principle of representative government and the attendant electoral process. While the idea of the "consent of the governed" must be rated as a fundamental principle of the American political system, it does not imply an unqualified endorsement of the judgment of the mass electorate in the short run. Eells and Walton cite the indirect election of senators and of the President, the rather cumbersome amending process, and appointment rather than election of federal judges as illustrations of this skepticism of the masses in the short run.[18]

The Rockefeller Panel Report offers a similar view:

> There is a fundamental error in the notion that a democratic government can be, or should be, merely the passive spokesman of the popular will. The error lies in assuming that a definite popular will actually exists in the absence of government, political parties, media of communication, and all the other agencies in society that register what is known as "public opinion." For these agencies do not simply reflect such opinion. They form and inform it and give it its direction and mode of expression.[19]

Thus, the power to govern is indeed contingent upon the consent of the governed, but we must also recognize that such consent is not formed in a vacuum; instead, it is largely influenced by the type of alternatives presented by the agencies in society which play the key roles in forming "public opinion."

Compromise

The conflict of diverse group interests should be resolved by peaceful compromise and not by violence.

Whenever people form social or economic groups it is to be expected that they will attempt to improve both their absolute and relative positions in society. In fact, the American ideals of incentive and competition have done much to promote effort along these lines. Yet, due to the interdependency among various social and economic groups and the scarcity of resources not all of these groups are likely to satisfy the entire spectrum of their needs.

Since we are a people opposed to the resolution of conflict by violence, the stage is set for compromise.

> Democracy depends on the ability of its citizens to negotiate peacefully with each other, to give as well as receive, and to arrive at understandings to which they will mutually adhere. . . .

---

[18] Eells and Walton, *op. cit.*, p. 502.
[19] "The Power of the Democratic Idea," *op. cit.*, p. 437.

Far from representing a lapse from principle, compromise thus represents one of democracy's most signal achievements. Compromise is incompatible with an unbending commitment to an abstract ideology; but it does not imply weak wills or fuzzy minds. Groups within a democracy may and do struggle hard for the achievement of their purposes; and if they do not achieve their full program at any given moment, they can continue to struggle until they do. The ethic of compromise does not call for them to abandon the struggle for their ultimate purposes. It calls for them only to carry on their fight at all times within the rules of the democratic process. They will use the courts, the press, peaceful public demonstrations, strikes, and elections; they will not use violence, slander, personal threats, or bribes.[20]

The American enterprise system is an excellent example of the principle of compromise at work. In our complex industrial society there no longer is the immediacy of relation between effort and productivity; thus, "equitable sharing" of increases in productivity is oftentimes only an abstract principle difficult to implement. The question of how much credit for increased productivity is attributable to labor, machines, and management has indeed been a perplexing problem especially prone to group biases. Despite the elusiveness of the "equity in productivity" concept the interests contributing to the increasing productivity of the American enterprise system have been able to resolve their differences in almost all cases by peaceful compromise rather than violence.

Economic Progress

Continuing economic progress is desirable as long as its pursuit does not invalidate other basic values.

In general terms, economic progress may be described as "the increase in human power to satisfy human needs."[21] What are the principal manifestations of economic progress? While others may be cited, most observers would likely include economic growth and development presumably reflected in a higher standard of living; economic stability; and an improved distribution of income. The national concern with these factors in economic progress is evidenced by the continuing debates over growth rates, Federal Reserve policies, tax reforms, unemployment, and so forth. Some attribute the growth of our economy to tradition and attitude dating back to the early development of this country. The Puritan ethic of hard work and thrift is often cited as one of the religious bases for the dynamism of the American economy. Religious beliefs may also be a restraining influence on economic activity. For example, it is generally acknowledged that the pursuit of economic gain is not an end in itself, but must find justification by the use to which the gain is put. This thought parallels the basic message of the value presented in this section, i.e., economic progress is not to be achieved at the expense of nonmaterial values. Economic progress achieved by the sacrifice of the other values presented earlier would presumably lead us into a totalitarian society—a consequence strongly resisted in this country up to this point in history.

[20] Ibid., pp. 415–416.
[21] Kenneth E. Boulding, "Economic Progress as a Goal of Economic Life," in *Goals of Economic Life*, edited by A. Dudley Ward (New York: Harper & Brothers, 1953) p. 73.

VALUE-PRESCRIBED RECOMMENDATIONS

Four basic objectives for external corporate reporting are suggested by the social values presented in this paper:

1. The managements of large business corporations have a reporting obligation to those segments of society affected by their decisions, i.e., investors, employees, consumers, suppliers, local communities, and the public at large.
2. Those groups with a legitimate interest in the corporation should be provided with information essential to arriving at rational judgments concerning the equitable sharing of corporate benefits.
3. In the interest of economic progress, those groups which are responsible for allocating resources in our economy should be provided with information which will promote efficient allocation.
4. In the interest of sustaining our basic values, information which is likely to influence socially desirable behavior and discourage undesirable behavior should be reported; e.g., calling attention to monopoly profits to preserve pluralism in the industrial sector of our economy.

Let us now examine the basis for the above-recommended objectives for corporate reporting. The first value suggests that individual freedom must be tempered by consideration for the over-all social welfare. The value thus sets the stage for the necessity of government in society. But more than that, it directs that governments function for the over-all social welfare, that is, in the "public interest."

The second value suggests that fear of the consequences of concentrated power has prompted the adoption of a pluralistic society, i.e., one in which governing power is diffused among as many decision-making centers as possible, consistent with the effective functioning of society. Just as the first value indicates the need for government, the second value establishes the need for diffusing the power to govern.

In our pluralistic society, individuals do not delegate certain freedoms of choice solely to public governments, reserving all other decision-making power to themselves as private persons. Instead, decision-making power is transferred to a variety of public and private governments.[22] Among private governments no form dominates the American scene as does the large business corporation. Recent statistics show that the one-hundred-thirty largest manufacturing corporations account for half of the manufacturing output in the United States. The five hundred largest business corporations embrace nearly two-thirds of all nonagricultural economic activity.[23]

The large business corporation is called a private government rather than a public government owing to the fact that individuals have transferred their decision-making power to private officials instead of public officials. Yet, the "public" versus "private" distinction can be extremely misleading when one con-

---

[22] Richard Eells, *The Government of Corporations* (New York: The Free Press of Glencoe, 1962) pp. 26–28. Eells describes the delegated decision making power as the "authority to act for otherwise free men on numerous issues that affect the lives and property of these individuals."

[23] Edward S. Mason, "Introduction," in *The Corporation in Modern Society*, edited by Edward S. Mason (Cambridge: Harvard University Press, 1961) p. 5.

siders the broad social significance of the corporation. Can we truly call business corporations which have the capacity to affect the lives and property of each of us a "private" affair?

I believe it is both accurate and useful to view the distinction between private and public governments as one which revolves around the central idea of creating the *kind* of organization (private or public) which best serves those social needs which require collective action. More significant than any differences which may exist between public government and a private government such as the large business corporation are their common impact on the public at large. The magnitude of the decisions of public governments upon our daily lives is undoubtedly profound. This is apparent if only one aspect of public governmental decision making is considered—the source and disposition of tax revenues.

As the principal form of economic organization, the large business corporation is one of the dominant institutions in our society, and consequently, it has broad implications for social policy. To gain some idea of the corporation influence we need only examine the capacities of the large corporation.[24] Consider, for example—

1. The capacity to determine when, where and how operations will be carried on. This can include the capacity to build new communities or to abandon existing ones.
2. The capacity to buy services, supplies, or raw materials. Such decisions affect the organizations and individuals who serve as suppliers for the corporation. For example, we may read of the decision of one of the major automobile manufacturers to produce a part previously supplied by other firms and in other cases the reverse decision is made.
3. The capacity to determine whether or not to produce a new product or service directly affects the range of products available to consumers.
4. The capacity to determine whether or not to expand affects the rate of economic progress as well as the level of employment and prices.
5. The capacity to decide whether to build up or reduce inventories may contribute to inflation or accelerate recession.
6. The capacity to determine how the mass media will be used for advertising and public relations purposes may influence our moral standards.
7. The capacity to transact business in foreign countries may promote international understanding or contribute to international tensions.
8. The capacity to determine to what extent profits shall be distributed, and to what extent these profits shall be dedicated to captial formation.
9. The capacity to make philanthropic contributions.[25]

The above list could well be expanded, but I believe it suffices to illustrate the social import of the daily decisions of large business corporations in this country. Does the broad social significance of corporate activity carry with it a corre-

---

[24] These capacities are not without restrictions. There are the constraints of legally enforceable obligations as well as nonlegal obligations largely dictated by public opinion and custom.

[25] A. A. Berle, Jr., *Power without Property* (New York: Harcourt, Brace and Company, 1959) pp. 82–83 and Howard R. Bowen, *Social Responsibilities of the Businessman* (New York: Harper & Brothers, 1953) pp. 3–4.

sponding obligation for social responsibility? This can best be answered by referring back to the first two values presented earlier. The first value suggests that individual freedom must be tempered by consideration for the public interest or welfare. Thus, it directs that those governments or decision makers who have the capacity to affect the public interest have a corresponding obligation to regard it as a public trust. This applies equally to private as well as public governments in a pluralistic society. After all, private and public governments are manifestations of a common value system and to ask that we be judged by the ideals inherent in our public governments without similar regard for such ideals in the government of the lives of men in the private sector would be sheer hypocrisy. Instead, our society requires a combination of public policies and voluntary private initiative to preserve our basic values.[26]

The law through its public agencies has to some extent determined the socially responsible behavior to be followed by business corporations. But the "law cannot always compel where it is good to go. Hence, legal duty may be lesser than moral obligation."[27] Thus, voluntary private action on the part of large business corporations is not only consistent with our value system, but is imperative if the pluralistic feature of our society is to long endure.

Having thus argued the case for social responsibility on the part of large business corporations via deduction from the first two values, the further implications to be derived from the third value may now be examined. This value established that the power to govern is a recallable trust subject to the consent of the governed. Indeed, from the American viewpoint, a government is judged to be responsible "only when those who make the decisions on which other men's destinies depend can be held effectively accountable for the results of their decisions."[28]

I believe it proper to deduce from the foregoing that corporate management has a reporting obligation to those segments of society affected by its decisions. Based on the earlier discussion of the present day social significance of the large business corporation, the old model of the corporation as an economic and legal instrument solely serving the property interests of its stockholders appears highly inadequate. Likewise, corporate accountability solely to stockholders is inconsistent with the contemporary model of the large business corporation. Based on the corporate capacity to affect the following segments of society, I believe managements have an obligation to report their stewardship to—(1) investors, (2) employees, (3) consumers, (4) suppliers, (5) local communities, and (6) the public at large.

It is beyond the scope of this paper to recommend specific accounting formats for corporate reports. Such recommendations should be supported by vigorous studies of the behavioral and communication context in which corporate reporting

[26] Peter F. Drucker in his study of General Motors, *Concept of the Corporation* (Boston: Beacon Press, 1960) p. 14, expresses the same thought—"The corporation as a representative institution of American society must hold out the promise of adequately fulfilling the aspirations and beliefs of the American people. A conflict between the requirements of corporate life and the basic beliefs and promises of American society would ultimately destroy the allegiance to our form of government and society."

[27] Walter Hamilton, "The Law, the Economy, and Moral Values," in *Goals of Economic Life* (New York: Harper & Brothers, 1953), p. 250.

[28] "The Power of the Democratic Idea," *op. cit.,* p. 405.

operates.[29] The last two value propositions do, however, afford us a general framework of further objectives to be served by corporate reporting.

The fourth value extols the virtue of resolving the problems associated with conflicting group interests by compromise. While managements more and more indicate their responsibility to preserve equity among corporate interests, it is the obligation of the independent public accounting profession to ensure that information relevant to this management responsibility be clearly reported. If corporate interests are to make sound judgments regarding their equitable share of corporate benefits, then they should be furnished with a free and comprehensive flow of information essential toward making such judgments. Indeed, if the whole range of problems associated with economic balance is not approached with the benefit of relevant information, then competing groups are doomed to pursue "equity" via the arbitrariness of ignorance.

The last value proposition emphasizes our society's belief in continuing economic progress as long as such progress does not invalidate other basic values. Indeed, it has been the pursuit of economic progress itself which has contributed so greatly to the emergence of the large business corporation as a significant instrument for economic and social policy. One of the keys to economic progress is undoubtedly the efficient allocation of resources. It is well established that accounting measurements *do* affect the investment decisions made in our economy. This is true of management, capital suppliers including consumers, and government investment decisions. In the interest of economic progress, it seems appropriate to suggest that corporate reporting include measurements which will induce an optimum allocation of resources.[30]

Conclusion

This inquiry rests upon two basic propositions:

1. Explicit and well conceived statements of corporate reporting objectives

---

[29] We may, for example, hypothesize that behavior is determined by the interaction of information and motives. Given that certain behavior is "desirable," that is, consistent with an established value system, then behavioral research can greatly facilitate decisions about "optimal" information design.

[30] Edgar O. Edwards and Philip W. Bell, *The Theory and Measurement of Business Income* (Berkeley: University of California Press, 1961), p. 5, contend that this type of data promotes both self-interest and the satisfaction of corporate social responsibility.

> Certain data are made available to tax authorities and regulatory agencies as a matter of law, but other external users cannot insist on data of any kind; rather they must be satisfied with what is offered them. Nevertheless, both a growing sense of social responsibility and an awareness of what may be considerable self-interest at stake are leading businessmen to be more and more concerned about the external users of accounting data. Further, many outside uses of accounting data may be of help to the businessman himself. Economists' research on business growth, efficiency, and relative profitability, for example, may contribute directly to the improvement of business decisions; business managers are coming to depend upon national income data, input-output tables, flow-of-funds reports, and the like in making plans for the future. Published accounting data should serve the other social functions as well: promoting a more efficient allocation of capital, calling attention to monopoly profits, and providing relative profitability figures to potential entrants into an industry, for example.

are essential prerequisites to the formation of a cohesive and useful theory of published corporate accounting reports.

2. Such statements are most appropriately derived from basic social values.

Given the acceptance of these propositions, this study offers *one* particular interpretation of the social values-corporate reporting relationship for the purpose of formulating a statement of reporting objectives. We urgently need active discussions to elicit alternative interpretations and statements. In this way, perhaps, the formulation of an authoritative statement concerning objectives for corporate accounting reports will be given early consideration by a recognized body such as the American Institute of CPAs or the American Accounting Association.

Once we have gained a consensus concerning corporate reporting objectives, "we have a framework that lets us investigate and conduct research in terms of carefully constructed objectives."[31] At such a point, significant research projects would likely include:

1. An analysis of the goals (compatible with social values) and the decision-making means by which these goals are achieved by the various decision makers representing the groups with a legitimate interest in published corporate accounting reports. Such research would facilitate an improved basis for determining the comparative relevancy of data, e.g., accounts stated at unadjusted historical cost, replacement cost, historical cost adjusted for changes in the price level, and so forth.

2. Research on new ways of transacting business, for example, in recent years the sale and leaseback of land, buildings, and equipment has been gaining popularity as an alternative to ownership.

3. Research on the "symbolics of information," that is, the symbols, concepts, and operations needed for the purpose of ordering and communicating information in a consistent and meaningful way. This requires inquiry into the fields of linguistics, logic, mathematics, philosophy of science and information theory.

4. Continuing research on the dynamic nature of society and consequent changes in social values which should properly affect the social phenomenon of corporate reporting.

Surely this list of research projects could be significantly expanded. The items in this list, or in a more comprehensive one, would inevitably share at least one common attribute—all suggested research projects need the guidance of a well developed concept of accounting purpose. Indeed, the formulation and agreement upon well conceived and explicit objectives for published corporate accounting reports represent both a challenge to the accounting profession to meet its social responsibilities and an opportunity to enhance significantly the theory and practice of corporate reporting.

[31] Devine, *op. cit.*, p. 399.

JOHN K. SHANK

JOHN K. SHANK (1940–   ), A.B. 62 Oberlin; M.B.A. 63 Pittsburgh; Ph.D. 69 Ohio State; CPA. Currently assistant professor of business administration, Harvard University. Contributor to *The Accounting Review*, *Journal of Accounting Research*, *Harvard Business Review*, and other journals.

Principal research interests: accounting for social costs, the relationship between planning and control systems, and the diffusion of innovations in corporate financial reporting.

CASE OF THE DISCLOSURE DEBATE

JOHN K. SHANK

FOREWORD

With the trend toward fuller corporate disclosure gathering steam, the debate whether to reveal the performance of segments of the business has been going on in many executive offices. Allied Machinery is no exception. Its four top executives and outside accountant find it difficult to reach agreement on the thorny issue.

The news that the Accounting Principles Board (APB) of the American Institute of Certified Public Accountants might impose the requirement of public product-line disclosure worried Martin Anderson. Allied Machinery Corporation (see the cast of characters), of which Anderson was president, had complied with the 1970 ruling of the Securities and Exchange Commission that made such disclosure mandatory in Form 10-K reports.

SOURCE: From the *Harvard Business Review*, Vol. 50, No. 1 (January–February, 1972), pp. 142–144, 146, 147, 150, 152, 154–156, and 158. Reprinted by permission of the *Harvard Business Review* © 1972 by the President and Fellows of Harvard College; all rights reserved.

Now, all businesses must disclose in the 10-K the sales and earnings for any "product or service" contributing 10% of total sales or earnings in either of the two preceding years. (For companies with sales of less than $50 million, the size criterion is 15%.)

Anderson was concerned about the stance that Allied should adopt in its an-

ALLIED MACHINERY AND ITS REPORTING PRACTICES

Now a conglomerate, Allied experienced spectacular growth during the 1960's. At the beginning of that decade, when its business was concentrated in appliances and electronic controls, sales were $74 million and net income was $4 million. By 1971, primarily through mergers and acquisitions, sales had reached $894 million and earnings totaled $44 million. The company had become a significant factor in such diverse industries as food distribution, pulp and paper, cement manufacturing, small computers, and defense contracting.

Each domestic division operates as a profit center, and the company places much emphasis on return on investment in evaluating divisional performance. The International Division is involved in joint ventures in several countries related to technology possessed by Allied and is also responsible for marketing Allied's various industrial and consumer products abroad.

Martin Anderson, the president of Allied since 1962, has engineered most of the expansion. His view of the job is very similar to that of a mutual fund manager; he thinks of Allied as a "portfolio of businesses" that can be expanded, contracted, or changed in the interest of ensuring steady growth in the price of the company's common stock.

For financial reporting purposes, Allied has always presented only aggregated information. Much space in the annual report is devoted to descriptions and pictures of the divisions and their products, but no financial details are revealed. Anderson has always said that investors can buy into Allied only as a whole, not piecemeal. So the financial results of the corporation as a whole were the only relevant figures for investors.

An estimated financial statement for the fiscal year ending February 29, 1972, and a comparative statement from the preceding year are shown in Table A. The format is that used historically in Allied's annual reports.

Table A INCOME STATEMENT FOR FISCAL 1972 (ESTIMATED) AND FISCAL 1971 AS TYPICALLY SHOWN IN ANNUAL REPORT (In millions of dollars)

	Fiscal 1972 (estimated)		Fiscal 1971	
Sales		$944		$892
Cost of goods sold*	$694		$647	
Selling, general, and administrative expenses*	199		169	
Taxes on income	22		32	
Total costs and expenses		915		848
Net earnings		$ 29		$ 44

* Including depreciation and amortization of $23 million in fiscal 1972 and $20 million in 1971.

Exhibit I DIVISIONAL BREAKDOWN OF SALES AND EARNINGS FOR FISCAL 1972 (ESTIMATED) AND FISCAL 1971 (In millions of dollars)

	Fiscal 1972 (estimated)		Fiscal 1971	
	Sales	Earnings	Sales	Earnings
Consumer Products				
Supermarkets	$ 47	$(3)	$ 41	$ 2
Home Appliances	141	12	131	9
Furniture	39	4	26	3
Recreational Land Development	9	(3)	6	1
Total	$236	$10	$204	$15
Industrial Products				
Pulp and Paper	$ 56	$ 3	$ 47	$ 4
Paperboard	58	4	50	5
Corrugated Containers	48	(2)	41	(2)
Electronic Controls	138	9	113	10
Business Systems	9	1	8	1
Cement Products	68	(1)	59	3
Total	$377	$14	$318	$21
Defense and Aerospace Products				
Electronic Systems	$ 95	$(7)	$130	$(6)
Marine Technology	28	3	20	2
Data Systems	66	6	94	9
Total	$189	$ 2	$244	$ 5
International				
Western Europe	$ 47	$ 4	$ 46	$ 4
South America	38	2	37	2
Asia	57	(3)	43	(3)
Total	$142	$ 3	$126	$ 3
Final total	$944	$29	$892	$44

Exhibit II PROJECTED INCOME STATEMENT TO BE FILED WITH SEC ON FORM 10-K FOR FISCAL 1972 (ESTIMATED) AND FISCAL 1971 (In millions of dollars)

	Fiscal 1972 (estimated)		Fiscal 1971	
	Sales	Earnings	Sales	Earnings
Electronic controls and related business system	$308	$ 9	$345	$14
Electric appliances	141	12	131	9
International	142	3	126	3
Other	353	5	290	18
Total	$944	$29	$892	$44

nual report for the year ending February 29, 1972, if the APB approved similar requirements for public reporting. Aware that the layout of Allied's report was almost under way, he decided to bring the matter up at the Executive Committee on January 3. He invited Earl Cunningham, partner of a "Big Eight" CPA firm in charge of the Allied account, to participate. As the playlet opens, the meeting is in progress in the board room.

Cast of characters

Martin Anderson .... President
George Trumball .... Executive Vice President, Operations
Robert Gooding .... Executive Vice President, Administration
Carl Fuller .... Executive Vice President, Finance & Accounting
Earl Cunningham .... Partner of Touche, Waterhouse & Sells, CPAs

Anderson: Moving now to the last item on the agenda, as I said in my memo to you, I'm concerned that the APB is considering issuing an opinion that will oblige us to break down sales and earnings by product line. We have to decide this week what to do for the annual report. I've asked Earl Cunningham to participate in the discussion. (*Anderson rises and goes to the door, opens it and speaks into the next room while standing at the threshold.*)

Anderson: Come in, Earl, won't you? Hope we haven't kept you waiting. (*A tall, gray-haired man enters and shakes hands with Anderson.*)

Cunningham: Not at all, Martin. I was busy reading the new *Harvard Business Review* that's on your lobby table. (*He waves casually to the others.*) Good morning, fellows. (*The others respond in kind, and Cunningham takes a proffered seat.*)

Anderson: As a point of departure, I've asked Carl to have copies made of a summary of estimated sales and earnings for our current fiscal year and the figures for last year, broken down by groups and divisions. For purposes of comparison, I've also asked him to prepare a projected 10-K report like the one we filed last year for fiscal '71. (*There is a shuffling of papers as the others produce their copies of the documents, which are reproduced in Exhibits I and II, page 110.*) Carl, do you want to make any comments about these?

Fuller: Yes, Martin, I do. First of all, the breakdown by products follows our internal organization and doesn't necessarily follow pure product-line categories. An obvious example is the International Group, since it handles most of our nondefense products. Also electronic controls are marketed by Home Appliances in the Consumer Group, by Electronic Controls in the Industrial Group, and by Electronic Systems in the D&A Group. And so on. I hope no one will argue that we should depart from our internal way of segmenting the business just to conform to a product-line categorization scheme.

Anderson: I don't think anyone would want to go that far, Carl. Go on.

Fuller: The second point I want to mention is that it's not possible to follow generally accepted accounting principles in a strict sense in preparing a breakdown like this. Internal transfers priced at market, rather than cost, and a very arbitrary allocation of general and administrative expenses are just two examples of departures from GAAP. This isn't really a problem since the disclosure wouldn't be part of the basic audited statements, but I thought I'd mention it anyway. The last point I want to mention is that the results for some units are misleading in a broad sense because of some cost allocations, though they do reflect actual revenues and expenses incurred. Electronic Systems, for example, has carried a large part of our R&D budget for several years because that way the expenses are partially recoverable under contracts. This results in the division's showing consistent losses, which wouldn't be true if corporate R&D expenditures were redistributed. To sum it all up, there are problems in—

Cunningham: May I interrupt for a moment, Carl? I'd like to add that, like most companies, Allied charges a lot of advertising to certain divisions that should really be considered as corporate advertising. Most of it is charged to one or two divisions in the Consumer Products Group.

Fuller: That's right, Earl. Thanks for mentioning it. So, gentlemen, you can see there are problems in splitting our operations into pieces like this, and the results have to be taken with a few grains of salt. On the other hand, of course, it's a good deal more accurate than the 10-K report.

Gooding: I think the issue here is more basic than accuracy of numbers, Carl. This schedule is all well and good for internal purposes, but I don't think we should be spreading information like this outside the company, even if it's completely accurate. I don't want our competition to know how profitable the Controls Division is. It's an open invitation for more people to get into that business. And I don't want competitors to find out how our Cement Products operation is deteriorating, either. That's also an open invitation for them to go after us.

Trumball: I'm also opposed to disclosing this kind of information, Martin. I don't think the average investor could grasp the reasons for profit differentials between Supermarkets and Paper Mills, for example. We'd spend half our time fielding silly questions about these differences. Also, I'm leery of the publicity seekers who would raise hell about some division that's losing money when we might have very good long-term reasons for taking the loss now. We could be showing a current profit in our Recreational Land Development operations, but we've agreed it can reach its potential faster if we invest heavily in expense dollars now.

Gooding: That's right. If we had to disclose those losses now, we might have to change our strategy, and that would hurt us in the long run. We shouldn't put ourselves in a position of being forced to defend all our product development strategies. Besides, Martin, you've always said the investor buys the whole package, not just the pieces.

Anderson: That's true, Bob. But this may be a new ball game. I don't really disagree with any of the objections you and George are raising, but it may be too late to worry about whether we should disclose or not. The SEC has ruled that we must in the 10-K, and perhaps the APB is going to do the same for the annual report.

Trumball: I think it's too *early* to worry, Martin. Even if the APB does issue an opinion on it, I'm not convinced that we'd have to bare our souls, so to speak. I did some checking around last week. I found out that 3M has become a one-product-line company since the new SEC regulations. Over 95% of their sales come from what they call 'scientifically applied coatings,' so they aren't going to show a product-line breakdown for the 10-K. They have hundreds of products, and for years they've been showing six major sales categories in their annual report. And take Honeywell. I don't have to tell you they're a very tough competitor of ours in controls and business systems, and they also have a broad range of other products. They've announced, though, that for earnings purposes they're in just one line of business—automation. Maybe if we put our heads together, we could come up with a caption for our whole product line, so we could become a one-product-line company again!

Gooding: I know you meant that facetiously, George, but it may be worth pursuing. I've heard that the auto companies are not going to show results for their different lines of cars. They're going to use an automotive–nonautomotive breakdown. Maybe we can't become a one-product-line company again, but we certainly can use that kind of approach to keep a lid on what we report. If we believe this kind of disclosure is bad for business—and I think it is—then we have a responsibility to the shareholders to use every available means to fight it.

Fuller: Bob, you've got this whole thing turned around. There is an awful lot of evidence that investors want and need information about segments of diversified companies, so they can make intelligent investment decisions. The trend is clearly toward more disclosure. The SEC is trying to move companies in this direction, and so is the APB. Many of our shareholders are also asking for product-line data. We can become a leader in providing this new information. I don't think we should view the SEC regulations as a threat. After all, anything that improves the way investors make buy and sell decisions has to be good for the economy in the long run. I'm old enough to remember the uproar that was raised when companies were first required to publish sales figures as well as gross margins. Would anyone still argue that this kind of disclosure is competitively disastrous?

Trumball: I agree that investors and analysts want more disclosure, Carl, but I'm not convinced they need it. Investors *always* want more information. And trying to keep up with requests from analysts is an endless job. I don't think anyone would argue that total disclosure is good anyway. This would mean inundating the public with reams of data, and the result would be chaos. Our annual report would be bigger than the Manhattan phone book! Some degree of summarization is necessary, and I'm not convinced that going beyond current levels of disclosure is beneficial to anyone. What we're doing for the 10-K is a nice, bland compromise, and I certainly wouldn't want to go any further than that for the annual report.

Gooding: Another thing, Carl. I don't buy that talk about what's good for the economy as a whole. Our first loyalties have to be with Allied, and it doesn't necessarily follow that what's good for the economy is good for individual companies. When it comes down to brass tacks, self-interest is what really makes the economy tick.

Fuller: I believe what you're referring to is *enlightened* self-interest, Bob. But I didn't mean to get us off on a tangent of economic theory.

Anderson: The points you were making, Carl, weren't based just on theory, though. Some large companies have been very open in disclosing product-line information and are quite happy about it. Westinghouse broke out sales and earnings for six product groups last year, voluntarily. Donald Burnham, the Westinghouse chairman, tells me he's very pleased with the results. Not only does it give investors a significant source of new information about the company which they at least want—if not actually need—but it's also stimulating some healthy rivalry among those groups. I'll be for anything that keeps our Group VPs on their toes! Westinghouse isn't the only one, either. I know that LTV and Textron have done it for several years. Textron even goes as far as to show earnings per share for each division.

Gooding: I've just been doing some figuring with Carl's schedule, Martin, and it looks to me as if 12 of the 16 divisions would technically qualify for segmentation under the 10% rule. George's comments about burying the investor with too much data really hit the target here. I just can't see putting in a schedule with 13 categories.

Fuller: I don't think one extra schedule in the annual report is going to bury anyone, Bob. Anyway, I'd like to make one other point in reference to something you and George spoke about earlier. Aren't you being a little naive about how much our competitors know about our performance? Anyone who's willing to invest the effort can get this kind of information now. All we're really talking about, therefore, is making it more readily available.

Anderson: I'd like to move the discussion along now and perhaps clear the air a bit. Earl, would you fill us in on the status of disclosure as far as the accounting profession is concerned?

Cunningham: Certainly, Martin. The APB has been on record for three years as favoring more product-line disclosure in annual reports, but so far it's been unwilling to impose precise ground rules. The Board would like to see more voluntary compliance on the part of companies so that legislation would not be necessary. A lot of people object to the accountants and the SEC making the rules for public reporting when the reports are actually a form of communication from management to the shareholders. They say that management should have responsibility for setting the ground rules, since it's management's story that's being told. I, for one, would have a lot more sympathy for this point of view if we had more evidence that managements are willing to accept this responsibility in a forthright way. The current situation with segmental reporting is a good example of the kind of foot dragging that can happen when there are no guidelines set by the APB or the SEC.

Anderson: Do you have any facts on the current situation, Earl?

Cunningham: Yes. I did some homework, and the figures I came up with are not very encouraging. *(He refers to a sheet of paper.)* In 1967, only about 50% of diversified U.S. corporations were disclosing sales by product line and only about 10% were disclosing product-line earnings. A recent survey showed that 1970 annual reports were not much better. Of the 614 manufacturing companies surveyed, only 64% show a breakdown of sales and only 27% show a breakdown of earnings. Now, that's better than the previous year, but when you—

Anderson: Excuse me, Earl. How much better was that in terms of earnings?

Cunningham: That compares with 15% the year before, Martin. But considering that the fiscal 1970 reports came after the SEC ruling, that isn't a very good record for the advocates of voluntary disclosure. This area of product-line reporting is a very significant test case for the concept of reporting standards determined by management. Unless there's a big increase in the level of voluntary compliance, the AICPA and the SEC will take the situation as evidence that voluntarily imposed standards won't work. Then we can expect another round of rule making by both of them. I don't like arbitrary, generalized rules any more than you do, but I'm not sure there's any workable alternative.

Trumball: You seem to be assuming that more is better in product-line disclosure.

Cunningham: Yes, George, I am.

Trumball: My God, Earl, you're really opening up a Pandora's box! The next thing we know we'll be broadcasting our R&D expenses and our order backlog. There's a limit to what an outsider is entitled to know.

Fuller: I'm not so sure we shouldn't go ahead and report such items as R&D or backlog, George. You know as well as I do that any company our size can move earnings up or down by as much as 25% to 30% for a year or two by just cutting back or accelerating discretionary expenditures such as R&D, advertising, or repairs and maintenance. The reader of the annual report would have a lot better idea whether earnings were pumped up or smoothed out in any given year if he could see the level of our discretionary expenses in relation to the norm. Maybe this product-line thing is a good chance to raise a much broader issue about what we should be disclosing in our annual report.

Anderson: Well, I agree that the real issue is much broader than just product-line information. But I don't want to fight all the battles at once! Let's stick to the issue at hand. Now let me try to summarize where we stand. Bob and George—

Cunningham: Could I say one more thing before you do that, Martin?

Anderson: Sure. Go ahead.

Cunningham: That is, there are some interesting results in another study comparing what companies are disclosing in their annual reports and the 10-Ks. Of 100 companies taken from the 500 biggest industrials, 39 gave the same sales and earnings breakdowns in both and 39 showed no breakdowns at all in their annual reports. The rest were in between in the disclosure spectrum.

Anderson: Hmmm. No uniformity there, either. Now, to sum up, Bob and George are opposed to more disclosure than is absolutely necessary, which would mean none for the annual report and as little as possible for the 10-K. Carl and Earl want us to grab the bull by the horns and take a big step toward broadening our disclosure for both the annual report and the 10-K. Earl also feels that we're likely to be stuck later with more rules in this area that we might find very distasteful, if we don't move on our own hook now. Carl thinks there are serious problems in splitting up our operations, but the problems are solvable if we're willing to accept a certain amount of arbitrariness. After all, we make such splits all the time for internal purposes. Is that a fair summary?

Gooding: I think you're somewhat overemphasizing the degree of conclusiveness of the ideas we've thrown out, but your summary does pretty fairly reflect our comments so far. (*The others nod in agreement.*)

Anderson: This discussion has been very helpful to me in clarifying the issues and your different points of view about them. Now, assuming that more product-line disclosure in annual reports is fairly likely in future years, I would like to hear some discussion as to whether we start in the current year or wait until next year, or even later.

Gooding: There are a couple of considerations that suggest waiting until at least next year, Martin. First is the chance to see how far other companies go in this area before we commit ourselves. We run the risk of being really out of step. The other thing is the fact that fiscal '72 isn't going to be a very good year for us. Several of the divisions are coming in with losses, and others are going to be well below par. I don't think we should go out of our way to air our dirty linen in public.

Trumball: Well, I don't feel as strongly about when we start as I do about starting versus not starting at all. But I think a case can be made for going ahead this year. A bad year is not necessarily a bad time to start. It sets up a very attainable benchmark for comparisons in future years. Also, everybody knows that '71 was a bad year, so there's no particular stigma in showing some red ink. If we're going to do it eventually, the chance to be one of the leaders in this disclosure thing is a big reason for going ahead right away.

Fuller: George is right on this one, Martin. Whatever it is we're going to do differently, we should go ahead and do it this year.

Anderson: At least we still have a perfect record as far as consensus goes today —absolutely none! Carl, if we did go ahead with some sort of product-line data in this year's annual report, would it be possible to give a breakdown of assets employed as well as sales and earnings?

Fuller: An approximation is certainly possible. As a matter of fact, I had the Controller's office work one up last week. The trouble is, it's often difficult to decide who has the asset. Most accounts receivable are centralized at the group level, for instance. Prepaid expenses, most investments, and some buildings are only identifiable at the corporate level. Also, the fixed asset numbers represent historical cost, less depreciation, and the purchases were made over a great number of years. We could use replacement cost data as we do for internal ROI calculations, but then the numbers wouldn't agree with the financial statements. The result is that comparisons of ROI across divisions aren't very meaningful. In fact, I think the whole asset breakdown isn't very meaningful.

Anderson: Do I understand correctly, Earl, that no asset breakdown is required by the SEC?

Cunningham: That's right.

Anderson: Is the APB likely to include a requirement on assets?

Cunningham: In my opinion, no.

Anderson: Well, gentlemen, it's getting late and I have a plane to catch, so let's bring the meeting to a close. Thanks for sitting in, Earl. I want to think about this product-line business a while longer before I decide to fish or cut bait.

QUERY TO READERS

If you were the president of Allied Machinery, what action would you recommend for the upcoming annual report? Would you show any segmented results? If so, would you go beyond the breakdown shown in the 10-K report? If so, how far would you go and how would you define the segments?

Take a few minutes to formulate your thoughts so that you can compare them with those of our panel of commentators. You may also want to consider the broader aspects of the issue since the commentators deal with more than just Allied's particular problem.

DISCLOSE OR NOT?

All three commentators are convinced that Allied should include some form of product-line disclosure in the upcoming annual report. Their rationales, however, differ. Leonard M. Savoie, Executive Vice President of the American Institute of Certified Public Accountants, is enthusiastically in favor of broader disclosure. He writes:

The more I hear the arguments for and against disclosure of product-line information in annual reports, the more I am convinced that the time has come for publicly owned corporations to make full disclosure of their operations to the investing public. Diversified companies like Allied should report sales and net income, at least, by line of business—refined to the extent that is practical and with full explanation of significant reasons for relative performances.

In this era of consumerism and concern over insider information, an enlightened management should absolutely insist on giving stockholders as much financial information as the SEC requires in a prospectus.

John E. O'Sullivan, Executive Vice President of Indian Head, Inc. is also a firm supporter of broader disclosure, partly because of the availability of information elsewhere. Part of his support also derives from a desire to avoid further unwanted regulation of corporate practices in this area. In his words:

By filing with the SEC, a company makes information available to those that want to go and read the SEC files. It is my belief, and it seems logical, that these data should be included in the annual report because Allied's shareholders, *employees,* analysts, the investment community, and the general public have every right to know how a company is doing by its major segments. This is what the SEC intended.

A diversified company attempting to circumvent this intent by claiming that all its products fall into one broad business category and that reporting by segment, therefore, does not apply to them invites government retaliation and, ultimately, extremely restrictive and unreasonable reporting requirements.

Allied Machinery, with nearly $1 billion in sales, would rank about No. 120 in *Fortune's* '500.' This large corporation's management is late with a capital *L* and lacks leadership in taking steps to follow the trend.

This trend is part of a broader trend toward more responsible stewardship by management. Ignoring the very real need for detailed financial information, particularly in the larger and more mature companies, is a disservice that shortchanges the company, its stockholders, and its employees. As corporations are subject to more and more scrutiny by vocal critics, it is necessary for companies to make fuller disclosure voluntarily. By taking such steps, they can, perhaps, make it more difficult for onerous and arbitrary requirements to be imposed.

John V. van Pelt, III, Vice President-Finance of Vulcan Materials Company, likewise believes that the tide is irreversible. He writes:

Martin Anderson must realize that disclosure of sales and earnings by product line is inevitable. Unless corporations use intelligence in responding to the public insistence for such disclosure, it is certain that the requirements will be dictated by governmental bodies.

The SEC has adopted a permissive approach so far. Extremists are thinking in terms of disclosure by S.I.C. codes, and some legislators have made public statements that the SEC is not doing an adequate job in this area.

COMPETITIVE IMPACT

None of the commentators is impressed with the claim of competitive disadvantage. Mr. Savoie states:

Particularly weak is Bob Gooding's argument that product-line disclosures in the annual report would give valuable information to competitors. Competitors have always had ways of finding out about each other's operations. Now they only have to look at the Form 10-K or a prospectus in order to get product-line information. Withholding it from the annual report only makes it relatively inaccessible to the stockholder.

Mr. van Pelt thinks that disclosure need not be revealing, after all:

> Anderson can satisfy himself that a breakdown by grouping will not help his competitors. Information on a broad group does not provide much help in deciding how well a company is doing with a specific product.

Mr. O'Sullivan wonders how meaningful such data are:

> The argument that fuller information can be damaging to the firm's competitive position doesn't hold water. You would be hard-pressed to find two companies—both complying with the spirit of the SEC requirements—whose data could be compared and meaningful market intelligence derived from them. Identical markets, products, distribution channels, product mix, and so forth, just don't exist in different companies.
>
> For example, General Electric's appliance consumer products group information would not be comparable to Westinghouse's. From such figures, one could not tell who has what percent of market shares for electric toothbrushes or mixers. There are many single-product companies competing with multiproduct companies who have not lost their competitive edge, despite their giving complete information in the annual report.

HOW MUCH DISCLOSURE?

In support of his contention that a breakdown by group is adequate, Mr. van Pelt asserts that it would satisfy the primary reader of the report at whom the company is "aiming":

> Before determining the breakdown. Anderson should know the primary audience he wishes to reach. It is not the average stockholder because he does not assimilate most of the information in the annual report and is rarely motivated by it in his investment decision. In terms of accounting data, Anderson is not really trying to reach the customer, though the report can be a selling tool. Obviously, his competitors, the government, publicly oriented organizations, and labor may be interested readers; but the objective of the report in these cases is primarily to create a good impression without disclosing too much.
>
> Basically, the report is written for security analysts, since they make the buy, hold, and sell recommendations for institutional investors and are the source of recommendations which brokerage houses make to their customers. Security analysts are a major factor in determining the price of a company's stock in relation to other issues being traded.
>
> Anderson should resolve to make the report a working tool in his relations with security analysts. They are impressed by management's efforts to paint a clear picture of its situation, and they have negative feelings when a company is obviously trying to hide pertinent information.
>
> A breakdown by class of customers, which in this case conforms to the orga-

nizational breakdown, would be meaningful. It wouldn't be necessary to break out each division, and in conversation it would be relatively simple for Allied's management to fend off disclosure of sales and earnings of the divisional elements that make up the groups publicly reported. Under present conditions the company has much latitude in meeting SEC requirements. On this basis, both the 10-K and annual report would show a product breakdown by consumer, industrial, defense-aerospace, and international groups.

Mr. O'Sullivan also proposes a procedure for the company to follow in making the appropriate breakdown:

> Allied Machinery's disclosure in the annual report should be more detailed than the breakdown it has for its 10-K but less than that in *Exhibit 1*. Before making that decision, however, management should draw up a schedule of the past five years' results—sales and profits—and also do pro forma projections for three to five years ahead.
>
> In this way management can see how a given approach to disclosure would work over a long period of time. It should try to anticipate any unusual swings or distortions that cannot easily be explained. The approach it finally takes should be one that it can live with for some time without major changes.

TECHNICAL PROBLEMS

Mr. O'Sullivan is not particularly concerned about the accounting problems involved in segmented disclosure:

> Certainly there are accounting problems in many companies for allocating costs, intracompany pricing, and so on, which makes this task difficult. But it can and should be done using good common business sense. As long as it is done on a logical basis—consistent from year to year—it can be very valuable information.
>
> If disclosure is done this way, comparisons will be meaningful and the investing community will know which segments are doing better or worse. If there are any unusually large expenses for research and development or special deferred-income items, then the company will have to decide whether the exception is material enough to disclose to the stockholders.

Mr. van Pelt favors minimizing the technical problems by dealing with available data and avoiding data based on one-time allocations:

> Interested security analysts are in constant verbal communication with more than one officer of the company. This puts a company at a disadvantage in view of the requirement that if it gives one party significant information, it must issue the information publicly. For this reason, it is better to stick to readily available information, as opposed to specially developed figures.
>
> If the annual report contains figures based on one-time allocations, the officers, when answering analysts' questions, will be constantly trapped in discrepancies between publicly reported figures and internal figures that do not include allocations. The exercise of reconciliation during the course of a conversation often reveals underlying divisional results.
>
> The solution is to report publicly without allocation, treating corporate cost as one lump sum. Taxes would be shown separately, or earnings reported on a pretax basis.

Mr. Savoie is also convinced that the accounting problems are not significant:

> Technical problems do arise in allocating common costs among segments and in accounting for intersegment transactions. The more of these a company has, the less likely it is to have separate lines of business. But the existence of some common costs and intersegment transactions should not be used as an excuse for the failure to report by lines of business that are really different.
>
> Every diversified company measures results of its various lines separately for internal management purposes. If it is worried about public disclosure because of questionable accuracy, that should be a spur to achieve greater accuracy, not an excuse for nondisclosure. In fact, the improved measurements might help management to run the business better.

Carl Fuller states that internal transfers at market price, rather than cost, and a very arbitrary allocation of corporate general expenses are departures from generally accepted accounting principles. I would state it in a different way—there are no standards in this area and, therefore, there are no departures.

My preference is to report internal transfers at market, thus recognizing a profit in the selling division. The interdivisional profit would be eliminated from the aggregate net income of all the divisions to arrive at net income as shown on the income statement.

ASSET BREAKDOWNS

Mr. Savoie's statement that management should provide shareholders as much information as is given in a prospectus implies going beyond product-line sales and earnings results. Details of R&D expenditures, promotion expenses, maintenance expenses, and order backlogs are regularly disclosed in prospectuses. Because of the higher order of technical problems involved, however, Mr. Savoie does not favor disclosure of divisional asset breakdowns.

Mr. van Pelt is more cautious about broadening the basis of disclosure in the annual report. He also opposes asset breakdown, but he goes further:

> Since the books do not provide a breakdown of jointly used plant assets, as well as cash and receivables, any intelligible breakdown would require substantial allocation. Furthermore, assets at depreciated cost may present a misleading picture in some of Allied's lines, such as Recreational Land Development.
>
> Under the circumstances there is no need to plow new ground in this area. Backlog data may be meaningful in Defense-Aerospace; but it is usually not so meaningful in Industrial Products, where there may be supply contracts with no specifically determinable amounts.
>
> Because of the lack of uniformity, every effort should be made to avoid formalizing this information as an overall company figure. But it may be necessary to explain in the text of the report the dollar amount of orders on hand for Defense-Aerospace.

REGULATORY ROLE

Mr. van Pelt and Mr. O'Sullivan have indicated that they want to avoid externally imposed standards and regulation by the SEC or the APB in this area. They place the responsibility for compliance on corporate management. Mr. Savoie, however, sees a positive role here for the APB:

The real obstacle to management's acceptance of product-line reporting is a lack of standards for disclosure. That is what the APB is attempting to provide in its proposed opinion. But this is not easy to do. Subsidiaries, divisions, and other organizational units often are not structured by separate industry.

The Robert Mautz research study on financial reporting by diversified companies concluded that more than one industry exists where segments of a company are subject to different rates of profitability, degrees of risk, or opportunities for growth. While this is a helpful analysis, it is hardly sufficient guidance to ensure that companies take a uniform approach to providing segmented information. A definition of 'separate line of business' is needed to set a uniform standard.

Earl Cunningham is perceptive in his recognition that management should have the responsibility for setting the ground rules and that management's foot dragging on voluntary disclosure will probably bring on rule making by the APB and the SEC. The APB would like to confine itself to issuing broad principles. But detailed rules are sometimes necessary in order to implement a principle, especially when managements do not adequately observe principles or even try to evade them.

C. **RELATIONSHIP BETWEEN ECONOMICS AND ACCOUNTING**

KENNETH E. BOULDING

KENNETH E. BOULDING (1910–), B.A. (hons.) 31, M.A. 39 Oxford; recipient of honorary degrees from 16 universities. Currently professor of economics, University of Colorado. Among his books are the following: *Economic Analysis* (1941, 1948, 1955, 1966), *A Reconstruction of Economics* (1950), *The Organizational Revolution* (1953), *The Image* (1956), *Principles of Economic Policy* (1959), *Linear Programming and the Theory of the Firm* (with Spivey, 1960), *Beyond Economics* (1968), *Economics as a Science* (1970), *The Economy of Love and Fear: A Preface to Grants Economics* (1972). Frequent contributor to many journals in the social sciences and humanities.

Served as professor of economics, Iowa State University (1943–46, 1947–49), McGill University (1946–47), University of Michigan (1949–67), and University of Colorado (since 1967).

Was vice-president, 1958, and president, 1968, of the American Economic Association. Has been a fellow of the American Academy of Arts and Sciences since 1958, and of the American Philosophical Society since 1960. Was recipient of the John Bates Clark Medal, presented by the American Economic Association, in 1949, and of the American Council of Learned Societies Prize for Distinguished Scholarship in the Humanities, in 1962.

ECONOMICS AND ACCOUNTING: THE UNCONGENIAL TWINS

KENNETH E. BOULDING

Economics and accountancy are two disciplines which draw their raw material from much the same mines. From these raw materials, however, they seem to fashion remarkably different products. They both study the operations of firms; they both are concerned with such concepts as income, expenditure, profits, capital, value and prices. In spite of an apparently common subject-matter, however, they often seem to inhabit totally different worlds, between which there is remarkably little communication. When I studied economics at Oxford a generation ago, it was not considered necessary for an economist to know any accounting at all. Indeed, as far as I recall, not even the opportunity to study accounting

SOURCE: From *Studies in Accounting Theory*, edited by W. T. Baxter and Sidney Davidson (Homewood, Ill.: R. D. Irwin, Inc., 1962), pp. 44–55. Reprinted by permission of R. D. Irwin, Inc.

was given. It was no doubt regarded as a pedestrian, commercial, workaday subject, quite unworthy of being admitted to those dignified halls. The situation, I am sure, is better at the newer institutions, both in Britain and the United States. Even in the United States, however, accounting is rarely integrated in any systematic or satisfactory way into an economist's education. The student of economics frequently has to pass a single required course in accounting, and that is the end of it. There is very little intellectual intercourse between economists and accountants at the professional level. The faults here may be more on the side of the economists than of the accountants. It is very rare to find an economist who reads the accounting journals. It is almost equally rare, however, to find an accountant who is well versed in economics.

This situation is all the more deplorable because many of the basic concepts of economics are, in fact, derived from accounting practice, and many accounting practices have been devised in an attempt to answer what are essentially economic questions. The concept of profit, for instance, is essentially an accounting concept. A large amount of the activity of accountants consists in the attempt to measure it. The concept of profit is likewise fundamental to economics. It is supposed to be the great motive power of a market system. It is supposed to account for the behavior of enterprises, and it is supposed to guide the allocation of resources among competing uses. The economist's concept of profit, however, and the accountant's concept often seem to have little in common. We do not, of course, have to have a single concept of profit for all purposes. The concept of profit will quite rightly differ depending upon the purpose for which we need it. The definition of profit for tax purposes, for instance, may differ considerably from the definition which is required for other forms of decision-making. What we need here is not a single definition of profit applicable to all cases, but a spectrum of definitions, in which the relationship of the various concepts is reasonably clear and in which the definition is fitted to the purpose for which it is to be used.

The point where accounting and economics come closest together is in what the economists call the theory of the firm. This is not surprising, as it is with a formalized and abstract description of the history of the firm that accounting is largely concerned, especially if we stretch the concept of the firm to include governmental and non-profit organizations of an economic character. The basic concept here both for accounting and for economics is that of the balance-sheet or position statement. This is essentially a description of the state of a firm or enterprise at a given moment of time. In its simplest form, what might be called the physical balance-sheet of an enterprise consists of a simple list of the values of all variables which are associated with it as they exist at a moment of time. This is a much larger concept, of course, than that of the accountant's balance-sheet. A great many variables which might be significant from the point of view of the state of the enterprise and especially from the point of view of its future, such as the quality of its management, or the morale of its work force, are quite rightly excluded from the accountant's balance-sheet. The accountant is interested in a limited aspect of the state of the enterprise, confined to those items which can be reduced by some rule or other to a value equivalent. What the accountant is doing, that is, when he constructs the balance-sheet, is essentially to make up a list of those items associated with the enterprise which can be valued, and he then proceeds to value them: he replaces the physical quantity of the item by so many dollars, pounds, or whatever the valuation unit may be. This he does by a variety of techniques, the end product of which is all the same—a sum of monetary values.

The ratio of the physical quantity of some item in the physical balance-sheet to the corresponding value equivalent may be called the "valuation coefficient." Frequently, the valuation process is performed by a rule which establishes a valuation coefficient, and then the value of a given physical quantity is obtained by simply multiplying the physical quantity by this coefficient. Thus if an enterprise has a stock of a thousand bushels of wheat, we value this stock at some price or cost per bushel, say $2 per bushel, which is the valuation coefficient, and the total value of the stock is then $2,000. Some confusion may be caused by the fact that certain items in the physical balance-sheet are already expressed as a sum of money, for instance, a loan or a bond. In this case, of course, the valuation coefficient is unity, but it still exists.

The accountant gives some such name as net worth to the total net value of an enterprise. This is the sum of all the value items, both positive and negative (*i.e.*, assets less liabilities). The accountant may not seem to attach much significance to net worth by itself, but he is very interested indirectly in the size of this total, since—as we shall see in Figure 2—the size of his profit figure depends on changes in net worth.

The difference in outlook of economists and accountants is perhaps one of emphasis rather than of principle. We may say, however, that accountants are primarily interested in the enterprise as it is now and as it has been in the past. The economist is interested in the "might have beens," as well as the actual situation. The accountant asks himself simply how profitable is the enterprise; the economist asks himself how profitable it might have been if it had done something different, and especially what it would have to do in order to make maximum profits.

Another possible difference, although the accountant might deny this, is that the accountant has a focus of interest in certain aggregates and totals, such as net worth or aggregate profit figures, whereas the economist is more interested in the structure of the enterprises. This interest in structure is admittedly soft-pedalled by many economists; it is a fair criticism of the theory of the firm, as set out in most economics textbooks, that the firm is depicted as acutely concerned with possible costs and revenues, and oblivious of asset structure—as having a profit budget but no balance-sheet.

To put the point in more mathematical language, the economist is interested in the balance sheet as a vector in n-space. The accountant is interested in reducing this n-dimensional vector to a simple scalar, that is a single number. Unfortunately, even though rules can be applied, that is principles of valuation, for reducing an n-dimensional vector to a single number, these rules are inevitably somewhat arbitrary, and different rules may give entirely different results. This principle can be illustrated in Figure 1 in which we take an extremely simple enterprise, which has only two assets which we will call wheat, measured along OW, and money, along OM. A point P in this field represents a position or state of the enterprise, that is, its physical balance-sheet. Thus, the point P represents an enterprise with NP bushels of wheat and VP shillings of money. If, now, we want to represent this position by a single figure, we have to value the wheat. If we suppose NK to be the value of the amount of wheat NP, then the valuation coefficient is $\frac{NK}{NP^1}$ which is the slope of the line KP. The net worth of the enterprise is then $ON + NK$, or OK. Consider now, two different positions of the enterprice, P and P^1 (the latter standing for more wheat and less money). The accountant wishes to know which of these two positions represents the larger value or net worth. If the valuation coefficient for wheat is the slope of KP and K^1P^1, then it is clear that P^1 represents the larger value, that is, the larger net worth, as OK^1 is larger than OK. Suppose, however, that we value the wheat at a lower price or coefficient equal to the slope of LP and L^1P^1. Now we see that the point P represents the higher value OL, whereas the point P^1 represents the lower value OL^1. Without knowing a set of valuation coefficients, therefore, we cannot tell whether the point P is "larger" or "smaller" than P^1. This is why the valuation procedure may properly be regarded as the heart of accountancy.

Both economics and accountancy are interested, not only in the state of an enterprise at a moment, but also in the course of the enterprise through time, that is, the sequence of position statements as they pass from one time period to the next. Suppose, for instance, that in Figure 2, in which the axes have the same meaning as in Figure 1, the point P_0 represents an initial position of the enterprise. Suppose now that the firm buys more wheat, moving from position P_0 to P_1. This means it gives up an amount of money equal to P_0Q and acquires an amount of wheat equal to QP_1. The price at which the wheat has been bought is $\frac{P_0Q}{QP_1}$ which is the slope of the line P_0P_1. Now suppose the firm sells wheat following the line P_1P_2, i.e., at a higher price. It is clear that in some sense a profit has been made. How much profit, depends on the valuation coefficients which are used. P_2 might even indicate smaller profit than P_0, if wheat were valued on both dates at a very high valuation coefficient, such as the slope of K_0P_0 and K_2P_2 (which reduces net worth from OK_0 to OK_2); but the accountant's bias towards conservatism will in general make for low coefficients, and so depress net worth where stocks of goods are high. In the course of successive periods, the enterprise will move to positions such as P_3, P_4, P_5, etc. If its opera-

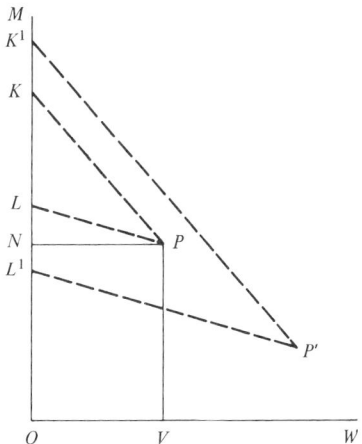

FIGURE 1

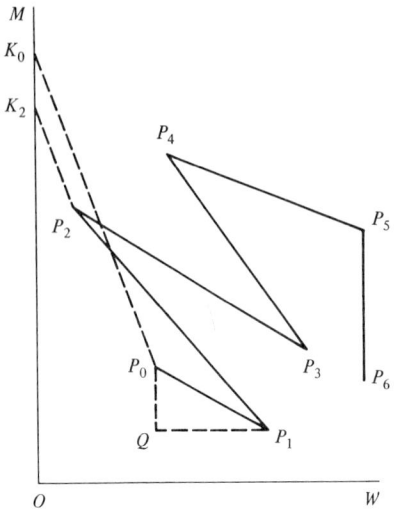

FIGURE 2

tions have been successful, the result of these various transformations will be to move its position in some sense further "out" in the field. Exactly what constitutes "out," however, depends upon the system of valuation.

Profit can always be defined, in some sense, to mean an increase in net worth. The calculation of profit, that is to say, always involves the calculation of net worth from the position statements of two successive periods.[1] The rate of profit is the rate of increase of net worth in some sense or another. The problem is complicated somewhat by the fact that there may not only be asset transformations in the course of the history of the enterprise, there may also be withdrawals, that is, simple deductions from assets of one kind or another. Thus from the positions P_5 in Figure 2, we could go directly downward to P_6 indicating a simple withdrawal of money from the enterprise. Yet a third event which may take place during the history of an enterprise is a revaluation—say, a change in the valuation coefficient by which physical assets are valued.

Virtually all events which are of significance to the enterprise can be classified in one of these three categories, either as an asset transformation, a revaluation, or a withdrawal. Asset transformations may be either through production or through exchange. When a miller grinds wheat into flour, for instance, he diminishes the quantity of wheat (raw materials) in the inventory shown in his position statement, and increases the quantity of flour (finished goods). When he exchanges flour, let us say, for accounts receivable, he diminishes the quantity of flour and increases the quantity of accounts receivable. The most fundamental concept of *cost* is that it represents the transformation ratio in *production*, that is, the ratio in which the input assets are transformed into the output assets. The most fundamental concept of *price* is that of the asset transformation ratio in

---

[1] This may not be obvious to accounting students trained to draft income statements *before* balance-sheets. But the costs and revenues in the former statement are all implicit in the changes in the latter, and are measured by these changes.

The accountant on occasion isolates some gains, *e.g.*, windfalls may be shown separately from operating profit. But such technicalities do not affect the main argument.

exchange. If wheat costs $1.50 a bushel, this means on the whole that resources or inputs equivalent to $1.50 have to be used up or destroyed in order to increase the stock of wheat by one bushel. If the price of wheat is $2 a bushel, this means that wheat can be transformed into money through exchange at this rate.

Withdrawals may also be of two kinds, positive and negative. A negative withdrawal consists usually of simply putting money into the enterprise. The initial capital of an enterprise represents a negative withdrawal which is usually the first event in its history from the accounting point of view. Interest and dividend payments, of course, represent positive withdrawals.

In accounting practice, revaluations frequently occur at the moment of sale. Inventory, for instance, will be valued at cost in some sense until the moment of sale, when the article is revalued to the sale price. At the moment of sale (that is, in the asset transformation) there is both a change of values from one item in the position statement to another, and an increase in values. The profit-making occurs essentially in the revaluation which takes place at the moment of sale. The fact that revaluation and exchange are bound up in a single transaction has often caused confusion, and it is necessary, analytically, to separate these two essentially dissimilar operations.

Another important difference between the accountant's and the economist's point of view, as we have seen, is that the accountant on the whole is interested in what is or what has been, whereas the economist is interested in what might be. In particular the economist is interested in the problem of what he calls "maximizing behavior." The accountant is interested, primarily, in what has happened to the enterprise in the past and in what is its position today; the economist is interested in the question of whether the enterprise could have done better. In accounting, for instance, price is largely treated as a datum and as a constant. In economics, price is usually treated as a variable. The economist asks himself what would have happened if there had been a different set of prices, exchanges, transformations, or withdrawals from that which actually occurred. Would the enterprise be better off now, or worse off? In particular, the economist is interested in the best pattern of behavior, that is, the pattern of behavior which places the enterprise in a position superior to that which can be reached by any other pattern of behavior. Achieving this best pattern is what the economist means by "maximizing behavior."

A good many of the propositions of price theory are based on the assumption that businessmen do, in fact, maximize profits. This is, of course, a highly dubious assumption. It is not only that there are always things for which businessmen are willing to sacrifice profits, such as security, respectability, liquidity, and so on, which means, of course, that they do not maximize profits. But a more fundamental difficulty is that the information which would enable a businessman to maximize his profits generally is not available to him. The difficulty here is a very fundamental one for the accountant and for the economist. Decisions are always made in the hope of the future, whereas information is always derived from the past. The theory of maximizing behavior assumes implicitly that we know all the possible patterns of the future and that we can select the best out of them. Our knowledge of the future, however, must be derived from our experience of the past, and our experience of the past is highly limited. Our image of the future or of the various possible futures is always dependent on some kind of projection of our past experience. These projections, however, are unreliable and they may be based on a very limited perception of the kind of dynamic system in which the enterprise operates. The basic difficulty here is that the future depends not only on the decision of one person, but on the decisions of all the decision-makers of a society. A man can control his own decisions within limits, but he cannot control the decisions of others even though he may attempt to predict them. Because of this, there are bound to be inconsistencies in the images of the future of different individuals, which means that some of them must be falsified. Maximizing behavior, that is to say, is something which cannot be universally applied by its very nature.

In spite of the practical difficulties in the way of maximizing profit, the economist's theory of maximization, which is known usually as the marginal analysis, has a good deal of merit. Its merit lies perhaps in the questions which it raises rather than in the answers which it is able to give. It is always useful to take a given situation and to ask, "Could we have done better?" It is also useful to ask, "What do we need to know in order that we could do better?" It is perhaps because of pressure from the economist that the accountant has in many instances become interested in the concept of what he calls "incremental cost" and what the economist calls "marginal cost." These two concepts are not perhaps identical but they are closely related. The economist looks at a given situation and asks himself "Suppose we did something a little different? Would the increase in revenue be greater than the increase in cost?" If it is, then profits are clearly not being maximized now, and we shall do well to make the change. If, on the other hand, a given change increases revenue less than it increases cost, not only are we very sure that we should not make the change but we have evidence that we should make a change in an opposite direction. Even though, therefore, we can seldom be sure that we are actually at the point of maximum profit, we can frequently tell whether a proposed change is likely to move us toward that point or away from it. The economist recognizes, of course, that marginal costs or receipts are hard to measure. They represent a "might be" rather than an "is" and they are, therefore, not perhaps congenial to the accountant's insistence on the measurement of the actual. It is potentialities, however, rather than actualities which are most significant in the making of decisions, and in so far as we regard the whole process of information collection and processing in the organization as essentially an aid to the making of decisions, these potentialities are even more important than the actualities.

We shall notice also that the accountant himself is not altogether free from the necessity of considering potentialities, and in particular he cannot avoid making certain projections about the future. This is implicit, in fact, in an evaluation process. The act of valuation, Janus-like, has two faces. It faces back into the past and forward into the future. On the one hand, we value assets by past cost, sometimes compounded; on the other hand, we value them as discounted future net receipts. The former is what we can most easily find out; the latter, however, is the truly significant figure. The accountant is wise to take the past accounts as the basis for his evaluations. He may sometimes recognize the uncertainties of the present and of the future by making write-ups or write-downs, as the case may be—periodically adjusting past accounts to the present knowledge of the future. If he does not do this, the stock market will tend to do it for him. A firm, for instance, which has sunk a lot of money into assets in a country undergoing the fervors of a revolution is likely to find that the stock market values its shares on future expectations rather than past costs. In economics, as Jevons once said, "Bygones are bygones." For the accountant, bygones are not bygones without a struggle. It is probably just as well that he struggles. Sometimes, however, the struggle must be abandoned and bygone costs must be written down (or up) in the face of present realities.

The implication of the above is that even the accountant's calculation of profit is essentially based on some expectations about the future. Profit is not simply a matter of past performance; it always has in it an element of future expectation. This is because profit depends upon revaluations, and these revaluations may have to be made in the light of changes in expectations in the future. A firm which suffers a diminution of the value of its assets by a million pounds for whatever reason also suffers a diminution of its current profit—in our fundamental sense—by a million pounds. Profit, therefore, is not merely a matter of trying to sell again at a higher price. Many of the elements of cost in fact involve future expectations. It has been said that we should call no man happy until he is dead; likewise perhaps we should call no firm profitable until it has been finally liquidated. Nevertheless, the accountant must give some kind of an answer to the question "What profits have been earned?" He must do this for legal as well as for decision-making reasons, for the law requires that, to some extent, the behavior of a firm conform to, or at least be limited by, its accounting results, especially for purposes of paying taxes or for distributing dividends.

The economist then looks on the accountant as a man who has to perform an impossible task. He has first to reduce what is essentially a multi-dimensional reality to a one-dimensional figure; and, in the second place, he has to do this on the basis of knowledge about the future which he cannot possibly have. Under these circumstances, it is not surprising that the economist regards much accounting procedure as in the nature of ritual. To call these procedures ritualistic is in no way to deny or decry their validity. Ritual is always the proper response when a man *has* to give an answer to a question, the answer to which he cannot really know. Ritual under these circumstances has two functions. It is comforting (and in the face of the great uncertainties of the future, comfort is not to be despised) and it is also an answer sufficient for action. It is the sufficient answer rather than the right answer which the accountant really seeks. Under these circumstances, however, it is important that we should know what the accountant's answer means, which means that we should know what procedure he has employed. The wise businessman will not believe his accountant although he takes what his accountant tells him as important evidence. The quality of that evidence, however, depends in considerable degree on the simplicity of the procedures and the awareness which we have of them. What the accountant tells us may not be true, but, if we know what he has done, we have a fair idea of what it means. For this reason, I am somewhat suspicious of many current efforts to reform accounting in the direction of making it more "accurate."

I am particularly suspicious of attempts to improve accounting by building into it an explicit recognition of the fact that the price level changes. It is easy to criticize accounting practice—and this is a criticism which economists have frequently made—on the ground that it assumes a monetary unit of constant value whereas in fact the monetary unit fluctuates constantly in purchasing power. The accountant's balance-sheet, it is argued, is reckoned in dollars of different ages, some of them perhaps of the year of the founding of the enterprise and others of last week. In the interim, however, the value of the monetary unit may have changed completely through the large social forces of inflation and deflation. This is almost as if we were trying to add feet to centimeters without reducing them to a common unit of length. A hundred feet plus ten centimeters is certainly not a hundred and ten anythings, and the accountant's balance-sheet total is not much better. It is argued also that because the accountant tends to perform valuation on the basis of historical cost, his measure of profit is inflated in a period of inflation and is correspondingly depressed in a period of deflation. Profits are made by selling things at a price greater than the cost. In an inflationary period, however, if the cost has been incurred at an earlier date, the price will reflect the general rise in prices as well as the relative price of a particular commodity. Hence, profits in accounts will be larger than they should be in terms of a dollar of constant purchasing power. Deflation destroys accounting profits in a similar way. An attempt is made to correct this distortion through valuing inventories by the last-in, first-out method, which is a more sophisticated substitute for the original first-in, first-out method.

The case for "constant dollar" accounting may be a strong one, but it is by no means invulnerable. The profits of inflation and the losses of deflation are not altogether illusory to the individual concern. Inflation, for instance, affects the real distribution of wealth away from those who hold liquid assets towards those who hold assets which are rising in price. Up to a point, the accounting profits of inflation reflect this, although they probably exaggerate it. Similarly, a deflation redistributes wealth towards those who simply sit tight with liquid assets, and the accounting losses therefore of those who trade and indulge in enterprise at such periods, again, are a partial reflection of this fact. There is something to be said also for a certain naïveté and simplicity in accounting practice. If accounts are bound to be untruths anyhow, as I have argued, there is much to be said for the simple untruth as against a complicated untruth, for if the untruth is simple, it seems to me that we have a fair chance of knowing what kind of an untruth it is. A known untruth is much better than a lie, and provided that the accounting rituals are well known and understood, accounting may be untrue but it is not lies; it does not deceive because we know that it does not tell the truth, and we are able to make our own adjustment in each individual case, using the results of the accountant as evidence rather than as definitive information.

My plea for naïveté, or at least for simplicity in accounting practice, does not preclude the hope that one day we may be able to set the whole information-collecting and processing operation of an organization on a somewhat more rational basis than now exists. At present one suspects that a great deal of information is collected and processed which actually is irrelevant to the making of decisions or the taking of any kind of action. The collection of such information is pure waste from the point of view of the organization even though it may have certain scientific value. Scientific information, however, is much better collected directly than as a by-product of other operations. By contrast, a great deal of information which is highly relevant to the making of decisions is neither collected nor processed. Nobody, to my mind, has yet developed an adequate theory of information collection and processing from the point of view of the decision-making process. When this is done, we may find that both accounting and economics may each lose their life in a larger science and a larger process. Until that day comes, one can only plead for more communication and understanding between the accountant and the economist, for each has much to learn from the other, especially if each recognizes the autonomy of the other. Their concepts are often different because the purposes for which they are used are different. These differences must be borne in mind if fruitful communication is to take place.

D. CONFLICT BETWEEN ACCOUNTING PRINCIPLES AND TAXATION

ARTHUR M. CANNON

ARTHUR M. CANNON (1911–1963), B.S. 33, M.A. 47 Oregon; CPA. Contributor to *The Journal of Accountancy*, *The Accounting Review*, and other journals. Book review editor, *The Accounting Review*, 1950–57, and served as editor or coeditor (with Walker) of the books and articles department of *The Journal of Accountancy*, 1954–59.

Was associated with Price Waterhouse & Co. and Whitfield, Stratford & Co. (now Haskins & Sells), 1933–40, in Portland, Oregon. In 1940, he became manager of a chain of wholesale bakeries in southern Oregon and northern California. Joined the University of Washington faculty in 1947, and in 1956 became vice-president of Standard Insurance Company, Portland, Oregon, a position he held at the time of his death.

Served as vice-president, American Accounting Association, 1955, and as president of the Oregon Society of Certified Public Accountants, 1962–63. He was a member of the AICPA Accounting Principles Board from 1959 to 1963.

TAX PRESSURES ON ACOUNTING PRINCIPLES AND ACCOUNTANTS' INDEPENDENCE*

ARTHUR M. CANNON

TAXABLE INCOME AND BUSINESS INCOME [1]

In the early days of income taxation the concept of "income" was imperfectly understood and tended to be confused with simple cash receipts or net cash increase, and some heritage of this confusion remains in our difficulties with the concept of realization. However with the 1918 expansion and re-examination of the tax the earlier simple cash-basis approach was deemed unworkable in broad

* The purpose of this article is to examine the effect of tax considerations on the application of accounting principles. Since 1952, there have been many changes in the law as well as changes in the tax rates. The current tax rates are reflected parenthetically; however, the more substantive changes are not reflected here. This article should be studied for its message concerning the conflict between accounting principles and taxation and *not* to understand *current* tax laws. [Eds.]

SOURCE: From *The Accounting Review*, Vol. XXVII, No. 4 (October, 1952), pp. 419–426. Reprinted by permission of the American Accounting Association.

[1] See Smith and Butters' *Taxable and Business Income* (New York: National Bureau

areas and the principle developed that income should be determined "in accordance with the taxpayer's regular method of accounting" if satisfactory to the Commissioner, and generally speaking on the accrual basis, and this remains the basic rule today.

Over the years and at an accelerating rate divergencies between taxable and business income have become so important and all-pervasive that the validity of the basic rule must be challenged outright, though it has been regarded as axiomatic or sacrosanct. Thus there has been an effort to maintain an unrealistic or impossible identity of what appear to be two different concepts. This effort is interfering with the proper understanding and development of both accounting principles and proper bases of taxation. The result is injustice and inconsistency between taxpayers. There also is exerted an unhealthy but powerful influence on accounting; tax law and enforcement are influencing accounting principles much more than the opposite. The time has come to recognize by divorce the separation-in-fact between taxable and business income, permitting each to go its way pursuant to the underlying purposes and nature of each.

Every man is his own tax expert these days and sometimes it seems that tax considerations are not just the most important but the only considerations at the top level in business policy determination. Everybody knows that income costs money—i.e. that *taxable* income costs money, and to nearly everyone this means that *accounting* income costs money. Most people realize in a vague sort of way that income before taxes is determined by various non-accounting considerations, largely in the market-place (except for regulated business); and that the accountant attempts to determine what that income was; but they also realize that what the accountant determines as income has a lot to do with what is left after taxes. Tax considerations give income-determining significance to accounting decisions. What powerful pressures are brought to bear on accounting principles with corporations at 52%–82% [today: 48%] and individuals at 22%–92% rates [today: 14%–70%]! If what accountants are trying to determine is something different from what Uncle is after and what the taxpayer is trying to hang on to, then the accountant, the "innocent bystander," is in an unnecessarily exposed position.

A review of the divergencies which have developed between taxable and business income is likely to surprise most accountants, legislators, lawyers, economists and certainly taxpayers.

Among the most important present differences are the following:

1. *Percentage depletion.* Depletion as a percentage of revenue unrelated to cost as now deductible for tax purposes by many extractive industries, is absolutely foreign to the matching of costs with revenue, accounting's central

---

of Economic Research, 1949), and the continuing series on *Effects of Taxation* from the Harvard Business School. See also the Business Income Study Group's *Changing Concepts of Business Income* (New York: Macmillan Company, 1952) and supplementary publications, and the splendid reviews thereof by George Husband in *The Accounting Review*, July, 1952, and by Eric Kohler in *The Illinois Certified Public Accountant*, March, 1952 and by Percival Brundage in *The Journal of Accountancy*, February, 1952. There is a considerable bibliography on the subject, lengthened by the effects of the business cycle in the 1930's and now again in the 1950's.

problem. The current free-enterprise prosperity of Texas is percentage-depletion prosperity.

2. *Accelerated amortization* (as of emergency facilities, etc.). Where the determination of useful life for depreciation purposes is made by administrative fiat—five year,—any relation to proper accounting depreciation is purely coincidental. In Britain a similar practice is a flat initial allowance—40% [today: variety of rates] the first year. Both provisions are in effect interest-free loans to encourage certain types of capital formation, the *total* depreciation being limited to cost. Yet this simple expedient, or subterfuge for a modest subsidy, has for the most part been carefully wrapped up in the accounts with resulting successive understatement and overstatement of profits.

3. *Inventory methods.* Anyone who thinks that the spectacular swing to LIFO comes from an equally sudden awakening of accountants to its intrinsic merits à la some of the rationalizations, has got his head in the sand. LIFO has been adopted for tax purposes. The Bureau in a holding action managed to limit the use of LIFO to those concerns regularly using it, in their accounts and statements, thinking that this limitation would effectively restrict use to industries to which LIFO had in generally accepted accounting principles been regarded as appropriate. How wrong they were! Where it has appeared tax-wise to use LIFO there has been no trouble at all in getting it into the statements. I do not argue the merits of LIFO. I simply point out that it has become incorporated into generally accepted accounting principles, as, i.e., for department stores, entirely as a result of certain tax advantages accompanied by a somewhat cynical Code provision which was consistent with the "basic rule" above cited. This has serious implications, to be dealt with more fully below.

4. *Pension plans and deferred compensation.* The reporting of cost has been in part or wholly dictated by deductibility for tax purposes, though perhaps in lieu of agreement on an alternative.

5. *Capital gains vs. "ordinary" income.* Here by reason of the 26% [today: 25%] tax limitation, one kind of income becomes more desirable than another. This is perhaps the principal tax consideration in contemporary business decisions. While the main influence is no doubt on the types of economic activities in which business men engage, there is also much influence on the *form* in which such activities are undertaken or described.

6. *Substituted, carried-forward, stepped-up and transferors' bases.* These special types of "cost" for tax purposes are related to tax-free exchanges, involuntary conversion, and to item 5 above; also included in the category are bases established as of March 1, 1913, and others. In the lumber industry we have a provision that in effect permits the lumberman to sell his cheap logs to himself at current prices, for a 26% [today: 25%] capital gain; then he sells them to his customers at a more modest gain taxable at 52%–82% [today: 48%]. All these maneuvers, though justified for tax purposes, have little or no relation to accounting concepts of cost.

7. *The "tax benefit" doctrine.* Entirely rational for tax purposes but devoid of meaning accounting-wise are the various provisions by which deductions in loss years (e.g. bad debts *et al.*) don't count.

8. *Tax exemptions.* Municipal bond interest, gifts and inheritances, proceeds of life insurance and related premiums, certain G.I. pay, etc. are given arbitrary statutory treatment, usually without accounting parallel.

9. *Miscellaneous provisions* exist to undermine cherished accounting contrasts of capital and revenue and expense: container deposits, instalment sales, prepaid rent, property taxes, bad debt reserves for banks, consolidated statements and intercompany dividends, reserves, research costs, exploration and development, "ordinary" and "extraordinary," surplus and profit-and-loss entries, etc.,—distinctions in one field or the other without carry-over, except for expediency.

10. Also mentionable are *artificial contractual relationships* such as the leasebacks, entered into to distort the form without changing the substance of a transaction. Accountants have been better able to deal with distorting effects on the financial statements, than with those on the tax returns. In the latter, accountants' hands have been tied by over-riding considerations, by lack of primary responsibility, and by assumed positions of advocacy.

WHY THE DIVERGENCIES BETWEEN TAXABLE AND BUSINESS INCOME

In part these differences are what we call "legalistic"—due to lack of understanding of economics, accounting and the concept of income by legislators and lawyers. In part they are administrative, to protect against loss of revenue by causing a tax to become payable when the taxpayer has the cash; also under this heading is the necessity as a practical matter for fairly definite and enforceable standards. As with the S.E.C., the Internal Revenue people have a hard time finding landmarks in a changing and uncertain field. There are too many "generally accepted accounting principles" for enforcement purposes—eleven different ways to amortize intangibles, for instance. With all the Institute's and the Association's accomplishments over years of effort, we still are without agreement on terminology, and though "general acceptance" is, and properly, the very basis of our discipline, we are quite prone to define "generally accepted" as "somebody tried it." Nobody could enforce a law that was without definition of terms or standards of procedure.

But these are minor. The main reasons for the differences between taxable and business income are the differences in the objectives for which each is determined. What are they?

The Nature and Purpose of Accounting

The purpose of accounting is to provide information.

Accounting is intellectual exercise but it is not *an* intellectual exercise. It is utilitarian. It is a language and a system of measurement. It is a body of convention and procedure and not a body of logic. Language is conventional and measurement is procedural. We are trying to transmit information; we are not investigating laws of nature, not constructing a science. It's an art, a means of expression.

Comparability and consistency are the prime requisites of such a system, so that the reader will receive the information the writer intended to transmit, and so that comparisons may be valid and trends and differences determined. The significance of accounting data is usually in relationships rather than absolutes. This year's profit for this company is significant only if we know last year's and the year before that and what other companies did. Of the gravest danger are tendencies that lead to inconsistency and noncomparability inasmuch as comparisons and trends might be assumed to be of substance when only of form. Thus the significance of the accountant's opinion that statements "fairly present financial position and results of operations in accordance with generally accepted accounting principles" consistently applied. The words "generally accepted" are to provide comparability between companies and "consistency" provides for comparability of data for different periods.

The duty of the accountant to the public in the preparation and certification of financial statements is that of an expert in difficult and complex concepts, often as an arbiter of adverse interests in the measurement of relative values. The core of his function is in impartial and honest and meaningful measurement and expression, only possible by adoption and use of consistent terminology and units of measurement, generally understood and applied. *Comparability and consistency* —these are the proper standards of accounting. It will be argued herein that noncomparability and inconsistency are of the essence both of the determination of taxable income and of tax saving.

The Objectives of the Determination of Taxable Income

Taxable income is the base of the income tax, which is a tax determined in part by the principle of "ability to pay"; the idea is to support the government by collecting taxes so as to minimize the total sacrifice by taxpayers. This concept is identical with that of charging "what the traffic will bear," or "getting the most feathers with the least squawking." Of course business income is only a part of, and not necessarily a good measure of ability to pay; e.g., unrealized appreciation in value though not business income may represent ability to pay. Certainly gifts and inheritances reflect as much taxpaying ability as earned income, maybe more; and so on. But business income is a part of it.

There are some other objectives of taxation than supporting the government according to ability to pay. First among them is the control of the price level— consciously applying the deflationary effects of taxation vs. the inflationary effects of government expenditure. The government has assumed far-reaching economic responsibility. An understanding of taxation would be very incomplete without a realization of the place of the Federal deficit or surplus in current economic thought and in public policy.

Taxes are used to accomplish other overt or covert social ends. Taxation is used to promote "brimful" employment, that sacred cow of modern politico-economic thought. It is notably used to promote or discourage certain types of economic activity (i.e. Texas vs. the rest of us). It is used to promote the investment of risk capital (via the capital gains provisions), or to discourage the same thing (via the interest deduction and dividend non-deduction). It is used to encourage a levelling of incomes via super-progressive rates and the abandonment of *quid pro quo*. The immense power of taxation can be used to enrich or to destroy. Taxation gives aid to some and discourages others; it rewards the politically powerful at the expense of the politically weak. Nor is this necessarily wrong; taxation is simply a weapon, and a powerful one, in the arsenal of government by which political means are used to accomplish economic ends. These are the aspects of taxation that are increasingly important. The rewards and penalties and hence the results of taxation at the present rates are swift and effective. They rest on discrimination, their objective being change. Let him think twice who would hold that "accounting principles" are going to make or long affect these social and economic policy determinations.

What Are the Prospects for Reconciling Taxable and Business Income?

Clearly income is not being determined "in accordance with the taxpayer's regular method of accounting" in some pretty important respects. Is it likely to become so? What will be the result of an effort to make it so? Take percentage depletion or replacement-cost depreciation for example. If percentage depletion to be deductible required an unqualified certificate that it conformed to "generally accepted accounting principles" would percentage depletion disappear from tax returns? Or would accounting principles be revised? The experience with LIFO provides a clue. The pressures are too great and they are unfair. But the public knows the answer and, I fear, so do the accountants. Here is a footnote from E. Cary Brown's *Effects of Taxation-Depreciation Adjustments for Price Changes* (Boston: Harvard Business School, 1952), p. 43, on the question of adjustments in accounts for replacement-cost depreciation if the latter should become acceptable for tax purposes: "The position of accountancy bodies would have had to change before this result could be widespread. But almost surely tax depreciation would have become acceptable for company reports. A number of 'unacceptable' accounting procedures have received sanction in this way."

Perhaps percentage depletion or replacement-cost depreciation should be proper for certain industries or certain companies or for everyone. The point is that their acceptance for tax purposes has nothing necessarily to do with the measurement of income for accounting or economic or other purposes. The tax purpose is to reduce the tax burden of some segment of the economy, presumably because social policy desired to encourage that segment—or because its Congressman was able to get it some selective relief. The determination of relative tax burdens is the province of Congress which may and does act not only with selective rates but also with special and selective methods of income determination. Such a selectively determined *taxable* income is not the comparable and consistent *accounting* or business income of which it is our duty to inform the lay and we hope the trusting public.

The legalistic and administrative differences between taxable and business income may not be too troublesome and in the long run may be removed by mutual education and improvement. Ability to pay may be reconciled with a proper determination of business income, the latter as a subdivision of the former kept in proper perspective (and there are many forms of ability to pay that are not now "accounted for"). But the social, economic and political objectives of tax policy are far too important—they are over-riding and they are not going to be abandoned. And they are selective in their very nature. They are entirely inconsistent and apart from the principles of description and measurement, comparability and consistency. They will not be subject to, or controlled by, what we may here refer to as "mere bookkeeping."

With the forces of government and economic advantage arrayed on the other side, efforts to maintain consistency between taxable income and "the taxpayer's regular methods of accounting" if the latter are based on accounting principles otherwise determined, will bring to bear absolutely irresistible pressures on accounting concepts of income. Distortions of accounting income to conform to or to resist political objectives of tax policy are inevitable. Business income will be politically determined and politically measured. Efforts to identify taxable and business income will inevitably result in changing the latter to agree with the former.

One further thought in this connection: Accountants regard it as their duty to state the "facts" (recognizing that we mean by "fact" an objective determination within a consistent framework of expression); management's duty is to take action. We have presumed that management's actions will tend more to be wise and timely with the facts than without, but at any rate we supply the facts and they take the action. Now management sometimes likes to ameliorate its problems by concealing them, especially in its relations with the government, customers, employees and stockholders in matters of profits. The *determination* of profits is our job; the *administration* thereof is management's. Pressures on management for profits that look high come from the four groups mentioned. The government wants taxes, the customers lower prices, the employees higher wages and the stockholders dividends. The management wants to "maintain capital." But the problem can be ameliorated at least in the short run if the *reported* profits can be held down. That brings pressure on accountants.

Of course nobody wants lower income. That's an easy way to avoid a problem of income administration but what is desired is the income without the problem. As to income taxes, it is the *reported* income that the tax is on; so the idea is to have the real income without the reported income. In the long run the total burden of taxes isn't going to be changed by the reported income. Only the rates would change. Taxes may be shifted between taxpayers, though, and thus real individual tax saving accomplished in the short run. Accounting determinations have income (after tax)-determining effect for the particular taxpayer but only at the expense of other taxpayers and not in total.

What Is the Solution?

In the first place taxable income should be generally recognized as a different thing from accounting or business income. The out-dated and undermined principle that income should be determined for tax purposes "in accordance with the taxpayer's regular method of accounting" will have to be appropriately qualified and restricted to details of procedure. The LIFO requirement which has so seriously inhibited full disclosure of financial position in published reports must be repealed. Different treatment of different taxpayers should be open and above-board and not buried in obscure distortions of revenue and expense concepts.[2]

Fictional correspondence of taxable and business income should not be forced. Accountants should resist all efforts to prostitute accounting principles to tax ends and should constantly remind themselves of the underlying precepts of consistency and comparability, which are foreign to the special-treatment tendency of taxation. Though we may as citizens decry and resist such special treatment in taxation, it remains the duty of accountants to resist its encroachment on accounting determinations. Unless accounting principles are determined independently of tax considerations, those principles can hardly provide an independent stand-

[2] The current Congress is in process of mumbling itself some tax-free income in the guise of traveling expense, buried in an irrelevant section. This is not different from some of the loophole-opening for constituents that burdens the Code. Let these things be done openly.

ard with which to appraise special deviations when they do appear in taxable income determination. However the tax be determined, it is simply one of the expenses in the accounting report; the rest of the report should be otherwise determined in accordance with an independent body of rules and procedures.

Accountants' reports should probably include a statement of taxable income and a reconciliation with reported income, much as provided in the corporation tax return and for the same reason: full disclosure of an important matter. While the phrase "two sets of books" is unacceptable, the necessity for supplementary records to record taxable as distinguished from accounting income will be unavoidable. We will eventually realize that there is no more reason for taxable income to determine accounting income than for assessed values to determine balance-sheet values; and we will report the discrepancy when it bears importantly on financial condition as it frequently does.

The alternative will be a fear or a realization on the part of the public that accounting reports may be distorted for tax purposes, with distrust of the impartiality, comparability and consistency and therefore usefulness, and reliability of certified statements and the certifiers, and a demand for someone else to do this important work. In modern experience a governmental agency would no doubt be a willing candidate for the job.

Full disclosure is not enough. The public needs and expects expert and independent assistance in this highly technical field with an independent judgment on the reliability of published statements. All the footnotes and qualifications in the world, all the "disclosure" that a long-form report can contain, are no substitute for this independent appraisal. I am reminded of Maurice Peloubet's story of the ice-cream vendor who, on passage of the Pure Food and Drug Act, complied with full disclosure as follows: "All my syrups and ice creams are highly adulterated." The principle is the same as that of the Institute's Auditing Statement 23[a] in which the accountant is required to express himself, not just hedge himself.

TAX PRESSURES ON ACCOUNTANTS' INDEPENDENCE

It has been pointed out that intense pressures may be brought on the determination of accounting income when that is identified with taxable income. When the accountant is a member or employee of management his determinations are those of management. In the sense that management's duty is to conserve the company's assets, it is natural and proper that management will determine close points in favor of the company, the tax burdens being as great as they are. But the situation for the independent public accountant is a different one. The same understatement of income that saves taxes also may defraud an otherwise uninformed minority interest—the bulk of the ownership in the case of publicly-owned corporations. The independent certified public accountant has a specific higher duty to the public than to his client. The essence of his professional position is in his independence. Therefore, since the pressure of tax saving is to minimize not the fact of income but the reporting thereof, he finds himself in some difficult positions where full and comparable reporting may be inconsistent with a tax position taken by management. Furthermore an important part of a public ac-

[a] This Statement was consolidated in *Codification of Statements on Auditing Procedure* (New York: American Institute of [Certified Public] Accountants, 1951). [Eds.]

countant's practice may be in the income-tax field; and he may find himself in an inconsistent position between himself as a tax consultant and as an independent certifier of financial statements.

It is very difficult for a tax consultant to avoid a position of advocacy. Indeed it has been well said that in tax practice accountants are the only ones who regard themselves as independent. Certainly the client does not regard the public accountant as a "government auditor"; neither does the government. There are many matters in which client's personnel, public accountants and even government auditors may work together to make a proper determination of fact. This is as it should be and it is important; the government's task would be greatly, impossibly increased otherwise. But there are other matters in which accountants, some more than others, find themselves making decisions which unavoidably are *for or against* a client's interest taxwise. Furthermore an accountant is frequently in a position, in tax practice, of defending a determination which he or the client has made; such a determination is always favorable to the client. The government's auditors are advocates of the government's position. As a group they are charged with maintaining the revenue. As individuals it seems quite likely that they will be graded at least in part on the additional taxes they bring in. Likewise will the independent accountant find himself in a position of advocacy. He too is graded at least in part on taxes—the taxes he saves for his client. When tax practice places an accountant in a position of advocacy rather than impartiality he is outside of and inconsistent with his position of independence in the public interest.

Independent public accountants will have to watch out for this pitfall. They will have to carefully segregate their practices in their own minds (this they can do), between tax advocacy and independent determinations. Staffs will have to be segregated; let the tax sections do the arguing; let the auditors make independent decisions. There will have to be full disclosure and open determination of disputed points, however unfair the government's auditors may sometimes appear in taking advantage of the information. When the position can not be disclosed, when only the favorable may be disclosed, then are the attorneys right in claiming the field for themselves. Theirs is the professional practice of advocacy; ours the professional practice of independence.

The independent accountant may certainly assist and advise in the determination of tax effect and tax liability; no one is so well qualified. But he must clearly differentiate in his mind taxable and accounting income and he must report the latter impartially and openly. The alternative will be government assumption of the independent accountants' task with the evils of inflexibility and bureaucracy, and the challenge to our way of life which that brings. Surely in recognition of the threat to orderly development of accounting principles and their usefulness to the public, and of the threat to their own essential attribute of independence, the public accounting profession will take the lead in the necessary separation of the concepts of taxable and business income.

SUMMARY

The differences between taxable and business income are so numerous and important that the two concepts must be regarded as essentially different. These differences are in part "legalistic" and in part administrative, but more importantly they reflect basic differences in the objectives of the determination of taxable income and of business income. The divergencies are not likely to be resolved. Therefore it becomes necessary to abandon the postulate that taxable income should be determined "in accordance with the taxpayer's regular method of accounting." Attempts to maintain a fictional identity of the two concepts can only lead to political determination of business income, as tax pressures are too powerful to be resisted by accounting principles otherwise determined.

Taxable income must be recognized as different from business income; accountants should resist efforts to prostitute accounting principles to tax ends; accountants' reports must be determined independently of tax considerations. Reports should include reconciliations of taxable and accounting income and necessary supplementary records should be maintained. Practicing accountants must carefully insulate their position of independence in preparation of certified statements from the position of advocacy sometimes assumed in tax matters. Recognition of the basic differences in concepts, and differentiation of the two types of professional practice, are required for the maintenance of public confidence in accounting statements and accountants' reports.

RELATED READINGS†

THE INSTITUTIONAL SETTING

This section deals with the institutional setting in which accounting principles (or standards) are authoritatively established. Knowledge of the political and economic environment in which these decisions are made is essential to an understanding and appreciation of the forces affecting the development of accounting practice.

Marshall S. Armstrong, "The APB and Corporate Accountability," *Financial Executive*, August, 1971, pp. 28–34. Discusses the Board's organization and structure.

Abraham J. Briloff, "The Accounting Profession at the Hump of the Decades," *Financial Analysts Journal*, May–June, 1970, pp. 60–67. Author suggests the reasons why the profession has failed to achieve agreement on a set of generally accepted accounting principles.

"A Challenging Look at the APB," a symposium with papers by Newman T. Halvorson, Glenn A. Welsch, and Walter F. Frese, and discussion, in *1968 Symposium for Educators* (Ernst & Ernst, 1968), pp. 3–46.

R. J. Chambers, "The Anguish of Accountants," *The Journal of Accountancy*, March, 1972, pp. 68–74. On the role of committees in achieving progress in accounting.

Howard M. Felt, "The Effort and Authority of the AICPA in the Development of 'Generally Accepted Accounting Principles'," *The International Journal of Accounting*, Spring, 1968, pp. 11–27. A survey.

Robert J. Freeman, "The Debatable Role and Status of APB 'Statements'," *The New York Certified Public Accountant*, July, 1971, pp. 501–506.

Dale L. Gerboth, "'Muddling Through' with the APB," *The Journal of Accountancy*, May, 1972, pp. 42–49.

Charles T. Horngren, "Accounting Principles: Private or Public Sector?," *The Journal of Accountancy*, May, 1972, pp. 37–41. Attempts to clarify the institutional setting in which the Accounting Principles Board functions.

K. C. Keown, "The Development of Accounting Standards around the World," *The Australian Accountant*, April, 1968, pp. 193–202.

Homer Kripke, "The SEC, the Accountants, Some Myths and Some Realities," *New York University Law Review*, December, 1970, pp. 1151–1201.

---

† The several groupings of Related Readings are intended to alert the reader to articles, monographs, and books appearing since 1968 that bear on the questions at issue. A few pre-1968 items are also included. No item appears in more than one grouping, although the editors readily concede that many articles and books overlap two or more of the subject areas into which the selections in this volume are divided. Many of the entries are annotated, and a deliberate effort has been made to point out colloquies in the literature and to interrelate items that are similar in content or approach. We hope this added information economizes the reader's time in making use of the Related Readings. The asterisk (°) indicates sources containing particularly rich bibliographies.

Argues, *inter alia*, that the SEC should not rely on the accounting profession to determine accounting principles.

David M. Lang, Jr., "The Dissenting Viewpoint," *The Price Waterhouse Review*, Winter, 1968, pp. 6–13. A review of the dissenting opinions expressed in AICPA pronouncements.

Maurice Moonitz, "Why Is It So Difficult to Agree upon a Set of Accounting Principles?," *The Australian Accountant*, November, 1968, pp. 621–631. Discusses the implications of the widening community interest in accounting principles. See also Walter B. McFarland, "Further Thoughts on the Search for Accounting Principles," *The Australian Accountant*, November, 1969, pp. 506–512, who comments on some of Moonitz's points.

———, "The Accounting Principles Board Revisited," *The New York Certified Certified Public Accountant*, May, 1971, pp. 341–345. Criticism of the APB's efforts to take a position on basic principles.

Kenneth S. Most, "Accounting Principles and Public Controversy," *The Accountant*, Nov. 20, 1969, pp. 682–685.

Alfred Rappaport and Lawrence Revsine (eds.), *Corporate Financial Reporting: The Issues, the Objectives and Some New Proposals* (Chicago: Commerce Clearing House, Inc., 1972), 251 pp. Proceedings from a conference at which the problems of establishing accounting objectives and fashioning accounting principles were critically reviewed.

Leonard M. Savoie, "Raising Accounting Standards," *Empirical Research in Accounting: Selected Studies, 1969*, Supplement to Volume 7 of the *Journal of Accounting Research*, pp. 55–62.

Lee J. Seidler, "Private Men in a Public World: The Accounting Principles Board in 1971," *The Accountant's Magazine*, April, 1972, pp. 170–178.

Edward Stamp, "Establishing Accounting Principles," *Abacus*, December, 1970, pp. 96–104. Proposes a *modus operandi* for developing accounting principles.

———, "Reforming Accounting Principles," in Edward Stamp and Christopher Marley (eds.), *Accounting Principles and the City Code* (London: Butterworths, 1970). A critical review of the process by which accounting principles have been developed in Britain and the United States.

Reed K. Storey, *The Search for Accounting Principles* (New York: American Institute of Certified Public Accountants, 1964), 65 pp.

Robert M. Trueblood, "Ten Years of the APB: One Practitioner's Appraisal," *Touche Ross Tempo*, September, 1969, pp. 4–8. Speech in which Trueblood proposes a 5- to 7-man APB on a full-time basis.

Lawrence L. Vance, "The Road to Reform of Accounting Principles," *The Accounting Review*, October, 1969, pp. 692–703.

Stephen A. Zeff, *Forging Accounting Principles in Five Countries: A History and an Analysis of Trends* (Champaign, Ill.: Stipes Publishing Co., 1972), 332 pp. Historical study of the institutional efforts in Canada, Mexico, England, Scotland, and the United States to develop accounting principles.

Establishing Financial Accounting Standards, Report of the Study on Establishment of Accounting Principles (New York: American Institute of Certified Public Accountants, March, 1972), 105 pp. Known as the "Wheat Report," this document lays the groundwork for the successor body to the Accounting Principles Board.

QUALITATIVE ATTRIBUTES OF ACCOUNTING INFORMATION

In this section, one finds readings on the factors that influence the measurement rules, statement format, and extent of disclosure in financial statements. Such factors as users' needs and the criteria by which one might be able to identify the attributes of accounting information have been accorded particular attention in the 1960s and 1970s. Some writers are interested in the motives that lay behind corporate directors' choices of accounting practices, and several studies have been done to test the hypothesis that such choices have the effect of "smoothing" income trends. Readers should also consult the Related Readings at the close of Parts 3 and 8.

Morton Backer, "Financial Reporting for Security Investment and Credit Decisions," *The New York Certified Public Accountant*, November, 1970, pp. 885–892.

―――――, "Financial Reporting and Security Investment Decisions," *Financial Analysts Journal*, March–April, 1971, p. 61 *et seq*. Results of a survey of the information needs of bank officers, security analysts, and senior company executives.

Max Block, "Improving the Credibility of Financial Statements," *The CPA Journal* (formerly *The New York Certified Public Accountant*), January, 1972, pp. 51–61.

Philip Brown, "The Impact of the Annual Net Profit Report on the Stock Market," *The Australian Accountant*, July, 1970, pp. 277–283. Research suggests that the market anticipates most of the annual net profit before it is reported.

John C. Burton (ed.), *Corporate Financial Reporting: Conflicts and Challenges* (New York: American Institute of Certified Public Accountants, 1969), 274 pp. Proceedings from a conference of practicing CPAs, financial executives, financial analysts, and bank credit officers.

R. J. Chambers, "What's Wrong with Financial Statements?," *The Australian Accountant*, February, 1970, pp. 19–28. A criticism of published accounts.

"Confusion on Reporting Corporate Profits," *Financial Executive*, November, 1971, p. 68 *et seq*. An exchange of correspondence between a controller and an economist on the difference between tax accounting and financial accounting.

Benny R. Copeland and Thomas P. Klammer, "Should the IRS Promulgate Generally Accepted Accounting Principles?," *The CPA Journal* (formerly *The New York Certified Public Accountant*), March, 1972, pp. 217–220.

Ronald M. Copeland, "Income Smoothing," *Empirical Research in Accounting: Selected Studies, 1968*, Supplement to Volume 6 of the *Journal of Accounting Research*, pp. 101–116. A review of prior research and a limited empirical study.

――――― and Ralph D. Licastro, "A Note on Income Smoothing," *The Accounting Review*, July, 1968, pp. 540–545.

A. Wayne Corcoran and Wayne E. Leininger, Jr., "Financial Statements—Who Needs Them?," *Financial Executive*, August, 1970, p. 34 *et seq*. Authors suggest a broader-gauge orientation.

T. K. Cowan, "The Trend Statement," *Accountants' Journal*, March, 1969, pp. 276–280.

Raymond C. Dockweiler, "The Practicability of Developing Multiple Financial Statements: A Case Study," *The Accounting Review*, October, 1969, pp. 729–742.

Geraldine F. Dominiak and Joseph G. Louderback III, "'Present Fairly' and Generally Accepted Accounting Principles," *The CPA Journal* (formerly *The New York Certified Public Accountant*), January, 1972, pp. 45–49.

John P. Fertakis, "On Communication, Understanding, and Relevance in Accounting Reporting," *The Accounting Review*, October, 1969, pp. 680–691.

Dale L. Gerboth, "Accounting Principles: Truth or Guides for Action?," *World* (PMM), Spring, 1971, pp. 12–15. The methodology of accounting argument.

Nicholas J. Gonedes, "Efficient Capital Markets and External Accounting," *The Accounting Review*, January, 1972, pp. 11–21. Argues that the market reaction to the disclosure of accounting numbers should be the gauge of their informational content.

Rudolph C. Greipel, "Review of APB Opinion No. 20–'Accounting Changes,'" *The CPA Journal* (formerly *The New York Certified Public Accountant*), January, 1972, pp. 17–24.

Merle M. Gynther, "Disclosure to Investors–For the Amateur or the Professional?," *The Australian Accountant*, May, 1968, pp. 268–74.

John R. Jordan, Jr., "Financial Accounting and Communication," *The Price Waterhouse Review*, Spring, 1969, pp. 12–22.

Robert S. Kaplan and Richard Roll, "Investor Evaluation of Accounting Information: Some Empirical Evidence," *The Journal of Business*, April, 1972, pp. 225–257. Analysis of the impact on share prices of changes in accounting methods.

T. A. Lee, "Utility and Relevance–The Search for Reliable Financial Accounting Information," *Accounting and Business Research*, Summer, 1971, pp. 242–249.

James J. Mahon, "Accounting Principles and Investor Confidence," *Lybrand Journal*, Vol. 48, Nos. 1 and 2 (1967), pp. 34–44. A reply to public criticism of accounting.

David Norr, "What a Financial Analyst Wants from an Annual Report," *Financial Executive*, August, 1970, pp. 20–23.

John L. O'Donnell, "Further Observations on Reported Earnings and Stock Prices," *The Accounting Review*, July, 1968, pp. 549–553.

Lyn D. Pankoff and Robert L. Virgil, "Some Preliminary Findings from a Laboratory Experiment on the Usefulness of Financial Accounting Information to Security Analysts," *Empirical Research in Accounting: Selected Studies, 1970*, Supplement to Volume 8 of the *Journal of Accounting Research*, pp. 1–48.

Lawrence Revsine, "General Purpose Reports and Users' Data Needs," *Financial Analysts Journal*, September–October, 1969, pp. 37–46. To what extent, the author asks, are present reporting practices responsive to users' needs?

Joshua Ronen and George H. Sorter, "Relevant Accounting," *The Journal of Business*, April, 1972, pp. 258–282. Authors propose that companies report discounted cash flows (with a risk index), exit values, and a historical measure.

Richard H. Simpson, "An Empirical Study of Possible Income Manipulation," *The Accounting Review*, October, 1969, pp. 806–817.

Surendra S. Singhvi and Harsha B. Desai, "An Empirical Analysis of the Quality of Corporate Financial Disclosure," *The Accounting Review*, January, 1971, pp. 129–138. Evidence that inadequate disclosures are likely to widen share fluctuations.

George J. Staubus, "Determinants of the Value of Accounting Procedures," *Abacus*, December, 1970, pp. 105–119. Emphasizes the importance of three attributes for assessing the value of accounting procedures: relevance, reliability, and effectiveness of communication.

Rosemarie Tevelow, "How a Security Analyst Uses the Annual Report," *Financial Executive*, November, 1971, pp. 18–21.

S. J. Titcomb, "An Investment Analyst Looks at Company Accounts," *The Accountant*, Jan. 29, 1970, pp. 153–157.

Anita I. Tyra, "Financial Disclosure Problems in the United States," *The Accountant's Magazine*, May, 1970, pp. 198–201. Historical survey.

William J. Vatter, "Progress in the Pursuit of Principles," *The International Journal of Accounting*, Fall, 1969, pp. 1–15. Reviews efforts of the last 35 years.

"What's Wrong with Financial Statements?," *The Australian Accountant*, July, 1968, pp. 385–396. Results of a questionnaire survey.

SEGMENTAL REPORTING

An accounting controversy that emerged in the 1960s, particularly in the United Kingdom, the United States, and Canada, concerns the measurement and disclosure of revenues and profits by product lines, divisions, or segments. These readings explore the political, economic, and accounting implications of "segmental reporting."

Newman T. Halvorson, "Accounting Aspects of Conglomerate Reporting," *The Business Lawyer*, January, 1968, pp. 549–560.

Robert E. Healy, "Reporting for the Diversified Company," *The Price Waterhouse Review*, Spring, 1968, pp. 6–13. A review of the issues and research done to date.

George Hobgood, "Voluntary Disclosure in 1968 Annual Reports," *Financial Executive*, August, 1969, pp. 64–69. Segmented reporting. Also see Hobgood's sequels: August, 1970, pp. 24–33, and August, 1971, pp. 18–22.

Patrick S. Kemp, "Contribution Margin Reporting for Diversified Companies," *Management Accounting* (US), May, 1968, pp. 14–17.

Thomas Edward Lynch, "Diversified Reporting: An Answer to Management's Objections," *Financial Analysts Journal*, November–December, 1968, pp. 67–73.

Robert K. Mautz, "Financial Reporting by Conglomerate Companies," *Financial Executive*, February, 1968, p. 52 *et seq.*

―――, *Financial Reporting by Diversified Companies* (New York: Financial

Executives Research Foundation, 1968), 390 pp. Results of a comprehensive FERF research study.

———— and K. Fred Skousen, "Common Cost Allocation in Diversified Companies," *Financial Executive*, June, 1968, pp. 15–25.

C. G. Peirson, "International Comparisons of Reporting for Diversified Companies," *The Australian Accountant*, August, 1969, pp. 359–363; see the comments in R. G. Walker, "Reports of Diversified Companies," *The Australian Accountant*, September, 1970, pp. 381–386.

*Alfred Rappaport, Peter A. Firmin, and Stephen A. Zeff (ed.), *Public Reporting by Conglomerates* (Englewood Cliffs, N.J.: Prentice-Hall, Inc., 1968), 154 pp. Proceedings from a conference.

———— and Eugene M. Lerner, *A Framework for Financial Reporting by Diversified Companies* (New York: National Association of Accountants, 1969), 61 pp.

———— and ————, *Segment Reporting for Managers and Investors* (New York: National Association of Accountants, 1972), 99 pp.

———— and ———— "Public Reporting by Diversified Companies," *Financial Analysts Journal*, January–February, 1970, pp. 54–64. Authors propose guidelines for the reporting of segmented financial information.

Leopold Schachner, "Accountability under Industrial Diversification," *The Accounting Review*, April, 1968, pp. 303–311.

Donald E. Schwartz, "Legal Implications of Product Line Reporting," *The Business Lawyer*, January, 1968, pp. 527–547.

A. A. Sommer, Jr., "Conglomerate Financial Reporting," *The Business Lawyer*, January, 1968, pp. 521–526.

* Indicates sources containing particularly rich bibliographies.

PART 3

INCOME DETERMINATION: GENERALLY

In recent years, conventional accounting practice has been the object of unprecedented criticism in academic journals. While in former years accounting educators debated the pros and cons of alternatives to traditional historical cost, with as many on one side as on the other, a veritable avalanche of opinion has formed behind current value since the middle 1960s. To many academics, it is no longer a question of whether historical cost or current value is superior, but only a question of which version of current value should be adopted. Several alternatives to traditional historical cost are analyzed in Parts 5 and 8. While it is important to formulate alternatives, it may be some time before they are implemented in practice. In the meantime, accounting practitioners and academics alike are actively discussing controversies within the realm of historical cost. An understanding of these controversies will furnish users of accounting information with a clearer perception of the strengths and limitations of the contents of accounting reports they receive.

All too frequently, accountants and readers of financial statements view particular accounting controversies, such as inventory valuation and the accounting for depreciation, intangible assests, and liabilities, as if each were capable of solution without reference to the others. But each of these problem areas is inevitably part of the larger task of determining periodic profit and placing a value on the firm's net assets. Reed K. Storey, in "Cash Movements and Periodic Income Determination," emphasizes the interrelatedness of asset valuation of income determination, and points out that specific problem areas are more susceptible to intelligent solution when they are viewed as special applications of the accountant's attempt to assign cash flows to specific time periods. In a world of perfect certainty, accountants, like economists, could value the firm by discounting future net cash receipts. But the existence of uncertainty obliges the accountant to develop criteria for ascribing a portion of the company's continually accruing profit to each of a series of discrete time periods. The gross receipts stream emerging from the sale of products and services is apportioned into a series of revenue figures of each of successive periods. The constant streams of expenditures for inputs contributing to revenue are also broken up into discrete amounts of expense for each successive fiscal period. The rules used by accountants to transform receipts into revenues and expenditures into expenses uniquely determine the moment when profit is recognized, and its amount. In Storey's words, it is the moment at which profit is allocated to the assets.

In the second article in this part, John H. Myers points out that revenue should be recognized when the "critical event" in the revenue-generating process occurs. The "critical event" is that which reduces to an acceptable minimum the risk inherent in the ultimate realization of the revenue. In particular, he argues that interest revenue should not be recognized evenly throughout the term of a loan, but at the time the contract is signed. The "critical event" is the negotiation of the loan contract, not the gradual expiration of the period during which the loan is outstanding. In his Accounting Research Study, *Reporting of Leases in Financial Statements* (1962), Myers advocates an approach to accounting for leases that is wholly consistent with his "critical event" theory. He argues that lessees should capitalize the present value at the time the lease agreement is signed, for it is then, he contends, that the lessor has fulfilled his contractual obligation.

In a pair of papers originally presented at a conference in 1970, Robert T. Sprouse and Alfred Rappaport espouse different frameworks for visualizing the place of financial statements in accounting theory. Once having identified the accounting entity, Sprouse proceeds to analyze all transactions in terms of their effect on the entity's assets and liabilities. The measurement of an entity's income, he argues, is a function of the measurement of its net assets. To Sprouse, this analytical relationship is central to an integrated accounting theory. Rappaport, contrariwise, advocates a user orientation in preference to Sprouse's structural analysis. He questions whether one may choose a theory construct, as Sprouse has done, without first proposing a user decision model. "In the absence of an explicit designation of user models," he writes, "there is no logical basis for either acknowledging or denying the validity of Sprouse's balance-sheet preferences." Rappaport suggests a further conception of the balance sheet which implicitly rejects Sprouse's axiom that the balance sheet and the income statement must articulate with each other. This exchange of views raises several questions that are too often ignored in discussions of theory: Regardless of whether one accepts traditional historical cost or any of the several conceptions of current value, are the balance sheet and income statement an effective "package" for the information which users require? Is it necessary that the balance sheet and income statement articulate with each other? Finally, must one inevitably choose between structural (Sprouse) and user (Rappaport) explanations of the nexus between the balance sheet and the income statement, or are they at least partially compatible?

A controversy that has permeated arguments for and against particular accounting practices is whether, and to what extent, comparability among the financial statements of different companies is achieved by the adoption of uniform, or more nearly uniform, accounting practices. Some assert that the application of uniform practices to demonstrably diverse circumstances will produce an artificial result. Others contend that interfirm comparisons are not possible when different accounting practices are used. A subcontroversy is whether a committee or board of a professional accountancy body has the right to impose uniform practices on companies, or whether such a decision is best left to the professional judgment of the independent auditor. Espousing an intermediate position, some suggest that it is proper for a professional body to specify criteria with which the independent auditor should make the determination. Thomas F. Keller inaugurates a tripytch of articles on this intensely debated controversy, by reviewing the evolution of the contrasting views since the 1930s. In quoting the arguments of the disputants, he suggests that the issues are clouded in a fog of imprecise terminology, and that it is frequently not clear that the parties are even discussing the same question. In the second article, initially presented as a paper at the 1970 Summer School of The Institute of Chartered Accountants of Scotland, Arthur Morison focuses on the diversity and uncertainty that confront the modern auditor. The proponents of uniformity, he asserts, have thus far failed to show that only one accounting treatment may logically be deduced for any one specific set of facts. He argues that the only rational alternative is to allow each company to choose the practices which it regards as appropriate to its circumstances, so long as it explains and justifies these practices in its financial statements. Quoting from Baxter, Morison writes, "No one else can decide this other than the company itself, and the reporting accountant who has to see that the choice is fair." In an appendix, Morison illustrates the criteria that might be used to determine which of several accounting treatments is appropriate in particular problem areas.

In the final article, Gary M. Cadenhead delineates "differences in circumstances" more narrowly than Morison. They should be confined, he asserts, to those factors that influence (1) the feasibility of particular accounting practices, and/or (2) the objectivity of the measures resulting from applying the accounting practices. Whether the attribute to be measured is historical acquisition cost, current replacement cost, net realizable value, or discounted future value is a matter of accounting principle, not the attendant circumstances. Until the profession is able to agree on accounting principles which provide for a ranking of attributes to be measured, as well as the accounting practices to be employed, Cadenhead believes that the invocation of "differences in circumstances" to justify an accounting practice will be little more than "clever rhetoric."

A. NATURE OF THE "ACCRUAL" APPROACH: WHY WE "MATCH" THE WAY WE DO

REED K. STOREY (1926–   ), B.S. 52 Utah; Ph.D. 58 University of California (Berkeley); CPA. Currently director of accounting research, American Institute of Certified Public Accountants, New York. Major publication: *The Search for Accounting Principles* (1964). Contributor to *The Accounting Review*.

Engaged in public accounting, 1949–52. Prior to joining the AICPA research staff in 1962, served on the University of Washington faculty for six years. Became director of accounting research in 1964.

REED K. STOREY

CASH MOVEMENTS AND PERIODIC INCOME DETERMINATION

REED K. STOREY

The determination of periodic net income is the most important function of financial accounting. In recent years the tenets of accounting income determination have been intensively scrutinized and re-examined as never before by both accountants and non-accountants. Although worthwhile progress has unquestionably been made, considerable confusion has been engendered by the piecemeal type of approach to the solution of accounting problems that has been employed by accountants and non-accountants alike. This approach, with some notable excep-

SOURCE: From *The Accounting Review*, Vol. XXXV, No. 3 (July, 1960), pp. 449–454. Reprinted by permission of the American Accounting Association.

tions, has been standard in accounting for many years. For instance, the Committee on Accounting Procedure of the American Institute of Certified Public Accountants has never attempted to formulate a comprehensive theory of income determination, but has dealt with specific topics of current interest and controversy. The *Accounting Research Bulletins* issued by the Committee over the last twenty years irrefutably constitute a major contribution to the accounting literature, but the secondary consequences of the process that produced the bulletins have been largely overlooked. This secondary effect has been the development of that peculiar, but common form of myopia—the inability to see the forest because there are so many trees—which afflicts those who concentrate on details without occasionally stopping to focus on the entire picture.

The practical result of this nearsightedness is twofold: (1) most of the problems remain at least partially unsolved, and (2) the multiplicity of "generally accepted" methods confuses non-accountants. For example, in spite of all the effort expended, first-in, first-out and last-in, first-out are both acceptable procedures. Similarly, both depreciation based on cost and depreciation based on appraised value may be used. In both cases cited, the alternative procedures are so conflicting as to be absolutely incompatible, yet, current practice approves their simultaneous use, not only for similar firms, but within a single enterprise. The desire for a larger degree of uniformity in accounting, not only in method and procedure, but also in agreement among independent authorities has been one of the moving forces behind the search for better income determination methods. Progress in this direction is frustrated, however, by the problem approach. Less uniformity exists, and more unsolved problems in income accounting remain than ever before.

The basic step in the solution of income measurement problems is therefore the achievement of an understanding of the nature of income and of the income determination process. Accountants must comprehend the fundamental framework of income determination in order to solve specific problems in proper perspective. The basic nature of the periodic income determination problem may best be studied by eliminating the most disturbing factor—i.e., uncertainty. Once the nature of the process is understood, we may judge any proposed solution to the problems of profit measurement. This is, of course, one of the functions of theory.[1] It permits the analysis of basic relationships under the assumption that other factors are held constant.[2]

Conceptually, the determination of income is relatively simple. Income is produced as a result of business operations. In barest outline, the process is as follows: (1) available cash assets are invested in the production process;[3] that is, cash outlays are made for productive assets—materials, labor, and other auxiliary goods and services; (2) the application of labor and the use of the productive facilities add

---

[1] Carl T. Devine, "Current Trends and Persistent Problems in Accounting Theory," in *The Controller*, Vol. X (July, 1942), p. 334. Cf. A. C. Littleton, *The Structure of Accounting Theory* (Urbana, Ill.: American Accounting Association, 1953), p. 132.

[2] This method is common to all science and is widely used in the analysis of economic problems. See Alfred Marshall, *Principles of Economics* (9th ed.; New York: The Macmillan Company, 1949), pp. 36–37.

[3] Inasmuch as the cash assets are "available," they are non-earning assets—idle cash balances—which must be invested to bring a return.

utility to the material, creating a product with increased economic value;[4] (3) the product is then converted from non-cash to cash assets, and the cycle begins again. If the utility added is positive, the resulting cash balance will be larger than it was before the investment was made. The conversion of cash assets into real or earning assets is known as an outlay; the conversion of real assets into cash assets is known as a revenue. The difference between the revenue and the outlay for a given investment is its profit or loss.[5]

The problem of accounting is not, however, the simple measurement of the difference between total revenue and total outlay over the life of an investment, but that of measuring the difference between revenues and expenses for a given segment of that life. Modern accounting breaks up a continuous stream of business activity into artificial segments known as accounting periods. This operation is designated as periodic income determination.

This problem of periodic income determination is inseparably connected with that of property valuation: "the problem of allocating the total profit of an enterprise over the years of its existence and the problem of estimating the value of the enterprise at any one moment of time are not two problems but merely different aspects of a single problem,"[6] for "all the various methods of valuation, whether used by accountants or not, are based on various methods of allocating profit."[7] The value of a non-cash asset is a combination of cost and allocated profit, and may be stated as follows: "the total capital invested up to any date may be defined as the sum of outlays incurred and profit allocated, less the revenues received, before that date."[8]

The following simplified illustration will demonstrate the relationships involved:[9]

A company is organized to purchase an asset whose life is known. The asset will

---

[4] This is true in both manufacturing and merchandising business. Both kinds of enterprise create utility since man cannot create material goods. He can merely rearrange and move goods so as to make them more serviceable. This is the service performed by both traders and manufacturers. See Marshall, *op. cit.*, pp. 63–64.

[5] Kenneth E. Boulding, *Economic Analysis* (3rd ed.; New York: Harper & Brothers Publishers, 1955), pp. 840–841. Cf. John B. Canning, *The Economics of Accountancy* (New York: The Ronald Press Company, 1929), pp. 94–95.

[6] Boulding, *op. cit.*, p. 849.

[7] *Ibid.*, p. 851.

[8] *Ibid.*, p. 842. Although stated in somewhat different terms than those to which accountants are accustomed, this concept of valuation is the one accepted in accounting. The difference between the accounting valuation for merchandise inventory or finished goods and accounts receivable is the gross profit which has been allocated to the receivable by the sale. Inventory is valued at the sum of outlays; receivables are valued at the sum of outlays plus an allocated profit. Similarly, the difference between the value of a note at present and at maturity is the amount of interest income that has been added to it, even though this interest is commonly shown in a separate Interest Receivable account.

[9] For more comprehensive treatments with examples, the reader is referred to: Boulding, *op. cit.*, Chapter 38; Canning, *op. cit.*, Chapters VI to XII inclusive; and Maurice Moonitz and Charles C. Staehling, *Accounting: An Analysis of Its Problems* (Brooklyn, The Foundation Press, Inc., 1952), Vol. I, Chapters 1 to 7 inclusive. Although the approach is somewhat different in each of these works, there is a remarkable degree of unanimity of opinion in the conclusions reached. The discussion herein is based on all three sources.

produce known revenues each year and will require known outlays each year. The asset will be sold at the end of the last year and the return will be included in the revenue of that year. The revenues and outlays will take place at the end of each year and the profit will be allocated to periods in such a way that all periods will have an equal *rate* of profit.[10] In order to further simplify the exposition, four additional limiting conditions are imposed which in no way affect the validity of the conclusions. These are: (1) all cash received from this business comes either from owners' contributions or from revenues; (2) all cash disbursed is either for operations or for owners' withdrawals; (3) the owners' contribution equals the original cost of the investment so that there is no excess cash in the business at its inception; and (4) all excess cash is withdrawn from the business as it comes in. The first two conditions eliminate the problem of borrowing; the latter two, the problem of non-earning assets.

The value of the asset when it is purchased will be equal to its cost because no profit will have as yet been allocated to it. This value will also be equal to the discounted value of the future net receipts from the asset, discounted at the profit rate. The value of this asset at the end of any period can be obtained in the same manner because in the situation in which all relevant amounts are known, the amount of capital invested always equals the present value of the investment, regardless of the method of profit allocation used.[11] Furthermore, the difference in value between the beginning and end of any period, the depreciation, may be determined readily.[12]

In the absence of capital contributions, the change in capital during the period is wholly explained by the profits and the withdrawals. Then, because withdrawals are defined to be the excess cash in each period (the excess of revenues over outlays), and because the change in capital value from the beginning to the end of the period is the depreciation, the profit for any period is equal to the revenue less the sum of the cash expenses and depreciation.[13] The sum of all depreciation charges

---

[10] Neither of the last two assumptions is necessary to solve the problem, but they simplify the calculations considerably by making possible the use of compound interest tables. The assumption of an equal profit rate is certainly a logical one, but it is not the only logical assumption that could be made. An assumption of a different rate of profit each period due to external factors is not unreasonable. The only requisite for solving the problems is that the method of profit allocation be known in advance, together with the amounts and time distribution of the revenues and outlays. In addition, if the rate is fluctuating, the rates applying to the various periods must be known; if the rate is constant, it can be determined from the problem itself. See Boulding, *op. cit.*, pp. 842–849.

[11] *Ibid.*, pp. 849–851.

[12] Depreciation may be either positive or negative in sign. Negative depreciation signifies that the value at the end of the period is greater than the value at the beginning of the period and is more properly designated appreciation.

[13] This somewhat complicated statement can be demonstrated easily with simple algebra. The change in capital value from the beginning to the end of the period, $(C_b - C_e)$, is explained by the profits, P, and the withdrawals, W.

$$C_b + P - W = C_e$$

But withdrawals are the excess cash, the difference between revenues, R, and outlays, O. Hence,

$$C_b + P - (R - O) = C_e$$

over the life of the asset is equal to the original cost of the asset.[14] It follows, then, that the total expense over the life of the asset (operating outlays plus depreciation) will exactly equal the amount of cash disbursed over the life of the asset, excluding capital withdrawals and repayments of borrowing.

A similar relationship exists between revenues and cash receipts. If owners' contributions and borrowing are excluded from consideration, the cash received over the life of the asset is exactly equal to the revenue. In fact, revenue is always identified with the conversion of real or earning assets into cash—with final fruition in money.[15]

The foregoing discussion reveals the following characteristics of the nature of periodic income and its determination:[16]

1. Over the life of a business, revenue is equal to the cash receipts from operations, and expense is equal to the cash disbursements from operations; the profit (positive or negative) is therefore equal to the difference between cash receipts and cash disbursements resulting from operations. This relationship is the most vital one in income determination.

2. For any period less than the life of the enterprise, revenue is equal to the cash that will be received (past, present, or future) as a result of the operations of the period, and expense is equal to the cash that will be disbursed (past, present, or future) as a result of the operations of the period.

3. Periodic income determination is essentially a process of asset valuation because the value placed on net assets at the beginning and end of an accounting period determines the profit allocated to that period, or conversely, the part of the total profit allocated to periods determines the value of the assets.

4. The rate of profit (whether it is assumed to be equal in all periods or not) is a rate of growth of capital value because it measures the proportion by which a given asset or group of assets increases in value during the period due to operations.

5. The value of an asset determined by the invested capital method (adding outlays and allocated profit) equals its value determined by the present value of net revenues method (discounting net revenues by the same profit-rates used in allocating profits under the invested capital method).

6. Income and asset valuation depend on the expected amount and time dis-

---

or

$$P = R - O - (C_b - C_e).$$

Then substituting depreciation, D, for $(C_b - C_e)$,

$$P = R - (O + D).$$

[14] Technically, depreciation will equal the original cost less the scrap value. From the very nature of the problem, however, scrap value must always be zero. One of the anticipated revenues from this asset is its scrap value at the end of its life. This amount is included in the revenue of the last year in calculating its cost. If all expectations are realized (as they will be in the absence of uncertainty), the capital value of the asset will be reduced to zero by the last revenue.

[15] Canning, op. cit., pp. 95, 101; Boulding, op. cit., pp. 841–842.

[16] See Edward G. Nelson, "The Relationship between the Balance Sheet and the Profit and Loss Statement," in The Accounting Review, Vol. XVII (April, 1942), p. 133.

tribution of cash movements which take place primarily in the future and are therefore subjective in nature.

The most serious problems encountered in the measurement of periodic net profit are the result of man's inability to foretell the future accurately. Inasmuch as the results of business decisions cannot be known, periodic income can only be estimated until such time as the effects of the decisions have all become apparent. The results of many decisions become intermingled until the accountant is faced with a continuous stream of business events which cannot be traced directly, and cannot entirely be separated into those relating to completed ventures and those relating to uncompleted transactions. In the actual world of uncertainty, the determination of periodic net income is not an easy matter.

The accountant's reaction to this uncertainty regarding estimates of income is to rely on accounting principles and conventions, especially those relating to the use of objective evidence as a basis for estimates, consistent treatment of items, and full disclosure of circumstances. Uncertainty and accounting conventions, however, do not change the basic *nature* of periodic income. They do not change the relationship between revenue and cash receipts or the relationship between expense and cash disbursements. Nor do they affect the relationship between income determination and asset valuation. They affect only the *accuracy* of estimates of revenue and expense and of asset valuation.

The estimating of income, under conditions of uncertainty as well as of certainty, requires that the accountant trace carefully the relation between income flows and cash movements:

> While it is true that there may not be an equality between the amount of revenue and the amount of cash receipts for any period less than the duration of enterprise existence, receipts are the elements with which we construct all measures of revenue. A dollar is received at *some time during the life of the enterprise* for each dollar of revenue exhibited during the fiscal period. The sum of the annual revenues for all fiscal periods is equal to the amount of ultimate total revenue. There may be no equality between the amount of expense and the amount of cash disbursements for the fiscal period and yet the two sums are equal for the life of the enterprise. A dollar is disbursed at *some time during the enterprise existence* for each dollar exhibited as expense of the fiscal period.[17]

The accountant's problem is essentially one of reconciling cash receipts with revenues and cash disbursements with expenses. That is, for every revenue recognized but not received in cash during the current period, an asset of equal value must be recorded (or a liability must be amortized); for every expense recognized but not paid in cash in the current period, a liability of equal value must be recognized (or an asset must be amortized).[18]

In actual practice, uncertainty precludes the assignment of revenues and expenses to accounting periods independently of each other. Either revenue or ex-

[17] Nelson, *op. cit.*, p. 133. Italics in the original.
[18] There is no place in the system for amortization of assets and liabilities under conditions of certainty. Asset and liability values are determined with reference to future events. With uncertainty present, however, some reference must be made to past events; hence, amortization is necessary.

pense must be chosen as the controlling factor and assigned to periods first. The other is then allocated to accounting periods on the basis of its relationship to the controlling factor. Although either element presumably could be chosen, accountants overwhelmingly agree that revenue is to be allocated first and then costs are to be matched against revenue.[19]

The problem of revenue estimation is one of estimating the cash that eventually will be received as a result of current operations. In practice, revenue may be recognized on the basis of cash receipt, sale, completion of production, or percentage-of-completion of production. The choice among these is usually based on practical considerations involving accuracy of estimate and reliability of evidence. All of these bases, if properly applied, result in an estimate of revenue that fulfills the requirements of the basic nature of the income determination process. Realization should occur at the earliest possible moment consistent with a reasonable degree of accuracy in estimating those values that will not ultimately be received in cash. If these realization bases are used under appropriate conditions regarding difficulty of estimation, each gives the best estimate possible under the circumstances of the eventual cash receipt.

Cost matching cannot be accomplished as satisfactorily as revenue estimation, and most of the income determination problems are found in this area. The choice of revenue as the controlling element in periodic profit measurement complicates cost matching. Income is accurately determined if all costs relating to the earning of the revenue allocated to the current period are charged as expenses of the current period, and all costs relating to revenue of future and past periods are eliminated from current expenses. Costs pertaining to future revenues must be carried forward as inventories, prepaid expenses, or fixed assets; costs pertaining to prior periods must be written off against prior periods' earnings. Liabilities must be set up for current expenses not yet paid. If the best possible measure of profit is to be attained, therefore, the accountant must make every effort to match costs with the revenues with which they are actually associated.[20]

The understanding of the relationships between cash movements, income, and asset value does not, of course, immediately and automatically solve all the problems of profit measurement. The assumption that the value of the measuring unit remains stable is implicit in the foregoing discussion. The price-level problem is therefore an example of an important problem which remains unsolved. This problem concerns differences between real and monetary income and the maintenance of capital. It cannot be solved by reference to realization and matching which are concepts derived from the relationship between cash movements and income and are themselves based on the assumption of stable prices.

But many of the perplexing problems of accounting do fall nicely into place when set in proper perspective against the background of the cash-income-asset relationships. Among these are the nature of bad debts and the status of such suggested solutions to accounting problems as LIFO, depreciation on replacement cost, re-investment depreciation, and others. The basic relationships between cash

---

[19] See George R. Husband, "A Critique of the Revised Statement of Accounting Principles," in *The Accounting Review,* Vol. XVII (July, 1942), p. 287, and W. A. Paton, *Advanced Accounting* (New York: The Macmillan Company, 1941), p. 458.

[20] *Accounting and Reporting Standards for Corporate Financial Statements and Preceding Statements and Supplements* (Columbus, Ohio: American Accounting Association, 1957), Supplementary Statement No. 6, December 31, 1953, pp. 36–38.

movements and income measurement lay out the path to real solution of income determination problems. Accountants should abandon the present practice which leads to so many dead-end detours and concentrate their efforts within the basic framework of income determination. An immediate consequence will be more uniformity of accounting thought and results, and less confusion among those for whom accountants prepare information. Myopia in accounting is curable if the right prescription is used.

B. CRITERIA FOR REVENUE "RECOGNITION"

JOHN H. MYERS

JOHN H. MYERS (1915–), B.S.C. 37, M.B.A. 38, Ph.D. 43 Northwestern; CPA. Currently professor of accounting, Indiana University. Major publication: *Reporting of Leases in Financial Statements* (1962). Contributor to *The Journal of Accountancy*, *The Accounting Review*, and other journals.

Was on the faculties of the State University of New York at Buffalo, 1939–45, and Northwestern University, 1945–68, prior to joining the Indiana University faculty. Served as research director, 1963–64, American Accounting Association.

THE CRITICAL EVENT AND RECOGNITION OF NET PROFIT

JOHN H. MYERS

The matching of cost and revenue has grown during the past fifteen or twenty years into a cardinal principle of accounting. We have learned to postpone or accelerate either cost or revenue, as the case might require, in order to get all the elements of a single transaction into the same period. In spite of such problems as price level fluctuations and requirements of governmental regulatory bodies, we have made considerable headway in sharpening the determination of net income. However, in this effort to sharpen the determination of net income we have given very little attention to the timing of income recognition. We have relied on a variety of rules for specific situations, not on an over-all principle. In

SOURCE: From *The Accounting Review*, Vol. XXXIV, No. 4 (October, 1959), pp. 528–532. Reprinted by permission of the American Accounting Association.

this paper I review both the economic concept of net income and the accounting procedure in a number of specific business situations, and then suggest a principle which is compatible with economic theory and at the same time coordinates most current accounting practice. I hope this discussion will provoke further thought on the subject leading to the ultimate refinement and acceptance of a principle which is both (1) as clear and uniform in its applicability as that of matching cost and revenue and (2) sound from an economics standpoint.

Economic theorists since the days of Adam Smith have spoken of land, labor, and capital as the three factors of production. Compensation to these factors has been known as rent, wages, and interest. Under a perfectly functioning system, these three factors receive all the income. Any residual that remains in an actual case is due to the imperfections of the system in the individual case at the particular moment of time. Later economists acknowledged a fourth factor of production: entrepreneurship. Its compensation is known as profit. Profit is the reward for bearing risk—the risk of enterprise, the risk of venturing in business, the risk of owning something in hope of selling it later. This profit may be positive or negative depending upon the entrepreneur's decisions as to the directions in which to risk his capital, his labor, and his land. This profit is very close to what the accountant calls profit.[1]

Let us assume for accounting purposes that profit is the same as the profit of the economist, a reward for having taken the risks of enterprise. This being the case, profit is earned by the operating cycle, the round trip from one balance sheet position back to that position, whether the starting point be cash or inventory or any other factor. Even in a simple merchandising business several steps occur; buying, selling, collecting. The question arises as to when during that cycle any profit should be recognized. Should the profit be recognized when a specific point on the cycle is reached, or should it be spread over that cycle in some manner? If it should be recognized at a point, what is that point? If it should be spread, what criterion should be used? In order to set some limits on this article, I have assumed that profit should be recognized at a single moment of time. This article will be devoted, therefore, to a consideration of the moment of time at which to recognize the profit. Perhaps after considering carefully the implications of the assumption we shall be in a better position to consider the question we have by-passed.

If profit is to be recognized at a moment of time, we must select that moment. The economist gives a clue in the function of entrepreneurship as the function of directing a business, bearing the pain of the risks, and reaping the rewards of astute decisions. This suggests that profit is earned at the moment of making the most critical decision or of performing the most difficult task in the cycle of a complete transaction. Just what event this is may not be easy to distinguish in many cases. Although in most types of business we recognize profit at the moment

---

[1] The accountant's profit includes, in addition to the economist's reward for bearing the risks of enterprise, "interest" on the owner's investment and, in some cases, "wages" to the owner of an unincorporated enterprise. However, these two variations do not negate the basic relationship between the profit of the accountant and of the economist. The wage element may be omitted for it is pertinent only in the unincorporated business, and even in such businesses there is a growing tendency to include a fair wage to the owner among the expenses. Interest is seldom if ever set out separately but in profitable corporations it may well be a minor part of the profit.

inventory is converted into accounts receivable, such timing is far from universal.[2]

Let us examine a number of different types of businesses (1) to determine what is done and the apparent theory behind such action and (2) to test the applicability of the critical function theory in that business. In so testing the theory, we must remember that it must not fall merely because the critical function is difficult to determine. A proposed accounting theory must provide the basic objective and leave room for developing means of implementing that theory. Objectivity is one of the desiderata of any means of achieving a goal, but it in itself must not be allowed to be the goal.

Merchandising is one of the most common businesses. The merchant generally performs three steps: (1) wise buying, (2) effective selling, and (3) efficient collecting. If "wise," "effective," and "efficient" permit, there is a profit. We recognize the profit at the time the second step, selling, is performed. Two reasons commonly are given for recognizing profit at this time: (1) an asset has been transferred for a valid claim (transfer); (2) the merchant's opinion as to value is not needed (objectivity). To claim that any profit was realized at the time of purchase would be contrary to our past heritage, but to defer profit until cash has been collected is not uncommon. Major reasons for deferring profit realization until receipt of cash are the risk of collecting in full and the possibility of incurring additional expense. Bad debt and collection expenses are common, but most businesses feel that they can set up adequate reserves for the estimated expense. Thus, it sounds as if the real principle behind current practice were certainty, but that cannot be so for we do prepare income statements in spite of such major uncertainties as unaudited income tax returns and renegotiable contracts.

The principle of the critical event seems to fit the situation of the merchant very well. Where collection is a critical problem (and I doubt if there are many cases where it is), profit may be taken up at collection time. For most businesses, most of us would agree that selling is the critical event and that profit should be recognized at that time. In rare cases buying might be critical, as where an extremely good price is paid for some rapid-turnover, staple item.

A manufacturer's business is much like that of a merchant except that an extra step is added, converting the purchased raw materials into salable units. This gives an extra point at which profit might be recognized, i.e. time of efficient manufacture. In general we do not use this time because of uncertainty as to eventual sale price. However, in the case of gold refining where the market is assured, profit is recognized at the time of manufacture. The same reasoning as in the case of the merchant seems to apply; again it is the certainty principle. The critical event principle is also pertinent: Selling is very important in most cases; in gold mining it is a mere clerical detail, for the market and the price are assured by the government.

However, in contracting and manufacturing goods to order, especially if the manufacturing time will extend over several fiscal periods, the situation is quite different. In many cases there is no assurance the goods can be made at the contracted price. Therefore, profit is recognized when it becomes certain, when the

[2] One clue to the most difficult or crucial task in the operating cycle may be the function of the business from which the president was selected. Was he in sales, manufacturing, collection or something else? A background in sales would tend to confirm most present accounting practice.

goods have been made. The critical event theory, if applied to this situation, might be construed to come to the same answer as the certainty theory. In many cases it probably will. However, there may well be cases when profit should be recognized at sale date before the goods are manufactured. If a manufacturer regularly makes standard items for stock, it does not seem right to defer profit recognition beyond sale date merely because the item is temporarily out of stock. Somewhere between these two extremes there will be a twilight zone in which determination of the critical event will be difficult, but knowing that such an event is the determining factor would clarify thinking considerably.

Some people argue that profit can be recognized only when a transaction has been completed, when both purchase and sale have taken place. They argue that both of these elements are necessary and that the sequence of the two is immaterial. This almost assumes that the normal position is to have nothing but cash and that any other position is one of risk. A merchant would consider himself on dangerous ground, assuming he plans to stay in business, if he did not have a stock of merchandise. Anyone who has maintained a heavy cash position in the last decade or so has been assuming a position in which risk (of price level change) has been high. Consider an individual who has accumulated more funds than needed for current living and for an emergency cushion. The normal position for him is to have an investment in stocks or bonds. When he is out of the market, he is assuming substantial risk until he reinvests. There is a real question if he is to measure profit from purchase to sale of a security or to measure from the time he gets out of the market until he again assumes his normal position with respect to the market. Point of view seems all important. What is the critical function in making a profit? This question may be a most useful over-all guide.

Profit is recognized by magazine publishers in the period when the magazines are distributed. In most cases sale occurs and cash is received at the time the subscription is booked. Manufacturing costs are incurred shortly before distribution date. Both advertising revenue and sale price are considered earned at the time of publication. There is serious question if this routine is correct even using the theory of certainty typically followed by manufacturers. Long in advance of publication date, the sales of magazines (by subscription) and of advertising are known. Printing costs are usually incurred under long-term contracts, so no element of uncertainty appears here. The only other element is the editorial one. Since most or all of the editorial staff will be paid fixed salaries, no uncertainty exists here. If the certainty theory is to be used, profit should be recognized at the time the subscription is sold. Among the currently used theories, only the completed contract theory explains the present practice.

Under the critical function theory we must determine whether sales of magazines, sales of advertising, or production of the magazines is the critical function. Without good advertising contracts, the firm cannot prosper. Since advertising rates are based on circulation, sales of magazines seems all important. However, unless the editorial work pleases the subscriber, he soon will fail to renew his subscription. The readers' response will be felt much more quickly in newsstand sales. Choice as to which of these functions is the critical one may well not be unanimous. If it is agreed that editorial work is critical and that editorial work culminates in publication, then the currrent practice is appropriate.

Lending agencies (banks, small loan companies, etc.) generally recognize profit over the period a loan is outstanding. When the note is discounted at the inception of the loan, the banker has, in a sense, collected the fee in advance. The fact that this fee is called interest might lead the unwary to assume that it should be spread over the period, because the payment is based on time. However, closer inspection shows that the theory behind the lending agency's recognition of gross income over the period of the loan is that many expenses (particularly interest paid on money loaned out and collection and bookkeeping expenses) are spread fairly evenly over the loan period. If expenses of setting up the loan are also spread over the collection period or are minor, the matching of revenue and expenses is well done. The resulting net income is spread over the loan period. In a sense the situation is somewhat comparable to the contractor and magazine publisher in that the customer has been "sold" at the beginning and only rendering of service is left to be performed. Profit is taken up as each piece of the service contract is completed. However, a fundamental difference exists: the manufacturer and banker have different responsibilities after "sale." The manufacturer or publisher must incur many costs to complete the service to the buyers. The banker's role is much more passive; he has only to wait for payments in the normal order of business.

The current practice of recognizing income during the period the loan is outstanding does not seem to agree with the critical function idea. The only things happening while the loan is outstanding are (1) the money borrowed to lend is incurring interest charges and (2) the economic situation is changing, especially as regards the borrower and his ability to pay. If the loan requires periodic payments there is an additional bookkeeping function. Perhaps in individual cases the critical function is the decision to loan or not to loan. If that is so, profit probably is earned at that time even though collection and exact determination of the amount might be delayed quite some time. This delay is, I am sure, one of the reasons profit is measured over the life of a loan. The service-rendered concept might be another reason for accruing profit over the life of a loan, but my experience is that the borrower receives the greatest service at the time he gets the money. Many merchants selling on the installment plan recognize all profit at time of sale of the merchandise and set up adequate reserves for loss. Their situation is only slightly different from that of a lending agency. The goods are sold and the loan is made in a single transaction. In the merchant's case, more rests upon this event than does in the case of merely making a loan. Nevertheless, a satisfactory or unsatisfactory lending policy, it seems to me, is the one thing that makes loans profitable or unprofitable.

A company owning and renting real estate presents an interesting case. Typically, rents are taken into income in the period to which the rent applies. Expenses are recognized as incurred. A major function of such a firm is providing various building services through payment of taxes, insurance, and the costs of maintenance, heat, and elevator operation. Rental of small dwelling units on a month-to-month basis is very different from rental of large areas for manufacturing or office use. Not only may more service be required for commercial purposes, but also the term of the lease will probably be considerably longer so that the tenant may feel justified in making many improvements to suit his operations. Even though the lease term may be short, there will be a strong presumption to renew because of the large expenses of moving. Under these circumstances, is profit really earned merely by serving the present tenants? When a major tenant occupying a whole floor or two is secured or lost, it would seem a renting firm would have real cause for a feeling of profitability or loss thereof. I would suspect the agent securing a long-term tenant would be well paid in recognition of his great service to the real estate company. The critical function theory would seem to demand that all profit for the term of the lease be recognized at this time. Practical difficulties of determining the ultimate profit from such a contract are large. The basic cause of the problem is the custom of determining profit at least annually. Although this custom is the root of the whole problem discussed in this paper, the problem is larger here because of the length of term of the contract. The practical difficulties of applying the theory in this case must not be the cause of rejecting the theory. If the critical function theory should be correct theoretically, then we must strive to find a way to apply it to the practical situation.

The theory of the critical event as the moment at which to recognize profit or loss on a transaction seems very useful. In the types of business which we have considered, it rather closely matches current practice and gives insight into the true nature of the business. It is a theory based on a fundamental economic process rather than upon such frequently used rationalizations as convenience, conservatism, certainty, tax timing, and legal passage of title. This theory may, at first, seem a radical departure from current practice. Upon further thought it does not seem so different. Perhaps this critical event theory will be rejected in favor of another, but the present status of relying upon many different theories of when to match revenue and expense cannot long stand in a profession. We need to give special attention to the development of a single theory for the timing of profit recognition.

C. INTERRELATION BETWEEN ASSET VALUATION AND INCOME DETERMINATION

ROBERT T. SPROUSE

ROBERT T. SPROUSE (1922–   ), B.A. 51 San Diego State; M.B.A. 52, Ph.D. 56 Minnesota. Currently member of the Financial Accounting Standards Board, Stamford, Conn. Major publications: *A Tentative Set of Broad Accounting Principles for Business Enterprises* (with Moonitz, 1962), *Accounting Flows: Income, Funds, and Cash* (with Jaedicke, 1965), *Essentials of Financial Statement Analysis* (with Swieringa, 1972). Contributor to *The Journal of Accounting Research*, *The Journal of Accountancy*, and other journals.

Served on the accounting faculty of the University of California (Berkeley), 1955–62, following which he was on the faculties of Harvard University, 1962–65 and Stanford University, 1965–73. He became a charter member of the Financial Accounting Standards Board in 1973. Was vice-president, 1969–70, and president, 1972–73, of the American Accounting Association.

Principal research interest: development of a conceptual framework for the analysis of financial accounting issues, and the application of that framework to the solution of unresolved practical financial accounting problems.

THE BALANCE SHEET— EMBODIMENT OF THE MOST FUNDAMENTAL ELEMENTS OF ACCOUNTING THEORY

ROBERT T. SPROUSE

The assertion is frequently made that in accounting's house the income statement is our most important product. To the extent that this is intended to mean that the attention of most users of financial statements tends to focus on the income statement, the assertion is acceptable. To the extent that the assertion refers to the most important elements of accounting theory, the assertion is delusory. This paper is written in support of an alternative proposition: the balance sheet embodies the most fundamental elements of accounting theory, from which the essential elements contained in the income statement are necessarily derived. Indeed, the income statement can properly be described as merely a summary of one class of transactions resulting in changes in one balance-sheet account.

SOURCE: From *Foundations of Accounting Theory*, edited by Williard E. Stone (Gainesville, Fla.: University of Florida Press, 1971), pp. 90–104. Reprinted by permission of the University of Florida Press.

I offer two forms of support for this proposition: (1) An analysis of two contending views of the components and function of the balance sheet that have emerged over time. The purpose is to demonstrate the fallacies and futilities of such opposing views. For convenience, let me designate these the sheet of balances view and the static funds statement view. (2) A positive case for reviewing the balance sheet as a statement of financial position which provides a basis for the measurement of a meaningful concept of income and which, at the same time, provides useful information in its own right. Each of these three distinguishable views has strikingly different implications for the construction of accounting theory—implications that are readily discernible in their application to the analysis of transactions and financial reporting.

THE SHEET OF BALANCES VIEW

The sheet of balances approach views the statement as a summary of debit and credit account balances that remain after the determinants of income have been decided upon and the retained earnings account has been adjusted for the amount of income that results. This is a "balance sheet" in the most literal sense of the term. Increasingly, this view has been adopted in accounting practice, as manifested by many of the pronouncements of the AICPA and by most of the financial statements published by corporations.

Accounting Terminology Bulletin no. 1 defines the balance sheet as "a tabular statement or summary of balances (debit and credit) carried forward after an actual or constructive closing of books of account kept according to principles of accounting."[1] An asset is "something represented by a debit balance that is or would be properly carried forward upon a closing of books of account according to the rules or principles of accounting."[2] Similarly, a liability is "something represented by a credit balance that is or would be properly carried forward upon a closing of books of account according to the rules or principles of accounting."[3]

Exaggerating only slightly, then, one might say that, according to this view, a balance sheet is a summary of debit and credit balances and that the primary difference between an asset and liability is the side of the account on which the balance happens to appear.

The sheet of balances view of the balance sheet stems from the notion that a valid and viable framework for accounting analysis—that is, an accounting theory —can be constructed on the basis of the pre-eminence of the income statement and the application of the "matching" concept. Which of these two—the pre-eminence of the income statement and the matching concept—is the chicken and which is the egg is difficult to determine. One might hypothesize that because both are sterile—at least as foundations for accounting theory—they were necessarily created simultaneously.[4]

Pre-eminence of the income statement is the offspring of confusion between the derivative information that decision-makers may find most useful and the fun-

---

[1] AICPA, Committee on Terminology, *Review and Resume*, Accounting Terminology Bulletin no. 1 (New York, 1953), p. 12.

[2] Accounting Terminology Bulletin no. 1, p. 13.

[3] Accounting Terminology Bulletin no. 1, pp. 13–14.

[4] Delmer P. Hylton comments on the concurrent ascendancy of the income statement and "the accounting convention known as 'matching revenue with expense'" in "On Matching Revenue with Expense," *The Accounting Review* (Oct. 1965), pp. 824–28.

damental elements of a framework for accounting analysis from which that useful information is derived. More about that later. First let me elaborate on the sterility of the matching concept as an element of accounting theory.

Without pretending to have traced its historical origin, it seems safe to say that the matching concept first began to receive widespread attention with the publication of *An Introduction to Corporate Accounting Standards*[5] by Paton and Littleton. There, as one of the basic concepts that constitute a suitable foundation for accounting standards, the authors cited the matching of effort and accomplishment. The economic concept of income as a change in wealth during a period of time was explicitly rejected, even as an ideal, and the notion of an income associated with each item of goods sold or service rendered was expounded. The authors stated that "if this conception could be effectively realized in practice, the net accomplishment of the enterprise could be measured in terms of units of output rather than of intervals of time. . . . Time periods are a convenience, a substitute, but the fundamental concept is unchanged. The ideal is to match costs incurred with the effects attributable to or significantly related to such costs."[6]

The implications of this approach become particularly vivid with the following statements: "Accrual and deferment are closely related phases of the process of matching. The full accrual of labor cost, under the terms of the various contracts in effect, needs to be recognized; otherwise the amount of labor-service received is incorrectly expressed. It is perhaps of secondary importance that wages earned but unpaid are recorded as part of the process. Deferred charges, broadly defined to include most assets, need to be recognized; otherwise the goods furnished or services rendered currently will be loaded with charges not significantly applicable. The flow of cost factors, in other words, needs to be appropriately divided between the pool of charges to be held back, deferred, and those representing elements from which the utility has been fully exhausted. Assets accrued but as yet uncollected should be recognized because, if they are ignored, services rendered will be incorrectly expressed."[7]

Note the relegation of the balance sheet to a sheet of balances created as a by-product of the matching process so that costs will not be incorrectly expressed. Although the deferred charges may include most assets, the objective is to avoid matching revenues with charges that are not significantly applicable and allow costs to be appropriately divided between deferred charges and expenses. This approach places a premium on judgment as to whether a cost is significantly applicable or inapplicable to a revenue and whether a division of a cost into amounts to be deferred and amounts to be expended is appropriate or inappropriate. Presumably, the matching process does not even require a concept of in-

---

[5] W. A. Paton and A. C. Littleton, *An Introduction to Corporate Accounting Standards* (Evanston, Ill.: AAA, 1940).

[6] Paton and Littleton, p. 15. The AAA's 1964 Concepts and Standards Research Study Committee—The Matching Concept adopted some of the same language (e.g., "costs constitute a measure of business effort, and revenues represent accomplishments coming from those efforts") and concluded "that it is desirable to emphasize the matching concept in financial reporting." The committee meticulously avoided any reference to assets and liabilities although at times it appears to have been a strain (e.g., losses are viewed as "product or service factors given up in return for a zero quantity of revenue"). "The Matching Concept," *The Accounting Review* (Apr. 1965), pp. 368–72.

[7] Paton and Littleton, p. 16.

come to serve as a basis for making those judgments. Instead, as suggested by some: "Time is what we measure with a watch. Income is what we measure with a profit and loss statement."[8]

Inevitably, of course, it is recognized that, even if it were conceptually desirable, in most cases the matching of costs and revenues is a practical impossibility. In practice, most costs are identified with a period of time in much the same way that even proponents of the matching concept identify revenues with a period of time. Nevertheless, the matching concept, based as it is on the pre-eminence of the income statement and relying heavily on subjective notions of correctness, applicability, and propriety, is responsible for those unique accounting products that one so frequently finds in today's sheet of balances: deferred charges that are not assets and deferred credits that are not liabilities.

In its Opinion 11, "Accounting for Income Taxes," the APB cited certain general concepts and assumptions as relevant in considering that problem. Among them, matching was recognized as one of the basic processes of income determination. The inherent sterility of the matching concept as a basis for resolving accounting issues is especially glaring, however, in the board's tautologous explanation that "expenses of the current period consist of those costs which are identified with the revenues of the current period and those costs which are identified with the current period on some basis other than revenue."[9]

Nevertheless, in rejecting the liability method, in rejecting the net of tax method, and in adopting the deferral method of interperiod tax allocation, the board stated explicitly that the "measurement of income tax expense becomes thereby a consistent and integral part of the *process of matching revenues and expenses* in the determination of results of operations."[10] In so doing, the board acknowledged that "deferred charges and deferred credits relating to timing differences represent the cumulative recognition given to their tax effects and as such do not represent receivables or payables in the usual sense."[11]

Elevated to "one of the most important principles in income determination"[12] and uninhibited by any meaningful concepts of assets, liabilities, and income, the matching concept may be deemed to supply adequate support for virtually any accounting procedure. As one author puts it: "In the minds of many accountants, this single convention outweighs all others; in other words, if a given procedure can be asserted to conform to the matching concept, nothing else need be said; the matter is settled and the procedure is justified."[13]

Obviously, the sheet of balances approach is operational; its everyday use is very much in evidence. At opposite extremes, however, this approach either permits maximum latitude in deciding which balances to carry forward, or it requires an ever increasing list of detailed rules and procedures to be promulgated designating which balances may properly be carried forward.

When new accounting problems arise—like the investment credit—this ap-

[8] John C. Burton, ed., *Corporate Financial Reporting: Conflicts and Challenges* (New York: AICPA, 1969), pp. 49–50, 225.

[9] "Accounting for Income Taxes," APB Opinion 11 (New York: AICPA, Dec. 1967), p. 160.

[10] APB Opinion 11, p. 169.

[11] APB Opinion 11, p. 178.

[12] Paul Grady, *Inventory of Generally Accepted Accounting Principles for Business Enterprises*, ARS 7 (New York: AICPA, 1965), p. 74.

[13] Hylton, p. 824.

proach either allows a variety of individual decisions to be made or requires that some recognized authority such as the APB designate by vote what is the best rule or procedure. The process is much like that of judges in a beauty contest where a winner is designated by vote based primarily on personal preference, there being no established concepts in determining beauty and in determining proper matching.

In keeping with democratic principles, the majority of such a group might "conclude that the allowable investment credit should be reflected in net income over the productive life of acquired property and not in the year in which it is placed in service,"[14] while the majority of another equally intelligent and experienced group might well conclude exactly the opposite.

One might ordinarily expect that an explicit concept of net income would be prerequisite to deciding what should be included in its measurement and what should not be included in its measurement. But, to my knowledge, no one has ever successfully managed to formulate a concept of income that is not directly or indirectly dependent upon the concept of assets and the concept of liabilities. It follows that the concepts of assets and liabilities are more fundamental than the concept of income. If this is the case, equal acceptability of three different methods of carrying forward deferred investment tax credit balances cannot be rationalized.[15]

In addition to the deferral method of accounting for tax allocation and the deferral method of accounting for the investment credit, the matching concept and the sheet of balances view are responsible for a variety of other balance-sheet anomalies. Unamortized bond discount, unamortized discount, issue cost, redemption premium on bonds refunded, and the LIFO method of inventory valuation are a few that are sometimes found among assets. Deferred gain on sale and leaseback, equity in net assets of subsidiary over cost, provision for replacement of LIFO inventories, and reserve for decline in conversion value of Canadian assets are examples of reported liabilities.

In summary, the sheet of balances approach, stemming from the pre-eminence of the income statement and the matching concept, necessarily relies on ad hoc decisions rather than on accounting theory—on independent value judgments rather than on consistent analysis.

THE STATIC FUNDS STATEMENT VIEW

A second approach to the balance sheet has emerged in recent years in which it is viewed primarily as a kind of static funds statement. A number of accounting textbooks describe the balance sheet in this way.[16] This development seems to have paralleled the increased attention given to reporting a summary of the

[14] "Accounting for the 'Investment Credit,'" APB Opinion 2 (New York: AICPA, Dec. 1962), par. 13, p. 7.

[15] APB Opinion 2, par. 14, p. 7.

[16] For example, Leonard E. Morrissey, *Contemporary Accounting Problems* (Englewood Cliffs, N.J.: Prentice-Hall, 1963), pp. 4, 44; Myron J. Gordon and Gordon Shillinglaw, *Accounting—A Management Approach*, 4th ed. (Homewood, Ill.: Richard D. Irwin, 1969), pp. 23, 497; Robert N. Anthony, *Management Accounting—Text and Cases*, 4th ed. (Homewood, Ill.: Richard D. Irwin, 1970), pp. 45, 325; Harold Bierman, Jr., and Allan R. Drebin, *Financial Accounting: An Introduction* (New York: Macmillan Co., 1968), p. 21.

transactions resulting in changes in working capital during periods of time—that is, to so-called statements of sources and applications of funds.

Raymond P. Marple has suggested in an article in *The Journal of Accountancy* that, to describe the balance sheet "as a statement of financial position, tells little about the balance sheet. It would be much more appropriate to refer to it as 'a statement of the sources and composition of company capital.'" According to Marple, "If this were done, and the form of the statement revised to better display the sources from which the capital was obtained and the forms in which it is held, the function of the balance sheet would be much clearer."[17]

In *An Inquiry Into the Nature of Accounting* Louis Goldberg contrasts the nature of the balance sheet according to the "commander" theory with the balance sheets of other theories. "If we allow ourselves to become imbued with the notion of ownership as the basis of accounting, the balance sheet becomes a statement of 'values' owned and owed; and the question of who owns and who owes is controversially but inconclusively raised. If, however, we adopt the position that the balance sheet is prepared by or on behalf of and from the point of view of a commander the chief executive officer, be he the proprietor himself or the small group of partners or the president or managing director—it can be seen as a statement of the sources from which he has (or they have) derived resources and the directions in which those resources have been applied, and it is therefore more directly a statement of stewardship than of ownership."[18]

Another proponent of the static funds statement approach to the balance sheet has attempted to analyze a specific accounting issue from that point of view. In a recent article in the *Financial Executive* David F. Hawkins has argued that considerable progress could be made in resolving the controversy surrounding income tax allocation if:

> financial accounting is regarded as being concerned with maintaining a continuing record of a company's flow of financial resources;
> the balance sheet is viewed as presenting a two-sided look at a company's capital (the left-hand side reflecting where the company's capital is lodged, the right-hand side showing the current status of capital obtained from creditors, owners, and other sources);
> net income is seen as measuring principally the funds available for dividends and reinvestment obtained through the use of capital in the operations of the company; and
> it is agreed accounting for deferred taxes should reflect (1) the way businessmen handle tax considerations in capital investment decisions, (2) the way they incorporate the deferral in their financial planning, and (3) the nature of income taxes.[19]

Earlier, in a similar article in the *Harvard Business Review*, Hawkins had hailed APB Opinion 11, "Accounting for Income Taxes," as one which seems to "Encourage, in its implicit move toward the sources and uses of funds approach, the aim of corporate executives and CPAs to find ways to make more understand-

---

[17] Raymond P. Marple, "The Balance Sheet—Capital Sources and Composition," *The Journal of Accountancy* (Nov. 1962), p. 58.

[18] Louis Goldberg, *An Inquiry Into the Nature of Accounting* (Evanston, Ill.: AAA, 1965), pp. 170–71.

[19] David F. Hawkins, "Deferred Taxes: Source of Non-Operating Funds," *Financial Executive* (Feb. 1969), p. 35.

able a number of items on the balance sheet which cannot be explained satisfactorily to stockholders by the more traditional accounting concepts."[20]

He criticized the opinion, not because of the board's conclusion in favor of comprehensive allocation—he supports that conclusion—but because the deferred tax account is not adequately rationalized. His analysis: "In the past the deferred tax issue has revolved around the question of whether the deferral should be treated as a liability, in the traditional accounting sense. But if the right-hand side of the balance sheet is regarded as presenting the current status of a company's source of funds obtained externally, then this argument becomes irrelevant. The question should be: Is the deferral a significant enough source of funds to be disclosed on the right-hand side of the balance sheet? By its support of comprehensive allocation, the Board has indicated that this is a meaningful source of capital and that it is misleading to include it in earnings."[21]

Of course, the amount of income taxes in question inevitably shows up on the right-hand side of the balance sheet either as deferred income taxes or as retained earnings.[22] But, using a "standard of meaningful and fair disclosure of invested capital," Hawkins argues that "the capital *retained* in the business through *postponement* of income tax payments" should be separately identified as a "source of invested capital."[23] His argument, however, is self-contradictory. Capital *retained* in the business through postponement of income tax payments must necessarily have had some other source; otherwise, the capital would not have been there to be retained.

The *nonuse* of funds is not the same thing as a source of funds. If sources were viewed as all those things for which funds were not used, rejected capital expenditure proposals and rejected union demands would qualify. Indeed, the possibilities boggle the mind. Furthermore, it seems unlikely that Hawkins' standard of meaningful and fair disclosure of invested capital has sufficient rigor to determine which transactions can be reflected in retained earnings and which require separate identification as a source of invested capital. For example, he states that the funds approach can be extended to include "profits on sale-and-leaseback arrangements."[24] Then, how about the gain on an outright sale? And, is it only the gain that is a source of funds, or is it the entire proceeds?

The observation has been made that, although the initial balance sheet of a newly formed concern may be a good statement of funds, "at some relatively early point along the way after operations have begun, the balance sheet, standing alone, begins to lose its function as a funds statement."[25]

Although for some purposes it may be useful to equate "funds" with assets, it is unfortunate that a term so commonly used as a synonym for cash and net working capital should be given this much broader meaning as well. And, even

---

[20] David F. Hawkins, "Controversial Accounting Changes," *Harvard Business Review* (Mar.–Apr. 1968), p. 20.

[21] "Controversial Accounting Changes," p. 30.

[22] This observation was also made by Lawrence Revsine in "Some Controversy Concerning 'Controversial Accounting Changes,'" *The Accounting Review* (Apr. 1969), pp. 354–58, where he examines Hawkins' analysis of accounting for income taxes in some detail.

[23] "Controversial Accounting Changes," p. 32.

[24] "Controversial Accounting Changes," p. 30.

[25] Maurice Moonitz, "Reporting on the Flow of Funds," *The Accounting Review* (July 1956), p. 376.

if funds and assets may properly be used synonymously, any attempt to describe the nature of liabilities as sources is at best diversionary and at worst fallacious.

Balance sheets do not report the sources of the assets on hand, except perhaps coincidentally, and describing balance sheets as though they do is likely to be misleading. Frequently, liabilities arise as a result of transactions that are not even remotely related to sources of funds. For example, none of the accrued liabilities such as accrued wages, accrued interest, and accrued taxes can properly be characterized as sources of funds. The declaration of cash dividends is properly reported in a statement of sources and applications of working capital as an application; the declaration of cash dividends is not a source of funds simply because it creates a liability. If a source of additional assets is being sought, the declaration of dividends with a concomitant increase in the amount of dividends payable is not likely to be fruitful. And one can be sure that liabilities resulting from legal actions, such as the antitrust actions against certain electrical equipment manufacturers a few years ago, are not viewed by the defendants as sources of funds.

Finally, the question of relevance must be raised. Even if it were possible to prepare a balance sheet reporting at a given point of time the funds on hand and where those funds came from, for what purpose might such information be used? The potential uses of measures of "flows of funds"—sources and uses of funds during periods of time—are widely proclaimed. For example, the board of directors of the Financial Analysts Federation has endorsed the publication of statements of sources and applications of funds in corporate reports to shareholders, stating that "the analysis of a company's past and projected flow of funds can provide valuable insight into such matters as: (1) future dividend policy, (2) the financing of capital expenditures and the extent to which additional debt and/or equities may be issued to finance same, and (3) the ability to meet debt service requirements. . . ."[26] Note the concern with flow of funds. Those purposes could not be fulfilled by measurements of the sources of the particular assets on hand at any given time. The relevance of the balance sheet as a static funds statement is not at all clear.

THE FINANCIAL POSITION VIEW

Viewed as a statement of financial position, the balance sheet represents the embodiment of the most fundamental elements of accounting theory and, at the same time, provides useful information in its own right. But the structure begins with the notion of an entity.

The concept of an entity is among the most primitive elements of accounting theory. In accounting, the entity may be defined as "an area of economic interest to a particular individual or group."[27] Neither a statement of income nor a statement of financial position is feasible without first circumscribing the entity for which an accounting is to be made.

[26] "News Report," *The Journal of Accountancy* (June 1964), pp. 9–10.

[27] An entity is fundamental to the sheet of balances and the static funds statement, as well. For a discussion of the fundamental nature of the entity concept and the development of this definition, see 1964 Concepts and Standards Research Study Committee—The Business Entity Concept, "The Entity Concept," *The Accounting Review* (Apr. 1965), pp. 358–67.

At the first level of derivation are the concepts of assets (expected future economic benefits, rights to which have been acquired by the entity as a result of some past transaction) and liabilities (the entity's obligations to convey assets or perform services, obligations resulting from past transactions and requiring settlement in the future). Once the entity is identified, one can contemplate accounting for its assets and its liabilities.

At the next level of derivation are the concepts of owners' equity or net assets (the residual interest in the assets of the entity) and income (the amount of any change in net assets during a period of time, assuming no additional investments or distributions to owners).[28] Of course, a variety of potential bases for measuring these concepts exist: invested cost in terms of numbers of dollars, invested cost in terms of purchasing power, current cost of replacing equivalent service potential, current cost of replacement in kind, current cash equivalent, etc. But, whatever the basis, it must be acknowledged that the measurement of income is dependent upon the measurement of net assets, which, in turn, is directly dependent upon the measurement of assets and liabilities.

According to this view, all transactions are analyzed in terms of their effect on assets, liabilities, and owners' equity. The measurement of income does not even require revenue and expense accounts; such accounts merely provide subsidiary information about charges in owners' equity in the same way that customers' accounts provide subsidiary information about the total amount of accounts receivable. This does not detract from the informational content of revenue and expense accounts. The information such accounts supply about the nature and extent of various operating transactions that give rise to changes in assets and liabilities and hence owners' equity can be extremely useful in making predictions about the results of the entity's future operations.

The financial position view does not eliminate all the problems and resolve all the controversies surrounding the analysis of accounting issues, but it does sharply limit the number of eligible alternatives and, most important, it focuses the resolution of accounting issues on fundamental concepts. As a result, it permits attention to be devoted to the refinement of those fundamental concepts rather than to the invention of new rationalizations for individual preferences.

As a statement of financial position that summarizes the assets, liabilities, and residual equity of the entity, the balance sheet is also an economic document providing useful information in its own right. The financial position of a business enterprise is the relationship of the resources available to the enterprise and the obligations of the enterprise that require the future utilization of resources. The resources reported in statements of financial position are necessarily limited to those assets that have been acquired as a result of past transactions, but the essence of reported assets is their ability to provide future economic benefits. Similarly, the liabilities reported in statements of financial position are necessarily limited to obligations that have been incurred as a result of past transactions, but the significance of reported liabilities lies in the future utilization of resources that their settlement will require.

Presumably, the financial statements supplied to current and prospective stock-

---

[28] These concepts of assets, liabilities, owners' equity, and income are adapted from Robert T. Sprouse and Maurice Moonitz, *A Tentative Set of Broad Accounting Principles for Business Enterprises*, ARS 3 (New York: AICPA, 1962).

holders and creditors are intended to provide information about two matters of critical importance: profitability and risk. Traditionally, the income statement has been the major source of information about the former and the balance sheet the primary source of information about the latter. These two statements, however, are inextricably related. Profitability cannot really be evaluated without reference to the resources employed in creating profits, and risk cannot really be evaluated without reference to the expected results of the firm's operations. Two firms with identical income streams are not necessarily equally profitable; two firms with identical financial positions do not necessarily involve equal risk.

Balance-sheet classifications—especially the current versus noncurrent classification—and the use of financial ratios in the analysis of financial statements frequently manifest concern with financial position.[29] For example, the current ratio is a measure of the relationship of the liquid resources available to an enterprise and its most pressing future obligations—obligations that will require the use of liquid resources. We are all aware of the widespread significance attached to the current ratio, the acid test ratio, the debt/equity ratio, the average cost of capital, and other ratios, each of which depends upon meaningful content and classification in the accounts reported in the balance sheet.[30]

The task of the analyst in evaluating financial position is bound to be complicated by the sheet of balances approach, where the balance sheet serves as a dumping ground for balances that someone has decided should not be included in the income statement. The analyst's necessary reclassification of such items in attempting to determine a firm's assets and liabilities is almost certain to be based on less information than was available to the accountant.

SUMMARY AND CONCLUSIONS

In summary, let me attempt to delineate the three alternative views of the balance sheet in terms of their consequences.

The sheet of balances view of the balance sheet is an outgrowth of the notion that, by employing the matching concept, the income statement can be made superior to the balance sheet—superior in content and superior as a basis for accounting analyses. The ultimate result of a continuing extension of this view is highly predictable; a precedent exists—the *Internal Revenue Code* and the *Regulations* which interpret the code. The similarities are most striking. Because no

[29] Roy A. Foulke, vice-president of Dun and Bradstreet and author of a well-known book on financial statement analysis, advocates the use of a set of fourteen financial ratios. The numerators or denominators for thirteen of the fourteen are taken from the balance sheet; for half of the fourteen ratios, both the numerators and denominators are taken from the balance sheet. *Practical Financial Statement Analysis* (New York: McGraw-Hill Book Co., 1961).

[30] In an empirical study, William H. Beaver tested the efficacy of thirty popular ratios in predicting the inability of a firm to pay its financial obligations as they mature. Of these, the best predictor—the cash-flow to total-debt ratio—proved to have excellent discriminatory power. Either the numerator or denominator was taken from the balance sheet for each of the top six predictors; for three of those six, both the numerators and denominators were taken from the balance sheet. "Financial Ratios as Predictors of Failure," *Empirical Research in Accounting: Selected Studies 1966* (Chicago: Institute of Professional Accounting, Graduate School of Business, University of Chicago, 1967), pp. 71–111.

concept of taxable income exists and individuals obviously have very different opinions about appropriate components and measurements, detailed rules for its computation must be promulgated. Amendments and revocations are commonplace, as judgments about the propriety of inclusions, exclusions, and measurements change. The role of the practitioner increasingly becomes one of checking the code to determine whether clients' treatments of transactions are acceptable according to the letter of the law.

This approach to financial reporting will work. Indeed, it may be the only feasible practical solution. But the costs are extraordinarily high—costs in terms of the time and talent that must be devoted to the promulgation of detailed rules and procedures and costs in terms of the sacrifice of intellectual stimulation and personal gratification that one normally associates with the professions.

The static funds statement view leads to a drastic departure from the balance sheet as we know it. This, in itself, is not necessarily fatal, but much work needs to be done in analyzing and explaining the consequences of such a departure. For example, in what way would the income statement be related to the balance sheet if this view were fully implemented? How shall guidelines be established to distinguish between transactions that may properly be reflected in funds from operations and transactions that should be separately identified in the balance sheet as a source of invested capital? And probably most important, who is interested in a static funds statement and for what purpose?

If there is to be a theory of accounting, among these three views the financial position view of the balance sheet provides the only hope. The theory calls for the identification of an entity and an accounting for the resources and obligations of that entity. The entity's income during any period of time is based on the changes in its resources and obligations during that period, and the basic distinction is between those transactions taking place between the entity and its owners and all other transactions. Obviously, this is oversimplified; the mere adoption of a particular view of the balance sheet will not solve all the problems of measuring financial position and income. It is, however, a necessary first step.

A few years ago one of the leading practitioners in the United States expressed his opinion that there is "a much bigger gap between the academic researchers and the practicing members of the accounting profession than in any other profession . . . including law, medicine and engineering."[31]

This gap has most likely widened still further since that statement was made. The academic emphasis is necessarily on theory, analysis, and logic—not on the memorization and unquestioning acceptance of rules that have been promulgated. The objective is to develop systematic, orderly thought processes that one can rely upon in striving to arrive at sound decisions about accounting issues as they arise and to insure that the solutions to such problems are consistent with the whole body of accounting thought. In other words, the objective of the academician is the development and application of accounting theory. To the extent that the primary intellectual ingredient in accounting is merely the experienced personal judgment of its senior practitioners, if there is no body of concepts and theories that can be utilized in the analysis of accounting problems, the study of accounting in the universities is rightfully in jeopardy.

[31] Herman W. Bevis, "Progress and Poverty in Accounting Thought," *The Journal of Accountancy* (July 1966), p. 39.

DISCUSSION OF "THE BALANCE SHEET—EMBODIMENT OF THE MOST FUNDAMENTAL ELEMENTS OF ACCOUNTING THEORY"

ALFRED RAPPAPORT

Biography appears on page 93.

Whenever Bob Sprouse, one of our most respected and articulate spokesmen, comments on the current scene in accounting, there is great interest in his observations. When I learned that Bob would be discussing the balance sheet, a statement relegated to obscurity by recent generations of accounting theorists, I awaited his manuscript with more than ordinary interest. I speculated at the time that, in the noblest tradition of good sportsmanship, Bob had decided to champion the cause of an underdog. The accuracy of this speculation was quickly confirmed when I read his manuscript. As a result, I find myself in the doubly unenviable position of being cast as a critic of Bob Sprouse defending an accounting underdog.

Sprouse's paper aims at providing support for the proposition that "the balance sheet embodies the most fundamental elements of accounting theory from which the essential elements contained in the income statement are necessarily derived." In support of this proposition, three views of the balance sheet (the sheet of balances view, the static funds statement view, and the financial position view) are examined. From this analysis, Sprouse concludes that one view, the financial position view, is superior to the other two. My purpose here is to examine briefly the claimed primacy for the balance sheet in accounting theory development and Sprouse's assessment of various balance-sheet approaches or views. In addition, I propose to offer for your consideration a fourth balance-sheet view.

Consider, first, Sprouse's initial proposition. It is important to recognize that this proposition is based on a structural or designer's view of the accounting system, not on the user's or consumer's view. Sprouse appropriately makes this distinction at the very beginning of his paper by accepting the primacy of the income statement in terms of user interest; on the structural or logical form level, he suggests that "concepts of assets and liabilities are more fundamental than the concept of income" since the latter depends upon the former. The relative merits of the structural-versus-user view of the accounting system will be discussed subsequently. First, let us turn our attention to Sprouse's structurally based argument on the primacy of the balance sheet.

The structural view offers no explicit user decision models or behavioral theory to provide guidelines for choice among alternative configurations of information. Instead, such a view in accounting is characterized by the implicit assumption that the duality framework per se, including the necessary articulation between

SOURCE: From *Foundations of Accounting Theory*, edited by Williard E. Stone (Gainesville, Fla.: University of Florida Press, 1971), pp. 105–113. Reprinted by permission of the University of Florida Press.

the balance sheet and income statements, is in some general sense useful and hence should be accepted a priori. Sprouse, using a structurally based argument, contends that the balance sheet embodies more fundamental elements of accounting theory than the income statement. The purported rationale for this contention would presumably include the following statements: (a) "the income statement can properly be described as merely a summary of one class of transactions resulting in changes in one balance sheet account"; (b) "the measurement of income is dependent upon the measurement of net assets which, in turn, is dependent upon the measurement of assets and liabilities"; and (c) "no one has ever successfully managed to formulate a concept of income that is not directly or indirectly dependent upon the concept of assets and the concept of liabilities."

For purposes of direct contrast, consider the following three alternative propositions:

a) The balance sheet can properly be described as a summary of stocks or residuals that results from income statement transactions.

b) The measurement of net assets is dependent upon the measurement of income, which, in turn, is dependent upon the measurement of revenues and expenses.

c) No one has ever successfully managed to formulate a concept of assets that is not directly or indirectly dependent upon a concept of income.

Is this set of three propositions more accurate than the Sprouse set enumerated earlier? Or is the Sprouse set perhaps more accurate? Adhering once again to the structural or logical form approach to accounting systems, we are necessarily indifferent about these two sets of propositions. Within the context of an explicitly defined analytical system such as the accounting double-entry system, one can define a given systems variable in terms of other systems variables. For example, a system with only two variables, a and i, can be described in terms of $a = f(i)$ or $i = f(a)$. If we were to adopt a somewhat oversimplified view of the accounting system, we would perhaps designate i to represent income and a, net assets. The two propositions $a = f(i)$ and $i = f(a)$ are analytic rather than synthetic propositions, since their validity depends solely on the definitions of the symbols they contain rather than on empirical observation.[1]

Returning for a moment to Sprouse's set of three propositions, note that the first two propositions are essentially two ways of asserting $i = f(a)$, while the third proposition is simply a logical consequence of the first two. As you would expect, the first two of my three alternative propositions assert that $a = f(i)$, and the third proposition is once again a logical consequence of the first two.

The important point to emphasize here is that the structural approach to accounting systems does not admit exogenously derived postulated systems objectives, and hence there is no logical basis for choosing one systems representation over another. For our specific purposes, the structural approach allows us no basis for choice between the Sprouse propositions and the alternative proposi-

[1] Alfred Jules Ayer, *Language, Truth and Logic* (New York: Dover Publications, 1952), pp. 78–79.

tions. Fortunately, we are not at an impasse, since Sprouse implicitly rejects the structural view as he begins his discussion of the three balance-sheet views.

Unlike the structural approach, the user approach to accounting theory is based upon some user decision model or models. While Sprouse does not explicitly present a user model, it is reasonable to assume that some underlying user model was employed to rank one approach to balance-sheet measures—the financial position view—above two alternative approaches—the sheet of balances view and the static funds statement view. In the absence of an explicit designation of user models, there is no logical basis for either acknowledging or denying the validity of Sprouse's balance-sheet preferences. In light of this, I propose to offer a number of general observations about the three balance-sheet views and then briefly discuss a fourth view based on a postulated user decision model.

Let us begin with the sheet of balances approach, which views the balance sheet "as a summary of debit and credit account balances that remain after the determinants of income have been decided upon and the retained earnings account has been adjusted for the amount of income that results." Surely the contention that this approach is not likely to result in a particularly useful statement is a foregone conclusion, assuming even a relatively wide spectrum of different user models. Is the basic problem simply the treatment of the balance sheet as a secondary or residual statement, or is there perhaps a more fundamental problem? I submit that the real answer lies in the futility of implementing the matching concept. As Sprouse forcefully states, "the matching concept necessarily relies on ad hoc decisions rather than on accounting theory—on independent value judgments rather than on consistent analysis." This observation is not only central to the Sprouse paper, but in large measure helps explain the difficulty facing accountants today. In light of its significance, I would like to elaborate on the measurement problems associated with the matching concept.

If we were to develop present-value financial statements under conditions of perfect certainty, the results would be identical whether we treated the balance sheet or the income statement as the residual statement. Residual approaches such as the sheet of balances approach affect results only when means of dealing with uncertainty are required.

What has been the accountant's response to uncertainty? Conservatism, consistency, increasing disclosure, and demands for objectivity as manifested by adherence to historical cost conventions represent key mechanisms for dealing with uncertainty. Consider the serious income-determination problems found in the cost-matching area. The cost-matching decision, that is the decision concerning the assignment of costs as deductions from revenue in specific accounting periods, reflects the accountant's broad perception of the relative risks associated with cost outlays. Accountants appear to be concerned with two types of risk— economic and measurement.[2] An economic risk may be viewed as the probability that an outlay will result in no net benefit to the firm. Where the economic risk is judged to be high, the outlay is treated as an expense in the same period as the commitment for the outlay is incurred. Costs associated with pure research

---

[2] The term "measurement" is used here only in the general sense of assigning numbers to real world phenomena according to rules.

serve as an outstanding example of a high-risk outlay generally treated as an expense.

Measurement risks are best characterized as the uncertainties of implementing the matching principle. High measurement risks occur when either it is difficult to identify the tangible benefits or revenues arising from certain costs (e.g., executive salaries paid largely for planning activities, campaigns to promote company name and products, executive and employee educational programs, administrative facilities such as buildings and information systems, philanthropic contributions) or when estimates of the magnitude and timing of benefits are subject to a significant degree of error (e.g., product improvement programs, patents, copyrights, new productive facilities). The accountant's reaction to the basic form of measurement risk can be summarized as follows:

Measurement risk	Measurement procedure
1. Difficult to identify revenues arising from a given cost.	1. Expense in current period.
2. Estimated time duration of expected benefit or revenue flow subject to significant measurement error.	2. Expense in current period.
3. Estimated time duration of expected benefits subject to relatively small margins of error, but magnitude and timing of benefit or revenue flows subject to significant measurement error.	3. Choice of a systematic write-off basis over the estimated time duration of expected benefits.

It should be clearly recognized that, while the three measurement-risk categories enumerated above may broadly indicate the basis for the accountant's choice of a measurement procedure, there is ample evidence to suggest that accountants evaluating a given cost outlay may in many cases not agree upon the appropriate measurement-risk category for the outlay. The accountant's subjective assessment of management's expectations for, say, research and development outlays will influence the choice between measurement risk no. 2 (expense in current period) and measurement risk no. 3 (systematic write-off). Furthermore, the choice of measurement risk no. 3 leads to a wide range of possibilities of systematic write-off patterns. Indeed, it is useful to view the basic income-determination alternatives as constituting the intersection between management-risk categories no. 2 and no. 3 plus the discretionary measurement alternatives available within measurement-risk category no. 3. Indeed, one can reluctantly view many of the controversies in accounting today as essentially a debate between uniform arbitrariness and flexible arbitrariness.[3] In summing up the sheet of balance view, I submit that its failings derive from, in Sprouse's words, "the matching concept (which) necessarily relies on ad hoc decisions rather than on

---

[3] For a comprehensive demonstration of the arbitrariness of accounting allocations, see Arthur L. Thomas, *The Allocation Problem in Financial Accounting Theory* (Evanston, Ill.: AAA, 1969).

accounting theory—on independent value judgments rather than on consistent analysis."

The static funds statement view, so named because it purports to show the sources and composition of company capital at a prescribed point in time, is rejected by Sprouse on grounds that it is not feasible, and, secondly, even if it were feasible, the relevance or usefulness of such disclosure is questioned. As is the case with the sheet of balances view, the lack of feasibility of the static funds statement view is clearly attributable to the accountant's difficulty in coping with uncertainty. The question of relevance is best deferred in the absence of an explicit user model.

Of the three balance-sheet views, Sprouse clearly prefers the financial position view. Indeed, he suggests that, "if there is to be a theory of accounting, the financial position view of the balance sheet provides the only hope." The evidence to support such a far-reaching assertion is far from apparent. Indeed, it is difficult to reconcile Sprouse's forceful presentation on the futility of the matching concept with his advocacy of the financial position view which depends directly on matching.

The distinctions between the financial position view and the other views proposed are not sharply delineated. For example, the description of the financial position view as "the relationship of the resources available to the enterprise and the obligations of the enterprise that require the future utilization of resources" is uncomfortably close to the static funds statement view of the balance sheet as "a statement of the sources and composition of company capital." Nor is it clear whether the financial position and the sheet of balances view are antithetical.

Sprouse suggests that stockholders and investors should be provided information about a firm's earning power and solvency. If we impose the constraints of current practice, that balance sheets and income statements must articulate with one another and that historical cost be employed, then it is quite possible to find important situations in which the goals of providing information about earning power and solvency may be in conflict. Consider, for example, the question of alternative inventory cost methods. Because LIFO, in most circumstances, generates a better matching of current costs with current revenues, it may result in a better indication of a firm's earning power than other methods such as FIFO or average cost. In a growing firm and under inflationary conditions, LIFO inventory cost appearing on the balance sheet may, however, be significantly less than current cost. The adoption of FIFO is likely to lead to the reverse situation. The advocate of the sheet of balances view would presumably choose the LIFO method since he is more willing to tolerate shortcomings in the balance sheet than in the income statement. Would the financial position advocate suggest FIFO under these conditions? Perhaps he would, but Sprouse has not set forth how he would logically assess information trade-offs between the balance sheet and the income statement.

One final observation concerning the financial position view warrants comment. Sprouse's preference for the financial position view appears to be based largely on the usefulness of balance-sheet outputs for assessing probable failure or insolvency. While this focus is particularly useful for creditors in extremely risky firms, there should be equal concern for the information needs of investors in the vast majority of going concerns. Whether this broader notion of the accountant's audience would change Sprouse's preference ordering is once again dependent upon postulated user models.

At this point I would like to note a fourth possible view of the balance sheet recently presented by the AAA 1966–1968 Committee on External Reporting. In its attempt to develop information useful to equity investors and creditors, the committee outlined the following steps:

1. Select normative investors' and creditors' valuation models. The committee selected a dividend model for equity investors.
2. Select a model for the prediction of dividends and other distributions to stockholders and creditors.
3. List object and activity inputs (potentially relevant identifications of items and events) and their related attributes and measurement concepts.
4. Evaluate each of the attributes of each object or activity input for relevancy (its ability to permit a prediction of a variable or relationship in the models).
5. List potentially acceptable measurement procedures.
6. Assess each procedure for each attribute in light of the standards of quantifiability, verifiability, and freedom from bias.
7. Select the attributes and measurement procedures that should be included in financial reports.[4]

Using the foregoing approach, some of the committee's broad recommendations are as follows:

1. External financial reports should include at least a statement of resources and commitments and a statement showing current monetary flows such as those suggested in Exhibits A and B. These two statements should complement one another in analyses for forecasting future cash flows. The statement of resources should include information regarding objects likely to contribute to future cash flows and the report of commitments should represent probable future outflows. The current monetary flow statement should represent an enumeration of changes in resources and commitments.
2. External financial reports should not be expected to "balance" or articulate with each other. In fact, we find that forced balancing and articulation have frequently restricted the presentation of relevant information.
3. Reported information should not be restricted to that which can be expressed in dollar terms. Wherever they meet the standards adequately, physical measures, classifications, and nonquantifiable descriptions should be included in reports in addition to monetary measurements.[5]

Perhaps at this juncture the committee's methodology is more interesting and useful than its recommendations. In my view, however, employing the user's approach to accounting theory, not the structural or designer's approach, holds the greatest hope for progress in accounting theory. The structural approach to accounting theory, which treats balance-sheet income statement articulation as

---

[4] "An Evaluation of External Reporting Practices: A Report of the 1966–68 Committee on External Reporting," *The Accounting Review*, Supplement to vol. 44 (1969), p. 80.

[5] "An Evaluation of External Reporting Practices," pp. 117–18.

Exhibit A ABC CORPORATION STATEMENT OF RESOURCES AND COMMITMENTS
DECEMBER 31, 19x0

Resources available

Monetary:
Cash	$ xx
Marketable securities—at current market price	xx
Accounts receivable—expected net realizable amount	xx
	$ xx

Operating:
  Inventory (by major classifications)—at historical cost, current replacement costs and current selling prices. Units should be expressed where feasible.
  Operating facilities—include data on capacity in terms of physical output and/or sales dollars, estimated economic life of principal facilities where mortality experience is available, relative status of facilities in light of current and predicted states of technology, and expected cost of replacing facilities in the near future.

Protective:
  Copyright, trademarks and patents—include information regarding products covered and duration.

Innovative:
  Description of major research and development programs to meet future needs of consumers. Include data on number and technical skills of research and development personnel.

Investment in other companies:
  Enumeration of companies, date(s) of investment, percent of outstanding stock owned, and current market value or current dividends being received.

Other resources:
  Sales backlog
  Selling and administrative facilities

Commitments

Due within one year:
Accounts payable	$ xx
Taxes payable	xx
Lease payments	xx
Pension payments	xx
Other (to be specified)	xx
	$ xx

Schedule of current commitments due after one year:

	19x1	19x2	19x3	19x4	19x5	19xx
Lease payments	xx	xx	xx	xx	xx	xx
Pensions						
Bonds payable						
(principal payments)						
Notes payable						
(principal payments)						
Other						

Schedule of new commitments planned for next three years:

	19x1	19x2	19x3
Lease payments	xx	xx	xx
Capital expenditures	xx	xx	xx
Other (to be specified)	xx	xx	xx

Shareholder's Rights:
  Number of shares outstanding of each class of stock with information regarding priority rights. Conversion rights of all senior securities and information regarding options outstanding or contemplated.

182 INCOME DETERMINATION

Exhibit B STATEMENT OF CURRENT MONETARY FLOWS FOR THE YEAR ENDED DECEMBER 31, 19x0

Operations—Major:
  Monetary asset inflows:
    Sales of goods or services (cash and charge) $ xx
  Less monetary asset outflows and current cash
    commitments:
    (1) Responsive to sales or production volume and mix:
      Material purchases $ xx
      Labor services   xx
      Other operating costs   xx
         $ xx

    (2) "Committed":
      Interest on debt $ xx
      Employee services   xx
      Lease payments   xx
      Pension payments   xx
      Property taxes   xx
         $ xx

    (3) Discretionary:
      Research and development (outlays by
        major programs) $ xx
      Advertising   xx
      Replacement of capacity   xx
         $ xx

    (4) Based on taxable income:
      Federal and state income taxes $ xx
      (classified by applicable rates)
  Net change in current monetary accounts resulting
    from major operations $ xx

Operations—Minor:
  Monetary asset inflows:
    Interest revenue $ xx
    Sale of securities   xx
       $ xx

  Less: Monetary asset outflows, and current cash
    commitments:
    Investment in securities $ xx
    Investment management expenses:
      Salaries $ xx
      Other   xx   xx
       $ xx

Net change in current monetary accounts resulting
  from minor operations $ xx

Financing:
  Monetary asset inflows:
    Sale of stocks and bonds $ xx
    Borrowing (classified by type)   xx
       $ xx

Less: Monetary asset outflows and current cash commitments:		
Retirement of securities	$ xx	
Repayment of debt	xx	
Management expenses	xx	
	$ xx	
Net change in current monetary accounts resulting from changes in capital structure		$ xx
Operating capacity:		
Monetary asset outflows and current cash commitments:		
Purchase of additional operating capacity*	$ xx	
Less: Monetary asset inflows		
Sale of plant, equipment and land*	xx	
Net change in current monetary accounts resulting from changes in capacity		$ xx
Distributions:		
Priority distributions:		
Preferred stock dividends	$ xx	
Residual distributions:		
Common stock dividends	xx	
Partial liquidation dividends	xx	
Total distributions		$ xx

* Include data as prescribed under "Operating facilities" in the statement of resources and commitments.

SOURCE: From Committee Reports Supplement to Volume XLIV of *The Accounting Review*, "Evaluation of External Reporting Practices—A Report of the 1966–68 Committee on External Reporting," pp. 119–122. Reprinted by permission of the American Accounting Association.

axiomatic, seriously limits the search for more useful information constructs. The fourth view of the balance sheet presented as exhibit A, which some may wish to refer to as the nonbalancing balance-sheet view, must, as any other proposed disclosure, meet certain empirical standards of usefulness. On the other hand, it should be noted that this, as well as other innovative departures from current practice, can be logically derived from the user's approach, but not the structural approach to accounting theory. Therefore, I submit that the question of whether or not the balance sheet as we know it today embodies the most fundamental elements of accounting theory is not as crucial as the question of what recommendations would result from rigorously developed accounting theory based on user needs. It is at least open to debate whether any of the conventional balance-sheet views would survive such inquiry.

In closing, let me emphasize that while Bob Sprouse and I may have some differences over research methodology, I am in absolute agreement with his fundamental observation that "if there is no body of concepts and theories that can be utilized in the analysis of accounting problems, the study of accounting in the universities is rightfully in jeopardy."

D. THE ROLE OF DIFFERENT CIRCUMSTANCES IN ACHIEVING COMPARABILITY

THOMAS F. KELLER

THOMAS F. KELLER (1931–), A.B. 53 Duke; M.B.A. 57, Ph.D. 60 Michigan; CPA. Currently professor of business administration, Duke University. Major publications: *Accounting for Corporate Income Taxes* (1961), *Intermediate Accounting* (with Meigs and Johnson, 1963; with Meigs, Johnson, and Mosich, 1968), *Advanced Accounting* (with Meigs and Johnson, 1966). Contributor to *The Journal of Accountancy* and *The Accounting Review*. Book review editor, 1971–72, and editor, since 1972, *The Accounting Review*.
 Joined the Duke University faculty in 1959, and was vice provost in 1971–72. Visited the faculties of the University of Washington, 1963–64, and Carnegie-Mellon University, 1966–67.
 Was vice-president of the American Accounting Association, 1968–69

UNIFORMITY VERSUS FLEXIBILITY: A REVIEW OF THE RHETORIC

THOMAS F. KELLER

How will the historian of accounting, looking back at you and me from A.D. two thousand and something, describe us?
 I suggest he might do worse than interpret the present state of accounting as a clash between two ways of thought—as yet one more example of the universal conflict between the man who wants to tug at the brake and the man who wants to step on the accelerator.
  —Baxter, Accounting Principles: The Conflict in Current Theory, *128 Accountant 699 (1953).*

SOURCE: From *Law and Contemporary Problems*, Vol. XXX, No. 4 (Autumn, 1965), pp. 637–651. Reprinted by permission of *Law and Contemporary Problems*.

The controversy among certified public accountants from Maine to California over "uniformity" versus "flexibility" has probably attracted more attention to the practice of public accounting than any other debate since the enactment of the Securities Act of 1933[1] and the Securities Exchange Act of 1934.[2] What lies behind this debate? Why are so many people involved? Why is the argument taken so seriously? At stake are matters no less critical than the reliability and comparability of published corporate financial statements accompanied by a standard CPA's certificate, which generally reads substantially as follows:

> In our opinion, the accompanying balance sheet and statement of income (and other statements included in the report) present fairly the financial position of XYZ Company at December 31, 19–, and the results of its operations for the year then ended, in conformity with generally accepted accounting principles applied on a basis consistent with that of the preceding year.

The importance of accurate and useful financial information in a dynamic economy can hardly be overemphasized. If, as has been claimed, the accuracy and utility of financial reporting are in doubt, the seriousness of the debate for the whole accounting profession is great.

The charge of those supporting "uniformity" is that there is no authoritative and generally recognized body of accounting principles to which the investor or the public can look when examining financial statements. Thus the confidence of the investor or other outsider must rest largely on his faith in the accountant's integrity, and the advocates of uniformity claim that this faith has been shaken. The most outspoken critics of current practice claim that financial reports at the present time do not provide adequate information presented in such a way as to allow the potential investor to make an intelligent choice among alternative investments. In short, the charge is that comparability between companies is lacking and that accountants are to blame. Those who support "flexibility" in general argue that meaningful comparability of financial data reflecting the affairs of diverse business organizations is a utopian goal and that, in any case, it cannot be achieved by the adoption of firm rules that do not take adequate account of differing factual situations.

I CHARGES AND PRESSURES FOR ACTION

Charges of the accountant's neglect of outsiders' interests and of his lack of independence from corporate management have come from many quarters. Steven Anreder, writing for *Barron's*,[3] cites specific examples of accounting practices that are not considered to be consistent with generally accepted accounting principles. Among these are Chock Full O'Nuts Corporation's capitalization of outlays for advertising, promotion, and research and development and Colgate-Palmolive's election to discontinue the amortization of good will. Anreder is, nevertheless, quite charitable in his remarks. He observes that

> The [Chock Full O'Nuts] incident serves as a timely reminder of something few investors bother to consider: that accounting is a very fluid practice. Ac-

---

[1] 48 Stat. 74, as amended, 15 U.S.C. §§ 77a-aa (1964).
[2] 48 Stat. 881, as amended, 15 U.S.C. §§ 78a-hh (1964).
[3] Anreder, "Pitfalls for the Unwary," *Barron's*, Dec. 24, 1962, p. 3.

counting varies from industry to industry. In fact, even among companies in the same field, practices are so diverse as to make comparisons of earnings less than meaningful.[4]

In the same section of his article Mr. Anreder states,

> Without question stockholders today are better informed than they used to be. . . . Gone are the days when a company could report what it wanted, whenever it cared to, or even refuse to report at all. Owing to enactment of the securities laws, more stringent regulation by stock exchanges and . . . a more responsible approach by management, the quality of financial data presented to U.S. investors is unrivaled anywhere in the world.[5]

In a news article published in January 1963, *Business Week* cited the 1957 annual report of Swift & Company as evidence of lack of consistency:

> Operating entirely within the framework of generally accepted accounting principles, Swift cut contributions to its pension plan to $1.1 million from $13.6 million the year before. The difference of $12.5 million amounted to over 90% of the net income that Swift reported for 1957. Thus, the company was able to keep its earnings on an even keel, despite the "unfavorable margins" that prevailed in the packing industry that year.[6]

Situations like these are embarrassing to accountants for the reason stated by Thomas G. Higgins of Arthur Young & Co., Swift's auditor, to the *Business Week* reporter: "There was nothing we could do—we had no firm guidelines to follow."[7]

Professor Robert N. Anthony cites a different type of situation: "General Motors and Standard Oil of New Jersey each recently sold its half ownership in Ethyl Corporation at a book gain of many millions of dollars. GM reported its fifty per cent of the gain as part of its net income for the year. Standard Oil left net income unaffected, crediting its fifty per cent directly to surplus."[8] Professor Anthony makes no judgment—he is merely pointing out the lack of accepted accounting principles that could be used to guide accountants in such situations.

In the above cited cases there is no charge that the published financial statements are in error. In the *Barron's* article, the reporter merely implies that unusual procedures were employed; in the particular case the procedure used may have been appropriate. But how can these statements be compared with similar enterprises that follow a procedure of classifying outlays like these as period expenses? Likewise, in the Swift & Co. case, the writer calls attention to a change in the method used to determine the annual pension cost, but this is not to say that the 13.6 million dollar figure was correct and the 1.1 million dollar figure erroneous. Nevertheless, there is no escaping the fact that a change in accounting method resulted in incomparable operating results for two consecutive years. Finally, Professor Anthony has pointed out how altogether different procedures were applied to a common situation. Which procedure was correct? There are

---

[4] *Ibid.*
[5] *Ibid.*
[6] *A Matter of Principle Splits CPAs*, Business Week, Jan. 26, 1963, p. 50, at 56.
[7] *Ibid.*
[8] Anthony, *Showdown on Accounting Principles*, Harvard Business Review, May–June 1963, p. 99, at 101.

opinions to support each, but some accountants would contend that there is no authority by which this situation can be finally resolved. Undoubtedly the accountants on either side of this question felt that their position was the sounder.

The recital of situations such as those discussed here has greatly aided the cause of the advocates of uniformity. On the surface at least there appears to be a need for more uniform practice. But this need may be more apparent than real. Whether this is the case is a major issue yet to be resolved by the accounting profession, and it may be the issue at the heart of the current controversy.

By calling attention to situations such as those cited above, the critics are in some sense issuing a mandate to the Securities and Exchange Commission to investigate the adequacy of the information provided to investors. If the information is found, or believed, to be inadequate, then the Commission might choose to exercise powers over accounting practices granted it in the Securities Act of 1933.[9] This act provides ample authority for the Commission to extend its regulation of the practice of accountancy by prescribing detailed rules and regulations for the presentation of financial information.

Accountants would like to avoid further regulation by the SEC, and they would like to have the confidence of the security analyst and the investor. Of almost equal importance is the fact that there have been an increasing number of lawsuits brought against accountants by investors who believe they have been damaged by relying on financial information which, in spite of the expressed opinion of the CPA, was not fairly presented.[10] For these and probably other reasons accountants are actively engaged in the debate regarding the standards of accounting practice.

II HISTORICAL BACKGROUND OF THE DEBATE

A. Early Views

In 1927, in discussing the practice of accounting, Professor Henry R. Hatfield mentioned that one of the achievements of accounting

> ... is the effort to introduce some unity into accounting theory instead of regarding its phenomena as diverse. For long it was generally considered that the investment of capital was in marked opposition to the payment of an expense. This view was crystallized in the phrase "capital expenditure or charge against revenue." It assumed that these two were radically different in nature, and one must never be confounded with the other. Today one sees a continuous gradation, land, building, machinery, raw material, expense of labor—each one of a series, each differing only as to length of the service which it renders, each paid for with the view of getting all possible use out of it in the productive process. The development of this point is, I believe, a real achievement in accounting theory—one not dreamt of in earlier centuries.[11]

Later in the same piece, Hatfield remarked that "accounting ... needs something

---

[9] § 19(a), 48 Stat. 85, as amended, 15 U.S.C. § 77s(a) (1964).

[10] *The Specter of Auditors' Liability*, Journal of Accountancy, Sept. 1965, p. 33.

[11] Hatfield, *What Is the Matter with Accounting?*, 44 Journal of Accountancy 267, 270 (1927).

more than a definite nomenclature. It needs above all else the formulation of sound theories, which can be crystallized into clear terminology."[12]

J. M. B. Hoxsey of the Committee on Stock List of the New York Stock Exchange, spoke in 1930 of stockholders' needs for more information supplied in a more understandable form. He discussed the problems that were likely to arise and the areas of greatest concern, stating that "the exchange is interested in the accounts of companies as a source of reliable information for those who deal in stocks. It is not sufficient for the stock exchange that the accounts should be in conformity with law or even that they should be conservative; the stock exchange desires that they should be fully and fairly informative."[13]

In 1932 George O. May, in a letter to M. C. Rorty, an organizer of the National Bureau of Economic Research, concerning the limitations of legislating accounting rules, advanced the idea that

> legislative provisions cannot be very effective—all that they can do is to establish a minimum standard which can be enforced universally without injustice.
>
> You and I agree that industrial activity does not lend itself to uniform accounting.... Accounts must at best be conventional, and in attempting to attribute profits to short periods of time we are doing violence to the facts. The fundamental distinction between capital and revenue which lies at the root of all profit accounting is ultimately only a question of degree....
>
> My idea would be that every corporation should adopt a method of accounting described in considerable detail. This method should be certified by its auditors as being in accordance with reasonable standards of business practice, and should be freely disclosed. The officers should then be guilty of falsification of accounts if they knowingly put forward any accounts not in conformity with the methods of accounting so adopted, and the auditors would be required to certify that the accounts were prepared in accordance with the corporation's official method....
>
> The trouble with an "official" system of accounting is, that while it is possible to lay down broad principles, wide variations are possible within the limits of such principles, and which variation should be adopted is a question on which one cannot rightly be dogmatic.[14]

The Committee on Stock List of the Stock Exchange, following discussions with members of the American Institute of Accountants (AIA), recommended, and the Stock Exchange and the AIA agreed, that the Exchange should attempt to achieve

> ... universal ... acceptance by listed corporations of certain broad principles of accounting which have won fairly general acceptance, and within the limits of such broad principles to make no attempt to restrict the right of corporations to select detailed methods of accounting deemed by them to be best adapted to the requirements of their business....[15]

The correspondence between the Stock Exchange and the AIA was filled with questions of terminology. The terms *practices, principles, conventions,* and *rules*

---

[12] *Id.* at 272.
[13] Hoxsey, *Accounting for Investors*, 50 Journal of Accountancy 251, 253 (1930).
[14] Memoirs and Accounting Thought of George O. May 61–62 (Grady ed. 1962).
[15] *Id.* at 68.

were used almost interchangeably. Mr. May quotes one exchange of letters that illustrates the terminological confusion. The Stock Exchange posed six questions, the last of which was this: "Whether such system in their opinion conforms to accepted accounting *practices,* and particularly whether it is in any respect inconsistent with any of the *principles* set forth in the statement attached hereto."[16] The accounting firms responded, "Your sixth question, apart from the specific reference to the *principles* enumerated, aims, we assume, to insure that companies are following accounting *practices* which have substantial authority back of them."[17]

B. Institutional Efforts

Accounting Research Bulletin No. 1[18] was issued by the AIA in September 1939. It set forth the conditions under which the Committee on Accounting Procedure intended to operate. As a matter of policy the Committee decided not to attempt an over-all coordinated statement of generally accepted accounting principles but rather to deal with particular questions or subjects as they seemed to require consideration.[19] In Bulletin No. 1, the Committee noted the change in the social system that permitted widespread ownership of securities and short-term holdings. In speaking of this change, the Bulletin stated,

> This evolution has also led to a demand for a larger degree of uniformity in accounting. *Uniformity* has usually connoted similar treatment of the same item occurring in many cases, in which sense it runs the risk of concealing important differences among cases. Another sense of the word would require that different authorities working independently on the same case should reach the same conclusions. Although uniformity is a worthwhile goal, it should not be pursued to the exclusion of other benefits. Changes of emphasis and objective as well as changes in conditions under which business operates have led, and doubtless will continue to lead, to the adoption of new accounting procedures. Consequently diversity of practice may continue as new practices are adopted before old ones are completely discarded. . . .
>
> The principal objective of the committee has been to narrow areas of difference and inconsistency in accounting practices, and to further the development and recognition of generally accepted accounting principles, through the issuance of opinions and recommendations that would serve as criteria for determining the suitability of accounting practices reflected in financial statements and representations of commercial and industrial companies.[20]

Twenty years later the American Institute of Certified Public Accountants (AICPA), the successor to the AIA, modified its approach to the development of accounting principles. In September 1958, the Special Committee on Research

---

[16] *Id.* at 74. (Emphasis added by May.)

[17] *Ibid.*

[18] Parts of this bulletin were incorporated into the *Introduction, Committee on Accounting Procedure, AICPA, Restatement and Revision of Accounting Research Bulletins* (Accounting Research Bull. No. 43, 1953).

[19] *Committee on Accounting Procedure, AICPA, Final Report* (1959), reprinted in part in Journal of Accountancy, Nov. 1959, pp. 70–71.

[20] *Committee on Accounting Procedure, AICPA, Restatement and Revision of Accounting Research Bulletins 7–8* (Accounting Research Bull. No. 43, 1953).

Program recommended an extensive revision of the procedures by which the Institute develops accounting guidelines. The Committee stated,

> The general purpose of the Institute in the field of financial accounting should be to advance the written expression of what constitutes generally accepted accounting principles, for the guidance of its members and of others. This means something more than a survey of existing practice. It means continuing effort to determine appropriate practice and to narrow the areas of difference and inconsistency in practice. In accomplishing this, reliance should be placed on persuasion rather than on compulsion. The Institute, however, can, and it should, take definite steps to lead in the thinking on unsettled and controversial issues.
>
> The broad problem of financial accounting should be visualized as requiring attention at four levels: first, postulates; second, principles; third, rules or other guides for the application of principles in specific situations; and fourth, research.[21]

The Accounting Principles Board (APB) was to be the official body of the Institute with the authority to issue opinions on acceptable accounting practice. To date the Board has issued six opinions. It was the second of these six opinions, issued in December 1962, that heightened the current controversy.

APB Opinion No. 2, *Accounting for the "Investment Credit,"*[22] was supported by fourteen members of the Accounting Principles Board; the Board is composed of twenty-one members, and a two-thirds majority (*i.e.*, at least fourteen) is required for the issuance of an opinion. Opinion No. 2 recognized only one method of accounting for the investment credit, while several members of the Board felt strongly that at least one other method was equally correct, based on accepted practice, as the one approved by the Board. The requirement that everyone, except regulated companies, adopt the specified method or justify departures from it ignited the debate. The issues were seemingly clear-cut: Does the Accounting Principles Board have the right to limit the practice of accounting to one procedure? Is the profession to have uniform or flexible rules?[23]

C. Attempts to Obtain Agreement on Fundamentals

One method of achieving a degree of uniformity would be to seek agreement on fundamental accounting concepts—postulates and principles, as they have come to be called by most—and it appeared for a time that the APB might be following this path to the desired goal. Professor Herbert E. Miller, speaking before the 1961 Annual Meeting of the Texas Society of CPAs, was optimistic about the acceptance of a set of broad accounting principles that were subsequently to be published as Accounting Research Studies Nos. 1 and 3. He expressed the opinion that "probably most accountants would say that research in the area of accounting principles was desirable in order to minimize any risk of

---

[21] *Special Comm. on Research Program, Report to Council* (1958), reprinted in Journal of Accountancy, Dec. 1958, pp. 62–63.

[22] *Accounting Principles Board, AICPA, Accounting for the "Investment Credit"* (Opinion No. 2, 1962).

[23] Opinion No. 2 was subsequently amended by *Accounting Principles Board, AICPA, Accounting for the "Investment Credit"* (Opinion No. 4, 1964), to permit alternative treatment of the investment credit.

loss of public confidence in financial statements."[24] And it is clear that he was using the term *principles* in the broad sense. He continued with this observation:

> There is some room for doubt, however, as to whether agreement about principles will remove the risk of loss of public confidence in the accounting process. Such doubt is based on a belief that a good share of the present-day variations appearing in financial statements may not be attributable so much to any sad state of accounting principles as it is to the existence of a variety of methods or ways in which accountants apply their principles.[25]

He then raised the crucial question:

> But how can this goal of achieving reasonable uniformity and comparability of accounting information be attained if we first of all permit the existence of a number of alternative ways to apply accounting principles and then go a step further and label all alternative ways of applying principles as being equally acceptable?[26]

As we now know, the principles set forth in Accounting Research Studies Nos. 1 and 3[27] have not been accepted by the profession nor has any other set of principles been accepted. Instead, members of the profession seem to have moved on to the alternative method of achieving uniformity suggested by Professor Miller—discussion of the desirability of eliminating alternative ways of applying principles.[28] As indicated earlier, this very point was at issue in 1932 in the discussions between George O. May and M. C. Rorty. At that juncture reliance was placed on consistent application of principles over time. There is some evidence, as in the case of Swift & Co. cited earlier, that even now accounting principles are not always applied consistently even though the auditor's opinion indicates that they have been. Ought consistency to remain the primary goal or has the profession of accountancy reached the stage where progress toward comparability can be made?

III THE CURRENT DEBATE

In order to gain some flavor of the debate, which has reached a higher pitch in the last few years, let us examine some of the arguments.

Thomas G. Higgins has stated the crux of the problem as follows:

> [W]hen we independent public accountants report that financial statements are presented in conformity with "generally accepted accounting principles,"

---

[24] Miller, "After There Is Agreement on Broad Accounting Principles—What Then?," Texas CPA, Sept. 1961, p. 3.

[25] *Id.* at 4.

[26] *Ibid.*

[27] Maurice Moonitz, *The Basic Postulates of Accounting* (AICPA Accounting Research Study No. 1, 1961); Robert T. Sprouse & Maurice Moonitz, *A Tentative Set of Broad Accounting Principles for Business Enterprises* (AICPA Accounting Research Study No. 3, 1962).

[28] For a full development of this history, see Sprouse & Vagts, *The Accounting Principles Board and Differences and Inconsistencies in Accounting Practice: An Interim Appraisal, infra,* pp. 706-26. [Appears in volume from which this article was taken—Eds.]

we cannot be sure what we mean, because the expression "generally accepted accounting principles" has never been satisfactorily defined.... [T]hose who issue the financial statements on which we report, and those who use them, do not know what we mean, either.[29]

Mr. Higgins believes that the APB is the group with the authority to define accounting principles. However, there is a difference of opinion among the members of the Board about how to proceed in this matter. Mr. Higgins finds that some

> Board members seriously question whether uniformity in accounting and comparability in financial reporting are desirable objectives. They feel that *complete* uniformity in accounting treatments and *strict* comparability of financial statements cannot be accomplished. Hence, they do not believe that the accounting profession, acting through the Accounting Principles Board, should move vigorously *toward* uniformity and comparability. They base their position in large part on the view that the responsibility of the directors of a corporation to account to stockholders through the medium of financial statements carries with it the authority to select the accounting methods to be followed by the corporation.[30]

Mr. Higgins finds this position contradictory. In his opinion, "defining the limits—providing the criteria for determining the accounting methods to be used—is . . . the proper function of independent public accountants."[31]

Hassel Tippit, speaking on the same occasion, propounded a contrary point of view. In his opinion,

> many people in our profession are groping for a panacea which would give them an immediate answer to any accounting problem. We have some in the profession who feel that alternative treatments should be eliminated on the theory that the gap in determining net income should be narrowed. Some people even go so far as to say that alternatives should be eliminated not because they are improper but because they contribute to undesirable flexibility.
>
> It is extremely bothersome to me that many people in our profession are striving for such a rigidity of treatment which, if accepted, would eliminate all the professional judgments we feel are necessary in today's financial reporting. . . . I am convinced that one inflexible set of rules could not deal adequately with the various business philosophies that are encountered in the complex financial world of today.[32]

Mr. Tippit continued with his argument by indicating his concept of uniformity:

> [I]t would be a tragic error for us to regiment accounting so that the answer to any question could be resolved quickly merely by turning to a given page in a book of rules and postulates.
>
> Isn't a profession by its very nature dependent upon the sound and reasoned judgments of its members rather than upon a restrictive codification of

[29] Higgins, "The Accounting Principles Board and Uniformity in Financial Accounting," in *Twenty-fifth Annual Institute on Accounting, Proceedings 67*, 71 (Ohio State University, 1963).
[30] *Id.* at 72.
[31] *Ibid.*
[32] Tippit, "Are We Expected to Eliminate All Alternatives?," in *id.* at 77, 78.

do's and don'ts? By making more rules and regulations, are we increasing or decreasing our professional status?

As you so well know, under present-day accounting there are numerous alternative treatments which are considered to be acceptable. . . .

. . . .

. . . [I]t seems to me to be ridiculous for the profession to say that, after all these years, we will now determine the one way to handle each of these items and insist on full compliance, with all the alternatives bundled up into a package and tossed out the window.

In many of the areas, any alternative selected—if consistently followed—will produce the same result in the aggregate over a period of years. This, to me, is the big reason for including the reference to consistency in our present form of certificate. If all the alternatives are eliminated, I assume there will be no need for the word "consistency" in our certifications.[33]

At the AICPA's annual meeting in 1960 a session was devoted to discussion of the controversy. This discussion highlighted many of the complexities of the current debate. On this occasion, Maurice E. Peloubet seemed to stress throughout his paper that the basic principles should be uniform but that the rules of implementation must of necessity be flexible to allow for different treatment of different factual situations. For example, with respect to the proposition that "the areas of difference in accounting must be narrowed," he stated, "This is a desirable end, provided that all we are proposing is that differences in accounting methods be narrowed. There is always, however, a tendency to describe different things or conditions in the same terms merely to be uniform."[34]

Leonard Spacek argued on the same occasion that accountants' principles are not accepted by the public or corporate stockholders but are merely tolerated. He appeared to use the term *principles* to refer to the detailed rules guiding the accountant in his work, which is somewhat different from the use made of the word by Mr. Peloubet. Mr. Spacek argued that accounting principles must be fair and that this fairness must be demonstrated. He implied that uniform principles (using his meaning of the word) are more likely to produce fair accounts than is flexibility. In discussing his idea, he stated,

> The objection has also been voiced that uniformity would eliminate flexibility in accounting principles. But to my knowledge, not one person has attempted to show where flexibility in the choice of alternative principles of accounting would result in financial statements that were fair to all segments of the business community. The arguments were only that flexibility was good, per se, and that the elimination of flexibility was bad, per se. Yet with respect to no single set of facts to be accounted for was the theory of flexibility applied and reasoning advanced to show why the "flexible" results were proper or fair.
>
> Assuming for the moment that flexibility of principles is needed for a transition period to permit improvement in accepted accounting principles, would not the proof of this contention demonstrate its merit by eventual elimination

---

[33] *Id.* at 78–79.

[34] Peloubet, *Is Further Uniformity Desirable or Possible?*, Journal of Accountancy, April 1961, p. 35, at 37.

of the less desirable practices? . . . Yet examination of the record shows that the alternative methods of accounting for intangible drilling costs . . . are each as old as the other. The alternative treatment of deferred income taxes is as old as the laws that permitted deferral of the taxes. The alternative treatment of pension costs is as old as the requirement that pensions be paid. Flexibility, as such, has not brought improvement; in fact, the less desirable practices have tended to drive out, or at least to retard, acceptance of the good.[35]

Professor Charles J. Gaa, in commenting on the papers presented by Messrs. Peloubet and Spacek, recognized the widely divergent meanings assigned to many of the words that are commonly found in the arguments about accounting problems and made a plea for standardization of terminology. He then turned his attention to the conflict between the speakers. He opined that "accounting 'principles' should be uniform for all profit-seeking enterprises, although there may have to be some allowable variations in detailed rules or practices. How to keep variations to an absolute minimum is the difficulty."[36] He continued,

> We should make every effort to achieve uniformity. . . . The closer we get to the bedrock of theory and the more general and fundamental we make our statements of "principles," the less likely they are to need change. As we get further out from this hard core into the area of detailed procedures, we are in the area of working rules which may need more frequent adjustment. Theory should not be used as a straitjacket, but instead as a core of logic, deviation from which must be justified convincingly and not by mere "nose-counting."
> . . . .
> If we are to change our rules to reflect different factual situations, we must be careful to explore all ramifications of the factual change and alter in a sound and consistent manner all of the rules affected. If we come to the conclusion that inflation and a general price increase is a factual change which justifies an alteration in our depreciation rules or methods, we should not stop there just because this one change satisfies our immediate desires to show less income, to encourage management to replace assets because they are depreciated on the books, or to reduce income taxes. Our reflection of the factual change, inflation, must be stated more broadly, perhaps as a "principle" plus a set of related rules only one of which applies to depreciation.[37]

Carman G. Blough, as chairman of the session, commented in his summary as follows:

> While I strongly subscribe to the idea that there should be a much greater narrowing of these areas of differences than has been possible to date, it seems to me it is, of necessity, a matter of evolution. Mr. Spacek hopes, along with most of the rest of us, that Congress will never lay down the principles that have to be followed. Yet, short of action by Congress or by some authority having absolute jurisdiction over all issuers of financial statements, the devel-

---

[35] Spacek, *Are Accounting Principles Generally Accepted?*, Journal of Accountancy, April 1961, p. 41, at 43.
[36] Gaa, *Uniformity in Accounting Principles*, Journal of Accountancy, April 1961, p. 47, at 50.
[37] *Id.* at 50–51.

opment of a comprehensive statement of accounting principles which will be universally accepted must be a long drawn out process. If we are ever to reach a point where the criteria are so well developed for any kind of transaction and so clear that they will always produce the same results when the situations are in fact identical, which Mr. Spacek feels is essential, and yet sufficiently flexible to meet differing situations, which Mr. Peloubet thinks necessary, there will have to be a great deal of give and take with earnest, honest, intelligent effort over a long period of time. A certain amount of impatience can be a useful spur but too much can lead to disaster.[38]

Herman W. Bevis, a staunch supporter of flexibility in the application of accounting principles and one who is often referred to as the leader of the opposition or the "laissez-faire" group, has taken a rather strong position that regulation of the accounting profession, either by the profession itself or by government through prescription of accounting practice, is bad. Mr. Bevis comments, "Some critics seem to feel that the CPA of the future will be lost if the APB or some other body does not: (1) do his thinking for him—e.g., give him a detailed check list of the accounting practices, methods and treatments which he must see that his client follows; and (2) threaten to penalize him if he does not take exception in his opinion when the check list is not followed."[39] He continues by adding the following admonition:

> Remember that the number one objective is that the financial statements themselves communicate the desired information, and that the use of certificates to convey information is not only second-best but often confusing to the reader as well. Therefore, the effectiveness of the important economic function of communication of data from the issuer of financial statements to users is now involved; no move that diminishes the effectiveness will long be tolerated.... [T]he CPA's opinion must remain his own. It is personal and its value ... has to depend ... upon the CPA's *own* competence and independence.[40]

Discussing generally accepted accounting principles, Mr. Bevis states: "In my opinion, there *is* a coherent and cohesive body of concepts behind present-day financial reporting, which not only gives meaning to the term 'generally accepted accounting principles' but is also the logic behind most (but not all) of the accounting treatments which are widely followed today by publicly owned corporations."[41]

Mr. Bevis also has some very definite ideas about the manner in which the areas of difference should be narrowed. He is opposed to any plan of uniformity for the sake of uniformity and would like to allow for the individual differences that exist between companies or industries:

> As to what the APB *should* do to narrow the areas of difference among significant accounting *methods*, my own view is that the most promising approach is industry by industry.... In the industry approach, and notwithstanding the

---

[38] Blough, *Principles and Procedures*, Journal of Accountancy, April 1961, p. 51, at 52.
[39] Bevis, *How to Improve Financial Reporting*, The Price Waterhouse Review, Autumn, 1963, p. 4, at 6.
[40] *Id.* at 6–7.
[41] *Id.* at 7–8.

significant differences in operations among companies in any given group, there are two distinct advantages. First, the principal accounting problems and methods can be visualized in far more practical terms than for the economy as a whole. Second, an industry approach makes more feasible arousing the interest and enlisting the assistance of industry management and accountants in analyzing problems. Constant pressure for the elimination of marginal or small minority practices would give real meaning to the phrase "narrowing the areas of difference."[42]

Mr. Bevis suggests that a part of the misunderstanding over the controversy about uniformity and flexibility is attributable to a misconception about what is meant by "greater comparability." He argues that

> the term is comparative, and suggests moving in a direction; but moving in the direction of the rainbow is quite different from grasping at the end of it the pot of gold that is *absolute* comparability. All this suggests that the APB through the Institute has a public enlightenment job to do, in terms of educating all concerned that it has not discovered that which has up to now eluded all mankind—the means of satisfying the natural human craving for certainty.[43]

Finally, W. T. Baxter, of the London School of Economics, has offered a slightly different view on the question of uniformity:

> Uniformity in presentation of published data... has strong arguments in its favour—provided it neither cramps honest business nor begs ideas. If a choice between words or methods clearly is arbitrary and free from any pretence of research, it is not likely to damage future thinking or to act as a straitjacket... Therefore, when we are attracted by uniformity, a good test is perhaps this: if a decision between possible terms or practices can be reached by tossing a coin or pulling words from a hat, then uniformity is unlikely to do harm.
> .... Rules for standard practice should not prescribe valuation methods. Even rules on how items should be grouped in a balance-sheet may impinge on principle....
> Perhaps "standard" should here mean "usual," *i.e.*, what is normal but not necessarily right.... An accountant should always reserve his right to depart from the standard, on giving notice, if he thinks the standard does not fit the particular case, or the reader's current needs, or his own views on theory.[44]

From the review of the arguments we can observe that the parties to the debate are often not debating the same issue. One is arguing that underlying principles are adequate guidelines, and another insists on a set of rules or regulations to which all must conform. The debate has been practically devoid of any discussion of what the underlying principles are or what specific rules should be adopted. Much of the debate has been emotional with little attempt to reason logically. The very mention of the words *uniformity* and *flexibility* will incite

---

[42] *Id.* at 8.
[43] *Ibid.*
[44] Baxter, *Recommendations on Accounting Theory*, in Financial Accounting Theory 427, 435–36 (Zeff & Keller ed. 1964). [Also reprinted in this edition—Eds.]

most accountants to do verbal battle. The battlelines are drawn and the slogan "I'd rather fight than switch" has become the byword. The great need at the present time is for operational principles or guidelines and methods by which to implement them.

IV SUMMARY AND CONCLUSIONS

The critics want financial statements which are comparable. Particularly, the analyst would like a basis for selecting the shares of A. Company rather than B. Company. How can two methods of accounting for research and development both be correct? One must be right and the other wrong. There appears to be almost no recognition that accounting data are surrogates for other attributes of "things" and "events."

There is the repeated plea that accountants should strive to make like things look alike and unlike things appear to be different. There seems to be no agreement as to whether this is best done by adoption of guidelines or rules. The debate seems to have bypassed an in-depth consideration of the objectives of financial statements. There are clearly a variety of users with a variety of needs. Can any one user be served by financial statements prepared to serve everyone but no one in particular?

Perhaps the statements are a report of the results of activities of the past which provide insight to the future. If this be the case, should one insist that LIFO is preferable to FIFO and that all firms should be required to adopt the same procedure? Or should one insist that the accountant accept only that method which provides the most appropriate base for an understanding of the past and from which the statement user can gain an insight into the relationships on which future results depend? Perhaps the argument is for accounting principles which can be understood by the statement user. Through his knowledge he can obtain a clear perception of the underlying events. George O. May proposed in 1932 that firms disclose the accounting methods used and apply those methods consistently over time.

The selection of an accounting method is complicated, however, by the high visibility of corporate management in the modern industrial society. The growth syndrome has clearly captured present day business. The key to growth appears to be cash. The providers of cash, including the Federal Government with its tax incentive plans, are looking at specific indicators of financial stability. The management, who is ultimately responsible for selecting the accounting methods, is under great pressure to take advantage of all means to obtain cash as cheaply as possible in order to attain the maximum rate of growth. Accountants undoubtedly find themselves in very uncomfortable positions as they attempt to explain to management that a lease agreement should be capitalized when management replies that if that option is followed the bond rating service will lower their rating from AA to A. Such an event may increase the cost of cash obtained via debt by ¼ of 1 percent.

There is little reason to be surprised that users are confused and concerned. There may also be little reason to believe that accountants can resolve this problem without enlisting the aid of a broader segment of society in the establishment of accounting guidelines.

A. M. C. MORISON

A. M. C. MORISON (1928–   ),
B.A. 52, M.A. 55 Cambridge; C.A.
(Scotland). Currently a partner in
Thomson McLintock & Co., London.
Major publication: *Understanding
Modern Business Mathematics* (with
Burden and Crabtree, 1971). Contributor to *The Accountant's Magazine*.
    Joined Thomson McLintock & Co.
in 1952 and was admitted to the
partnership in 1961.
    Principal research interests: profit
forecasts, accounting "standards"
and their relation to the theory of
accounting, and the use of analytical
and philosophical techniques in accounting theory.

THE RÔLE OF THE REPORTING ACCOUNTANT TODAY—PART I

A. M. C. MORISON

I—INTRODUCTION

1. It is fashionable these days to question, fundamentally, what someone else is doing, and to tell him, frankly and in his own best interests, that he is not doing it very well. I may therefore seem a trifle square to question what *my own* profession is doing, and shall certainly be counted a complete has-been if I conclude that we are doing it not too badly. We must move with the times. Reappraisals must be agonising, investigations searching and in-depth, differences of opinion nothing less than rows, conclusions shocking at the very least. I shall try not to fail you in these things; but truth is sometimes stranger than journalism.

2. Certainly the tide of unfavourable criticism directed towards our profession has been rising of late, and this has made many practitioners unhappy. They feel that things can never again be quite what they were:—

> But no longer at ease here, in the old dispensation.

SOURCE: From *The Accountant's Magazine*, Vol. 74, No. 771 (September, 1970 and October, 1970), pp. 409–415 and 467–478. Reprinted by permission of the author.

For a profession whose acknowledged standing is its sole *raison d'être* any criticism, however absurd, can cause unpleasant twinges of anxiety.

3. The predominant reason for the spate of recent attacks has simply been the fashion of the times: it is smart to criticise everything, so why not accountancy? With rising standards of living there are now more people than there used to be who can be persuaded that reading about finance is fun, especially if presented in capsules of succulent gossip and tantalising innuendo. There are also more people now in the communications industries, whose occupations make them understandably anxious to create some stir in the world. We need scarcely be surprised that criticism has resulted.

4. What is more interesting is to bear in mind the underlying misconceptions which have made this possible. These may be summarised (in a suitably simplistic way) as follows:—

(i) Auditors are wholly concerned with the past: we are interested in the future. Their contribution is therefore negative and pointless.

(ii) Accounting principles permit differing treatments of the same set of facts. This is wrong: most accounting disputes (*e.g.,* on catastrophes and take-overs) stem from it.

(iii) Modern information systems produce all the required figures automatically: the accounts are simply the mathematically-predetermined output of a computerised model, so what need of accountants? And what need of auditors?

(iv) Auditors are paid by the companies they report on, and are selected by their directors. They must therefore from their very nature be corrupt and their opinions valueless.

(v) Who cares if an auditor thinks the figures are fair? We want to know if the company is efficient.

5. I do not propose to answer these comments formally. It is more helpful to consider the problems afresh: what *really is* the nature of accounting? And what *really is* an auditor trying to do? (I hope you will appreciate the urgency of those italics—we are of course taking a long hard look at the subject.) But it will be wise to bear our critics in mind while we ponder, with considerable calmness, what our profession is all about.

6. I mean by "reporting accountant" one who gives his opinion on financial statements (whether relating to past or future) prepared by others. I speak throughout, needless to say, in a wholly personal capacity. And I try to avoid the shilly-shallyings of "on the one hand" and "on the other" in order to make the issues clear, and to keep them so.

II—THE NATURE OF ACCOUNTING

7. Let us first consider what the reporting accountant reports on. It is impossible otherwise to understand what he is trying to do.

8. . . . an accountant is an artist. He finds a subject; he studies it; he must be moved; and then he endeavours to portray his subject faithfully. The main principle is one of truth. . . .

In accountancy the term profit has no absolute meaning. It is simply a measurement of the success or failure of a business to achieve what it has set out to achieve. The measurement is a subjective one in so far as it depends upon the view taken as to what the business has in fact set out to achieve. Thus the term profit as used by accountants can never have that absolute meaning which lawyers, economists and Revenue officials seek to attribute to it.

The absence of any absolute meaning to the term profit in accountancy, however, does not absolve the accountant from explaining what the word purports to mean in relation to the statement which he produces. On the contrary, the acknowledged empiricism of accountancy makes it absurd for accountants to talk of profit without definition. Moreover the very flexibility of the term profit as used in accountancy makes it essential for the accountant to have some personal conception of how the success or failure of any particular business should be measured, some simple guide by reference to which it can be seen whether the chosen conventions are operating satisfactorily. The test which accountants apply for this purpose, I suggest, is simply that of commercial common sense, the test of considering whether the pattern of profits thrown up over a period of years by the chosen conventions in fact reflects how the business "is doing" during that period. The choice of conventions is subordinate to that test and no convention can over-rule it. . . .

If the term "profit" is no more than a standard for measuring success or failure—and our clients will never believe that it is anything else—it is important that we give more thought to choosing the right standard of success or failure for the right client. For if we choose standards that are too high, clients may become dispirited without cause; whereas if we choose standards that are too low, they may fail and become slack, not because they are incapable of better things, but simply because they have been given the wrong standard of success. . . .

9. If I quote from a remarkable Summer School paper prepared by an "associated person" of mine,[1] it is because it is not easy to find elsewhere so clear and unequivocal a statement of the essentially *descriptive* nature of accountancy. It is a record of what a man *sees*. Accountants express a view, an opinion. The reporting accountant expresses an opinion on *them*.

10. "To me accounting is a language, the language of business."[2] The concept of a language is helpful here. A language is a set of conventions for conveying meaning. While the set of conventions is circumscribed, what we can say with them is not. Linguistic rules exist for what individual words may mean and for how we may join them together, but no such rules prescribe what statements we may properly make. Language is the vehicle of thought, not the substance of it.[3]

11. The analogy of a picture is helpful, too. Accounts present a picture of eco-

---

[1] R. M. Morison, M.A., C.A.: "A Critical Review of Recognised Accounting Conventions," presented to the 10th Summer School of The Institute of Chartered Accountants of Scotland, on September 1, 1962. Reproduced in *The Accountant's Magazine*, September and October 1962, at pages 661 and 783 respectively.

[2] From a paper prepared for a New Zealand accounting seminar by P. B. Sinclair in 1967.

[3] It is the criterion of triviality in communication that the medium should be the message.

nomic facts. Pictures are drawn by human beings, and therefore vary. There may be many pictures of the one object, each of them true, each life-like and each different: consider a miniature, a presentation portrait, a holiday snap, a caricature. We do not condemn the activity of portraiture because different artists present different views of the same thing; indeed, we only condemn it when they do conform to a single imposed view. "Truth sits at the top of a mountain", it has been wisely said, "and there are many ways up".

12. I think these are fair illustrations of what accounting at present is. We shall consider later whether this is what it ought to be. There are at present a great many permissible accounting conventions which the accountant can choose from; nothing in the logic of the discipline itself prescribes which one he shall choose. And the area of the permissible is itself continually changing. The object is simply to present a picture of the facts; the means are a set of conventions using both figures and (may we not forget) words. The restraints on what is said are therefore empirical and subjective, not logical or demonstrative. First, what *are* the facts? Secondly, what picture will most fairly present them? The concern is wholly with the truth. The concept of truth is not a mathematical, but a moral one. It is *charity* that rejoiceth in it. And it was jesting Pilate, we may recall, who asked "What is truth?" and would not stay for an answer.

13. The object of the balance sheet is to present an estimate of where the business now is, and the object of the profit and loss account is to present an estimate of how it is doing. An estimate is something which *ex hypothesi* one does not exactly know; there may be many careful estimates (many pictures) of one fact, and they may all be wrong. This does not prove that the people who made them were felons; it suggests that some facts are difficult to know and to describe. "Where a business now is" and "how a business is doing" are things which are *very* difficult to define, know or describe. They depend as much on the future as on the past: this is the key difficulty. One is seeking to convey a picture of things that (in any complex case) *cannot* possibly be fully known until long after they have ceased to matter. The hall-mark of accounting, as of all commercial activity, is uncertainty.

14. If profit is scarcely ever uniquely determinable at the time it is earned (which is when we want to know it), it follows that there are likely to be as many current views of it as there are accountants to prepare them. This is only shocking to those who have not closely grappled with the real-life problem before. Businessmen are not shocked by it; they are accustomed to see their best forward estimates regularly disproved over an amazingly wide bracket of variability. This does not make them despair. I suggest that our financial commentators should take heart, too. Profit is difficult to measure for precisely the same reasons as those that make it difficult to earn: we do not know what other people are going to do. It is no accident that the two most subtle concepts on which every free economy rests—profit and money—depend for their value on the actions of others.

15. If profit is not uniquely determinable, it clearly becomes vital to know *who* has determined it. What is his interest in producing a rosy result rather than a sombre one? What evidence has he collected to support the picture he paints? What skill does he have in painting such a picture at all? As soon as we get a firm grasp of the kind of thing a set of accounts is, we begin to get a clearer idea of the rôle of the reporting accountant. His function is to *lend credibility* to the financial statements. There are good reasons (he states) why this view of the facts

should be believed, trusted and acted upon. His is most definitely *not* a seal of certainty; rather, a sanction of fairness. The auditor stakes his all (very much so, these days!) not on the assertion that this view of the facts is right, but on the claim that it is reasonable to believe it. That is a difficult enough task, in all conscience. It is also an indispensable one.

III—AUDITING: THE REASONS WHY

16. Why does anyone bother to have an audit? It is, when one reflects on it, a surprising thing to do. No other human activity that occurs to me is quite comparable. A report prepared by X describing the state of his affairs is attested by Y, and is only then issued to third parties so that it can be acted on by them. Other self-regarding documents designed to influence the conduct of others seem to escape the preliminary vetting; the general law of deceit and misrepresentation, for example, operates only after a document has been issued and acted upon. Government press-releases, political manifestos, autobiographies, advertisements, *curricula vitae*, lovers' letters, newspaper editorials, propaganda produced by the public relations industry—if the object is simply to prevent people being misled, why should these not be audited, too?

17. No doubt the short answer is that people are prepared to appraise and act on these other kinds of documents, however loaded they may be, without having them independently assessed; therefore there is no need. Investors, however, are not so frivolous. They will not part with their money unless they are going to be told, reliably, what has happened to it. In a free society the prerequisite of investment is trust, and the price of obtaining this trust is an independent audit. The audit enables the wheels to go round.

18. It is significant that this argument does not extend to the government-controlled sections of the economy (currently estimated at 48.9% in the United Kingdom).[4] The entrepreneur cannot function unless he persuades his backers to go on trusting him; the government, however, whatever its political complexion, can spend the economic resources within its control whether the electorate continues to trust it or not. The alarming implications of this would form the subject of a separate, rather more sinister, paper.

19. What, then, is it that the investor fears in the absence of an independent audit? What horrors does he hope we will save him from? I consider this under five headings:—

(i) Uncertainty about the future.
(ii) Difficulty of conveying the truth.
(iii) Unintentional errors.
(iv) Fraud.
(v) Different bases of accounting.

(i) Uncertainty about the Future

20. I think that the uncertainty which necessarily attaches to any set of accounts (especially those of a trading concern) has so far been altogether under-

---

[4] Based on proportions of capital expenditure in 1968: *Annual Abstract of Statistics* (1969), table 301.

estimated by the public and the press. Perhaps we as a profession have been at fault in not making this clearer to those who use our accounts.[5] Uncertainty is the hall-mark of business; accounting cannot and should not do other than reflect the uncertainty inherent in the very thing it sets out to describe. With the increased pace of change and development in the modern world, this element of uncertainty is growing very fast. A shoe-manufacturer in 1870, say, would have experienced little difference in his products, his customers or his techniques either 20 years earlier or 20 years later; a shoe-manufacturer today is likely to run the whole gamut from Indian sandals to kinky boots in two or three years.

21. All assets, whatever the basis on which they are stated in the accounts, represent sources of *future* benefit. That is how an asset may be defined. Productive capacity, office space, raw materials, the right to use a process or publish a book, the right to obtain cash, cash itself—all are benefits, and the benefits are all in the future. There can be no certainty that the firm will ever receive these things, or that the eventual benefit it does receive will equal the expected one. Liabilities likewise represent sources of future detriment, and many are subject to the same kind of uncertainties.

22. Examples are not difficult for accountants to think of: –

How long will the plant last?
How long will the product be saleable—at this price?
Will customers make their own instead of buying ours?
Is this new project going to be a success? If so, when? (Look what happened to the last one!)
What are we going to find when we dig these foundations?
When will chunky jewellery have had its day?
Are the back-room boys right?
Are we going to be able to raise another £ 1 million or not?
How many customers' rinses turned green instead of blue?
How much longer will the war in Vietnam last?
S.E.T., betterment levy, value-added tax, investment grants—who will win the next election?
Is our principal customer doing well (answer only after applying all these illustrative uncertainties to *his* business, also)?

And so on. Such uncertainties govern the value of fixed assets, the rate of depreciation, the saleability of stock, the value of research and development expenditure, the benefit or otherwise of long-term contracts, the liability to be sued, the collectability of debts, the question whether you are going to be in business this time next year or not. And all these things affect profit.

23. The auditor's rôle in the face of these uncertainties is not to make them less uncertain; that cannot by the nature of the problem be done. He is concerned with the view taken of them, with the assessment made of what is by definition not known. Is it fair? Does it take account of past experience? Does it

[5] The point was, however, admirably brought out by the [then] President of The Institute of Chartered Accountants in England and Wales, Mr R. G. [now Sir Ronald] Leach, C.B.E., F.C.A., in his reply to Professor E. Stamp, M.A. (Cantab.), C.A. (Canada), head of the Department of Accounting and Business Method at Edinburgh University and a very fierce critic of our profession (*The Times,* September 22, 1969).

allow for the changes that we believe are going to occur? It is much more difficult for management to judge these things dispassionately; they are committed to one view of the future the minute they take the decision to invest. And all the subsequent psychological pressures militate against the independence of their judgment; reputations, wives, mistresses, fortunes, all are at stake. "Perhaps if we run the risk just a *little* bit longer . . . ?" Executives are conditioned to deal in uncertainties, to run them deliberately as risks; risk-taking is the essence of their lives. And they well know how the forecasts produced by even the most elaborate information systems can, on individual plants and products, be wildly out (of course the larger the company, the more it benefits from averaging the ups and downs). But they are accustomed to deal in risks as the basis of *decisions;* once the decision has been taken they are saddled with it. This does not make it any easier for them to be impartial when it comes to the crunch, when it is necessary to judge fairly whether the risk is *still* a reasonable one to run now that everything depends on it—and whether it is still a reasonable one not to disclose. The auditor's rôle is thus to check the view taken by management with his essential independence of judgment. He would naturally like his client to do well, but it is no part of his interest to improve this year's results at the expense of next year's. His rôle gives him no bias towards anything other than the truth.

24. I think that this is the most important part of the auditor's function in the modern world. It is often the least understood part. Management find it difficult to believe that their own view can be anything other than impartial, and the outside world has little idea that the uncertainties even exist. Most of the accounting *causes célèbres*, I suspect, have turned on this point—not on the difference in accounting principles, but on the different views of the facts reflected by differing estimates of the future. The continuing trend towards speeding up the production of accounts increases its importance, as it makes the area of uncertainty even greater.

25. Profit depends on the view taken of the future. The only actual *evidence* of the future, however, that we ever have in any kind of human activity is what has happened in the past. All science, social or physical, rests on this method of arguing—the inductive method, the assessment of future probabilities from past experience. A clearer understanding of this would, I think, help the layman as well as the accountant to grasp more firmly the kind of claim, and the only kind of claim, that an audited set of accounts can make. I quote from a classic work on probability[6]:—

> The fundamental connection between Inductive Method and Probability deserves all the emphasis I can give it. . . . But it has been seldom apprehended clearly . . . that the validity of every induction, strictly interpreted, depends, not on a matter of fact, but on the existence of a relation of probability. An inductive argument affirms, not that a certain matter of fact *is* so, but that *relative to certain evidence* there is a probability in its favour. The validity of the induction, relative to the original evidence, is not upset therefore if, as a fact, the truth turns out to be otherwise.
>
> The clear apprehension of this truth profoundly modifies our attitude towards the solution of the inductive problem. The validity of the inductive

[6] J. M. Keynes: "A Treatise on Probability" (Macmillan, 1921), at pages 220–221.

method does *not* depend on the success of its predictions. Its repeated failure in the past may, of course, supply us with new evidence, the inclusion of which will modify the force of subsequent inductions. But the force of the old induction *relative to the old evidence* is untouched. The evidence with which our experience has supplied us in the past may have proved misleading, but this is entirely irrelevant to the question of what conclusions we ought reasonably to have drawn from the evidence then before us.

(ii) Difficulty of Conveying the Truth

26. First, the difficulty of knowing the facts; secondly, the difficulty of describing them. It is well understood nowadays that the record of events cannot be dissociated from the recorder; there is no history without bias. We are familiar with the phenomenon from the newspapers, especially if we are wise enough to read two: in one we find a searing account of angry demonstrators, police brutality, prostrate bodies; in another a good-humoured report of some idealistic young people, a few tolerant policemen, a wet Sunday afternoon. Which is true? We can only report what we see, and what we see is inevitably coloured by what we are conditioned to expect. The difficulty in communication in no way exempts a set of accounts.

27. The problem extends to the selection of the figures as much as to the words. An accounting convention that works well when things are going smoothly may not necessarily give a fair impression when things are going ill. For example, suppose a successful contracting company prudently provides each year for the full loss to completion on its infrequent bad contracts (*i.e.* the direct loss plus the bad contract's share of allocated overheads necessary to complete it). Now suppose that the company runs into a really bad patch, and all its uncompleted contracts show losses. If it provides for the full overheads required to complete those jobs, this will be consistent and will faithfully reflect the real loss in the year the contracts were entered into; but next year's results (if the company is still in business next year) will look remarkable—the overheads will already have been provided for. Year I will show a large loss and Year II a break-even, although in both years the same contracts are being worked on. What is the fair treatment? There can, I think, be no rule about it. It depends on how badly the company has been hit and on how likely it is to survive. But it is an interesting illustration of the way that mere consistency may not be enough to produce a consistently sensible result. One has to select the accounting treatment, I suggest, which best measures the extent of the disaster.

28. Clients are no doubt accustomed to find their auditors much more severe when things are tough than they are when times are good, and this is surely right; bad times must of their nature make it probable that assets will not bring as much benefit as they did "in younger, happier days". One has to convey what has happened to the company by the figures presented. For similar reasons it is right to be sceptical of the treatment of items which affect the *trend* of profits; the truth about the way the business is going is conveyed by more than one year's results.

29. The other half of the problem is the right use of words. This is not a talent which everyone has, and these days one may justifiably conclude that fewer people have it than before. Many of the matters to be communicated in a set of accounts are of their nature difficult or obscure (*e.g.* most things to do with tax);

some are highly delicate (*e.g.* liabilities under guarantees or contingencies); some are, as explained above, simply uncertain, and to convey an exact shade of uncertainty is a searching test of verbal skill. Auditors have an essential rôle to play in agreeing on the drafting of these matters. They represent the layman's views as opposed to the insider's, and can therefore more readily anticipate how a shareholder will react. They are familiar with problems of this kind from daily experience and know how other companies are solving them. Above all, they act as umpires of fairness. In a complicated set of accounts the drafting of the narrative can cause quite as much difficulty as the computation of the figures. For this reason the tendency of the press to concentrate on the figures alone is sadly unhelpful. The information contained in a complete set of accounts cannot be meaningfully boiled down into one surrogate figure, such as the year's profit or the P/E ratio or the earnings-per-share; it is as relevant to know how a profit has been computed and what it is made up of as to know how much it is.

(iii) Unintentional Errors

30. The third reason for having an audit is the possibility of unintentional error. This is one of the traditional reasons, but two points spring to mind in the light of practice today.

31. First, the modern audit stems from a systems review and directly relates the audit work carried out to the system that the company is supposed to be operating. The auditor's report to management on this system can be of great assistance in improving it and in keeping it up to scratch. Few systems are incapable of improvement, fewer still remain the same for any length of time; men change and decay, machines are introduced and wear out, customers come and go. The people at the top of a business of any size rarely have full and accurate knowledge of what goes on below them. There must therefore be some method of reporting to them—and a report on anything must be independent to be of value (does anyone outside Russia rely on *Pravda?*). The management letter written by the auditors is accordingly a highly valued part of the whole audit function today; it is a pungent, far-ranging document[7] often of great commercial value (*e.g.* on how to eliminate errors and waste) and very different from the somewhat finicky carpings of earlier days.

32. The second point is that modern computerised accounting systems do not eliminate (as is sometimes fondly suggested) the possibility of error. All men are fallible, not only rogues. The probability of error should no doubt diminish with the number of built-in checks in a system, but it never approaches zero or anywhere near. Anyone who has ever audited a computerised system is likely to be struck by the irrepressible and endearing propensity of human nature to err, however much it is hedged around with the most admirable controls. An intelligent review of what actually goes on and what is actually produced as output rarely fails to produce a pleasing crop of oddities. The specialist computer auditor, with wide experience of computerised systems in action, is also well placed to advise on the design of suitable controls for new ones; he is likely to have examined more *working installations* than most. The advent of computers, then, does not mean the end of unintentional errors; it requires more exacting and expensive skills in the auditor to detect, correct and prevent them.

---

[7] Sometimes *too* pungent for the recipient!

(iv) Fraud

33. Accounting literature has sometimes appeared to suggest that the prevention or discovery of fraud is not the purpose of an audit.[8] Not surprisingly, this view is scarcely shared by the laity or the press, who consider that if an audit is not meant to uncover major frauds then it must be of very little use. The first object of an audit is to say that the accounts can be *relied on*, that they are "all right"; it is absurd to say that they are all right subject of course to the possibility that undetected fraud may have made them all wrong. An audit can never give a guarantee against fraud—"auditors are not insurers"; but it must provide grounds for honestly holding the opinion that material fraud has not taken place. The main business of the profession is precisely to report on the "truth" and "fairness" of other people's accounts: this means, at the end of the day, are they *honest?*

34. The concept of reasonableness must here, as elsewhere, prevail. The auditor is not obliged to develop a neurosis about it. He need not approach every entry in the books as though it must be treated as fraudulent until proved otherwise, like an old lady perpetually searching for robbers under the bed. But he cannot forget about the possibility. The whole theory of internal control is designed to prevent errors, and errors may be deliberate no less than accidental. All the work of the audit is designed to prove that the system works and the results it produces are right: active criminality would mean that the system did not work, and the results were not right. The auditor is therefore not starting from the premise that in the particular case there *is* fraud (as say the police acting on information would do), but he assumes that there *may* be fraud; if it is material his audit ought to be effective to find it.

35. The criterion of materiality is vital in this as in most other aspects of auditing. The possibilities of small frauds are widespread in many organisations. Frequently it is not worth the expense of guarding against them, and even the best audit cannot usually be expected to unearth them. Contrast the occasional catastrophe: half the stock is not there, or three-quarters of the liabilities have been left out, or £250,000 of defalcations have been charged off to profits. Plainly these are matters which go to the root of the true and fair view; they make the accounts fundamentally wrong. We can thus distinguish the category of fraud which an audit *is* designed to discover or prevent: it is the big ones.

36. Another source of confusion relates to the size of audit samples. Any opinion which is based on a sample can only ever be a probability: there is no certainty short of a 100% check. But a sample *does* give a statistical probability of finding an error, if there is a certain percentage of errors in the population. It is worth recollecting that for a fraud to be a big one there must either be a small number of high-value manipulations or a large number of low-value ones; the second possibility falls within the scope of random checking and, as such entries must by definition be numerous, they afford a reasonable chance of being caught. Of course the random test *may* not succeed; any sample *may* be unrepresentative. But it is intended to have a sporting chance. On this argument a transactions

---

[8] *E.g.* "Montgomery's Auditing", 8th edition, 1957, at pages 27–30. V. R. V. Cooper: "Manual of Auditing", 2nd edition (Gee, 1969), though naturally much concerned with internal control, does not emphasize the distinction between intentional and unintentional error; the word "fraud" is not mentioned in the index.

audit which is restricted to a "walk-through" (of two or three items only), which some authorities recommend, scarcely seems to me to be acceptable.

37. I mention computers in this context, because the prospects are frightening. When a clever criminal makes use of a highly developed accounting system in order to carry out his defalcation, the amounts lost can be enormous. There has, I suspect, so far been little experience of such prodigies in this country, with the consequence that systems analysts and management executives still tend to pooh-pooh the auditor's fears as being alarmist, and his careful controls as being a useless and outdated expense. But the auditor is right to persist in his warnings. Human nature does not change with the advent of data processing; "for it needs must be that offences come". These particular offences, when they do come, are going to be cataclysmic.

38. There are of course many shades of dishonesty before one reaches the out-and-out fraud. In practice the problem of *bona fides* is more often met with in the grey areas—a change of accounting basis in a bad year, a view of the future that seems too good to be true, an over-great reluctance to write off a dud investment. Dishonesty frequently starts as simply a negligent attitude to the truth; we do not know that what we are saying is false, but we have not taken the steps that would have shown any reasonable man that it was. (Your real rogue never thinks he is lying; he has long ago ceased to check his opinions with any evidence at all.) It is perhaps not too saturnine a comment on the contemporary business scene to suggest that the grey area is now rather larger than it used to be. Life is everywhere a little less gentlemanly; standards of conduct are correspondingly less nice, less scrupulous. Management today are certainly more knowing about what can be done with figures in order to suit their book—*e.g.* on a take-over, or on the various kinds of start-up expenditure. There is less agreement that the only respectable view is the most prudent one (investment grants have had something to do with this). Less sense of commitment, too, to shareholders, creditors, customers and staff; anything goes as long as the cash flow is right. The large international corporations reflect the same lack of commitment, controlled as they are conceived to be by nobody quite knows whom—the nameless, classless, conscienceless executives who determine the quality of all lives in Brussels, Osaka or Detroit. In such a climate the traditional rôle of the auditor as the keeper of the businessman's conscience does not grow any less. His fundamental concern must always be with *motive:* what is the company's reason for wanting to say this? The inherent uncertainty of business gives a wide scope to the ill-intentioned. But it would be much wider still without an audit. The real justification of our profession is not the changes we have obtained in the accounts actually presented to shareholders; it is the remarkably different sets of accounts that shareholders *would* have been presented with if there had not been going to be an audit at all.

THE RÔLE OF THE REPORTING ACCOUNTANT TODAY—PART II

A. M. C. MORISON

Biography appears on page 198.

(v) Different Bases of Accounting

39. I now come to perhaps the juiciest part of the subject. If I treat it more extensively, it is because the problem has been frequently misunderstood and also contains the most food for thought; it is not because I think that it has in fact caused the major accounting furores (paragraph 24 in Part I).

40. The substantive argument is this. Accounting principles ought to be uniform, but are not. If they were, everything would be much better, shareholders would be happier, financial analysts would be able to do their sums to some purpose. Let us accept, as a body of accountants, that accounting principles are not now, and no doubt never have been, uniform. Then let us examine the argument with care; it is more interesting than one may so far have been led to suppose.

41. First, we should be clear that it is an argument solely about what *ought* to happen. It is therefore no kind of reply to say that uniformity does not happen now, and never has. We are here concerned with which of two proposals is *better*, the relevant criteria of "good" and "better" being at large. Accordingly, if you think it tautologous to establish that people *ought* to be doing what in fact they *are* doing, please bear in mind that this is the only logical refutation there can ever be of the argument that they ought to be doing something else.

42. The substantive argument can, on closer analysis, mean one of two mutually-exclusive things (some furious critics of our profession may well mean both):—

> (a) Accounting theory should be constructed so that for any one set of facts only one accounting treatment can possibly be deduced.
>
> (b) Accounting theory should admit more than one accounting treatment for any one set of facts, but out of this set of possible treatments *one only* should be authoritatively selected as being permissible.

I shall call the first the "only one possible answer" school, and the second the "let's settle for one view anyhow" school.

(a) Only one possible answer

43. With the first of the two arguments I am wholly in agreement. Accounting ought to be deductive. Every branch of knowledge ought to be. A mathematical treatment is the developed form of every science because, as a branch of logic, it is both clear and exact; it allows the greatest number of possible conclusions to be drawn from the observed data and hence permits the greatest number of possible predictions to be made. Prediction is (I take it) the *use* of science. Further,

SOURCE: From *The Accountant's Magazine*, Vol. 74, No. 772 (September, 1970 and October, 1970), pp. 409–415 and 467–478. Reprinted by permission of the Institute of Chartered Accountants of Scotland.

it puts the conclusions and predictions into quantified form so that they are easy to verify. The scientist is looking for testable hypotheses; mathematical treatments provide them. If accountancy is the quantified representation of economic reality I can see no reason in principle why a strictly mathematical model should not one day be constructed.

44. Of course it will not be easy to get the model right. It never is. Every person, animal, country, government, corporation and thing in the entire universe would need somehow to be included—all in motion, all waxing and waning, striving and achieving and failing, buying and selling, making and using, planning and being planned, persuading and being persuaded, taxing and being taxed, eating and being eaten. But when we have reached that highly desirable point, then for every set of economic facts the inevitable accounting treatment should be instantly deducible. It will follow as surely as the night the day, by the force of logical necessity rather than the revolution of the spheres. There will by then be no need for any more accountants; but at least we shall know where we are.

45. We have not—in spite of much effort devoted to economic model-building —quite reached that point yet. Only the physical sciences, I believe, have so far been developed to a highly mathematical degree, and those which have to do with living things are in a more rudimentary state than those that deal with the inanimate world; the social sciences (including economics) are in the most rudimentary state of all.[1] This is in no way to suggest that the latter are useless; human behaviour is as much the proper province of scientific method—if contemporary philosophers will allow us to use the expression—as anything else. But these are very early days. The topics are still in their infancy. It is not yet very clear what *kind* of enquiry will be fruitful, what *kind* of explanation will meaningfully explain a wide range of data. In such an intellectual climate—the intellectual climate of the kindergarten—we need not be in the least surprised that accountancy is likewise in a very rudimentary state. It is the common lot.

46. We are nowhere near being able to deduce from a given set of facts one single accounting treatment *to the exclusion of all others*. That is the critical point in this argument. What is implied is not merely that such and such an accounting treatment can be logically inferred for a given body of financial data, but that no other treatment can be: the cause is to be not merely necessary, but sufficient. It is a big implication to justify.

47. I am not aware (but may easily be in ignorance) that this problem has yet been solved. Two projects have at least approached it. The first is the attempt of the American Institute's research group to infer "postulates" (the proper word in the logical analysis of a science) from empirical accounting data.[2] They examined how people accounted for things in real life and sought to generalise some of the common assumptions that would have led them to behave in such a way. This procedure was apparently carried out with a long-term view to enhancing uniformity. It is clear, however, that in logical terms it cannot possibly do so if one starts from the premise—which we granted here at the outset—that current ac-

---

[1] This is partly conditioned by the nature of the subject-matter. In physics, for example, the principle of randomness appears to apply only at the molecular level: in economics it applies every time a housewife goes shopping.

[2] Maurice Moonitz, Ph.D., C.P.A.: "The Basic Postulates of Accounting" (1961), and its companion volume, Robert T. Sprouse, Ph.D., and Maurice Moonitz: "A Tentative Set of Broad Accounting Principles for Business Enterprises" (1962).

counting practice is *not* uniform. In that event one can only infer from the empirical data such inclusive principles as will permit people to do whatever variety of things they are doing already. I can see no way in which such a process could ever lead us to infer *only* those postulates that would lead to *only* one solution for each set of facts. If we do make such a partial inference we are simply choosing those principles we like out of all the ones that are possible, but in an unusually elaborate way.

48. The second approach to the problem is on more rigorous lines. This is Professor Ijiri's elegant example of how the elements of accounting theory may be treated in purely logical terms.[3] He first defines a set of axioms, then applies a set of measurement rules for computing the monetary effect of transactions and hence deduces some of the general rules of conventional accounting practice. Accounting treatment is on this view deductively certain, like geometry or Boolean algebra: no choice, intuition, or judgment. The difficulty is that on the particularly simple axiom set he has chosen (no doubt rightly for his purpose of fundamental exposition), only historical cost is allowed for; valuation is deliberately omitted. The system was never intended to distinguish between the actual alternatives that prevent uniformity in real life.[4]

49. It would be theoretically possible to develop a logical system such as Professor Ijiri's so that it *did* distinguish deductively between differing accounting treatments. Straight-line depreciation, for example, would be a logically inferrable consequence of the system, and reducing balance would not be; similarly with any other matter where opinions differ. But it would (I suspect) be enormously difficult. The number of axioms would grow rapidly, so that the number of theorems (*i.e.* the number of accounting treatments) deducible from them would grow even more rapidly. In general the utility (like the beauty) of a logical system is inversely proportionate to the number of axioms it is built on. But the world is full of examples of suspicions such as mine being proved wrong; a beautifully-simplifying assumption, as yet unknown to me, could do it in a moment. I hope someone will try.

50. A further difficulty, however, would remain. The real problem would only have been deferred. It would still be necessary to decide *which axioms to select*— i.e. the ones that favoured straight-line depreciation as against the ones that favoured reducing balance, and so on. This route therefore eventually brings us back, just as the American research group's postulates did, to the question of *selecting* one treatment out of a number of possibilities—to the "let's settle for one view anyhow" school.

51. I am sure that no subject is more worth the while of academic accountants everywhere than to try to establish beyond cavil the logical foundations of accounting. This is the way to make our profession not merely useful, but intellectually respectable (a great comfort to the fastidious). Whether such a solution can ever be found is not yet apparent, but the seeking for it would inevitably clarify minds—and that is all we can ask of a truly philosophical enquiry. Most of us would be prepared to forgo quite a number of substantial volumes on in-

---

[3] Yuji Ijiri: "Axioms and Structures of Conventional Accounting Measurements", *The Accounting Review*, January 1965. A later version appears in a rather more pretentious work, "The Foundations of Accounting Measurement" (Prentice-Hall, 1967).

[4] Professor Ijiri has confirmed in private correspondence that while he has endeavoured to axiomatise a valuation method, he has not yet succeeded in doing so fruitfully.

come determination, changing price-levels, theories of depreciation, managerial economics and so on while the necessary thinking was done.

(b) Let's settle for one view anyhow

52. We have reached this point: there can be and often is a variety of permissible accounting treatments for a given set of facts, and no one of them can be logically inferred to be more desirable than the rest. The view which we are now to consider makes a briskly unembarrassed response. "Right! Let us select *one* out of all the various possibilities for each situation. We will call this selected method the *best* (or the *recommended,* or the *normal,* or the *preferred,* etc.). All accountants will be required to follow this best, etc. method, or if not, they will have to disclose in their accounts what the effect would have been if they had. That will fix it! Soon no-one will go to the trouble of using any other method than ours." I put the matter crudely because the thought itself is so crude. Such a thought may well not be a wise thing to say in words as plain as these,[5] but let us ask a more rewarding question: is it even a wise thing to think?

53. First, let us be clear that, by the stated terms of the problem, the method which is fortunate enough to be chosen as the preferred one can have no in-built superiority over its rivals; *ex hypothesi* all the permissible choices were indeed permissible, and none could be inferred from accounting theory as being better. This is not therefore a dispute between two arguments, one true and the other false; both are by definition neither true nor false, but reasonable. The criterion of fairness does not enable us to choose between two alternatives both of which are fair. Why should it? The preferred method would therefore only be the preferred one simply because it *was* preferred; the object of the exercise would be by its very nature not to choose the best (where all were equal) but just to plump for one. When this point is fully grasped the exercise looks much less attractive. It would be a thin reply to a critic, for example, to say that the merits of the case were irrelevant; the choice had been made on the grounds of which method the selecting body had been able to agree on.

54. A second reason for doubt is less abstract. Attention would immediately be engrossed by the question "Are the figures in accordance with the rules?", instead of "Are the figures in accordance with the facts?".[6] The auditor would have a hard time of it if the rules in any particular case did *not* produce a fair result. In recent years certain firms in this country have shown a growing reluctance to argue controversial questions *de novo* with their clients, but have sheltered behind official pronouncements or even their own manuals of procedure: "Well, that's what the book of rules says and our policy is to follow it." This does not strike me as a very persuasive line for an auditor to take (nor do I think his clients find it so). The interesting, difficult and relevant questions are:—"Are those rules right for these facts? What figures will fairly represent the underlying realities? What figures would represent them best?"

55. A third reason for doubt is the difficulty of getting authoritative pronouncements well enough written. If they are broad enough to cover the variety

---

[5] See for example, the English Institute's *Newsletter* of December 1969, where the proposal to carry out just such a plan is put into rather different words.

[6] This I believe to have been the practical effect in America, where of course the S.E.C.'s regulations and prescribed accounting procedures are mandatory.

of circumstance, they become platitudinous and admit the very disparity of treatments they were designed to avoid; if they are narrow enough to exclude this, then all sorts of hard cases will end up with a silly result. They should therefore *never* be mandatory. Differing opinions reflect difficult problems, which do not cease to be difficult just because one party to the debate has been outlawed. There is, further, great and natural reluctance to change such pronouncements when it later becomes clear that they ought to be changed: either the change is made and there is loss of face, loss of the very authority which it was intended to enhance (this has recently happened to both the American Institute—investment credit—and the English Institute—investment grants);[7] or the change is not made, and good judges cease to regard the pronouncement as either a helpful or reliable guide to what best practice is.[8] It is clear that we must always have two Institutes (at least), so that the debate can be kept open. No progress is possible when points of genuine interest are lost to sight in the bleak Siberian wastes of mindless uniformity. In a telling phrase of T. S. Eliot's, "The danger of freedom is deliquescence; the danger of strict order is petrifaction". The subject makes us turn, instinctively, to Mill:—"Not the violent conflict between parts of the truth, but the quiet suppression of half of it, is the formidable evil; there is always hope when people are forced to listen to both sides; it is when they attend only to one that errors harden into prejudices, and truth itself ceases to have the effect of truth, by being exaggerated into falsehood."[9] I accordingly hope that the Scottish Institute will from now on extend its co-operation with our neighbours in this kind of way, not merely by agreeing in advance some of the things that they are going to say, but also by contesting stoutly a number of the things that they have already said. It is no part of true friendship to connive, in serious matters, at what is muddled or mistaken.

[7] First Opinion of the A.I.C.P.A. Accounting Principles Board on investment credit, December 1962; S.E.C. Accounting Series Release No. 96 in January 1963 permitted an alternative treatment; Second Opinion of the Accounting Principles Board in March 1964 allowed both treatments. English Institute interim recommendation on investment grants, March 30, 1966; Scottish Institute research paper recommending a different treatment, September 1966; English Institute final recommendation permitting both treatments, April 14, 1967.

[8] For example, the English Institute's statement on auditing numbered U5, criticised severely from a Scottish viewpoint in "Subsidiaries Not Audited by Us", *The Accountants' Magazine*, February 1966, at pages 90–99.

[9] John Stuart Mill: "On Liberty" (1859). The whole of the second chapter of this miraculous little book—"Of the liberty of thought and discussion"—could well be required reading for any body of any kind that was feeling tempted to promulgate its opinions as authoritative. On a more recent note, it is fascinating to find rigorous modern philosophers beginning to have their doubts about even the well-established orthodoxies of scientific empiricism for just the same reasons as Mill's:—". . . However, this background theory, like any other theory, is itself in need of criticism. Criticism must use alternatives. Alternatives will be the more efficient the more radically they differ from the point of view to be investigated. . . . Hence *the invention of alternatives in addition to the view that stands in the centre of discussion constitutes an essential part of the empirical method.* . . ." The passage continues under the heading "The self-deception involved in all uniformity". (From P. K. Feyerabend: "How to Be a Good Empiricist—A Plea for Tolerance in Matters Epistemological" (1963), reprinted in "The Philosophy of Science" edited by P. H. Nidditch, O.U.P., 1968).

56. The main piece that has been missing from accounting thought up to now, in my opinion, is not an agreed codification of principles—"if that is your problem, here is your answer"—but a clear understanding of which *kind* of principle should be chosen out of a number of possibilities, and *why*. The criteria of appropriateness are wholly to seek. The existing choice of treatments, after all, is not just the result of capriciousness or ignorance, nor does it rest merely on the proposition that whichever basis maximises the profit should invariably be chosen: the trouble with cynicism is that it misleads. The variety of treatments reflects the variety of human experience; a number of people in the past have felt that things should be shown in this way, and a number of others have felt otherwise. This should not be so very shocking, even to such an illiberal age as ours. Accountants have been more concerned to give the picture that *they* felt was true and fair in *their* circumstances than to follow the rule set by someone else as being true and fair in *his*. In this, I submit, they have been wholly right. The object of a set of accounts is to tell the truth.

57. What considerations, then, should affect the decision on which of several possible treatments to choose? My answer is implicit in everything said above about what a set of accounts purports to be: one should choose whichever treatment gives the fairest view of the way the business is going. Should profit be taken now or later? That depends on whether profit is in fact being earned now or later. Should expenditure be written off now or later? Again, that depends on which period will really benefit from it. The accounts paint a picture of the facts; it is therefore the facts that determine the figures. Above all, the procedure adopted in previous years should not be allowed to become an incubus preventing all future change if in fact a fairer picture could be painted by following a new procedure; the same applies to the treatments followed elsewhere in the group if the circumstances there are quite different. The actual basis adopted in the accounts should be the subject of rational choice and justification year by year.

58. I have set out in an appendix some common examples of different accounting treatments, and have suggested which kind of situation might be better recognised by which accounting treatment. I have no expectation that these examples will be agreed by any substantial portion of the Summer School, and of course a hypothetical case-study cannot really simulate the whole flavour of a company's past, present and future, its personnel, products and problems, which would influence the decision in real life. But I hope that these examples may at least stimulate discussion and focus attention on the critical point: what *kind* of factor ought to influence the choice of this accounting treatment rather than that?

59. When accounts are prepared in a really serious way along the lines suggested here—that is, attempting to give the best view of the facts and not just any old view—the proposal to codify accounting principles can be seen to be irrelevant. The treatment actually adopted will be the *best* for representing fairly the fortunes of that company during that period: why then state how much more or less the profit would have been if some other accounting treatment had been used? By definition, "some other treatment" must in these circumstances be less good than the "best". The only reasonable implication would be that the results would have been different if the facts had been different. I can see little point in treating shareholders to metaphysical speculations of that kind.

60. All the "Let's settle for one view anyhow" proposals depend on a single

insupportable premise: they suppose that it is a matter of indifference in any particular case which out of a number of competing accounting principles is used. It is very far from being a matter of indifference to the company itself. Proposals for codification are directed to the right problem, but have come up with the wrong solution. We do not want a Procrustean bed, nor is it material to know what the results would have been if the world had been a different place; but we do want to know what has been done, and even more, we want to know *why* it has been done. *Why* does company A think it right to include overheads in stock? *Why* does company B not think it right? I dispute no-one's privilege of applying his honest judgment in the way he thinks right, but I do think he incurs the corresponding responsibility to say *why* he takes that view rather than some other equally possible.[10] This I believe would do more to bring forward the rational debate on accounting principles than many a learned tome and tedious lecture. There would be chapter and verse from the real-life world: *this* is what they did there and *this* is why they did it.

61. Two reasons I should rule out as being totally unacceptable:—

(a) We chose this principle because we have always done so;

(b) We chose this principle because it was appropriate to the circumstances.

The question being asked is, *why* was it right always to use it? And *why* is it appropriate to the circumstances? The power of free and rational argument remains, I am old-fashioned enough to believe, the best road to the truth in human affairs. I would therefore give companies the maximum freedom to present their accounts in whatever way they thought fit, and would then require them to *explain* and *justify* the course they had taken.

62. The auditor's task—no light one!—would be to ensure that they did. And to see that they did it fairly.

IV—INDEPENDENCE

63. It is clear that independence is the key to the auditor's rôle. If he is not independent he is nothing. It is therefore sad to read recent allegations that the auditor cannot possibly be independent because his remuneration is fixed by the directors of the company he reports on.[11] It is also a little surprising, for if the auditor's opinions have not been worth a groat all these years, why has society bothered to go on getting them?

64. The real answer to this accusation is very simple, and it is known to every practitioner and company of whom at least I am aware: it is not true.

65. Such criticisms of the auditor's integrity tend to spring from a transatlantic background, where the auditor's position is less regarded and less secure. From experience obtained on both sides of the Atlantic, I rather doubt whether Ameri-

---

[10] This is not far removed from one of Professor Stamp's more persuasive suggestions, "The public accountant and the public interest", *Journal of Business Finance*, Spring 1969, at page 41. [Reprinted in this volume—Eds.]

[11] *E.g.* Professor Stamp in *The Times*, September 11, 1969. "There went a smoke out in his presence: and a consuming fire out of his mouth, so that coals were kindled at it."

can practice and procedures in all respects measure up to British ones. Understandably for a new country with an immigrant population, the ethos of their society has been traditionally geared towards putting a value, not so much on *excellence,* as on *conformity* (for which they are paying a sadly high price now); the professions in the two countries reflect the different societies that have produced them. I accordingly should not care to see the increasing Americanisation of some of our leading U.K. firms carried any further. A significant point on this was succinctly made by an American accounting professor at the Summer School here last year.[12]

66. The auditor is appointed by the shareholders. He is paid out of their funds. And he reports to them. I cannot see what in this arrangement vitiates his independence; it is entirely as it should be. Auditors of public companies in this country also enjoy a degree of practical security once they have been appointed, for changes can lead to awkward questions (*e.g.* the very significant City of London Real Property affair of some years ago). This assists their independence. The directors as the shareholders' agents of course fix the quantum of the auditor's remuneration, but the parameters are not really very wide. The company must have an audit and it must (eventually!) pay the market rate in order to get it; I have never heard of any company attempting to pay *more.* Indeed, all the evidence points to auditors being prepared to go to remarkable lengths, often without hope of adequate remuneration, in order to deal fully and fairly with difficult situations. The duty to shareholders is ranked uncommonly high. The sort of innuendo made above does not look very likely to me. The auditor's reputation is far too precious to him. It is his only permanent asset, the only reason he stays in business. And he backs that reputation, every time he reports on a set of accounts, by putting everything he has at risk.

67. I do not see that if all auditors were civil servants, as has been noted, they would have quite the same interest in maintaining this degree of independence. (I in no way refer to the admirable Exchequer and Audit Department, who are concerned more with the efficiency and legality of expenditure than with expressing an independent opinion on the truth and fairness of the accounts and forecasts of trading concerns.) It is already deeply disturbing to consider how many public employees are now called on to make absolute and discretionary decisions, subject to no independent outside verification or control, which vitally affect the financial interests of companies and of private citizens. One party which a government employee (not protected by judicial immunity) can never be wholly independent of is government itself; this could be highly relevant to the rôle of reporting accountant. Who would know the degree of independence attaching to a government employee's view, for example, of companies in an industry that the government itself confessedly disapproved of, or especially favoured, or was busy "restructuring", or whose prices it was reviewing? We have seen many examples in recent years of public bodies whose appearance of independence has scarcely borne examination: the body can never be more inde-

[12] Lee J. Seidler, A.B., M.S., C.P.A.: "A Comparison of the Economic and Social Status of the Accounting Profession in Great Britain and the United States of America," reproduced in *The Accountant's Magazine,* 1969, at page 489: a sample of U.K. stockholders and analysts considered that British auditors would get their own way in a material dispute with a client, while a similar sample in the United States considered that U.S. auditors would not.

pendent than those appointed to it.[13] A further doubt is whether civil servant auditors would attain quite the same quality as the leading members of the profession; it is the independence that attracts outstanding men. The standard of financial reporting achieved by some government bodies in recent years does not measure up to what would be expected in the profession.[14]

68. An interesting question is whether the rendering of services other than auditing to the same client interferes with the independence of the audit function. In my view this is unlikely to be so; the partners and personnel are usually different, and services *for* management do not constitute management itself. It is the results of management, not the skills it uses or the efficiency it shows, that the independent auditor reports on. I leave on one side the intriguing question of management auditing (to which this topic leads), as this was fully discussed at a Summer School two years ago.[15]

V—INVESTIGATIONS AND REPORTS

69. A discussion of the reporting accountant's rôle today would not be in any way complete without referring to the many reports he makes other than as an auditor—particularly full-scale reports for purchasers of businesses, loan creditors and banks, issuing houses, on mergers and amalgamations, and on negligence claims and frauds. This is a highly important part of any large and busy practice in the U.K. (though not so much, I believe, in America). The varieties of accounting treatment and the uncertainties of business life referred to earlier make clear the need for such investigations.

70. There has been some discussion in the past on whether an independent accountant's investigation was really essential for a purchasing company, which may consider itself not ill-equipped to make an investigation itself, or may prefer to rely wholly on published information and not-too-exacting discussions in the cigar-scented parlours of merchant banks. Not surprisingly, some very bad bargains have been made, and complaints have been voiced that the view of the facts taken by the vendors in their accounts was by no means the view that the purchasers would have taken. I trust that the idea of what accounting really is, discussed in the course of this paper, will make this reaction seem surprising to

---

[13] "Every function superadded to those already exercised by the government causes its influence over hopes and fears to be more widely diffused, and converts, more and more, the active and ambitious part of the public into hangers-on of the government, or of some party which aims at becoming the government. If the roads, the railways, the banks, the insurance offices, the great joint-stock companies, the universities, and the public charities, were all of them branches of the government; if, in addition, the municipal corporations and local boards, with all that now devolves on them, became departments of the central administration, if the employés of all these different enterprises were appointed and paid by the government, and looked to the government for every rise in life; not all the freedom of the press and popular constitution of the legislature would make this or any other country free otherwise than in name."—Mill *op. cit.*, from chapter V.

[14] See, for example, the criticisms elaborated in "The Reports of the Prices and Incomes Board", *The Accountant's Magazine*, 1967, pages 158–164.

[15] E. J. Baden, M.A., C.A., A.T.I.I.: "Management Audit", reproduced in *The Accountant's Magazine*, 1968, pages 520–529.

no-one. It must therefore be a wise precaution (to put it no higher) to have the vendor's view of the facts independently examined by a reporting accountant on the purchaser's behalf; it can save many heartaches. More persuasively, it can save hundreds of thousands of pounds. And from the opposing point of view of a sale or raising more capital, it can turn an indecipherable shambles that nobody would touch into a highly-marketable entity that will be immediately snapped up.

71. The point is this: an investigation report has to be extremely well done to be of use. A good one is invaluable: there is no place for the merely routine. And it has to be very well written if it is to achieve its purpose. Not all accountants (alas!) bear this in mind. I believe that maintaining really high standards of reporting, in an age which is increasingly given over to the superficiality of mass-market journalism and TV, is an essential part of what our profession can give to society. To be negligent of how one reports—of adducing the evidence, distinguishing comment from fact, making clear what one knows and what is hearsay, allowing opportunity for replies to criticism, being precise, scrupulous and fair—is simply to be negligent of the truth; and that is the beginning of falsehood. One cannot dissociate what is said from the way it is said.

VI—PROFITS FORECASTS

72. We come to the vital and growing rôle of reporting on profits forecasts. I expect this work to grow even more in the future. Why give shareholders more information at the time of a take-over than they get during the rest of the year? Each investor's decision at any time to buy, sell or retain his holding is his own personal takeover problem, and he is entitled to as much relevant information. I therefore expect that companies will regularly publish their profits forecasts for the coming year in their annual reports, together with a comparison between last year's forecast and the actual results achieved, and that these forecasts will be covered in the auditor's examination. Much kudos—and no doubt an improved market rating—awaits the first large concern that is prepared to take the plunge.

73. This would go a long way towards removing the severer difficulties felt at present. First, profits forecasts would be a *regular thing*, not a nine days' wonder; they would attract less bally-hoo. Secondly, they would be made and issued at the right time of the year, when reliable audited figures for the year just finished are to hand, instead of being prepared and issued at the drop of a hat often on someone else's initiative. Thirdly, the comparison of forecasts and achieved results over a period of years would show how risky the business was, what kind of unexpected events affected it, how successful its forecasting had been in the past. Fourthly, not being made in connection with a bid, they would be subject to no special bias in favour of optimism rather than prudence. Fifthly, there is nothing like a regular annual discipline to improve the *quality* of a company's forecasting—and equally, I do not doubt, the quality of the auditor's examination of those forecasts. Finally, the management of every sizeable company these days prepares forecasts for their own use and guidance, so why should the shareholders not have them, too?

74. Regularity of public forecasting would help to deflect the spotlight away from only *one* year's results. This has caused much trouble. A sensible view of a company's worth cannot be formed simply by applying an arbitrary and ill-thought-out multiplier to the expected results of a single year. An investor buy-

ing an equity share is buying a variable perpetuity, with expectations that it will increase and fears that it will diminish; the current year's results form merely one chapter in a long saga, and not by any means (he trusts) the final one. It is the short-term views of professional market men, peering myopically into the middle of next week, that have lent this wholly false importance to the current year's results. Regularity in forecasting would concentrate attention on the *trend*, and would emphasize the wide uncertainties that all forecasts are subject to.

75. If such a system became standard, then there would be something to be said for not allowing any extra *ad hoc* forecasts to be made at any other time of the year.[16] The directors could still say whatever they liked about the future, but they would not be permitted to quantify it; the odds against making a fair impartial forecast in the heat and dust of a contested take-over battle are too great. The attention of the parties would also be less distracted from the real point at issue—namely, what would the *benefit* of the merger be?

76. Reporting on a company's forecast does not present any different kind of problem from reporting on its accounts; I hope this will be clear from the views expressed earlier on uncertainty and probability. Of course the document reported on is subject to a much, much greater *degree* of uncertainty; the probability of forecasts being wildly out compared with the annual accounts is extremely high. But the same principles of evidence and reasonableness apply. One can only ever reach a probability in either case; and the view taken at the time does not cease to be reasonable because the event turns out to be different. There is much less to go on, but the method of proceeding is the same.

77. The auditor's report on a forecast should therefore, I suggest, be an expression of opinion on fairness and reasonableness—a statement going to the *bona fides* of the document. I am not sure that the English Institute's otherwise extremely helpful note on the latest take-over code goes quite to the root of the matter.[17] It is true that the reporting accountant is required under the City code to report only on "the accounting bases and calculations for the profit forecasts, as distinct from the assumptions"; but how can he stop there? Suppose he thinks that the assumptions are nonsense—would he allow his name to go forward? That being so, might it not be better to state in the report that he *has* examined the assumptions on which the forecast is based and they were such that a reasonable man could fairly hold them, and then go on to give every qualification about the inbuilt uncertainty of the whole exercise? (So much trouble is caused because people are tempted to conclude that a forecast's proving to be wrong is evidence that it was wrong to make it.) It is the breeding-ground of confusion if something is tacitly understood to have been done but is not stated. The practice under the previous take-over code suffered conspicuously from this defect.[18] The same point is met with on prospectuses, where reporting accountants satisfy themselves (and everyone else connected with the issue) on the reasonableness of the forecast, although no word of this appears in the document. Plain things are best. If the reporting accountant will not give his certificate with-

---

[16] But forecasts quickly go out of date; if a company is regularly reporting its profits half-yearly or quarterly, it would need to publish its revised forecasts at the same time.

[17] "Accountants' Reports on Profits Forecasts"—statement S15, April 1969; this was prepared in consultation with the Scottish Institute.

[18] Reporting accountants had to examine the forecasts but were to permit no word of this examination to appear in the circular—Statement S11, July 1968.

out looking at the assumptions and being satisfied that they are at least not nonsense, it would be clearer to everyone if he said so.

78. The problem of how to convey the degree of uncertainty that attaches to a forecast remains, I think, unsolved. As far as my limited knowledge of the subject extends, mathematical probability theory does not help. Classical statistics is wholly based on the concepts of repeated identical trials and the counting of chances, where (at least in theory) something may or may not happen a great many times. Bayesian statistics rests on subjective *a priori* probabilities and their modification by the results of subsequent trials. But in a profit forecast there is only ever going to be *one* trial in total; this estimate is going to have to be made by these people at this time in the light of these facts and these expectations *once only*. Earlier and later forecasts are not identical. There are no chances to count.

79. Recognising that this is so, I still think it would be better to borrow the imagery of probability theory, even though we cannot borrow the method of reasoning. Forecasts should be presented in the form of a range of expected results, and matched with the subjective probabilities that the directors consider to be right for the various parts of that range. Nothing else will so readily convey the idea that the whole exercise is conceived in uncertainty.[19] The range and related probabilities need only be broadly indicated. I would like to see a forecast looking like this:—

Range of forecast profits, £ million	Directors' subjective probability distribution
Less than .5	.1
.50 to 1.00	.1
1.00 to 1.25	.6
1.25 to 1.5	.2
Greater than 1.5	0
(The sum of all possibilities is conventionally taken as unity)	1.0

The only certainty is that something is bound to happen. This seems to me to convey the real flavour of a forecast more poignantly than just a bald point-estimate and "subject to unforeseen circumstances". The directors here say that they think it most likely—and likelier than not—that the profits will be between £1 million and £1¼ million; they think they are as likely to be more than that as less; but if profits are more, they judge they are likely to be only a little bit more—if they are less, they judge that they are as likely to be a lot less as a little.

80. Forecasting along these lines would help to educate the public in what the exercise really means. It would bring out into the open a difficulty that at the moment is swept under the carpet: beyond a certain level, the higher the figure of profit that is forecast, the less likely it is to be achieved. It would make everyone in an organisation, big or small, apply their minds to uncertainty in an organised way; the directors of the parent company would need to specify the probability distribution in advance, so that subsidiaries and divisions could forecast

---

[19] It would of course be consistent that accounts of completed periods should be presented in the same way, too, but this might be rather fatiguing.

their own range of individual results in accordance with that scale. And it would diminish one of the great practical difficulties of forecasting at present, which is the very human tendency to keep a little bit up one's sleeve—nobody likes to be found "wrong". As I have tried to show, the fear is itself erroneous, because this is never what a failure to meet a forecast "proves" at all.

81. I would see nothing wrong or improper in an independent accountant reporting on the fairness and reasonableness of a profits forecast that was presented in this form. Qualifications would no doubt be more frequent than they are on accounts, but this would help to remind everyone that an opinion is by definition something that one may not agree with. And I think it would be clearer and more candid than what we are required to do now.

SUMMARY

In presenting the above Paper to the Summer School Mr. A. M. C. Morison said:—

(1) I am conscious of having to present to you a paper so orthodox that a contemporary gathering is likely to find it almost unreadable. Our professional iconoclasts have fed us on such a diet of over-ripe prose that we confidently expect, when we open the page, to be stupefied immediately. I can only hope that, where revolution has become part of the daily round, the statement of the obvious (which is all I have attempted) may itself provide just a tincture of novelty. For we are certainly here to argue about *something!*

(2) The current fever of debate about the nature of accounting is, in my view, quite a good thing. That is not to say that, at least so far, it has been a very good debate; indeed, it has been rather indifferent. So often one finds today that it is not the subject that is boring, but the speaker: not the question, but the tone of voice. You cannot be anything we could legitimately describe as "interesting" in the straitened confines of a couple of columns of newsprint, or a three-minute interview on TV; the fact of the discussion presupposes that the subject is interesting, but the conditions in which it is conducted ensure that hardly anything interesting will be said. This is of course, I am sure, quite what our admirable convener had in mind in asking me to speak to you now for no more than 15 minutes: it is a convention developed in the interests of the general contentment, and I am delighted to benefit from it as much as you.

(3) The proper nature of accounting is a *difficult* question, and difficult questions do not admit easy answers—or perhaps any answers. It is for that reason wholly proper to go on asking them. All we can reasonably hope for is the clarification of minds. It is good that this Summer School should be meeting, in a place with a rigorous intellectual tradition, to discuss the fundamentals of our profession. It is perhaps the weakness of practical men and women—which I can see at a glance we all unquestionably are— . . . very well, *if* practical men and women *have* a weakness, it is that they tend to shy away from abstract thought. "This is what we did last year", or "That is what they did there", or "Oh well, never mind first principles as long as we get an answer we can accept"—we can all recognise the pragmatist voice that seduces us, in the hurly-burly of everyday life, from taking the trouble of *thinking things out.* I hope that that voice, alone among all those possible, will not venture to be heard here today. For the rôle of the reporting accountant is wholly dependent on what the nature of accounting

is; and as we are continually being told these days (with suffocating tiresomeness), if accountants as a profession cannot make more intelligible what they are trying to do, there are others who will seek to do it for them. It is these others who are for ever telling us so; what they don't tell us is that they are likely to do it considerably less well.

(4) When writing my paper at the beginning of the year I thought that I was perhaps giving too much weight to the question of uniformity of accounting principles, a topic that intrigued me. In the light of later events, however, I do not think this is so, and as it is the key to the other questions I will consider it now. But I hope that you will also find something of interest to discuss on profits forecasts, because that chestnut will surely return, with all its amusing power to confound the laity, before very long; it will be well to be steady and resolved in one's mind on what one's attitude is going to be. It would be interesting to learn, by the way, how the proponents of "cash flow accounting"—whatever that may be: I do hope we have some here?—how they propose to establish their discounted estimates of future receipts and outgoings with any greater degree of assurance than any other forecasts of the future; it seems curious to attack the unavoidable uncertainties of conventional accounting with a proposal which is by several degrees more uncertain. A clear recognition of the uncertainty of *any* method would more naturally lead one, I should have thought, to prefer for every-day use the method that was least uncertain.

(5) The central issue on uniformity is this. *Here* we have a number of different accounting treatments; *there* we have a number of different companies in different sets of circumstances: how do we fit the one to the other? Let us admit right at the start that if anyone can show us how to *deduce*, by logical means alone, one, and *only one* treatment, for any specific set of facts, then the question is answered and we can all go home. I do not know how to do this; and it seems to me that the proponents of uniformity have not yet applied themselves with sufficient rigour to ask the question at all. But I do hope that anyone here who can tell us how to do it will not be in any way shy.

(6) If we cannot find a logical rule, implicit in the nature of accounting itself, for selecting the right treatment to fit the facts, then we are obliged to fall back on some other rule which is not such a logical rule. (I forgo the extreme possibility of selecting our accounting treatment by a random process—though surely we must eventually reach the great day of stochastic accountancy?—and also the other extreme of always reporting *every* set of facts by means of *every* possible accounting treatment.) What rule of selection, then, shall we use? On one side you have the big battalions—and may I say that they are of course quite as distinguished and fully as impressive as the big battalions nearly always are?—who say: "*We* will choose, for each set of facts, the most appropriate rule, and everyone else will follow it. It will—er—take a little time, perhaps, to get round all the different sets of circumstances, and—um—of course we can only indicate the broad lines of what is likely in the ordinary case to be the best sort of thing, but still, our committees are turning out authoritative guide-lines and fundamental first principles and—er—things at a very great rate now, and if only we all resolve to *pull together* we shall present such a broad united front that our critics will be silenced". On the other side you have the redoubtable figure of Professor Baxter, who I am delighted to see is with us today, and apart from him—well, it some-

times seems, practically only me, who says: "The right accounting treatment depends on *all* the facts of the individual company and not merely on a selection of them (which is what uniformity implies). It depends on what the business is trying to do, on how well it is doing it, on whether it is growing or static or declining, on what view it can reasonably take of its own future. No one else can decide this other than the company itself, and the reporting accountant who has to see that the choice is fair. The character of a business is as various and as subtle as the character of a human being (on which indeed it very much depends). The arbitrarily-prescribed accounting approach remains about as remote from the truth as an Identikit mock-up is from a photograph, or an application for a driving licence from the maniac who will drive the car. The accounts have to tell the truth about the facts, and only the man who knows the facts can know what he believes the truth to be."

(7) But it will be said against me—indeed I trust it will be said here loud and clear and strong: "Surely, whenever you have the same set of facts, it is reasonable to choose the same accounting treatment to describe them?" My answer is: "Yes, of course it is; but how often do you actually meet the same set of facts— the same set, that is, in all its elements? Can you think of any two sizeable independent companies which you know at all well that can in any meaningful sense of the word be said to be the *same?*"

(8) Let me take the strongest example against me that I can think of (as a devotee of John Stuart Mill I cannot do otherwise): namely, the four major clearing banks, who have recently adopted a uniform basis of accounting. First, let us bear in mind that in a most material particular—namely, the interest rate on deposits—they do not overtly compete with one another (at least only in very roundabout ways); the same factors that affect one are therefore naturally likely to affect the others in a similar sense. It is of course competition more than anything else that produces the difference in circumstance between one business and another that it is the precise function of accounting to record and portray. Next, let us concentrate on one feature only of the banks' uniform accounting—the computation of the charge for bad debts based on a five-year average. Now let us suppose that *one only* of the big four had—*horresco referens!*—a really shocking year for bad debts, so that such a computed charge was no longer enough, and that the other three miraculously avoided the cataclysm. Would the uniform basis of accounting still be the right basis for *it?* Indeed one of the banks already points out in its accounts that if the formula does not give a fair answer in any later year they will not use it. Or, if you find that prospect altogether too alarming, take the less extreme point which will presumably be of relevance from now on: each year the computed bad debt charge will for each bank be nearer to, or further away from, the true charge that would have been required on an actual basis. In some years the reported profits will be less, and in others more, than that which an assessment based on the facts would have given. I have no doubt at all that such a rule as the present one, in the scale and type of business that the clearing banks carry on, will give a perfectly reasonable approximation to the true profit in any year that one is at all likely to foresee, but do we not see *which* view of the two—the actual basis and the formula—we mean by the "true" one? For the purpose of clarifying the reasoning, extend the argument more widely, to a wider class of accounting rule and a wider class of company: how about the

bad debt provisions in hire-purchase companies, or stock provisions in the manufacturers of fashion goods? Would we fancy a *general* formula for them? We intuitively feel a concept of the "true" or "real" profit which is something *other than* the result of applying an arbitrary rule. The rule gives one result and the facts give another. Uniformity of treatment accordingly entails variability of truthfulness; it pre-empts the one question that is the most essential to ask—*which* accounting treatment would portray *these* facts *best?* That is the kernel of the topic that I hope you will be discussing today. . . . [Appendixes begin on p. 225]

APPENDIX
EXAMPLES OF SOME DIFFERING ACCOUNTING TREATMENTS AND THEIR USE

	Varieties of accounting treatment	Effects of these treatments	Example of facts suited to these treatments	Reasons why
Depreciation	Straight-line	Even charge to profit over life of assets	Well-established large-scale company in basic (non-fashionable) industry	Use and benefit of asset likely to be as much in one year as another; competitors would need to be similar large-scale companies also
	Reducing balance	Heavier charge in early years, getting smaller later on	New product expected to do very well for short time, less well when competitors come in	Total effective earning period quite uncertain; only thing clear is that early years will earn more than later years
	Sinking fund	Lower charge in early years, getting bigger later on	Property company amortising premium on a long lease	Loss in value in early years, if any, is negligible; in later years it accelerates
	In accordance with projected cash flow profile used in D.C.F. etc. decision to invest	Cost is written off in proportion as cash is expected to be received	Where expected cash profile is irregular and does not follow a conventional pattern	Some proportion of each £1 of income is treated as recovery of fixed cost every year (assuming projected cash profile is right!)
Stock				
(a) *Effect on cost of sales*				
	Actual	Actual profit taken on each transaction	Where items in stock are identifiable and non-homogeneous —*e.g.* a jeweller or property dealer	Unexceptionable method, only possible in such cases
(Not really happy about this distinction)	F.I.F.O.	Stock is valued near replacement cost, cost of sales at less (assuming rising prices)	Where prices rise only slowly or time-cycle is short—*e.g.* retail shop	Difference between two prices is small

APPENDIX
EXAMPLES OF SOME DIFFERING ACCOUNTING TREATMENTS AND THEIR USE (continued)

	Varieties of accounting treatment	Effects of these treatments	Example of facts suited to these treatments	Reasons why
(Not really happy about this distinction)	Average	Stock is valued some way below replacement cost, cost of sales likewise (do.)	Where prices rise fast, or timecycle is necessarily long—*e.g.* timber	Reduces pure inflationary element in profit without removing it altogether
	Base stock (or L.I.F.O.)	Stock is valued below actual cost, cost of sales at near replacement cost (do.)	Where prices fluctuate, and object of business is *not* dealing, *e.g.* processor of a base metal	Stock profits (where quantity is constant) are restricted to price movements within the one accounting year
	Market value	Unrealised profit is reported as profit	Where stock is instantly disposable—*e.g.* commodity-dealer with world-wide market, banker holding foreign currency	Decision not to sell stock is policy one, not impossibility of finding customers at present

(b) *Overheads*

	Varieties of accounting treatment	Effects of these treatments	Example of facts suited to these treatments	Reasons why
	Direct cost only	Profit varies with sales, not with production	Strongly market-oriented products, where real difficulty is selling rather than manufacture	How the business is going depends on the real difficulty being surmounted—*i.e.* on getting the customers
	Full manufacturing overheads	Profit varies with production as well as sales	Rapidly expanding company where growth in production and overheads necessarily *precedes* growth in sales	Otherwise company may well show a loss when it is in fact doing very well

Long-term contracts

(a) *Overheads*

	Included in w-i-p	Profits charged with overheads when work is completed, not when work is done	Contractor with small number of long-term contracts	No continuing flow of completions to provide regular gross margin for charging overheads against
	Written off as incurred	Profits charged with overheads when work is done, not when work is completed	Contractor with large number of short-term contracts	Opposite to above

(b) *Profit on incomplete work*

	Excluded from w-i-p	Profit is shown as earned when work is completed	Contractor with small number of very long-term contracts (lasting several years)	Impossible to estimate profit until final account is agreed and all extras and claims settled
	Included in w-i-p	Profit is shown as earned when work is done	Contractor with large number of short-term contracts	Feasible to estimate final profit on short-term jobs, and benefit of averaging a number of estimates

Research, development and know-how

Write off when incurred or paid for	Profits of later years benefit from the research without being charged with the cost	Where benefit is totally uncertain—*e.g.* fundamental research on pharmaceuticals	Doing such research is simply a cost of staying in business; profits vary with exploitation of successes, but expenses are continuous
Carry forward and write off when benefit received	Costs and benefits are matched in one year	Where benefit is reasonably certain—*e.g.* development costs on new vintage car	Such expenses are discontinuous, and are tolerably likely to result in a saleable product

APPENDIX
EXAMPLES OF SOME DIFFERING ACCOUNTING TREATMENTS AND THEIR USE (continued)

Varieties of accounting treatment	Effects of these treatments	Example of facts suited to these treatments	Reasons why
Consolidation goodwill			
Carry forward until company acquired is wound up or sold	Shows where and how the group's funds have been invested	Where business acquired has been retained in *status quo*—e.g. subsidiary of a conglomerate	Relevant to judge management of group by (*inter alia*) how much of group funds they have used in buying profits rather than assets
Write off against reserves when acquired (Not really happy about this distinction)	Shows as the group's assets only those which are employed in earning the profits (not amounts paid to acquire the right to *enjoy* those profits)	Where business bought has long ceased to retain its management, customers or identity—e.g. subsidiary becoming part of large manufacturing group	Only real question now is, what are the assets earning these profits?
Write off out of income over a period	Treats goodwill as a deferred expense (n.b. not allowed for tax until disposal)	Where "goodwill" acquired really represents wasting assets—e.g. aggregate-bearing land	When wasting asset is used up, the "goodwill" will have gone. (cf. procedure popular in America of writing off out of profits goodwill which does *not* represent wasting assets: can anyone see any justification for it?).

GARY M. CADENHEAD

GARY M. CADENHEAD (1940-), B.A. 62, B.B.A. 62 Southern Methodist; M.B.A. 64 Harvard; Ph.D. 68 Stanford; CPA. Currently secretary and treasurer, and secretary to the senior fellows, Center for the Study of Democratic Institutions, Santa Barbara, California. Major publication: *Using Accounting Information: A Simulation* (with Label, 1972). Contributor to several journals.

Was a member of the UCLA accounting faculty, 1968–70, prior to joining the Center for the Study of Democratic Institutions.

Principal research interest: as a branch of humanistic psychology, a concern for how people can relate and care for each other, both more effectively and affectively.

"DIFFERENCES IN CIRCUMSTANCES": FACT OR FANTASY?

GARY M. CADENHEAD

The need is not for uniformity (in financial reporting) without regard to circumstances. Rather, it is the elimination of variations which cannot be justified by differences in circumstances. (Emphasis added.)

Alvin R. Jennings[1]

This appeal to "differences in circumstances" is central to and pervades the dialogue between the advocates of "uniformity" and the proponents of "flexibility" in financial reporting. Rarely does a discussion concerning the stated objective of the Accounting Principles Board, "to narrow the areas of differences and inconsistency in practice",[2] not include the caveat "differences in circumstances". But, as Thomas D. Flynn, 1965–6 President of the AICPA, asked, "What do we mean by 'differences in circumstances'?".[3] The AICPA Special Committee on Opinions of the Accounting Principles Board made a strong recommendation to the Accounting Principles Board concerning this issue:

SOURCE: From *Abacus*, Vol. 6, No. 1 (September, 1970), pp. 71–80. Reprinted by permission of *Abacus*.

[1] Alvin R. Jennings, "Opinions of the Accounting Principles Board", *Journal of Accountancy*, Vol. 118, August 1964, p. 31.

[2] AICPA, Special Committee on Research Program, "Report to Council", *Journal of Accountancy*, Vol. 106, December 1958, p. 63.

[3] Thomas D. Flynn, "Uniformity in Financial Accounting: A Progress Report", *Law and Contemporary Problems*, Vol. 30, Autumn 1965, p. 634.

· The Board should move toward the reduction of alternative practices in accounting by adopting policies under which it will:

(a) Recognize the objective that variations in treatment of accounting items generally should be confined to those justified by *substantial differences in factual circumstances.* (Emphasis added.)

(b) Set forth in its opinions the criteria for application of such acceptable variations.

(c) In an Opinion dealing with a situation which the Board believes justifies alternatives even though there is no significant difference in factual circumstances, set forth the treatment to be preferred, and require disclosure of the treatment followed.[4]

Despite the special committee's recommendation to the Accounting Principles Board, despite the frequency with which one encounters the phrase "differences in circumstances", despite its importance in narrowing differences in reporting practices, and despite the recognition of its ambiguity by prominent members of the accounting profession, no systematic attempt has been made to clarify the meaning of the phrase nor to isolate the circumstances which might justify different accounting practices. As recently as May 1968 a subcommittee of the Accounting Principles Board declared:

The most important unsolved problem is the use of alternative accounting practices or methods under circumstances which themselves do not appear to be sufficiently different to justify different accounting treatments.[5]

However, only a few inquiries into the nature of circumstantial differences have been made.

Related Research

Professor Graham classified Paul Grady's list of "alternative methods of implementing generally accepted accounting principles"[6] into three categories based on differences in circumstances:

Category 1: Situations in which alternatives are available even though there are no significant differences in circumstances;

Category 2: Situations in which alternatives are available where there are significant differences in circumstances but in which circumstances are ordinarily ignored in selecting the alternative to be employed; and

Category 3: Situations in which alternatives are available where there are significant differences in circumstances that are now quite generally considered in selecting among the alternatives.[7]

[4] *Report of Special Committee on Opinions of the Accounting Principles Board,* American Institute of Certified Public Accountants, New York 1965, p. 16.

[5] *APB Subcommittee Draft of Opinion on "Basic Concepts and Accounting Principles Underlying Financial Statements of Business Enterprises",* American Institute of Certified Public Accountants, New York 1968, pp. 114–15.

[6] Paul Grady, "Inventory of Generally Accepted Accounting Principles for Business Enterprises" in *Accounting Research Study No. 7,* American Institute of Certified Public Accountants, New York 1965, Ch. 10.

[7] Willard J. Graham, "Some Observations of the Nature of Income, Generally Accepted Accounting Principles, and Financial Reporting", *Law and Contemporary Problems,* Autumn 1965, p. 669.

Unfortunately, Graham did not specify the criteria he used in classifying the alternative methods into the three categories. For example, he placed inventory valuation into Category 2 but failed to designate the "significant differences in circumstances" which "are ordinarily ignored in selecting the alternative to be employed".

Following an approach similar to Graham's, Professor Langenderfer asserted that there are two types of diversity:

1. Diversity arising from a *free* choice among alternative methods in those cases where the choice is *not* governed or justified by significant differences in circumstances.

2. Diversity arising from the *considered* choice among alternative methods in cases where the choice *is* governed and justified by significant differences in circumstances.[8]

Langenderfer, however, neither identified the kinds of differences in circumstances he used in classifying alternative methods nor the circumstances which he thought would justify different methods.

This article is a response to the continuing need for a systematic exploration of the meaning of the phrase, "differences in circumstances", and of the relationship between differences in circumstances and the multiplicity of alternative accounting methods.

Circumstantial Variables Defined

The phrase, "differences in circumstances", is cumbersome, and its meaning is ambiguous. To obtain greater precision, the term "circumstantial variables", which will be used throughout the article, is introduced and explained.

Circumstantial variables are environmental conditions which vary among companies and which influence (1) the feasibility of accounting methods and/or (2) the objectivity of the measures resulting from applying the accounting methods.

In this context an environmental condition is similar to the concept of the environment as Churchman uses it in *The Systems Approach*.[9] In Churchman's framework for a system, the system's environment refers to the fixed constraints; the environment is outside the system's control but determines in part how the system performs. Similarly an environmental condition is outside the control of the manager or accountant but affects the output of the accounting or measurement system. For example, the non-homogeneous nature of the end products into which beef carcasses are broken is beyond the control of the accountant; and, if the accountant attempts to determine the historical cost of beef primal cuts, the non-homogeneous nature of beef carcasses has a profound effect on the accountant's measure of historical cost. Two questions can be used to identify environmental conditions. "Can the accountant or manager do anything about it?" and "does it affect the results of the accounting process?" If the answer to the first

---

[8] Harold Q. Langenderfer, "A Problem of Communication", *Journal of Accountancy*, Vol. 123, January 1967, p. 36.

[9] C. West Churchman, *The Systems Approach*, New York 1968, pp. 28–37.

question is "No" but to the second is "Yes", then "it" is an environmental condition.

The first requirement for an environmental condition to be a circumstantial variable is that it varies among companies either within the same industry or among industries. For example, the Internal Revenue Service's requirement that LIFO be used for financial reporting purposes if LIFO is used for income tax calculations is not a circumstantial variable because this requirement applies to all companies in all industries, i.e., it does not vary among companies. On the other hand, the predictability of disposal costs does vary among companies and does influence the feasibility of the net realizable value method of valuing inventories and the objectivity of the resulting estimates of net realizable value; therefore, predictability of disposal costs is a circumstantial variable.

The second requirement for an environmental condition to be a circumstantial variable is that it influences the feasibility[10] of accounting methods and/or the objectivity[11] of the estimates resulting from applying the accounting methods. The unit value of inventory items is a circumstantial variable which affects the feasibility of inventory valuations based on acquisition costs under the specific identification method. For example, valuing the inventories of a hardware or variety store using the specific identification method is not feasible because of the high costs of the record keeping compared with the low unit value of the inventory items. The circumstantial variable, "unit value of inventory items" suggests a retail inventory method if the unit value is "low"; a perpetual inventory method if it is "high", and a periodic inventory method if it is "medium".[12]

The existence of a ready market with regularly quoted prices is a circumstantial variable too, because this condition facilitates inventory valuation based on current market prices and, accordingly, produces estimates of net realizable value which are highly objective. Another circumstantial variable which influences the objectivity of accounting measures is the relationship between inputs and outputs. For example, if an input is joint with respect to two non-homogeneous outputs, as crude oil is with respect to gasoline and kerosene, inventory valuations based on the costs of inputs require arbitrary allocations which reduce the objectivity of the resulting cost estimates.

Considerations other than circumstantial variables do influence the choice of methods of accounting for inventories. Managerial attitudes, such as one management's preference for conservative income statements as opposed to another's desire to report the maximum profits possible, are not circumstantial variables because they are not environmental conditions and they do not influence either the

---

[10] As used here, "feasible" means "capable of practicable and economic implementation". This definition is from *The Measurement of Property, Plant, and Equipment in Financial Statements*, Harvard Business School Accounting Round Table (Robert T. Sprouse, Reporter), Boston 1964, p. 22.

[11] Objectivity is used here in the Ijiri-Jaedicke sense: "objectivity of a measurement system gives the degree of consensus in the results. . . ." Yuji Ijiri and Robert K. Jaedicke, "Reliability and Objectivity of Accounting Measurements", *Accounting Review*, Vol. XLI, July 1966, p. 476.

[12] For a discussion of considerations in choosing a basic inventory system *see* Joseph Buchan and Ernest Koenigsberg, *Scientific Inventory Management*, Englewood Cliffs 1963, pp. 26–8.

feasibility of accounting methods or the objectivity of the estimates and measures resulting from applying a method. Similarly, a difference of opinion concerning which accounting theory or which concept of income is preferable is not a circumstantial variable.

CIRCUMSTANTIAL VARIABLES AND ACCOUNTING PRINCIPLES

Circumstantial variables exist in relation to accounting principles. Under the principle that inventories should be measured at net realizable value, predictability of disposal costs is a circumstantial variable which affects the objectivity of the resulting measures of net realizable value. On the other hand, under the principle that inventories should be valued at historical acquisition cost, predictability of disposal costs is not a circumstantial variable because it affects neither the feasibility of performing the measurements nor the objectivity of the resulting measures.

An accounting principle specifies a preferred attribute, such as historical acquisition cost, to be measured; but the existence of one or more circumstantial variables may make measuring the attribute unfeasible or may reduce the objectivity of the measure. Several alternative methods may be available for measuring a particular attribute, and the methods may produce measures which vary in objectivity. In measuring a specified attribute, circumstantial variables may make unfeasible using the method which could produce the measure of highest objectivity; in such a case, if another acceptable method which measures the same attribute is available, it could be used. To obtain a measure of the preferred attribute, the accountant may be willing to accept some reduction in the objectivity of the measure. In other cases, the influence of circumstantial variables may be so strong that no methods provide acceptable measures of the preferred attribute; and the accountant must settle for a measure of a different and inferior attribute. According to this viewpoint, accounting principles should specify and rank attributes and specify and rank methods for measuring the attributes beginning with the preferred method for measuring the ideal attribute.[13] Then deviations from the preferred method for measuring the ideal attribute would be justified only when circumstantial variables result in the preferred method being unfeasible or producing measures of unacceptable objectivity.

To illustrate this viewpoint, consider a principle of inventory valuation which specifies and ranks attributes and accounting methods. This illustration intends to demonstrate the nature of the relationship of circumstantial variables to accounting principles, not to argue for nor to recommend this particular ranking of attributes and methods. Assuming that measures of any attribute must satisfy certain feasibility and objectivity criteria, the nature of the relationship of circumstantial variables to accounting principles is independent of the particular rankings of attributes and methods prescribed by different principles.

Illustrative principle of inventory valuation: Given the following ranking of

[13] This concept of a principle as a set of rank-ordered attributes and accounting methods is an extension of the concepts used by Canning and Sprouse and Moonitz. John B. Canning, *The Economics of Accountancy*, New York 1929, Ch. XI. Robert T. Sprouse and Maurice Moonitz, "A Tentative Set of Broad Accounting Principles for Business Enterprises", *Accounting Research Study No. 3*, American Institute of Certified Public Accountants, New York 1962, pp. 27–32, 57.

attributes and accounting methods, select the first method which in the circumstances is feasible and produces sufficiently objective accounting measures:

A Discounted Future Value (attribute)
1. Estimated net sales proceeds discounted at the cost of capital (method)
B Net Realizable Value
1. Current sales price less costs of disposal
C Replacement Cost
1. Input factors at current prices
D Historical Acquisition Cost
1. Specific identification
2. FIFO

Under restrictive but possible conditions, for example, goods manufactured under contract at predetermined prices with specified payment dates, objective measures of the preferred attribute, discounted future value, would be feasible, and method A1 would be selected. If such circumstantial variables were not present, method B1 of measuring the next attribute, net realizable value, would be attempted. To obtain objective measures of net realizable value, current market prices must be determinable and costs to complete and dispose must be predictable. Such conditions prevail in the meat packing industry. For a particular cut and grade of beef, market price can easily be determined; and disposal costs, consisting mainly of transportation costs, are predictable. In industries where neither of the above sets of conditions is present, following the above principle, method C1 of measuring the next attribute, replacement cost, should be considered.

To base inventory valuations on replacement cost, current prices of all inputs must be objectively determinable. This requirement is a necessary but not a sufficient condition for objective estimates of replacement cost. Innate to basing inventory values on input values, whether current or historical, is the joint cost allocation problem resulting from inputs being common to more than one output. In some cases the number of arbitrary allocations required to determine an inventory cost estimate is so great as to reduce significantly the objectivity of the resulting cost estimate; for example, what is the cost (replacement or historical) of a barrel of crude oil to a crude oil producer? In other cases the influence of common costs may not be so pervasive or bothersome.

If the circumstances were such that objective estimates of current prices were not determinable, under the above principle, method C1 of measuring replacement cost should be rejected, and method D1 of measuring the next attribute, historical acquisition cost, should be attempted. "Under most conditions the specific identification method comes closest to describing the actual historical cost, and therefore, it is the least biased in measuring this attribute".[14] Because of the nature of the manufacturing process or because of the costs of determining cost, the specific identification method is not feasible in all situations. If the specific identification method were not feasible, method D2, the FIFO cost method, should be used to measure the attribute historical cost.

[14] "An Evaluation of External Reporting Practices—A Report of the 1966–68 Committee on External Reporting", *The Accounting Review*, Vol. XLIV, Supplement 1969, p. 100.

The foregoing illustration demonstrates the nature of the relationship of circumstantial variables to an accounting principle. If accounting measures of any attribute must satisfy feasibility and objectivity standards, the nature of the relationship of circumstantial variables to accounting principles is independent of the particular rankings of attributes and measurement methods prescribed by different principles. The rankings prescribed by different principles will determine the circumstantial variables which are operative but not the manner in which they operate. Under any accounting principle which ranks and orders attributes and measurement methods, circumstantial variables determine the highest method which meets the feasibility and objectivity criteria. Exhibit 1 shows examples of circumstantial variables in accounting for inventories and the attributes with which they are likely to be associated.

Circumstantial variables, as defined in this article, should not influence the decision as to which accounting principle (ranking of attributes and measurement methods) is preferable. Rather this decision should be made assuming that measures of the competing attributes which satisfy both feasibility and objectivity criteria are obtainable. In other words, the ranking of the attributes should be made on the intrinsic value of the attribute, not on whether an objective measure of the attribute is obtainable in all circumstances. The choice among the attributes should then be based on fundamental assumptions regarding the purposes

Exhibit 1 **EXAMPLES OF CIRCUMSTANTIAL VARIABLES IN ACCOUNTING FOR INVENTORIES**

If the preferred attribute is	These circumstantial variables may affect the feasibility of accounting methods and/or the objectivity of the accounting measures	
	General category	Specific Example
Historical acquisition cost	Unit value of inventory items	Specific identification method or method incorporating flow assumptions (FIFO)
	Prevalence of joint costs	Crude oil, beef primal cuts
Current replacement cost	Determinability of current prices of major inputs	Daily transactions and published reports on prices for major raw materials: steel, aluminum, copper
	Prevalence of joint costs	Gasoline
Net realizable value	Determinability of current sales prices	Daily transactions and published reports on prices: crude oil, aluminum ingot
	Predictability of disposal costs	Insignificant disposal costs or pattern of non-fluctuating historical disposal costs: crude oil, beef primal cuts
Discounted future value	Predictability of future sales price	Goods manufactured under contract at predetermined prices
	Predictability of future costs	Product with historical pattern of relatively constant costs

of financial statements, how they are likely to be used, and by whom. Presumably the attributes would be ranked according to their usefulness to the assumed user groups. Although circumstantial variables are not relevant to the ranking of attributes and measurement methods, they are relevant to the uniformity-flexibility controversy.

IMPLICATIONS FOR THE UNIFORMITY-FLEXIBILITY CONTROVERSY

The quotations presented at the beginning of this article suggest that specifying differences in circumstances would, at least partially, resolve the uniformity-flexibility controversy. Within the context of these quotations uniformity means identical accounting treatment except where circumstances differ.[15] Accordingly, if accounting methods or treatments could be matched with circumstances on a one-to-one basis, accountants would be able to specify the appropriate method for a company after examining the circumstances in which the company operates; and variations in accounting methods among companies which were not justified by different circumstances would be eliminated.

This line of reasoning implies that researchers should attempt to correlate circumstances with accounting methods. But this approach is fraught with difficulties. Firms differ along an infinite number of variables from the types of market in which their products are sold to management attitudes to number of employees per rest room. No multiple regression analysis could possibly include all of these variables. In addition, some variables such as management attitudes and objectives, probably do influence the choice of accounting methods,[16] even though many accountants, investors, and other users seem to prefer financial statements free from management biases. The matching of accounting methods with circumstances does not provide a rational method either by reducing the infinite set of variables to a manageable number or for identifying unacceptable "causes" of diversity.

Within the framework of this article, differences in circumstances have no significance outside the context of an accounting principle, which identifies and ranks the attributes to be measured and the measurement methods to be used. Within the context of such a principle, circumstances (that is circumstantial variables) which prevent objective measurement of the preferred attribute can be identified and given as grounds for the use of one accounting method rather than another. Until agreement exists as to a ranking of attributes and methods, the use of "differences in circumstances" to justify an accounting method can be little more than clever rhetoric.

It seems, therefore, that the Accounting Principles Board should direct its attention back to the fundamental issues concerning the objectives and uses of accounting information and strive to formulate a ranking of attributes to be meas-

[15] For an examination of this viewpoint see Weldon Powell, "Putting Uniformity in Financial Accounting Into Perspective", *Law and Contemporary Problems,* Vol. 30, Autumn 1965, pp. 677–83.

[16] Evidence exists which suggests that managements choose accounting methods which tend to have the effect of smoothing over time the incomes of their respective companies. For example, see Myron J. Gordon, Bertrand N. Horwitz and Philip T. Meyers, "Accounting Measurements and Normal Growth of the Firm" in Robert K. Jaedicke, Yuji Ijiri, and Oswald Nielsen (eds), *Research in Accounting Measurement,* American Accounting Association, 1966, pp. 221–31.

ured and a ranking of methods for measuring the attributes. To do so would at least be consistent with the earlier quoted recommendations of the AICPA Committee on Opinions of the Accounting Principles Board, specifically paragraph (c) which reads in part "... set forth the treatment to be preferred...."[17]

The phrase, "differences in circumstances", continues as a major rationalization, of both accountants and managers, for the existing diversity of accounting methods. In addition to differences in circumstances, other factors such as differences in reporting objectives or philosophies, differences in traditions (or inertia), differences in emphasis given to income tax considerations,[18] and allegiances to conflicting accounting theories, also contribute to the multiplicity of accounting methods found in practice. Until accounting principles are developed which rank the attributes to be measured and until the accounting methods for measuring the attributes are formulated and generally accepted, it will be impossible to know whether the phrase "differences in circumstances" has reference to identifiable external conditions or is merely a cloak for idiosyncratic diversity.

Summary

1. Although the phrase, "differences in circumstances", is central to the accounting profession's efforts to reduce the number of alternative accounting methods in practice, the meaning of the phrase had not been systematically explored and was ambiguous.

2. To replace "differences in circumstances" with a less cumbersome phrase and to obtain greater precision, the term, "circumstantial variables" is introduced and defined as "environmental conditions which vary among companies and which influence (1) the feasibility of accounting methods and/or (2) the objectivity of the measures resulting from applying the accounting methods".

3. If accounting principles were formulated to specify and rank the attributes to be measured and to specify and rank the accounting methods for measuring the attributes, then deviations from the preferred method for measuring the ideal attribute would be justified only when circumstantial variables cause the preferred method to be unfeasible or to produce measures of unacceptable objectivity.

4. Searching for circumstantial variables without considering accounting principles is a fruitless process which will not resolve the uniformity-flexibility controversy.

5. The Accounting Principles Board should direct its attention back to the fundamental issues concerning the objectives and uses of financial statements and strive to formulate accounting principles which specify and rank attributes and accounting measurement methods, respectively.

6. Until accounting principles which rank-order attributes and accounting methods are formulated and generally accepted, "differences in circumstances" is an empty justification for diversity of accounting methods.

---

[17] *See* the quotation which is referred to at footnote 4.

[18] Butters concluded that expected income tax saving was the major motivation for companies which adopted LIFO. He also noted, "Management inertia and ignorance have been the major reason that LIFO has not been more extensively employed". J. Keith Butters, *Effects of Taxation: Inventory Accounting and Policies*, Boston 1949, p. 90.

RELATED READINGS

These articles focus on the manifold problems of income measurement, with special emphasis on the uniformity versus flexibility controversy and the predictive ability of financial reports. An extension of the latter question, explored in the article by Morison, is the policy question of whether companies should disclose profit forecasts or even general budgetary information. Readers should also consult the Related Readings at the close of Parts 2 and 8.

A. D. Barton, "Accounting Principles, Why Uniformity?," *The Australian Accountant*, January, 1969, pp. 615–630, and comments by R. L. Mathews, pp. 630–633.

W. P. Birkett, "Accounting Inputs," *Abacus*, December, 1968, pp. 164–173. Analyzes various interpretations of transactions and other events that enter accounting records.

George S. Bissell, "A Professional Investor Looks at Earnings Forecasts," *Financial Analysts Journal*, May–June, 1972, pp. 73–78.

*R. Gene Brown, "Ethical and Other Problems in Publishing Financial Forecasts," *Financial Analysts Journal*, March–April, 1972, pp. 38–45, 86–87.

Dudley E. Browne, "Progress in Corporate Financial Reporting," *Management Accounting* (US), July, 1969, p. 7 *et seq.*

Lanny G. Chasteen, "An Empirical Study of Differences in Economic Circumstances as a Justification for Alternative Inventory Pricing Methods," *The Accounting Review*, July, 1971, pp. 504–508. A study based on a sample of 300 companies shows that significant differences in economic circumstances do not exist among companies using different inventory methods.

Almand R. Coleman, "Controversial Areas of Corporate Reporting Practices," *Financial Executive*, October, 1969, pp. 36–41. Review of eight areas of controversy.

Eugene E. Comiskey and F. A. Mlynarczyk, "Recognition of Income by Finance Companies," *The Accounting Review*, April, 1968, pp. 248–256.

W. W. Cooper, N. Dopuch, and T. F. Keller, "Budgetary Disclosure and Other Suggestions for Improving Accounting Reports," *The Accounting Review*, October, 1968, pp. 640–648.

R. Austin Daily, "The Feasibility of Reporting Forecasted Information," *The Accounting Review*, October, 1971, pp. 686–692.

Eunice M. Filter, "Accounting Practices of Major Computer Companies," *Financial Analysts Journal*, May–June, 1971, pp. 44–52. Financial analyst recasts the earnings per share of eight computer companies to conform to the accounting practices of the industry leader, IBM.

*James Finnie, "Business Income," *The Accountant's Magazine*, June, 1968, pp. 280–294; July, 1968, pp. 345–357. A comprehensive, prize-winning essay.

C. G. Gillette, E. L. Hicks, and J. W. Nicholson, "Guidelines for Recognition of Profit on Real Estate Sales," *The Arthur Young Journal*, Summer, 1971, pp. 3–15. Includes 15 hypothetical cases.

M. N. Greenball, "The Predictive-Ability Criterion: Its Relevance in Evaluating Accounting Data," *Abacus*, June, 1971, pp. 1–7. "To attempt to apply

---

* Indicates sources containing particularly rich bibliographies.

the predictive-ability criterion to accounting is to try to fit a square peg (hypothesis testing in a positive science) into a round hole (accounting, which is *not* a positive science)."

Ernest L. Hicks, "Accounting for Transactions Not at Arm's Length," *The Arthur Young Journal*, Autumn, 1970, pp. 6–11.

Thomas L. Holton and Olden J. Hoover, "The Accountant's Stand on Franchise Reporting," *World* (PMM), Summer, 1970, p. 17 et seq.; reprinted in *The New York Certified Public Accountant*, January, 1971, pp. 49–56.

Orace Johnson, "Some Reservations on the Significance of Prospective Income Data," *The Accounting Review*, July, 1968, pp. 546–548.

Donald P. Jones, "Management Freedom in Annual Reports," *Financial Executive*, August, 1971, pp. 23–26. In part, an argument for giving greater flexibility to company managements.

James J. Klink, "Mergers and Acquisitions: Their Effect on Comparability," *The Price Waterhouse Review*, Spring, 1969, pp. 50–58.

R. M. Lall, "An Enquiry into the Nature of Assets," *The New York Certified Public Accountant*, November, 1968, pp. 793–797.

T. A. Lee, "Goodwill: An Example of Will-o'-the Wisp Accounting," *Accounting and Business Research*, Autumn, 1971, pp. 318–328. Argues that companies should publish cash transaction forecasts together with the assumptions on which they are based.

Herbert F. Leisy and Robert D. Milne, "What Are Bank Earnings?," *Financial Analysts Journal*, March–April, 1968, pp. 89–94; reply by Charles R. Wolf, "Reporting Gains and Losses on Bank Securities," *Financial Analysts Journal*, January–February, 1969, pp. 86–90; and rejoinder by Leisy and Milne, *ibid.*, p. 91.

Joseph G. Louderback III, "Projectability as a Criterion for Income Determination Methods," *The Accounting Review*, April, 1971, pp. 298–305. "The projectability criterion does not articulate with the position that income is relevant to investor decisions."

Archibald E. MacKay, "Accounting for Initial Franchise Fee Revenue," *The Journal of Accountancy*, January, 1970, pp. 66–68, 70–72. An influential article on this controversial subject, having the support of the SEC. Also see Robert R. Leone, "Franchising Business Benefits and Accounting Problems," *LKHH Accountant*, Fall, 1970, pp. 10–19, which criticizes the MacKay article.

Robert K. Mautz, "An Approach to the Uniformity-Flexibility Issues in Accounting," *Financial Executive*, February, 1971, pp. 14–19. Preliminary conclusions of an FEI empirical study.

R. W. Metcalf and G. D. Welch, "Basic Accounting Theory: A Set of Three Postulates," *Management Accounting* (US), June, 1968, pp. 3–7.

Sybil C. Mobley, "Measures of Income," *The Accounting Review*, April, 1968, pp. 333–341. Reviews several concepts of income.

Thornton O'glove, "Finance Company Accounting—Variations and a Solution," *Financial Analysts Journal*, January–February, 1968, pp. 37–44.

R. A. Rayman, "An Extension of the System of Accounts: The Segregation of Funds and Value," *Journal of Accounting Research*, Spring, 1969, pp. 53–89.

———, "Accounting Reform: Standardisation, Stabilisation, or Segregation?," *Accounting and Business Research*, Autumn, 1971, pp. 300–308.

Lawrence Revsine, "Predictive Ability, Market Prices, and Operating Flows," *The Accounting Review*, July, 1971, pp. 480–489.

R. W. Schattke, "An Analysis of Accounting Principles Board Statement No. 4," *The Accounting Review*, April, 1972, pp. 233–244.

John K. Simmons and Jack Gray, "An Investigation of the Effect of Differing Accounting Frameworks on the Prediction of Net Income," *The Accounting Review*, October, 1969, pp. 757–776.

K. Fred Skousen, Robert A. Sharp, and Russell K. Tolman, "Corporate Disclosure of Budgetary Data," *The Journal of Accountancy*, May, 1972, pp. 50–57. Results of a questionnaire study of corporate executives, financial analysts, and practicing CPAs.

Howard J. Snavely and Allan H. Savage, "Clean Surplus vs. Current Operating Performance—Gaps in APB Opinion No. 9," *The New York Certified Public Accountant*, February, 1970, pp. 124–129.

George J. Staubus, "An Analysis of APB Statement No. 4," *The Journal of Accountancy*, February, 1972, pp. 36–43.

Robert R. Sterling and Richard E. Flaherty, "The Role of Liquidity in Exchange Valuation," *The Accounting Review*, July, 1971, pp. 441–456.

Edward L. Summers, "Observation of Effects of Using Alternative Reporting Practices," *The Accounting Review*, April, 1968, pp. 257–265. Accounting diversity as shown by the financial statements of 23 United States air line companies.

Iain W. Symon, "Business Income: Some Reflections on Its Principles and Measurement," *The Accountant's Magazine*, August, 1968, pp. 414–426.

A. Carl Tietjen, "Financial Reporting Responsibilities," *The Price Waterhouse Review*, Spring, 1970, pp. 6–9; reprinted in *The Journal of Accountancy*, January, 1971, pp. 69–73. Proposes an approach to the diversity problem in accounting by reliance more on professional standards than on detailed techniques.

Lauren M. Walker, Gerhard G. Mueller, and Fawzi G. Dimian, "Significant Events in the Development of the Realisation Concept in the United States," *The Accountant's Magazine*, August, 1970, pp. 357–360.

Don Wharton, "Accounting & Reporting for Companies in the Development Stage," *The Arthur Young Journal*, Summer, 1970, pp. 3–15.

What is Profit?, papers presented at the Summer Course, Churchill College, Cambridge, Sept. 16–20, 1970 (London: The Institute of Chartered Accountants in England and Wales), 196 pp. Among the authors and panelists are practicing accountants from England and the United States, a financial journalist, and a security analyst.

Theodore L. Wilkinson, "Designing an International Companies Act," *The Price Waterhouse Review*, Winter, 1969, pp. 6–14. Discusses several basic accounting concepts in the face of international diversity.

Arthur R. Wyatt, "Comparability in Accounting," *Management Accounting* (US), July, 1969, pp. 10–14.

PART 4

VALUATION OF SHORT-LIVED "TANGIBLE" COST FACTORS

Conventional accounting is predicated on the belief that income is best measured by apportioning the entity's continuous stream of activities into a series of overlapping cash cycles. Cash is received from investors or lenders and is used to acquire productive resources. These resources, in turn, are employed to produce goods or services which are eventually sold, cash being ultimately received from customers. The resulting net increase in cash, modified by an arbitrary allocation of the cost of long-term resources, is labeled as profit or income for the fiscal period in which the cash cycle reaches its final phase.

The measurement of profit by reference to the rotation of cash has been the object of a rising crescendo of criticism in the last few decades. Initially, the complaint was that conventional accounting failed to adjust for the changing purchasing power of the monetary unit. William A. Paton, Henry W. Sweeney, and Ralph C. Jones were among those who championed this cause. But in more recent years, writers have urged that the historical cost/revenue realization convention be supplanted by an approach that recognizes changes in current value. Historical cost and current value have been contenders for many years, and accounting practice has come to reflect a gradual infiltration of current-value thinking in the guise of historical cost. More than forty-five years ago, a perceptive observer of accounting practice said,

> The trouble is that in the balance sheet as we know it today there is a constant struggle between two basic ideas ... which are practicably incompatible, and we veer from one to the other. The first idea is that the balance sheet

should show the distribution of, or physical embodiment of, a certain amount of capital that has been put into the business—it should show its destination—that the balance sheet should be a faithful record of what has happened to it; but that is considerably modified from time to time by the other basic idea that the balance sheet should show what the business really is, what the assets are, what they are worth, and what "going value" it has—what it is worth and so on. These two ideas are contending for the mastery, and whereas the first still stands paramount, the tendency of the last few years has been to modify it by introducing the other.[1]

As testimony either to the prescience of the author or to the slowness with which change occurs in accounting, much the same can be said today. Accounting has become a half-breed, containing elements of both historical cost and current value. The elements of current value, however, are sometimes identified as *genus* historical cost. The adoption of LIFO by companies experiencing a secular movement in the prices of their inventoried goods would seem to be in point. In order to match approximately current costs against current revenues in the income statement, the residue in the balance sheet becomes a motley assortment of outdated figures. There is a view among accountants that the *relevance* of the balance sheet can be sacrificed to that of the income statement, as if the information content in both financial statements were not pertinent to the decision needs of users. We thus have the paradoxical situation in which accountants talk of the income statement as being the "more important" of the two financial statements, as if earning power could be assessed without knowing something of the magnitude of resources employed to generate the earnings.

In the opening article in this part, Charles E. Johnson adopts the view that accounting income is based on a "recovery of monetary investment" concept of income. He regards the monetary outlay as a reasonable representation of asset value prior to the moment of realization. In his opinion, there are two major reference points available to the accountant for testing the logic of alternative "flow" assumptions. One is that the asset represents service potential to the firm. The other is the assumption that the firm "is as well off when it has recovered—in some sense—its past monetary investment." While these statements are admittedly broad and not definitive, they are sufficient, in Johnson's view, to make it unnecessary to accept *any* arbitrary amortization or write-off of asset costs.

In spite of Johnson's belief about the nature of accounting, there is an increasing number of accountants who argue that inventory should be valued at other than historical cost. F. K. Wright builds a case for an opportunity-cost analysis styled as the "value of the goods to the firm." A choice would be made between replacement cost and realizable value in view of demand and supply factors and the relative levels of replacement cost and realizable value. This suggestion is discussed further by Stamp in Part 8 (B).

Notwithstanding Johnson's view that there is a rational ground for choosing among alternative procedures of cost allocation, accountants continue to disagree on how the cost associated with inventories should be allocated. Each method of allocation assumes a different flow of *costs* through the enterprise. That a last-in, first-out (LIFO) flow of *goods* is demonstrably invalid for a particular enterprise

---

[1] Sir Josiah Stamp, "Accountants' Problems of To-day: An Outsider's Reflections," *The Accountant*, Oct. 31, 1925, pp. 685–686.

is of no concern to the advocates of LIFO. The larger question of matching dollars of current purchasing power against revenue dollars of roughly the same purchasing power is said to be sufficient reason for LIFO, for this procedure will allot the cost of the most recent purchases—whether in fact the goods were sold or not—to the income statement. It is admitted by most LIFO advocates that the resulting balance-sheet figure for inventory is archaic, but H. T. McAnly, among others, prescribes a remedy [Part 4 (B)].

LIFO is a procedure that originated in the United States and is usually found only in American financial statements. Its widespread use in the United States springs from its acceptability for federal income tax reporting, an instance of accounting principles being affected profoundly by income tax legislation.

Is LIFO an attempt at "income smoothing" (to use Hepworth's term)? Or is it an appropriate method of accounting for inventoriable costs in periods of changing prices? Initially, LIFO was advocated by corporations that were subject to sharp cyclical swings in materials' prices. Today, corporations that are in much more stable markets also employ LIFO. Is LIFO appropriate to both situations? A confrontation of the two divergent philosophies of the place of LIFO is found in the Moonitz and McAnly articles.

Maurice Moonitz reviews the developments leading up to the acceptance of LIFO as an inventory-pricing technique. He then examines the rationales of LIFO, both pro and con. He finds that LIFO does not do what is claimed for it and that the method is internally inconsistent. McAnly argues in rebuttal that LIFO does state income realistically and that it is applicable to any industry. These two articles represent the conflicting views of the theoretician and the practitioner. On the one hand there is a search for theoretical validity and consistency, and on the other there is a plea that the effect on income is the important consideration. A thorough understanding of both sides of the controversy is necessary for a full appraisal of LIFO.

Aside from the argument over cost flow, another controversy concerns the composition of inventory cost. Should fixed costs, those that appear to be related more to the expiration of time than to actual production, be included in the cost of inventory or be considered as an expense of the period in which the plant capacity is available? As John R. E. Parker points out, the central issue is the proper matching of revenues and expired costs. Should all factory-related costs, other than inefficient expenditures, be eventually assigned to the inventory of work in process or finished goods, or should only the variable costs be associated with the inventory?

Howard Greer sees three possibilities (p. 295) which could be considered:

1. Write off all fixed charges (direct costing).
2. Include all fixed charges in product cost (absorption costing).
3. Include normal fixed charges in product cost and write off any excess due to subnormal production (standard costing).

Greer draws attention to the difficulty of satisfactorily dividing costs into fixed and variable classifications. He argues that a standard cost of the produced article, including an apportionment of fixed costs, would be the most useful type of information for most purposes.

A. THE VALUATION PROBLEM: GENERALLY

CHARLES E. JOHNSON

CHARLES E. JOHNSON (1920–1969), B.B.A. 42, M.B.A. 48, Ph.D. 52 Minnesota; CPA. Major publications: *Accounting: The Basis of Business Decisions* (with Meigs, 1962 and 1967), *Intermediate Accounting* (with Meigs and Keller, 1963; with Meigs, Keller, and Mosich, 1968), *Advanced Accounting* (with Meigs and Keller, 1966), *Financial Accounting* (with Meigs and Mosich, 1970). Was a frequent contributor to *The Accounting Review* and other journals.

Joined the accounting faculty of the University of Oregon in 1952. He became dean of the College of Liberal Arts in 1963 and was acting president of the university from 1968 until his death.

Served as vice-president of the American Accounting Association, 1960.

INVENTORY VALUATION: THE ACCOUNTANT'S ACHILLES HEEL*

CHARLES E. JOHNSON

Most of the everyday problems which plague practicing accountants in the realm of inventory accounting are somewhat divorced from the theory of inventory valuation and its inevitable relationship to income determination. With the practical inventory problems of verification, accountability, and control, you as practitioners are far more familiar than am I, and I shall not presume to burden you

* This paper was given at the Second Northwest Graduate Accounting Study Conference sponsored by the Washington Society of Certified Public Accountants, the School of Business Administration of the University of Washington, and the American Institute of Accountants, held at Harrison Hot Springs, September 24–26, 1953.

SOURCE: From *The Accounting Review*, Vol. XXIX, No. 1 (January, 1954), pp. 15–26. Reprinted by permission of the American Accounting Association.

this morning with any ivory tower advice on the subject. Instead I should like to entice you to stand back and take a bird's-eye look at some questions currently at issue in the field of inventory valuation—and in particular to look at them in their perspective against the background of some fundamental theoretical concepts in accounting.

Any accountant worth his salt has learned long ago to shy away from the word "value." The "value" of something implies its worth, and you don't have to be a timid soul to shudder at the insuperable problems which surround an attempt to determine the worth of anything.

In part this is because value, like beauty, lies in the eyes of the beholder. Examine the horrible abstract painting which adorns a friend's living room and then note the obvious satisfaction he gets from owning it. Remind yourselves of the times you have seen a seller and a buyer walk away from a transaction—each feeling that he has stolen the other blind.

In the business world, however, this individualistic viewpoint plays a lesser role in making value a treacherous concept than does the fact that determining the money-worth of an asset- its value—is essentially a speculation about the future. This is a lesson you all learned early in your training or experience—that essentially the monetary value of any productive asset is the present discounted worth of the *future* net returns to be expected from its use. Cost, replacement cost, physical quantities, operating characteristics—all are secondary to a careful, well reasoned forecast of future earning power.

Looking at the asset side of a balance sheet, we are reminded that in this sense the accountant does come pretty close to valuing some assets. Cash, for example, causes us almost no trouble, given a confidence in the banking system. We view receivables clearly as the present right to receive money at some future date, after discounting the ability of some debtors to pay. We could come even closer to the correct value of receivables were we to apply a discount factor to allow for the fact that $1 due in 30 days is not now worth $1, and if we adjusted for prospective shrinkage through the taking of sales discounts. In most cases these factors are not material, and we are thus justified in saying that accountants *value* receivables.

Turn now to the question of inventories—product, partially completed product, raw materials, and supplies—all awaiting the ultimate fruition of the sales transaction. Value theory tells us that such inventories must be worth the present discounted amount of the net receipts which will ultimately flow into the business as a result of their sale. Roughly, this is what Accounting Research Bulletin #29 [a] refers to as "net realizable value," but it is discussed only as one element of the "lower of cost or market" rule. Accountants do not normally "value" inventories on a net realizable basis. Why?

The barrier which stands between value theory and the accounting treatment of inventories is essentially the *realization* convention. Let's take a brief look at just what is involved in this concept of realization. Realization, as I understand it, is a set of rules devised as a guide in determining when the *quality* of the evidence with respect to prospective net revenues is such that they may be directly valued as an element of the firm's financial position. In support of this position it is argued that the primary operational problem facing a firm holding an inventory of goods

---

[a] Bulletin No. 29 was superseded (with no major change in substance) by Chapter 4 of Accounting Research Bulletin No. 43 (in 1953). [Eds.]

is to find a buyer at an acceptable price. The mere existence of an inventory and of past transactions is thus not considered good enough evidence to warrant estimating the ultimate net selling price and discounting that back to an inventory value—there are too many slips 'twixt the cup and the lip. The accountant's position is to remain neutral with respect to these prospects until better evidence is available. Now, when a sale takes place, or where production under a fixed contract occurs, or where production of goods which sell on an organized market at given prices is completed—in all these cases the accountant is willing to grant that the evidence is satisfactory. Uncertainty has been reduced to a point where the value of the prospect of future net receipts warrants recognition as an asset on the records. To put it another way—these events are deemed to constitute realization.

Now if the rule is to postpone valuing inventories until realization takes place (and they are transformed in essence into receivables), what course do accountants follow in the meantime? The answer might be that we establish a *valuation* for inventories. This, you say, is the academic mind playing with words. I think the distinction between value and valuation is, however, a useful one. By valuation I mean only that a useful relationship has been established between the monetary unit and some element of property or property rights. Valuation in this context must be judged primarily on the basis of its usefulness—if it serves well the purpose for which it is intended, and everyone understands that purpose, it is a useful valuation. The relationship between physical inventories and the monetary outlay necessary to bring them to their present status is a useful valuation, to be compared with a later selling price to establish a gain or loss. If the selling price turns out to be greater than expected, it may also be useful to determine that a speculative price gain has been realized as well as the normal operating margin. Thus a whole series of valuations may be used in accounting for economic events to furnish information to those concerned. The choice among methods of *valuation* rests not on any proof of the correctness of one valuation over another—but on questions of logic, usefulness, and measurability.

This gives us only a highly subjective basis for judging various methods of inventory valuation. If we wish to estimate what inventories are worth—it seems evident that the best evidence is the discounted estimated future net selling price. If we agree not to do this until realization occurs, then the primary issue must be the purpose to be served by inventory valuation. The answer seems evident: we are interested in attaching a valuation to inventories in order to determine periodic realized monetary income—and we must then ask ourselves, what do we mean by income?

An English economist, J. R. Hicks, published in 1946 a highly theoretical treatise called *Value and Capital*.[1] He would no doubt have been surprised had he known that his discussion therein of the nature of income would receive a great deal of attention by accountants and others who were giving renewed attention to various possible concepts of business income. No doubt you have all stumbled across Hicks' definition of income in the recent literature. As applied to a business enterprise it runs something like this: *Business income is the maximum amount a company could distribute during a given period of time and remain as well off at the end of that period as at the beginning.*

Now, that definition is not operational in the sense that if we were all to agree

[1] Second Edition (London: Oxford University Press, 1946).

upon it this would solve all our problems in income determination. I think as a definition it is useful because it expresses the essence of what is meant by business income. The element with which I am particularly concerned here, however, is this basic assumption that the process of arriving at income involves determining whether the business unit at the end of any period is better off, worse off, or as well off as at the beginning. Note that the definition does not say—"The maximum amount the firm could distribute without forgoing expansion, selling assets, or borrowing money. Merely could dispose of and remain as well off—in a comparable position."

There are, of course, many different meanings which could be attached to the phrase "as well off"—each involves essentially a different concept of income—but we are here concerned with the meaning inherent in the *accounting* concept of income.

Accounting income is based on what I would call a "recovery of monetary investment" concept of income. The income earning activities of a business are viewed as a series of overlapping investment and realization cycles in which available funds are committed by management in the expectation of realizing future net receipts having a present value equal to or greater than the outlay. The success of these expectations is tested periodically by comparing realized receipts with that portion of the past investment which is deemed to be related thereto. Those investments which have not reached fruition are carried forward from one period to the next to be tested for recovery against future revenues. And—a firm is generally considered as well off as before when it has recovered its monetary investment in any particular turnover of assets.

The major conceptual weakness of this approach to income is that there exists no provable theoretical basis for determining the portion of any given investment which has expired during any period. Strictly speaking the revenues of any period are a joint product of the entire resources of the firm—and there is thus no immutable principle which may be applied in determining what portion of any given revenue dollar represents a recovery of past investment and what portion is realized gain.

This does not mean that we must accept *any* arbitrary write-off of past investments. There are two major reference points available for testing the logic and usefulness of various "flow" assumptions. The first is the fact that the essence of any asset is that it represents a future service potential. Every business expenditure presumably results in the acquisition of some useful service. If at any point in time some portion of this service remains as a source of future advantage to the business, the monetary outlay involved in its acquisition, it would appear, should be a reasonable representation of the asset which exists, prior to realization. The second reference point is this underlying assumption that the firm is as well off when it has recovered—in some sense—its past monetary investment. There is no point to matching revenues and costs in a vacuum—these points of reference constitute the basis for a reasoned preference for one method over another.

All this is pretty fundamental. At the risk of belaboring the obvious, I have been trying to make the point that questions of inventory valuation go back ultimately to some very basic assumptions behind the accounting process.

In the time remaining I should like to examine, in the light of the groundwork just laid, two currently significant problems in the area of inventory valuation—first the variable cost assumption which has been given a great deal of recent attention under the title of "direct costing"; and secondly, the LIFO assumption in inventory pricing, which is once more in the spotlight as a result of current attempts to gain acceptance for "lower of LIFO cost or market" for tax purposes.

VARIABLE COSTING

The term "direct costing" is actually a misnomer—"variable costing" would be a more accurate and descriptive name for the idea. But, as is the case with many pieces of terminology, an ill-fitting handle originally attached by Jonathan Harris in 1936 has somehow stuck. The idea of distinguishing between fixed and variable costs is not a new one. Professor Dohr claimed, in a recent *Journal of Accountancy* article, to have discussed the idea in a 1924 edition of his text, and economists would probably claim much earlier antecedents. The essence of the system being referred to currently as "direct costing" is that this distinction between fixed and variable costs should be built into the accounting records. The system itself is quite simple—it goes something like this:

All cost and expense accounts are divided into their two elements: those which are fixed or "period" costs and those which vary directly with changes in volume of output or operations, i.e. variable costs. This distinction is maintained in the records, and only variable costs are assigned to the product and carried through the various inventory accounts—work in process, finished product, and eventually into cost of sales. The difference between Sales and "direct" cost of sales for any period is labeled "marginal income," which replaces gross profit on the income statement. (The same classification between fixed and variable may be maintained in selling and administrative expenses and a marginal income computed after the variable portion of such costs is deducted.)

From marginal income so computed is deducted fixed costs of operations to arrive at operating income. The net effect is that all fixed costs are charged off in the period in which they are incurred, as a function of time rather than as a function of sales volume or revenues.

It should be carefully noted that, in theory at least, the distinction between fixed and variable costs differs from the distinction between *direct* and *indirect* costs. Direct costs, defined as those costs which may be associated directly with a given product or process, will be largely variable, but not entirely. There are important costs directly and solely attributable to the output of a particular product or process which are *fixed* within wide ranges of volume of operation. Likewise there are numerous elements of indirect cost which change with variations in volume over fairly narrow ranges of operation. It must be remembered that the use of direct costing involves the assumption that it is possible to distinguish objectively from among both direct and indirect costs, those costs which are fixed and those which are variable—as a function of *volume of operation*.

The advantages claimed for such a method of costing are numerous. Cost-volume-profit relationship data needed by management for profit planning are readily available from the accounts. Marginal income figures facilitate the relative appraisal of products, territories, and departments. Variable costing ties in nicely with standard cost systems and flexible budgets. In general, the effect on income will be to reduce reported income during periods when physical inventories are being increased (i.e. production is outrunning sales) and to increase income during periods when physical inventories are being depleted (i.e. sales are outrunning production)—this reduction and increase being in comparison with the effect of "*absorption costing,*" the term now given to conventional costing methods.

In considering variable costing in its relationship to inventory valuation and thus to income determination I should like to focus attention on two points. The first is the problem of establishing some reasonably objective meaning of the concepts of fixed and variable. The separation of all costs into their fixed and variable elements is not as simple and straightforward a task as it sounds. Depreciation, for example, when charged on a straightline basis appears to be a fixed charge; yet for the most part only the obsolescence element of depreciation is truly fixed. With modern methods of "mothballing" almost the entire wear and tear element of depreciation may well be considered variable. In some industries wear and tear may be a negligible factor in useful life, in others it will be highly significant. On the other hand restrictions in current wage contracts make large portions of direct labor cost fixed in nature. If the guaranteed annual wage becomes widespread, a substantial portion of direct labor cost may in effect become a fixed charge which does not vary with volume. Are these costs to be excluded from inventory?

Some consistent assumption must be made as to the range of volume variation within which the fixed and variable assumption is framed. In the range from 0–100% of capacity, only standby costs are truly fixed. On the other hand in the 80–100% range, a large number of salary and service department costs become essentially fixed. It is obvious that if each firm makes different assumptions in this respect the results will vary widely. Another element for decision is the time factor. What is fixed with respect to monthly variations in volume may be variable with respect to annual volume variations.

Workable assumptions are being made on these points for internal accounting today, and any assumption which satisfies management is satisfactory for managerial accounting. In order to accept the results for corporate reporting, however, the public accountant must be satisfied that some standard can be derived which can be objectively verified and consistently applied. If not we may find we are approaching the "*sayso*" inventory method—inventories are what the company says they are.

There remains the question whether variable costing produces meaningful and useful financial statements for the use of outsiders. This question must ultimately revolve around the relationship between inventory valuation and income determination—and we are back to the reference points described earlier in this discussion.

Absorption costing involves the assumption that all cost traceable to the existence of inventoriable goods and services should be allocated thereto and carried forward as a representation of the future services inherent in its ownership. Variable costing involves the assumption that only those costs which vary with volume shall be carried forward. This requires the assumption that period costs are associated entirely with the passage of time and not with the existence of inventories; i.e. fixed costs are somehow the cost of providing production facilities of a given capacity and thus unrelated to the amount of product turned out. The corollary assumption is that the firm must recover these fixed costs from the revenues of any period before it is better off—or conversely that a failure to recover them makes the firm worse off, without regard to the amount of saleable product which is on hand at the end of any given period.

This, it seems to me is regression not progression in inventory valuation. If the essence of an asset is that it represents service potential to the company, there is no logical reason which can be deduced why that service potential is best or even adequately represented by only that portion of the past investment which will vary with volume of output. Were that particular assumption to become the basis for the decision between capital expenditure and revenue charge, we should approach the cash basis of accounting in a hurry. What we are asked to do, it would seem, is to transfer what is a highly desirable idea from one basic purpose to another. As a managerial device I have nothing but acclaim for variable costing. It can be devised to fit whatever assumptions management cares to make—and these assumptions not only can but perhaps should be inconsistent from year to year as the problems facing management change. For most managerial decisions are matters of alternatives, and the fixed costs which have a tendency to be irrelevant to such decisions change with the alternative, while different kinds of variable costs come into the ascendency. In reporting progress over time however we should keep our methods of asset valuation firmly rooted in the idea that an asset represents a future service potential and that a firm which has invested in such future services is not worse off for having done so as long the prospect exists that net realizable receipts will exceed that investment.

LIFO

Now let's turn to a method of inventory valuation designed to cope, not with fixed and variable costs, but with changing prices. LIFO, which is essentially a variation on the older base-stock method of inventory accounting, has been rationalized under a whole series of arguments in the past, and we should perhaps first clear away the deadwood to get down to current issues.

The idea of LIFO as some approximation to the actual flow of inventories from stock into production or sales has long since been abandoned. The idea that the investment in inventories is somehow irrevocably fixed is inconsistent with its classification as a current asset on the balance sheet. In tax legislation dealing with the "involuntary liquidation" of inventories during 1941–47 it was assumed that taxpayers could replace such liquidated inventory before the end of 1952—a not unreasonable presumption. Yet in the June, 1953 *Taxes*, Ray Hoffman of Price Waterhouse points out "taxpayers have not only been unable to obtain goods to replace *wartime* liquidations but have suffered further involuntary liquidations."[2] The ability to maintain an expanded volume of business while remaining in a state of "involuntarily liquidated inventories" would seem to indicate that the so-called fixed quantity of inventory necessary for operations is a very elastic concept, and certainly bears no relation to the quantity of inventories on hand at LIFO adoption date.

The idea that LIFO is some sort of evolution away from the use of historical costs may appear at first glance plausible, since under "dollar value" LIFO the result may be to price the inventory at costs which were never in fact actually incurred by the firm. Nevertheless LIFO *is* a *cost* method, in the sense that it involves an allocation of the actual past investment in goods and services between inventories and cost of sales—no more and no less than actual monetary outlay is allocated.

[2] R. A. Hoffman, "Tax Shortcomings of the LIFO Provisions," *Taxes*, June, 1953, p. 407.

A more persistent line of argument is that LIFO is somehow a part of an evolutionary movement from monetary income to *real* income. This argument has a distinct advantage in that it puts your adversary on the defensive—if *you* are dealing with reality, *he* must be arguing for something unreal and non-genuine.

In examining this argument, however, we must remind ourselves that the distinction between monetary and real is a distinction between a measuring unit and what is being measured. Changes in the general level of prices are evidence of changes in the size of the measuring unit—the value of money—and it is *this* which produces the divergence between *monetary* and *real*. Looked at in these terms it seems clear that LIFO has no strong claim to reality. In the first place LIFO results in neutralizing only those price changes affecting some given quantity of inventory which happened coincidentally to be on hand at the time the adoption was made. But even more important—those who argue for LIFO as reality fall into the well populated pitfall of confusing *any and all* price changes with changes in the *general* price level. To say that a company should price its 1953 inventories at 1938 prices because they represent approximately the same physical quantities and therefore the company is no better or worse off than before, ignores the possibility that this collection of goods almost certainly has a different significance in the economy in 1953 than in 1938. The divergence in the movement of *specific* prices in relation to the over-all average is a well known phenomenon. If the price of copper has tripled while the general level of prices has doubled, something has happened to the significance of copper in the economy. To ignore this possibility is like telling the fellow who owned a uranium mine in 1929 and still has it today that his position has not changed and therefore he is no better off in "real" terms. Something may have happened to uranium in the meantime!

Take a close look at this inherent assumption behind the decision to freeze prices as of LIFO adoption date, and you begin to see that the argument that LIFO is *realistic* has some gaping holes in it. Fortunately, many respected authorities have abandoned it.

That leaves two major strongholds left for supporters of LIFO. The first is a highly practical one. If adopted at the right time and under certain conditions the use of LIFO will almost certainly reduce total income taxes paid over a period of time. The possibility of reducing *property* taxes also exists. If an unsophisticated assessor grabs for book values, the LIFO user may find an extra incentive for its use when he examines his property tax bill. The only answer to this, I suppose, is educating tax assessors.

In advising businesses within the present structure of our tax laws the accountant is derelict in his duty if he does not advise his clients to use LIFO whenever conditions are such that it will produce a probable tax advantage. Since at present the law requires that tax-LIFO must likewise be used in corporate reporting this automatically puts LIFO on the books. Arthur Cannon has effectively battered one-half of this position by pointing out that questions of equity and governmental fiscal policy which govern taxable income have no counterpart in questions of business accounting, and he therefore urged a clearer delineation between taxable and business income.[3] If the inference is drawn from this, however, that the solution then is to *remove* the requirement that tax-LIFO must be accom-

---

[3] A. M. Cannon, "Tax Pressures on Accounting Principles and Accountants' Independence," *The Accounting Review*, October, 1952, p. 423.

panied by the use of book-LIFO, it should be pointed out that arguments for the use of LIFO for *tax purposes alone* are weak.

Several recent studies on the problem of business taxation have reached the conclusion that LIFO as a tax device is undesirable.[4] I am not going to speculate as to how many staunch LIFO advocates would fall by the wayside were its use denied for tax purposes. Nor do I have time to fully develop the position that it *should* be denied. Briefly the conclusion rests on two major considerations. The first is intertaxpayer equity. LIFO is not a device to reduce the total tax load—therefore it must necessarily shift the burden from one class of taxpayers to another. Since some businesses and most individuals have no compensating device to reduce taxes in times of rising prices, it appears inequitable to allow such a device to one group of taxpayers. To quote Moonitz on this point "the accounting profession should be wary, now and in the future, of new 'principles' of accounting whose major objective is to shift the burden of income tax from one group of clients to another."[5]

But an even stronger argument against LIFO for tax purposes is that its use produces results which are at odds with the presumed desirability of counter cyclical fiscal policy. The desirability of increasing the tax load and running a government surplus during periods of prosperity and inflation, and conversely decreasing the tax load promptly and incurring deficits in periods of deflation and recession is, I think, well agreed upon in principle, however inept we have been in putting it into practice. The use of LIFO operates in the *opposite* direction—by decreasing taxable income in periods of rising prices and increasing taxable income in periods of declining prices. Thus it may well be argued that as professional advisors we should inform clients of the tax advantages inherent in the use of the LIFO device; but as well informed citizens, accountants should take the lead in opposing that particular element of the tax law.

Instead through our official representatives we find ourselves urging the adoption of lower of LIFO cost or market for tax purposes.

It is interesting to note the line of argument being used. In the very nature of the proposition it is possible to transfer the debate away from the merits of LIFO as good or bad tax policy and to base the case on questions of *equity*. Some companies were able to adopt LIFO at a low point in the price cycle, while others through legal barriers, lack of foresight, or pure inertia failed to do so. Now these companies are barred from getting on the bandwagon by the thought that if prices fall below the LIFO inventory price, such price losses cannot be deducted under present rulings.

At the time the original extension of the use of LIFO was being argued before Congress there were those who said that its supporters would never face the logic of their arguments when prices turned downward. They may now wear a satisfied "I told you so" smirk—but they've been outsmarted. The inevitable retreat in the face of the implications of falling prices is being handled with tactical genius. Instead of retreating over the terrain by which they advanced the beleaguered

---

[4] Richard Goode, *The Corporation Income Tax* (New York: John Wiley & Sons, 1951), p. 171. E. C. Brown, *Effects of Taxation: Depreciation Adjustments for Price Changes,*" (Boston: Division of Research, Harvard Graduate School of Business Administration, 1952). "The equity considerations for LIFO are nearly the same as for replacement-cost depreciation" (p. 76). "Our general conclusions are that historic-cost depreciation is more desirable than replacement-cost depreciation for tax determination" (p. 17).

[5] M. Moonitz, "The Case against LIFO," *Journal of Accountancy*, June, 1953, p. 687.

advocates of LIFO are being flown out over the ruins of their arguments in an equity helicopter.

In my opinion the real solution to the lower of LIFO cost or market argument is to eliminate the LIFO device for everyone for tax purposes. I have no real hope that this will be done—I'm merely exercising my inalienable right to fight a hopeless rear guard action. This is one of the ever present dangers facing program chairmen—whenever you give a number of people a platform, one darned fool among them is almost certain to start exercising his inalienable rights.

To those who argue for LIFO as a matter of accounting principle without regard to tax questions—the final stronghold is the question of *realization*.

This was the cornerstone of Mr. McAnly's case for LIFO in a recent issue of *The Journal of Accountancy*.[6] I think I state his position fairly, if briefly, as follows: LIFO is a device to keep unrealized income out of the accounts. As prices rise it costs more to maintain the same inventory of goods on hand. To the extent that funds are used for this purpose they do not represent realized income, for "certainly no realized profit *or loss* results from mere fluctuations in the value of things we must continue to own in order to be a going concern." Because under LIFO we do not recognize income to the extent it is represented by a gain in inventory prices, we thus do not have to report a loss when it is represented by a fall in inventory prices. Thus LIFO stabilizes earnings as they should be. Anyone who can't see this doesn't understand the realization principle in accounting.

Let's examine this reasoning in the case of a price decline. The firm has made a commitment in inventory at $1 a unit, let us say, expecting to sell for $2. Current cost is 60¢ and the selling price has fallen to $1.20. Following through on Mr. McAnly's argument, the inventory should be carried at $1 rather than at 60¢ since this decline in the investment in inventory is an unrealized loss. The firm must always carry this basic investment in inventory—which it can buy now for 60¢ per unit. Therefore the difference between its original investment ($1) and current cost (60¢), or 40¢ is freely available as disposable income without the necessity of reducing the scale of operations.

If this argument sounds somehow strange it is because I have deliberately reversed its usual direction—the case of rising prices. But if gains which must be reinvested in inventories are unrealized, it follows that losses which need not be reinvested in inventory are likewise unrealized. And if the balance sheet inventory figure is to be a meaningless residual incapable of interpretation, there seems no reason why it cannot as well be meaninglessly high as meaninglessly low. And if the problem can be solved by showing current cost parenthetically on the balance sheet, this seems as true if current cost is *below* LIFO cost as above. Furthermore there is no good reason in logic why LIFO for accounting purposes should not be adopted at the top of the price cycle as at the bottom. Inventory price losses will then not be reported and this will relieve the company of the necessity of reporting inventory price gains when they occur. In past history there is more support for the statement that pricewise what goes down must come up than for the converse that what goes up must come down—the trend of prices throughout history has been in an upward direction.

If proponents of LIFO would argue along these lines, I would still not be won over, but I would have a great deal more respect for their position as a valid differ-

[6] H. T. McAnly, "The Case for LIFO," *Journal of Accountancy*, June, 1953, p. 691.

ence of opinion as to whether *earned* income or *disposable* income should be used in business reporting. Looked at from this direction, however, the argument loses much of its flavor. Mr. McAnly in particular abandons this unpalatable hot (if not burned) potato and moves over to sample the equity argument for dessert. When prices decline, he argues, it is inequitable to deprive the firm of a deduction for these unrealized losses.

The basic flaw, in all this, it seems to me, is the assumption that we can produce *meaningless* balance sheets and *meaningful* income statements at the same time. One of the motivations behind the development of accrual and inventory accounting was to get away from the idea of income as a disposable cash balance —yet we are again and again, in the name of progress, referred back to this idea that if a dollar of revenues must be reinvested in more valuable assets it somehow should be removed from realized monetary income.

Let's start with the premise that the most recent costs are the most relevant *cost* figures which can be attached to any given collection of goods and services on the balance sheet, until such time as evidence that a reasonably certain sum of money will be realized from their disposal warrants revaluation and recognition of income or loss.

Now what is the effect of price changes on the results which will follow in the income statement? First off we should recognize that because of the time lag between an investment in resources and their ultimate disposal a business is always in a position to gain from a rise in prices and suffer from a fall, unless this risk can be hedged. For most firms there exists no future market through which any substantial hedge can be made. Now if prices do in fact change between the time the commitment is made and the time that the ultimate sale restores the liquidity of the original investment in inventories, the monetary margin between cost and selling price will be composed of two elements: An operating margin consisting of the difference between current cost and current selling price, and a price gain or loss consisting of the difference between actual costs and current costs—i.e. costs as they are at the time the sale takes place.

I reject the assumption that this price gain or loss is not realized, since once the firm's liquidity is restored any new commitment in inventory must be made primarily because management expects net realizable value to be equal to or greater than cost. The concept of periodic realization through turnover seems to me a more useful one than the assumption of a fixed dollar investment to be congealed at some nominal figure picked out of the past, largely by accident, providing it is low enough.

But it may well be that it would be useful to disclose separately these two elements of monetary profit—the operating margin and the price gain or loss. A proforma statement illustrating how such a separation might be presented (not only for inventories but for all elements of operating cost) is shown in Exhibit I. This is not a new idea—it has been in the literature for some time—but I think this is a good time to give it serious consideration.

Such a statement will show that during rising prices most firms will make an operating gain and a price gain. During price declines the operating gain will be offset to some extent by a price loss. Whether these price gains and losses will offset each other over the long run thus remains clearly to be seen by all who read financial statements. The management which shows foresight in adjusting its position to the vicissitudes of the price cycle will receive their credit when it is evident that price gains are maximized and price losses minimized. But even if it is shown that price gains and losses tend to cancel out in the long run, this does not warrant a failure to disclose them. Corporations may go on forever but the outsider's interest in their financial affairs is often ephemeral. Persons who read financial statements have a right to information concerning the impact of *all current* operating conditions on the corporation's position.

Exhibit I AN ILLUSTRATION OF THE SEPARATION OF "OPERATING MARGIN" FROM PRICE GAINS AND LOSSES

Statement of Operations
Year Ended December 31, 19XX

Total Revenues		
Sales (Net of Sales Discounts, $XX; Sales Returns & Allowances, $XX)		$XXX
Miscellaneous Revenues		XXX
Interest Earned		XXX
Total Revenues		$XXX
Contemporaneous Costs (Actual Goods & Services Used Stated at Current Period's Prices):		
Materials and Supplies		$XXX
Employees' Compensation Including Contributions Toward Retirement, Unemployment & Accident Insurance		XXX
Depreciation		XXX
Purchased Services		XXX
Taxes Other Than Income		XXX
Interest on Borrowed Funds		XXX
Total Contemporaneous Costs		$XXX
Current Operating Margin		$XXX
Estimated Monetary Gain or Loss Due to Price Changes		
Excess of Contemporaneous Costs Over Actual Costs		
Depreciation	$XXX	
Purchased Services	XXX	
Excess of Actual Costs Over Contemporaneous Costs		
Materials and Supplies	(XXX)	
Add Net Price Gain		XXX
Net Income Before Taxes		$XXX
Deduct Taxes on Income		XXX
Net Income for the Year		$XXX
Deduct: Dividends to Preferred Shareholders	$XXX	
Dividends to Common Shareholders	XXX	XXX
Amount of This Year's Income Retained in Business		$XXX
Balance of Retained Income at Jan. 1, 19XX		XXX
Total Retained Income Dec. 31, 19XX		$XXX

By adopting this approach the accountant is placed in the defensible position of having made a full disclosure of all information available to him. For those who believe that price gains and losses are unrealized—the data on disposable income is available to them for whatever use they wish to make of it. Those who reject this position likewise have the kind of information they desire in forming their judgment of corporate affairs. Those who wish to derive supplemental computations of "real" income have a solid foundation on which to build such analysis through the use of an index of the general price level.

I think the outstanding results of adopting this kind of disclosure would be the impact in restoring or building (depending on how pessimistic one is) public confidence in financial statements. Management, which is deeply and personally concerned with the need for additional funds to finance replacements and expansion, is understandably enamored with any accounting device which will result in lowering income during price rises. It is entirely understandable why—pressed with higher costs, higher taxes, and demands for increased wages and dividends,—corporate management should feel strongly that a dollar which must be reinvested in more valuable inventory is not available for distribution—and thus, somehow not income. It is not quite so understandable why the dollar which need not be invested in lower priced inventories is apparently still not available for distribution.

Nevertheless, if the word independent has real meaning, the public accountant should balance this position against that of investors and other public users of accounting information. I doubt seriously whether any real service is done by acceding to management's demands and failing to disclose the amount of inventory price gains and losses. The comparability of financial statements is to a material extent destroyed, since even those companies using LIFO have adopted at different dates and therefore their base prices have been set at different points in time. Furthermore sophisticated users of financial statements will often attempt a rough adjustment of income to add back the unstated price gains—and if they are prejudiced in the opposite direction from management the result will be misinformation. Finally the omission of this information cannot help but stimulate cries of subterfuge—which appear only too plausible to the layman who sees an inventory valuation of 8¢ per pound which "fairly presents the financial position" on an item currently being exchanged on an organized market at 26¢.

On these grounds I believe the case for LIFO falls. If you tell me you are for LIFO because it reduced taxes, and Lord only knows taxes are too high—I will respect that for an honest opinion. If you tell me you are for LIFO because it is an income smoothing device, and anything which knocks off the peaks and valleys of reported income is a good thing—I recognize the usefulness of averages. I cannot respect the logic of the argument that LIFO results in a more realistic, more accurate, more truthful, or more factual presentation of periodic business financial information.

We have been presenting income statements in which price gains and losses and operational gains and losses are lumped together. To the extent that LIFO has gained a foothold, we are currently in the position of omitting some portion of inventory price gains and losses from the financial picture altogether. Rather than encourage this device even further by allowing its users to have their cake and eat it both—now may well be the time to carry the evolution to its logical conclusion, and to fully disclose both *price* and *operational* gains and losses as elements of the most useful measure of *monetary* income we can at present devise.

F. K. WRIGHT

F. K. WRIGHT (1925–), B.Met.E. 46, B.Com. 47 Melbourne; F.A.S.A. Currently professor of commerce, University of Adelaide. Contributor to *Abacus, Journal of Accounting Research*, and other journals.

Was employed as a works accountant with Massey-Ferguson Ltd. (Australia), 1957–58, and as a management consultant with W. D. Scott & Co. Pty. Ltd., 1958–62, prior to joining the University of Adelaide faculty as a senior lecturer in 1962. Three years later, he was named to the chair in commerce.

A THEORY OF INVENTORY MEASUREMENT

F. K. WRIGHT

Generally accepted accounting principles require inventories of most businesses to be valued at cost of acquisition, except where the lower of cost and market rule calls for departure from historic cost. In some industries, however, inventory measurement at net realizable value (current selling price less expected costs of realization) is acceptable. Thus Accounting Research Bulletin No. 43 of the American Institute of Certified Public Accountants recognizes the acceptability of stating inventories at net realizable value if those inventories consist of "precious metals having a fixed monetary value with no substantial cost of marketing" or "other exceptions" characterized by "inability to determine appropriate approximate costs [and] immediate marketability at quoted market price."[1] In practice,

---

SOURCE: From *Abacus*, Volume 1, No. 2 (December, 1965), pp. 150–155. Reprinted by permission of *Abacus* and the author.

The author is grateful to Professor R. L. Mathews and Professor R. J. Chambers for helpful comments on earlier drafts of this paper.

[1] Committee on Accounting Procedure, *Restatement and Revision of Accounting Research Bulletins*, Accounting Research Bulletin No. 43, American Institute of Certified Public Accountants, New York, 1953, p. 34.

net realizable value is commonly applied to such staple products as cotton, grain, soy beans, raw sugar, coffee beans, and crude oil.[2]

Sprouse and Moonitz have argued that measurement of inventories at net realizable value, instead of being classified as exceptional, ought to be "the preferred method whenever the measurement is objectively determinable."[3] They recognize, however, that in many cases inventories cannot be satisfactorily measured in this way, and for those cases they recommend the use of current replacement costs.[4]

Edwards and Bell have pointed out that there are in theory no fewer than eighteen possible bases of asset valuation.[5] Of these, they consider that six merit further discussion,[6] and eventually they recommend two of these, net realizable value and current replacement cost, for use in measuring business income. Which of these two is to be used, they say, depends on the purpose for which business income is to be measured: net realizable value leads to a short-run concept of business income, while current replacement cost is more relevant to the long-run point of view.[7] Chambers, however, has questioned the relevance of their distinction between the short and the long runs.[8]

The Committee on Concepts and Standards—Inventory Measurement, sponsored by the American Accounting Association, has criticized the net realizable value method as "generally impractical" and has, by majority, decided in favour of replacement cost, provided that this amount can be determined objectively. At the same time, the Committee recognized that obsolete goods, for instance, "will not be replaced in kind, and their net realizable value must be substituted for their cost."[9]

Bennett, Grant and Parker have taken a similar position: they recommend "valuing inventories at either their current replacement price or their net realizable value, whichever is the lower."[10] They stress that this recommendation, despite its superficial resemblance to the lower of cost and market rule of conventional accounting, is not a concession to the doctrine of conservatism, but represents an attempt to measure "the value of the goods to the enterprise." They justify their recommendation by the following argument: If current replacement cost exceeds realizable value, goods will not be replaced, so that their value to the enterprise is determined by their net realizable value. Conversely, when realizable value exceeds replacement cost, the goods are worth no more to the

---

[2] R. T. Sprouse and M. Moonitz, *A Tentative Set of Broad Accounting Principles for Business Enterprises*, Accounting Research Study No. 3, American Institute of Certified Public Accountants, New York, 1962, p. 27.

[3] Ibid., p. 28.

[4] Ibid., pp. 100–1.

[5] E. O. Edwards and P. W. Bell, *The Theory and Measurement of Business Income*, University of California Press, Berkeley and Los Angeles, 1961, p. 77.

[6] Ibid., pp. 78–9.

[7] Ibid., pp. 100–1.

[8] R. J. Chambers, "Edwards and Bell on Business Income", *Accounting Review*, October 1965.

[9] Committee on Concepts and Standards—Inventory Measurement, American Accounting Association, "A Discussion of Various Approaches to Inventory Measurement—Supplementary Statement No. 2", *Accounting Review*, July 1964, pp. 708, 710.

[10] J. W. Bennett, J. McB. Grant and R. H. Parker, *Topics in Business Finance and Accounting*, Melbourne, Cheshire, 1964, p. 79.

enterprise than it would cost to replace them; in this case, therefore, the value of the goods to the enterprise is determined by their replacement cost.[11,12]

Thus there seems to be a reasonable amount of agreement, at least in academic circles, that net realizable value and current replacement cost are the most appropriate bases for inventory measurement. There is only limited agreement, however, on the circumstances in which each should be applied.

The object of the present paper is to put forward some criteria for deciding which of these two measures should be used in any particular instance. Such criteria can only be established on the basis of some assumptions about the purposes of accounting.

THE PURPOSES OF ACCOUNTING

Any statement of the purposes of accounting is necessarily subjective and may or may not command wide assent. Perhaps a writer cannot do much more than put forward, by way of assumption, those purposes which he considers most plausible, and hope that at least some of his readers will agree with his assumptions sufficiently to be interested in his conclusions.

In what follows, it will be assumed that the principal purposes of accounting are (1) to assist managers and investors in making decisions of an economic nature; and (2) to help them evaluate the performance of a business in relation to the (assumed) goal of wealth maximization.[13] Fortunately, we shall find that there is no conflict between these two purposes so far as inventory measurement is concerned.

But before we enter upon a detailed examination of how these purposes may best be served, it will be necessary to justify a further assumption on which our discussion will be based: the assumption of continuity.

THE CONTINUITY ASSUMPTION

Few accountants will dissent from the proposition that, for a firm in the process of liquidation, net realizable value is the most appropriate basis of asset measurement. A different basis of measurement may well be desirable, however, for a firm which intends to stay in business for an indefinite period. Without prejudging the question of what the basis of measurement in such a firm should be, let us suppose that it differs from that appropriate to a firm in liquidation.

Now consider the case of a firm which may or may not go into liquidation. The firm is currently a going concern, but at any time the owners may decide (as is their prerogative) to put it into liquidation. In order to decide whether or not they should do so, they will need (among other data) the value of the firm's assets on *both* bases: they will want to know the value of the assets to the firm if it stays in business, *and* their value on a break-up basis.

But unless accounting is to provide continuously two distinct valuations of all

---

[11] Ibid., pp. 79–80.

[12] A very similar stand has been taken by T. K. Cowan, "A Resources Theory of Accounting", *Accounting Review*, January 1965, p. 12.

[13] M. J. Gordon, "Postulates, Principles, and Research in Accounting", *Accounting Review*, April 1964, pp. 257–8.

assets, it can provide only part of this information. If we accept the usual limitation that accounting provides only one valuation in respect of each asset, a choice must be made between valuing on a liquidation basis or on a going-concern basis. Since the decision to continue in business is made far more frequently than the decision to liquidate, it seems eminently sensible for accountants to value assets normally on a going-concern basis. In this way the information provided will be relevant whether or not liquidation is to be considered, though it will need to be supplemented by break-up values (obtained from outside the books of account) whenever liquidation is regarded as a serious alternative.

Having thus justified the continuity assumption of accounting, we shall ignore the possibility of liquidation in the remainder of this article and concentrate our attention on the problems of inventory measurement in a firm which intends to stay in business.

VALUE TO THE FIRM

It will be argued that the most appropriate basis of inventory measurement in such a firm, for either of the above-mentioned purposes of accounting, is the "value of the goods to the firm",[14] where this expression is defined to mean the amount of cost or loss which the firm is able to avoid through having those goods. Thus, in order to assess the value of an article to the firm owning it, we need to consider what difference it would make to the firm if that article were lost or destroyed. If there is only one alternative to ownership of the article, then clearly the cost of that alternative represents the value of the article to the firm. Where there are several things the firm could do on losing the article, we may assume that management would try to minimize the costs or losses resulting from the disappearance of the article, so that we need only consider the most favourable course of action. The value of the article to the firm will then be measured by the *minimum or unavoidable financial loss which disappearance of the article would cause to the firm.*[15]

We shall now try to show that this concept of value is relevant to the principal purposes of accounting. In relation to the first of those purposes, economic decision-making, its relevance is almost self-evident. The management of a firm, faced with the need to make a decision about its inventory—how much to insure it for, or whether to accept a certain price for it—should clearly be guided in its decision by the value of the inventory to the firm. Similarly, the owners of the firm, in making decisions about the firm as a whole, will find it very useful to know the value to the firm (as a going concern) of its inventory.

For the purpose of evaluating the performance of a business firm in relation to the goal of wealth maximization, the most useful definition of asset value would again seem to be "value to the firm". For, under the continuity assumption, we must suppose that the firm will continue to operate as a profit-seeking organiza-

---

[14] Instead of this rather awkward expression, the writer would have preferred to use the term opportunity cost. Unfortunately, however, that term has been used by Edwards and Bell as a synonym for current net realizable value. (See their definition on p. 80.) In order to avoid being misunderstood, therefore, the writer has found it necessary to eschew that term in the present context.

[15] A. J. Merrett and A. Sykes, *The Finance and Analysis of Capital Projects*, Longmans, Green & Co. Ltd., London 1963, p. 466.

tion, and that the management of the firm will make its decisions in accordance with this objective. On these assumptions, "value to the firm" as defined above seems the most appropriate measure of the wealth represented by inventory.

This concept of value will now be applied to the problems of inventory measurement.

MEASUREMENT OF TRADING STOCK

Suppose that a firm has ten vases in stock. The purchase price of a vase is $5 and the selling price $6. For simplicity, assume that buying and selling expenses are negligible, and that replacements are available without delay. How ought this firm to value its stock of vases?

To answer this question, we need to consider what difference it would make to the firm if it lost a vase—if one were irreparably damaged, for instance. As we have seen, we may assume that the firm would act to minimize its loss. In the usual case, where the volume of sales is determined by demand rather than by supply, the appropriate action to minimize loss would be to order a replacement before shortage of stock leads to lost sales. Given that action, the breakage would make no difference to sales; but it would increase by one the number of vases the firm must buy in order to earn the same revenue. In other words, the minimum loss to the firm is, in this instance, identical with the cost of replacing the broken vase. It follows that the value of a vase to the firm is its current replacement cost, $5.

If we now drop the simplifying assumption that replacements are available without delay, we have to recognize that the loss of a stock unit may involve some risk of a lost sale. It would seem to follow that, in these circumstances, a vase should be valued at somewhat more than current replacement cost, though at less than net realizable value. Since the risk of a lost sale is difficult to assess, however, this approach would not yield an objective measurement; it is thus very unattractive from an accounting viewpoint. To avoid this result, therefore, we might stipulate that inventory value for accounting purposes is not to be measured by the effect that a sudden, unpredictable disappearance might have, but by the effect of its loss in circumstances which give the firm time to minimize the adverse consequences.

Now consider another product, mousetraps, of which the firm has one hundred in stock. These mousetraps have been bought at $2 each from a manufacturer who is willing to supply, at short notice and at the same price, any further quantities that may be required. Unfortunately, however, the firm has been unable to sell these mousetraps, and thinks it will be lucky to get rid of them for $1 apiece.

If one of these mousetraps became broken, the effect would be to reduce the firm's future revenue by (say) $1, and to reduce the firm's future selling expenses by a small amount. The value of a mousetrap to the firm would therefore be $1, less any expenses the firm would save by not having to sell the mousetrap, and perhaps discounted for the expected delay in receiving that revenue. In short, we have here a clear case for the application of net realizable value; this is recognized in ordinary accounting practice by the use of the lower of cost and market rule.

Next, let us look at the case of a smelter producing bullion for sale on the world market. We shall assume that there is no restriction on the amount of bullion that can be readily sold at current prices, so that sales are limited only by the amount which the smelter can produce. Under these circumstances, the loss of a ton of bullion would cause a reduction in revenue equal to its selling price, offset by any savings in selling expenses. Once again, therefore, the value of the stock to the firm is its net realizable value; and as we have seen, this method of valuation would be acceptable under conventional accounting.

MEASUREMENT OF MANUFACTURING STOCKS

So far, we have considered only goods intended for sale and in a saleable condition; the argument must now be extended to cover raw material and work in process.

Where the value of finished goods is equal to their current replacement cost, measurement of raw materials and work in process presents no special problem; clearly, these stocks should be measured at current replacement cost also. Where production limitations cause stocks of finished goods to be measured at net realizable value in excess of their replacement cost, however, there may be some difficulty in deciding how far back along the production line this measurement principle should be carried. Common sense suggests that goods almost in saleable condition should be measured at net realizable value also, that is, at the net realizable value of the finished product less the costs to convert those goods into finished form. But this approach hardly seems applicable to raw materials, or to work in process which has not progressed very far from the raw material stage.

In theory, the dividing line between measurement at net realizable value and measurement at replacement cost should be drawn at that process which effectively limits total production. For example, if the production of a smelter were limited by the capacity of its blast furnace, it would be logical to value ore, concentrates, and sinter at current replacement cost until they reached the blast furnace, and to value all metal which had gone through the blast furnace at net realizable value. In the case of a custom smelter, it could well be that its level of activity depends mainly upon the quantity of concentrates it is able to buy; in that case, all metal owned by the smelter, in whatever form, should be carried at net realizable value. The implied assumption "that all income or loss arises through the acquisitive activities of the business entity"[16] would be substantially correct in this instance.

CONCLUSION

The implications of our assumptions for the measurement of inventories may therefore be summed up as follows:

1. If sales are limited by demand rather than supply, and if the selling price is above replacement cost, the value of all stocks is equal to their current replacement cost.
2. If the stock is dead or slow-moving, or is unlikely to be replaced when sold, it should be measured at net realizable value, since in this case the loss of revenue represents the most favourable alternative to owning the asset.
3. Where the level of activity is controlled by supply rather than demand, net realizable value should be used as the measure of inventory.

[16] Committee on Concepts and Standards—Inventory Measurement, loc. cit., p. 706.

B. LIFO AGAINST THE FIELD

MAURICE MOONITZ

MAURICE MOONITZ (1910–), B.S. 33, M.S. 36, Ph.D. 41 University of California (Berkeley); CPA. Currently professor of accounting, University of California (Berkeley). Major publications: *The Entity Theory of Consolidated Statements* (1944), *Accounting: An Analysis of Its Problems* (with Staehling, 1950; with Jordan, 1963–64), *The Basic Postulates of Accounting* (1961), *A Tentative Set of Broad Accounting Principles for Business Enterprises* (with Sprouse, 1962), *Significant Accounting Essays* (edited readings, with Littleton, 1965), *Public Accounting—1980* (editor, 1971). Contributor to *The Journal of Accountancy*, *Journal of Accounting Research*, *The Accounting Review*, and other journals. Was coeditor, *California Management Review*, 1959–60.

After serving on the faculties of the University of Santa Clara (1937–42) and Stanford University (1942–44), joined the staff of Arthur Andersen & Co., for three years. In 1947, became a member of the accounting faculty at the University of California (Berkeley), serving also as associate dean of the Graduate School of Business Administration from 1955 to 1959. He was founding director of the Lingnan Institute of Business Administration, Hong Kong, 1966–68.

From 1960 to 1963, he was the director of accounting research of the American Institute of Certified Public Accountants, New York. He was a member of the AICPA Accounting Principles Board from 1963 to 1966. In 1958, he was vice-president of the American Accounting Association.

Principal research interests: the process by which accounting principles are established, and the problem of diverse scales of measurement in accounting especially price-level accounting.

THE CASE AGAINST LIFO AS AN INVENTORY-PRICING FORMULA

MAURICE MOONITZ

In recent years, the LIFO method of inventory pricing has increased in popularity as a result of the tax advantages it confers; at the same time, its inadequacies as a measure of assets and of net income have become more prominent. This article seeks to review the history and rationale of LIFO in this country in order to lay bare the reasons for the rising tide of opposition to its continued presence in the goodly company of generally accepted accounting principles.[1]

SOURCE: From *The Journal of Accountancy*, Vol. VC, No. 6 (June, 1953), pp. 682–690. Reprinted by permission of the American Institute of Certified Public Accountants.
[1] The types of objections raised to LIFO can be traced in one or more of the following items: W. A. Paton, *Advanced Accounting* (New York, 1941), pp. 145–147; G. R.

In order to narrow the area of discussion and to minimize misunderstandings as to what is being attempted, it should be emphasized that this article does not attempt to encompass the whole area of the accounting treatment of price-level changes. For example, a method of reflecting "replacement cost of goods sold" has long been described in the literature.[2] More recently, the use of index numbers to convert accounting data to a common-dollar basis has been urged.[3] These and other similar devices are not the central preoccupation of this article; it is immediately concerned with LIFO, as that method is described in the Internal Revenue Code and the Income Tax Regulations.[4]

Developments prior to 1938. Until the middle and late 1930s, LIFO was not an important method of pricing inventories and cost of goods sold. According to testimony submitted to a Congressional committee, six companies had used "LIFO or similar methods" in their corporate accounts prior to 1920; five additional companies appear in the 1920s; fifteen more are included in the list during the early 1930s.[5] That more than these 26 companies used or had used LIFO prior to 1938 is probable, since the list referred to was compiled from readily available data, and was restricted to the larger companies. But the evidence is unmistakable that LIFO was of no consequence until the Great Depression had run its course. As careful and painstaking an author as Hatfield, for example, does not even mention the method in his *Accounting*, published in 1927.[6] The 1934 edition of Finney's *Principles* is likewise silent on this topic.[7]

Husband, "The First-in, Last-out Method of Inventory Valuation," *Acctg. Rev.*, Vol. 15, No. 2 (June, 1940), pp. 190–196; E. B. Wilcox, "The Rise and Fall of LIFO," *JofA*, Feb48, pp. 98–103; J. E. Walter, "Last-in, First-out," *Acctg. Rev.*, Vol. 25, No. 1 (January, 1950), pp. 63–75; J. Pagani and W. O. Jones, "Price and Mortality Expectations and Valuation of Inventories," *Acctg. Rev.*, Vol. 25, No. 3 (July, 1950), pp. 315–319; Study Group on Business Income, *Changing Concepts of Business Income* (New York, 1952). LIFO is discussed throughout this report, and, on balance, is mildly censured. A careful reading of pages 39 to 44 should be required of anyone seeking a license to discuss LIFO.

[2] C. F. Schlatter, "Market Profits on the Operating Statement," *Acctg. Rev.*, Vol. 17, No. 2 (April, 1942), pp. 171–178. A similar discussion is also contained in Dean Schlatter's books on cost accounting.

[3] Committee on Concepts and Standards Underlying Corporate Financial Statements of the American Accounting Association. Supplementary Statement No. 2, "Price Level Changes and Financial Statements," *JofA*, Oct51, pp. 461–465; also *Acctg. Rev.*, Vol. 26, No. 4 (October, 1951); Study Group on Business Income, *op. cit.*

[4] Regulations 111, Sec. 29.22(d), "Gross Income—Inventories under Elective Method." The "elective" method now includes the "dollar-value" method of adjustment by the use of price indexes as well as "LIFO" in the older sense. See Sec. 29.22(d)-1. In Section 29.22(d) of the regulations is found the requirement that a taxpayer must employ the "elective" method in his records, accounts, and financial statements if he wishes to employ the same method in his tax return.

[5] Senate Finance Committee, Hearings on the Revenue Act of 1938, 75th Congress, 3d Session, on H. R. 9682 (Govt. Printing Office, 1938). Pages 143 to 167 of these hearings contain the statements of M. E. Peloubet and others on behalf of LIFO. The statistics cited appear on page 164.

[6] H. R. Hatfield, *Accounting: Its Principles and Problems* (New York, 1927).

[7] H. A. Finney, *Principles of Accounting: Intermediate* (New York, 1934).

The clearly discernible features which distinguish the 1930s from earlier decades all center around the federal income tax. Although income taxation has been an integral part of the American scene since 1913, the rates of tax applicable to business corporations were not of sizable proportions until the 1930s. An excess-profits tax had been in effect during World War I, but it was short-lived, and the 1920s were years of relatively mild taxation. The rise in rates after the Great Depression was great enough to constitute a qualitative as well as a quantitative change in terms of the impact of the tax on business.

Against a backdrop of fluctuating prices, the problem assumed sizable proportions. Prices had risen sharply during World War I, had dropped abruptly a few years thereafter, had held reasonably stable during the twenties, had broken catastrophically in the Great Depression, were on the rise in uneven fashion after the spring of 1933, and were expected to drop again in the near future, as they did in fact in 1937 and 1938. It is significant that there was no averaging provision in the tax law in the early and middle thirties, such as the carry-back or carry-forward of operating losses. As a consequence, a company which paid taxes on large profits during a price rise could look forward to no "relief" or offset if a subsequent price decline should result in net losses.

In 1936, permission to use LIFO had been requested of the House Ways and Means Committee and of the Senate Finance Committee, but the petitioners had been referred to the Commissioner of Internal Revenue who, they were told, had authority to legalize the use of LIFO for tax purposes. But the Treasury refused to budge in its traditional opposition to the "normal stock" methods of inventory pricing in general, and to LIFO in particular.[8]

The problem of an inequitable tax burden could have been solved by a change in the tax rules (*i.e.*, averaging of gains and losses over a period of years, for tax purposes, according to some workable formula) or by a change in the accounting rules (*i.e.*, a new theory or formula for determination of profit). Taxpayers got both. The Revenue Act of 1938 permitted the use of LIFO by a few types of businesses; the scope of LIFO was liberalized somewhat in the Revenue Act of 1939. The latter act also restored the "net operating loss deduction." Both features have been in the federal tax structure ever since. The root of the difficulty created for accounting is the unique provision of the income-tax law which requires that LIFO must be used for reporting purposes if it is to be accepted for tax purposes. In other words, a generally applicable accounting rule was formulated by act of Congress.

In order to obtain some perspective on later developments, the conditions under which LIFO was originally thought to be appropriate, according to its proponents, are summarized at this point.[9]

1. The investment in inventories must be large, relative to other assets.

2. The inventory must consist of a few basic materials which form a substantial part of the cost of the product sold.

3. The spread between raw material cost and selling price must be relatively constant.

(The discussion of Statement 4 in Accounting Research Bulletin 29, as originally issued in July, 1947, contained the following sentences: "These methods

[8] Hearings, *op. cit.*, p. 143.
[9] Hearings, *op. cit.*, pp. 154–55.

recognize the variations which exist in the relationships of costs to sales prices under different economic conditions. Thus, where sales prices are promptly influenced by changes in reproductive costs, an assumption of the 'last-in first-out' flow of cost factors may be the more appropriate. Where no such cost-price relationship exists, the 'first-in first-out' or an 'average' method may be more properly utilized." The committee on accounting procedure, in the process of codifying the Accounting Research Bulletins, voted some time ago to eliminate these sentences from Bulletin 29.) [a]

4. Inventory turnover must be slow because of the length of the period of process.

5. The company involved must customarily make purchases of raw materials to fill specific orders.

Furthermore, it is abundantly clear that LIFO was viewed, in 1938, primarily as an adaptation to cyclical price movements. Witness the following statement by Peloubet:

> Over a period of years total income will be the same under any method of accounting consistently applied, and if taxed at a flat rate the aggregate tax will be the same. . . . There is one thing that I might bring out. Of course we are not asking for privileges, we are not asking for anything exceptional, and there is nothing in this method which will reduce revenue over a period. . . . Our people are perfectly willing to take the consequences either way (*i.e.*, rising prices or falling prices). The only thing is we do not want to pay taxes 2 or 3 years before we make any profits just because we must write up inventories which we cannot sell.[10]

INFLATIONARY TREND SINCE 1938

Developments since 1938. Instead of a series of cyclical price movements about some reasonably stable norm, the last decade or so has witnessed a marked inflationary trend. Prices have moved unevenly upward, with only minor and sporadic interruptions. During the same period, income-tax rates moved to levels formerly unknown, the peak being reached during the war period under the excess-profits tax. Especially during the war years, liquidation of a part of the basic or normal LIFO inventory became extensive enough to constitute a new problem. This liquidation occurred because of the disruption of usual sources of supply and the consequent difficulty of replacing inventories as fast as they were consumed. It is significant that liquidation occurred even among companies which had asserted that their basic or normal inventory was essential to operations, that it was "fixed" by technical considerations and could not be liquidated without suspension of activity. Still they continued to operate, and on a high level. It is also significant that these companies were *not* willing to take the consequences, taxwise, of their use of low-valued inventories in a period of high

---

[a] Bulletin No. 29 was superseded (with no major changes in substance) by Chapter 4 of Accounting Research Bulletin No. 43 (in 1953). The three quoted sentences were indeed omitted from Chapter 4, constituting perhaps the most significant change in substance. [Eds.]

[10] Hearings, *op. cit.*, pp. 145, 147.

prices. The result was an extension of LIFO to include "next-in first-out," to permit the deduction of the cost of units *subsequently* acquired from revenues *previously* realized and wholly unrelated to the replacement of the "involuntarily-liquidated" basic stock.

In 1947, the Tax Court handed down a decision, later accepted by the Commissioner of Internal Revenue and incorporated in his regulations, which removed the last legal barrier to the use of LIFO by any taxpayer in any line of activity in which inventories were used for tax purposes.[11]

The combined effect of these developments has been to stimulate the adoption of LIFO—adoptions which have been dominated by tax considerations. This point is made crystal-clear by an analyst of the LIFO method: [12]

> Since 1939 few management decisions on LIFO have been made without reference to their tax effects. Decisions as to whether to use LIFO, how to apply it, and even as to the industries in which the method constitutes acceptable accounting practice, have been dominated by tax considerations. It would be difficult to cite other instances in which management considerations on matters of broad policy and general economic significance have been more strongly influenced by tax requirements.
>
> Undoubtedly the opportunity to reduce tax liabilities has been by far the most powerful motivation leading to the widespread adoption of LIFO during the past decade. The combination of sharply rising prices and high excess profits taxes gave managements in many industries a strong tax incentive to shift to LIFO during the early war years. The large postwar price increases caused some companies to make the shift as late as 1946 and 1947, though the risk of ultimate tax penalties was then greater because of the height to which price levels had already risen.
>
> As to non-tax reasons for electing LIFO, Butters states (p. 9), that "many executives who recalled the severe inventory losses of 1920 and 1921 were also anxious to provide a 'cushion' to protect themselves from the necessity of reporting similar losses in the event of a price collapse at the end of World War II. They saw in the availability of LIFO an opportunity to accomplish this objective and at the same time to make substantial tax savings."

WHY MORE COMPANIES DON'T ADOPT LIFO

Why haven't more companies adopted LIFO for the tax advantages involved? Apparently there are two main reasons (other than inertia). The first reason is based on the fact that in a period of rising prices, and all other things being equal, reported profit under LIFO will be less than reported profit under FIFO or average cost. As a consequence, a shift to LIFO may involve less income, less

---

[11] *Hutzler Bros.*, 8 T.C. 14 (1947).

[12] J. Keith Butters, *Effects of Taxation: Inventory Accounting and Policies* (Boston, 1949), pp. 6, 8. See also R. W. Button, "The LIFO Bonanza?" *The Balance Sheet*, February, 1948, and subsequent articles on LIFO in the March, 1948, and April, 1948, issues of the same journal, published by the Controllers' Congress of the National Retail Dry Goods Association.

dividends, less management compensation where that compensation varies with reported profit, and may result in a default under a bond contract. The second reason stems from expectations as to price movements in the near future. If prices are expected to decline sharply, any advantages under present rules and regulations obtained by a shift to LIFO will be minor, or nonexistent.

But this is not the end of the story. Under existing tax regulations, LIFO is a "cost" method; a taxpayer who elects LIFO must stay on LIFO. He cannot employ "cost or market, whichever is lower," as can a taxpayer on FIFO or average cost. In other words, as long as prices are stable or are rising, real or potential tax advantages exist; but if prices should fall substantially, the LIFO taxpayer will at that time report higher profits and pay higher taxes than a taxpayer not on LIFO, but otherwise in identically the same situation. For the time being, then, those who expect price declines will stay away from LIFO. Meanwhile, representations are being made to the appropriate Congressional committees to amend the Internal Revenue Code to permit LIFO cost or market, whichever is lower.

The recommendations for amendment of federal tax laws, submitted to Congress by the committee on federal taxation of the American Institute of Accountants, contained the following statement, as summarized in *Journal of Accountancy*, Dec., 52, p. 720:

> Section 22(d). The Code should be amended to permit taxpayers using the LIFO inventory method for income-tax purposes to value their inventories at the lower of cost or market while the Excess Profits Tax Act of 1950 is in force, and for five years thereafter.[b]

If Congress obliges, highest-in first-out can then be added to the list of "generally accepted accounting principles."

ANALYSIS OF LIFO

Later the arguments for and against LIFO are to be considered. The discussion in this section remains on the descriptive and historical level in order to round out the picture of LIFO in actual operation.

The salient effect of LIFO is the smoothing of reported profits in the face of continued changes in prices. Technically, the relative stabilization of profit is obtained by an increase or decrease in recorded cost of goods sold as prices rise and fall. Two effects of the relative stabilization of reported profit are immediately apparent. One is the failure to report all gains (and losses) from changes in prices; the result of buying cheap and selling dear, or of buying high and selling low is not recorded. Good merchandising is obscured. It is not a question of isolating or earmarking these gains or losses for special treatment or disclosure; the LIFO method simply ignores them, and leaves no trace of them in the financial statements. The other effect, in terms of actual experience since 1938, is the gross

---

[b] Although Congress did not follow this suggestion and has never accepted the principle of "LIFO cost or market, whichever is lower," it has allowed special relief for taxpayers who, because of materials shortages during World War II and the Korean conflict, were forced to deplete their LIFO inventories. If certain conditions were met, these taxpayers did not, ultimately, have to pay tax on the excess of the *actual* replacement cost over the cost originally assigned to the LIFO inventory. [Eds.]

understatement of inventory values among the assets in the balance-sheet. This attribute of LIFO has long been recognized by its advocates. Indeed, as long ago as 1934, W. A. Staub commented that "if such a cost formula or method (*i.e.*, LIFO cost or market) were generally adopted in an industry, it would be desirable to show as a memorandum on the balance-sheet the current replacement market-value for the inventory."[13] But to date the instances in which companies reporting inventories on LIFO also disclose current replacement costs are all too few.

A further result of LIFO, then, is to weaken, if not to destroy, comparability among the published financial statements of different companies, or indeed, the comparability of financial statements of one company over a period of years. For example, the calculation of inventory turnover involves a comparison of cost of goods sold or of sales, on the one hand, with inventory, on the other. But the inventory figure, under LIFO, bears no relationship to current conditions; consequently, the calculation of inventory turnover in such cases is a useless exercise in arithmetic. A similar effect is observable with respect to the current ratio, and other analytical devices involving inventory data. In this respect, then, the usefulness of published financial statements has diminished in recent years.

Despite the high hopes of its proponents that LIFO would reduce the inequities in the federal tax structure, the method has actually increased them. In the face of rising prices and rising tax-rates, the LIFO companies have been a favored group; a substantial burden has been shifted from them to taxpayers not on LIFO. This is no reflection on the taxpayer who elected LIFO and was permitted to use it for tax purposes; under the prevailing rules of the game, anyone may use every available legal means to see that someone else foots the bill. But the experience with LIFO and the federal tax bill should serve as an object-lesson to the accounting profession. No one will seriously maintain that the size of the federal tax load on the whole community has been reduced by LIFO, or by any other scheme of tax "minimization." The profession should be wary, now and in the future, of new "principles" of accounting whose major objective is to shift the burden of the income tax from one group of clients to another group.

RATIONALE OF LIFO—PRO AND CON

Over the years, the arguments advanced in support of LIFO as a superior method of inventory pricing have changed. As the current euphemism has it, there has been "evolution" in the concept of LIFO, and the process of evolution is not yet complete.

Originally, much was made of the point that LIFO reflected results of operations as though "hedging" had been practiced successfully. For example, assume that, at the time a contract for future delivery of metal products is made, a quantity of metal is purchased to replace the amount which will be consumed in filling the order. The assertion is made that, under this set of circumstances, fluctuations in the price of metal as raw material are irrelevant to the calculation of gain or

---

[13] Quoted in *Hearings, op. cit.*, pp. 157–58. Staub pointed out that replacement value would be needed to assist credit-granters, and to facilitate comparison among industries. He also urged the disclosure of replacement value under other methods of inventory pricing.

loss on the contract.[14] In a perfect hedge, the facts bear out the assertion; gains and losses on the simultaneous sale and purchase of commodities cancel each other. But a perfect hedge requires, by definition, no speculation in commodities. In the cases, however, in which LIFO was urged as a more appropriate method of pricing, substantial quantities of basic commodities were carried, against which there was no offsetting "hedge." As a consequence, to the extent of these basic stocks, the business was exposed to the effects of price fluctuations. In order to bolster the "hedging" argument, the further point was made that the fabricator, in effect, acts as a buying agent for his customer, and not as a dealer in metal; as a consequence, it is alleged, no gain or loss on the metal accrues to the fabricator.[15] To accept this argument, however, is to ignore the actual relationship between the dealer and customer and to substitute a fictional relationship. If the agency relationship is in actuality more realistic, it would appear to be a relatively simple matter to change the formal contracts and other arrangements to bring it into being; if this were done, there would be no need to invoke LIFO, since the fabricator would have no materials' inventory to price.

In these days of "dollar-value LIFO" for department stores, the points just discussed appear archaic, and are no longer relied on as major elements in the theory behind LIFO. Instead, three other points appear more frequently as buttresses of the structure:

1. To an extent varying with technical conditions in each industry, inventories represent an involuntary, fixed commitment, analogous to a fixed asset.
2. LIFO is a method of adjustment to price level changes.
3. Increases in the unit prices of inventory items represent unrealized and unrealizable inventory profits, and therefore should be excluded from the accounts, by means of LIFO.

The first point, the one with respect to an "involuntary commitment" of inventory, need not detain anyone long. Even if the point is accepted as valid, its impact is with respect to the classification of the inventory item, not its pricing. If it were decided to show some basic quantity of materials, for example, among the fixed assets, the problem would still remain as to the appropriate pricing formula. No one has ever, in a published statement, so treated inventories; consequently, there is no evidence as to the concrete, operational meaning of the assertion that some portion of inventories is "fixed."

LIFO DOES NOT ADJUST PRICE LEVEL CHANGES

For obvious reasons, the second point asserting that LIFO is a method of adjustment of price level changes, is in vogue these days. But the point is invalid, for two related reasons.

First, LIFO fails miserably and completely in making adjustments of inventory values for *any* type of price change. Arthur Dean has this to say on the point under discussion:

> There are, however, obvious shortcomings to LIFO as a solution of the problems presented by the decline in the value of the dollar. While it does in certain circumstances . . . have the effect of revaluing goods *sold* in terms of depre-

[14] *Hearings, op. cit.*, p. 143.
[15] *Hearings, op. cit.*, p. 152.

ciated dollars, it does so by ascribing to *unsold* goods the old monetary costs, resulting in a corresponding undervaluation in terms of current dollars of inventories on hand.[16]

Witness also the following comment of Gilman:

> While both LIFO and accelerated depreciation may accomplish a desired effect on the income statement, they influence the balance-sheet oppositely, and conceivably, below the limits of reasonable conservatism.
>
> This effect contradicts our general thesis relating to decreased purchasing power of the dollar. It is inconsistent in that it provides "inflated" costs in the income statement and correspondingly "deflated" asset values in the balance-sheet—a paradox which should cause concern to the certified public accountant who is requested to give as his opinion that his client's balance-sheet presents fairly the client's financial position.[17]

In the second place, LIFO does not even adjust for price level changes in the income statement. What LIFO does do under the procedures usually prescribed by its advocates is to reflect in cost of goods sold the latest costs paid for the *specific* commodity dealt in.

These latest costs may or may not be close to the current replacement costs of the commodity involved; in the case of seasonal buying the last cost paid may be quite different from current replacement cost. As a consequence, LIFO eliminates only an undetermined part of the effects of specific price fluctuations.

But even if it is conceded that LIFO, on the average, does eliminate the effects of fluctuations in the prices of specific commodities, the problem of the effect of price level changes is still left unsolved. The price movements of any given commodity bear no necessary relationship to the movements of the general price level or of its reciprocal, the purchasing power of the dollar.[18]

As to the "unrealized profit" argument, an early proponent of LIFO has made the following statement:

> These inventory profits may be called unrealized inventory profits—that is, profits represented by unsold inventories rather than cash. In fact, to a going concern, most of the inventory profits are not only unrealized but they are also unrealizable if the concern is to continue in business. Even though inventories are constantly being turned over, a certain quantity of inventories is a part of the capital equipment of the business. Increases or decreases in inventory values are analogous in every essential to unrealized capital gains or losses.

---

[16] Arthur H. Dean, *An Inquiry into the Nature of Business Income under Present Price Levels* (New York, 1949), p. 24 (Emphasis supplied).

[17] Study Group on Business Income, *Changing Concepts of Business Income* (New York, 1952), p. 120.

[18] For more detailed discussion of the problems involved in adjusting for price-level changes, see Supplementary Statement No. 2 of the American Accounting Association's Committee on Concepts and Standards, "Price Level Changes and Financial Statements," *Accounting Review*, Vol. 26, No. 4 (October, 1951), and the report of the Study Group on Business Income, *Changing Concepts of Business Income* (New York, 1952). [Also see APB *Statement No. 3*, "Financial Statements Restated for General Price-Level Changes" (June 1969) and *Accounting Research Study No. 6*, "Reporting the Financial Effects of Price-Level Changes" (1963).]

Inventory profits, as here defined, cannot be converted into cash profits without a net liquidation of inventories.[19]

This quotation makes abundantly clear the extent to which LIFO depends upon a crude "cash balance" concept of profit, without reference to changes in other assets or debts. The quotation also makes clear that the primary technical objective of LIFO is to avoid the credit to balance-sheet net worth which would result if inventories were to be carried at a figure close to their current value, as measured by prices actually prevailing in the market in the current period.

WHAT ABOUT "UNREALIZED PROFIT"?

But what is to be made of the point as to "unrealized profit"? Observe that the unrealized profit is "represented" by unsold inventories. Accordingly, in a period of rising prices, inventories must, under LIFO, be progressively understated as compared with the same inventories stated at current prices actually prevailing in the market; total reported assets and reported proprietary investment are also correspondingly and progressively understated. The defense of LIFO must then take the uncomfortable form of a defense of a statement of financial position which is known to be inaccurate, and, what is worse, wherein the approximate magnitude of the inaccuracy is known but usually undisclosed. This type of defense is put forward in many forms and under numerous guises; probably the most common form is the oft-repeated assertion that the income statement is more important than the balance-sheet, and therefore it doesn't make too much difference what appears in the latter statement. But this leaves unanswered the important query as to how it is possible to have reasonably accurate statements of income accompanied by a series of admittedly inaccurate balance-sheets. Where is the difference buried, and of what significance is it? In other words, the advocates of LIFO have formulated no theory of income or of financial position which will meet the practical test of making understandable that which is going on in the real world.

One type of argument frequently advanced in defense of LIFO states essentially that a ton of steel, for example, has the same economic and business significance today as a ton of steel did last year, and in 1940, and in 1890. If, then, a concern has need for at least 1,000 tons of steel at all times in order to operate, the corresponding inventory valuation should not be affected, so it is asserted, because of increases or decreases in the price of steel. This type of primitive economic argument is advanced despite the clear-cut recognition of changed buying prices for steel, of changed selling prices for steel products, of changed market conditions confronting the industry of which the concern is a part, of changed technology, wage rates, labor relations, and so on. The plain fact of the matter is that the economic or business significance of any given quantity of any specified commodity changes from day to day, in response to a whole constellation of forces; any accounting procedure which fails to reflect in some degree the effect of these forces cannot claim to be realistic and practical. The manner in which accounting can, and usually does, reflect the effect of these forces can be sketched in broad outline, somewhat as follows.

[19] H. B. Arthur, "Inventory Profits in the Business Cycle," *American Economic Review*, Vol. 28, No. 1 (March, 1938), p. 28.

HOW ACCOUNTING REFLECTS ECONOMIC FORCES

By definition, units of inventory are acquired, processed, and held for sale to customers; each repurchase is an independent decision, as to time, type, and quantity, or whether to repurchase at all; at each turnover of the inventory, the resultant receipts from customers restore the liquidity of the investment in inventories, thereby making possible a new set of decisions as to the amount and direction of investment. If the proceeds of sale are used to acquire, process, or hold additional units of inventory, it is because management expects future sales to be at a price equal to or (usually) greater than current cost; to assume otherwise is to postulate deliberate dissipation of resources by management. Any inventory is worth what the quantity of goods actually on hand will bring on the market at orderly sale; under the cost rule, then, and in the absence of physical deterioration or obsolescence, an inventory is realistically priced when it is carried at some cost prevailing in the last turnover period (*e.g.*, FIFO and possibly some forms of average costing) or at some net selling price expected to prevail in the next turnover period (*e.g.*, cost, not in excess of net realizable value). In brief, profit emerges not later than the time of sale or collection from customer; reinvestment in similar items has no bearing on whether a profit was or was not realized on the investment and liquidation of items previously held.

The validity of the preceding observations is independent of the movements of the price level. That is to say, inventories should always be reflected in terms of prices currently prevailing; if the price level has changed appreciably then *all* relevant statement data should be adjusted in some systematic manner. The assault on common sense offered by LIFO, which requires the assertion on a balance-sheet that an inventory is "fairly presented" at three cents a pound when the level of prices actually prevailing in the current period is around fifteen cents, is thereby avoided.

SUMMARY AND CONCLUSION

The case against LIFO as an inventory-pricing formula can be readily summarized:

1. On historical grounds, the original reasons for its adoption are no longer present; a reading of the early testimony before the pertinent Congressional committees amply demonstrates this point.

2. As it has worked out, LIFO is primarily a device for reducing or deferring the amount of income tax payable by a given concern, not a device for measuring its business income.

3. LIFO does not even have the virtue of adjusting for price level changes; in fact, it has a perverse effect on the inventory figure appearing in the balance-sheet.

4. LIFO suppresses realized market gains and losses; it assigns a nonexistent stability to earnings and to inventories.

In fact, LIFO presumes a type of business and economic system which does not exist. In the world in which we live, prices do go up and down, profits do change from year to year, dividends vary; as a result, stockholders, trade union leaders, and tax collectors may misunderstand what is going on. Therefore, says LIFO, let us write down the story as it does *not* happen; if we shut our eyes to reality, maybe it will go away.[20]

But despite all the marshalling of facts, arguments, logic, and analysis, the popularity of LIFO increases. Given permission, as seems more than possible at the moment, to use "LIFO cost or market," many more taxpayers will adopt LIFO. This "popularity" rests solely on the unique provision of the Internal Revenue Code requiring the use of LIFO in all published statements and reports if a taxpayer wishes to use LIFO for tax purposes.

What is sorely needed is a declaration of independence by the profession from the exigencies of income taxation as the arbiter of business income. Specifically, two recommendations are submitted:

> 1. For the immediate future, the current cost of inventories on LIFO should be revealed in financial statements.
>
> 2. For the longer term, LIFO should be abandoned for reporting purposes, provided the mandatory provision of the Internal Revenue Code is modified, as it should be in order to restore to accounting its function of defining and measuring business income.

These steps seem to be the least that can be taken in order to preserve the rational basis of modern accounting.

[20] "To summarize, if one grants that the traditional accounting statement of profits is subject to dangerous misinterpretation, the alternatives are to change present accounting practices or to change the public. The former would seem to be infinitely more feasible than the latter." Butters, *op. cit.*, p. 136.

HERBERT T. MC ANLY

HERBERT T. MC ANLY (1898–), LL.D.(h.c.) 59 Wittenberg University; CPA. Currently retired. Anthology: H. T. McAnly, *Selected Writings on Accounting and Related Subjects* (Ernst & Ernst, 1963). Was a frequent contributor to *The Journal of Accountancy* and other journals.

Joined Ernst & Ernst in 1920, becoming a partner in 1936. He assumed firmwide direction of management services in 1948, and retired from the partnership in 1964.

Was a member of the Federal Trade Commission's advisory committee on cost justification, 1954–56.

McAnly has been closely identified with the literature on the LIFO method of inventory valuation, and was primarily responsible for developing the "dollar value" procedure of adapting LIFO to inventory pools.

THE CASE FOR LIFO: IT REALISTICALLY STATES INCOME AND IS APPLICABLE TO ANY INDUSTRY

H. T. McANLY

An increasing number of professional accountants believe, as I do, that LIFO is a major step in the evolutionary development of sound accounting. The primary objective of those who have been active in the promotion of the broad application of LIFO has been to arrive at a more realistic profit determination for all purposes. I am sure that none of us believe that LIFO is a solution to the price level problem. Thus, in the beginning paragraphs of Professor Moonitz' article, the emphasis on the effectiveness of LIFO as a solution to the price level problem would seem to have little bearing on the ultimate conclusions reached.

SOURCE: From *The Journal of Accountancy*, Vol. VC, No. 6 (June, 1953), pp. 691–700. Reprinted by permission of the American Institute of Certified Public Accountants.

Professor Moonitz implies that LIFO has failed as a means of reflecting profit and loss based upon a current replacement cost of sales. As a matter of fact, the LIFO method makes no claim to substitute replacement cost for historical cost of sales. It simply matches the latest incurred costs against sales, rather than the earliest. In other words, in a rising market it charges the added cost of carrying the same inventory necessary to continue the business as a charge against operations in the year it occurs. Since the inventory cost value has not been increased when prices go up, there is no corresponding reduction needed when prices go down. To this extent LIFO tends to level out or stabilize earnings as they should be, for certainly no realized profit or loss results from mere fluctuations in value of the things we must continue to own in order to be a going concern. To some extent LIFO approaches the expression of cost of sales on a replacement cost basis but the degree to which a cost of sales resulting from LIFO and one expressed on a replacement cost of sales basis coincide, depends, of course, on the extent of the lag between actual acquisition costs and the current replacement costs.

The statement is made that the LIFO method of inventory pricing has increased in popularity because of the tax advantage it confers. While there is no doubt that the tax angle rightfully has a tremendous bearing on anything which deals with the determination of income, the tax picture can hardly be considered as the primary reason for the use of LIFO. Many companies have adopted LIFO or its approximate equivalent—reserves to eliminate price increases from inventories—in order to state their corporate profits more correctly even though they deferred its adoption tax-wise because of an inequity (dealing with timing of adoption) contained in the present tax law which establishes the beginning cost level as a floor for all future tax determination.

It should be obvious to everyone that the introduction of income taxes (1913) has been a tremendous factor in the development of accounting. Equally obvious is the fact that the higher the tax rates (such as resulted during both World War periods and as exist at the present time) the greater the need for all business to have a more accurate method for determination of realized profit subject to those taxes. Since taxes are a primary factor in the disposition of earned income, the use of an inventory method which produces a more realistic statement of realized income certainly should have wide popularity but since it is something which is available to everyone, it can hardly be placed in the category of a tax advantage. It is merely a method of inventory pricing which will result in more nearly stating the income which has actually been realized and is available for distribution in taxes, dividends, profit-sharing, wage increases, and possible price reductions.

At the present time, an American Institute of Accountants committee has been appointed at the suggestion of the chairman of the House Ways and Means Committee, for the express purpose of working with the Treasury in the development of a statement of accounting principles for income-tax purposes. In other words, they are trying to establish a closer relationship between the determination of corporate and taxable income. Thus any suggestions which appear to widen the gap between corporate and taxable income, such as would result should LIFO be permitted as a tax device but not be required in the statement of corporate income, would seem to be at variance with the trend.

The primary objective of accounting should be to report profits on a strictly factual basis. This is a fundamental obligation to stockholders, to the government, to employees, and to the general public. If there are various methods by which profit can be computed and which result in different answers, profit reporting can hardly be considered factual but one of choice.

LIFO ARGUMENTS BASED ON DIFFERENT CONCEPTS

The arguments pro and con about the soundness of LIFO are based upon different concepts of income. Should income represent profits which reflect latest costs against current sales and which in reality are available for distribution (last-in first-out basis) or be a combination of these available profits, plus or minus an amount which represents the changing value of a continuing investment in the inventory (first-in first-out basis)?

There certainly will be disagreement generally among the accounting profession with the statement that "there is a rising tide of opposition to the continued presence of LIFO in the goodly company of generally accepted accounting principles." While it is true, as the article points out, that certain individuals have expressed some objections to LIFO, there certainly is an increasing trend toward the acceptance of LIFO by industry and the accounting profession generally.

The types of objections raised in the references noted again all deal with a concept of profit, and from the trend as to the adoption and interest in LIFO, it would appear that there is a narrowing of the concept of profit to mean actual available or realized income since the disposition of that income, to a great degree, no longer rests with business management. Taxes take substantially more than half—actually up to 82 [now 52] per cent of income. Section 102 [now 531 to 537] of the Internal Revenue Code puts pressure on dividend distributions. Demands for wage increases are geared to reported incomes, and both consumer and government pressures exist for price reductions as reported profits increase. Thus, the method of describing what is available as a realized profit is vitally important.

If members of the teaching profession can convince industry that it is wise to use a concept of profit which adds to the realized profit under LIFO, the fluctuations in value of the necessary inventory, then the trend toward LIFO adoption will cease. However, as indicated by a recent study of annual reports of 600 corporations conducted by the American Institute of Accountants, LIFO was being used by 31 per cent of the companies surveyed as compared with 19 per cent two years prior to that time. It would appear, therefore, that whatever rising tide of opposition exists, it must be confined to those who are largely removed from business and to others in the accounting profession who are still seeking justification for their adverse pronouncements made early in the LIFO picture due primarily to their failure to comprehend broad LIFO objectives and application.

Members of the accounting profession who are familiar with the problems which confront business generally, concede that the percentage of industry using LIFO is not indicative of the interest or desire to use it. The great majority of industries recognize that profits reflected under LIFO are more realistic. It is also well known that little is accomplished by using LIFO corporate-wise and not using it tax-wise, since those who interpret corporate figures for purposes of wage demands, renegotiation, etc., merely add back to the correctly reported income, nondeductible reserves which have been set up in an attempt to more clearly reflect the income.

The first reason advanced by Professor Moonitz for more companies not adopting LIFO—that management desires to show greater earnings to support general management profit-sharing, etc.—I am sure is without foundation. Certainly it is contrary to the opinions of those in the profession who have been actually engaged in meeting with management, in their consideration of LIFO during the latter years of the current inflationary trend, when they learned that practical methods of LIFO were available to them. The real obstacle, of course, to the broad use of LIFO is the cost restriction contained in the present revenue law which establishes cost as of the year of adoption as a floor for future tax determination. Thus, until we straighten out the tax law, we cannot expect industry, at what appears to be a high cost level period, to begin to use the tools to more clearly reflect income, which were supplied by Congress in 1939 but not endorsed by the Bureau of Internal Revenue until 1949.

The original regulations interpreting LIFO implied that its use was restricted to companies having simple inventories. These narrow interpretations continued in effect for ten years. It was not until there were three Tax Court decisions recognizing practical mechanics of application which make LIFO practicable for any inventory, regardless of its complexity, that the regulations were modified. And in the interim, prices had more than doubled. Industry has been forced to write up as profit the increase in cost of carrying the same inventory quantities, and industry rightfully does not want to give up the right to write down this cost to the extent prices recede in the future. To adopt LIFO at too high a cost level would take away from industry the right to recoup taxes that have been paid on the write-up in inventories which they were forced to do, since they were prevented from using LIFO because of the narrow interpretations of the law originally contained in the regulations under the present tax law. The adoption of LIFO will continue to be postponed in the event of further price increases, by the majority of industries waiting for some future time when cost levels reach a lower point. In the meantime, the overstatement of inventories and profits and the confusion in the comparison of reported profits will continue. Thus, it may well be said that the number of companies using LIFO at present is no indication of the tremendous interest and desire on the part of industry to use this method to more clearly reflect their profits for *all* purposes.

LIFO WILL NOT DESTROY BALANCE-SHEET

The arguments advanced in Professor Moonitz' article relative to the destruction of the balance-sheet because of LIFO's inadequacy as a measure of assets are not valid as regards the determination of income. While it has been recognized that the determination of income is primary and the balance-sheet more or less secondary, there is no reason for stating that the use of LIFO in the income statement prevents the construction of a balance-sheet in which inventories are expressed at current cost levels. To date most of the emphasis has been placed upon the need for LIFO to reflect income more clearly. Possibly it is time that we got around to the construction of a balance-sheet which carries all of the essential information relative to the financial position of a company on a current basis. That this can be accomplished easily will be shown in the latter part of this article.

It is particularly significant to note that the U.S. Department of Commerce in its determination of national business income, develops inventory valuation adjustments which, in effect, put all industry on a LIFO basis. Its 1951 income supplement, on page 39, makes the following statement: "The LIFO method of inventory accounting yields results most akin to national income practice." In other words, to determine income on a sound basis, the Department of Commerce feels it necessary to exclude from income any amounts which result from mere price fluctuations in continuing inventory investment.

The references used in the historical background section of Professor Moonitz' article would appear to have little bearing on the current status of LIFO. Certainly the fact that it was not commented upon by certain authors as far back as 1927, can hardly be construed as a valid argument that it is an unsound procedure. All of us use many procedures today which only a few years ago did not exist.

The first indications of the use of the base stock method in Europe were in England in the latter part of the Nineteenth Century. In this country it was used in the early part of the present century and LIFO came into being after the base stock method was disallowed tax-wise (in 1930) correcting the provisions of the base stock method which the court criticized. The base stock method was disallowed because it contained an arbitrary price applied to an arbitrary quantity. LIFO, which in effect legalizes the base stock idea, defines the acceptable quantity as the quantity on hand at the end of the year equal to the beginning quantity and calls for pricing that quantity at cost.

Income tax has been an integral part of our system since 1913 but the rates were not of sizable proportions until the short-lived excess-profits tax during World War I. During this short-lived period, a great many companies operating without LIFO built up tremendous inventory inflation profits during the war period on which taxes were paid and dividends distributed, only to suffer tremendous inventory write-downs in the early Twenties which represented a reversal of those previously reported profits. For example, the inventory values of a group of 468 companies declined approximately 26 per cent from 1920 to the end of 1921. Dun's index of commodity prices showed a decline of approximately 28 per cent. A group of 38 "blue chip" listed companies had inventory write-downs to market of approximately $300,000,000 in the early Twenties over the high points reached in 1919 and 1920. One of our largest corporations had set up a Reserve Against High Cost of Inventories of $93,755,698 during the period 1917 to 1920 so this company only had to take an additional write-down of $14,000,000 in 1920. Incidentally, this company has been on LIFO since it was made available.

LIFO NEEDED AFTER WRITE-DOWNS OF 1931

In 1931, additional write-downs took place—another group of 15 companies suffered write-downs at this time of about $100,000,000. The need for LIFO became evident at that time. However, reference to the price chart in Exhibit I on page 134 clearly shows that we had an upward trend in prices from the beginning of the century through 1920, most of it occurring since 1913. Thus, most of this price inflation occurred in a period after the introduction of income taxes, and the existing accounting principles, which were still in the development stage, generally made no provision to keep inventory price increases out of profits. After the severe decline in 1921, there was a stabilization of prices for a few years and then a further drop in the early Thirties to about the same level as those existing in 1913. During this ten-year price-decline period—1921 to 1931—the need for corrective accounting measures became apparent. Also, during this period, the base

Exhibit 1. Wholesale Price Index (All Commodities), 1801–1951

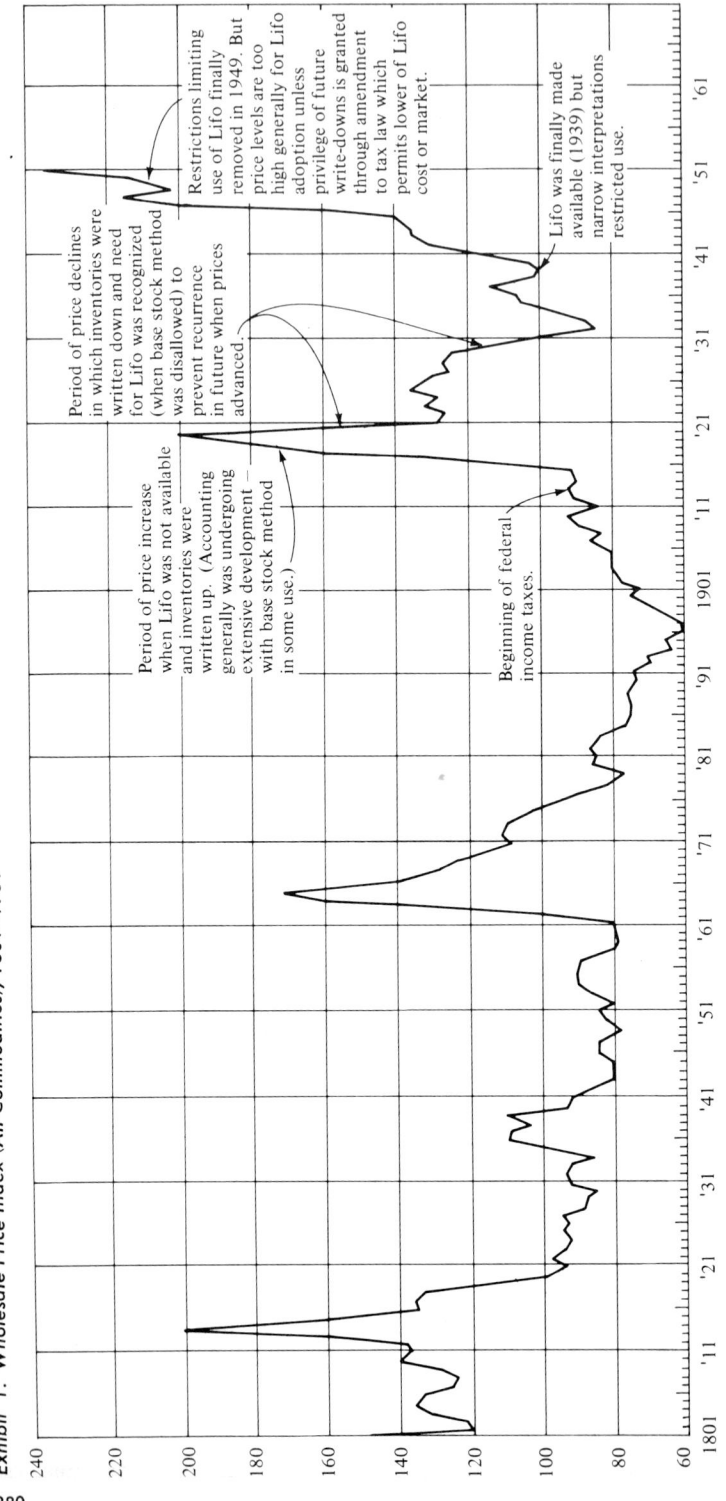

Note: Index numbers, January 1939 =100. Comments on sections of the chart are those of the author.
Sources: Bureau of Labor Statistics; Warren & Pearson; plotting through 1951 by the Conference Board.

THE CASE FOR LIFO   281

stock idea gained some headway only to be ruled out by a Supreme Court decision. LIFO was finally put into the tax law in 1938, in effect correcting the features of the base stock plan which were criticized by the Supreme Court. The development of the LIFO technique was the result of efforts of a small group, covering companies with simple inventories, headed by Maurice Peloubet, New York CPA. Thus the LIFO principle was born at the beginning of the current inflationary trend and supposedly has been available to all since 1939.

Unfortunately the lack of understanding of application to a complex inventory situation of a means of keeping out of profits the inventory price inflation, coupled with the narrow interpretation of the Bureau, prevented many companies from adopting LIFO during this period. It was not until 1949 that the dollar value method was actually recognized in the regulations, and as mentioned before, the requirement of the law of using cost price levels of the year of adoption as a floor for future tax determination continues to cause many companies to defer adopting it until they have had an opportunity to write down the price inflation in their inventories which they have previously been forced to write up and call realized income available for taxes and dividends. Obviously there would be little historical information on the development of an inventory pricing procedure which has as its objective the elimination of price fluctuations in the inventory investment in a period of price declines such as existed from about 1920 through 1932, for it was in this period that business was gradually writing down its inventory investments to new low cost levels which represented a reversal of the write-ups taken in the previous ten years. So it is of little significance to point out that articles appearing on accounting principles in those early years did not contain references to LIFO. Certainly no one would be advocating the introduction of LIFO during a period of price declines, thus freezing beginning inventories at higher levels than those existing at the end of a period. It is easy to understand why, when LIFO was finally introduced, its use gained slowly but steadily as it became understood in the inflationary period since 1939. It is extremely unfortunate that this broad application was not clearly understood nor accepted in the tax regulations in the early Forties. The various discussions and pronouncements as to the type of industry to which LIFO would apply make apparent the fact that it was not properly understood.

LIFO PROVES VALUABLE IN INFLATION

As Professor Moonitz points out, a gradual evolution in our thinking has occurred. LIFO has come to be recognized as a means of eliminating from profit any increase in the value of the same quantity of inventory that existed at the beginning of an accounting period. In a long period of continued inflation, such as we have been experiencing since 1940, in which cost levels generally have more than doubled, the real value of LIFO has become apparent. Companies which have not been using LIFO have been required to call as profit this increase in the cost of their basic inventories. None of this increase, of course, has been realized, and should prices level off, the increased capital required to carry the same inventories will have been classed as a realized profit even though it must be recognized that until such time as the inventories are reduced or eliminated, it will never be actually realized as profit.

Thus, it would seem that the objections to LIFO contained in Professor Moonitz' article are based primarily upon the concept of profit. We are either going to call the change in the cost value of the inventory a part of realized profit or we are going to eliminate it. The comments in the article about liquidations below the basic or normal essential to operations are further evidence of a lack of understanding of the intention of LIFO. The creation of an abnormal profit through liquidation of a base stock which is only temporary and which results in charging against income for a period a low cost value which will be replaced when the merchandise or materials are available certainly is something which should be recognized as unsound in setting up profits for a short period of a business cycle. While LIFO does not actually result in reflecting a full replacement cost against current sales value, it approaches this since it takes the latest costs incurred as those first construed to be shipped out. Thus, to the extent that latest costs have been incurred, it does match these against sales. The resultant profit is, therefore, more closely a true trading profit than one which includes a charge against operations for a low assigned value to a base stock which has been temporarily liquidated. The whole idea of base stock or LIFO contemplates a normal basic inventory. When this normal basic quantity is invaded for a temporary period, certainly profits are more truly expressed if the involuntary liquidation situation is recognized as such and provisions are made for the difference between the base stock assigned value and the replacement cost which more closely represents values upon which selling price levels are predicated.

PREVENTING WRITE-DOWN TO MARKET IS UNJUST

Professor Moonitz' comments about the proposed modifications of the tax statute covering LIFO to permit the lower of cost or market again clearly indicate that he does not understand the reasons for this revision. While the proponents of LIFO have always recognized that the profits of the period should not be influenced by fluctuations in the basic inventory value, either up or down, they also recognize that unless there is some protection from the effects of freezing the beginning price level, LIFO will continue to be an elective method adopted by the individual companies at such time that they guess to be a reasonably low price level, in order that they do not find themselves at a temporary tax disadvantage at some future time. The provision of the present law not permitting write-downs to market is particularly unjust to those companies which were misled from adopting practical applications of LIFO in the early Forties due to the narrow interpretations of the Bureau. After the ten-year period during which the Bureau was forced to accept the LIFO dollar method—(after the several Tax Court decisions in its favor)—many companies with complex inventories found LIFO available to them but prices had more than doubled in the interim. Certainly they should now be able to adopt LIFO at present cost levels to prevent further inflation of profits if prices continue to rise without losing the right to adjust their beginning cost level if prices go below that point in the future. They would only be retaining the privilege they now have under FIFO. Thus, under the proposed amendment, these companies will be permitted no greater inventory write-offs against profits in periods of price decline than would be permitted if they continued to operate under the FIFO or market basis. Without the amendment, they no doubt will continue on the FIFO lower of cost or market basis and when a low point is reached at some future time, they will then adopt LIFO. Other companies that have come into existence or expanded materially in a period of high cost levels will hesitate, without the amendment, to adopt LIFO until prices decline. Thus the indecision and resulting confusion will continue. The justification for the introduction of market in the LIFO formula is merely one of straightening out the inequities which have developed from lack of understanding of the practical LIFO application until it was too late, coupled with the need for a provision in the law which makes it possible for any company to adopt LIFO at any time in the future without having to give consideration to the possibility of a future unfavorable tax position.

The proposed amendment to permit lower of LIFO cost or market has the backing of the American Institute of Accountants committee on federal taxation and many industry associations, including: Tax Committee of the National Association of Manufacturers; the Department of Manufacture Committee of the U.S. Chamber of Commerce; the American Retail Federation (includes National Retail Dry Goods Association); the American Iron & Steel Institute; the American Cotton Manufacturers Institute; the Commerce and Industry Association of New York.

OBJECTIONS BASED ON TURNOVER UNREALISTIC

The comments in Professor Moonitz' paper relative to turnover appear to be somewhat unrealistic since turnover is based on the relation of the average inventory to cost of sales, and it is obvious that the determination of the inventory average must be based upon current costs during the year, to match current cost of sales. There is no reason why current values of the inventory cannot be disclosed on the balance-sheet even though LIFO is used in the profit-and-loss statement. Instead of ruling out LIFO, which is now generally recognized by the majority of industry as more correctly reflecting income, let us take steps to express both the profit-and-loss statement and the balance-sheet on a current value basis. This can readily be done and is possibly the needed step to cover what is being put forth as an inadequacy of LIFO. Instead of turning backwards, the accounting profession would do well to look ahead so that the usefulness of all published financial statements, as well as the profit-and-loss statements, will increase rather than diminish.

Before embarking upon a discussion of the development of the balance-sheet as well as the profit-and-loss statement at current cost levels, we must recognize that practical mechanics exist today which make it possible for any company having an inventory to express it on a LIFO basis. Thus, there is no favored group among companies which must recognize inventories in the determination of profit. Professor Moonitz' contention that LIFO means that a ton of steel, for example, has the same economic and business significance today as it did last year and in 1940 and in 1890, is certainly another indication of a lack of understanding of LIFO application. LIFO, as it is understood today, deals with "dollars of inventory investment," regardless of the character of the product units in which these dollars are invested—as they change LIFO merely preserves the cost price level of the materials, labor hours, and burden content of the basic inventory dollar investment.

Under the dollar value application, the inventory is considered as units of dollars of investment at a specific price level. Regardless of the character of that inventory investment, and whether or not a company has the same identical type of material in the inventory, or whether the investment is made up of rapidly changing items, we are dealing with the fixed monetary investment and freezing it at a price level so that the charges to operations representing cost of sales pick up the latest cost price levels which have been incurred. Under this concept, it is immaterial whether the reinvestment is in similar items or new items, for whatever investment is required it is carried forward in the inventory at the beginning price levels to the extent that the quantity of the aggregate investment is comparable with the beginning.

LIFO DOLLAR METHOD APPLIES TO ANY INDUSTRY

Professor Moonitz' paper also implies that the dollar value LIFO method is for department stores. The LIFO dollar method is applicable to any industry. It just so happened that the first test case tried before the Tax Court was a department store application. An increasing number of industrial companies with complex inventories have adopted very simple LIFO dollar value applications which involve the development of specific company indices of price changes. LIFO is merely a method of preventing price changes in the fixed inventory investment from affecting profits for the short period. Thus, when it is pointed out that LIFO fails miserably and completely in making adjustments of inventory values for any type of price change, it is apparent that the true objective of LIFO is not understood and, of course, when an attempt is made to widen the scope of LIFO beyond its purpose, criticisms which result are without foundation.

The argument is advanced that while LIFO might accomplish the desired effect on the income statement, it influences the balance-sheet oppositely and conceivably below the limits of reasonable conservatism. In view of this, it is suggested that we should give up the desired effect on the income statement rather than correct the balance-sheet.

Let us now consider how we can continue to use the LIFO principle of pricing which is being accepted by industry in ever-increasing numbers, and at the same time take steps to preserve the balance-sheet so that it too represents current values.

Let us assume in the simple balance-sheet in Exhibit II that we have an inventory priced at LIFO which is $300,000 under the current acquisition cost.

The adjustment of the LIFO inventory to the lower of incurred cost or market represents the net additional after applicable income taxes. The current assets of the company already reflect the tax reduction resulting from the application of LIFO. The net addition to the inventory is offset by a credit to a Reserve to Prevent Impairment of Capital Covering the Inventory Cost Increase.

In order to complete the picture, possibly we should also introduce the need for recognizing the depreciation deficiency, which exists in periods of rising prices when historical costs only have been used for depreciation purposes, and the adjustment of plant assets to current values. Thus, the following suggested balance-sheet treatment brings all costs to current levels. Let us assume in this balance-sheet that we have an inventory priced at LIFO which is $300,000 under the current acquisition cost and also that the company's plant assets expressed at current price levels equal twice the original acquisition cost, and all plant assets were acquired as of the same date. (See Exhibit III.)

The accumulated depreciation to date on a cost basis was $500,000. On a current cost basis, this accrued depreciation would be $1,000,000. Thus accumulated earnings or surplus have been reduced by $500,000 depreciation deficiency (not deductible tax-wise under present law) and this likewise has been credited to a Reserve to Prevent Impairment of Capital Covering Accumulated Depreciation. The appreciation in the net plant assets of $500,000 has been credited to Unrealized Appreciation Account.

Exhibit II

Assets		
Cash		$ 150,000
Receivables		250,000
Inventory—LIFO cost	$ 400,000	
Excess of lower of incurred cost or market over LIFO (300,000) less applicable federal income taxes (156,000)	144,000	544,000
Plant Assets	$1,000,000	
Less: Allowance for depreciation	500,000	500,000
		$1,444,000
Liabilities		
Payables		$ 400,000
Capital Stock		200,000
Reserve to Prevent Impairment of Capital * Covering Inventory Cost Increase		144,000
Earned Surplus		700,000
		$1,444,000

* In the opinion of some, under the present LIFO tax law, including this reserve in the equity section might be construed as an indirect violation of the prohibition against expressing earnings on other than a LIFO basis. To forestall this possibility, this reserve could be shown above the stockholder's equity section of the balance-sheet.

Exhibit III

Assets		
Cash		$ 150,000
Receivables		250,000
Inventory—LIFO cost	$ 400,000	
Excess of lower of incurred cost or market over LIFO (300,000) less applicable federal incomes taxes (156,000)	144,000	544,000
Plant Assets (original cost adjusted to current price levels)	$2,000,000	
Less: Allowance for depreciation	1,000,000	1,000,000
		$1,944,000
Liabilities		
Payables		$ 400,000
Capital Stock		200,000
Reserves to Prevent Impairment of Capital:		
Covering Inventory Cost Increase	$ 144,000	
Covering Accumulated Depreciation	500,000	644,000
Unrealized Appreciation in Net Plant Assets		500,000
Earned Surplus		200,000
		$1,944,000

The foregoing balance-sheet thus represents all assets and liabilities expressed in current values. Earnings have been reduced to cover the inventory cost increase and likewise accrued depreciation charges against earnings have been adjusted to reflect depreciation recovered on a current dollar basis. The appreciation in the residual value of the plant assets is an unrealized appreciation and has been so set up.

If it is desired to express the inventory at current market rather than incurred cost, should the market prices be higher, the additional amount representing the increase of market over incurred cost could likewise be set up as an unrealized appreciation.

The Reserves to Prevent Impairment of Capital are a part of the capital structure. They represent charges against revenues to cover the increased costs incurred in maintaining basic inventory investment and to provide the additional current dollars needed to cover the portion of the investment in plant facilities which has expired. The unrealized appreciation represents the increase of the residue of the investment in plant assets to current price levels. It merely reflects the additional capital requirements which will be needed to continue the existing assets at the current price levels. This unrealized appreciation will be a charge against future earnings as the assets expire if the current price levels continue. Thus, since the adjusted depreciation to cover price level changes is provided for out of accumulated or current earnings, corresponding amounts should be transferred from the unrealized appreciation account to the Reserve to Prevent Capital Impairment. Therefore, as the depreciable assets are used up, the capital required to replace them in excess of the depreciation on original cost would be accumulated in the Reserve to Prevent Capital Impairment Account. Also, as price levels change, the net plant asset accounts would be adjusted with an offset in the Unrealized Appreciation Account.

LIFO results in reflecting earnings on the basis of current incurred costs during the period. With the depreciation deficiency provided for, the items on the profit-and-loss statement represent current values incurred during the period. The introduction of a few simple reserves in the balance-sheet, such as have been suggested in the preceding comments, should serve to overcome the objections that **LIFO** or any other improvement needed to more clearly reflect income destroys the balance-sheet.

In conclusion, I would like to suggest that we continue to take only forward steps in the evolution of accounting. We need agreement on a concept of profit which eliminates the effect of fluctuations in the value assigned to the basic inventory investment in the determination of realized factual profit (**LIFO**). We need to recognize the introduction of lower of **LIFO** cost or market as a requisite to correct inequities which have existed and will continue to exist unless given this relief. Then we should turn our combined efforts toward correcting the balance-sheet.

C. DIRECT COSTING

JOHN R. E. PARKER

JOHN R. E. PARKER (1931–   ), B.Com. 52 Dalhousie; M.B.A. 59 University of Washington; C.A. (Ontario). Currently professor in the Faculty of Administrative Studies, York University, Toronto. Major publications: *Professional Accounting* (with Bonham, 1965), *Accountancy: A Sourcebook of Readings* (edited readings, 1971). Contributor to Canadian journals.

Principal research interest: measuring and reporting earnings per share: an empirical analysis of Canadian accounting practice.

GIVE CONSIDERATION TO DIRECT COSTING FOR EXTERNAL REPORTING

JOHN R. E. PARKER

Direct costing has earned the acceptance of many accountants and businessmen, particularly those in industry. Nevertheless, the status of the method as to general acceptance is clouded with uncertainty. Financial statements that include inventories valued at direct cost may be subject to qualification by external auditors if the valuation differs materially from what it would be under absorption costing. Furthermore, direct costing is not likely to be recognized for tax purposes. Because of these uncertainties, direct costing is often confined to purposes of internal reporting. In these cases, external financial statements prepared from accounts based on direct costing are converted to an absorption cost basis. However, the adjustments that restore the applicable amount of fixed overhead to inventory are neither involved nor difficult.

SOURCE: From *NAA Bulletin* (now *Management Accounting*), Vol. 45, No. 2 (October, 1963), pp. 3–9. Reprinted by permission of *Management Accounting*.

On the other hand, some accountants believe that direct costing procedures, in addition to aiding management, yield more useful results to external users of financial data. Upwards of forty percent of the companies that use direct costing internally also use the method in external financial statements.[1] Moreover, among the remaining companies that use direct costing—despite the ready adjustment referred to above—there is a strong preference for external reports that are in agreement with the internal financial statements.

DISTINGUISHING MARKS OF DIRECT COSTING

The separation of fixed and variable costs has been stressed as the principal characteristic of direct costing. However, this is almost mandatory for many managerial purposes. Such segregation is basic to direct costing but not exclusive to it. In other words, the separation of costs can be useful in absorption costing, although not basic to the method. The point to be emphasized is that direct costing incorporates the separation of costs in the recording phase of the accounting process. Through redesign of the income statement, the separation of fixed and variable costs becomes the basis of the direct cost reporting system.

But direct costing also limits inventory valuation to variable costs. Herein lies the fundamental difference between direct and absorption costing for financial statement purposes. Conventional procedures of absorption costing exclude selling, general and administrative expenses, interest and similar items from inventory value. They may also omit variations from standard cost which represent inefficiencies in the use of materials, manpower and plant. To these exclusions from inventory valuation direct costing adds all fixed manufacturing costs.

In general terms, absorption costing emphasizes the distinction between production costs and all other costs. On the other hand, direct costing emphasizes the distinction between fixed and variable costs. Each values inventory accordingly. Absorption costing, with a balance-sheet emphasis, includes all costs believed to add to inventory value, and therefore applies fixed manufacturing costs to inventory. Direct costing, with an income-statement emphasis, excludes from inventories these fixed manufacturing costs as having been applied against income of the period. These costs are value added from an absorption costing viewpoint. From a direct costing viewpoint, they are costs which cannot properly be deferred.

THEORETICAL SUPPORT FOR DIRECT COSTING

Direct costing claims theoretical support by virtue of the generally accepted accounting concept that period costs should be recognized in the income account of the period in which they are incurred. Only those costs which are a function of output should be deferred as inventory costs and matched against future revenue. The proponents of direct costing suggest that the individual product does not incur fixed overhead; fixed manufacturing costs are incurred on a time basis, regardless of the volume of production or sales. The question to be answered concerns the nature of fixed overhead: Are fixed costs really period costs?

[1] Wilmer Wright, *Direct Standard Costs for Decision Making and Control*, McGraw-Hill, 1962, p. 214.

Those who favor direct costing claim that the fixed portion of manufacturing overhead is not really a cost of production but only a standby cost which facilitates production, and which must be incurred regardless of the level of production or sales. In theory, direct costing views the fixed overhead of a business as a constant quantity that is incurred during a period of time. When the time period expires, the fixed costs incurred expire with it. Accordingly, the whole of the fixed overhead must be allocated to what has been sold in the period, as this is the only source of revenue from which the fixed costs can be recovered. The next accounting period will incur its own fixed overhead; therefore, it is regarded as irrational to defer in the inventory account any portion of the previous period's fixed costs. Moreover, fixed costs are the result of a special kind of management decision; hence it is reasonable to accord a different accounting treatment to the fixed and variable portions of manufacturing overhead.

Attempts have also been made to justify direct costing on the basis of what is termed "contribution theory." Each sales dollar is said to consist of two parts: (1) a reimbursement of total variable costs and (2) the remainder of the sales dollar which contributes to the coverage of fixed costs and profits. As applied to the measurement of income, this accords with the economists' concept of the margin which clearly demonstrates that profit does not accrue on a unit basis. No profit, regardless of price, is realized until fixed costs are fully recovered.

Profit, then, accrues in a manner that is not revealed by the margin between selling price and full unit costs, fixed and variable. The difference between the aggregate value of sales and the aggregate variable cost of the products sold provides a fund of contribution from which to discharge the fixed costs and provide for the profits of the entity. After fixed costs have been recovered, the sale of an additional unit of product results in an addition to total revenue which, in the final analysis, increases net profit by an amount equal to the difference between the selling price and the unit's variable cost.

DIRECT COSTING AND GENERAL ACCEPTANCE

Is direct costing a generally accepted method of accounting? This question can be answered with no more authority than an informed opinion.

At the outset, it must be recognized that a compendium of generally accepted accounting principles does not exist. As a result, many accounting practices have simply evolved on an *ad hoc* basis. This is significant because, in audit reports, the profession is committed to the existence of generally accepted accounting principles. However, it is not clear to whom accounting principles must be acceptable or to what extent acceptance is necessary. Furthermore, the process of accepting alternative practices is so uncertain that one may question how improvements can be made, if such improvements are not permissible until generally accepted![2]

As they presently exist, generally accepted accounting principles are incomplete in terms of fulfilling the need for an integrated and comprehensive structure of accounting theory. The bulletins of the American Institute of Certified Public Accountants, together with the various releases of other professional accounting

---

[2] George R. Catlett, "Relation of Acceptance to Accounting Principles," *The Journal of Accountancy*, March 1960, pp. 34 and 35.

organizations, probably represent the best evidence of general acceptance. However, such statements lack the absolute authority to be binding on all accountants under all conditions. Moreover, these bulletins and other pronouncements have been directed more to accounting practices than to the underlying principles. Therefore, they generally lag behind the problems they purport to solve.

In this case, there is a minimum of help to be gained from "official" pronouncements. Organizations of professional accountants in North America have maintained silence with respect to direct costing. There is nothing in the bulletins of the American Institute of Certified Public Accountants that can be used with any degree of certainty to either support or reject the use of direct costing in external financial statements. The same can be said of the bulletins issued by the Canadian Institute of Chartered Accountants.

However, a 1957 pronouncement by the Committee on Concepts and Standards of the American Accounting Association states that "the cost of a manufactured product is the sum of the acquisition costs reasonably traceable to that product and should include both direct and indirect factors. *The omission of any element of manufacturing cost is not acceptable.*"[3] Although this statement implies a lack of acceptability to direct costing for external purposes, inasmuch as published financial statements were under discussion, it is significant that two of the seven members who comprised the committee dissented from the majority position. Their published dissent expressed the opinion that "direct costing is at least as acceptable in accounting theory as is the conventional 'full costing' concept."[4]

Favorable implications from official statements are tenuous at best. In Accounting Research Bulletin No. 43, which superseded all previous bulletins, the American Institute of Certified Public Accountants does not speak of direct costing but states that "the exclusion of all overheads from inventory costs does not constitute an accepted accounting procedure."[5] Although certainly not intended as such, this statement has been interpreted in terms favorable to direct costing. While admitting that it is not proper to exclude all overheads from inventory costs, proponents of direct costing contend that it is proper to exclude fixed overhead. There is also the statement of the Committee on Accounting and Auditing Research of the Canadian Institute of Chartered Accountants in its Bulletin No. 5:[6]

> Sometimes certain costs are excluded in determining inventory values. Usually expenditures arising out of abnormal circumstances, such as rehandling of goods and idle facilities, are not included. *Similarly, in some cases, fixed overhead is excluded where its inclusion would distort the profit for the year by reason of fluctuating volume of production.*

It is possible to read into this statement an implication of acceptability for

---

[3] American Accounting Association, "Accounting and Reporting Standards for Corporate Financial Statements, 1957 Revision," *The Accounting Review*, October 1957, p. 539 (emphasis provided).

[4] *Ibid.*, p. 545.

[5] Committee on Accounting Procedure, *Restatement and Revision of Accounting Research Bulletins, ARB No. 43*, American Institute of Certified Public Accountants, 1953, p. 29.

[6] Committe on Accounting and Auditing Research, *The Meaning of the Term Cost as Used in Inventory Valuation, Bulletin No. 5*, Canadian Institute of Chartered Accountants, 1950, p. 2 (emphasis provided).

direct costing. However, Bulletin No. 5 does not mention direct costing; as a result, the position of the Institute is not clear.

A somewhat more positive expression comes from across the water. Statement on Accounting Principles N 22, issued by the Institute of Chartered Accountants in England and Wales, recognizes the acceptability of direct costing as follows:[7]

> Where, however, the levels (of production or sales) are subject to material fluctuation and are not kept in balance, it may be decided to exclude these (period) expenses from stock on the ground that, as they would be incurred whatever the levels of production or sales, their inclusion in stock has the effect of relieving the profit and loss account in the period when they are incurred of expenses which it should fairly bear and of charging these expenses in a later period to which they do not properly relate.

The above position is based on the premise that no one method of accounting for manufacturing overhead is suitable for all businesses. It should be recognized that British philosophy supports maximum freedom in accountancy, together with consistency in the application of accounting principles or full disclosure of departures from consistent application where the effect of the departure is material. This philosophy is in contrast with what seems to prevail in North America, where there is evidence of a desire for greater uniformity and comparability in financial reporting, narrowing the areas of difference and inconsistency.

BASIC ACCOUNTING THEORY AND DIRECT COSTING

From a practical point of view, all costs incurred by a business entity are intended to produce revenue. In strict theory, therefore, all costs attach to the product or service that provides the source of revenue from which costs are recoverable. However, as pointed out by Professors Paton and Littleton, "Not all costs attach in a discernible manner, and this fact forces the accountant to fall back upon a time-period as the unit for associating certain expenses with certain revenues."[8]

The concept of period costs is well established in accounting practice, even though the same authors further state that "time periods are a convenience, a substitute, but the fundamental concept (remains) unchanged."[9] Accounting is an art that is generally regarded as being utilitarian by nature. Therefore, accounting principles are closely related to the way in which accountants do their work in practice. This close relationship between use and principle serves to explain the recognition of period costs in accounting theory. Here is an example of conflict where the practical difficulties of cost allocation override what appears to be sound accounting theory.

The adoption of the fiscal year as a convenient period for financial reporting is basic to the accounting process. The related concept of period costs is primarily

---

[7] Council, *Treatment of Stock-in-Trade and Work in Progress in Financial Accounts, Accounting Principles N 22*, Institute of Chartered Accountants in England and Wales, 1960, p. 3.

[8] W. A. Paton and A. C. Littleton, *An Introduction to Corporate Accounting Standards*, American Accounting Association, 1940, p. 15.

[9] *Ibid.*

the result of a practical need to minimize the incidence of cost allocation. Accounting theory recognizes that there is no practical solution other than period-cost treatment in the case of selling and administrative costs. If period-cost treatment is sound for certain costs that have a closer affinity to time than to activity, it is sound for all such costs, regardless of the functional relationships that may exist. The fact that fixed manufacturing overhead is essential to production does not necessitate allocating this cost to each unit of output.

Fixed costs, by definition, relate to the capacity and organization provided, which is not necessarily the same as the normal level of activity. As a result, a joint-cost situation arises under absorption costing, in that fixed manufacturing overhead can consist of product-cost and period-cost components. Conventional procedures of absorption costing frequently involve the problem of separating the cost of product from the cost of unused capacity. Period-cost treatment of idle capacity is widely recognized in accounting theory. Therefore, it is not difficult to agree with Raymond P. Marple that it takes "a considerable amount of stretching to jump to the conclusion that costs which are charged against the period when the capacity is not used can . . . be transferred into effective and deferrable product costs when management decides to use, as compared with not use, the provided capacity."[10]

The test to be applied in deciding whether an item of cost is a proper period charge involves determining that the item represents an expenditure from which only the current period will benefit. The concept of future benefit is widely accepted by accountants in explaining the nature of an asset.[11] Referring to asset expiration, the Committee on Concepts and Standards of the American Accounting Association states: "Expired costs are those having no discernible benefit to future operations."[12]

Future benefit is a useful criterion for determining those costs that should be treated as product costs. Under the going-concern or continuity postulate, inventory valuation is, by nature, much more a process of cost deferral than a process of valuation. To the extent of variable manufacturing costs, inventory produced but unsold in one accounting period relieves subsequent periods of further outlays. Thus, the future benefit of cost obviation clearly exists in the case of variable manufacturing costs.

Since the fixed costs incurred during one accounting period have no bearing on reincurring the same kind of fixed costs in subsequent periods, the cost obviation test for future benefit fails when applied to fixed manufacturing overhead. Also, it is difficult to explain why the production of an additional unit necessitates charging to that unit a normal share of costs which are incurred even if the unit is not produced. Assuming that capacity is available, the decision to produce an additional unit does not increase fixed costs, nor does it reduce the costs of subse-

[10] Raymond P. Marple, "There is a Fundamental Error in Absorption Costing," *The Controller*, July 1961, correspondence, p. 318.

[11] For a more complete treatment of future benefit and cost obviation, see David Green, Jr., "A Moral to the Direct Costing Controversy," *Journal of Business*, July 1960, pp. 222–223; and Charles T. Horngren and George H. Sorter, "Direct Costing for External Reporting," *The Accounting Review*, January 1961, pp. 84–93.

[12] American Accounting Association, *op. cit.*, p. 541.

quent periods. The only logical conclusion is that fixed manufacturing costs are irrelevant in such circumstances and, therefore, do not represent asset values under the going-concern concept.

It must also be recognized that potential future revenue is implicit in the recognition of assets. In the absence of revenue-producing potential, an item of cost that might otherwise represent an asset cannot benefit future operations and, therefore, becomes an expired cost. On the other hand, in circumstances where potential future revenue exists, this fact is nothing more than *per se* evidence that an asset exists. It is still necessary to determine the value that should be assigned to that asset.

There is, of course, an inevitable lag between the production of goods and their ultimate sale. The resulting delay in revenue recognition means different things to different people. Those who favor absorption costing believe that the matching process necessitates that full costs, fixed and variable, be matched with the recognition of revenue at the time of sale. Under direct costing, fixed manufacturing overhead of prior periods is not considered a proper charge against future revenue. In the opinion of Louis H. Jordan, "the matching process degenerates into mere subtraction: from revenues for the period determined in a variety of ways are subtracted expenses also determined in a variety of ways."[13]

Direct costing procedures produce a concept of inventory valuation that is at least as acceptable in accounting theory as the conventional absorption cost concept. Inventories valued on the basis of variable costs reflect the amount of working capital tied up in unsold products. Under the going-concern assumption, such a concept is consistent with a deferred-cost interpretation of inventory and fully recognizes the nature of assets as "service-potentials available for or beneficial to expected operations."[14]

THE DUPLE MOTOR BODIES CASE

The House of Lords decision in the case of *Duple Motor Bodies v. Ostime* ranks as an interesting and authoritative treatment that, in substance, rejects absorption costing in the circumstances that prevailed. A tax case, the decision establishes that the inclusion of overhead in inventory results in a disallowance of deductible expenditures in the period in which they are incurred. However, their Lordships also recognized the importance of consistency and the fact that no change in the method of inventory valuation is justified unless there is a good reason, such as a change in circumstances.

It is interesting to note that Lord Simonds found the absorption cost method undesirable because it could lead to absurd conclusions. In an article that appeared in the *Canadian Tax Journal*, Gwyneth McGregor states, "In arriving at the cost of work in progress it was 'undesirable to indulge in what is no better than guesswork': and a large part of the (absorption cost) method appeared to the learned judge to involve 'the wildest guesswork.' "[15]

[13] Louis H. Jordan, "A Discussion of the Usefulness and Theory of Direct Costing," *NAA Bulletin*, March 1962, p. 60.

[14] American Accounting Association, *op. cit.*, p. 538.

[15] Gwyneth McGregor, "Accountancy in the Lords," *Canadian Tax Journal*, July–August 1961, p. 269.

FURTHER INQUIRY NEEDED

The central issue in the direct costing controversy involves the process of matching costs with revenue, particularly in terms of timing the release of fixed manufacturing costs to expense. Under absorption costing, fixed overhead is matched with revenue when the products to which the fixed costs relate are sold. Direct costing writes off the fixed portion of overhead to revenue on a time basis as incurred. Considered from a more fundamental point of view, the direct costing controversy revolves around the definition of an asset and the costs that should be included as such in the balance sheet. As a corollary, the nature of expense is also involved.

The uncertainty that exists with respect to direct costing makes it impossible to conclude that the method conforms with generally accepted accounting principles. In fact, the majority of informed opinion may hold the opposite view. However, the theoretical structure of direct costing appears to be sound. Furthermore, the statements of professional accounting organizations do not clearly rule out the acceptability of direct costing.

In the context of financial reporting, public accountants do not object to the use of direct costing where the external financial statements are adjusted to reflect the applicable portion of fixed costs in inventory or where the effect is not so material as to require adjustment of the statements for external reporting. Moreover, there is still sufficient doubt concerning the acceptability of direct costing that qualification may not result even in circumstances where inventories are materially different from what they would be under absorption costing. The decision to adopt direct costing for external reporting is likely to result in a consistency qualification in the year of change, because it cannot be stated that accounting principles have been applied on a basis consistent with the preceding year.

It is apparent that direct costing and absorption costing involve two different concepts of inventory valuation. Two methods of inventory valuation, one of which omits a significant portion of the cost included in the other, cannot both be recognized as conforming with generally accepted accounting principles. One method or the other has to be the proper practice to follow. In the long run, no useful purpose is served by ignoring this fact. However, further research and experience are required in order to develop the insight needed to resolve the direct costing controversy.

HOWARD C. GREER

HOWARD C. GREER (1894–), A.B. 15 Northwestern; CPA. Currently retired. Major publications: *Chain Store Accounting* (1924), *A Uniform System of Accounts for Retail Furniture Dealers* (1926), *How to Understand Accounting* (1928), *Packinghouse Accounting* (1929), *Problems in Cost Accounting* (with Willcox, 1931), *Accounting for a Meat Packing Business* (with Smith, 1943). Was a leader in formulating the American Accounting Association's *Tentative Statement of Accounting Principles Underlying Corporate Financial Statements* (1936). Frequent contributor to *The Journal of Accountancy*, *The Accounting Review*, *Management Accounting* (U.S.) (formerly *N.A.A. Bulletin*), and other journals.

After three years with Arthur Young & Company, in 1922 he joined the Ohio State University faculty, where he served as director of the Bureau of Business Research. From 1927 to 1939, he was an executive with the American Meat Institute, Chicago. Was vice-president and general manager of Kingan & Co., Indianapolis, from 1939 to 1949, following which he was vice-president–finance of Monon Railroad, Chicago (1949–58), and vice president–finance of Chemstrand Corp., New York (1950–58).

He delivered the Dickinson Lecture for 1951–52, "Prices and Costs in a Free Economy," and "Prices and Costs Under Government Regulation." Served as secretary-treasurer (1926–29), vice-president (1930–31 and 1936), and president (1932) of the American Accounting Association. Was a member of the Study Group on Business Income, 1948–52.

ALTERNATIVES TO DIRECT COSTING

HOWARD CLARK GREER

The vigor and enthusiasm of the current debate on direct costing is unmitigated by the fact that it is not at all clear just what is being debated. The proponents of direct costing describe it in such diverse terms that it is difficult to determine exactly what one is accepting or rejecting in lining up for or against the proposition. Of the contentions advanced by direct cost advocates, some are plainly true and some are extremely doubtful. It is going too far to demand their acceptance on an "all or none" basis.

This paper presents the results of an effort to separate the several elements of the direct cost philosophy and examine them individually for merits and defects, and also to relate them to other cost procedures of longer standing. After such a study of this new philosophy, there is a temptation to suggest that what is good about it is not new and what is new about it is not good. That, however, would be unfair. Several valid and important conclusions have received needed empha-

SOURCE: From *NACA Bulletin* (now *Management Accounting*), Vol. 35, No. 7 (March, 1954), pp. 878–888. Reprinted by permission of *Management Accounting*.

sis from the direct costing approach. It has thus served a very useful purpose, whether or not it deserves an all-inclusive acceptance.

DIRECT COSTING—WHAT IS IT?

There seems to be no simple straight-forward definition of direct costing. The available descriptions of the procedure are vague and rambling, with the authors by no means precise as to the essentials or the boundaries of the suggested method. The more dubious aspects of the theory are introduced as optional and secondary, but so emphasized as to make them appear fundamental. This is confusing.

However, there appear to be two principal elements in the philosophy, one having to do with cost analysis for management control and price comparison purposes, and the other with cost assignment for inventory valuation and profit determination purposes. Some of the recent pronouncements on the subject, though not following any such clear-cut lines, can be separated into these two primary idea groups. For example, the statement of "essential characteristics" quoted with approval in the Association's excellent research study on this subject[1] can be rearranged to emphasize the basic association of ideas, as follows:

Cost analysis	Cost assignment
"Direct costing should be defined as segregation of manufacturing costs between those which are fixed and those which vary directly with volume.... The point to be emphasized is that direct costing is primarily a segregation of expenses and only secondarily a method of inventory valuation."	"Only the prime costs plus variable costs are used to value inventory and cost of sales. The remaining factory expenses are charged off currently to profit and loss.... By this approach, full attention can be devoted to the effect which direct costing has on the profit and loss statement and supplementary operation reports."

In case you do not understand that, you can proceed through the following paragraph, in which the researchers explain what they think is meant:

"... the prime objective of the plan is provision of information about cost-volume-profit relationships . . . not a reversion to earlier costing practices which omitted some or all indirect costs from product costs because accountants did not then know how to allocate them or failed to see their importance as product costs."	"Direct costing has sometimes been described as a plan for eliminating fixed costs from inventories. This description stresses an incidental feature.... Under direct costing, variability with volume determines whether a manufacturing cost should be classified as a product cost or as a period cost."

If this leaves the definition still somewhat obscure, one may turn to the papers on this subject presented at the most recent National Cost Conference[2] which again offer contrasting concepts of the essentials of direct costing, in such comments as the following (language altered slightly for sake of brevity):

[1] N.A.C.A. Research Series No. 23, *N.A.C.A. Bulletin,* April 1953, pp. 1079–80.
[2] 1953 Conference Proceedings, *N.A.C.A. Bulletin,* Section 3, July 1953, pp. 1534–35, 1546–47.

"Direct costing... is designed to satisfy the need for a simple presentation of operating results, clearly indicating the cost-volume-profit relationships... adheres to concept of the break-even chart in providing marginal income figures to measure profit value of changes in sales volume."

"Basic concept is . . . to make a careful classification or division of expenses between fixed and variable, and then pull all fixed expenses out of product costs and treat them as costs of the period... only variable costs will be included in cost of sales ... difference between cost of sales and sales is marginal contribution to period costs."

BASIC PROPOSITIONS

Mind-reading is a hazardous occupation, but it appears that these authors, and others, are advancing two basic propositions which may be stated briefly in the following language:

In the presentation of cost comparisons, the essential distinction, for all purposes, is between expenses considered as variable and expenses considered as fixed.

In the determination of profits and inventory values, only variable expenses may be included in product costs, and all fixed expenses must be treated as period costs.

The validity of these propositions can be better assessed if they are reframed in the form of questions, as follows:

1. Is a simple distinction between apparently variable and supposedly fixed expenses all that is necessary for managerial cost control, pricing policy, operations planning, etc.?

2. Is periodic profit measurement improved by charging all fixed expenses against current sales revenues, regardless of production volume, inventory accumulation, etc.?

The answer to both these questions is obviously, "No." Cost problems are far from being that simple, as even the most ardent advocate of direct costing would doubtless agree. To clarify the problem, two additional questions may be posed:

3. In pricing, is it essential to distinguish between (a) marginal income contribution (excess of sales revenue over direct out-of-pocket costs) and (b) net income contribution (excess of sales revenue over fully apportioned costs)?

4. In operation, is it essential to distinguish between (a) controllable expenses (those related to the degree of departmental activity and efficiency), and (b) fixed expenses (those resulting from factors and decisions beyond the influence of the departmental supervisor)?

The answer to both of these questions is clearly "Yes." If that is what the proponents of direct costing are trying to prove, there should be no one to dispute their contention, even if there is nothing strikingly novel about it.

Since the issue has been joined on both grounds, it may be worthwhile to explore the entire field somewhat further, to determine what elaboration of conventional procedures is desirable and how management decisions can be improved through consideration of facts developed by direct cost presentations.

VARIABLE COSTS—VARIABLE WITH WHAT?

Management difficulties in adjusting selling practices to direct cost facts are complicated by accounting difficulties in developing the facts. These arise from the impossibility of making a clear distinction between variable and fixed costs.

Proponents of marginal income calculations, break-even charts, and similar devices, usually start with the convenient assumption that every expenditure, in relation to the volume of output, either varies directly with that volume or is completely independent of it. Grant the assumption and numerous conclusions become easy. Unfortunately for theory, the assumption is manifestly false in most cases.

While certain costs obviously are influenced by volume to a greater extent than others, it is broadly correct to say that over the entire potential volume range (from maximum to zero) almost no costs are precisely uniform per unit of output or per unit of time. At the one extreme, even such supposedly fixed costs as insurance, taxes, and depreciation can be reduced when there are radical reductions in output. At the other extreme, even such direct costs as materials and labor may be larger per unit when volume is down.

This well-understood fact is not, itself, a bar to the establishment of "variable" and "fixed" as broad classifications of costs, however rough and arbitrary they may be. Within rather narrow ranges of over-all volume (e.g. 60–80 per cent of capacity) assumptions as to relative variability and fixity can be made without risk of serious error, but, in a large manufacturing operation, there are further complications.

Production on a broad scale entails not merely the conduct of the direct operations of processing the materials into finished products, or parts, but also the performance of numerous auxiliary functions of independent character. For example, there may be power plants, pumping stations, waste disposal units, analytical laboratories, mechanic shops, medical facilities, cafeterias, plant guard forces, fire-fighting units, etc. There also may be supervisors, personnel men, time study engineers, inspectors, paymasters, and others.

Each of these activities may comprise variable and fixed expenses—variable with the service performed by that unit or fixed in relation to it, but not necessarily bearing a similar relationship to the output of any product item or production center. Informative classification of such costs can become a very intricate and puzzling affair.

Even within a production center, variations in volume have often unpredictable effects on cost incurrence. Discontinue the output of one machine from a battery of ten and supervision cost may be unaffected, but discontinue one whole battery from a group of three and supervision may be cut one-third. Volume increase up to the point of maximum single-shift output may leave overheads fixed, but the addition of a second shift may suddenly magnify such overheads in a startling manner. Maintenance costs often are higher when volume is down and machinery available for repair.

Thus, even the direct cost of a given activity often cannot be determined unless it is known what other activities are going to be conducted at the same time. Numerous classes of expenses are sometimes fixed and sometimes variable, depending on conditions. When major decisions are to be made, it becomes necessary to make a forecast of results through the entire manufacturing operation, with integrated assumptions as to both the amount and the character of the anticipated output, before a safe conclusion can be reached.

This does not weaken the direct cost argument. It merely broadens its scope and exposes the dangers of oversimplification of either the analyses or the conclusions they suggest. The problem is still one of combining in one enterprise a group of productive activities which in the aggregate will produce the largest possible return on investment. This end is not to be achieved by seeking uniform profit margins over fully apportioned costs, but neither is it to be attained by treating certain cost components as unalterably fixed or undeviatingly variable under all possible manufacturing conditions.

ADEQUATE COST AND EXPENSE CLASSIFICATION

The most important contribution of the direct cost philosophy is its emphasis on more intensive analysis and more effective presentation of product costs and operating expenses. It has been apparent that many cost accountants, in their preoccupation with the assignment of all classes of costs to individual units of output, have failed to give adequate emphasis to the nature of the cost components themselves.

The first step in classification is the selection of suitable primary expense categories. This is sometimes assumed to consist solely of establishing a single "code of accounts," in which analysis is extended merely by establishing further subdivisions of the categories initially selected.

In a large operation, the inadequacies of such procedure are soon apparent. Intelligent managerial study of expense data requires that they be classified not merely according to one characteristic (e.g. expense type), but also according to possibly two or three others (e.g. function, controllability, basis of assignment). There must be, not just a one-way expense analysis, but a two-way or three-way summary, analyzing the various aspects of the outlays made, for the various interpretations requisite to effective management.

A two-way classification, so universally needed that it is fast becoming standard practice, identifies expenses first by type and second by function. Through this device, a distinction can be made between such expense-type groups as materials, labor, security, supplies, outside services, insurance, taxes, and depreciation, and such functional activity subdivisions as production, utilities, maintenance, supervision, etc. Separate recognition of both characteristics prevents either from obscuring the other.

This, however, is only the beginning of an adequate analysis of costs and expenses. As to each activity (cost center), a distinction must be made between direct and apportioned charges, between standard and allowable expense, between fixed current and fixed sunk costs, and between those outlays which are presently controllable at the local level and those which reflect management decisions made at some earlier time or in some higher echelon.

Such analyses give rise to a series of internal cost reports which are vital to intelligent control of activities and evaluation of results, while, at the same time, contributing the elements necessary to a calculation of product costs, stated in whatever terms may be most useful for the management's immediate purposes. A glance at the report for any individual cost center will show the probable cost influence of any additions to (or reductions in) the volume of any product utilizing the facilities of that center and will suggest the advantage or disadvantage of any price decision of either short range or long range import.

This supports, but again modifies, the direct costing contention that cost elements must be known when price and profit calculations are made. The important point is that margin contributions must be measured, not simply in their relation to some simple composite cost figure (supposedly comprising only the two elements of direct-variable and overhead-fixed expense), but rather in their relationship to an overall production and sales program, and to other similar income contributions obtainable at the same time. It would be convenient if the simpler concept would suffice, but unhappily it often does not, and its indiscriminate acceptance may be more dangerous than constructive.

DIRECT COSTING IN PRICING AND SELECTIVE SELLING

What cost information is needed for pricing purposes? Is a single fully apportioned cost figure sufficient as a guide to sound pricing policy? If not, what additional facts will be most useful to the price-maker?

It is plain to every manager that any sale which covers the out-of-pocket cost of the goods sold and contributes something toward the general overhead of the business will add to the total profit of the enterprise. It usually is also plain that all products cannot be expected to provide income contributions of exactly equal amounts. Thus the extent of the contribution of each becomes a management fact of major significance.

It follows that the management should be informed of the out-of-pocket cost of each product as distinguished from its fully apportioned cost. This out-of-pocket cost presumably will consist of the expenditures for material and direct labor, which will occur only if this product is made, plus such additional expenditures for manufacturing and selling activities as tend to vary directly with the volume of production and sales.

The importance of isolating and reporting these facts is now well recognized. It has been emphasized in another fine Association research study,[3] in one of the author's own previous literary efforts,[4] and in numerous other recent contributions to cost literature.

Does the direct costing technique add substantially to our effectiveness in dealing with this problem? If it brings essential facts to management attention more effectively, yes. If it merely gives bookkeeping expression to a set of already familiar calculations, probably not.

A point which seems to be overlooked by direct costing advocates is that cost-price decisions are made not on the basis of periodic cost summaries, but from individual unit cost data, developed from moment to moment as circumstances require. The desired price is one insuring a full overhead contribution and a liberal profit. If this is not obtainable, what lesser price can be considered? The question must be answered for each item separately, according to its own cost-price-volume characteristics.

It can be taken for granted that any concern which approaches the pricing problem scientifically will have developed a "standard" cost for each product. If

[3] N.A.C.A. Research Series No. 24, *N.A.C.A. Bulletin*, August 1953, pp. 1671–1729.
[4] Harvard Business Review, July 1952, pp. 33–45.

the establishment of the standards has been through careful and thorough cost analysis, each unit cost should disclose its components—prime cost, variable expense, fixed overhead, etc. If this has been done, the facts necessary for intelligent pricing are already at hand.

Recasting the general income statement in the same form adds little to management comprehension of price relationships. It is a common error to suppose that analytical data used in making decisions are comparable with post-facto summaries of the results of those decisions. The purpose of periodic recapitulations is not to aid in current decisions but rather to "prove out" the validity of the standard cost data used in the day-to-day conduct of the business and thus lay a groundwork for accuracy in such future cost calculations as become necessary.

Selective selling, concentrated on profitable items, can be an important aid to expanded profit. Most product lines contain a variety of items with differing profit potentialities. Identification and promotion of high-margin items is often a vital management function. It is a little naive, however, to suppose that managements deprived of direct cost data have remained in ignorance on this subject.

Most companies, in most industries, are vigorously attempting to develop more business in their more profitable lines, through their more profitable channels, in their more profitable trade areas, etc. They are striving, in other words, to improve the sales pattern, or "mix," to obtain the maximum total profit contribution. They have been long aware, from the conventional cost data furnished to them, or by other means, what pays best. A precise measure of the differences in marginal income contribution is less important than some ingenuity in applying the information already available.

What are the management actions to be taken when analysis discloses that a given item stands high (or low) in profit contribution? If it is a high-margin item, how do you sell more of it? The very availability of a high margin may indicate the difficulty of selling it, the small quantities in which it normally moves, the large expenditure it entails in costs of stocking, solicitation, order-filling, delivery, etc. Margins often reflect hidden cost components and, if any such costs are mistakenly treated as "fixed" or "general" overhead, the analysis may lead to the wrong conclusion.

When it comes to dropping or subordinating low-margin items, an even more difficult task presents itself. These unsatisfactory articles may be by-products, companion items, "fill-ins," high-turnover staples, etc. The same is true of customers. Small-volume buyers may be adjacent to large ones and thus servable at low incremental cost. Any revenue is welcome from a freight car that would otherwise move empty.

All this is not to decry the value of full exposition of the margin contribution from each item of product and each class of trade, but merely to point out that the whole problem of selective selling is immensely complicated, and not to be quickly solved, even with the best of cost-price analyses.

WRITING OFF FIXED COSTS—A FORWARD OR BACKWARD STEP?

This brings the inquiry down to the final question of whether profit measurement is improved and management facilitated by treating all fixed expenses as period costs rather than product costs (i.e. charging them in total against revenues from current sales, rather than against revenues from sales of the product manufactured during the period to which the costs relate).

The principal arguments for this procedure seem to be that the benefits of fixed costs expire with the passage of the period to which they relate, and they must therefore be absorbed by the revenues of that period, and that it is simpler and more understandable to treat all fixed expenses as profit-reduction items than as value creating items.

These contentions again greatly oversimplify the problem. Do all fixed costs in fact relate to periods of time rather than units of output? This is not demonstrable. Charges for insurance, taxes, maintenance, and depreciation are commonly treated as relating to such short-term periods as individual months, but this is largely a matter of convention and convenience. The costs of facilities usage may be as logically apportioned to units of output as to periods of time. Either basis is arbitrary and largely theoretical. Are vacation costs related to the period when the vacation is taken, or to some other period, or to the output of some other period? Answers reflect preference rather than fact.

It seems clear, however, that even if the "period" argument is accepted, it is the *production* of the period rather than the *revenue* of the period that supplies the test of the benefits obtained. Machine rental may relate to a specific time period, but it is hardly arguable that the company has sustained a loss of the amount of the rental because the product made in that period was not sold in that period. Facilities are utilized to create values, not to reduce profits. The values stored up in manufactured goods are sacrificed when the goods are sold, not lost when the goods are produced.

Concededly, it might be simpler merely to write off all fixed charges as incurred and management might readily understand what had been done. Simplicity, however, is not the exclusive or even the major goal of cost analysis. If it were, it would be very simple to write off all costs as incurred, carrying inventories at zero value. Simpler, still, all cash disbursements might be treated as expenses, and all cash receipts as revenues. These seem like logical extensions of a philosophy that charges should be treated as losses whenever it is easier to do it that way.

Would management be helped or strengthened by adoption of the "immediate write-off" theory? It is hard to see why or how. The profit and loss variations which normally accompany the rise and fall of sales volume would be exaggerated by the deduction from revenue of a heavy burden of fixed manufacturing expense, in addition to the normal burden of fixed selling expense. Months of low sales volume would bring criticism from owners, even though a busy factory might presage expanding profits in the near future. There could be pressure for greater sales during unfavorable market conditions, unreasonable optimism during seasonal sales peaks, etc.

Illustrations of supposed improvement in interpretation of results, under direct costing, are unimpressive. Under certain conditions, the emphasis on deficient sales revenue might be constructive, but often it could be merely confusing. A factory which produces in the spring and summer for sale in the fall and winter would show startling losses for six months and illusory profits for the next six, contrary to logic and reason. Facilities usage does not involve a loss if the goods manufactured are worth what they cost, including the fixed-charge component. Why tell people it does?

MORE THAN TWO ALTERNATIVES

In the argument for direct costing, that method is often contrasted with what is termed "absorption" costing, with an accompanying inference that the only alternative to charging off the total of period fixed charges is the inclusion of the total of such charges in the cost of the goods produced, with a pro rata share finding its way into inventory valuations.

This, of course, is not the common practice in the handling of fixed charges, under conventional cost procedure. Most manufacturers employ something in the nature of standard or other pre-determined unit costs for inventory valuation purposes, and such unit costs include not more than a "normal" fixed charge component, based on production at some selected level (maximum, average, expectable, budgeted, or what have you). Costs are "absorbed" in inventory values only to that extent.

When production is less than the amount on which the standard cost is based, some portion of fixed overhead expense remains "unabsorbed," and thus is charged off to profit and loss as a production variance. To this extent, conventional procedure parallels the direct costing approach, the difference being that conventionally the profit and loss charge represents only the amount of fixed cost not assignable to production, while, under direct costing, the profit and loss charge would include all fixed charges, whether production was at maximum or at zero.

The choice then lies among three alternatives rather than two, as follows:

1. Write off all fixed charges (direct costing).
2. Include all fixed charges in product cost (absorption costing).
3. Include normal fixed charges in product cost and write off any excess due to subnormal production (standard costing).

It is difficult to discover either theoretical or practical considerations which make the first of these procedures preferable to the third.

Apologists for the direct costing approach concede that the exclusion of fixed overhead from inventory costs is not yet an "accepted method of accounting," and with good reason. They have injected an occasional suggestion that such exclusion was unwarranted when it occurred because the accountant once did not know any better but that it may be appropriate now that he has thought up a more elaborate defense of his action in valuing inventories at prime cost plus "variable" expense.

Perhaps this is intended to be humorous. It is doubtful that a method esteemed wrong when adopted for one purpose, can become right when adopted for another. Auditors have trouble enough with objective measurements. They can hardly be expected to certify to the mental state or intellectual attainments of the fellow who did the figuring. The question is whether the procedure contributes to a better understanding of results and more constructive management decisions. Direct-cost inventory valuation seems unlikely to do so.

ALTERNATIVES TO DIRECT COSTING

Alternatives to direct costing as commonly defined may be stated as follows:

1. Emphasize the marginal income contribution of any present or prospective piece of business, at any proposed selling price, by calculating the excess of the additional costs it will entail.

2. Maintain the data required for such calculations in the form of detailed reports, by cost centers, designed to facilitate the quick computation of changes in total costs which will result from any major change in the production and sales pattern.

3. Classify expenses as to type and function, for all activities, so that the relative fixity or variability of each can be determined for any prospective operating condition or volume level, for each cost center affected.

4. Retain the orthodox practice of absorbing in product costs and inventory values only such fixed charge component as is reasonably related to the facility utilization reflected in actual manufacturing operations for the period in question.

With these modifications, the direct costing philosophy can make an important contribution to better management, while retaining the advantages of presently accepted methods of inventory valuation and profit determination.

RELATED READINGS

The following readings pertain to the conceptual issues in inventory measurement. Since the inventory problem may be viewed as a special case of the historical cost versus current value controversy, readers should also consult the extensive list of readings at the close of Part 8.

C. Richard Cox and Carl L. Glassberg, "LIFO: Analysis and Review," *World* (PMM), Summer, 1971, pp. 42–48. A review of tax aspects of LIFO together with a survey of the evolution of LIFO.

William L. Ferrara, "Relevant Costing: Footnote to a Controversy," *Management Accounting* (US), January, 1970, pp. 45–47.

George J. Foster, "Mining Inventories in a Current Price Accounting System," *Abacus*, December, 1969, pp. 99–118.

Raymond A. Hoffman and Henry Gunders, *Inventories: Control, Costing, and Effect upon Income and Taxes*, Second Edition (New York: The Ronald Press Company, 1970), 444 pp.

Daniel J. Kelly, "Accounting for Start-up Costs," *The New York Certified Public Accountant*, November, 1968, pp. 773–778.

P. N. McMonnies, "Stock and Work-in-progress," *The Accountant's Magazine*, January, 1968, pp. 9–11. Summary of the analysis and findings of an empirical research study on the measurement and reporting of inventories. The full report is *Valuation of Stock and Work-in-progress* (Edinburgh: The Institute of Chartered Accountants of Scotland, 1968), 32 pp.

PART 5

VALUATION OF LONG-LIVED "TANGIBLE" COST FACTORS

In the case of short-lived cost factors, one can at least observe a physical transfer of the product from the seller's warehouse to the buyer's receiving dock, even if the measurement of the accounting magnitudes is determined without reference to the actual physical flow of the goods. Within the producing enterprise, one can also monitor and record the consumption of short-lived cost factors in the evolution of the finished product, although, even in this sphere, arbitrary judgments cannot be avoided. But this reliance on physical phenomena is more tenuous for long-lived cost factors. The moment when buildings, machinery, and automotive vehicles are first available for productive use can, it is true, be approximated on the basis of physical observation. But the consumption of their economic services in the fashioning of goods and services may be unaccompanied by an observable physical change, and the change which can be observed may be irrelevant to the phenomena which accounting undertakes to measure.

Depreciation is not concerned with "physical wear and tear." It is, instead, a measure of the degree to which the limited capacity of a "tangible" economic resource has been spent in the process of creating value in other things. Traditionally, depreciation accounting has been an apportionment of historical cost to the fiscal periods in which economic benefit arising from the use of depreciable assets is reflected in revenues. Depreciation, it has been asserted, is a process of allocation, not of valuation. Although accountants have been adjured to select patterns of allocation, or depreciation methods, that are "systematic and rational," it has been argued that no choice is free from arbitrariness.[1] The literature is well stocked with articles on the merits of particular depreciation methods. In recent years, time-adjusted methods have had a fair amount of attention. (See, e.g., the article by Anton in *Financial Accounting Theory*–Volume II.)

In the first article in this part, D R Scott warns accountants not "to make depreciation a term of art peculiar to an accounting cult...." Depreciation cannot be conceived and understood apart from the real-world experience to which it relates. Scott's concern with defining and accounting for depreciation was prompted by the publication of a terminology committee report in 1942 by the American Institute of [Certified Public] Accountants, which included a discussion of the nature and meaning of depreciation. This report, as slightly amended in 1953, continues to be Institute policy today. The process of accounting for depreciation is, in Scott's opinion, a function of revenue realization. The problem is to apportion the cost of the asset between its realized usefulness and its potential usefulness. Although Scott confines his discussion largely to the allocation of historical cost, he is not doctrinaire. "The writer is not disposed to argue for the general assertion that depreciation should be based on current values. But he is even less inclined to subscribe to the dictum that it must always be based upon cost."

George O. May, who was chairman of the American Institute committee that issued the report of which Scott was critical, once captured the essence of the accounting problem of separating capital from income expenditures. In 1937, he wrote,

> The distinction in accounting today between capital expenditure and income expenditure does not rest on any essential difference in the nature of the property acquired.... It rests, rather, upon the relation between the length of the useful life of the property acquired and the length of the accounting period for which income is being determined.... If the accounting period were increased from the customary year to a decade, most of what is now treated as capital expenditure would become chargeable to income; while if the period were reduced to a day, much of what is now treated as current maintenance would become capital expenditure.

While the ascertainment and allocation of cost are key determinations in conventional accounting, many writers today believe that the preoccupation with historical cost is not unlike the attempt to fine-tune a receiver when the channel selector has been set to receive another frequency. While historical cost is the value implicit in a transaction, should the reckonings made in future periods all be predicated on this initial measure of value? This question is more critical for long-lived assets than for inventories because of the much greater possibility of major fluctuations in market value over the lives of the former.

Edgar O. Edwards and Philip W. Bell, the authors of *The Theory and Measurement of Business Income*, discuss, in separate articles, the roles of general-price-level adjustments and current values in the measurement and reporting of accounting results. Edwards focuses on the application of general and specific price adjustments to depreciable assets, argues that their roles are complementary

---

[1] The most extensive argument may be found in Arthur L. Thomas, *The Allocation Problem in Financial Accounting Theory* (Evanston, Ill.: American Accounting Association, 1969.)

and not competitive, and demonstrates how they might be reflected in the accounts. Bell reviews the debate over "entry" and "exit" prices in the selection of the one best notion of current value. Central to his defense of the Edwards-Bell preference for entry prices is his assertion that "accounting must measure past events, and to be useful, it must measure those which might happen if a firm does something other than that which was planned." Bell also examines the "value to the firm" analysis of Solomons and Parker-Harcourt, further discussion of which may be found in the articles by Wright and Stamp in Parts 3 and 8 (B), respectively, of this volume.

Herbert E. Miller considers the use of "quasi-reorganizations" in circumstances other than when a corporation is in "trouble." Since the early 1930s, the United States accounting profession has approved of quasi-reorganizations when (1) a company's assets are overvalued in relation to current price levels, (2) the overvaluation is expected to persist well into the future, (3) operating losses are in prospect, and (4) the company's retained earnings would not be sufficient to absorb the indicated adjustment. Writing in the late 1940s, when the American Institute's Committee on Accounting Procedure was actively considering a bulletin to authorize *upward* quasi-reorganizations when a company's assets were seriously understated, Miller asks whether quasi-reorganizations might not be used as a "device enabling a fresh start to be achieved in extraordinary situations *whenever* a continuation on the established basis would produce accounting statements susceptible to widespread, gross misinterpretation." In 1950, in fact, the Committee on Accounting Procedure unanimously approved a bulletin embodying this suggestion, but it was thwarted by the determination of the Securities and Exchange Commission to oppose all departures from traditional historical cost (except in circumstances justifying *downward* quasi-reorganizations). Miller proposes a set of circumstances in which an upward quasi-reorganization should be seriously considered.

The final selection in this part consists of extracts from the 1961 and 1967 annual reports of the Sheraton Corporation of America. Ernest Henderson, the late chairman of the Sheraton Corporation, firmly believed that traditional historical costs failed to depict his company's true progress. Owing to the SEC's antipathy toward current-value accounting, Sheraton was unable to depart from conventional accounting in its audited financial statements. Instead, Henderson experimented with a novel approach to current values in his letter to stockholders, thus escaping the censure of the SEC. The Sheraton philosophy of current-value accounting was, to our knowledge, unique among United States companies. Certainly, no other United States company has offered its stockholders a more elaborate analysis of the impact of specific price changes on its assets and earnings. While many companies in Great Britain and Australia have revalued their assets in their audited financial statements, they have not attempted, as did Sheraton, to translate the unrealized appreciation into a measure of economic performance. One might argue, of course, that the Sheraton analysis is more germane to a hotel chain than to a manufacturer. Henderson, moreover, had his motives. The current-value analysis showed his company in a more favorable light than did the historical-cost approach. The Sheraton experiment came to an end in the late 1960s, upon the company's entry into the conglomerate stable of International Telephone & Telegraph Corporation.

B. DEPRECIATION

D R SCOTT

D R SCOTT (1887–1954), B.A. 10, B.S. 10 Missouri; Ph.D. 30 Harvard. Major publications: *Theory of Accounts* (1925), *The Cultural Significance of Accounts* (1931). Biographies and anthologies: "Accounting Related to Social Institutions: The Theoretical Formulations of D R Scott" (*Accounting Research*, January 1958), *Collected Publications of D R Scott* (edited by Kvam and Bauer, 1964). Contributed over two dozen articles to *The Accounting Review* and other journals.

Since his given name consisted only of his father's initials (for David Roland), Scott adopted a signature of "D R" without stops.

From 1911 to 1912, he was on the political economy faculty of the University of Michigan, following which he worked for two years on the *Detroit Times*. In 1914, he commenced a 40-year term on the University of Missouri faculty, beginning in the economics department and proceeding to the department of accounting and statistics, of which he was chairman for ten years.

Served as vice-president of the American Accounting Association in 1941 and as first vice-president of the American Association of University Professors from 1952 to 1954.

Reflecting the influence of Thorstein Veblen (1857–1929), Scott endeavored to relate accounting to the evolving social order, so that accounting might ultimately become a controlling factor in economic activity. He was one of the early advocates in the U.S. of the use of replacement cost in balance sheets.

DEFINING AND ACCOUNTING FOR DEPRECIATION

D R SCOTT

All theoretical formulations, like institutions, derive their significance from their contribution to the concrete process of human living. Many times in the course of the world's history peoples have built up systems of law and religious creeds which eventually lost their vitality because they lost contact with the concrete, everyday living of the peoples concerned. Those legal and religious formulations

SOURCE: From *The Accounting Review*, Vol. XX, No. 3 (July, 1945), pp. 308–315. Reprinted by permission of the American Accounting Association.

DEFINING AND ACCOUNTING FOR DEPRECIATION 311

have developed out of man's experience in what is described above as the concrete process of human living. They have remained vital so long as and to the extent that they have interpreted and illuminated that experience.

But when men in their search for truth have turned away from the concrete world of their experience and have centered their attention exclusively upon polishing and perfecting their own formulations, they thereby have initiated an atrophy of their ideas. It was this truth which Bacon had in mind in his declaration that it is the first distemper of learning "when men study words and not matter."

The Report of the Committee on Terminology of the American Institute of Accountants on Depreciation, dated October, 1942, and the definition of depreciation based on that report and published in September, 1943, in the *Journal of Accountancy* are open to criticism along the line of the foregoing introduction.[a] They confuse an economic fact with the process of accounting for it. Indeed they undertake to identify the two. The result is that the concrete phenomenon of depreciation drops out of the picture entirely. Acceptance of the proposed definition would mean that, with respect to the depreciation problem, accounting would lose touch with the everyday world of economic affairs in a fashion precisely similar to the way in which religious, legal, and political systems have so often lost contact with the concrete process of human living.

After quoting several definitions, the committee report presents the following paragraph:

> These definitions treat depreciation, broadly speaking, as a money cost or loss due to exhaustion of usefulness. The term is sometimes used to describe the exhaustion itself; however, it seems desirable to emphasize the money-cost or loss concept as the primary if not the sole accounting meaning of the term. "Depreciation" corresponds to "wages" rather than to "labor."

Later in the discussion is the following paragraph:

> The various methods of computing depreciation in use obviously rest on materially different basic assumptions. The fact that methods are employed which produce as widely different allocations as (a) the diminishing balance method; (b) the sinking fund method; and (c) a unit cost method, emphasizes the truth that the allocation bears no close relation to change in value and does not attempt to measure the exhaustion which actually takes place within a given period—an important truth that is not always fully understood. All that the various methods have in common (which is all that could be embodied in a definition) is that they are designed to distribute the estimated total depreciation incurred or to be incurred during the useful life of a unit or group of units over that life in a systematic and equitable manner.

If we define depreciation as an accounting cost which is arrived at by the use of methods which do not "attempt to measure the exhaustion which actually takes

---

[a] This statement on terminology was incorporated in *Accounting Terminology Bulletins: Review and Resumé* (in 1953), pp. 20–55. Although some change in wording is evident and certain of the original material was omitted in the second writing, for purposes of this article the Institute's position in 1953 with respect to depreciation was the same as in 1942. [Eds.]

place within a given period," we thereby divorce the depreciation problem from the everyday world of business experience in which managerial decisions are made. Unquestionably, managements in their selection of depreciation methods have sometimes had purposes in mind other than an accurate accounting for depreciation. They have sometimes been motivated by an undue regard for financial conservatism. Even aside from the selection of methods, their depreciation policies have sometimes brought accounting results which have been positive misrepresentations of the facts. However, the accounting profession cannot afford to countenance such practices and still less can accountants afford to make them a basis for their own analysis of the problem of depreciation.

The fact that managements have used methods of depreciation with different ends in view does not mean that the different methods rest upon basically different assumptions. If the use of different methods is limited to the legitimate purpose of accounting for depreciation, there is no reason to assume that they rest on different basic assumptions. Different types of assets used under widely varying conditions do in fact depreciate at widely divergent and varying rates. The fact that methods which afford such different results continue to survive is due to the wide variation in ways in which depreciation takes place. The use of correspondingly divergent methods, therefore, indicates an attempt to measure actual depreciation rather than the reverse.

If we have a machine built specially to produce a good for which the demand rests upon a current fad or style, the depreciation of the machine may well depend upon the demand for its product rather than upon physical considerations limiting the time in which it can be used to produce the product. If demand for the product is currently at its peak, and is expected to fall off rapidly over a period of fifteen months, the decreasing value of the machine may well justify calculation of depreciation as a fixed percentage of the diminishing book value.

An opposite type of situation confronts us when we turn to consideration of a hydro-electric plant. The operation of such a plant involves relatively small costs in labor and ordinary repairs. The result is that capital costs, such as interest on capital and the depreciation of capital assets, make up a relatively large proportion of total operating costs and thereby a premium is put upon an accurate statement of such costs. It is in this sort of situation that the use of a compound interest method of calculating depreciation is justified.

Some assets are used irregularly. An airplane may be flown several times as much in one month as it was in the previous month. It may well be desirable to calculate the depreciation of its engine in each period in terms of working hours. Other assets may be used under varying conditions at different times, and their service output may be better than any other basis for calculating their depreciation.

As a final illustration let us take the problem of a dairy farmer's allowing for the depreciation of cows in his herd. A dairy cow usually is put into production when she is two and a half or three years old. She does not reach maximum production until she is about seven years old and after that peak is passed there is a slow, gradual falling off in her production. However, as the farmer well knows, she reaches her maximum value at about five years. The farmer also knows her probable productive life and her probable ultimate sale value. His practical computations may not go beyond a comparison of current prices for different grades of cows of different ages but if pressed for an explanation of his valuations he goes back to these underlying considerations which are so obvious to him that they are taken for granted.

Any method of calculating depreciation which started to amortize the initial cost of a cow while she was still increasing in value would strike the dairy farmer as foolish and impractical. And he would be right. The problem of setting up a suitable method for the systematic calculation of the depreciation of a dairy cow is a simple combination of mathematics and accounting. It is a problem well within the constructive responsibility of accountants.

The dairy-cow example is unusual but in a sense it is typical of the whole depreciation problem. There are technical peculiarities connected with the utilization of many assets. If we make the flat statement that depreciation is indeterminate and that methods of calculating depreciation do not undertake to present actual periodic depreciation, we thereby advertise the accountant's ignorance of that technical familiarity with the conditions under which assets are used which businessmen need and typically do have as a basis for their managerial decisions.

It can not be argued in defense of the committee report here under discussion that "indeterminate" means merely not determinable in an exact or absolute sense. Most costs are indeterminate in that sense. A far better statement, and one which would be essentially true instead of essentially false, would be that depreciation is determinate within the limits necessary for the selection of a proper method of its allocation. And to this statement might well be added the further assertion that it is a responsibility of accountants to select a proper method and, if necessary, to adjust the method selected to any peculiar technical situation in which the assets to be depreciated are being utilized.

VALUE AND DEPRECIATION

In a price system values are in proportion to utility or usefulness. Price and value are the terms in which businessmen commonly make comparisons and decisions. When the price system breaks down, men resort to barter or a sytem of direct exchanges of goods and services. But so long as the price system works effectively such a resort to barter is awkward and costly.

When assets are new, businessmen and accountants both appraise them in terms of cost. This is not because that cost is significant *per se*. It is not. The importance attached to it arises from the fact that it is a present appraisal or evaluation of the total usefulness of the asset in question. This point is illustrated when we have to account for an asset which is acquired as a gift or in some other way which does not permit a direct allocation of cost. Under such circumstances we assign to the asset a valuation which corresponds as closely as possible with what it would cost under usual market conditions.

The cost new of an asset is a valuation of its usefulness just as any market price is such an evaluation. The process of allowing for depreciation by one method or another writes down the book value of the asset from cost new to scrap value. The appropriateness of the method chosen and the equitableness of the result which it affords depend upon the degree to which the writing down of the book value corresponds with the actual change in the value of the asset from cost new to scrap value.

Those who define depreciation in terms of loss of value and those who define it in terms of an exhaustion of usefulness are of course referring to precisely the same set of facts. Those in the first group are content to stop with the terms of a dollars-and-cents appraisal in which market operations, business transactions, and the accounting record run. Those in the second group appeal to the technical serviceability of assets which lies back of every market price attached to them. They do this in an attempt to avoid the responsibility for making monetary valuations which do not rest directly upon business transactions. However, they do not in fact avoid such a responsibility so long as they undertake to select proper and equitable methods of calculating depreciation. The appeal to exhaustion of technical usefulness brings needless complexity into the discussion. It tends to create confusion even in the thinking of those who resort to it. Its use in accounting discussion is parallel to the error of which we would be guilty in our economic conduct if we were to insist upon using the technique of barter when the effective operation of a price system was available.

HOW DEPRECIATION TAKES PLACE

As long as we have assets which are as different as a dynamo, a dairy cow, and an airplane engine, we shall need different methods of calculating periodic depreciation. The endless variety of assets in business use is not a constant. New assets and new conditions under which old assets are used are continually arising. If the accountant is to keep abreast of these changing conditions he must be open-minded with respect to the technique of calculating periodic depreciation. He must be ready to devise new methods when needed and to adapt old methods to new conditions.

When we ask how depreciation takes place, the obvious answer is that it takes place in a never-ending variety of ways. Nevertheless there are some factors bearing on the problem which are of such general significance that it is worth while to point them out. They help to guide the accountant in selecting or devising a method of calculating periodic depreciation for a specific situation.

One of the factors affecting depreciation is the distribution of income over the expected life of an asset. If an asset has half of the years of its useful life left but only one-fourth of its total usefulness or income, a method of depreciation which kept it on the books at half of its original cost would be grossly inequitable.

There are many assets which do have an uneven distribution of income expectation. The dairy cow is one of them. If we build a factory building too large for present needs in expectation of a growth of business, and are unable to use or rent out the excess space, this fact should be taken into account in any precise allocation of depreciation cost.

A second factor which always bears on the accrual of depreciation is interest. The influence of interest may be so overshadowed by other considerations that the only practicable procedure is to ignore it, but it is always present.

In economics we learn that the value of a production good is a present appraisal of its future services or the incomes which its use affords. In the process of arrival at a present value, those incomes which are most remote in time suffer the largest discount. The truth of this proposition may be illustrated very simply if we ask ourselves which is worth more, assuming equal security, a three-year annuity paying $1,000 at the end of each year or a group of three separate notes for $1,000 each due one year from now. By way of an oversimplified example, let us assume an asset which will last ten years and have no scrap value. Assuming an even distribution of income over the ten years and disregarding other disturbing factors, this asset's depreciation will follow the curve of amortization of a ten-year annuity.

In our past treatment of depreciation the effect of interest has not been given much consideration. The reason is obvious. Our allowances for depreciation typically have been such rough approximations that a refinement like an attempt to allow for the effect of interest has not been worth while.

A third general influence upon the way in which depreciation takes place is the distribution of repair costs necessary to keep the asset in working order. Repair costs are a direct burden upon the services or income afforded by the asset. In periods when repair charges are high the net return available from the use of the asset will be correspondingly reduced, and depreciation will be lower because such periods represent smaller fractions of the asset's total net usefulness. Other things being equal, when repair costs are high depreciation is relatively low and when repair costs are low depreciation is relatively high.

In the past treatment of depreciation, recognition of repairs has been mainly of two types. One is as an argument by proponents of the straight-line method in opposition to proponents of compound-interest methods. The argument is that repairs tend to become heavier with the advancing age of the asset and so would tend to offset the effect of interest.

The second recognition of repairs has been in their combination with depreciation. Total repair costs for the life of the asset have been estimated and have been added to depreciation, that is, to cost new minus scrap value. The sum of the two has then been spread on a straight-line basis as "depreciation expense." The method sometimes affords a more accurate distribution of total expense than would be obtained by treating repairs as expense when made and allocating depreciation on a straight-line basis. However, still greater accuracy can be obtained by a more precise treatment of the relations between repairs and depreciation.[1] The present writer agrees that it is better to preserve separate expense accounts for depreciation and repairs.

Irregularity of use may bring about irregularity both in the realization of income and in the effects of wear and tear upon depreciation. Idle assets do not bring in profits. If assets are used very irregularly the only rational procedure may well be to calculate their lives in terms of hours used or output produced and to charge depreciation in proportion to their utilization as measured in those terms.

All the foregoing factors have a common fundamental basis. They all go back to income realization: to the proportion between the value of realized usefulness and the value of potential usefulness still embodied in the asset. Attempts to select a suitable or accurate method of calculating depreciation are attempts to adjust the periodic depreciation expense to an actual loss of value.

WHAT WE ACCOUNT FOR

The problem of depreciation will be clarified if we differentiate as distinctly as possible between the definition of depreciation and the accounting process of giv-

[1] Cf. DR Scott, "Depreciation and Repair Costs," *The Accounting Review*, June, 1929, p. 116.

ing recognition to it. This statement holds, notwithstanding the approach of the Committee on Terminology of the American Institute.

What do we in fact account for in making periodic allowances for depreciation? The prevailing answer to this question is that we account for a fraction of that part of the original cost of the asset which is not covered by its scrap value. The cost of an asset is not depreciation. That is obvious. Hence depreciation must be the process of accounting for that cost. If we approach the question in this way, we can readily understand the disposition of members of the American Institute committee to identify depreciation with the accounting item of periodic depreciation expense. This view reflects the traditional accounting distrust of processes of valuation other than the *bona fide* business transaction.

However, the common-sense approach to depreciation views it not as an item in the accounting record but as an objective phenomenon—as a change in the value of assets which takes place regardless of whether or not it is reflected in the accounts. And the accounting distinction between depreciable and nondepreciable assets appears to lend conclusive support to this common-sense view.

Management takes the common-sense view of depreciation rather than the proposed, sophisticated accounting view. In order to make the best use of the assets at its disposal, management needs to know how those assets do in fact depreciate under the actual conditions of their utilization.

If we accept the view that depreciation is a loss in value of an asset occasioned by the utilization or exhaustion of potential services embodied in it, we are confronted by the difficulty that the values of those services still remaining at any given date may not remain the same as they were expected to be when the asset was acquired. If there is a general price rise and an increase in the money value of services to be rendered, this change will be reflected in an increased value of the asset. Further exhaustion of the remaining services in it will then give rise to a different schedule of losses in value.

Most accountants meet this problem with a cutting-of-the-Gordian-knot solution. They hold that the calculation of depreciation should be based upon cost and not upon present values. In short, they hold that depreciation is not depreciation of an asset in the common-sense meaning of the term but is rather an accounting amortization of its original cost.

The writer is not disposed to argue for the general assertion that depreciation should be based upon current values. But he is even less inclined to subscribe to the dictum that it must always be based upon cost. At an earlier point in the discussion, it was suggested that the accountant should undertake to adjust depreciation methods to a never-ending variety of changing conditions under which assets are used. It seems reasonable that the question of adjusting depreciation charges to changed values in any particular case should be included in the general responsibility of the accountant to select or devise an appropriate depreciation technique.

A COMMON-SENSE DEFINITION

In the common-sense view, depreciation is an accruing loss of value which begins with cost new and ends with scrap value at the end of the asset's useful life. When the Committee on Terminology of the American Institute holds that "'Depreciation' corresponds to 'wages' rather than to 'labor'," it deprives the term of realistic meaning. No one would argue that depreciation corresponds to labor. In fact, in a wage system there is no parallel to depreciation to be found in the labor contribution to production. Under a slave system the diminishing value of a slave would be depreciation in the common-sense meaning of the term. And the calculation of a slave's depreciation would involve some of the problems encountered in the depreciation of a dairy cow.

Of course not all losses of asset values commonly suffered by business enterprise are to be treated as depreciation. Losses by fire, wind, and many adverse weather conditions may be provided for by taking out insurance. Premiums paid constitute costs of the periods in which they accrue. If a company elects to carry its risk of fire loss instead of taking out insurance, it may properly make periodic charges to expense to cover that risk and thereby accumulate a reserve against which to charge losses when they occur. But neither the loss nor the periodic expense charge is depreciation. Any attempt to apply the term "depreciation" in such a situation would only result in confusion without any compensating advantage.

If special constructions or installations are necessary to the fulfillment of any contract it is entirely proper to spread their net cost over the work of that contract. And no objection is to be raised to the application of the term "depreciation" to such costs. This procedure may in specific cases be applicable to war contracts, but war production often involves special difficulties of forecasting the length of time and the amount of work for which the facilities will be used, and sometimes also a problem of determining the extent to which wartime facilities can be salvaged for peacetime production. Business prudence and proper accounting require that provision be made for the cost of such special facilities, but the difficulties involved in arriving at periodic charges may well justify a practice of calling the periodic provision "amortization" rather than "depreciation." Whatever the term used it is important to keep it separate from regular depreciation: to treat it as the special case which it is.

If we build a building on leased property knowing that we shall have to give it up ten years hence at the expiration of the lease, we have a problem which is comparable with that of special facilities for a specific contract. The value of the building on our books must be reduced to zero in the ten years and the necessary periodic charge may well be called depreciation expense.

But should the term "depreciation" be applied to the accounting for patents and leaseholds and to losses from obsolescence and inadequacy? The answer to this question is not important so long as we think clearly about the problems in question and make sure, for example, that "depreciation of patents" is not confused with or combined with the depreciation of tangible assets.

In general, clear and precise terminology is conducive to exact and fruitful thinking. However, we need always to remember that a living language grows out of common usage and that even technical terminology must retain a realistic contact with the concrete data to which it is applied. That accounting terminology is best which best serves to promote clear thinking about the concrete problems with which accounting and business management are concerned. Precision of terminology is too dearly bought when its price is a sacrifice of realism. The proposed definition of depreciation does not pass this test.

Too many of the present generation of leaders in accounting are too much governed by the past general practice of the profession. Conversely, they are too little influenced by new factors in accounting such as new problems of management, the increasing use of statistical methods, and the rise of what is generally called cost accounting. Future development of the problem of depreciation depends much more on these new influences than it does upon the traditional accounting of the past.

The definition of depreciation which is criticised in the foregoing discussion was formulated to fit in with a preconceived theory of the nature of accounting, whereas definitions in accounting, as in other fields, should be arrived at in the spirit of an open-minded approach to the subject matter and the problems which are to be considered. This error arises from uncritical habits of thought which are moving in the direction of making accounting theory a closed and perfected system. The dictum that accounting is essentially a record of historical costs divorces the viewpoint of accounting from that of management. The present attempt to make depreciation a term of art peculiar to an accounting cult would, if successful, widen still further the breach between accounting theory and the everyday sphere of concrete economic affairs in which management must act.

The greater the degree to which accountants are willing to think in terms which are peculiar to their own field, the easier it will be to eliminate loose ends of theory. The temptation to take that road is always present in every field of knowledge and especially in those dealing directly with human affairs. When a movement once starts in that direction it is prone to continue at an accelerated pace. The proposed definition of depreciation should be a clear warning to open-minded students of accounting not to take that road. The definition is an illustration of that distemper which Bacon pointed out so long ago.

A. IMPACT OF CHANGING PRICES

EDGAR O. EDWARDS

EDGAR O. EDWARDS (1919–   ), B.A. 47 Washington and Jefferson; M.A. 49, Ph.D. 51 Johns Hopkins. Currently economic advisor, Asia and Pacific Program, The Ford Foundation, New York. Major publications: *The Theory and Measurement of Business Income* (with Bell, 1961), *The Nation's Economic Objectives* (editor, 1964). Contributor to *The Journal of Business, Southern Economic Journal,* and other journals.

Was on the economics faculties of Princeton University, 1950–59, and Rice University, 1959–70, prior to joining The Ford Foundation. Between 1964–1968, he was principal economic advisor to the Ministry of Economic Planning and Development, Government of Kenya.

Principal research interests: development theory and the employment problems of developing countries.

DEPRECIATION POLICY UNDER CHANGING PRICE LEVELS*

EDGAR O. EDWARDS

The feeling has increased in recent years that the traditional accounting technique of computing depreciation on the basis of the original cost of fixed assets is inadequate, particularly during periods of rising prices. Some of the best evidence of this can be found in the efforts of business firms to find an acceptable way to increase the annual depreciation charge, preferably as a reduction in profits in order to reduce tax and perhaps wage liability, but as a reservation of profits in

* This paper is an outgrowth of research done under the auspices of the Organizational Behavior Section at Princeton University. The author is deeply indebted to Professor Philip Bell of Haverford College who has made many suggestions for improving the quality of the article.

SOURCE: From *The Accounting Review,* Vol. XXIX, No. 2 (April, 1954), pp. 267–280. Reprinted by permission of the American Accounting Association.

any case in order to facilitate the maintenance of real capital.[1] Witness, also, the amazing number of pamphlets, books and articles in both accounting and economic journals on the subject.[2] For further evidence one need only observe the increasing concern of the government with depreciation both as a tax problem and as a means, via accelerated depreciation, of encouraging defense production.

These concerns are genuine. Straight-line depreciation based on historic cost is inaccurate, if not grossly misleading, during periods of rising prices. Furthermore, despite the tendency for some accountants to favor traditional depreciation accounting during periods of falling prices, that policy is equally misleading. In fact, so long as the general price level or the prices of the fixed assets being depreciated are changing in either direction, straight-line depreciation on original cost yields unrealistic estimates.

Various remedial techniques have been developed for the rigidity of historic cost depreciation and the resulting difficulties of measuring economic profit, taxable profit and funds necessary for replacement. Some of these involve changes in the timing of depreciation charges; others require special reservations of profit; those techniques, however, which break substantially from traditional methods make use of depreciation bases other than historic cost, usually the current cost of fixed assets, the historic cost adjusted by a general price index or the actual cost at the time of replacement. Which of the first two methods is the "better" has involved some controversy. Both are often referred to as approximations of the third.

It is my purpose in this paper to suggest that both current cost and adjusted historic cost have an accounting role to play, that these techniques are essentially complementary rather than competitive, and that actual cost at the time of replacement is a concept which properly should be abandoned for depreciation purposes. In the process of establishing these points one possible approach to depreciation under changing price levels will be developed which utilizes both the current fixed asset cost ("current cost") and historic cost adjusted by a general price index ("purchasing power cost") as bases for depreciation. This approach, considerably simplified for expositional purposes, has as its primary aim a meaningful statement of economic profit, but appears to have advantages for computing taxable profit and taxable gains, and for making replacement, properly considered, possible.

The application of this technique would involve certain practical difficulties but I do not believe them to be insurmountable. Even crude attempts should result in an improvement over present depreciation practices. During periods of rapidly changing prices crude measurements of a relevant item are likely to be much more meaningful than accurate measurements of an irrelevant one (in this case, historic cost).

---

[1] The annual reports of DuPont and U.S. Steel since the end of World War II provide two interesting examples of this kind of development.

[2] A notable effort to reconcile accounting and economic views of depreciation and profits is reported in Study Group on Business Income, *Changing Concepts of Business Income* (New York: The Macmillan Co., 1952).

THE DEFINITION OF ECONOMIC PROFIT

The economic definition of income as the amount which one can consume during a period and still be as well off at the end of the period as at the beginning [3] is not, I think, appropriate for this problem.

First, the values which must be compared at the beginning and at the end of the period are subjective values. They have meaning to the individual but very little significance for anyone else. For most economic purposes, business profit must be measurable according to market criteria; for tax purposes income should, for obvious reasons, be computed in some uniform fashion. A computation of corporate profits according to an objective set of rules should furnish valuable information to the outside analyst or to the prospective entrant into the industry because the basis for the reported figures can be clearly understood. Subjective estimates have their place in the decision-making process of each firm (though this is less clear in the case of large corporations), but objective tests of profitability will continue to have more value for the outsider so long as the bases for subjective valuations are either not disclosed (if they could be) or are subject to bias in the process.

Second, it is useful to regard economic profit as being related to current production rather than to anticipated production. A comparison of subjective asset values at the beginning and end of a period is essentially a comparison of past revenue-cost expectations with current revenue-cost expectations. Thus, income is derived from expected profits (or net receipts) and represents essentially a smoothing out of a series of future profits. Profit is, therefore, a more fundamental concept than income. Further, the measurement of profit, as contrasted to the measurement of profit expectations, is concerned with past, as opposed to future, events. Hence, profit on a current production basis measures the difference between the identifiable value of current output and the value of identifiable current inputs. On the level of the individual firm or industry, these profit figures are meaningful for evaluating the allocation of resources and the composition of output. The aggregate of these figures would be consistent with the concept of profits toward which national income accountants appear to be working.

The identification of inputs and their values is crucial to this view of profit. Identification must be as exhaustive as possible. All inputs (whether the return each receives is a direct payment or an imputed one) that can be identified and for which values can be discovered must be deducted as a cost of current production.

Following this line of reasoning we shall define profit as a residual. It is that part of revenue which cannot be identified as a cost of any particular factor of production. To determine "economic profit," revenue must be measured in current prices and compared with all identifiable costs measured in current prices as well. The current prices applicable to revenue are those which could be *received* in the

---

[3] J. R. Hicks, *Value and Capital*, Second Edition (Oxford: Clarendon Press, 1946), pp. 172ff. See also Sidney S. Alexander, "Income Measurement in a Dynamic Economy," *Five Monographs on Business Income* (New York: Study Group on Business Income of the American Institute of Accountants, July 1, 1950) in which the author leans heavily on this concept.

market during the period. Thus long-term sales contracts, for example, might result in a deviation of actual revenue from revenue at current prices. The current prices applicable to costs are the current market prices which the firm might *pay* for the goods and services the firm uses during the period. Long-term buying contracts and fixed assets purchased in a prior period may give rise to a discrepancy between actual money costs and costs at current prices.

By current cost we mean the cost of purchasing (if such a market exists) the actual factor services used in current production—not the cost of the most efficient factors that might have been used. Hence, technological change creates a problem only if it destroys markets for now-outdated factor services. Other sources of cost estimates must be found in that event—presumably opportunity cost.

Economic profit, then, is the difference between current revenues and current costs. It represents the difference between the *economy's* current valuation of the goods and services *rendered* by the firm and its current valuation of the goods and services *used* by the firm. Profits computed in this fashion could be aggregated into meaningful totals for industries and would be consonant with the concept of profits desired for national income purposes.[4]

This concept of profit is basic to the argument to follow. Concepts of taxable profit and of relevant replacement cost will be developed in the course of the discussion. We shall assume that the only possible source of deviation of taxable profit from economic profit is the use of fixed assets by the business firm. Other sources will not be considered explicitly, but the treatment accorded fixed assets can be generalized for other kinds of deviations as well.

THE SIMPLE CASE: NO PRICE CHANGES

The hypothetical data in Table I may be used to illustrate depreciation, profits and taxes in a stable price situation. It is assumed that fixed assets having a life of 5 years are purchased by a firm for $1,000.00 and are depreciated according to the straight-line method. We abstract from technological change and assume that prices throughout the economy do not change.

Table I DEPRECIATION, PROFIT AND TAXES: STABLE PRICES

Period	1	2	3	4	5	Total
Revenue before Depreciation	$500	$500	$500	$500	$500	$2,500
Depreciation	200	200	200	200	200	1,000
Profit	300	300	300	300	300	1,500
Taxes (40%)	120	120	120	120	120	600

In this simple and highly unrealistic situation, depreciation presents no problem. It is the same amount whether computed on current cost or on historic cost; therefore, the use of original cost to compute depreciation coincidentally yields

---

[4] Solomon Fabricant has indicated some of the elements of business income which must be adjusted if consistency with national income measurements is desired. "Business Costs and Business Income under Changing Price Levels," *Five Monographs on Business Income, op. cit.*, pp. 143–154.

the proper figure.⁵ So far as depreciation affects them, economic profit and taxable profit are identical. Further, there are no capital gains to contend with. Finally, the funds equivalent to the depreciation charge are sufficient to provide exact replacement at the end of the fifth period if the firm chooses to reserve them for that purpose.

PROPORTIONATE CHANGES IN PRICES

Let us look at another equally unrealistic but more enlightening situation—one where it is assumed that *all* prices change proportionately at the beginning of each period. Different depreciation techniques now yield different results. The hypothetical data in Table II are based on the current cost criterion set forth above; i.e., depreciation is computed each year as 20 per cent of the current cost of fixed assets which is an estimate of the current cost of services rendered.

Table II DEPRECIATION, PROFIT AND TAXES: PROPORTIONATE PRICE CHANGES

Period	1	2	3	4	5	Total
Price Index	100	125	150	175	200	
Current Cost of Fixed Assets	$1,000	$1,250	$1,500	$1,750	$2,000	
Revenue before Depreciation	500	625	750	875	1,000	3,750
Depreciation (Current Cost)	200	250	300	350	400	1,500
Economic Profit	300	375	450	525	600	2,250
Taxes (40%)	120	150	180	210	240	900
Depreciation (Original Cost)	200	200	200	200	200	1,000
Present Taxable Profit	300	425	550	675	800	2,750
Taxes (40%)	120	170	220	270	320	1,100

It will be noted that taxable profit, as it is computed today, exceeds economic profit by the difference between depreciation on current cost (which is here identical to depreciation on purchasing power cost) and depreciation on historic cost. If we explore the nature of this difference, we may find a clue to its proper treatment for tax purposes under the circumstances depicted here.

Monetary Capital Gains Realized through Use

In dollar terms the difference between current cost depreciation and historic cost depreciation represents a capital gain realized through retention and use rather than through sale.⁶ When the fixed asset depicted in Table II, for example, was purchased for $1,000, the real purchase was the acquisition of the future

---

⁵ The cost which should be deducted in arriving at economic profit is the current cost of the services *provided* by the fixed assets which would undoubtedly differ from straight-line depreciation on the current cost of the asset itself if only because the latter reflects, in part, the value of *anticipated* services as well as of current services. This refinement, though desirable, must await better estimation techniques than are now available.

⁶ Sidney Davidson, "Depreciation and Profit Determination," *The Accounting Review*, January, 1950, p. 49, notes that realized capital gains and losses may arise in this fashion. He argues against their recognition for tax purposes because of enforcement difficulties.

services of the asset at a cost of $200 per period.[7] But the value of the services rendered by the asset in subsequent periods (at then current prices) exceeds their original cost by $50 in Period 2, $100 in Period 3, $150 in Period 4 and $200 in Period 5, each amount being the difference between current cost depreciation and historic cost depreciation. These amounts represent dollar capital gains realized through use (if receipts cover depreciation in addition to other costs). They represent, also, the amortization of asset appreciation.

In the present case, where all prices are rising in proportion, the taxation of these dollar capital gains would, in reality, fall on real capital. To avoid this, depreciation must be taken in each period on the basis of cost adjusted for price level changes. Whether current cost or purchasing power cost should be used as the depreciation base for tax purposes is a question which will be discussed in a later section on differential price changes.

Replacement: A Management Decision

Even the exemption from taxation of monetary capital gains would not satisfy those who might argue that depreciation funds held in the form of cash should be sufficient to effect actual fixed asset replacement. If held in the form of cash, the amount available for replacement at the end of the fifth period, $1,500, is $500 short of the amount necessary for actual replacement in kind. It is essentially for this reason that E. Cary Brown discards current cost depreciation for the single asset firm.[8] He specifies continuous replacement equal in each period to the depreciation charge as the condition necessary for the method to yield the anticipated results (maintenance of real capital) in terms of replacement. This line of reasoning is quite correct *so long as funds equal to the depreciation charges are held in the form of cash when not used for immediate replacement.*

This, I submit, assumes an unnecessary rigidity in the decision-making process of the individual firm. There seems little justification for assuming that the firm must invariably select a particular mode of holding funds. Holding funds in the form of cash is but *one* alternative open to the firm. There are innumerable other choices that could be made. The firm, instead of holding cash, might hold a commodity or set of commodities, stocks or purchasing power bonds—anything whose price appreciation keeps pace with the general price level. It might choose to turn over continually the funds at its disposal. In any event, given a certain amount of funds there must be a variety of forms in which these funds can be held so that purchasing power will remain intact.[9] While holding cash is one way of attempting this, the purchase of fixed assets, whether as replacement or as new investment, can be regarded as another.

Whatever the method the firm chooses, the outcome of the choice is a legitimate test of the effectiveness of the decision-making process in the firm. Considered in this way, the amount of depreciation charged in each period on the basis of historic cost adjusted for changes in the general price level indicates the amount of funds which must be retained out of current receipts *in some form*

[7] Consistent with the practice of straight-line depreciation, discounting and interest accumulation are ignored.

[8] E. Cary Brown, *Effects of Taxation: Depreciation Adjustments for Price Changes* (Boston: Harvard Business School, Division of Research, 1952), pp. 100–101.

[9] We are ignoring possible legal restrictions on the choices open to the firm. In general, however, the firm is probably not unduly circumscribed in its range of choice.

(*open to choice*) in order to maintain undiminished the value of the firm's assets in terms of purchasing power.[10]

If all prices do not change proportionately, the opportunity exists to increase the purchasing power of a given amount of cash through judicious investment. When prices are falling, whether proportionately or not, the opportunity exists to increase purchasing power simply by holding cash. If the firm is wise enough (or lucky enough) to make such decisions, an advantage will accrue to the firm. This advantage is the direct result of *choosing* one of a set of successful alternatives. The selection of alternatives of this sort is, I submit, a proper function of management. If this is acknowledged, the case for exempting the full cost of actual replacement from taxation is buried.[11]

In the case of proportionate price changes, economic profit, which is obtained by deducting current cost depreciation, is identical to taxable profit, which, it will be argued, should be obtained by deducting depreciation on purchasing power cost. The propriety of this technique for tax purposes can be checked by deflation for price changes. The data in Table II, if deflated to prices prevailing in Period 1, for example, would be identical to those in Table I except that those data which are based on historic cost would be revealed as meaningless. Revenue, depreciation, profit and taxes, when computed on a current cost basis, are identical in each period in terms of purchasing power. If the depreciation charge does not reflect rising prices, however, reported profits and taxes rise with the passage of time. Total costs are understated, profits are overstated and taxes are levied, in part, on real capital rather than on real profit alone.

DIFFERENTIAL PRICE CHANGES

The more realistic situation where the price of particular fixed assets does not move identically with other prices introduces some further complexities which merit examination. The hypothetical data in Table III are based on the assump-

Table III DEPRECIATION, PROFIT AND TAXES: DIFFERENTIAL PRICE CHANGES

Period	1	2	3	4	5	Total
General Price Index	100	100	100	100	100	
Fixed Asset Price Index	100	125	150	175	200	
Current Cost of Fixed Assets	$1,000	$1,250	$1,500	$1,750	$2,000	
Revenue before Depreciation	500	500	500	500	500	2,500
Depreciation (Current Cost)	200	250	300	350	400	1,500
Economic Profit	300	250	200	150	100	1,000
Taxes (40%)	120	100	80	60	40	400

tions that price changes are restricted to those fixed assets which the firm employs and that these changes are not sufficient to alter the general price index. Depre-

---

[10] It should be noted again that eventual replacement in kind is itself but one of many alternatives available to the firm. This decision should be taken on the same basis as any other. The maintenance of the real value of total assets does not require replacement in kind.

[11] The argument that current cost depreciation should be exempt from taxation will be discussed in a later section.

ciation is again computed according to the current cost criterion and price changes are assumed to occur at the beginning of each period.

Economic profit again indicates the amount by which revenue at current prices exceeds identifiable current costs. Specifically, the trend of economic profit spells out the decreasing profitability of using these kinds of fixed assets in this particular way in this industry. The insider can take heed, while the outsider, too, is not so likely to be misled by profit reports and enter the industry, making it even less profitable for everyone.

The tax situation, as it now stands, is a more pleasant one. The business firm is paying over to the government fewer units of purchasing power than it was in either of the preceding cases. This is a direct result of the transference of $500 in total from the category of economic profit to depreciation as a result of the rise in the price of fixed assets while all other prices remained stable.

Real Capital Gains Realized through Use

If the fixed assets had been sold during their lifetime, the firm would have realized a real capital gain which would have been taxed (and properly so). The use of the fixed assets by the firm is an alternative way of realizing a similar gain.[12] Table III takes no account of this kind of gain (or loss) which the individual firm may receive.

If after the price changes which occur at the beginning of the second period (see Table III), the firm's fixed assets (now one period old) have a market value of $1,000 as compared to a book value of $800, there is a capital gain of $200 which is as yet unrealized. This gain is potentially real and not monetary because it has resulted from a change in fixed asset prices unaccompanied by any change in other prices. If the indicated change in fixed asset prices between Period 1 and Period 2 were the only price change to occur during the life of the asset, the $200 capital gain would be realized through use at the rate of $50 per subsequent period, the excess of current cost depreciation over historic cost depreciation in each period.

The firm could be asked to pay a tax on that part of its depreciation charge which represents the use of appreciated purchasing power. While these gains and losses should not be included in economic profit or in national income, the fact that individuals and firms do receive them and that purchasing power is augmented thereby justifies their taxation.[13] It can be argued that these gains are really a part of the higher cost of doing business and should be exempt from taxation on that ground, but this confuses the fact of the gain with the particular manner in which the firm chooses to use it. If the higher price of the fixed assets is the result of increased demand in other industries or uses, it probably indicates the advisability of finding a cheaper substitute in this industry. This is a choice the firm must make and the necessity of making the decision should not be confused with the fact that the purchasing power derivable from these assets has risen. The way in which the firm chooses to utilize the purchasing power is a management decision and the economic profit derived from this use is a legitimate

[12] The gain may not be the same, however. The market in which the firm can sell may not be the same (if one exists at all) as that in which it buys. Further, the price of new assets may not be related to the price of second-hand assets as simply as straight-line depreciation implies.

[13] See Brown, *op. cit.*, p. 135.

test of decision-making ability. Table III should include, therefore, the following data in order to present the full tax picture:

Period	1	2	3	4	5	Total
Real Capital Gains Realized	—	$50	$100	$150	$200	$500
Tax on above (40%)	—	20	40	60	80	200
Total Taxes	$120	120	120	120	120	600

The real capital gain realized in each period is the difference between depreciation on a current cost basis and depreciation on a purchasing power cost basis (in this example, the latter equals depreciation on historic cost). It indicates the amortization of real fixed assets appreciation. When these real gains are taxed, the firm pays total taxes of $600, the same amount in purchasing power units that it paid in the other cases we have considered.

It will be noted that one criterion for the taxability of gains is that the gain be realized. Yet purchasing power is potentially augmented by unrealized gains. Taxes, however, must be paid in cash. If gains or losses are not reflected in changes in holdings of reasonably liquid assets, their taxation may force a company to make decisions regarding the liquidity of its assets which it would not otherwise deem advisable. A firm may be forced to realize the gains through sale. Ideally, unrealized gains and losses should be recognized for their effect on tax *liability*, but their effect on tax *payments* should be deferred until the gains and losses are realized. So long as this distinction is not made, gains and losses should be recognized for tax purposes only when realized.

Replacement

Providing for actual physical replacement is even more difficult in this case. Total depreciation funds, $1,500, are not only insufficient, if held in cash, to effect replacement in kind, but the opportunities to invest the funds to yield the necessary replacement amount at the end of the fifth period are limited to these particular kinds of assets because they are the only commodities rising in price. Provision for exact replacement seems almost impossible. When that part of total depreciation which represents a real capital gain is subject to taxation, exact replacement with depreciation funds becomes even less feasible.

But the fact must again be emphasized that replacement in kind, when replacement is due, is but one alternative among many. If prices of these fixed assets have risen relative to other prices it is possible that the firm would choose other alternatives regardless of the funds at its disposal. If exact replacement is made, the firm has chosen an alternative which requires more purchasing power than its original investment represents. If exact replacement cost were exempt from taxation when the prices of these fixed assets were rising faster than other prices, the firm would make a non-taxable gain. The particular use to which the firm chooses to put the gain does not alter the fact. On the other hand, if specific fixed asset prices were falling relative to other prices, the taxation of profits based on current cost depreciation would not exempt sufficient funds to maintain general purchasing power. The use of inefficient assets might be prolonged because funds sufficient to take advantage of other alternatives may not be available.

If the firm is permitted to retain its *general* purchasing power free of taxation, the firm is free to make any investment decision it wishes. At the same time, its taxable gains and losses are equitably computed. The criterion for tax purposes of maintaining general purchasing power also avoids placing actual replacement cost on a pedestal and makes it clear that replacement in kind is but one of a host of alternatives. Hence, while current cost depreciation is necessary to obtain a statement of economic profit, depreciation based on historic cost adjusted for changes in the general price level is the proper deduction for tax purposes.[14] It might be desirable, of course, to tax economic profit and real capital gains at different rates.[15]

THE PRACTICAL APPLICATION OF THE METHOD

Four bases have been considered on which depreciation can be computed—original cost, current cost (cost at current market prices of the assets when used), purchasing power cost (historic cost adjusted for changes in the general price level), and cost at the time of actual replacement. The first and the last of these have been discarded for purposes of computing both economic profit and taxable profit. The use of current cost has been suggested as most appropriate for determining economic profit while purchasing power cost has been advocated for tax purposes.[16] The division of taxable income into economic profit and real capital gains not only serves analytical purposes but also permits the application of differential tax rates.

[14] See Arthur M. Cannon, "Tax Pressures on Accounting Principles and Accountants' Independence," *The Accounting Review*, October, 1952, pp. 419–426, for a good discussion of the need to distinguish between taxable and business income.

[15] If real income is to be the tax base for corporations, the question arises as to whether it should not be the tax base for others also. Ideally, the answer must be "yes" from the equity point of view. To assure equity to all, taxes should be levied on real gains and real income because only in this way can differentials in real income be fully allowed for in the tax structure. The practicality of making these adjustments in other areas must, of course, be considered. Even if it is not practical there, however, equity might best be served by the adoption of a real basis wherever possible. Uneven application can gradually be corrected and temporary inequities can be roughly adjusted through differential tax rates. Improvement must be gradual if it is not to be revolutionary; the discarding of an improvement because it cannot be applied all at once simply rigidifies existing errors. (See Brown, *op. cit.*, pp. 76–78 for some opposing arguments.)

[16] Current cost and purchasing power cost have vied for the attention of accountants. An excellent case for current cost depreciation is presented by W. J. Graham, "The Effect of Changing Price Levels on the Determination, Reporting, and Interpretation of Income," *The Accounting Review*, January, 1949, pp. 15–26. Myron J. Gordon applies current cost in the accounts in "The Valuation of Accounts at Current Cost," *The Accounting Review*, July, 1953, pp. 373–384. K. Engelmann in "The Realization Basis of Determining Income Would Eliminate Distortions Caused by Inflation," *Journal of Accountancy*, October, 1950, pp. 321–323, also presents an appeal for current cost. Donald L. Raun in "Income: A Measurement of Currently Added Purchasing Power through Operations," *The Accounting Review*, July, 1952, pp. 352–358, presents a good case for the purchasing power basis. The combination of the two bases in a system of accounts seems to have escaped detailed analysis in recent years. Sweeney treated replacement cost in his system in a somewhat different fashion. (*Stabilized Accounting*, New York: Harper & Brothers, 1936, Chapter III.)

The Index Number Problem

To record the information suggested two indexes would be required: A general index of purchasing power and an index of the prices of fixed assets used by each firm. The former could be constructed objectively and independent of the firm; the latter would have to be constructed by (or for) each firm (or industry) according to objectively determined standards and rules. Fixed assets, classified by year of purchase, could be adjusted by the internal index for the purpose of determining the amount of depreciation to be deducted in arriving at economic profit. The general price (or external) index could be applied to the original cost of these assets to determine the amount of depreciation deductible for tax purposes. A comparison of this charge with the charge based on current cost would disclose the amount of real capital gain or loss realized during the period.

The difficulties involved in computing an appropriate general price index should not be minimized.[17] Changes in quality are especially difficult to comprehend. The difficulties involved in computing an internal index are of a different order. It should apply to the particular assets of the firm. Current prices are needed on those particular assets. If identical assets are no longer made and marketed, difficulties multiply. Cost of production would be too high a figure to use (if it were not, there would most likely be a market and a market price). Some substitute price would have to be found, probably on the basis of opportunity cost. Despite these difficulties, the results obtained should be more accurate and more equitable than figures computed on the basis of known but generally irrelevant historic cost.

Application in the Accounts: An Illustration

As the information developed in the accounts should include balance sheet data as well as profit and loss data, unrealized gains and losses must be recognized as they accrue. The net amount of these gains and losses shown on the books at any one time could be termed a revaluation surplus. The true nature of this "surplus" is more accurately revealed, however, when it is designated as unrealized gain or loss. It will be advantageous to segregate these gains and losses as they accrue into real and monetary portions. The distinction must be made when these gains and losses are realized; the real part, which is taxable, must be distinguished from the monetary part, which is not taxable. To illustrate briefly one way of doing this we shall use the data in Table IV. Price changes are assumed to occur at the beginning of each period.

The amounts of realized capital gain can be determined as amortizations of unrealized gain. The dollar value of the assets after the price change at the beginning of Period 2 is $1,200 (current cost minus current cost depreciation for one period). Subtracting the book value ($800) yields the estimated capital gain, $400, which would be realized if the assets were sold. Until sold or used, however, it represents an unrealized capital gain. If prices did not change further, the capital gain would be realized through use at the rate of $100 per period for the remaining four periods. As prices rise again at the beginning of Period 3

---

[17] See Brown, *op. cit.*, pp. 131–136 and Solomon Fabricant, *Capital Consumption and Adjustment* (New York: National Bureau of Economic Research, 1938), pp. 159–160 and ff.

a further unrealized gain accrues, this one amounting to $300—new current cost depreciated, $1,200, less the current cost of last period depreciated to date, $900 ($1,500 less depreciation for two periods, $600). This gain will be realized through use at the rate of $100 per period for the remaining three periods. Another unrealized capital gain amounting to $200 accrues at the beginning of Period 4 and one of $100 accrues at the beginning of Period 5, each the result of further price changes. Each of these gains would be realized in a fashion similar to the others. The sum of the gains *realized* in each period is equal to the difference between current cost depreciation and historic cost depreciation, i.e., the realized gains can be represented as amortizations of asset appreciation.

Table IV DEPRECIATION, PROFIT AND TAXES: DIFFERENTIAL PRICE CHANGES

Period	1	2	3	4	5
General Price Index	100	120	140	160	180
Fixed Asset Price Index	100	150	200	250	300
Revenue	$500	$600	$700	$800	$900
Depreciation (20%) (Current Cost)	200	300	400	500	600
Economic Profit	300	300	300	300	300
Taxes (40%)	120	120	120	120	120
Unrealized					
Capital Gain	0	400	300	200	100
Monetary	(0)	(160)	(120)	(80)	(40)
Real	(0)	(240)	(180)	(120)	(60)
Realized					
Capital Gain	0	100	200	300	400
Monetary	(0)	(40)	(80)	(120)	(160)
Real	(0)	(60)	(120)	(180)	(240)
Tax on Real Gain (40%)	0	24	48	72	96
Total Taxes	120	144	168	192	216

If both the general price index and the fixed asset price index are based on the year in which the fixed assets were purchased, the total unrealized capital gain which accrues at any time can be approximated by the following formula:

$$\Delta C = N_{t-1}(F_t - F_{t-1}) \tag{1}$$

where ΔC is the unrealized capital gain (change in money value), N is the remaining book value of the assets as computed with the historic cost method, and F is the fixed asset price index divided by 100.

This amount is an unrealized gain or loss. It can be further divided into its potentially real and potentially monetary parts. The purely monetary unrealized gain or loss is given by

$$\Delta C_m = N_{t-1}(G_t - G_{t-1}) \tag{2}$$

where G is the general price index divided by 100. The real segment of the unrealized gain or loss can be determined by subtraction. It is given by

$$\Delta C_r = N_{t-1}(F_t - F_{t-1}) - (G_t - G_{t-1}). \tag{3}$$

The amount of the total capital gain or loss *realized through use* in each period is the difference between current cost depreciation and historic cost depreciation.

That part of the realized gain or loss which is purely monetary can be determined as the difference between depreciation on a purchasing power cost basis (historic cost multiplied by the general price index) and depreciation on the historic cost basis. The difference between current cost depreciation and purchasing power cost depreciation represents the real gain or loss realized during the period.

Table V SKELETON ACCOUNTS SHOWING THE DEPRECIATION TECHNIQUE APPLIED

Fixed assets				Allowance for depreciation			
(0) 1,000						(1a) 200	
						(2b) 200	
						(3b) 200	
						(4b) 200	
						(5b) 200	
Fixed asset value adjustment				Unrealized real gain or loss		Unrealized monetary gain or loss	
(2a) 400	(2b) 100			(2c) 60	(2a) 240	(2d) 40	(2a) 160
(3a) 300	(3b) 200			(3c) 120	(3a) 180	(3d) 80	(3a) 120
(4a) 200	(4b) 300			(4c) 180	(4a) 120	(4d) 120	(4a) 80
(5a) 100	(5b) 400			(5c) 240	(5a) 60	(5d) 160	(5a) 40
Realized real gain (taxable)				Depreciation		Retained earnings	
To P&L 60	(2c) 60			(1a) 200	To P&L 200		(2d) 40
To P&L 120	(3c) 120			(2b) 300	To P&L 300		(3d) 80
To P&L 180	(4c) 180			(3b) 400	To P&L 400		(4d) 120
To P&L 240	(5c) 240			(4b) 500	To P&L 500		(5d) 160
				(5b) 600	To P&L 600		

The skeleton accounts in Table V indicate how this information might be recorded in each period as it pertains to depreciation and related accounts. The circled numbers indicate periods in which entries are made while the letters designate particular entries. Starting with a new purchase of fixed assets having a five-year life and a cost of $1,000, depreciation is recorded throughout on the historic cost basis in the Allowance for Depreciation account. Adjustments for price changes are handled in additional accounts.

Entry (1a) records historic cost depreciation only, because prices have not changed during Period 1. Entry (2a) records, as a debit, the total increase in the value of the fixed assets at the beginning of Period 2 and, as credits, the unrealized real gain and the unrealized monetary gain. Entry (2b) records current cost depreciation at the end of Period 2, carries historic cost depreciation to the Allowance for Depreciation account and records that part which represents realized gain as a credit to the Fixed Asset Value Adjustment account (a separate account might be established for this additional "allowance"). Entry (2c) transfers the realized real gain from the unrealized account to the realized account from where it would be closed to the Profit and Loss account.[18] Entry (2d) transfers the realized monetary gain directly to the Retained Earnings account as it reflects a purely monetary change and is not taxable. Entries for subsequent periods can be traced in similar fashion.

On the balance sheet fixed assets might be shown as follows at the end of Period 2:

Fixed Assets (Historic Cost)	$1,000
Less: Allowance for Depreciation	400
Remaining Historic Cost	600
Add: Fixed Asset Value Adjustment	300
Current Value of Fixed Assets (estimated)	900

The proprietorship section of the balance sheet would show the amount of unrealized real gain or loss and the amount of unrealized monetary gain or loss, the sum of the two being equal to the amount of the fixed asset value adjustment.

Should the assets be discovered to have value after the estimated life has expired, this value should be written up in the value adjustment account and in the Unrealized Real Gain or Loss account. Depreciation should continue to be recorded on a current cost basis so that profit figures would not be misleading. The credit entry for depreciation would go to the value adjustment account. The whole amount would be realized gain and should be transferred to the Realized Real Gain or Loss account. In this way both the balance sheet and the profit and loss statement would record vital economic data while taxable income could be easily identified and classified.

CONSISTENCY AND CONSERVATISM

Conservatism in accounting frequently demands inconsistency and this is nowhere more apparent than in the accounting profession's positions on the appropriate accounting techniques applicable in periods of rising prices as compared to those techniques advocated for use in periods of falling prices. Consistency is not necessarily a hallmark of accuracy but where a technique is conceded to be accurate in periods of rising prices, there should be at least a presumption that it will be accurate if consistently applied in periods of falling prices. The possibility should be recognized that what may be parading under the banner of conservatism is nothing more heroic than group self-interest, not accuracy.

Where conservatism is blindly adhered to even at the expense of good accounting, it is being carried too far. Conservatism, of itself, is not a virtue. It is a good residual, or background, rule. Where the course is not otherwise clear, resort to conservatism. Conservatism is no excuse, however, for failure to furnish owners and managers with essential 'economic data'.[19]

Certainly for decision-making as well as analytical purposes accurate reporting should take priority over conservative reporting. Accounting for depreciation

[18] It should, of course, be shown separately on the profit and loss statement where economic profit, realized capital gains and losses, and total taxable income should be carefully identified.

[19] Herbert F. Taggart, "Sacred Cows in Accounting," *The Accounting Review*, July, 1953, pp. 313–319.

under changing price levels is not an area where sound reasons for exception can be found. Yet the expressions of many business and accounting groups on the price level problem have become most pronounced during periods of rising prices and even then their observations are frequently hedged by adherence to historic cost as a basis for depreciation during periods of falling prices whenever the use of this basis will result in higher depreciation estimates.

George O. May has presented such a depreciation proposal.[20] Briefly his position is that historic cost should form the basis for each annual depreciation charge. If the *general* price level rises, a special reserve would be established to which an additional amount of depreciation would be credited to bring the total charge up to the current general price level. When prices are generally falling the reverse procedure would operate until the special reserve is extinguished after which depreciation on historic cost would be reestablished. If current or carry-over expenditures for plant fall short of the depreciation charge, the amount allowed as a charge would be reduced but not below that computed on the historic cost basis.

This differs from the proposal presented here in two major respects: (1) it takes no account of current fixed asset cost and (2) it posits depreciation on historic cost as a minimum charge so long as full historic cost has not been exhausted. The second point requires further consideration.

May recognizes that theoretical considerations do not support his exceptions [21] and relies on two practical appeals to support his case for historic cost depreciation as a minimum charge: (1) failure to provide for recovery of cost would deter investment and (2) established principles of income taxation require that cost recovery be permitted and that total accumulated reserves do not exceed total accumulated cost.[22]

The matter of tax principles has received considerable attention from others in recent years.[23] It should be clear, therefore, that tax "principles" as embodied in the law may not be principles at all but merely expediencies. Hence, if changes in depreciation accounting are warranted for accounting, business, economic and social reasons, laws should be changed to conform to principles. Realism requires not only an appreciation of the law but also an awareness that it can be and often should be changed.

The effect on investment incentives of placing both depreciation and taxation on a real instead of a purely monetary basis is not clear. If such a system were

---

[20] George O. May, *Business Income and Price Levels: An Accounting Study* (New York: Study Group on Business Income of the American Institute of Accountants), July 1, 1949, Appendix V, "Proposal for Depreciation of Current Costs," pp. 105–109.

[21] *Ibid.*, p. 107.

[22] *Loc. cit.*

[23] "The tax laws have unduly and unintentionally tended to influence the development of corporate accounting in that to some extent legislative concessions in measuring taxable income have been adopted into accounting practice without justification in principle." (Committee on Concepts and Standards Underlying Corporate Financial Statements, "Accounting Principles and Taxable Income," Supplementary Statement No. 4, *The Accounting Review*, October, 1952, p. 429).

The following statement appears in the same journal: "Accountants should resist efforts to prostitute accounting principles to tax ends; accountants' reports must be determined independently of tax considerations." (Arthur M. Cannon, *op. cit.*, p. 426).

initiated during a period of falling prices (which seems highly unlikely) the money illusion might have a deadening effect on investment. Businessmen might view a depreciation charge lower than that which the historic cost basis would provide as a means of transferring capital recovery to the category of taxable profits. If they are so easily misled by money figures, however, they should succumb as easily to the more pleasant and more real effect on reported profits. As depreciation charges are reduced, reported profits rise and what businessmen may have mistaken for losses may now be recognized as smaller losses or even profits. The perception of their true profit status may encourage investment. Which of the two effects would prove the stronger is difficult to determine.[24]

If businessmen are not misled by accounting figures computed on the historic cost basis, they may be aware of the subsidy hidden in historic cost depreciation during periods of falling prices. These charges reduce reported profits and therefore taxes. It should be clear, however, that the subsidy is realized only if profits are positive. Further, if it is felt that subsidization is necessary in such a period, perhaps an open subsidy independent of depreciation policy might be preferable. (Businessmen frequently extol the virtues of the open subsidy in the case of supports for farm income!) Further, if a subsidy is needed when profits are positive, it would appear to be more necessary when they are negative.

Businessmen do not appear to be led astray by money measures during periods of rising prices. If depreciation in real terms were initiated in such a period (which is more likely), their knowledge that money measures are often illusory should be strengthened. Then if the money illusion should be resurrected during periods of falling prices, it can be tabbed for what it is—a search for a hidden subsidy.

CONCLUSION

Regardless of how one may feel about the present practicality of recording depreciation on the books so as to reflect the results of price movements, it is difficult for anyone to deny the trend toward realistic accounting. Recognition is spreading that easily determinable dollar figures are not realistic if they are inaccurate. Viewed in this fashion, those accounting techniques which are most practicable are often the most unrealistic. The increasing concern with this fact is evidence that the search for more accurate accounting methods is well underway and is not likely to be halted by those who preach impracticality. Improvement in accounting is to be achieved by making accuracy more practical.

The techniques suggested in this article deviate in many respects from the ideal. I think, however, that they represent a realistic compromise between proponents of accounting for general price changes and those who support accounting for specific current costs. The compromise lies in the fact that both are used; it is a realistic compromise, however, because both are truly needed. If the forces supporting each can be joined, perhaps changing price levels will be recognized in practice as well as in theory.

[24] While arguing against replacement cost depreciation, A. R. Prest concedes that its use means higher profitability and higher savings because of the tax effects. ("Replacement Cost Depreciation," *Accounting Research*, July, 1950, pp. 385–402.) See also S. P. Dobrovolsky, "Depreciation Policies and Investment Decision," *American Economic Review*, December, 1951.

PHILIP W. BELL

PHILIP W. BELL (1924–), B.A. 47 Princeton; M.A. 49 University of California (Berkeley); Ph.D. 54 Princeton. Currently professor of economics, University of California (Santa Cruz). Major publications: *The Sterling Area in the Postwar World* (1956), *The Theory and Measurement of Business Income* (with Edwards, 1961). *Economic Theory: An Integrated Text with Special Reference to Tropical Africa and Other Developing Areas* (with Todaro, 1969). Contributor to economics journals and several collections of papers.

Was on the economics faculty of Haverford College, 1952–57 and 1960–62, flanking three years of service at the University of California (Berkeley). In 1963–65, he was on the economics faculty of Makerere University College, Uganda, and served for one year as dean of the social science faculty. In 1965–66, he was on the faculty of Fisk University, and in 1968 he joined the economics faculty of the University of California (Santa Cruz). Between 1968 and 1972, he served as provost of Merrill College.

ON CURRENT REPLACEMENT COSTS AND BUSINESS INCOME

PHILIP W. BELL

I. HISTORIC COSTS VERSUS CURRENT COSTS

The issue of whether historic costs or current costs should be used in the measurement of business income has been discussed so widely, particularly in the literature of the last ten years, that both sides are probably tempted simply to fall back on the Disraeli principle of always ending an argument in which he could neither convince his antagonist nor his antagonist convince him with one word, an exasperated "Perhaps." Still, it seems worthwhile in terms of the overall aims of this symposium, as I understand them, to stress three points on the current cost side and then move on.

First, the use of current cost data, at least as Professor Edwards and I have employed them,[1] does *not* need to exclude historic cost data from accounting records. End-of-period adjustments are made to historic cost figures on the basis

---

SOURCE: From *Asset Valuation*, edited by Robert R. Sterling (Lawrence, Kans.: Scholars Book Co., 1971), pp. 19–32. Reprinted by permission of Scholars Book Co.

[1] Edgar O. Edwards and Philip W. Bell, *The Theory and Measurement of Business Income* (Berkeley, California: University of California Press, 1961).

of current cost values, but *both* are then reported in somewhat rearranged form in finished accounting statements—nothing is lost and a great deal, we feel, is gained. The other two points I wish to stress, then, relate to what is thereby gained.

One very important improvement in the records of the enterprise is that the resultant data properly separate operating from holding gains of the firm, something that use of historic cost information clearly does not do.

The other, less widely recognized but equally important advantage of using current costs in developing accounting records for the firm is that by so doing, one can recognize in the accounts all gains of the enterprise *as they accrue, as well as* when they are realized. *Not* counting gains when they arise has the unfortunate consequence that when such gains are in fact realized, the gains earned over the full span of time during which the assets were held are attributed entirely to the period in which the gains are realized. This difficulty carries with it two implications: First, it means that even though absolutely identical events occur in two periods, accounting data will normally yield a different figure for profits reportedly earned in the two periods, because the data for each period are influenced by data of past periods. Second, if holding gains are only reported when realized through sale, there is no way to determine in what periods holding activities were successful and in what periods they were unsuccessful.

Before briefly illustrating these points, let me re-emphasize what I stressed at the outset: the use of current costs in accounting records in order to achieve the above advantages does not have to obviate employment of historic costs; indeed, the methods we employ build upon traditional accounting principles and keep track of historic costs both in daily internal records and in finished balance sheets and income statements. Surely no one can complain of more, rather than less, information when he can accumulate the additional information at very little time and cost, and when the additional information permits statements which have the above advantages, which statements he (and others) can use or not as they see fit.

At a risk of seeming to vastly oversimplify and exaggerate, let me give a brief, much truncated illustration of the above arguments. A small enterprise, the XYZ Corporation, earns sales revenues over a three-year period of $40,000, $50,000, and $60,000, respectively. Its costs include payment of wages and salaries, which rise slightly each year. Under present historic cost methods of accounting, it computes its materials costs in accordance with some generally accepted principle (such as FIFO or LIFO) which is related to a completely artificial assumption about physical movements of goods and which, if there are physical changes of inventory stocks as in the LIFO case, does not accurately reflect the current costs of materials used in production when there are price changes. Depreciation cost of machinery used is another cost: machinery is purchased at the beginning of operations in Year 1 for $80,000 and is to be depreciated on a straight-line basis over a ten-year period, no salvage value, at $8,000 per year. Similarly, we shall assume that land and building are depreciated over a twenty-year period on the same basis, having been acquired also for $80,000. These costs are subtracted from revenue each year, and the income which traditional accounting practices yield, as shown in Figure 1A, suggests that the enterprise is doing very well, with income rising from $7,000 to $15,000 to $21,500. With no additional outlay of capital, the data suggest that this might be a good enterprise to invest in, or expand investment in.

Revenues are going up for this enterprise, perhaps because of larger output, perhaps because of rising prices—let us assume that it is largely the latter and that prices of materials, machinery, land, and building are also rising, in this case at a more rapid rate than what is being sold. Actual data do show sharp differences in movements of prices of individual assets from those of the general wholesale price index, both in this country and abroad.[2] Specifically, for ease of illustration, let us assume in the case of machinery that, if purchased in the second year rather than the first it would cost $140,000, and $180,000 in the third year. Further assume that the replacement cost of land and buildings in Years 2 and 3 would have been $120,000 and $180,000, respectively. We also assume that the true current cost of materials used also differs somewhat from those arrived at by our artificial inventorying methods.

Using current costs of operation, rather than historic costs, our income statement would appear as in Figure 1B. The purchase price of machinery being used is, in Year 2, $140,000 rather than the original $80,000. The current cost of using

Figure 1A THREE YEAR INCOME STATEMENT FOR ENTERPRISE XYZ (TRADITIONAL HISTORIC COST ACCOUNTING METHODS)

	Year 1		Year 2		Year 3	
Revenue	$40,000		$50,000		$60,000	
Cost						
Wages & Salaries	$14,000		$15,000		$17,500	
Materials	7,000		8,000		9,000	
Depreciation, machinery	8,000		8,000		8,000	
Depreciation, land & building	4,000		4,000		4,000	
		33,000		35,000		38,500
Income		$ 7,000		$15,000		$21,500

Figure 1B THREE-YEAR OPERATING INCOME STATEMENT FOR ENTERPRISE XYZ (CURRENT COSTS MATCHED WITH CURRENT REVENUES)

	Year 1		Year 2		Year 3	
Revenue	$40,000		$50,000		$60,000	
Cost						
Wages & Salaries	$14,000		$15,000		$17,500	
Materials	7,000		9,000		11,500	
Depreciation, machinery	8,000		14,000		18,000	
Depreciation, land & building	4,000		6,000		9,000	
		33,000		44,000		55,000
Income		$ 7,000		$ 6,000		$ 5,000

[2] See, for example, Edwards and Bell, p. 20; D. H. Whitehead, "Price-Cutting and Wage Policy," *Economic Record*, No. 39 (June 1963), p. 189; W. A. H. Godley and C. Gillion, "Pricing Behavior in the Engineering Industry," *National Institute Economic Review*, No. 28 (May 1964), pp. 50–52.

it in that year is then $14,000 on a ten-year depreciation basis, not $8,000, and a similar adjustment must be made for the rising cost of land and buildings. With our three outdated cost items adjusted to the true current cost of using those items (wages and salaries, like revenues, are presumably already based on current prices of the year in question), our income statements come out very differently than that shown with traditional accounting practices. Figure 1B shows that income on operations is actually *declining* year-by-year, rather than increasing nicely, as suggested by traditional accounting methods as shown in Figure 1A.

Now we have shown, of course, only part of what has actually been taking place by utilizing current costs to measure operating gains or losses. The gently rising material costs and sharply rising fixed asset costs not only involve rising *operating costs,* when measured in terms of current prices to make them comparable to other items on the income statement, but also involve *holding gains,* or preferably we may term them *cost savings.* Given the assumption that machinery, new, rose in value suddenly at the beginning of Year 2 from $80,000 to $140,000, the difference between current cost depreciation and historic cost depreciation in Year 2 of $6,000 is a cost saving realized during the year, from using machinery purchased originally for $80,000 but now costing $140,000.[3] Looked at over a longer term, machinery which was worth $72,000 at the end of the first year ($80,000 less $8,000) and $112,000 at the end of the second year ($140,000 less $28,000) as well as use value during the second year of $14,000 would involve total realizable (realized and unrealized) cost savings of $54,000 at the end of Year 2, of which $6,000 was actually realized through use in the second year, and another $6,000 will be used up in each of its subsequent eight years of life if held to maturity and assuming no further price changes. In Year 2, we feel that *both the realized and unrealized cost savings* of that year should be reported, so that they can be distinguished separately, on the income statement for that year. This is done in Figure 2, having made similar adjustments necessary for items other than those of the machinery account.[4] Only if this is done will the two advantages from utilizing current cost data cited at the beginning of this section be incorporated in the accounts. Operating gains are correctly separated from realized holding gains on the left, although the *total* of realized income is the same as that reported using traditional historic costs. The *total earned income* on the right (realized and unrealized) is the amount, and the only amount, which will prove to be the same when identical events, with respect to operations and individual price changes, occur in the life of the enterprise.[5]

---

[3] We have used abrupt price changes for this much simplified example, rather than measurement of income in terms of average prices for a period, a practice criticized by Professor Chambers. In Edwards and Bell, we try to show rigorously why we think that an averaging process is quite acceptable (see Chapters V and VI, particularly pp. 144–147, with respect to inventories). Russell Mathews has also tried to answer Professor Chambers' criticism, particularly with respect to consistency of income and balance sheet statements. See his, "The Price-Level Controversy: A Reply," *Journal of Accounting Research* (Spring 1967), pp. 116–118.

[4] How such adjustments are handled in practice in ledger account adjustments at the end of the year, providing consistency in income and balance sheet accounts, is detailed in Edwards and Bell, Chapters V and VI.

[5] For a particularly telling example of this, affecting LIFO inventory valuation methods, see Edwards and Bell, Table 7, p. 156, and explanation, p. 158.

Figure 2 YEAR 2 COMPREHENSIVE INCOME STATEMENT FOR ENTERPRISE XYZ

Revenue		$50,000
Costs		
Wages & Salaries	$15,000	
Materials	9,000	
Depreciation, machinery	14,000	
Depreciation, land & buildings	6,000	
		44,000
Current operating income		$ 6,000

Current operating profit		$ 6,000	Current operating profit	$ 6,000
Realized cost savings on cost of			Realizable cost savings on	
materials	$ 1,000		inventories	$ 500
On depreciation,				
machinery	6,000		On machinery	54,000
On depreciation,				
land & buildings	2,000		On land & buildings	38,000
		9,000		$92,500
Realized income		$15,000	Earned income	$98,500

This is as much as we can say here about the historic cost-current cost controversy, for we must move on to other issues. We will touch on the feasibility of acquiring sound current cost data for income statements, such as that shown in Figure 2, at the end. Let us now turn to the problem of dealing with price-level changes. The use of a simple adjustment for general price-level changes, rather than for individual price changes—as suggested by many accountants—is an adjustment which can readily be tacked on to the current cost data which we have suggested. However, we can only honestly say, that such an adjustment is an aberration of the first magnitude if applied without introduction of current costs, i.e., if it is applied to simple historic cost data.

II. THE PROBLEM OF PRICE-LEVEL CHANGES

I gladly concede that it is a digression from the subject of this paper, and indeed from the general subject of this symposium, to discuss general *price-level* changes. But we are forced into the matter because of the well-known monograph published by the American Institute of Certified Public Accountants in 1963 entitled *Reporting the Financial Effects of Price-Level Changes*.[6] Though it was not the intention of the authors, I fear the effect of this monograph was to lead some accountants to believe that making a single price-level adjustment to historic cost data served to deal with changing prices in the economy and thus obviated the need for current cost adjustments, such as we have been proposing here. Nothing could be further from the case. Once meaningful data have been accumulated on operating income and holding gains, *then* a general price-level adjustment may be

---

[6] Staff of the Accounting Research Division, American Institute of Certified Public Accountants, *Reporting the Financial Effects of Price-Level Changes*. Accounting Research Study No. 6 (New York: American Institute of Certified Public Accountants, Inc., 1963).

made in assets and liabilities on the balance sheet and a "real" income figure consistent with these values may be readily computed. Such an exercise adds relatively little to the usefulness of accounting data for decision-making by internal and external users, which we feel should be the primary concern of the accountant.[7] But unless cost figures are first adjusted to current values, i.e., account taken of *individual* price changes, one is left with "meaningless data," as R. L. Mathews put it in his, to my mind, excellent critique of the ARS 6.[8] "Data which are measured in different units to begin with cannot be converted to a common basis of measurement merely by applying a common conversion factor," Mathews correctly argues.[9] Indeed, because prices of individual assets may frequently move *opposite in direction* to a general consumer price index in the economy,[10] a general price-level adjustment to historic cost asset values may, in fact, move one *away from* rather *than toward* a true current cost income picture.

But, we would argue, the price-level adjustment approach to problems of income measurement is bleaker still. The utility of adjusting even meaningful income data for changes in the value of the dollar is really quite limited. Issues with respect to the payment of dividends and maintenance of real capital are, of course, the primary ones put forward for the importance of a proper measurement of real income. To the extent that management substitutes growth in real capital for profitability as a goal, the additional information would, of course, affect decisions, although such a goal would be difficult to rationalize, whether to owners, investors, or others interested in general economic decisions with respect to the allocation of resources in an economy. In fact, if fund retention is based on profit alternatives available to the firm, the identification of real profit should not alter the amount paid in dividends, even if real capital is impaired by payment. Even the "going concern" convention does not suggest that a concern must continue at a constant or expanding level of real capital if owners are thereby pushed into putting earned profits into what should, on economic grounds, be a declining business firm.

This is not to suggest that real income data are of negligible significance, for clearly, movements in the general price-level have a bearing on a firm's access to funds and on other considerations which may influence its total economic situation, including taxes paid on what may be thought of as fictional (as opposed to real) gains. (There is little doubt, in my mind at any rate, that the hope to lower corporate taxes has served as the primary impetus underlying the interest in adjusting business data, however compiled, for changes in the general price-level.) The fact of the matter is that comparisons among firms at a moment of time, and of trends in one firm over time serve as the primary valid reason for adjusting properly constructed income and balance sheet data for changes in the value of the dollar.

So much for corrections in accounting information for changes in the general price-level—adjustments which can readily be made to our current cost data if

---

[7] See Edwards and Bell, Chapter VIII, especially pp. 264–269.

[8] R. L. Mathews, "Price-Level Changes and Useless Information," *Journal of Accounting Research* (Spring 1965), pp. 133–155.

[9] *Ibid*, p. 147.

[10] As found by Whitehead, *op. cit.*, for Australia in 1954–58, for example, and as was true for electrical machinery vis-a-vis consumer prices in the United States between 1961 and 1966.

this is desired. We now turn to what we believe is a much more relevant and perhaps divisive issue at this conference—the question of how current costs are to be defined if they are to be used in accounts, or more specifically, the question of whether entry or replacement cost values are to be used (or exit or opportunity cost values) in measuring current costs.

III. ENTRY (REPLACEMENT COST) VERSUS EXIT (OPPORTUNITY COST) VALUES IN THE MEASUREMENT OF CURRENT COSTS

In our book, we delineated eighteen different concepts which might be relevant to the valuation problem in accounting, based on past, current, or future entry and exit values on the one hand, and on the form of what was being valued (initial inputs, present form, or ultimate form) on the other, in one grand matrix, and I am sure that the matrix did not exhaust all the possibilities.[11] But here I wish to dwell on only two of those eighteen concepts or matrix entries: (1) the current entry or replacement costs of initial inputs versus (2) the current exit or opportunity costs of the present form of existing assets.

In thinking about the basic issue, I could not help but reflect on an experience I had in East Africa in 1963–64, when I served as one of the three members of an Economy Commission for the University of East Africa—a commission designed to somehow cut $300,000 out of a 1.5 million dollar budget for a new federal University being designed for the countries of Kenya, Tanzania, and Uganda. At Makerere University in Uganda (the older, more experienced entity of the three being joined together, and indeed the pearl of the widespread University of London network in overseas colonies) we were given a budget for expenditures broken into various categories for 1961–62, 1962–63, and 1963–64. I asked if we might have the actual expenditures, using the same categories, for the years then past, and was told, "No, we do not have those." "But then how do you make up your budget for the succeeding year?" The answer came back, "On the basis of the budget of the preceding year." It turned out that actual expenditures were never compared with planned or budgeted expenditures in devising future plans!

The essence of my argument here is that first things must come first, and that the first task of any enterprise is to measure the profitability or performance of plans and decisions *which were actually made for some period ahead,* and thus evaluate performance against the expectations one originally had. Certain assets were purchased with a plan of operations in mind. That plan, those operations, indeed those people who developed that plan, must first be evaluated before alternatives about the future can be considered, and it is the accountant's task to provide the data for that evaluation. Once this is done, *then* one can compare the cost of continuing to use the assets for the purposes for which they were originally acquired, as opposed to acquiring and using some other assets for these purposes (a measure involving use of the cost of best alternative services as a measure of current cost, as proposed by R. H. Parker and G. C. Harcourt,[12] and/or selling the assets and using the cash received for some other purpose, i.e., using

---

[11] Edwards and Bell, p. 77.

[12] R. H. Parker and G. C. Harcourt, *Readings in the Concept and Measurement of Income* (Cambridge, England: Cambridge University Press, 1969), p. 19.

opportunity cost as a measure of current cost as proposed by Chambers.[13] Let me make clear that both of these alternatives are relevant to the decision-making process. But a meaningful concept of profit, as we see it, is the measurement of performance in terms of what was originally intended. Only after this plan is evaluated can one proceed to the next stage of deciding whether or not performance should be changed.

In these terms, Professor Chambers' concept of profit, if we understand it correctly, would have to be that a business plan would always have to be one of maximizing the acquirable cash equivalent of assets over successive short-run periods. This would seem to be where using the exit value or opportunity cost value of assets, period-by-period, to compare with current revenues leads us. For a firm dealing with anything more than the simplest retail or wholesale trading operations, that is, for one involved in any kind of production, such a view of the enterprise, its objectives, and its mode of thought, would just not seem to be applicable.[14] Current user cost, or the current replacement cost of assets the firm has, in fact, chosen to employ in its plan of operation would, we suggest, be the relevant data to match against current revenues to measure the relative success or failure, i.e., performance of the enterprise, both for internal and external users of such accounting data. Therefore, current user cost would be the cost of primary concern to the accountant in carrying out his function for the firm and for the world at large. Once the performance has been measured, *then* the accountant, in conjunction with cost engineers, business planners, or what not, can go ahead and help to assess how to modify the existing or present plan of operation, or support the firm in adopting a new one.

While briefly put forward, that is really the essence of our argument for using entry, rather than exit, values as the proper measures of current costs, which we feel are so essential for accounting records. Under certain ideal conditions, there may exist no difference in the two measures of current cost, of course, but such ideal conditions, like most ideal conditions, never actually prevail in practice. The ideal conditions would be the following:

1. There must exist a large number of identical assets traded on one market so that market prices are known for both new and used assets;
2. The firm must have nondiscriminatory access to both the buying and selling sides of that market;
3. There must be no transportation or installation costs involved in either the purchase or the sale of the particular asset in question.

Now, such conditions rarely, if ever, exist in the real world, so we are talking about two different concepts of current cost here. David Solomons has treated

---

[13] For example, he writes: "The current cash equivalents of the assets of a going concern are the sums obtainable in the short-run in the ordinary course of business; that is, market resale prices in the short-run. The measure of the cost of using an asset is its then market resale price." See R. J. Chambers, *Accounting, Evaluation and Economic Behavior* (Englewood Cliffs, New Jersey: Prentice-Hall, 1966), p. 218.

[14] Professor Sterling, who also rejects entry for exit prices, would seem to be treating almost exclusively a rather simplified trading entity. See Robert R. Sterling, *Theory and Measurement of Enterprise Income* (Lawrence, Kansas: University Press of Kansas, 1970), especially pp. 328–330.

this whole issue with considerable care,[15] and his argument for use of current replacement costs (entry values) rather than opportunity costs (exit values) has been very briefly but, we think, well summarized in the Parker-Harcourt volume.[16] What Parker and Harcourt show, following Solomons, is that current replacement cost (entry value) use, as opposed to opportunity cost (exit value) use, generally has more economic meaning to the firm under most circumstances. Replacement Cost (RC) is almost invariably the upper limit to current cost, as opposed to Net Realizable Value (NRV) or the Present Value (PV) of the expected net cash receipts from the asset where this may differ from RC and NRV because of, perhaps, the existence of Goodwill or for some other reason. Parker and Harcourt argue that there are six hypothetical possible relationships among these three values of RC, NRV, and PV, viz.:

1. NRV > PV > RC
2. NRV > RC > PV
3. PV > RC > NRV
4. PV > NRV > RC
5. RC > PV > NRV
6. RC > NRV > PV

They then proceed to divide these cases into two groups according to whether the asset should be held for use or resale as follows:

Use	Resale
3. PV > RC > NRV	1. NRV > PV > RC
4. PV > NRV > RC	2. NRV > RC > PV
5. RC > PV > NRV	6. RC > NRV > PV

Deducting all NRV's from the "use" group as irrelevant and all PV's from the "resale" group as irrelevant, and also remembering that the upper limit of value to the firm is RC, the six cases can be written as follows:

Use	Resale
3. RC	1. RC
4. RC	2. RC
5. RC > PV	6. RC > NRV

The final rule which arises from this little exercise is that the value of an asset to the firm = RC, except where RC > PV or RC > NRV, where value to the firm = PV or NRV, whichever is greater.

But, we would argue for current replacement cost as opposed to opportunity cost on simpler grounds related to measuring performance cited earlier rather than on the above, rather sophisticated theoretical argument. Accounting must measure past events, and to be useful, it must measure those which actually happened, not those which might happen if a firm does something other than that which was planned. As we have said, measure what has actually happened, then compare with what might happen now or in the future. It is really on this basis that our case for entry values rests, and we shall leave it at that and see what the discussion brings out.

[15] See David Solomons, "Economic and Accounting Concepts of Cost and Value," *Modern Accounting Theory*, ed. Morton Backer (Englewood Cliffs, New Jersey: Prentice-Hall, 1966).
[16] Parker and Harcourt, pp. 17–18.

IV. FLEXIBILITY, FEASIBILITY, COMPLEXITY AND RELIABILITY: A SUMMING UP

We have tried to present a flexible plan for the measurement of the income of an enterprise—one which loses nothing in terms of present practices but adds a great deal. A key stumbling block to its acceptance in the profession would seem to be what we regard as mistaken notions as to its *feasibility*, its *complexity*, and its *reliability*. Let us treat the first two issues together.

We know of two examples where the Edwards-Bell data have been formulated in their entirety, i.e., involving many more adjustments than suggested in our grossly oversimplified example used for this paper, for business enterprises over several years time. In both cases, the results on operating profit, and of course on earned income, differed significantly from those arrived at by using traditional historic cost data, even though the works concentrated on operations in the early 1960's, which was a period of relatively mild price changes compared with the period of 1965-69.

Peter Dickerson, in a monograph published by the Institute of Business and Economic Research,[17] revised comprehensively the data for a "small producer of moulded plastic articles located on the West Coast," in operation only since 1956. He found for this *new firm* (wherein differences would not be expected to be as large as in older firms) that over a seven-year period (late 1950's and early 1960's) and a five-year period (1963-1968), when the consumer price index rose 11 percent and 14 percent, respectively, the use of current costs actually *raised* current operating income from $82,000 to $94,000, or slightly under 15 percent, whereas a general price-level adjustment of historic costs would have *reduced* the figure to $78,000. What is *more important* in many ways to the misunderstood issue of complexity, however, is that in adjusting the whole array of data for this firm to conform to that shown in Figure 2 above (except that the number of items to be adjusted were enormously more intricate and complex, with the computations very carefully done and with income and balance sheets produced in both "money" and "real" terms for the seven-year period) Mr. Dickerson reported that he spent a total time of only 95 *hours of work* on the data, 40 of which were spent examining and analyzing the enterprise's books, i.e., getting used to them. What may seem to be quite difficult and complex at first blush is really not so at all, we feel, once the system is understood. Yet, as indicated, much more realistic and relevant data are supplied to internal and external users.

The other attempt to employ the Edwards-Bell approach reported in available (in this case, unpublished) literature that I am aware of was done here in Kansas by Robert Hollinger of Kansas State University. The application was to a wholesaling firm only over a three-year period (1964-66, also a period of relative price stability). Over this period, the rise in income in accordance with the conventional accounting practices involving use of historic costs was $1,845,000, or 72 percent, whereas true operating income, in our sense, rose only by $440,000, or 16 percent. The residual or difference between these two figures, of course, actually involved holding gains rather than operating gains—gains which might be expected to be especially significant for a wholesaling firm.

---

[17] Peter J. Dickerson, *Business Income—A Critical Analysis*, Institute of Business and Economic Research (Berkeley: University of California Press, 1965).

We turn, finally, to the last issue which bothers many accountants a great deal, that of feasibility. Current cost figures on inventories are relatively easy to arrive at, but what about fixed assets—can current data on them be arrived at in reliable fashion? For those accountants hopelessly wedded to that "sacred cow" of accounting—the "objectivity principle"—perhaps not. Certainly, there are now available a wide range of official Government indices on fixed asset prices of various kinds, and there is always the possibility of appraisals and/or checking back with suppliers. But our principal answer to those who we think worry excessively about "objectivity" and not enough about "realism and relevance" is that one can hardly help but come *closer* to good, meaningful data through use of current as opposed to historic cost. If a system is feasible, reasonably simple, and very likely to be much more relevant and useful for decision-making by both insiders and outsiders, why not adopt it?

HERBERT E. MILLER

HERBERT E. MILLER (1914–), A.B. 36, M.A. 37 Iowa; Ph.D. 44 Minnesota; CPA. Currently partner in Arthur Andersen & Co., Chicago. Major publications: *Principles of Accounting, Introductory* (with Finney, 1953, 1957, 1963), *Principles of Accounting, Intermediate* (with Finney, 1951, 1958, 1965), *Principles of Accounting, Advanced* (with Finney, 1952, 1960), *C.P.A. Review Manual* (editor and contributor, 1951, 1956, 1966; with Mead, 1972), *Principles of Financial Accounting A Conceptual Approach* (with Finney, 1968). Contributor to *The Accounting Review*, *The Journal of Accountancy*, and other journals. Book review editor, *The Accounting Review*, 1945–48.

Was on the faculties of Simpson College, 1937–38; the University of Minnesota, 1938–44; the State University of Iowa, 1945; the University of Michigan 1946–61; and Michigan State University, 1961–70, prior to becoming a partner in the home office of Arthur Andersen & Co. He visited the Stanford University faculty in 1960 and 1962.

Served as vice-president, 1957, and president, 1965–66, of the American Accounting Association, and was chairman of the Association's special committee to formulate a revision, in 1948, of *Accounting Concepts and Standards Underlying Corporate Financial Statements*. Was grand president of Beta Alpha Psi, 1961–62, and served as a member of the AICPA Committee on Accounting Procedure, 1956–59, and Accounting Principles Board, 1959–63.

QUASI-REORGANIZATIONS IN REVERSE

HERBERT E. MILLER

The recent discussion among accountants concerning reinstatement of fully amortized emergency facilities was, in some respects, too late. It is tempting to use hindsight and observe that perhaps a more useful and timely framework within which to handle the question of reinstatement might have emerged if the profession had started to think about and to discuss the problem earlier. Although it is freely admitted that in the nature of things many ramifications of any given accounting problem cannot be foreseen, a practice of attempting to anticipate major accounting problems on which there is considerable unsettled opinion should be encouraged. Often urgency does not stimulate objective thinking.

SOURCE: From *The Accounting Review*, Vol. XXIII, No. 2 (April, 1948), pp. 154–157. Reprinted by permission of the American Accounting Association.

Many of the urgent problems that confront the profession from time to time have a common issue: Is a departure from the established basis of accounting justified? Without meaning to suggest either that our generally applicable accounting concepts and standards have or have not reached a stage of acceptable refinement or clarification, may it not be a fact that insufficient attention has been devoted to the investigation and development of acceptable "departures" from an established basis of accounting? If there is some merit to the above question, then a discussion of the problem of quasi-reorganizations may be warranted since this device, characterized by a break in the continuity of the accounting statements, quite definitely entails a departure from the established basis of accounting.

One of the basic problems relates to the scope or limits of a quasi-reorganization. Should it be restricted to "fresh start" cases where the corporation is in "trouble," or may it be used as a device enabling a fresh start to be achieved in extraordinary situations *whenever* a continuation on the established basis would produce accounting statements susceptible to widespread, gross misinterpretation? In other words, should "fresh starts" be restricted to an environment dominated by losses and deficits or may the process of quasi-reorganization be used as a device to introduce some element of flexibility into the accounting process?

In the more traditional use of the concept, some combination of the following circumstances is generally held to be condition precedent for a quasi-reorganization. These conditions do not *require* a quasi-reorganization; accounting readjustments of this type are optional.

Conditions Precedent

1. Overvalued properties.
2. Credible evidence to support an opinion that the decline to the present level is a relatively permanent affair.
3. An unlikelihood that future earnings could recoup the unrecognized losses within a reasonable period.
4. Operating losses, past and prospective.
5. The earned surplus would be at least exhausted by the recognition of losses.

Should a quasi-reorganization be warranted, there are several requirements and limitations that should be recognized before the readjustment can be described as having satisfied generally recognized standards.

Requirements and Limitations

1. Stockholder approval.

See the American Accounting Association's 1941 Statement of Accounting Principles Underlying Financial Statements. Also *Accounting Research Bulletin #3*,[a] American Institute of Accountants.

2. Disclosure required.

The corporation "should make a clear report to the stockholders of the restatements proposed to be made, and obtain their formal consent." *Accounting Research Bulletin #3*.

---

[a] Bulletin No. 3 was superseded (with no major change in substance) by Chapter 7(a) of Accounting Research Bulletin No. 43 (in 1953). Also consult Bulletin No. 46, "Discontinuance of Dating Earned Surplus" (1956). [Eds.]

3. Earned surplus should emerge with a zero balance.
"It seems essential that earned surplus be exhausted." W. W. Werntz: "Some Current Problems in Accounting," *The Accounting Review*, June, 1939, p. 121.

4. Subsequent earned surplus should be dated. See the Statement of Accounting Principles Underlying Corporate Financial Statements.

5. "The effective date of the readjustment . . . should be as near as practicable to the date on which formal consent of the stockholders is given, and should ordinarily not be prior to the close of the last completed fiscal year." *Accounting Research Bulletin #3*.

6. "The readjustment of values should be reasonably complete." *Accounting Research Bulletin #3*.

7. As readjusted, the "assets and liabilities should be so stated that no artificial credits will arise from realizations of the assets or discharge of the liabilities." *Accounting Research Bulletin #3*.

8. After a quasi-reorganization has been consummated, "The company's accounting should be substantially similar to that appropriate for a new company." *Accounting Research Bulletin #3*.

Actually, the above summary only lays the foundation for the main question: What is the *essential* justification for readjusting the recorded amounts through a process of quasi-reorganization? It is quite possible that the moving force behind this concept stems from a loss of or deterioration in the significance of financial statements. Where a continuation on the established basis produces financial statements that, in the opinion of interested parties, do not correctly report the position and progress of the enterprise, a pressure is created to revise the basis of accountability. If the financial statements were adequately reporting on the position and progress of a given enterprise, there would be neither justification, nor, in most cases, an active pressure to disturb the accounts. Users of accounting statements are entitled to expect enough realism of the accounting process to permit the use of accounting data as a basis for formulating judgments and opinions. There is no assurance that an adherence to recorded costs will always achieve this objective. Since the environment in which a business operates may be subjected to wide and significant changes, a rigid adherence to recorded amounts may substantially undermine and even discredit the accounting function.

Traditionally, the quasi-reorganization device has been applied during periods of business depression. In the depression situation the recorded amounts were written down in an attempt to restore current reality to the accounting process. May not a reverse quasi-reorganization be every bit as justified under opposite conditions? Must the undermining always take place on the down side?

The suggestion that the quasi-reorganization device may appropriately be applied in reverse has the support of a number of accounting authorities. For example, George O. May has written that,

> In the case of downward adjustments, the concept of quasi-reorganization has been developed, and it would seem desirable that it should be applied, also, to recognition of increases in value.[1]

In *Contemporary Accounting*, Professor Paton clearly suggested that in the event of a long period of advancing prices in the postwar period the mechanism of

[1] *Financial Accounting* (New York: The Macmillan Company, 1943), p. 99.

quasi-reorganization might be used "to afford a basis for a 'fresh start,' with significant figures." [2] His definition of quasi-reorganizations admits adjustments in either direction:

> . . . a means by which recorded data may be restated when major changes have occurred which render the figures resulting from the ordinary processes of accounting inadequate and misleading from the standpoint of the purposes accounting is supposed to serve.[3]

Professor Dohr can be listed as a supporter for an "expanded" quasi-reorganization concept.[4]

The most exhaustive article justifying reverse quasi-reorganizations to come to the writer's attention appeared in a recent *Arthur Andersen Chronicle*. In that article the author, D. J. Erickson, stated that

> Despite the common tendency to associate this procedure with a concept of unabsorbed losses and earned surplus deficits disposed of to capital surplus, it is believed that the principles may be availed of where significant changes in the character of business operation have occurred, where changes in the location of principal plants have been brought about, where significant subsidiaries have been sold or acquired, where major portions of the business have been disposed of and operations are continued on a reduced scale or where significant economic changes, such as inflation or deflation, have made carrying values unrealistic in relation to current price levels.[5]

It is incorrect to conclude from the above quotations that reverse quasies are widely supported. Many accountants, after reviewing the record of the pre-1929 appraisal adjustments upward and the subsequent quasi-reorganizations of the 1930's, are understandably doubtful of all departures from recorded cost, up or down. Our previous performance does not offer an encouraging precedent. Other accountants, conservatively inclined to accept write-downs, object to the prospect of quasi-reorganizations in reverse because of their opposition to any and all write-ups. They believe there is more danger to the accounting process in the write-up of assets than in the perpetuation of unrealistic recorded amounts. Admittedly, there is a real danger that reverse quasies open some opportunities for abuse. For that matter, any *departure* from the regularly established basis of accounting, or any major revision of accounting policy, is open to abuse. As it has often been observed, it does seem peculiar to view revisions in one direction as good and in the other direction as bad, *per se*. Actually, a write-down is no less subjective than a write-up. Each may be abused. The application of any group of accounting concepts requires a high degree of integrity and competence on the part of practicing accountants. If accountants lack the above characteristics, abuse is bound to prevail.

Accountants have long recognized that an emphasis on recorded costs may be too rigid, particularly under conditions of substantial and rapid price changes.

[2] *Contemporary Accounting*, Chapter 2, p. 2. American Institute of Accountants, 1945.
[3] *Ibid*.
[4] James L. Dohr, "Cost and Value." *The Journal of Accountancy*, March, 1944, pp. 193-6.
[5] D. J. Erickson, "Quasi-reorganizations and Related Tax Effects," *Arthur Andersen Chronicle*, July, 1946, page 175.

It has been repeatedly pointed out that accounting has adopted a unit of measurement which is in fact not stable. Gradual or small changes in the value of the dollar do not significantly impair accounting results, mainly because the turnover and replacement of assets keep the accounting data current. But a stage can be reached where an element of flexibility is needed and justified if accounting is to serve its intended purposes. This element of flexibility may be provided by permitting, in extraordinary situations, a departure from the established basis.

Changes in the value of the dollar are not the only justification for departing from or revising the accounting basis. Expropriation, accident, loss of markets, accretion, or discovery, to mention some of the more significant, could provide equally important justifications for revising the basis of accounting for the resources and equities of a corporation.

If we label an upward departure as a reverse quasi-reorganization, what are the conditions precedent to its application? Would the conditions precedent mentioned earlier in connection with traditional quasi-reorganizations, slightly modified, provide a starting basis?

Conditions Precedent for a Reverse Quasi-reorganization

1. Assets understated.
2. Credible evidence to support an opinion that the present level is a relatively permanent affair. (Whatever the reason for restatement, the new bases cannot be justified unless it is possible to demonstrate adequately that they have a good chance of remaining significant.)
3. An absence of general economic instability.
4. An unlikelihood that future reported earnings, after deducting average, regular dividend distributions to shareholders, if reinvested in the business could do more than maintain the corporation's present, relative position in regard to productive capacity.

It would seem that the same set of requirements and limitations should apply as well for a reverse quasi. This includes the requirement that previously earned surplus be clearly differentiated from subsequently earned surplus. The writer is inclined to the view that any earned surplus carried forward should be capitalized in order to have the statements comparable to the "fresh start" of a new enterprise. Requirement 7 might be amended to suggest that the "assets and liabilities should be so stated that no artificial credits *or debits* will arise from realizations of the assets or discharge of the liabilities."

There is considerable justification for arguing that some of the most pressing problems currently facing accountants, namely, depreciation on a replacement cost basis, the use of inventory reserves, and the practice of expensing a portion of current capital outlay, have as their common origin a feeling that currently the accounting process is producing inadequate and, perhaps, misleading financial statements. A common fault of each of the three practices just mentioned is that they are "piece-meal" approaches to the problem of presenting currently significant accounting statements. There is not the slightest intention to argue that *now* is the time for quasi-reorganizations, in reverse or otherwise, but it does appear that *now* is the proper time to investigate, discuss, and settle upon the limits of accounting reorganizations. The relevant conditions precedent may not be far distant.

SHERATON CORPORATION OF AMERICA: ANNUAL REPORT 1961

Letter to Stockholders: Further Comment

AN INTERESTING LOOK AT DEPRECIATION

A new ten million dollar building, normally assigned a 50-year life, would require—if straight line depreciation of 2% a year were used—$200,000 each year for depreciation. In fifty years the building, having then presumably reached the end of its economic life, could in theory be replaced by funded reserves which would amount to the ten million dollars originally invested in the building.

However, the money set aside does not in practice lie idle. If reinvested at 4% after income taxes compounded annually for fifty years, these cash reserves, instead of the original $10,000,000, could aggregate $30,533,000, a very generous sum even after taking into account increased reproduction costs expected in an inflationary economy.

Assuming the depreciation reserves are earned, as they have been in Sheraton's past twenty-four years' experience, and that these reserves are not required for debt amortization (on the theory that when property values are maintained, debt amortization is customarily replaced with new debt), and assuming that the annual depreciation reserves can continue to be readily invested and reinvested profitably during the fifty-year life of a new property at a rate better than 10% annually,—then the cash ultimately realized from these reserves would amount to more than $232,781,000. At a 15% rate, which corresponds more closely to Sheraton's past twenty-four-year actual experience, the amount becomes much larger, taxing the capacity of Company calculating machines. Utilizing one of several available forms of accelerated depreciation calling for larger reserves in earlier years, makes the figures resulting from this compounding process even more impressive.

As a further illustration, consider only the first year's depreciation reserves of approximately $800,000 actually taken on an accelerated basis on the new Philadelphia Sheraton (building only) in the year 1958. If this sum were invested in the business, at a rate of only 10% after taxes compounded annually for fifty years, without the benefit of setting aside any additional depreciation reserves during the remaining forty-nine year life of the building, then the principal and interest accumulated in fifty years would amount to $93,912,000. This alone would be six times the amount required. If providing funds for replacing the building fifty years later was the primary objective for setting up depreciation reserves, the amount of $133,000 set aside once for the first year only, would have been, if compounded annually, sufficient to attain this objective in fifty years. This amount of $133,000 would be less than a single year's depreciation allowance called for when using the straight line depreciation method.

The effective reinvestment of depreciation reserves accounts in a large measure for the rise of Sheraton's total assets during the twenty-four years that the Com-

SOURCE: From *Sheraton Corporation of America, Annual Report 1961*, pp. 4, 7, 8, 14–18, and 22. Reprinted by permission of Sheraton Corporation of America.

pany has operated hotels and other real estate. The reinvestment of these reserves and consequent increase in asset value has broadened the credit base of the Company permitting further growth through debt financing up to the Company's stated objective of approximately 50% of total assets at estimated values, less current liabilities. The Officers of the Company believe that this program has been primarily responsible for the increase in total assets during this period from less than $1,000,000 to more than $400,000,000 at estimated values.

The picture, of course, is not always as rosy as suggested by these illustrations. They do not tell the complete story. In practice a portion of the depreciation reserves may be necessary for amortization of debt to the extent it may not be replaced by new financing. However, the value of depreciation reserves reinvested in the business does furnish a possible clue to the interesting past growth record of the Company. It does explain our emphasis on cash flow, as well as certain advantages of owning rather than leasing hotels.

CASH FLOW AND NET ASSET VALUES VERSUS "REPORTED EARNINGS"

Some shareholders may be unaware of the relative impact of cash flow and indicated net asset values on the one hand, and reported earnings, on the market performance of Sheraton shares. Sheraton shares seem to follow the former fairly closely, and appear to be influenced relatively little by the latter.

Looking back over a ten-year period we find year-end quotations of Sheraton shares on the New York Stock Exchange were $3.04 a share in 1951 (corrected for stock splits, etc.) as against $17.75 in 1961. The rise was 5½-fold. During this same period estimated net asset value and cash flow increased approximately three-fold. However, this was in the face of a thirty per cent *decline* in reported earnings (with a similar drop in income taxes) during this same period. It would appear from this ten-year record that net asset values and cash flow rather than "reported earnings" are the principal influence affecting Sheraton market performance. Reported earnings are perhaps too closely related to such matters as maintenance expenditures, and to Company policy with respect to depreciation.

Sheraton depreciation reserves in 1947 were 2.3 per cent of total assets at estimated value, and 5.2 per cent of total sales. By 1961, these percentages had risen to 4.5 and 8.8 respectively, advances of about 100 and 69 per cent in the rate at which depreciation reserves were being set up. Taking an average increase in depreciation in relation to the growth of the Company, means that currently, in relation to our practice fourteen years ago (representing period covered by table, p. 354), our depreciation reserves were relatively higher by over $7,000,000. This is equivalent to over $1.33 a share on Sheraton stock for the year just ended.

Actually, on account of the improved physical condition of our hotels today, and due to the higher proportion of new buildings in the system, it would appear that perhaps a lower rather than a higher rate of depreciation might be more appropriate for 1961.

* * *

SHERATON'S FINANCIAL PHILOSOPHY

Net Asset Value Calculations

Earlier in the President's Report we referred to "adjustments" to basic earnings used to measure indicated net asset values. By basic earnings we mean earnings before interest, depreciation and income taxes. The adjustments to basic earnings attempt to take into account certain nonrecurring events and expenses. We allow for deficiencies or excesses, if any, from normal repairs and maintenance expenditures. We attempt to reflect the trend of occupancy and earnings. We also try to make appropriate allowance in advance for anticipated competition if new hotels are likely to provide serious competition.

Our figures for capitalizing basic earnings, or the earnings multipliers as they are sometimes called, vary according to many factors, including age and location of the property, money rates, type of financing available, and the luxury status of a hotel. Investors in hotels are willing to pay a relatively higher price for any given basic earnings of luxury hotels in large American cities.

Our multipliers usually range between eight and ten, which corresponds to capitalizing basic earnings on a ten to twelve and a half per cent basis. Due to our approximate fifty per cent debt ratio, the Company enjoys a certain leverage which raises this level of basic earnings to a rate of approximately fifteen per cent per annum. Long term leaseholds, not as readily mortgaged, frequently call for a slightly lower multiplier. We normally apply to leasehold earnings, after these are reduced by appropriate amortization, a multiplier of 6¾.

It should of course be pointed out that the multipliers themselves sometimes change with changing economic conditions in the real estate market. These factors we believe have all been carefully weighed and taken into account when indicated net asset values are calculated.

In recent years rising interest rates, coupled with increasing reluctance on the part of financial institutions to make mortgage loans except to larger companies willing to provide parent company guarantees, have been noted. This disadvantage has been partially offset by a noticeable upward trend in the multipliers being applied in the industry to basic earnings, the yardsticks by which valuations are customarily arrived at both by the industry and by Sheraton. Both of these factors are of course beyond the control of management. Fortunately both have tended in the past to some extent to offset each other.

Some inquiries have been received as to the reliability of estimated property values used in determining our indicated net asset values. Sales of Company properties over a long period of years were always made at sales prices in excess of the latest estimated values determined prior to the sales.

In connection with many of these sales transactions, the Company received second mortgages on the disposed properties as a part of the proceeds. The second mortgages are usually recorded on the books at discounted value, which reflect the terms of the respective mortgages.

There were in fact a few instances of hotels being sold when, after setting up reserves of 25 per cent against second mortgages taken in part payment, these properties brought slightly less than our latest estimated values. This however was more than counter-balanced by higher amounts realized in the majority of instances when properties were sold. On some $44,000,000 of property sales, comprising some fifteen transactions, such excesses over estimated values exceeded the losses by over a million dollars. Furthermore, the 25% reserves themselves have proven in practice to be too high. A recovery of over two million dollars from these excessive reserves is currently indicated, now that the second mortgages have been materially paid down or sold.

This discussion is presented in order to clarify the record with respect to this controversial subject of net asset values.

VALUATION OF LONG-LIVED TANGIBLE COST FACTORS

GROWTH CONSOLIDATED IN THOUSANDS OF DOLLARS

Years ended April 30	Total assets at estimated values (a)	Total assets at book values	Gross income	Depreciation	Cash flow (b)
1961	$400,445	$276,741	$205,701	$18,181	$20,249
1960	390,620	273,401	204,882	16,833	19,656
1959	346,910	245,503	171,474	14,144	17,494
1958	304,007	217,325	159,014	14,164	17,896
1957	304,645	219,866	153,792	11,920	16,668
1956	243,697	172,468	121,672	8,098	12,534
1955	193,033	134,543	89,376	5,390	9,504
1954	132,520	89,568	72,771	4,507	7,924
1953	129,475	91,313	68,142	3,857	6,772
1952	113,524	82,459	62,773	3,490	6,062
1951	101,861	74,982	56,071	3,253	6,156
1950	87,874	73,029	39,739	2,626	4,594
1949	60,279	54,541	31,605	1,795	3,698
1948	55,710	47,643	28,663	1,569	3,177
1947	49,860	42,332	21,511	1,128	2,141

(a) Estimated by Company Officers.
(b) Net Operating Income plus Depreciation.
(c) Before Interest, Depreciation and Income Taxes.
(d) After Minority Interests.
(e) After Minority Interests and Preferred Dividends.

Those shareholders who have a further interest in this subject and in the subject of "Net Worth Accounting" are asked to turn to page 355.

* * *

A "Hidden Asset"

Sheraton has an important asset previously referred to, which, though currently virtually non-income producing, is presently believed nonetheless to be worth over five million dollars. For eleven years this investment has been carried at virtually no book value, and during these years it has recorded only nominal earnings, since nearly all operating income received, close to $850,000 a year, had to be applied during this period to rental charges and to modernization of the property. This investment represented our interest in the large Sheraton-Whitehall Building, an office building in New York often referred to as "the first building on the right as you enter New York Harbor." Situated on the southern tip of Manhattan Island, it enjoys a superb view of the water front.

Eleven years ago we sold this building for $6,500,000 cash to a life insurance company, and leased it back for a period of sixty years, with the proviso that rental payments should be reduced after the first eleven years to coincide with the anticipated termination of the probable useful life of that building. No book value was recorded for this leasehold since we sold the property for full market value.

In December of this year, the rental payments required of us will be reduced

"Basic" earnings (c)	Reported net operating income (d)	Other credits	Net profits on capital transactions (d)	Total reported net income and net profits (d)	Net worth profit (a) (e) (f)
$32,399	$2,068	$...	$1,166	$3,234	$ 8,469
32,962	2,823	...	270	3,093	18,854
29,267	3,350	...	2,001	5,351	19,651
29,405	3,732	...	1,101	4,833	7,257
28,150	4,748	...	654	5,402	18,263
21,748	4,436	...	2,215	6,651	18,239
16,622	4,114	...	4,760	8,874	23,111
14,302	3,417	...	1,878	5,295	11,261
12,625	2,915	...	1,007	3,922	11,295
11,096	2,572	414	1,196	4,182	7,174
10,629	2,903	816	1,191	4,910	16,701
7,898	1,968	139	1,457	3,564	13,440
5,779	1,903	...	1,470	3,373	2,723
5,389	1,608	...	68	1,676	2,378
3,946	1,013	...	1,161	2,174	7,924

(f) Represents Total Net Income and Profits including changes in Estimated Net Asset Values and differences arising from sales and purchases of Common Stock at more or less than Estimated Net Asset Values. For information regarding Net Worth Accounting see page 355.

by approximately four hundred and seventy-five thousand dollars a year at the very time when tenants, due to major improvements we have made to the property, especially in recent months, will be paying substantially higher rentals. These tenants now include some of the nation's foremost corporations.

Probable basic earnings of seven or eight hundred thousand dollars a year after reduced rental obligations to the lessor next December indicate a present market value for this leasehold of over five million dollars.

The asset value of this leasehold, reflecting its fair market value, has been building up gradually over eleven years when rental costs and expenses of modernization were absorbing nearly all the income of the property. While neither book values nor earnings were reflecting this gradual rise in value, our indicated net asset values were reflecting more accurately the economic consequences of this sale and lease-back transaction. This is an illustration of how significant expenditures for modernization and improvements can extend the useful life of a building for many years, and thereby create values not otherwise reflected by ordinary financial statements.

Net Worth Accounting

As basic accounting procedures, particularly with reference to depreciation, are employed by Sheraton in connection with the preparation and certification of the Income Statement, we believe that the earnings disclosed therein are not a true measure of economic performance. For example, a part of Sheraton's depreciation,

VALUATION OF LONG-LIVED TANGIBLE COST FACTORS

"ECONOMIC PERFORMANCE" PER COMMON SHARE*

Years ended April 30	Estimated net asset values (a) (g)	Cash flow (b)	Quoted market price	Depreciation	Cash dividends paid during year
1961	$32.70°	$3.84	$17.75	$3.45	$.60
1960	31.70°	3.80	18.14	3.25	.59
1959	28.85°	3.60	17.78	2.91	.57
1958	25.76°	3.66	10.72	2.90	.56
1957	24.88°	3.40	11.66	2.43	.48
1956	21.84°	2.55	10.38	1.65	.41
1955	18.67°	1.93	11.66	1.10	.27
1954	15.86	1.59	5.39	.90	.21
1953	13.80	1.33	4.40	.76	.18
1952	11.76	1.17	3.68	.68	.18
1951	10.55	1.20	3.04	.64	.18
1950	7.44	.88	2.37	.51	.12
1949	4.92	.70	1.63	.35	.12
1948	4.52	.59	1.78	.30	.12
1947	4.18	.39	2.11	.22	.10

° Adjusted for stock dividends and stock split-ups, and Estimated Net Asset Values at April 30, 1955 to 1961. Allow for exercise of Warrants and conversion of 4¾% Debentures.

(a) Estimated by Company Officers.

in accordance with applicable federal and state regulations, has been established on an accelerated basis. This accelerated depreciation, and frequently our straight line depreciation, do not necessarily relate to the economics of any given year.

Therefore to provide a system of accounting that can reflect from year to year with reasonable accuracy economic facts that are not ordinarily revealed by conventional accounting procedures, we rely on what we call a system of "Net Worth Accounting."

Under this concept, we compute each year changes in market values of our various properties and other assets, including leasehold property interests. We determine at the beginning and end of each accounting period the fair market value of each property through the application of the appropriate multiplier (price earnings ratio) to the adjusted basic earnings for the preceding year. Purchasers of income real estate usually pay little attention to basic earnings of earlier years except to establish a trend. This may appear drastic, but it conforms to practical experience. Our asset valuations of leasehold interests merely reflect the fair market value of future earning power, duly discounted at a rate which ordinarily runs at twelve per cent or more per annum until such time as future earning power becomes fully available. This becomes significant in many sale and

Increase in estimated net asset value during year	"Economic performance" i.e., asset value increase plus dividends paid (includes estimated appreciation)	Price cash flow ratio (shows ratio of market price of shares to cash flow)	Reported net operating income and other credits (e)	Net profits on capital transactions (d)	Total reported net income and net profits (e)
$1.00	$1.60	4.6	$.39	$.22	$ .61
2.85	3.44	4.8	.55	.05	.60
3.09	3.66	4.9	.69	.41	1.10
.88	1.44	2.9	.76	.23	.99
3.04	3.52	3.4	.97	.13	1.10
3.17	3.58	4.1	.90	.45	1.35
2.81	3.08	6.0	.83	.97	1.80
2.06	2.27	3.4	.69	.37	1.06
2.04	2.22	3.3	.57	.20	.77
1.21	1.39	3.1	.57 (h)	.23	.80
3.11	3.29	2.5	.72 (h)	.24	.96
2.52	2.64	2.7	.40 (h)	.28	.68
.40	.52	2.3	.35	.28	.63
.34	.46	3.0	.29	.01	.30
1.42	1.52	5.4	.17	.22	.39

(b) Net Operating Income plus Depreciation.
(d) After Minority Interests.
(e) After Minority Interests and Preferred Dividends.
(g) After Liabilities, Minority Interests and Preferred Stock.

lease-back transactions where high lease rentals during the early years virtually eliminate all operating earnings.

After determining the change in market value during a given year, capitalized improvements made during the period are taken into consideration in the following manner. If a decline in market value has been determined for any property for a given year, this amount plus the cost of improvements becomes the measure of actual loss and is deducted as a "depreciation substitute" from operating income in place of conventional depreciation reserves. If the value of the property for some reason rose during the year, over and above the investment in improvements, this depreciation substitute is *added* instead of being subtracted in determining earnings. In the latter case, the "depreciation substitute," which for convenience we might call the "net worth factor," becomes a "negative" deduction, and hence an addition to earnings. Under this method of accounting, adjusted earnings are referred to as "net worth profit."

This procedure actually corresponds to some extent, to the practice of manufacturers when taking annual inventories—except that the concept of "the lower of cost or market" is not applicable. This is because, unlike manufacturers' inventories which are periodically revalued through the process of frequent turnover, hotels are often held for many decades without ever being sold.

Under the concept of net worth accounting, the role of depreciation reserves becomes limited to measuring the income tax liability. The depreciation substitute, or "net worth factor" replaces the more theoretical annual depreciation or deterioration with a much more scientific measure of the actual changes in market value—either up or down—of *all* the various fluctuating assets of a business. With several hundreds of millions of assets required in Sheraton's business, nearly all subject to major variations in value—an approach of this nature is clearly essential.

The importance of a "depreciation substitute" is evident when considering the value of one of the larger, and one of the oldest Sheraton hotels. This hotel next year would normally reach the end of its original fifty-year life. Annual depreciation reserves would then have served to "write off" the entire original cost of the building. The problem of normal accounting procedure is illustrated by the fact that this hotel, whose theoretical value should be approaching zero, is actually recording close to the highest earnings—both basic and reported—in its forty-nine-year history. The property at fair market value is presently worth nearly twice what it originally cost to build nearly fifty years ago. Under "net worth accounting," reported earnings, instead of being penalized each year by unrealistic depreciation reserves, would have been augmented by the appropriate depreciation substitute, or "net worth factor."

Ultimately—so that net worth accounting can be protected against possible abuse, independent net worth audits based on these principles of net worth accounting would develop. Eventually perhaps, a new professional corps of independent "certified public evaluators" will arise so that recognized evaluation certificates can be attached to evaluation statements, just as certificates of independent certified public accountants presently validate audited financial statements. In the meantime Sheraton's concept of "gainings" must remain in the same category as unaudited company financial statements.

Evaluation Certificates may eventually become almost indispensable to companies such as paper, lumber, or petroleum companies which maintain in the form of growing forests or underground oil reserves extensive assets which—since their value is not periodically redetermined through market "turnover," may be changing materially in value.

Changes brought about by inflation, or recessions; changes due to good or poor maintenance; and changes brought about by new competition are all duly reflected through the medium of net worth accounting. These are among the reasons for Sheraton's interest in net worth accounting, and in the proposed depreciation substitutes or net worth factors.

The following illustration presents a comparison of application of principles of net worth accounting and ordinary accounting relating to transactions of the Company for the ten years ended April 30, 1961.

It can be observed from the tabulation below that earnings are 93 million dollars greater as determined in accordance with the net worth accounting concept. It is apparent that this substantial difference can be related largely to the depreciation reserves provided under ordinary accounting which do not always reflect true economic performance. A net worth factor has been substituted, based on Company officers' estimates of changes in market value—realized or unrealized during the period—of real estate as well as other assets of the Company.

This net worth factor increases reported earnings (becomes a negative quantity) when net appreciation in values is indicated.

TEN-YEAR PROFIT & LOSS
To April 1961

	According to	
	Net worth accounting	Ordinary accounting
Gross income	$1,310,000,000	$1,310,000,000
Operating costs and expenses	1,081,000,000	1,081,000,000
Basic earnings	229,000,000	229,000,000
Interest	52,000,000	52,000,000
Income taxes	37,000,000	37,000,000
Minority interests	5,000,000	5,000,000
Depreciation		101,000,000
Net worth factor (note 1)	−8,000,000	
Net worth profit (note 2)	$143,000,000	
Income from operations		34,000,000
Realized capital gains		16,000,000
Income from operations plus realized capital gains		$50,000,000

Note 1: Takes into account changes in estimated asset values, realized capital transactions, and differences arising from sales and purchases of common stock at more or less than net asset value. Adjusted for minority interests. Not adjusted for income taxes on unrealized appreciation as amounts are based upon a continuing business theory and sale of properties or liquidation is not ordinarily contemplated.

Note 2: See tables on pages 354 and 355.

The improvement in operations reflected by net worth accounting results largely from the fact that the market value of Sheraton properties and other assets held in 1951, together with the cost of subsequent acquisitions, additions and improvements,—instead of declining to the extent suggested by depreciation reserves of $101,000,000 that were recorded—actually appears to have increased an indicated $8,000,000 in value as measured by the net worth factor. Accordingly, all in all, the depreciation reserves provided during the ten-year period were substantially unnecessary, therefore becoming the equivalent of retained earnings. Such an indicated discrepancy, we believe, should be recognized from year to year if shareholders are to be properly informed on economic developments affecting the Company.

It is for this reason that under the concept of "net worth accounting" we would substitute for a $101,000,000 theoretical, and in this instance seemingly unrealistic depreciation reserve set up for contingencies which did not materialize, a much more scientific "net worth factor." It is not hereby contended that aging, obsolescence, and shrinkages in values due to competition and other causes, are not a very real and ever present force constantly affecting adversely the value of income real estate. We believe these ever present deterrents can be partially, and in our ten-year (and prior) experience, more than offset by constructive developments such as good maintenance, effective merchandising, and especially by investing the amounts represented by our large depreciation reserves in improvements, additions, or new acquisitions. The added earnings from these improvements when capitalized, usually add enough more, over and above their cost, to the value of Sheraton properties to compensate at least in part, and frequently more than compensate for aging, obsolescence, etc.

An example is our experience with another of our larger Sheraton hotels. We purchased it fairly recently for approximately 3¾ million dollars and have since invested some six million dollars in improvements, additions, etc. This investment of six millions has added over twelve millions to the fair market value of the property as a going business, as measured by capitalizing the increased basic earnings.

There are, of course, instances, frequent in the industry, though fortunately rare for Sheraton, when inadequate maintenance, competition, or other factors caused properties to decline in value even faster than was compensated for by depreciation reserves. In such instances the net worth factor could exceed any normal permissible depreciation. Ordinary accounting often obscures such danger signals, sometimes causing costly repercussions, whereas net worth accounting highlights such developments.

We believe an important task facing the Company is to clarify to shareholders and to the financial community the basic philosophy behind Sheraton's major objective of building up net asset values. Sheraton cannot be judged by yardsticks applicable to companies whose principal product is constantly revalued through the process of periodic market turnover; nor can the Company's progress be judged by reported earnings, due to the variables involved in determining the large depreciation reserves. It is our belief that Sheraton's rate of growth can only be measured accurately by true economic changes in net asset values, or measured approximately, by its cash flow.

✧ ✧ ✧

SHERATON CORPORATION OF AMERICA
COMPARATIVE CONSOLIDATED BALANCE SHEET
ASSETS

	April 30, 1961	April 30, 1960
Current assets		
Cash		
Demand deposits	$ 14,690,933	$ 11,806,792
Restricted deposits	345,045	334,543
On hand	1,561,147	1,504,228
	16,597,125	13,645,563
Securities—marketable—at cost		
U. S. Treasury bonds	328,275	355,207
Other	64,645	67,113
(Market values $377,874 and $392,645)	392,920	422,320
Accounts and notes receivable	17,026,292	16,793,257
Less: Estimated uncollectible accounts and notes	606,522	520,766
	16,419,770	16,272,491
Accrued Interest Receivable	54,245	56,197
Mortgages receivable—payments due within one year (below)	744,277	618,556
Inventories—at cost	5,837,055	6,764,884
Prepaid expenses	2,643,814	2,392,960
Total current assets	42,689,206	40,172,971
Investments—at cost		
Securities—other than marketable		
***(Officers' estimated values $3,919,299 and $3,920,327)	3,973,409	4,073,409
Securities of subsidiaries—not consolidated	619,906	315,500
***(Estimated values $738,000 and $673,500)		
***Mortgages receivable	7,261,666	7,709,266
(Officers' estimated values $8,899,767 and $10,105,124)		
Less: Mortgage payments due within one year (above)	(744,277)	(618,556)
Total investments	11,110,704	11,479,619

Property, plant and equipment (Note 3)

Land and leaseholds	50,954,545	55,595,472
Buildings and improvements	181,919,270	170,048,095
Leasehold improvements	5,456,237	4,285,087
Furniture and equipment	78,742,413	70,659,552
	317,072,465	300,588,206
Less: Depreciation to date	99,701,085	84,552,912
Total property, plant and equipment	217,371,380	216,035,294

*** (Officers' Estimated Values $340,500,000 and $331,500,000)

Other assets

Options and deposits on contracts	5,000	5,000
Notes and contracts receivable—Due after one year	304,989	174,152
Unamortized debt discount and expense	2,944,835	3,030,085
Security and other deposits	763,836	665,932
Life Insurance—cash surrender value	276,921	261,128
Other	1,274,437	1,576,806
Total other assets	5,570,018	5,713,103
Total assets	$276,741,308	$273,400,987

See Notes to Consolidated Financial Statements [only Note 3 reproduced].
*** Asterisks denote items of importance.

NOTES TO CONSOLIDATED FINANCIAL STATEMENTS

3—Property, Plant and Equipment

Substantially all of the real estate and furniture and equipment are pledged to secure mortgages and other long-term debt.

Officers' estimated values are based primarily upon earnings before deducting interest, depreciation and income taxes, and after adjustment for unusual repairs. These earnings are capitalized at varying rates (generally 10% to 12½%), depending upon the type, age and location of the property, competition, debt financing and other factors.

SHERATON CORPORATION OF AMERICA: ANNUAL REPORT 1967

LETTER TO STOCKHOLDERS

It is with considerable pleasure that we announce the highest operating earnings in the Company's 30-year history. Sheraton earned 91 cents per share from operations which is double last year's earnings of 45 cents and thus continues our recent favorable trend of earnings.

The progress has been to a large extent the result of management's success in developing techniques to control operating expenses. As the chart on pages 372 and 373 shows, profit margins had dropped to 16% from a level that had reached 21%. We have already recovered half of those five percentage points, and we are presently developing new techniques to regain, and possibly exceed, the profit margins formerly enjoyed.

Reflecting this progress, the Board of Directors in May of this year increased the regular quarterly dividend to $.12½ a share from the $.10 quarterly dividend previously paid on common stock.

Gross Sales have increased in each of the 30 years since the first Sheraton hotel was acquired. This growth has come principally from the reinvestment of large sums represented by depreciation reserves set up to offset shrinkages in property values which in many instances did not materialize.

o o o

Much of the past decade has seen a comparatively stable dollar; however, we see indication of rising inflationary pressures. Sheraton's equity in its real estate should benefit from inflation especially due to the leverage provided by mortgage indebtedness.

This coming year looks promising. The backlog of convention sales is not only at an all time peak but is 11% above last year. This, coupled with the Company's plan for further improvement in profit margins as well as increased sales, should improve next year's earnings.

On the basis of such yardsticks as sales volume, total assets at estimated market value, cash earnings, and number of hotel rooms owned, Sheraton is presently the world's largest hotel corporation. This carries with it responsibilities which our Sheraton staff of over 26,000 is prepared to assume. The Company's ambitious training and development programs are a measure of its recognition of these responsibilities. Our new five-year plan is especially designed to achieve a sustained long-range growth of earnings.

We hope and sincerely believe that next year we will again be able to report substantial improvement in our net income. Your patronage of Sheraton hotels and motor inns will help us to achieve that goal.

For some years we have attempted to develop a method of accounting which will provide a satisfactory measure and a realistic appraisal of our management

SOURCE: From *Sheraton Corporation of America, Annual Report 1967*, pp. 2–7, 12. Reprinted by permission of Sheraton Corporation of America.

objectives, performance, and accomplishments. Stockholders may be interested in studying the following presentation of a concept which we refer to as "Modified Earnings."

ERNEST HENDERSON III
President

"MODIFIED EARNINGS"

The adverse effect of excess depreciation on the reported earnings of Sheraton is a matter that may be of interest to shareholders of the Company, especially because of the magnitude of the reserves permissible under present accounting practice and because of certain provisions of existing treasury rulings.

Although some corporations, notably public utilities, meet the problem posed by high allowable depreciation reserves by reporting differently for purposes of income taxes and when reporting to shareholders, this procedure is not generally practical for certain reasons for a hotel enterprise. Accordingly, Sheraton follows the practice of setting up maximum depreciation reserves both for tax purposes and when officially reporting to shareholders.

It is true that heretofore somewhat more realistic earnings figures have been included in Company annual and semi-annual reports under the heading of "adjusted earnings." Such earnings are based on a formula that in practice tends to reduce depreciation reserves by approximately 25%. This latter approach, however, still provides excessive depreciation. The resolution of the problem of needed depreciation can determine whether operating earnings of 91 cents a share for fiscal '67 as reported are the correct amount, or whether $1.94 a share (after provision for possible added income taxes) is more realistic. Based on actual experience over the past 15 years, the net amount of depreciation needed in order to maintain constant Sheraton's property values can be demonstrated to be only about half of the $210 million provided out of current earnings for this purpose during these 15 years. If this conclusion is correct, the higher earnings figure should be accurate.

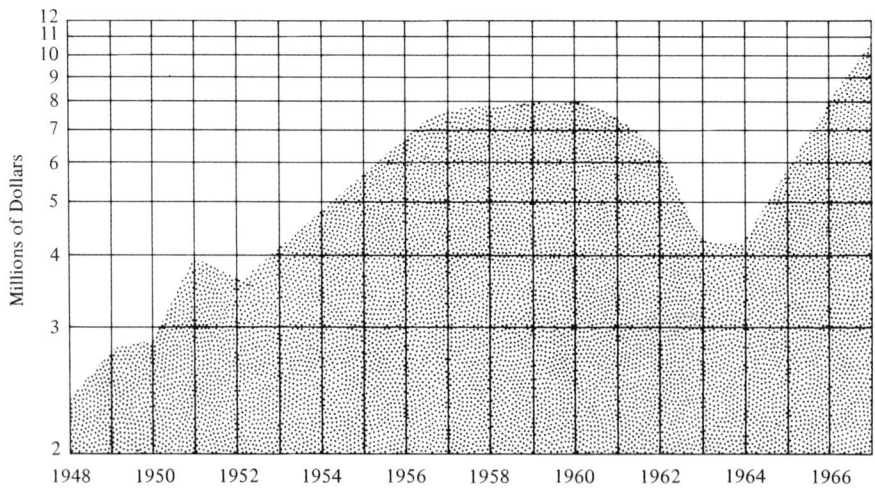

Modified Earnings (Ratio Chart). (See discussion in Chairman's comments.)

The conclusion that depreciation reserves are excessive is supported in part by the fact that fifteen years ago the total gross assets of the Company at indicated market values were only $113 million, or in fact $82 million if taken at book values. Especially since substantial non-depreciable items such as land, cash, and accounts receivable were included, it is unlikely that a $210 million reserve could have been needed to cover losses from aging or obsolescence during the following 15 years!

Since actual computations establish that depreciation reserves have been taken at almost twice the level required to maintain constant the market values of Sheraton properties, we have this year discontinued showing "Adjusted Earnings" in the tables and have substituted what we call "Modified Earnings" (columns 12A and 12B, pages 367 and 369). These are arrived at by simply reducing each year the provision for depreciation by a calculated amount which equals approximately one half the allowable depreciation set up on the books of the Company. The remaining depreciation reserves still provide, we believe, an ample and scientifically correct allowance to cover any net losses from aging, obsolescence, etc., likely to be encountered in coming years, especially if averaged out over good and bad years.

The reason for anticipating future depreciation requirements at a rate no higher than those of the preceding 15 years, is that heavy shrinkages in Sheraton property values did occur during fiscal '62 and '63, due to losses in those years which necessarily affected property values. The resulting abnormal depreciation requirements for those two unsatisfactory years were included in the calculations of actual depreciation needs covering the past 15 years. It is anticipated that the losses of '62 and '63 will turn out to be largely of a non-recurring nature and may thus to a considerable extent be avoided in the future. Such expectations are materially strengthened by the consistent sales growth indicating the essentially non-cyclical nature of the hotel business. (See column 3A, page 366.)

During the past year, Sheraton's cash earnings from operations before depreciation reserves, but after income tax, referred to as Cash Flow (column 6A, page 366) amounted to $24.6 million. Of this amount $19.6 million was set aside for depreciation, leaving $5.0 million, or 91 cents a share (column 9B) as reported operating earnings. The question is frequently asked: why should nearly 80% of the Cash Flow be set aside for possible shrinkage in the value of Sheraton properties when such losses are clearly not realistic. The reason seems to lie in the limitations of generally accepted accounting procedures, in the intricacies of our tax structure, and especially in the *dual function* that depreciation reserves are expected to perform.

The two purposes that depreciation reserves are designed to serve are quite distinct and largely unrelated. They are:

(1) A measure of allowable reserves under treasury regulations. These are designed to provide tax free income for the "recapture" of the original investment in properties such as hotel buildings, etc. which have a theoretically measurable useful life. Such allowable reserves are sometimes modified to serve as a tax incentive to stimulate construction and related industries, and accordingly may bear little relationship to actual requirements for offsetting aging and obsolescence. Such reserves, being tax deductible and to some extent discretionary, are usually maximized in order to reduce tax burdens.

(2) Depreciation reserves also serve a second purpose: to make meaning-

20-YEAR GROWTH RECORD CONSOLIDATED (000's omitted)

Years ended April 30	1 A Total assets at estimated values (a)	2 A Total assets at book values	3 A Gross income	4 A Book depreciation	5 A Modified depreciation (b)	6 A Cash flow (c)
1967	$392,691	$282,777	$286,676	$19,559	$10,101	$24,637
1966	366,184	282,569	276,303	19,661	9,943	22,206
1965	343,031	274,885	248,372	19,446	9,736	19,598
1964	328,934	264,396	232,925	18,845	9,410	17,490
1963	346,554	281,961	227,885	18,129	9,114	17,078
1962	393,984	280,580	215,199	18,887	9,417	19,691
1961	400,445	276,741	205,701	17,828	8,849	20,092
1960	390,620	273,401	204,882	16,511	8,194	19,623
1959	346,910	245,503	171,474	13,735	6,838	17,430
1958	304,007	217,325	159,014	13,693	6,804	17,547
1957	304,645	219,866	153,792	11,690	5,783	15,979
1956	243,697	172,468	121,672	8,098	4,034	12,534
1955	193,033	134,543	89,376	5,390	2,619	9,504
1954	132,520	89,568	72,771	4,507	2,137	7,924
1953	129,475	91,313	68,142	3,857	1,846	6,772
1952	113,524	82,459	62,773	3,490	1,646	6,062
1951	101,861	74,982	56,071	3,253	1,534	6,375
1950	87,874	73,029	39,739	2,626	1,237	4,619
1949	60,279	54,541	31,605	1,795	844	4,069
1948	55,710	47,643	28,663	1,569	737	3,495

The amounts shown above have been adjusted to give effect to changes in income resulting from Federal Income Tax examinations for prior years.

(a) Estimated by Company Officers. *Although estimated asset values and "Modified Earnings" represent the best judgment of the Officers these nonetheless are based on methods of determination that have not as yet become generally accepted. They should not be given undue weight until subjected to more critical evaluation by independent and knowledgeable authorities.*

(b) "Modified Earnings" represents Net Operating Income adjusted by substituting for depreciation recorded on the books a charge equal to 47% of hotel book depreciation so as to take into account only the indicated "net" depreciation needs necessary to maintain property values, using calculated depreciation requirements averaged out over

ful to an investor the amount of earnings being currently generated. Obviously when depreciating assets are involved, there must be adequate reserves taken out of current earnings to offset any trends towards declining property values, before true earnings can be reported. Otherwise attrition of capital could take place, and reported earnings would be meaningless. On the other hand excessive allowable depreciation can also be misleading. Reported earnings under such circumstances are unduly penalized and therefore unrealistic. Such excess would eventually appear in the form of rising net asset values growing out of

7 A	8 A	9 A	10 A	11 A	12 A
				"Economic	
	Reported			performance"	
	net	Net profits	Total	i.e., estimated	
	operating	on capital	reported	net asset	
Basic	income	trans-	net income	value increase	"Modified
earnings	(Loss)	actions	and net	plus dividends	earnings"
(d)	(e)	(e)	profits (e)	paid (f)	(a) (b) (e)
$39,601	$5,078	$ 355	$5,433	$33,292	$10,753
36,311	2,545	3,205	5,750	20,685	8,376
31,423	152	238	390	5,510	5,978
29,956	(1,355)	5,271	3,916	3,961	4,306
30,811	(1,051)	1,295	244	(42,675)	4,358
32,601	804	317	1,121	(6,674)	6,486
32,512	2,264	1,166	3,430	8,377	7,652
33,260	3,112	270	3,382	17,744	8,103
29,267	3,695	2,001	5,696	17,000	7,833
29,405	3,854	1,101	4,955	7,113	7,987
28,150	4,289	654	4,943	17,201	7,833
21,748	4,436	2,215	6,651	17,561	6,874
16,622	4,114	4,760	8,874	15,150	5,777
14,302	3,417	1,878	5,295	11,327	4,839
12,625	2,915	1,007	3,922	11,319	4,122
11,096	2,572	1,196	3,768	7,184	3,678
10,629	3,122	1,191	4,313	16,694	4,153
7,949	1,993	1,436	3,429	13,449	2,826
5,896	2,274	1,470	3,744	2,686	2,845
5,481	1,926	68	1,994	2,378	2,425

a fifteen year period. Income taxes calculated on the excess depreciation have been deducted in determining the "Modified Earnings" even though these provisions may not eventually be required. The concept of "Modified Earnings" should not be confused with "Adjusted Earnings" reported in previous years and which have not been computed in this report. See discussion in Chairman's letter, beginning on page 363.

(c) Net Operating Income plus Depreciation.
(d) Before Interest, Depreciation and Income Taxes.
(e) After Minority Interests.
(f) Represents "Economic Performance" for outstanding Common Shares at the end of the respective years. Excludes amounts allowed for exercise of Warrants and conversion of 4¾% Debentures.

reserves in excess of requirements. The amount of such appreciation in net assets, (after allowing for any retained reported earnings) can be a measure of the excess depreciation provided. From an investor's point of view, earnings figures can only be fully meaningful when depreciation reserves reflect accurately the trend of change in the market value of depreciable property by supplying a realistic provision for replacement of net losses in property valuations.

Fortunately there are many forces which tend to reduce, and sometimes even

20-YEAR RECORD OF PERFORMANCE PER COMMON SHARE*

	1 B	2 B	3 B	4 B	5 B	6 B	7 B
Years ended April 30	Estimated net asset values (a) (g)	Quoted market price	Book depreciation	Modified depreciation (b)	Cash flow (c)	Cash dividends paid during year	Increase (or decrease) in estimated net asset value during year
1967	$30.52	$17.00	$3.54	$1.83	$4.45	$.44	$5.59
1966	24.93	11.25	3.53	1.79	3.98	.42	3.30
1965	21.63	9.63	3.49	1.75	3.51	.42	.57
1964	21.06	9.50	3.43	1.71	3.17	.40	.32
1963	20.74	8.58	3.29	1.66	3.09	.54	(8.29)
1962	29.03†	14.18	3.42	1.71	3.55	.57	(1.78)
1961	30.81†	16.73	3.19	1.58	3.59	.56	.94
1960	29.87†	17.09	3.00	1.49	3.57	.55	2.68
1959	27.19†	16.76	2.66	1.32	3.37	.54	2.91
1958	24.28	10.10	2.64	1.31	3.38	.53	.84
1957	23.44	10.99	2.25	1.11	3.07	.45	2.86
1956	20.58	9.78	1.55	.77	2.40	.38	2.99
1955	17.59	10.99	1.03	.50	1.82	.26	2.64
1954	14.95	5.08	.85	.40	1.50	.20	1.94
1953	13.01	4.14	.71	.34	1.25	.17	1.93
1952	11.08	3.46	.64	.30	1.10	.17	1.14
1951	9.94	2.86	.60	.28	1.17	.17	2.93
1950	7.01	2.23	.48	.23	.83	.11	2.37
1949	4.64	1.54	.33	.15	.72	.11	.38
1948	4.26	1.68	.28	.13	.61	.11	.32

The amounts shown above have been adjusted to give effect to changes in income resulting from Federal Income Tax examinations for prior years.

* Adjusted for stock dividends and stock split-ups, and Estimated Net Asset Values at April 30, 1955 to 1966 allow for exercise of Warrants and conversion of 4¾% Debentures.

† Influenced by abnormal demand for income real estate presumed to have been caused by real estate syndicators.

(a) Estimated by Company Officers. *Although estimated asset values and "Modified Earnings" represent the best judgment of the Officers these nonetheless are based on methods of determination that have not as yet become generally accepted. They should not be given undue weight until subjected to more critical evaluation by independent and knowledgeable authorities.*

(b) "Modified Earnings" represents Net Operating Income adjusted by substituting for depreciation recorded on the books a charge equal to 47% of hotel book depreciation so as to take into account only the indicated "net" depreciation needs necessary to

SHERATON CORPORATION OF AMERICA: 1967

8 B	9 B	10 B	11 B	12 B	13 B
"Economic performance" i.e., estimated net asset value increase plus dividends paid	Reported net operating income (loss) (h)	Net profits on capital transactions (e)	Total reported net income and net profits (h)	"Modified Earnings" (a) (b) (h)	Price- "modified earnings" ratio (ratio of market price of shares to "modified earnings") (a) (b) (h)
$6.03	$.91	$.06	$ .97	1.94	8.8
3.72	.45	.57	1.02	1.50	7.5
.99	.02	.04	.06	1.06	9.1
.72	(.26)	.96	.70	.77	12.3
(7.75)	(.20)	.23	.03	.78	11.0
(1.21)	.13	.06	.19	1.16	12.2
1.50	.40	.21	.61	1.36	12.3
3.23	.57	.05	.62	1.47	11.6
3.45	.71	.39	1.10	1.52	11.0
1.37	.74	.21	.95	1.54	6.6
3.31	.82	.13	.95	1.51	7.3
3.37	.85	.43	1.28	1.32	7.4
2.90	.79	.91	1.70	1.11	9.9
2.14	.65	.35	1.00	.91	5.6
2.10	.54	.19	.73	.76	5.4
1.31	.46	.22	.68	.67	5.2
3.10	.57	.22	.79	.76	3.8
2.48	.35	.27	.62	.50	4.5
.49	.39	.27	.66	.50	3.1
.43	.33	.01	.34	.42	4.0

maintain property values, using calculated depreciation requirements averaged out over a fifteen year period. Income taxes calculated on the excess depreciation have been deducted in determining the "Modified Earnings" even though these provisions may not eventually be required. The concept of "Modified Earnings" should not be confused with "Adjusted Earnings" reported in previous years and which have not been computed in this report. See discussion in Chairman's letter, beginning on page 363.
(c) Net Operating Income plus Depreciation.
(e) After Minority Interests.
(g) After Liabilities, Minority Interests and Preferred Stock.
(h) After Minority Interests and Preferred Dividends.

eliminate the need for depreciation, even if these forces do not in any way affect the amounts properly deductible for tax purposes. Among the forces that tend to reduce from an investor's point of view the amount of net depreciation needed, are the following:

(1) The quality of property maintenance provided, and the effectiveness of provisions for modernization.

(2) The impact of inflation on property values, augmented by the leverage provided by mortgage indebtedness.

(3) The effect of rapidly rising land values, especially in desirable downtown areas where many Sheraton hotels are located. High downtown land values, by discouraging competition in the area, are generally reflected in the level of attainable room-rates.

(4) The influence on the level of hotel values of improved operating techniques, of expanding referral business, and other benefits resulting from large scale operations.

An interesting illustration, by no means unique, of unneeded depreciation reserves is the experience of the Sheraton-Plaza in Boston, originally built as the Copley Plaza in 1913 at a cost of $4 million. Today, 54 years later when its assigned 50 year life has more than run out, the present value arrived at by capitalizing the equity earnings at 9% is actually far in excess of the original cost. Obviously the annual charge for depreciation reserves set up was unrealistic. The charges were an unnecessary penalty on earnings.

All the forces tending to counteract the effects of aging, obsolescence, etc., outlined in the above summary, thus diminish—and in some instances eliminate, as in the case of the Sheraton-Plaza—the need for depreciation reserves, which might otherwise be needed to compensate for shrinkages in values. From the Sheraton-Plaza illustration, although it is not typical, it can be seen that there can be a substantial difference between the amount of depreciation used quite properly for book purposes, and for the determination of net depreciation required in order to make earnings figures meaningful to an investor. For the latter, any provision for depreciation in excess of the amount needed to maintain property values constant, introduces a distortion in the earnings picture. Any excess reserves should be considered reserves to meet a contingency which simply did not arise.

The Company's theoretical earnings in a given year, based on actual depreciation required for that particular year, can of course be readily determined. This we refer to as "Economic Performance" for the year. It takes into account the increase in net asset value for the year and adds thereto the amount of dividends paid (columns 11A and 8B, pages 367 and 369). Because of excessive fluctuations from year to year such "Economic Performance" figures although interesting, are of limited value in establishing trends. Depreciation requirements in order to be practical and thus more useful, should be determined on the basis of average needs over a number of years. This procedure will tend to smooth out earnings which might otherwise fluctuate excessively. To be meaningful, both good and bad years should be included in the interval used as a base period. A 15-year span seems adequate to meet these requirements. Determining depreciation requirements averaged out over a 15-year period, forms the basis for what we call

"Modified Earnings." The sum of the amounts of annual "Economic Performance" figures added up for the 15 years since 1952 will equal in general the total of "Modified Earnings" for the same period. The only significant differences between "Economic Performance" and "Modified Earnings" are that in determining the latter, not only have depreciation needs been "averaged out," but provisions for possible future income taxes (in the amount of $42 million) have been made.

Actually, for any specific year or period of years, depreciation requirements from an investor's standpoint can be easily determined by means of the Tables presented on pages 366–373. We can simply subtract from the Cash Flow generated for one or more years (columns 6A and 5B) the "Economic Performance" (columns 11A and 8B) for the same period. The resulting figure is the correct amount of net depreciation required. (In the event that any substantial repurchases or distributions of the Company's common stock had taken place, these should be taken into account. Likewise the operations of the Company's major subsidiary Thompson Industries engaged in the manufacturing business should be excluded.) The indicated excess depreciation based on a simple calculation of appreciation in Sheraton net assets during the past 15 years is $107 million compared with $210 million provided, or 51%. By taking into account purchases and issuance of Sheraton stock during the 15 year period, and eliminating Thompson Industries, the figure becomes 50%. The latter more precise measure of excess depreciation is being used in the calculations of "Modified Earnings."

Applying this formula to the period since 1952, shows that actual depreciation requirements were $105 million, or approximately 50% of the reserves of $210 million recorded on the books, which means that excess reserves of $105 million were not needed. These excess reserves were in fact essentially comparable to any other reserves set up for contingencies that did not materialize. They should thus, we believe, be added back to the reported earnings from operations. This would indicate that for the fiscal year just concluded total earnings, referred to as "Modified Earnings" (column 12A page 367) were $10.7 million, or $1.94 a share compared with actual reported earnings of $5 million, or 91 cents per share, arrived at in accordance with prescribed accounting procedure. ("Modified Earnings" for the past year were after a provision of $3.8 million for possible future added income taxes.)

Although some of these added earnings do show up occasionally in the form of capital gains in the event that properties are actually sold, in most instances Sheraton hotels are retained as long-term investments.

With reference once more to "Adjusted Earnings" tabulated in earlier reports, it should be noted that this concept, based on depreciation reserves equal to 6% of hotel sales, is still retained for determining property valuations. For this purpose, the Company's equity in a hotel over and above mortgage indebtedness is measured by capitalizing at 9% the so-called "Adjusted Earnings" before income tax (after interest, and depreciation using the 6% of sales formula). Sheraton, having sold many hotels over the years, has found its measurements of market values to be quite reliable, erring if at all on the side of understatement.

The seeming contradiction of using close to 50% of allowable depreciation in determining Sheraton's "Modified Earnings" and a figure equal to six per cent of sales, amounting to approximately 75% of allowable depreciation, when calculating indicated market values, is nonetheless quite logical. It reflects the fact that depreciation reserves ordinarily needed by the industry, tend to be somewhat

VALUATION OF LONG-LIVED TANGIBLE COST FACTORS

RATIO OF LONG-TERM DEBT TO TOTAL ASSETS AT ESTIMATED VALUES LESS CURRENT LIABILITIES (000's omitted)

April 30	Total assets at estimated value (a)	Less current liabilities	Net
1967	$392,691	$43,820	$348,871
1966	366,184	45,956	320,228
1965	343,031	48,790	294,241
1964	328,934	40,743	288,191
1963	346,554	43,247	303,307
1962	393,984	40,825	353,159
1961	400,445	35,565	364,880
1960	390,620	36,853	353,767
1959	346,910	28,641	318,269
1958	304,007	24,345	279,662
1957	304,645	26,028	278,617
1956	243,697	20,865	222,832
1955	193,033	16,746	176,287
1954	132,520	12,199	120,321
1953	129,475	10,899	118,576
1952	113,524	11,375	102,149
1951	101,861	9,260	92,601
1950	87,874	12,396	75,478
1949	60,279	6,803	53,476
1948	55,710	7,760	47,950

(a) Estimated by Company Officers. *Although estimated asset values represent the best judgment of the Officers these nonetheless are based on methods of determination that have not as yet become generally accepted. They should not be given undue weight until subjected to more critical evaluation by independent and knowledgeable authorities.*

(b) Ratios in this column are determined on long-term debt excluding 6½% Income Debentures and 7½% Capital Income Debentures.

higher than the net amount required by a major hotel system which generally has above average facilities for maintaining and improving properties, and for developing increased earning power. In establishing indicated market values of real estate holdings, it is the presumed earning power under generally prevailing operating conditions in the industry that ordinarily governs market values; not necessarily the somewhat more favorable conditions experienced by a large hotel system. Thus the somewhat more generous depreciation reserves equal to 6% of hotel sales are considered both realistic and have the added advantage that they are easily determinable.

To adopt the concept of "Modified Earnings" as the official method of reporting Company income would presumably require the sanction of the Company's certified public accountants, the Securities and Exchange Commission and perhaps others. The fact that this change in the method of reporting Sheraton income is not feasible at the present time does not detract from the need to inform

Long-term debt including income debentures	Ratio—including income debentures	Ratio—excluding income debentures (b)	Profit margin Percentage of gross income (c)
$177,253	50.8%	39.9%	18.5%
177,392	55.4	43.3	17.7
168,444	57.2	43.4	16.8
165,138	57.3	42.8	16.5
182,618	60.3	45.9	16.2
180,941	51.2	38.7	17.9
178,830	49.0	38.9	19.0
176,321	49.8	39.2	19.2
159,615	50.2	40.7	19.8
137,410	49.1	45.8	20.4
140,524	50.4	47.3	20.5
99,584	44.7	43.9	20.9
68,267	38.7	38.7	20.4
36,394	30.3	30.3	21.2
43,085	36.3	36.3	20.2
35,266	34.5	34.5	19.3
32,483	35.1	35.1	20.6
30,171	40.0	40.0	20.5
22,776	42.6	42.6	18.7
20,202	42.1	42.1	19.2

(c) Represents Basic Earnings before Rent Expense stated as a percentage of Gross Income. Percentages shown for Profit Margins exclude operations of Thompson Division and International Hotel Supply Corporation, the latter is a merchandise distributor to outside companies.

stockholders as fully as possible of the inadequacies of present depreciation concepts in measuring the performance of a real estate company such as a hotel enterprise. We take comfort in noting that a partner of a leading national accounting firm (see *New York Times* June 17, 1967, page 38) has recently advocated revisions in proposed legislation so as to require "value reporting" by companies especially as a means of informing stockholders who have to pass on proposed mergers and tender offers. He notes that "as a workable accounting method, value reporting has been successful for investment companies for more than twenty-five years." He further notes that the "value reporting principle should apply to all assets owned and not just to securities."

The Company's present net worth of some $168 million arrived at on the basis of an estimated $30.52 a share of net asset value, would indeed be difficult to explain on the basis of operating earnings reported over the 30 years' life of the Company, since such earnings have amounted to less than $60 million, and most of these were distributed as cash dividends. Since the Company's net worth 30 years ago was under ¼ million dollars, and only a modest amount of retained earnings from operations were available to contribute to the present indicated net worth, clearly the Company's growth from $¼ million to $168 million cannot have come from these relatively small reported earnings. Only through some concept such as that of "Modified Earnings" based on the recapture of close to one half the depreciation reserves set up on the books, could the retained earnings be sufficient to account realistically for the present indicated net worth of the Company.

ERNEST HENDERSON
Chairman of the Board

SHERATON CORPORATION OF AMERICA
COMPARATIVE CONSOLIDATED BALANCE SHEET
ASSETS

	April 30, 1967	April 30, 1966
Current assets		
Cash		
Demand deposits	$ 11,017,695	$ 14,036,926
Time deposits	785,400	4,800,000
Restricted deposits	868,788	530,947
On hand	1,909,313	2,107,229
	14,581,196	21,475,102
Securities—marketable—at cost		
U. S. Treasury bonds	72,026	72,026
Other	4,670	307,479
(Market values $66,549 and $487,985)	76,696	379,505
Accounts and notes receivable	26,492,916	24,973,688
Less: Estimated uncollectible accounts and notes	1,314,946	1,329,800
	25,177,970	23,643,888
Accrued interest receivable	23,779	25,129
Mortgages receivable—payments due within one year (below)	475,314	644,869
Inventories—at cost	9,884,464	11,807,851
Prepaid expenses	3,037,744	3,175,627
Total current assets	53,257,163	61,151,971
Investments—at cost		
Securities—Other than marketable	61,870	1,067,830
(at values of $97,700 and $1,461,729)		
Securities of subsidiaries—not consolidated	689,218	689,218
(Underlying equities $820,100 and $872,400)		
Mortgages receivable	1,086,940	1,645,484
(Principle Amounts $1,471,915 and $2,369,015)		
Less: Mortgage payments due within one year (above)	(475,314)	(644,869)
Total investments	1,362,714	2,757,663
Property, plant and equipment		
Land and leaseholds	49,500,971	48,324,414
Buildings and improvements	231,999,839	218,945,450
Leasehold improvements	8,403,404	8,115,696
Furniture and equipment	86,148,343	84,939,743
	376,052,557	360,325,303
Less: Depreciation to date	154,303,487	148,318,363
Total property, plant and equipment	221,749,070	212,006,940
(See discussion of Estimated Values in prior section of report)		
Other assets		
Notes and contracts receivable—due after one year	404,739	349,566
Unamortized debt discount and expense	2,595,442	2,793,034
Security and other deposits	574,649	519,194
Life insurance—cash surrender value	470,141	449,841
Other	2,362,932	2,540,491
Total other assets	6,407,903	6,652,126
Total assets	$282,776,850	$282,568,700

RELATED READINGS

Like those on inventory valuation, the following readings on depreciation also form a subset of the historical cost versus current value controversy. Readers are therefore advised to consult the extensive listing of readings shown at the close of Part 8.

Russell M. Barefield and Eugene E. Comiskey, "Depreciation Policy and the Behavior of Corporate Profits," *Journal of Accounting Research*, Autumn, 1971, pp. 351–358. Evidence that straight-line depreciation can contribute to a smoother earnings stream.

W. T. Baxter, "Depreciating Assets: The Forward-looking Approach to Value," *Abacus*, December, 1970, pp. 120–131. An approach to selecting the right depreciation method. Also: *The Accountant's Magazine*, April, 1971, pp. 159–165.

———, *Depreciation* (London: Sweet & Maxwell, 1971), 176 pp.

——— and N. H. Carrier, "Depreciation, Replacement Price, and Cost of Capital," *Journal of Accounting Research*, Autumn, 1971, pp. 189–214.

Eugene F. Brigham, "The Effects of Alternative Depreciation Policies on Reported Profits," *The Accounting Review*, January, 1968, pp. 46–61. Simulation analysis.

Eugene E. Comiskey, "Market Response to Changes in Depreciation Accounting," *The Accounting Review*, April, 1971, pp. 279–285. More evidence that the market seems not to be fooled by changes in accounting method.

Joseph D. Coughlan and William K. Strand, *Depreciation: Accounting, Taxes, and Business Decisions* (New York: The Ronald Press Company, 1969), 327 pp.

Joe J. Cramer, Jr., and William J. Schrader, "Depreciation Accounting and the Anomalous Self-insurance Cost," *The Accounting Review*, October, 1970, pp. 698–703. Suggestion that expected casualty losses be considered in group depreciation calculations.

Louis Goldberg, "Depreciation: A Critical Moment," *The Accountant's Magazine*, December, 1969, pp. 664–667.

Yuji Ijiri and Robert S. Kaplan, "Probabilistic Depreciation and Its Implications for Group Depreciation," *The Accounting Review*, October, 1969, pp. 743–756.

Charles W. Lamden, "Depreciation: A Credibility Gap," *World* (PMM), Autumn, 1971, pp. 29–34; reprinted in *The Journal of Accountancy*, April, 1972, pp. 67–70. A review of the controversy and the issues by the author of a forthcoming AICPA research study on the subject.

P. N. McMonnies, "Depreciation: Its Meaning, Purpose and Accounting Treatment," *The Accountant's Magazine*, February, 1969, pp. 73–85. A study based in part on a survey of Scottish chartered accountants in industry.

John H. Myers, "Depreciation Manipulation for Fun and Profits," *Financial Analysts Journal*, November–December, 1967, pp. 117–123; and September–October, 1969, pp. 47–56.

John Pick, "Concepts of Depreciation—Business Enterprises," *The New York Certified Public Accountant*, May, 1970, pp. 369–380.

Robert R. Sterling, "A Test of the Uniformity Hypothesis," *Abacus*, September,

1969, pp. 37–47. Argues that accountants' anxiety over different depreciation methods is misplaced, that attention should be turned instead to variations in factor estimates, particularly that of useful life.

Jeri Trawczynski and Walter Fesmire, "Historic Cost Versus Current Cost for Fixed Asset Valuation," *Cost and Management*, May–June, 1971, pp. 32–37.

°Harry I. Wolk, "Current Value Depreciation: A Conceptual Clarification," *The Accounting Review*, July, 1970, pp. 544–552.

° Indicates sources containing particularly rich bibliography.

PART 6

GOODWILL, OTHER "INTANGIBLES"

The problem of accounting for goodwill and other intangibles is like that which the accountant faces in connection with tangible cost aggregates: What is the cost of the asset, and how should this cost be treated subsequent to incurrence? Why, then, is there a difference in the solutions to the two problems if in fact the problems are basically the same? Some accountants have suggested that since we cannot observe an intangible asset, there is no concrete evidence to establish the fact that the asset exists. Others have argued that the future usefulness or value of the asset is so nebulous that an attempt to capitalize and amortize the cost is futile.

What is the nature of this thing we call goodwill? One description is that it is the present value of the expected income stream in excess of that required to justify the investment in the accompanying tangible assets. How is it created? The business enjoys the favorable attitudes of its customers, employees, creditors, and suppliers, and possibly of politicians. These favorable attitudes did not arise without the incurrence of cost. The cost may be composed of many outlays for different purposes, such as advertising, quality control, the premium price paid for a particular location, public relations, and employee relations. The major problem is to determine what part of these various outlays is applicable to creating favorable attitudes for the future and what part is applicable to current operations. Thus one of the major differences between plant assets and goodwill is apparent in many cases: There is no one outlay or series of outlays which can be unequivocally identified with the cost of goodwill. Hence, to avoid interminable arguments and to preserve objectivity, accountants recognize goodwill only when it is purchased.

The event which occasions the recognition of goodwill is the acquisition of a going concern by another enterprise. If the acquisition is considered a "pooling of interests," then the assets of both companies are carried forward at book value. No goodwill is recognized as a result of the transaction. This accounting result does not imply that no goodwill exists. If the transaction is considered as a "purchase," the cost of goodwill is measured as the difference between the purchase price and the sum of the assigned costs of the tangible and identifiable intangible assets acquired, less liabilities assumed.

If accountants can agree on the cost of the intangible, the next major question is the number of periods in which the asset will provide useful service. Since the asset cannot be observed, accountants find it difficult to determine by experience just when the asset loses its ability to contribute to the production of revenue. If the intangible is purchased, or its cost is otherwise determined (in the case of intangibles other than goodwill), what part of current outlays is considered maintenance and what part is considered a capital cost to be consumed in future years? Even though the higher level of earning power is maintained, we are never certain whether it is the result of the intangible purchased in an earlier period or the result of current outlays being made to perpetuate the income stream.

It is perhaps significant that of the several countries in which the accounting profession has been issuing authoritative statements of accounting principles, in only one, the United States, has a pronouncement appeared on goodwill. The American Institute's most recent statement, APB Opinion No. 17, takes a firm position that the costs identified with intangibles should be amortized in a systematic and rational manner over the period to be benefited. The pronouncement provides, however, that this period may not be longer than forty years. Neither the Canadians nor the English have taken a position on goodwill. Even in the controversial 1971 exposure draft on business combinations, issued by the Accounting Standards Steering Committee, goodwill is effectively ignored. This silence on goodwill is not due to its lack of importance. Rather, it is the result of the institutes' inability to arrive at an agreement on how goodwill should be treated in the accounts. That goodwill may not be amortized for income tax purposes in many countries has not facilitated a solution of the accounting problem.

George O. May, here in the throes of intensive cross-examination, reveals the difficulty of establishing a value for goodwill. His testimony suggests that, although accountants know in theory how the value of goodwill should be calculated, there are many variables which may affect the final valuation. The testimony also shows that a valuation of goodwill, other than when purchased, can be devilishly difficult to defend.

William A. Paton approaches valuation in a similar manner, but he treats the intangible value as the residual between the value of the enterprise and the value of the tangible assets. He posits two approaches to the problem of valuation—cost and income. While cost is an acceptable basis for individual asset valuation, the income approach is necessary for the valuation of the enterprise. Indeed, finding the cost of individual assets is a matter of estimating the present value of the future net receipts to be received from their productive use.

Robert H. Nelson argues that goodwill is the price paid for momentum. As this momentum is lost, the future usefulness of the goodwill expires, and the cost should be amortized. He illustrates this theory by applying it to many of the more common types of intangibles. Nelson contends that a payment of dividends when the intangible assets have not been amortized may result in an effective erosion of capital. If the purchased goodwill is considered to be a permanent asset, then the risk of ultimate realization rests on the creditors. In Nelson's opinion, there really is no such thing as permanent goodwill.

George T. Walker attempts to show why goodwill should be amortized. In the first place, amortization is necessary to achieve a proper matching of costs and revenues. Secondly, there is equally as much logic for this as there is for systematic depreciation of plant assets; and, thirdly, he agrees with Nelson that there is no such thing as permanent goodwill.

A. THE VALUATION PROBLEM

GEORGE O. MAY

GEORGE O. MAY (1875–1961), FCA (England and Canada); CPA. Major publications: *Improvement in Financial Accounts* (1937); *Financial Accounting: A Distillation of Experience* (1943); *Business Income and Price Levels: An Accounting Study* (1949). Biographies and anthologies: *Twenty-five Years of Accounting Responsibility, 1911–1936* (collected essays ed. by Hunt, 2 vols., 1936); *Contributions of Four Accounting Pioneers: Kohler, Littleton, May, Paton* (synopses prepared by Edwards and Salmonson, 1961); *Memoirs and Accounting Thought of George O. May* (collected essays and reminiscences edited by Grady, 1962). Contributor of over 100 articles to *The Journal of Accountancy*, *The Accounting Review*, *Quarterly Journal of Economics*, and numerous other journals.

Joined staff of Price Waterhouse & Co., London, in 1897 and was transferred in the same year to the staff of Jones, Caesar & Co., who represented the former in New York City. Became member of staff of newly formed New York City office of Price Waterhouse & Co., in 1901, attaining partnership status the following year. Became senior partner in 1911, retaining administrative responsibility until 1926. Retired from active participation in the firm in 1940, but continued to act as its consultant until his death.

Was vice-president of American Institute of Certified Public Accountants, 1917–18, and vice-president of the American Economic Association, 1930. Played a prominent part in launching the first International Congress on Accounting, 1904. Was director-at-large, National Bureau of Economic Research, 1924–41. Served as research consultant to Study Group on Business Income, 1948–52. Delivered first Dickinson Lecture, for 1936–37, on Improvement in Financial Accounts. Was elected to Ohio State University's Accounting Hall of Fame, 1950. Beginning in 1927, was instrumental in gaining cooperation of New York Stock Exchange and later, of Securities and Exchange Commission, with the Institute. In the course of this endeavor, he served as chairman of the Institute's Special Committee on Cooperation with Stock Exchanges, 1930–35, and chairman of Institute's Special Committee on Development of Accounting Principles, 1933–36, and was consultant to New York Stock Exchange in late 1920s and early 1930s. He said, "I regard the correspondence from which extracts are given [in *Audits of Corporate Accounts, 1932–34*] as the most important contribution I have made to the Accounting profession." (*Memoirs*, p. 78) Was chairman (1937–39), vice-chairman (1939–41), and member (1941–44) of Institute's Committee on Accounting Procedure.

Best known for his leadership in establishing the Institute as the organization which should determine and promulgate "accepted principles of accounting." Also contributed substantially to the early formulation of these principles, the evolution of the phraseology in the accountant's audit report, and the wider publication of audited financial statements. Possessing unflagging energy and drive, keenness of insight, and a firm grasp of the complexities of financial accounting theory and its manifold applications, Mr. May was an indispensable figure in the adolescent and early maturation stages of the accounting profession in the U.S.

THE VALUATION OF GOODWILL

TESTIMONY OF GEORGE O. MAY

Question: Coming to the question of the value of the goodwill, will you please tell us how you estimated that value?

Answer: The value of the goodwill was a very difficult problem indeed. In the first place, I adopted the method that has been used in numerous cases which have come to my notice in the sale of goodwill, of determining the value solely on the basis of the earning capacity or of the past earnings. Some time before May 20, Mr. Ordway asked me a question on that subject, and I worked out the value of the goodwill for him on the basis of deducting from the earnings interest on the investment, tangible assets, and then capitalizing the excess on the basis of five years' profits. Now, taking the profits for the five and a half years ending January 31, 1910, I arrived at a value of eight hundred and fifty thousand dollars, allowing seven per cent interest on tangible assets, or a million dollars allowing six per cent. In considering the question on May 20, I used that calculation as a starting point, and considered what seemed to me to be the modifying factors. First of all, the profits for the year 1909 had amounted to only three hundred and ten thousand dollars, or seventy thousand dollars less than the average which I had used in the earlier calculations, so that if the last year's profits were taken as the basis I figured the result would be to reduce the value of the goodwill by a sum of three hundred and fifty thousand dollars. Then the other factors which I considered were first of all as regards the wholesale department. There had been considerable discussion of a proposed sale of the wholesale department without any payment for goodwill, and in the course of discussion on that subject I learned that there was some doubt as to the permanency of that business, and furthermore that it was a question whether the goodwill of the wholesale department did not inhere to a large extent in the two managers who had direct charge of the business and who were in personal touch with the manufacturing houses and the trade. Then a further element that detracted from the value of the goodwill seemed to me to be the dissension amongst the management, which was undoubtedly operating adversely to the business. Then again, there was the fact that most leases of the premises expired in 1914, so that there was the prospect of having to move the business. Of course it is not possible to assign specific weights to each one of these considerations, but weighing all of

SOURCE: Excerpt from testimony given to referee, *In the Matter of the Estate of E. P. Hatch, Deceased* (1912). The questioner was evidently attempting to establish that the executor had acted imprudently in disposing of some 8,000 shares of Lord & Taylor common stock at $27 per share, when there were indications that the "true value" per share might have been as high as $110. The referee's decision, which upheld the executor, was appealed twice, and (with respect to this aspect of the case) was denied both times. *In re Titus, et al.,* 148 NYS 359 (1914); 156 NYS 509 (1915).

This testimony was originally reprinted in Bishop Carleton Hunt (ed.), *Twenty-five Years of Accounting Responsibility, 1911–1936* [selected writings and utterances of George Oliver May]; (New York: Price Waterhouse & Co., 1936), 2 vols., I:237–46. It is reproduced here without changes.

them together—I do not know whether I should go any further—I think I have probably answered your question.

Q. Did you take into consideration the efficiency of management in the retail department?

A. Yes. Of course the retail department—the ratio of profit in that department had been so much reduced that at that actual time I should say the profits being earned in the retail department would not have justified any payment for goodwill of that business as it stood, although of course the established name does give the goodwill a value in strong hands.

Q. Did you also take into consideration the lack of working capital?

A. Well, that was a factor not so much in the valuation of the goodwill as in the desirability of the proposed sale as a whole, the lack of working capital; it was a very important element in that.

. . . .

Q. Had you any immediate or direct knowledge with regard to the inefficiency of the management of the retail department?

A. Well, I had a number of criticisms of it, but the main factor to my mind was the low ratio of profit. That, it seemed to me, must be evidence of inefficiency somewhere.

Q. Where did you get at the figures of the ratio of profit in the two departments?

A. Well, various statements were prepared.

Q. Were they the result of any researches which you made in the books of Lord & Taylor or were they based upon reports which came to you from others?

A. Do you mean that I made personally?

Q. Yes.

A. Or through my representatives?

Q. That you made personally.

A. Not on those that I made personally, except in part they were figures according to the books and in part they were figures made up by my subordinates.

Q. Not from the books?

A. Well, from the books with adjustments. Some of them were absolute book figures.

Q. When you speak of adjustments do you mean adjustments in this sense, that somebody took up the accounts as they stood on the books, and they from time to time made, so to speak *nunc pro tunc*, reservations and deductions as you would have made if you had been there at the time?

A. Yes, that is what I mean by adjusted figures.

Q. Take, for instance, in 1910, you assumed a certain adjustment made for the year 1906, which in point of fact had not been made in 1906, is that the idea?

A. Yes, that is what I referred to.

Q. And so on all through the years in succession?

A. Yes, but then I also considered the unadjusted figures. I have here a statement.

Q. As regards the working capital, should you say to us the same thing that you said in regard to all those other elements of your judgment, that you attributed to it no particular value in the deductions which were to be made?

A. I think "particular" is an unfortunate term to use, because saying "no particular value" might be considered as meaning "no material value." I attached no specific value to it, although I did attach considerable importance to it.

Q. You think that "specific" in this relation might have a different meaning from "particular"?
A. Well, I do not think it would be so ambiguous.
Q. Have you now told us all that you are able to recollect with regard to the —if you do not object I shall use the same word again—particular value that you assigned to these different elements of diminution?
A. Yes.
Q. Now, lumping them all together as you have done, what was their aggregate value as a figure to be deducted from the figure at which you started?
A. Well, I did not feel it quite necessary to put an aggregate value.
Q. Did you simply guess at it?
A. No, I did not.
Q. Did you make an accurate computation?
A. No—
Q. You did not?
A. I took—
Q. One moment. Did you make an accurate computation?
A. No, I did not.
Q. And you did not guess at it?
A. No, I did not guess at it.
Q. And you did not average it?
A. No, I did not average it.
Q. Then will you tell us precisely what you did with it?
A. Well, I took the maximum value for the stock as determined by my starting point, and the value that I was asked to consider for the common stock, and asked myself the question: Is the difference between those two values, those two figures, sufficient, in the light of all those circumstances and of the whole proposed arrangement, to justify you in advising the executors not to make the proposed sale? That is substantially how I dealt with the question.

. . . .

Q. Mr. May, in this question I do not mean to make any imputation at all upon your purposes, but should we not be quite right in understanding that when you certified the balance sheet as of January 31, 1910, you believed that balance sheet which you certified to be correct?
A. Yes, certainly. Perhaps I ought—if you will allow me, I will elaborate that.
Q. You say you did understand it to be correct?
A. Yes, it is correct.
Q. What you said was, "We certify that the above balance sheet correctly sets forth the financial condition of the company at January 31, 1910."
A. Yes.
Q. Did you believe that statement to be true?
A. I believed that to be true, yes.
Q. Do you now believe it to be true?
A. I still believe it to be true.
Q. When you signed that statement in those words were you making any mental or other reservations?
A. Well, I do not know quite what you mean by that. The way I would—
Q. Have you not heard the expression of saying a thing with a mental reservation?

A. Yes.

Q. Well, you know what the phrase means, don't you?

A. Well, it has a rather sinister sense, in which sense of course I had no mental reservations.

Q. You do not now wish to express any mental reservation, do you?

A. No, of course a balance sheet is always a question of opinion.

Q. It was your opinion, was it not, that this balance sheet correctly sets forth the financial condition of the business?

A. Yes, it was—

Q. Was it your opinion or not?

A. It was my opinion that—

Q. Can't you answer my question yes or no?

A. I think not without giving rise to misunderstanding.

Q. I understand you to say that you are not able to say categorically either yes or no to the question I put to you, whether in your opinion this balance sheet correctly sets forth the financial condition of the company; is that so?

A. Well, of course I can say it is a correct statement, but I do not know that that is the whole answer. At the same time I do not want to inject anything.

Q. Now, Mr. May, when you make that remark are you not really telling us that you made that certification with some mental reservation?

A. No, all I mean by that: for instance that balance sheet might have been made up to show a surplus of two hundred and fifty thousand dollars less, and I would still have said that it showed the correct position of the company.

Q. Now, how will you explain that discrepancy? You have certified that when you showed a surplus of four hundred and eighty-six thousand dollars that statement was correct; now you say that if you had certified to a surplus of two hundred and thirty-six thousand dollars, that also would have been correct.

A. Yes, that is—

Q. Now, they both would have been correct?

A. Well, I think they would have been both correct in that they would be both fair expressions of opinion; and that is all a balance sheet ever is.

Q. Oh, you do not regard a balance sheet then as representing a state of fact, but as representing a state of mind, is that the idea?

A. Well, I would state my position exactly as Lord Justice Buckley stated it, that it is necessarily a question of estimate and opinion, every balance sheet.

Q. Did he say that about your opinion?

A. He did not say that about my opinion, he said that about every balance sheet; and the greater of course includes the less.

Q. We all recognize the influential value of expressions of opinion by Lord Justice Buckley, we do not at all mean to disparage that, but of course you know, Mr. May, that the opinion which we are now dealing with is Mr. May's opinion.

A. Exactly. But I did not feel that I could improve on the language of the Lord Justice nor did I care to plagiarize it without acknowledging the source.

Q. Now, then, you tell us that it would have been just as true to certify to a surplus of four hundred and eighty-six thousand dollars as it would have been to certify to a surplus of two hundred and thirty-six thousand dollars?

A. Both would have been certified and both would have been correct statements.

Q. So you might have cut off two hundred and thirty-six thousand dollars, might you not?
A. Yes.
Q. And leave no balance?
A. Oh, a further two hundred and thirty-six thousand?
Q. Yes.
A. Well, I do not know how far one could go, but I just took the figures of the two hundred and fifty thousand less as representing in my mind the reasonable limit of the opinions.
Q. Now, if you could with propriety certify to a surplus of two hundred and fifty thousand dollars less than you have certified to, might you not with propriety have certified to a surplus of two hundred and fifty thousand dollars more than you certified to?
A. No, I am quite satisfied as to that.
Q. Then your opinion would only be justified in the descending scale?
A. In the case of this particular balance sheet.
Q. Once again, if it would have been equally true to say that the surplus was two hundred and thirty-six thousand dollars as it was to say that the surplus was four hundred and eighty-six thousand dollars—once again, would it not have been equally true to say that the surplus was nothing at all?
A. Not necessarily. No, not in fact, I think.
Q. Where would you draw the line between two hundred and thirty-six thousand dollars and nothing at all?
A. Well, I would not draw a hard and fast line anywhere; but in that balance sheet there are at least—
Q. Wait a minute. I am not talking about that. I am asking you to give us an answer to my question. You say you would not draw a fast and hard line anywhere; now, give us a wavy line somewhere.
A. Well, it is very hard to do.
Q. Is it too hard for you to do?
A. Well, it is too hard for me to do offhand without careful consideration.
Q. You mean that in order to do it you would have to sit down with that large bundle of papers that you have beside you and work out some mathematical computations?
A. No, I would have to sit down and consider what I considered the limits of value—of reasonable difference of opinion as to value of certain assets in that balance sheet.
Q. If I follow you, that would not then be a mathematical computation but it would be an evolution of opinion, is that it?
A. That is it, purely an expression of opinion and judgment.
Q. So that when we are talking about this balance sheet of January 31, 1910, when you certified that the correct financial condition of the company shows a surplus of four hundred and eighty-six thousand dollars, are we to understand that that figure merely represents the evolution of your opinions up to that time?
A. No, I think that would be an erroneous impression. But it is our opinion that it is correctly adjusted and it is correctly stated in respect, of course, to the majority of items, in my opinion; but there are certain items, as I said before, that are of doubtful value, and in those cases, as I said before, we have accepted values placed upon the properties by the Finance Committee or officers of the

Company; and in regard to those assets there is room for a certain latitude of opinion.

* * * * * * *

Q. Will you tell me once again what you mean by tangible assets of this concern?

A. The excess of all assets, excluding goodwill and trademarks, over liabilities. Net tangible assets is the expression I would use.

Q. You have not used that word "net" heretofore when I asked you the questions.

A. Well, I used the same phrase, the investment in tangible assets.

Q. If you leave out net, and we are talking about tangible assets, you would regard, wouldn't you, the whole amount of merchandise as a tangible asset?

A. Yes.

Q. And all the horses and wagons as tangible assets?

A. Yes, certainly.

Q. And fixtures?

A. Yes.

Q. Would you regard accounts receivable as a tangible asset?

A. Yes, I would include everything on the assets' side of the balance sheet except the goodwill.

Q. Is it customary in your profession to call an account receivable a tangible asset?

A. Yes.

Q. What is the meaning of the word tangible as it is used in your profession?

A. Well, I think it is—unfortunately the whole terminology of my profession and of finance generally is pretty loose, but I think its significance is best reached by saying that it is everything that is not intangible, and intangible includes goodwill, trademarks, patents, franchises, and that class of property.

Q. I infer, Mr. May, from your experience and from the degrees which you hold of which you have told us, that you know what in ordinary speech the word tangible means, don't you?

A. Yes.

Q. Well, what do you understand it to mean in ordinary speech?

A. Something that can be touched, I imagine.

Q. Like merchandise?

A. Yes.

Q. You can touch merchandise or horses?

A. Yes.

Q. Can you touch an account?

A. You can touch the debtor.

Q. Is that the basis on which you include the debtor's debt as tangible?

A. It had not occurred to me before, but possibly it is.

WILLIAM A. PATON

WILLIAM A. PATON (1889-   ), B.A. 15, M.A. 16, Ph.D. 17 Michigan; recipient of honorary degrees from four universities; CPA. Currently professor emeritus of accounting and of economics, University of Michigan. Major publications: *Principles of Accounting* (with Stevenson, 1916), *The Economic Position of the United Kingdom, 1912-18* (1919), *Accounting Theory: With Special Reference to the Corporate Enterprise* (1922), *Accounting* (1924), *Accountants' Handbook* (editor and principal contributor, 1932, 1943), *Corporate Profits as Shown by Audit Reports* (1935), *Essentials of Accounting* (1938, 1949; with Dixon, 1958; with Dixon and Hepworth, 1966), *An Introduction to Corporate Accounting Standards* (with Littleton, 1940), *Advanced Accounting* (1941), *Dickinson Lectures in Accounting* (with May and Halsey, 1943), *Asset Accounting* (with Paton, Jr., 1952), *Shirtsleeve Economics* (1952), *Corporation Accounts and Statements* (with Paton, Jr., 1955), *Corporate Profits* (1965), *Assets—Accounting and Administration* (with Paton, Jr., 1971). Biographies and anthologies: *Contributions of Four Accounting Pioneers: Kohler, Littleton, May, Paton* (synopses prepared by Edwards and Salmonson, 1961), *Paton on Accounting* (collected essays edited by Taggart, 1964). Contributor of approximately 150 articles to *The Journal of Accountancy, The Accounting Review, Michigan Business Review,* and other journals. Editor and founder, *The Accounting Review,* 1926-28.

With minor interruptions, has been on the University of Michigan faculty since 1914. In 1947, was one of some ten University of Michigan faculty members who were designated as "university professor." Became professor emeritus in 1959, one year after retirement from the teaching faculty. Has visited the faculties of the University of Minnesota, 1916-17; University of California (Berkeley), 1921 and 1937-38; and the University of Chicago, 1924 and 1960-61.

Was president, 1922, vice-president, 1921, secretary-treasurer, 1920, and research director or codirector (with Littleton), 1937-39, of the American Accounting Association. Elected to the Ohio State University Accounting Hall of Fame, 1950. Delivered the Dickinson Lecture for 1939-40 "Recent and Prospective Developments in Accounting Theory." Was a leader in the formulation of the American Accounting Association's *A Tentative Statement of Accounting Principles Underlying Corporate Financial Statements* (1936). Was a member of the AICPA Committee on Accounting Procedure, 1938-50. Was presented with an award for distinguished achievement in 1968 by the Michigan Association of Certified Public Accountants.

Has appeared as an expert witness or testified before state and federal commissions and courts, and Congressional committees on scores of occasions.

Of Paton, Hatfield wrote in 1925 and again in 1942, ". . . there is, perhaps, no other accountant who equals him in keenness of insight, careful analysis and penetrating interpretation."

VALUATION OF THE BUSINESS ENTERPRISE

WILLIAM A. PATON

With the development of large-scale activity, elaborate technical processes, and the corporate form of organization the business enterprise has become in many cases a highly complex economic institution, and the valuation of the facilities and conditions of production in terms of the enterprise in its entirety is accordingly a bafflingly difficult problem, a problem which comprehends substantially all phases of accounting analysis and all types of value determinations. The business enterprise, it is scarcely going too far to say, is truly an organic entity, a something capable of being contemplated for its own sake and valued in its own right. The enterprise in other words, and as has often been pointed out in utility valuation cases, is an integrated, functioning, continuing establishment, and not a mere bundle or aggregation of separate elements or parts. And the value of the enterprise, it follows, may be more or less than the sum of the values of the constituent factors, considered singly, in apparent violation of one of the more obvious mathematical axioms. Further, in view of the extent now-a-days to which both small and large blocks of securities evidencing enterprise ownership are transferred from one party to another, including the practices of acquiring whole businesses through merger and consolidation, to say nothing of the matter of proper periodic measurement in the interest of the various equities, it appears that there is some excuse for urging that more systematic and discriminating attention be given to the question of enterprise valuation as opposed to other forms of appraisals.

Speaking broadly there are two main approaches to the problems of valuation in business:

1. Cost
2. Income

The cost avenue to value has two divisions labeled on the one hand "original" or "historical" cost and on the other "replacement" or "reproduction" cost, either of which may be modified by estimates of depreciation or other forms of expiration. It needs to be emphasized, however, that all varieties of cost measurement are in essentially the same pew. That is, there is no basic divergence of doctrine between those who glorify actual cost and those who are enthusiastic for replacement cost; in both cases the search is for cost, with disputation arising only with respect to the question of what constitutes the proper method of expression or measurement. Incidentally, there is some truth in the paradoxical observation that the replacement cost school is insisting upon the use of cost values more emphatically than is the historical cost school, since replacement cost is of course likely to express actual economic commitment or sacrifice in terms of current dollars more

SOURCE: From *The Accounting Review*, Vol. XI, No. 1 (March, 1936), pp. 26-35. Reprinted by permission of the American Accounting Association.

VALUATION OF THE BUSINESS ENTERPRISE 391

closely than does original recorded cost. The second approach, the income route, accepts the view emphasized by many economists to the effect that present values of production facilities and other objects of valuation represent the sum of the values of the uses or results which may be expected to flow from such facilities or objects through the term of their effective existence, appropriately discounted to date.

This statement may seem to oversimplify the situation somewhat, particularly in that it makes no definite provision for liquidation or salvage values and a number of other special problems. The writer believes, however, that all so-called bases of valuation and types of values can reasonably be listed under the two general heads indicated. The enterprise under consideration in this discussion, it may be added, is the typical going concern, not the business on the verge of liquidation.

The emphasis upon cost values in accounting is inevitable. The accountant's raw materials are particular transactions and relationships, and the values of the enterprise he is serving first come to his attention for the most part in the form of explicit costs attaching to specific factors and facilities. It is the accountant's function, to begin with, to assist in the process of effective internal administration of the business, and this evidently requires the tracing of the funds of the enterprise as they become represented by definite terms and classes of materials, equipment, etc. Further, the accountant must concentrate upon costs for the reason that no other approach is practicable in the majority of situations with which he must deal. It may be entirely proper as a matter of underlying theory, and may even be helpful in the formulation of policy, to conceive of a specialized factory machine as the embodiment of the series of uses which the machine may be expected to yield during its economic life, and to view the value of the machine at any point of time, correspondingly, as the amount of the prices of such uses, discounted to date; but it is surely quite obvious that conditions are seldom such as to make it feasible to measure machine values in this manner for the purpose of making records and reports. A specific productive facility cannot, as a rule, be interpreted as the equivalent of an interest-bearing contract with the customers of the enterprise. All we know about the economic character of the machine is its cost at various points of time coupled with facts as to its use and condition. The business concern in acquiring a unit of equipment of course assumes that there is at least a reasonable expectation of profitable utilization, but there is no precise matching of a discounted series of incomes with cost in reaching a conclusion. It is recognized that each productive facility, as an element in a complex of factors, should make its contribution to business income, but it is also recognized that it is usually mere assumption to assign any particular segment or amount of business income as realized to the specific facility. Even our cost accountants—who have more nerve in general than anyone else in the accounting field—do not attempt this hopeless task. The gap between enterprise income in a particular period and individual contributing factors is too wide to be bridged by any scheme of accounting, however elaborate. And even were this problem to be met successfuly it would still leave us with the difficulty of estimating the future incomes of specific factors! It may be added that any interpretation of business assets primarily in terms of income concepts is bound to be unsatisfactory and inadequate for purposes of accounting.

When, however, interest is shifted from the value of the particular facility to that of the going concern as a whole the significance of the cost approach fades appreciably and income assumes a position of importance. It is precisely at this point, in fact, that the contrast between asset valuation and enterprise valuation lies. The business enterprise, not the particular facility, is the essential unit in terms of which business income blooms; it is the enterprise, not the individual asset, which produces profits in our system of organization. This is not to deny that earnings may sometimes be reckoned departmentally and that some enterprises in the strict legal sense may not be significant units for income measurement. The enterprise, a conglomerate of facilities, has no value in itself except that which flows from its power to earn. The valuation of the enterprise, accordingly, is essentially the problem of estimating and discounting enterprise income; and the bare statement of the problem gives an indication of the difficulty of dealing with it effectively in actual affairs.

In the case of an established business the first step is a study of past earning records. In this study the period considered should be neither too long nor too short. A period of less than three years is probably too brief, as a rule, to throw much light on prospective earning power. For one thing the difficulties in the way of measuring periodic net income, familiar to all accountants, are so great as to make it unwise to place great faith in a short-term picture, however carefully limned. In this connection one cannot but marvel at the effect on stock-market prices of the announcement of the earnings of a single quarter. Apparently in speculative circles the tendency is naïvely to project the "latest dope," either good or bad, into the future in perpetuity. On the other hand, in our continuously changing economic fabric, it is to be doubted if a record of greater length than ten years, at the most, augments our powers of divination. It is cold comfort for the common stockholders of the Illinois Central Railroad, for example, to recall that their enterprise had an unbroken dividend record from the 1850's to the 1930's, as this fine showing augurs very little for the future. The trends evidenced in past performance, especially where persistent, are of course important in estimating future earnings, although here too caution must be exercised. The widespread notion that long-continued trends in human affairs may be expected to be forever maintained is in general without much foundation, whether the subject be divorce rates or profit rates. Further, in studying past profit records for the light which they may throw upon the future, scrutiny of valuation and accounting practices is important. Recorded net earnings are notoriously unreliable and of varying significance depending upon the circumstances of their determination. Among matters requiring special attention in this connection are: (1) treatment of organization and developmental charges; (2) inventory policies; (3) maintenance and depreciation, depletion, and amortization. The subject of unusual losses and profits, and of changes in the nature of the activities of the enterprise during the period under review, should also be investigated.

For a new enterprise there is of course no earning record to serve as a guide in valuation. In this situation, however, helpful data may sometimes be gleaned from the past records of other concerns engaged in the same or a similar line of activity.

The second step is the translation of the record of the past, carefully studied and interpreted, with proper weighting for trends, and tinctured by judgment in the light of plans and prospects, into an estimate of the earning power of the future. To begin with, the effort should be directed to setting up a range of estimates within which earnings will probably fall for a limited period of say five to ten years. Here is the crux of the problem, and in the nature of the case the estimates prepared often can be little more than intelligent guesses. Even when dealing with stable industries and very strongly situated companies, it is not safe to be too positive as to forthcoming events and especially as to that very special construction of coming events—the net earnings of the particular enterprise. The need for conservatism at this point is so great as to suggest that the public accountant has the ideal temperament for the task of making these estimates. Presumably this step will involve the preparation of underlying calculations of the volume of business and expenses, taxes, and other deductions, in more or less detail, care being taken to make proper adjustment for the increasing or decreasing charges which may accompany changes in gross revenue and methods of production.

Assuming that a range of careful estimates of future earnings has been compiled, the task arises of converting these data into a judgment as to present value or worth of such earnings to an interested buyer. In this connection it is necessary to raise the question of the proper definition or conception of net enterprise income for the purpose in hand. There are two main possibilities (and a number of minor variations, which need not be listed here). On the one hand earning power may be expressed in terms of the final amount, after all charges, accruing to the residual proprietary interest, in general that of the common stockholder in the case of the corporation; on the other hand earning power may be stated from the managerial, all-capital point of view, the point of view of the enterprise in its entirety as an economic institution. In attempting to value the enterprise, the first conception is not fully satisfactory, and this is true even where the final definite object of valuation is the common stock. The value of the enterprise as a whole, which must be estimated as a preliminary step in placing a value on the stock, is not affected by the nature of the sources of the funds supplied, by the form of capitalization, except as it be assumed that continuity of operation is jeopardized by the nature of the rights of those who supply the requisite economic capital. It must of course be granted that the value of the stock in a particular situation may be affected by the financial structure of the enterprise, but it may still be insisted that the significance of "trading on the equity" is a special and subordinate fact. Borrowing business capital is really an acute form of speculation in the value of money, and in general there is little relation between the worth of a shoe manufacturing business, for example, and the value of the ability to secure creditor-capital. The writer believes, incidentally, that the possibility of increasing earnings on a residual interest through the issue of bonds and preferred stock is more limited than has often been assumed, and that where such possibility exists it is usually a very temporary phenomenon.

The treatment of taxes, particularly income taxes, is a special problem here. From a strict management standpoint it may be argued that the net earning power of the enterprise includes the amount which is produced, after due allowance for all costs of operation, as the share of the Federal Government and any other governmental units levying upon earnings. However, from the standpoint of private capital the value of the enterprise as a producer of taxes is not subject to purchase and hence may be ignored. A more serious complication concerns the treatment of the capital represented by the current creditors not explicitly entitled to share in income. It seems fair to assume, in general, that implicit interest on such capital, at the prevailing commercial-paper rate, is buried in operating charges and that an adjustment is in order by which the estimated amount of such interest is included in earning power as otherwise determined.

The next step is a critical appraisal of all the tangible assets of the enterprise as they stand at the time that the value of the enterprise as a whole is being determined. It would be rather pleasant to us as accountants if some way of avoiding this ordeal could be found, but it is indispensable, as I shall try to show later. Book figures may be reasonably satisfactory for current assets, but the recorded data of fixed property are usually inadequate for the purpose of a qualitative analysis of earning power. As to how such an appraisal shall be made no suggestions will be offered here beyond indicating that the general approach should be that of a prospective buyer who sees the enterprise in its present setting and who is assuming that operations will be continued in an effective manner. The appraiser must of course bear in mind the purpose of the valuation and make special adjustments for nonoperating assets or property which for any reason cannot be expected to have an effective bearing on future activity.

Finding the "reasonable" or "fair" or "representative" or "significant" rate of return for economic capital under the conditions prevailing in the particular industry, a further requirement of enterprise valuation, is a troublesome matter and at the best nothing more than a rough estimate or range of estimates is possible in most situations. Even to define reasonable rate is not easy. It is obviously not the average of existing rates under similar conditions; it is presumably not the lowest rate that appears to be holding capital in the field. Probably the proper conception of the rate of return to be used in capitalizing earning power as a basis for determining a fair bid for a business enterprise is substantially that commonly employed in utility rate cases—a rate sufficient to maintain capital in the particular field and to attract additional funds as needed for the normal growth of the industry, in view of all the conditions recognized as attaching to the particular situation—with a little margin added to be on the safe side. Fortunately there are sufficient data available in government publications, trade association compilations, and elsewhere with respect to rates of return experienced by various enterprises and groups of enterprises to make it possible to avoid blind guesses. Needless to say, care must be taken in interpreting reported rates and in making use of such rates in a particular valuation project.

Comparison of estimated average future earnings with the average amount of tangible assets which it is expected will be associated with or required in the activities leading to such earnings is next in order. If the amount of such assets, at the significant rate of return which has been determined, more than absorbs the estimated earning power, the estimated value of the enterprise is less than the amount of the so-called tangible facilities, even if it be assumed that the work of appraising tangibles has been done with the utmost of care and discrimination. In this case the maximum bid which can reasonably be made for the business is the present value of the average estimated earnings in perpetuity capitalized at the estimated significant rate of return. If on the other hand the estimated average earnings are more than sufficient to clothe the tangible assets with adequate earnings, we are confronted with superior earning power, or a condition of intangible assets, and the measurement of the present value of such anticipated differential income must be undertaken.

Before proceeding with a discussion of the final stage in enterprise valuation, a number of "accrued" complications should be noted. Often the earnings of the future, like those of the past, may be expected to appear as a fluctuating series rather than as a stable stream. The assets to be associated with the various periodic increments of income may likewise be assumed to vary somewhat in character and amount. To attempt, however, to take these features into account in the valuation process, other than as elements in rough averages, would be clearly unreasonable in view of the inherent limitations involved. It should also be remembered that in the final computations adjustment must be made for the difference if any between the amount of the average tangible assets assumed for the future and the amount of such assets actually available to be taken over by the buyer. In this connection the matter of non-interest-bearing current liabilities may again be referred to. If the estimated future earning figures employed do not include an allowance for the implicit interest on the average of such liabilities assumed for the future, the average amount of the tangible assets used in the calculation of differential earning power should be reduced by the amount of such liabilities.

Another complication is the matter of excess working capital. It is a familiar fact that a concern may possess items of plant which are in whole or in part unutilized or ineffectively utilized, and assuming that this condition may be expected to persist such assets, even if they are to be taken over at salvage value, should not be considered in the qualitative measurement of earning power. Similarly an enterprise may have a large backlog of purchasing power in the form of marketable securities and bank balances which can hardly be said to be effectively employed, in total, in the main activities of the business. In such circumstances an estimate must be made, as in utility valuation cases, of the amount of working assets which can reasonably be assumed to be required in connection with the realization of the estimated income in the future. Then in estimating future earnings any income earned on excess current resources should be excluded, and if the excess resources are actually to be taken over in the acquisition of the business a corresponding amount must be added to the estimated fair purchase price as otherwise determined. The estimate of working capital required, it may be added, should be liberal and should recognize the need of substantial cash reserves. A reasonable cash balance, under the circumstances which make it good management to maintain such a balance, is as productive and as vitally connected with operations as the necessary stock of raw materials.

Let us now return to the question of the valuation of differential or superior earnings. The first consideration to be emphasized is the fact that earnings in excess of a reasonable rate of return on the tangible assets to be employed are likely to persist for only a short period, or, to put the matter more pointedly, that an investment can safely be made in anticipated excess profits only on the basis of a very conservative judgment as to the duration of such profits. There is such a thing as competition, and the hazards of business operation in other respects are commonly very real. Long-standing exceptional profit rates—ignoring those artificially produced by arbitrary treatment of assets and expenses—are a rarity. Further, the persistence of superior earnings in a given case may be due not to the conditions and factors which were present a few years before when the business was acquired, but to new circumstances and developments; and while a buyer may reasonably be willing to pay in cash or equivalent for the peculiar momentum which a business has achieved to date, he is not justified in investing in future earnings which may result from conditions not present at the time of purchase, especially where these may require additional effort and expenditure later. Accordingly the layer of anticipated excess earnings, isolated as outlined above, should in general be given a life of five years or less.

What rate should be applied to the series of estimated differential incomes in discounting the series to a present value? The reasonable rate applicable to tangible asset requirements, or a rate commensurate with the greater risk which may be assumed to be involved? If the duration of the top layer of earnings is very conservatively estimated, it might be held that the investment in such earnings is no less secure than the investment in the layer matching the tangible assets and that the same rate of return may therefore be assumed in both cases. On the other hand, there is something to be said for the view that excess earnings are always more perilously situated than normal incomes and that a double dose of conservatism is desirable in estimating amounts which may reasonably be invested in prospective earnings of this type. From this standpoint the application of a substantially higher rate in the process of discounting the top layer is justified.

In these comments on the process of valuing the enterprise the view is accepted that the so-called intangible assets—Canning's master valuation account—represent merely the excess of the value of the enterprise as a whole over such part of this value as may be imputed to the recognizable or tangible assets. According to this view, in other words, the intangibles are the reconciling element between the sum of the values of the business taken in terms of definite objective elements, item by item, and the value of the organized institution. The view has also been accepted that intangibles are based on a residuum of income, that no intangibles exist where the entire earning power is absorbed by the ordinary assets. It is of course theoretically possible to conceive of a business (as the Board of Tax Appeals seems to have done in a few cases) which has an earning power of less than a reasonable return on assets and which nevertheless has actual intangible values, but this means the exclusion of active and necessary assets from normal relation to earnings and appears to be an unworkable approach. One of the many natural sequence assumptions of accounting is that which considers income as first to be imputed to capital requirements as reflected in typical assets and second to imponderable circumstances and conditions inhering in and focusing upon the particular enterprise in its peculiar setting.

(This statement of the situation may be objected to on the ground that it draws too sharp a distinction between tangible and intangible assets as ordinarily understood. As Professor Hatfield has pointed out, even land might be viewed as an intangible since land ownership consists simply of certain rights granted with respect to the use of a specified portion of the earth's surface. It is no doubt true that such definite factors as franchises, patents, and other recognizable monopolistic privileges may be independent objects of valuation under some circumstances and may be assumed to have a relation to earning power not utterly different from that indicated for the tangible assets.)

In concluding this rough outline I would like to emphasize the fact that the measurement of intangibles, the appraisal of corporate securities,[1] and the valua-

---

[1] It is recognized that the market value of a stock in a particular company may be affected by the dividend policy, and various other factors not given attention here.

tion of entire business concerns are essentially a single problem. In each case the same estimates are required, the same factors must be considered, the same computations must be made. Further, an appraisal of tangible assets is a necessary part of the process, particularly in connection with the qualitative interpretation of earning power.

May I also emphasize the need for more critical and conservative appraisals of business concerns both in connection with outright purchase and sale of entire enterprises and in connection with investment activities as exemplified in the organized markets for securities and elsewhere. Certainly careless overevaluation was in evidence on every hand during the so-called boom period of 1925–1929, and the inclination to don the rose-colored glasses is again apparent in financial circles. In many of the cases of merger and consolidation, of course, the nominal price paid for constituent companies was not on a cash basis, and the inflation was accordingly more apparent than real; nevertheless the actual prices paid—especially in terms of the market values attached to the new securities issued—were often ridiculously high. No wonder that the owners of a host of small, local corporations were tempted to dispose of their companies to those who were quite sure that two plus two was much more than four!

B. THE DISPOSITION PROBLEM

ROBERT H. NELSON

ROBERT H. NELSON (1921–   ), A.B. 44 Detroit; J.D. 50, M.B.A. 51 Harvard; member of the Michigan and Federal Bars; CPA. Currently attorney at law, Farmington, Michigan. Contributor to *The Accounting Review*.
Was a staff accountant with Peat, Marwick, Mitchell & Co., 1951–55.

THE MOMENTUM THEORY OF GOODWILL

ROBERT H. NELSON

The purpose of this article is to analyze purchased "goodwill" with a view to seeing whether it ought to be amortized by charges to income, and in general to present a case for amortization, a case however which is contrary in some instances to *Accounting Research Bulletin 43*, Chapter 5,[a] as it now stands.

The term, "goodwill," is used in its broad aspects, while the term, *goodwill*, will

SOURCE: From *The Accounting Review*, Vol. XXVIII, No. 4 (October, 1953), pp. 491–499. Reprinted by permission of the American Accounting Association.

[a] The author's original references were to ARB No. 24, which was superseded (1953) by Chap. 5 of ARB No. 43. Other than for a quotation from Bulletin No. 24 that the editors have changed to fit Bulletin No. 43, Chap. 5, it is the editors' opinion that all of the author's statements are as applicable to the former bulletin as to the latter. All subsequent references to Bulletin No. 43 apply to Chap. 5 only; each appearance of "43" in the reprinted article is the editors' replacement for "24" in the article as originally printed. ARB No. 43, Chap. 5 has been superseded by APB Opinion No. 17, "Intangible Assets," (Aug. 1970). The conclusions of this opinion differ from those cited for ARB No. 43. The conclusions of APB No. 17 can best be stated by citing para. 9: "The Board concludes that a company should record as assets the costs of intangible assets acquired from others, including goodwill acquired in a business combination. A company should record as expenses the costs to develop intangible assets which are not specifically identifiable. The Board also concludes that the cost of each type of intangible asset should be amortized by systematic charges to income over the period estimated to be benefited. The period of amortization should not, however, exceed forty years." [Eds.]

be used for references in the more literal sense. "Goodwill," as meant here, is approached by Leake:

> In its true economic meaning the term "commercial goodwill" covers a vast field of rights growing out of all kinds of past effort in seeking profit, increase of value, or other advantage which may be capable of future profitable development. These rights are legally protected under various names, both by statute law and by common law, for the use and benefit of the owner. Commercial goodwill may include any or all such property as business connection associated with names, persons and places of business, trade marks, patents and designs, copyright, and the right to exercise monopolies. The exchangeable value of goodwill is based on anticipation, and the character of the anticipation always is that the owner of any of these rights will earn future profit, increase of value, or other advantage in excess of the normal reward of any capital and human effort (which includes labour) needed to carry on the undertaking.[1]

The analysis will proceed by a discussion of each of the various items which are commonly thought to constitute "goodwill": *goodwill*, customer lists, organization costs, costs of development, trade names, secret processes, patents, copyrights, licenses, franchises, superior earning power, and going value.

GOODWILL

Goodwill, usually the most important item of "goodwill," refers to favorable attitudes toward an enterprise. Thus, it would include the favorable attitudes of customers, employees, credit grantors, investors, suppliers, governmental regulators, politicians and the general public. Other descriptive terms for *goodwill* are reputation and customer habit. Usually *goodwill* is transferred only on the sale of the entire concern. However, there are cases where the *goodwill* involved in a patent, copyright, secret process, or trade mark is transferred with the patent or other item without selling the entire business.

Goodwill is about as fickle as the human nature of which it is an aspect. Some human habits are strong, but customer habit is usually not one of them. Reputations fade from memory unless the reputation is fed or replenished by new feats or reminders. Fickle or not, it is hard to build up, so the buyer of a concern will often pay a large sum of money for the *goodwill*. The reason is that he wants this starting "push" in his new enterprise, rather than to start fresh in a similar business and devote much effort and money over a long period of time to develop such *goodwill*, especially since his profits are likely to be meager until *goodwill* is developed. According to what I shall call the Annuity Theory,[2] the buyer is investing in a series of excess earnings—an analogy to an investment in an annuity. But isn't it only on rare occasions that this may be the case? A better hypothesis would seem to be that businessmen are not buyers of annuities but buyers of a marketing or promotional "push."

This "push" which the buyer receives for his investment in *goodwill* is not a continual, everlasting one, but rather it is like momentum or a running start.

---

[1] P. D. Leake, *Commercial Goodwill: Its History, Value, and Treatment in Accounts*, v (4th ed. 1948).

[2] Proponents: Leake, *op. cit.*, at 76–81; W. A. Paton, *Advanced Accounting* 409–410, 435 (1st ed. 1947); *Accountants' Handbook* 849 (Paton ed. 1947).

He has to feed in new energy to keep from slowing to a standstill. Thus arises the Momentum Theory which, it is hoped, will be distinguished from the Annuity Theory. The Momentum Theory is the hypothesis that a businessman purchases a promotional push instead of an annuity and that the "push" dissipates like momentum. The assumption that an asset may exist in perpetuity is very risky, to say the least. It follows that the investment ought to be charged against income over the estimated life of the momentum, the period during which it will be contributing its "push" or benefit. As a corollary the buyer should not write off his investment by a charge direct to retained earnings, unless an unfortunate turn of events should wipe it out. It also follows that the investment should not be written off by a charge to capital surplus. The money which is spent on *goodwill* is just as good as the money spent on plant and equipment, and the representation (as to assets purchased) which is put on the balance sheet should be made accordingly.

Due to the nature of this momentum, it seems that the amortization would, in most cases, be over a life of from two to ten years. The Annuity Theory would call for a shorter life than the Momentum Theory hypothetically, since excess earnings would cease before all the "push" was dissipated.

Estimating the life of the purchased momentum would be more difficult than estimating the life of a lathe or a foundry building. There could be no reliance on a table stating past experience on useful life. Nor would it be possible to correct the estimate of the life of the *purchased* momentum as the end of the estimated period approached. The buyer's estimate of the life should be controlling, according to the Momentum Theory. The estimate should be the one on which the buyer based his top offering price. Thus, where the buyer makes an estimate of the life of the momentum, say, 5 years, and uses this estimate in calculating his top offering price, he has, in effect, decided to incur an annual charge amounting to twenty per cent of the purchase price against his income accounts for the next five years. He acts on this decision when he closes the deal, and this decision and action of management should be reflected in the accounts. The buyer's outlay in this situation is analogous to an outlay for five years of insurance on his plant or for a five-year lease. The arrival at the price would probably be based more on "hunch" than on any Annuity-Theory calculations, but one factor in the "hunch" would almost always be an estimate of momentum life, and this estimate should be used. The fact that the payment might equal four years' purchase because of a hard-driven bargain would not mean he should amortize over four years since the estimated life was five years—unless he were purchasing a series of future incomes and then the Annuity Theory would apply. The straight-line method of amortization should be used, it seems, in view of the meagerness of our knowledge about the dissipation of this momentum.[3] Where the Annuity Theory applies, a compound-interest method of amortization is called for.

Accounting Research Bulletin 43 classifies "goodwill generally," as against "goodwill as to which there is evidence of limited duration," as a type (b) in-

---

[3] Some beginnings have been made in this area. See Hollander, "A Rationale for Advertising Expenditures," *Harvard Business Review,* January, 1949, p. 79 at pp. 85–87, and Lathrop, "Industrial Applications of Operations Research," *Quality Control Conference Papers,* 1953, American Society for Quality Control, p. 295 at pp. 304–305.

tangible, for which non-amortization is favored. It seems questionable whether this is correct.

Bulletin 43 sets forth two requirements, both necessary, for an intangible's classification as a type (b) intangible instead of type (a), for which amortization is required:

> 1. term of existence not limited by law, regulation, or agreement, or by the nature of the intangible (limitation by *nature*), and
> 2. no indication, at time of acquisition, of limited life (*evidence* of limitation).

Therefore, it is submitted for consideration that *goodwill* should be classified as a type (a) intangible, because in view of the foregoing analysis there is a limitation by *nature*, even though there may not be, at the time of acquisition, any *evidence* of limitation.

Bulletin 43 also says:

> In determining whether an investment in type (b) intangibles has become or is likely to become worthless, consideration should be given to the fact that in some cases intangibles acquired by purchase may merge with, *or be replaced by*, intangibles acquired or *developed* with respect to other products or lines of business and that in such circumstances the discontinuance of a product or line of business may not in fact indicate loss of value. (Italics supplied.)

Thus, it would seem that *Bulletin 43* would allow the buyer to carry the investment in purchased *goodwill* on his books without amortization, even after the momentum had dissipated, as long as the buyer had developed momentum to replace it. Since the amount on the books cannot represent the purchased momentum which has been used up, it must represent self-developed *goodwill*.[4] It is submitted that this procedure is inconsistent with the condemnation of the recognition of self-developed *goodwill*. Perhaps such recognition of self-developed *goodwill* is not so dangerous as an "out-and-out" recognition, since the figure on the books has undergone the commercial test of actual cost incurred. Yet the figure allowed to remain on the books is likely to be just as inaccurate a measure of the self-developed *goodwill* as any figure newly placed on the books in the type of "out-and-out" recognition which is so uniformly condemned. It was arrived at on the basis of different factors and at a different time than would a present valuation of *goodwill*.

The proposition that purchased *goodwill* should be amortized even though self-developed *goodwill* is not recognized may have a certain practical consistency.

---

[4] The Annuity Theory reaches the same conclusion: "It is urged against the writing off of the cost of goodwill—and often it is a fact—that the goodwill of a prosperous undertaking earning large surplus profits is worth no less now than it was when it was purchased ten or twenty years ago. The question is asked: 'Why, therefore, should the goodwill be written off?' The answer is that the present goodwill is, in the main, not the goodwill which was bought ten or twenty years ago. At that time—ten or twenty years ago—the now existing goodwill (which is the present value of super-profit expected to arise in still future years) would, owing to the effect of annual interest, have been worth next to nothing." Leake, *op. cit.*, at 77.

Take the case of a company which wants to start into a certain line of business. It has two courses open to it. One is to start from scratch and develop the business, and the result will be large charges in its income statement for the next few years. The other course is to buy out an established business, and the result again, will be large (amortization) charges in its income statement for the next few years. If it does not amortize its purchased *goodwill* however, it will not have these large charges, and the second course of action will seem more profitable, although the costs of getting into the line of business may have been the same under either course of action. Breaking into a new line of business is costly one way or another, but doesn't non-amortization tend to hide this fact?

Bulletin 43's position, by way of hypothesis, may be merely a holdover from the days when the emphasis was on the balance sheet. Time was when even self-developed *goodwill* was placed on the books. Abuses led to *goodwill* being considered a tainted asset, and some companies wrote it down to $1.00 while the generally accepted accounting practice became on the whole that which is stated by *Bulletin 43*. It was strictly a utilitarian rule to prevent abuses, since both purchased and self-developed *goodwill* should be shown on balance sheets which are intended to show financial condition and value. But those days are gone and it seems accounting practice should be consistent and insist on amortization, for the stress today is on the income statement instead of the balance sheet. (In fact, George O. May recently remarked that we're now in a third era where the stress is on the footnotes.)

Customer Lists

Customer lists or a file on customers is another item of "goodwill" which can be a valuable asset. A new selling organization has to spend a great deal of time and money collecting information on prospects and then finding out which prospects are good potentialities. Hence, the acquisition of a file on customers will enable a new management to start selling and thereby turning over inventory from the beginning, and to save on salaries paid to collect such information. According to the Momentum Theory it's an investment in an organizational type of momentum. Customer lists, though they are not *goodwill*, are related to *goodwill*. The purchaser can take advantage of the *goodwill* more readily if he knows exactly where to tap it. Customer lists tell him where.

It seems a fair statement that the customer lists which are purchased are a temporary benefit, not perpetual. After a few years they become almost wholly a self-developed advantage. In view of these characteristics it seems that the investment in customer lists ought to be amortized over a few years. It is submitted that *Bulletin 43*'s classification as a type (b) intangible may be incorrect.

Organization Costs

Organization costs include expenditures for promotion, incorporation and raising capital. Accountants are not in agreement as to the nature and treatment of these costs in the hands of the organizing management. Most seem to agree, as a practical matter, on treating them as a deferred charge subject to early amortization, while at the same time there is the feeling that in theory the benefit of such costs will last as long as the corporate existence.[5] *Bulletin 43* classifies

---

[5] *Accountants' Handbook* 128–129 (Paton ed. 1947).

organization costs as a type (b) intangible. But is this correct? The Momentum Theory would say no while the Annuity Theory would not seem to apply.

The treatment of these costs as a deferred charge subject to early amortization seems to be preferable, but not merely as a matter of expedience or conservatism. These costs seem to be in the nature of an expenditure of energy to overcome inertia and impart momentum. Every enterprise has to have a start, and human inertia, which can be considerable, has to be overcome. The important point is that the organizational momentum thus imparted will last only a short time. This point is contrary to legal doctrine about incorporation and subsequent legal life (perpetual), but there is little reason to be guided here by the implications of such doctrine. The buyer of an enterprise, years after its organization, will not pay a cent for the initial momentum. He pays only for the momentum existing at the date of purchase. After all, it's the only momentum he gets. An argument against this viewpoint is that the management wanted the limited-liability advantage, paid part of the costs of organization for it, and continues to receive this advantage throughout the corporate existence, therefore the costs should not be amortized. Since momentum is the major factor of value, however, it would seem the entire expenditure should be amortized.

Costs of Development

Costs of development include, and should be limited to, specific expenditures for preliminary advertising, collecting information on customer prospects, exploration, training personnel, and similar developmental costs. These expenditures are for organizational and promotional momentum to get the concern really going; the initial organizational momentum involving organization costs is not enough.

In general, accountants are opposed to treating as an asset costs of development in the going-value sense—excess of (all) charges over revenue during the developmental period. For treatment as a deferred charge, there must be unmistakable legitimacy, i.e., specific expenditures identifiable with building organizational and promotional momentum.

Trade Marks, Trade Names, and Brands

Trade marks and trade names are another item of "goodwill." Probably because there is no time limitation on the legal protection given to trade names as there is to patents and copyrights, *Bulletin 43* lists trade names as an example of a type (b) intangible.

What is the nature of the value of a trade name? One element in this value is the monopoly element, i.e., the legal protection given to exclusive use. There is also an element of promotional momentum, the "push" or assistance given by the reputation or customer habit involved in the trade name, i.e., *goodwill*. It seems that this promotional momentum is the major element in the value. To a businessman, the price he pays will be low if there is little *goodwill* and high if there is much. Hence, the investment is mostly a purchase of *goodwill*. In some trade names there is a third element of value, name attractiveness. But even the attractiveness of names becomes "old hat." It would seem that the investment in a trade name ought to be amortized by charges against income over the estimated life of the promotional momentum, the *goodwill*.

Secret Processes and Formulas

Another item of "goodwill" is the secret process. *Bulletin 43* classifies it as a type (b) intangible, probably because there is no time limitation on the legal protection given to the secrecy and because successful secrecy can mean an exclusive use lasting indefinitely.

However, it seems that there are other elements of value than the monopoly element (exclusive use) in a secret process. The process or formula would have value in the case of a delicious candy bar or perfume whether the process were secret or not, so it seems that there is a product-desirability element in the value. Both the product-desirability element and the monopoly element help in building up *goodwill,* the former helping to develop favorable attitudes, reputation and customer habit, and the latter helping to keep this *goodwill* from dissipating to competitors. *Goodwill,* developed by these or other means such as advertising, would become an element in the value of the secret formula. If the secrecy should be lost, or if a competitor worked up a similar process or formula, the product-desirability element in the value would still remain and so would the *goodwill*. These factors, especially the *goodwill,* would continue to help the product to sell well. It should be pointed out that the product-desirability element of value in a secret process may not be a perpetual thing, since tastes may change or there may be a possibility of obsolescence.

There is a question as to whether the buyer of a secret process should amortize his investment. Assuming that he could allocate his investment to (1) the product-desirability element, (2) the monopoly element and (3) the *goodwill* element, how would he treat each of these? Since there is no time limitation involved in (2), it seems that that part of the investment should not be amortized, but it would seem to be a small part of the investment. The rest of the investment should be amortized. If allocation is impossible, the buyer might, as a practical expedient, try to determine which is the major or predominant element of value. Since the major factor will probably be the *goodwill,* it seems the entire investment should be amortized.

Patents

A patent is another item of "goodwill." Since the legal protection given for exclusive use is limited in time, *Bulletin 43* classifies patents as a type (a) intangible.

The value of a patent can be increased, in cases where the major element of value is the product-desirability factor, by advertising and other items building up *goodwill.* Thus, in many cases where a patented article has been marketed for several years, a buyer of the patent may be paying for the following elements of value: exclusive use, product-desirability and *goodwill.* It is agreed that the buyer of a patent must amortize his investment, but it would also seem that where the patent is running out shortly and there is much *goodwill,* the amortization period might be longer than remaining patent life.

Copyrights

A copyright is another "goodwill" item which is mainly thought to be a monopoly factor due to the legal protection given to exclusiveness of use. Since the legal protection is limited in time, *Bulletin 43* classifies copyrights as a type (a) intangible.

Here again, however, just as in the case of other "goodwill" items previously discussed, it seems that the time factor in the legal protection should not be slavishly followed in matters of amortization. Due to the fact that the product-desirability of most copyrighted items endures but a few years at most, the investment in a copyright should not be amortized over the full copyright period. Rarely does a book, including the most popular of best-sellers, turn out to be great enough to live even for the copyright period. Walter A. Staub recommends spreading the cost on a unit basis of sales in each fiscal period as compared with the expected total sales, with frequent revisions in the light of the actual sales.[6]

Licenses

A license may be issued under a patent or copyright or under governmental police power (e.g., liquor license). *Bulletin 43* classifies a license as a type (a) intangible. Where a lump sum is paid instead of royalties or fees, the accounting treatment would be generally covered by the ideas discussed under the topics: patents, copyrights and franchises.

Franchises

Franchises confer on the grantees varying degrees of monopoly. *Bulletin 43* classifies fixed-term franchises as a type (a) intangible and perpetual franchises as a type (b) intangible. In the case of the fixed-term franchise grantee, the costs of acquiring the franchise would clearly seem to be a deferred charge. In the case of the perpetual franchise grantee, the costs of acquiring the franchise would seem to be in the nature of organization costs, costs of initiating organizational momentum, since enfranchised businesses usually require either monopoly conditions or official approval or both.

As for the buyer from, or assignee of, the franchise grantee, we might distinguish between public and private franchises. Since heavy utility regulation in recent years has tended to reduce earnings, it seems that in many cases companies buying up a utility and its franchise will not be buying any excess earnings, and thus the Annuity Theory could hardly apply, whereas in the case of private franchises or licenses (for example, an exclusive marketing territory), a built-up territory probably has superior earnings and the Annuity Theory might possibly apply. Again, in all cases where the investment is in various types of momentum it should be amortized.

Superior Earning Power

There seems to be general agreement that there is a relationship between "goodwill" and superior earnings. However, the relationship does not always seem very clear. On the one hand, if we find that a company has superior earnings, we can usually say that "goodwill" is present. On the other hand, if we find that a company is established and has a large group of regular customers, we can also say that the *goodwill* item of "goodwill" is present. Yet it is said that "the mere existence of an established concern, and favorable attitudes on the part of

---

[6] Staub, "Intangible Assets" in *Contemporary Accounting* Ch. 8, p. 4 (American Institute of Accountants, 1945).

customers, employees, and others associated therewith, does not demonstrate the existence of intangible property." [7] This would seem to be a premise of the Annuity Theory. Favorable customer attitudes however are favorable attitudes, and they can give a push, momentum, and it does not seem you can deny the existence of *goodwill* just because there are no superior earnings. People have been known to pay money for "goodwill" in such a case. Also, it is known that on occasion patents are purchased in order to rid the buyer of a nuisance, there being no question of superior earnings from the purchased patents.

And just as the existence of "goodwill" does not always mean the existence of superior earnings, so also, the existence of superior earnings does not always mean the existence of "goodwill." The superior earnings might be due to factors other than "goodwill." For example, they might be due to luck, as by a foolish laying-in of a huge inventory subsequently given the touch of Midas by a war shortage, or due almost wholly to entrepreneurial and managerial ability.[8]

Even where there are excess earnings it should be questioned, it seems, whether the value of "goodwill" is in most cases the present value of estimated future excess earnings. It is true that the purchase price of "goodwill" is *calculated* sometimes in terms of the present value of estimated excess earnings. The reason for calculation in such terms may be that "goodwill" is very difficult to evaluate, and such terms are about the only rational basis. Often, however, the buyer is agreeing to a price on the basis of a "businessman's hunch" in view of all the circumstances. This phenomenon, an examination of the facts and analysis of the factors followed by a "feeling in the bones" as to the proper decision, is quite common.[9] Also, the give-and-take of bargaining often leads to decisions on price which the Annuity Theory does not fit. And sometimes the buyer wants the business but has little use for the "goodwill," wants to do things a lot differently than the old crowd, but the old crowd demands and gets a payment for intangibles. In this case, the buyer has been willing to make an entrance payment or a payment for organizational momentum. The Momentum Theory does not seek to rationalize in a neat, logical manner the calculation of the amount of the purchase price, hence fits all these cases.

Price decisions not explainable on any rational grounds have frequently been very successful, but at the same time these decisions have often been explained to others by means of some sort of rationalization, usually in terms of present value of earnings, though, again, this does not mean that in many cases the range of offering prices is not arrived at through the use of such calculations. However, just because such calculations are used either to help make the decision or to rationalize "hunch" decisions, does it follow that the value of "goodwill" is the present value of estimated future excess earnings and that the buyer of "goodwill" is buying an annuity?

Going Value

Bulletin 43 lists going value as an intangible. The term may mean various things. First, it may mean the going value of physical assets, i.e., the value-in-use

---

[7] *Accountants' Handbook* 840 (Paton ed. 1947).

[8] See G. O. May, *Financial Accounting* 106 (1943).

[9] See, for example, Washburn v. National Wall-Paper Co., 81 Fed. 17, 23 (2nd Cir. 1897).

to a going concern, as against scrap or liquidation value. In this sense, it is not an intangible asset, since intangibles are value over and above the going value of physical assets. Second, it may mean developmental value, i.e., the excess of costs of development and other charges over current revenues during the period of establishment, discussed above under Costs of Development. Third, it may mean the value of superior earnings, just discusesd.

Does *Bulletin 43* refer to going value in this third sense? It is submitted that *Bulletin 43* is not clear on this point. This third meaning comes the closest, of the recognized meanings, to the idea of an intangible asset. Yet *Bulletin 43*'s classification of going value is type (b). Going value, as a measure of *all* intangibles, could not have a type (b) sort of implication, it is submitted, since *all* intangibles include not only type (b) intangibles but also type (a) intangibles.

There is, possibly, a fourth sense of the term. Organization costs and costs of development express the *costs* of developing organizational momentum but there is no term expressing the *value* of the organization momentum which is purchased from the developer. "Going value" might well perform the function. However, there are already so many different and confusing meanings of "going value" as to make one mindful of the Tower of Babel. Perhaps the term, "going-organization value," might serve.

POLICY ARGUMENTS

An argument may be made for the amortization of purchased "goodwill" on the ground that such treatment will better effectuate the general policy of the law of dividends. This objective might be stated as the restriction of dividends to protect creditors, senior shareholders and even junior shareholders. Creditors, especially, need protection, because a corporation enjoys limited liability.

If purchased "goodwill" be an investment in assets which are used up in the process of helping to produce income, then part of the earnings which come subsequent to the purchase will be a return of investment. To let these earnings be paid out as dividends is to pay dividends out of capital. It is submitted that this is inconsistent with the policy of dividend law. The accounting profession seems to have a responsibility here. The reason is that accounting practice carries great weight with the courts.[10]

Even if purchased "goodwill" be considered an investment in a permanent asset, it seems that the asset is too unstable to permit the risk of its ultimate realization to fall on the creditors, as would happen if the asset were left unamortized. Also, write-downs can too easily come too late to protect creditors. It is not only very difficult to tell when and by how much there must be a write-down, but also, there would be a human tendency to delay the write-down. The fact that amortization is less difficult and probably more accurate than such write-downs makes a practical argument in favor of the amortization position which should appeal to the auditor who has to argue with a client for a write-down.

Another practical aspect is the fact that *Bulletin 43*'s allowance of the op-

---

[10] *Cf.* Pardee v. Harwood Electric Co., 262 Pa. 68, 72, 105 Atl. 48, 49 (1918), Indiana Veneer & Lumber Co. v. Hageman, 57 Ind. App. 668, 681, 105 N.E. 253, 257 (1914); Ballantine, *Corporations* 529 (2nd ed. 1946).

tional amortization of type (b) intangibles would, as to companies which amortize, help to leave them open to the charge that they are concealing income. This would seem especially true in view of the fact that *Bulletin 43* encourages the non-amortization side of the option.

The conclusion which may be warranted from an analysis of "goodwill" and from these policy arguments is that all or almost all of the items of purchased "goodwill" ought to be amortized by charges to income.

GEORGE T. WALKER

GEORGE T. WALKER (1913–   ),
B.A. 35 Northwestern State (La.);
M.S. 36, Ph.D. 48 Louisiana State.
Currently president of Northeast Louisiana University. Contributor to *The Journal of Accountancy*, *Journal of Business Education*, and other journals.

Served as a member of the business faculties of several Louisiana universities prior to becoming professor of business administration and dean of the School of Applied Arts and Sciences, Northwestern State University (La.). Was appointed to the presidency of Northeast Louisiana University in 1958.

WHY PURCHASED GOODWILL SHOULD BE AMORTIZED ON A SYSTEMATIC BASIS

GEORGE T. WALKER

How to handle goodwill in accounting has long been a thorny problem. This author argues that purchased goodwill should be written off on a systematic basis without regard to the profitableness of the enterprise during a given year or period of years. Such amortization should be made a charge to current operations. He intends that the present discussion will stimulate a new approach on the part of accountants to goodwill and its amortization treatment.

Goodwill (like other assets) often appreciates in value after a bona fide purchase has been made. However, since goodwill takes recorded form only upon the event of an actual purchase, sound accounting procedure dictates that appreciation of goodwill not be recorded in the accounts. There has been general agreement to this effect for a long time.[1] On the other hand, there is not general agreement on the depreciation of goodwill and its treatment in the accounts. Though accountants agree that goodwill does not depreciate in exactly the same sense as tangible fixed assets, they do agree that goodwill may depreciate. But whether or not depreciation of goodwill should be shown on the books has been a moot question. Granting that goodwill in a given case has not depreciated, the question as to whether or not it should be written off may still arise.

SOURCE: From *The Journal of Accountancy*, Vol. VC, No. 2 (February, 1953), pp. 210–216. Reprinted by permission of the American Institute of Certified Public Accountants.

[1] For a comprehensive analysis of the basis for not recognizing appreciation of goodwill in the accounts, see George T. Walker, "Nonpurchased Goodwill," *Accounting Review*, Vol. 13, No. 3, September, 1938, pp. 253–259.

In analyzing the principles involved, one may well review the reasoning of those who say that it is not necessary to write down the goodwill account. Among the group holding that it is unnecessary or improper to write off goodwill are Montgomery, Esquerré, Kester, Staub, Couchman, Dicksee and Tillyard, May, and Cole. Thus Montgomery says:

> It is not the practice and it is generally impractical to attempt to depreciate goodwill.[2]

Esquerré expresses an even stronger view, as follows:

> There is no reason why it [goodwill] should be amortized, depreciated, written down, or otherwise deprived of its vitality and meaning.[3]

Kester says:

> There is usually no logical basis for writing it off. When profits are large, goodwill is a very real asset. To write it off then is not logically consistent. When profits are small and goodwill has declined, it would hardly be logical to write off any portion less than its decreased amount yet the profits at such a time are rarely sufficient to stand so heroic a treatment.[4]

Staub, following closely the outline and reasoning of the 1943–1944 committee on accounting procedure of the American Institute of Accountants in Accounting Research Bulletin No. 24,[a] says:

> . . . there is no basic reason for, or scientific method of, writing off or amortizing the cost of Type B intangibles (including goodwill), the value of which is continuing. To require the compulsory amortization of intangibles, the value of which is being currently maintained or even enhanced, seems a departure from the "going concern" concept of financial statements and an attempt to provide for losses which may be sustained upon termination or liquidation of an enterprise at some time in the future. If, however, a corporation decides to amortize the cost of a Type B intangible, as to which there is no present indication of limited existence or loss of value, by systematic charges

---

[2] Robert H. Montgomery, *Auditing Theory and Practice* (6th ed.; New York: Ronald Press Company, 1940), p. 498.

[3] Paul-Joseph Esquerré, *Accounting* (New York: The Ronald Press Co., 1927), p. 191.

[4] Roy B. Kester, *Advanced Accounting* (4th ed., New York: The Ronald Press Co., 1946), p. 369. One may ask why it is sound to determine charges in terms of "sufficient profits"? The reader will note also the conflict between the above quotation and the following from the same page: ". . . the best course for all purposes seems to be to retain goodwill in the accounts at a nominal amount as evidence of its legitimate existence and right to consideration."

[a] Bulletin No. 24 was superseded (with certain changes in substance) by Chap. 5 of ARB No. 43 (1953). The former permitted, but discouraged, write-offs of goodwill to be charged against capital surplus in certain circumstances, but this practice is prohibited by Chap. 5. ARB No. 43 Chap. 5 has been superseded by APB Opinion No. 16, "Intangible Assets," (August, 1970). The conclusions of APB No. 17 differ from those cited for ARB No. 43. The conclusions of APB No. 17 are: "The Board concludes that a company should record as assets the cost of intangible assets acquired from others, including goodwill acquired in a business combination. A company should record as expenses the costs to develop intangible assets which are not specifically identifiable. The Board also concludes that the cost of each type of intangible asset should be amortized by systematic charges to income over the period estimated to be benefited. The period of amortization should not, however, exceed forty years." (para. 9) [Eds.]

in the income statement, long established custom indicates such procedure to be permissible despite the fact that expenditures are being made to maintain its value.[5]

The lack of consistency in reasoning is evident when one substitutes "building" for "intangibles" and "depreciation" for "amortization" in Staub's statement. The paraphrased statement reminds one immediately of early practice when little, much, or no depreciation was charged off in terms of the amount of profit. It is as incorrect to relate amortization to the value of intangibles as it is to relate depreciation to the value of fixed assets.

Other accountants take a slightly different position, but they apparently follow the same line of reasoning. Probably Couchman's statement is the most significant in this respect. He says: ". . . if you can write it down, you need not; if you cannot, you should!"[6] This reasoning, even though accepted and quoted by many accountants, is illogical and unsound.

BASES FOR NON-AMORTIZATION POLICY

The weight of accounting authority probably is to the effect that goodwill, when properly brought into the accounts, need not or should not be written off the books. One may briefly summarize the major points which might be given in support of this position.

First, it is overconservative to write goodwill off the books when it has not depreciated in value below the purchase price. To write off goodwill in such case creates a secret reserve. To recognize this reserve is thought to be unorthodox accounting.[7] Goodwill suffers no actual decline in value so long as the earning capacity of the enterprise is maintained.[8]

[5] Walter A. Staub, in *Contemporary Accounting* (New York: American Institute of Accountants, 1945), Chap. 8, p. 5. It should be noted that "customary practice" apparently kept the Institute committee from issuing an unequivocal statement on the amortization of goodwill and one in which logic is consistent with treatment of other assets.

[6] Charles B. Couchman, *The Balance Sheet* (New York: American Institute of Accountants, 1924), p. 138. See also Lawrence R. Dicksee and Frank Tillyard, *Goodwill and Its Treatment in Accounts* (4th ed.; London: Gee & Co., 1920), pp. 88–96; George O. May, *Financial Accounting* (New York: Macmillan Co., 1943), pp. 152–159.

[7] "To put on the books what is paid for goodwill purchased, however, is to show costs, and one must show what was got for what was given—unless, indeed, one wishes to charge some nominal account and thus create a secret reserve (which, of course, is bad accounting, for the purpose of accounting is not to hide the truth but to show it)." William M. Cole, *The Fundamentals of Accounting* (New York: Houghton Mifflin Co., 1921), p. 368.

"If profits have continued or increased, the goodwill value has not diminished; to write off the goodwill creates a secret reserve, understating the net worth and accumulated profits, a procedure that may be prejudicial to the interest of stockholders wishing to market their holdings." H. A. Finney, *Principles of Accounting* (Rev. ed.; New York: Prentice-Hall, Inc., 1934), Vol. I (Intermediate), p. 317. It is pertinent to note that Finney takes quite a different position in the 1946 edition of the same book; he agrees that it is logical to amortize purchased goodwill on a systematic basis. See 3rd edition, pp. 384–387.

[8] Thomas H. Sanders, Henry R. Hatfield, and Underhill Moore, *A Statement of Accounting Principles* (New York: American Institute of Accountants, 1938), p. 68.

Second, when goodwill has actually depreciated, it is not necessary to record that depreciation in the operating accounts. The degree to which goodwill exists is best shown by the profit-and-loss record. Its value fluctuates according to expected future earning possibilities of the enterprise. It is permissible to write goodwill off the books when it is declining in value or when it has lost its value, but amortization is not required.

Third, it is impossible to determine accurately the extent to which the goodwill has depreciated. This fact has been accepted by some accountants as one of the major reasons why it should not be brought into the accounts, unless purchased. The owner of a business cannot make an impartial estimate of the extent to which goodwill has depreciated. Consequently, since appreciation of goodwill is not recognized in the accounts, neither should depreciation be charged.

Opposing the group who say that purchased goodwill should not or need not be written off the books is a group of accountants, possibly a smaller group, who hold that goodwill should be amortized regardless of which way earnings fluctuate. Among these contentions, the treatises on the subject by Paton, Leake, Littleton, and Finney are especially commendable.

PATON THINKS GOODWILL SHOULD BE WRITTEN OFF

Paton makes the following significant statement:

> It is sometimes held that since the existence of intangibles depends upon earning power the cost or value of goodwill may be maintained on the books undisturbed so long as the level of income does not fall below that implicit in the original purchase or valuation. This position is objectionable in that it is inconsistent with the assumptions ordinarily made in determining the intangible value. If the amount of goodwill as acquired is conceived as the present worth of a terminable series of special incomes it would seem to follow that the asset should be written off against revenues through the period in which such incomes are expected to be realized.[9]

A part of the theory behind the quotation from Paton is brought out in a statement by Leake, as follows:

> It is urged against the writing off of the cost of goodwill—and often it is a fact—that the goodwill of a prosperous undertaking earning large surplus profits is worth no less now than it was when it was purchased ten or twenty years ago. The question is asked: "Why, therefore, should the goodwill be written off?" The answer is that the present goodwill is, in the main, not the goodwill which was bought ten or twenty years ago.[10]

The line of reasoning presented is made more complete by the following statement from Paton and Littleton:

> The cost of goodwill included in the purchase price of a going concern is essentially the discounted value of the estimated excess earning power—the amount of the net income anticipated in excess of income sufficient to clothe

---

[9] W. A. Paton, *Advanced Accounting* (New York: Macmillan Co., 1941), p. 435.
[10] P. D. Leake, *Commercial Goodwill* (2nd ed.; London: Pitman & Sons, Ltd., 1930), p. 77.

the tangible resources involved with a normal rate of return. Thus purchased goodwill represents an advance recognition of a debit for a portion of income that is expected to materialize later. It follows that the amount expended for goodwill should be absorbed by revenue charges—during the period implicit in the computation on which the price paid was based—in order that the income not paid for in advance may be measured.[11]

The viewpoint as represented by these quotations is to be distinguished from the view of those accountants who hold that goodwill should be written off as soon as current revenues and/or surplus balances are sufficient in amount to make the write-off feasible. This practice is unsound in theory and practice. Still, with only "custom" to support it, the practice prevails with many accountants as evidenced in corporation annual reports and as the following quotation indicates:

> The writing off of such intangible assets as goodwill evokes scarcely any protest, even when it is recognized that substantial goodwill exists. The general distrust of goodwill and the knowledge that it has been widely used to capitalize exaggerated expectations of future earnings leave an almost universal feeling that the balance-sheet looks stronger without it. When actual consideration has been paid for goodwill, it should appear on the company's balance-sheet long enough to create a record of that fact in the history of the company as presented in the series of its annual reports. After that, nobody seems to regret its disappearance when accomplished by methods which fully disclose the circumstances.[12]

The present writer contends that the cost of purchased goodwill should be written off or amortized on a systematic basis, without regard to the profitableness of the enterprise during a given year or even a period of years. At the time that goodwill is brought into the accounts, a decision should be made as to the length of period over which annual charges are to be made to operations. The method or plan of amortization can be as scientific or objective as any plan for charging depreciation on fixed tangible assets.

WHAT IS GOODWILL?

By definition, goodwill has no accounting significance except in terms of an earning capacity which is estimated to be above normal. A price is paid for goodwill—a price above the value placed on the other assets—because profits in excess of a normal return on the investment are anticipated. In other words, an enterprise is purchased, not primarily as a means of securing a group of assets, but as a means of securing a stream of income in the future. If the expected stream of income is a normal amount or at a normal rate, all factors considered, no payment is likely to be made for goodwill. If the expected income stream is in excess of normal earnings, a payment will probably have to be made for goodwill. Then, it may be said that the payment for the expected stream of income in excess of a normal return is a payment for goodwill, and that the payment for the ex-

---

[11] W. A. Paton and A. C. Littleton, *An Introduction to Corporate Accounting Standards* (Chicago: American Accounting Association, 1940), pp. 92–93. See also H. A. Finney, *Principles of Accounting, Intermediate* (3rd ed.; New York: Prentice-Hall, Inc., 1946), pp. 385–387.

[12] Sanders, Hatfield and Moore, *op. cit.*, p. 14.

pected stream of income equal to a normal return is a payment for the other assets.

Both of these payments represent charges against future income. Each payment represents a cost of future operation.[13] Since purchased goodwill is, by definition, the present worth of an anticipated future income stream, logic dictates that the cost be written off against the income over the period for which the excess earnings are expected to be realized. For example, if the purchase price placed on goodwill of $100,000 assumed an annual excess income of $10,000 for a period of ten years, goodwill should be amortized at the rate of $10,000 annually for a ten-year period.[14]

REASONS FOR SYSTEMATIC AMORTIZATION

In support of the systematic amortization of purchased goodwill and in partial explanation of the many conflicting and confusing pronouncements on goodwill write-offs, a few summaries may be made.

1. In accordance with a primary function of accounting to match costs and incomes, the cost of purchased goodwill should be amortized as a means of matching the cost of securing the income against the income actually received. All purchases, whether for advertising, stationery, buildings, machinery, employee services, goodwill, or the use of money or machinery, are made for the purpose of an income return greater than the output, or as an aid to that goal. The cost of these purchases is matched with that part of the income stream for which each cost is applicable. The matching is not in terms of the changed value of each of the assets.

2. In the past, accountants have often sanctioned the writing off of goodwill as one charge or as soon as earnings or surplus would permit, because goodwill, in terms of a worthwhile accounting concept, never existed or was not obtained through a bona fide purchase. This policy is still sound in cases where goodwill has been brought into the accounts without justifiable reason, but it is unsound with reference to the writing off of bona fide purchased goodwill.

3. The basis for the most confusion on the question of amortizing goodwill can be traced to the word "value." Though accounting is not a process of valuation, writers continue to reach conclusions with reference to the treatment of goodwill on the thesis that its present value has changed or has not changed.[15] Depreciation charges are not made in an attempt to show present value, but as

---

[13] Exception may be taken to this general statement in the case of land purchased for certain purposes.

[14] The procedure might be made more scientific if the $100,000 item is amortized by the compound-interest method of say 5 per cent per half-year for a ten-year period. It is doubtful, however, that usual practical circumstances require this refinement in calculating the amortization charges. Just as in calculating depreciation, straight-line, compound-interest, annuity, or other methods may be used. For an illustration of the use of the compound-interest method in amortizing goodwill, see W. A. Paton, *op. cit.*, p. 435.

[15] A type of erroneous reasoning which is easy to find in the literature of the field is the following: "While exact agreement with real values cannot be attained, yet accounts will be more respected in proportion as they avoid arbitrary or fictitious values, and reflect real values as nearly as possible."—Sanders, Hatfield, and Moore, *op. cit.*, p. 17. What is "real" value, anyway?

a means of allocating the cost of the asset over the period of its estimated usefulness. Goodwill amortization charges are of the same nature. The fact that the value of the building or the goodwill has increased during the year is beside the point. In general, asset values have skyrocketed during the past fifteen years, but this increasing of values did not eliminate the need for depreciation charges on buildings and the systematic amortization of purchased goodwill.

4. It has been argued that there is no scientific method for the amortization of goodwill, since it is impossible to determine accurately the extent to which goodwill exists or has depreciated. It is readily admitted that the purchase price of goodwill is based on an estimate of the value of future expectations. However, the same is true for the building, advertising, equipment, and all other items which are purchased. Likewise, practically all cost and income matching items are based on estimates. Any difference is one of degree and not of kind.

5. Accountants, as a rule, bring goodwill onto the books only when a purchase of that asset has been made, therefore they take the position that a firm should not bring goodwill into the accounts as it is created. According to this view, then, if the purchased goodwill has depreciated and a new goodwill has been built up, the new goodwill should not be allowed to appear as an asset because it is nonpurchased goodwill. And it is certain that goodwill does not exist in perpetuity. Owing to the operation of economic forces, excess earnings can never exist permanently. Purchased goodwill expires, sometimes very quickly. Management must always be making expenditures for the purpose of maintaining or increasing goodwill. The cost of the purchased goodwill which expires and the expenditures which are later made in an effort to maintain goodwill must ultimately be matched against income. Similarly, the original cost of a building and current repair and maintenance costs are matched against income over a period of years.

On writing off goodwill on a systematic basis as urged in this paper, or at irregular intervals, the question arises as to the account to be charged. When purchased goodwill is amortized on a periodic basis, what account should be debited and what account should be credited? When purchased goodwill is written off at irregular intervals or at one time, what accounts should be debited and credited? When nonpurchased goodwill is written off, what accounts should be debited and credited? The remainder of this discussion is devoted to a consideration of these problems.

QUESTION OF WHERE TO AMORTIZE GOODWILL

In view of the many conflicting and confusing statements which have already been referred to, it is not surprising that there is a difference of opinion on these questions. However, very few writers have considered the question of whether amortized goodwill should be charged to current profit and loss or to surplus directly.

Among those who believe that goodwill should be amortized directly to a surplus account are Sherwood and Culey, and Montgomery. Sherwood and Culey maintain that it should be written down through a "charge to surplus, not operating expenses, as such a charge has nothing to do with the cost of producing the product, whatever that product may be." [16] Montgomery says: "If any adjustment in the book amount of goodwill is made, the off-setting debit or credit should be to earned surplus or capital surplus, whichever is appropriate." [17]

On the other hand, Paton handles the cost as a revenue charge. Thus, he states:

> If it were possible to segregate the special layer of earnings as realized for which goodwill represents the amount paid the amortization charge would properly be assignable to such earnings. Since this is generally out of the question the periodic amortization should be included in expenses. . . .
>
> In any event the charge for amortization of goodwill should be clearly segregated in the income statement.[18]

Paton and Littleton say:

> It follows that the amount expended for goodwill should be absorbed by revenue charges—during the period implicit in the computation on which the price paid was based—in order that the income not paid for in advance may be measured.[19]

The 1943–1944 committee on accounting procedure makes the following policy statement:

> . . . the cost (of intangibles) may be amortized over a reasonable period of time, by systematic charges in the income statement. . . . Such amortization is within the discretion of the corporation and is not to be regarded as obligatory.
>
> . . . the committee recognizes that in the past it has been accepted practice to eliminate type (b) intangibles (including goodwill) by writing them off against any existing surplus, capital or earned, even though the value of the asset is unimpaired. Since the practice has been long established and widely approved, the committee does not feel warranted in recommending, at this time, adoption of a rule prohibiting such disposition. The committee believes, however, that such dispositions should be discouraged, especially if proposed to be effected by charges to capital surplus.[20]

Walter A. Staub, who served as chairman of the committee referred to above, quotes sections of the report, including those above, and comments as follows:

> . . . in the opinion of the writer, it is desirable that the amortization charge be set forth as a deduction from, or appropriation of, income after the net income from operations of the period is shown.[21]

---

[16] J. F. Sherwood and R. T. Culey, *Auditing Theory and Procedure* (Cincinnati: South-Western Publishing Co., 1940), p. 206.

[17] Montgomery, *op. cit.*, p. 273.

[18] W. A. Paton, Editor, *Accountants' Handbook* (3rd ed., New York: The Ronald Press Co., 1943), p. 850.

[19] Paton and Littleton, *op. cit.*, pp. 92–93.

[20] "Accounting for Intangible Assets," *Accounting Research Bulletin No. 24* (New York: American Institute of Accountants, December, 1944), p. 197.

[Para. 28 of APB Opinion No. 17 (superseded Chap. 5 of ARB No. 43 which superseded Bulletin No. 24) states that the cost of intangibles should not be written off in the period of acquisition. APB No. 17 also requires that the cost of all intangibles be amortized over a period to be determined by an analysis of all the factors but that the period may not exceed 40 years. Eds.]

CHARGE TO CURRENT OPERATIONS URGED

These references set forth the varying opinions on the treatment of amortization charges. Which procedure represents the best practice in theory? The present writer maintains that when purchased goodwill is being amortized according to a systematic plan, a charge to current operations is the only type of charge which is consistent with the definition and meaning of goodwill and the functions of accounting. The cost of the goodwill represents a cost of securing income in the same sense that the costs of machinery and rent are costs of securing income. The annual amortization charge should be matched with the income for the year in the same manner as other costs of current operation.

The suggested journal entry is:

    Goodwill amortization expense   xxx
        Allowance for amortization of goodwill   xxx
    (Annual charge—1/10 of original cost of goodwill)

In general practice the credit is made directly to the goodwill account instead of to an allowance or off-set account. Accountants universally recognize that it is preferable to credit a Reserve for Depreciation account instead of making the credit directly to the fixed tangible asset account. The same procedure should be followed with goodwill. It should be emphasized, however, that "allowance" is used in the suggested account title in preference to "reserve." The word "reserve" when used in this sense is a misnomer; the account is not intended to show that something has been reserved. The connotation of the word "allowance" is consistent with the facts.

REGULAR AMORTIZATION CHARGES NOT MADE

Many of the corporations which have amortized goodwill, purchased or non-purchased, have not followed a policy of making regular amortization charges, often amortizing a large or small amount depending upon the ability of net profits or surplus to bear large or small charge-offs. The adjustment of such a policy to conform with the recommendations in this paper may require that a portion of the charge be to current profit and loss and a portion to a surplus account. The writer is an advocate of a clean surplus statement. Typical entries are given below.

If, in correcting the failure to amortize goodwill in the past, goodwill is charged to surplus, one may naturally ask, to which surplus account should the charge be made? The origin of the goodwill determines whether the charge should be to Earned Surplus, Capital Surplus, or Revaluation Surplus.

DEBITING PURCHASED GOODWILL

Purchased goodwill that is written off to a surplus account should be debited to Earned Surplus.[22] Over the period in which purchased goodwill expires, its

---

[22] The writer recognizes that not all accountants classify surplus as shown above. *Capital* surplus is a misnomer, but still the term is commonly used. However, regardless of the classification or titles of the several surplus accounts, the charge should be to the surplus account into which current profit or loss is closed.

cost should be balanced off against the realized excess incomes, if any. Indirectly the Earned Surplus account is debited when amortization expense is brought on the income statement as an operating expense; therefore when amortization charges have not been made on a systematic basis to current income, any lump-sum charge made to the surplus account for the estimated amortization for a period of years should be to Earned Surplus.

Suggested entry types:

Earned Surplus	xxx	
Allowance for amortization of goodwill		xxx
(Goodwill which was not charged off during the period for which payment was made for expected excess profits.)		
Goodwill Amortization Expense	xxx	
Earned Surplus	xxx	
Allowance for amortization of goodwill		xxx
(Annual charge to expense—1/8 of original cost of goodwill; 5/8 to Earned Surplus, since annual charges were not made in five previous years; remaining 2/8 to be charged off in future—1/8 each of next two years.)		

If the amortization of nonpurchased goodwill is in question, a different procedure should be followed. If the nonpurchased goodwill should not have been brought into the accounts in the first place, as is likely the case, the entire amount should be written off immediately. The charge should be to the surplus or capital account that was credited when the goodwill was brought into the accounts.[23,b]

If there had been some compelling justification for bringing the nonpurchased goodwill into the accounts, it might be amortized systematically over the period implicit in the original valuation. Nonpurchased goodwill, like purchased goodwill, cannot exist in perpetuity. The charge-off of nonpurchased goodwill cannot be classified as a cost of operation, since there is no cost involved in the acquisition of such an item that is not otherwise included in the cost category. Any such charge should be to the account that was credited when the goodwill was brought into the accounts.

CONCLUSION

The stature of the accounting profession has grown remarkably in the minds of the general public in recent years. This growth has come in part from the successful efforts of the profession to rethink and to clarify its body of principles. The American Institute of Accountants, through its members and committees, has been primarily responsible for the progress which has been made in the evolution of a more acceptable body of principles. Probably because of the fact that goodwill is of relatively minor importance, the accounting treatment of goodwill has barely been touched by attempts to broaden the consistent application of accounting principles.

[23] "If appreciation has been recorded on the books, no matter under what title, it is proper to make write-downs against the account containing the appreciation to the amount of the appreciation included therein." Raymond P. Marple, *Capital Surplus and Corporate Net Worth* (New York: The Ronald Press Co., 1936), pp. 175, 117–118.

[b] See editors addition, footnote 20.

The Institute's Bulletin No. 24 was a step in the right direction, but the committee apparently permitted "customary practice" to outweigh logic and consistency. A statement in the accountant's certificate to the effect that "generally accepted accounting principles" have been applied is meaningless in so far as goodwill is concerned. The present writer suggests that there should be a "rethinking" of the whole question of the amortization of goodwill and revision of Bulletin 24.

RELATED READINGS

This section deals not only with goodwill and other intangible assets but also with the general subject of accounting for business combinations. The existence of goodwill for accounting purposes uniquely depends on the choice between the "purchase" and "pooling of interests" interpretation of a merger or acquisition, although it is suggested by some that even in a "purchase" situation, goodwill should be subtracted from stockholders' equity. The subject of human resource accounting is also covered by readings in this section.

Robert Beyer, "Goodwill and Pooling of Interests: A Re-assessment," *Management Accounting* (US), February, 1969, pp. 9–15; reprinted in *Touche Ross Tempo*, March, 1969, pp. 18–27.

Abraham J. Briloff, "Distortions Arising from Pooling-of-interests Accounting," *Financial Analysts Journal*, March–April, 1968, pp. 71–80.

———, "The 'Funny-money' Game," *Financial Analysts Journal*, May–June, 1969, pp. 73–79. How to buy without paying.

Ronald M. Copeland and Joseph F. Wojdak, "Valuation of Unrecorded Goodwill in Merger-minded Firms," *Financial Analysts Journal*, September–October, 1969, pp. 57–62.

Leonard S. Douglas, "Quasi-Pooling," *LKHH Accountant*, Spring, 1970, pp. 7–9. A new approach to pooling.

Nabil Elias, "Some Aspects of Human Resource Accounting," *Cost and Management*, November–December, 1971, pp. 38–41.

Samuel P. Gunther, "The Current Status of Accounting for Mergers and Acquisitions," *LKHH Accountant*, March, 1968, pp. 11–15.

———, "Part Purchase–Part Pooling: The Infusion of Confusion into Fusion," *The New York Certified Public Accountant*, April, 1969, pp. 241–249.

———, "Poolings–Purchases–Goodwill," *The New York Certified Public Accountant*, January, 1971, pp. 25–37. A critical analysis of APB Opinions 16 and 17.

David Perry Harmon, Jr., "Pooling of Interests: A Case Study," *Financial Analysts Journal*, March–April, 1968, pp. 82–88.

Homer Kripke, "Accounting for Corporate Acquisitions and the Treatment of Goodwill: An Alert Signal to All Business Lawyers," *The Business Lawyer*, November, 1968, pp. 89–114.

Baruch Lev and Aba Schwartz, "On the Use of the Economic Concept of Human Capital in Financial Statements," *The Accounting Review*, January, 1971, pp. 103–112. See the later exchange between Eric G. Flamholtz and the authors, *The Accounting Review*, January, 1972, pp. 148–154.

A. T. McLean, *Accounting for Business Combinations and Goodwill* (Edinburgh: The Institute of Chartered Accountants of Scotland, 1972), 85 pp. A Scottish Institute research study.

Samuel A. Martin, Stanley N. Laiken, and Douglas F. Haslam, *Business Combinations in the 60's: A Canadian Profile* (The Canadian Institute of Chartered Accountants and The School of Business Administration, University of Western Ontario, [1970]), 87 pp.

Shaun F. O'Malley, "Accounting for a Purchased Business," *The Price Water-*

adequate. The problem is that statement users are not able to place a value on lease obligations owing to the insufficiency of published information. At the present time, Axelson writes, "The lack of generally accepted methods of estimation and lack of detailed information on leases opens the way for substantial errors in judgment." He argues that the conservatism of creditors results in a bias against companies which use leases extensively to finance property rights. Penney's approach is to report its estimate of the present value of all future minimum payments as the value of its obligation arising from property rights being used by the company. This amount is considered the equivalent of unamortized mortgage debt. The major problem of accounting for leases is, in Axelson's opinion, one of measurement.

The second major problem facing accountants in the liability category is the treatment accorded deferred federal income taxes. This problem arises because of provisions in the Internal Revenue Code which permit taxpayers to include certain items in the determination of taxable income in periods different from those in which these same items are included in the determination of accounting net income. The definition of a liability expressed by Moonitz is very important to this discussion. There appears to be no legal basis for arguing that a tax deferred in this manner is an obligation of the enterprise prior to the year in which the law requires the payment to be made.

Sidney Davidson does not rely upon legal considerations to support his case for not recognizing a liability arising from the deferral of taxes. Instead, he argues that the timing differences are not, in reality, temporary. They do not reverse, but rather the differences become permanent. He bases his case on the aggregate balance concept, arguing that the growth or maintenance of the enterprise's stock of depreciable assets will result in a perpetual deferral of the tax obligation. In effect, therefore, the deferral is converted into a tax reduction. This concept, he argues, is consistent with the going concern assumption.

Thomas F. Keller, an advocate of tax allocation, argues that the income tax is a levy on the business income of the corporation. When the income is earned, a liability for the payment of the tax accrues. The *payment* of the tax may be delayed under any number of specific circumstances; however, a strict application of the accrual concept requires that the expense and the corresponding liability be recognized. Contrary to Davidson's thesis, the argument does not depend on any particular pattern of economic activity. Payment of the tax depends on a reversal of the timing difference which gave rise to the deferral in the first place. The aggregate balance of the deferred tax liability is important only insofar as it represents the sum of the tax payments deferred and as yet unpaid.

A. PROBLEM OF DEFINITION

THE CHANGING CONCEPT OF LIABILITIES

MAURICE MOONITZ
Biography on page 263.

Apparently the concept of liabilities is undergoing a change. We have seen a great deal of activity recently involving the credit side of the balance sheet. For example, recent years have seen a great deal of discussion concerning the reflection of deferred taxes, the proper disclosure of pension costs, and the short but significant life of "reserves for estimated expenses" in the 1954 Internal Revenue Code. In the discussions of these and related topics, there seems to be a lack of rigorous separation between the debit and credit aspects of the transaction under scrutiny. The impression remains that most of the thought and analysis has gone into the determination of the debit, the charge to income, with the credit introduced as an afterthought. Some indication is also at hand of "bootstrap lifting," that is to say, the practice of introducing expenses or other charges into the determination of income without first analyzing the situation to determine whether or not an asset has been used up, or a liability incurred. As a result, we see fairly frequently the spectacle of expenses paired off with credits to some element of proprietary interest.

Problems of this type are not new, of course, since they are merely one aspect of the continuing problem of the relationship between the balance sheet and the income statement. But the number of examples appears to be increasing, and their importance is definitely on the upgrade. The problem of definition is explored at some length later, but here we note that current usage is clearly not able to cope with the situation. For example, we cannot agree as to whether a "deferred tax" is a real tax or not, and if it is, whether it is to be shown as a liability or "netted" against an asset. All liabilities are indeed "credits" in the balance sheet, but some credits (e.g., allowance for depreciation, allowance for bad debts) are not liabilities. As a result, we need some way to tell us which credits belong under liabilities and which do not.

These reasons seem sufficient to justify an inquiry into the nature of that which we call liabilities. Of even more importance, however, is the question as to whether we are prepared to cope with new problems as they arise, problems which will involve, among other things, some answer to the question of the presence or absence of a liability.

THE DIVERSITY OF LIABILITIES

As reported in *Accounting Trends and Techniques,* the following items have appeared as liabilities, so labeled, in recent published financial statements, under

SOURCE: From *The Journal of Accountancy,* Vol. CIX, No. 5 (May, 1960), pp. 41–46. Reprinted by permission of the American Institute of Certified Public Accountants.

a caption which clearly excluded them from proprietary elements. I am responsible for the classification employed below; it is clearly designed with an eye to the discussion which follows. The specific examples under each class are taken from recent editions of *Accounting Trends and Techniques;* I have merely paraphrased the account titles reproduced literally in that source:

(A) cases involving an outlay of cash in the near future: (1) estimated collection costs on receivables; (2) additional costs on completed contracts; (3) estimated additional costs under a performance-guarantee clause; (4) estimated costs of product or service guarantee

(B) cases involving part of an outlay in the near future: estimated loss on purchase commitments

(C) cases involving a future outlay under certain conditions: estimated sales returns and allowances

(D) cases involving future outlays, current and noncurrent: payments under a leasehold contract

(E) cases involving a possible future outlay: deferred Federal tax on income including the case of the deferred tax on installment sales

(F) cases involving financing arrangements: billings on uncompleted contracts

(G) cases involving items that are probably not liabilities at all: (1) reserve for self-insurance; (2) minority interest in a consolidated balance-sheet; (3) reserve for furnace rebuilding and relining; (4) reserve for repairs

The diversity and variety of "liabilities" listed above raise a real question as to the common thread or threads which hold them together. Later in this article we submit a framework to hold most of them.

We are not directly concerned with the question of whether liabilities include some forms of capital stock. Most of the issues involved in this inquiry would still exist even if we included all proprietorship in the liability category. We will assume, however, that a distinction between liabilities and proprietorship is made, as in fact it is in most published statements. Whether or not preferred stock is better treated as a liability than as a proprietary element becomes a secondary matter. The only necessary condition for our purposes is that someone outside the entity itself owns the residual interest.

We may decide that some of the items listed above are not really liabilities under any acceptable definition of liabilities. Certainly a revenue agent would take this position. The following propositions may help as a point of departure in discussion of the reasons for lack of agreement on what constitutes a liability. (These propositions are based on some material in Dohr, Thompson, and Warren, *Accounting and the Law*):

1. Based upon experience, accountants for the most part assume "normal" developments in the future in assessing the presence and magnitude of debts. For example, accountants assume ordinarily that contracts entered into will be honored by the participants, as in fact they are in most cases. Breach of contract is not contemplated as normal or usual. The "allowance for bad debts" measures our estimate of the extent to which this assumption is inaccurate.

2. Lawyers, in the nature of their profession, must be concerned primarily with what happens if participants do *not* live up to their agreements or, what

amounts to the same thing analytically, disagree as to the meaning of the contracts made. As a consequence, the law (to the extent that it is influenced by this attitude) tends to recognize debts only when a rather rigorous set of conditions has been satisfied.

3. The income tax is influenced greatly by both law and accounting but, in addition, must recognize the demands of administration. For example, certainty and accuracy of income and of deductions may be more important than the equity of the results. Also, income tax rules and regulations must always be influenced by the Treasury's interest in protection of the revenues.

WEAKNESSES IN PRESENT DEFINITIONS

If we compare various definitions of liabilities, some surprising results emerge, enough so to reinforce our hunch that the concept is neither simple nor well-understood.

Accounting Terminology Bulletins: Review and Resumé, published by the American Institute of Certified Public Accountants in 1953, covers the topic as follows:

> Similarly, in relation to a balance sheet, *liability* may be defined as follows:
> "Something represented by a credit balance that is or would be properly carried forward upon a closing of books of account according to the rules or principles of accounting, provided such credit balance is not in effect a negative balance applicable to an asset. Thus the word is used broadly to comprise not only items which constitute liabilities in the popular sense of debts or obligations (including provision for those that are unascertained), but also credit balances to be accounted for which do not involve the debtor and creditor relation. For example, capital stock and related or similar elements of proprietorship are balance-sheet liabilities in that they represent balances to be accounted for, though these are not liabilities in the ordinary sense of debts owed to legal creditors."
>
> Consideration of the facts noted in the last sentence of this definition has led some accountants to the view that the aggregate of *liabilities* as contemplated in this definition should be referred to as the aggregate of *liabilities and capital*, and that the balance sheet consists of an asset section, a liability section, and a proprietary or capital section, with the monetary amounts represented by the first shown as equal to the sum of those represented by the other two. The committee feels that there is no inconsistency between this view and the suggested definition (pages 13–14).

This definition says in effect that if you want to know what a liability is, ask an accountant. But I am an accountant, and you are an accountant. Whom do we ask?

Kohler (*A Dictionary for Accountants*, 1952) defines "liability" as:

> 1. An amount owing by one person (a debtor) to another (a creditor), payable in money, or in goods or services; the consequence of an asset or service received or a loss incurred; particularly, any debt (a) due or past due (current liability), (b) due at a specified time in the future (e.g., funded debt, accrued liability), or (c) due only on failure to perform a future act (deferred income; contingent liability).

The Committee on Concepts and Standards of the American Accounting Association (1957 Revision) discusses liabilities under the general category of "equities":

The interests or equities of creditors (liabilities) are claims against the entity arising from past activities, or events which, in the usual case, require for their satisfaction the expenditure of corporate resources. . . . Equities should be accorded accounting recognition in the period in which money, goods, or services are received or obligations incurred, and should be measured initially by the agreed cash consideration or its equivalent. The elimination of an equity should be recognized in the period in which it ceases to exist.

This definition is fairly loose. The one point worthy of comment at this time is that the Committee apparently identifies "liabilities" with "creditors." Since the determination of who is a creditor and who is a debtor is entirely a legal matter, the Committee apparently clings closely to the law to determine what should and what shouldn't go into the liability section of the balance sheet.

Corpus Juris Secundum summarizes the legal attitude in Vol. 53, p. 17:

The term (liability) has been variously defined as meaning amenability, or responsibility to law; . . . the state of being bound or obliged in law or justice to do, pay, or make good something; . . . the state or condition of one who is under obligation to do at once or at some future time something which may be enforced by action. (*White* v. *Green,* 105 Iowa 181, 74 N.W. 929 adds: "It may exist without the right of immediate enforcement.") It is a condition which creates a duty to perform an act.

In a restricted sense, liability is that which one is under obligation to pay to another, that for which one is responsible or liable; that which one is under obligation to pay, or for which one is liable; one's pecuniary obligations, or debts collectively.

The first paragraph of this legal definition is surprisingly broad. If, however, we look for a legal definition of "debt," the picture changes.

. . . debt may generally be identified as an obligation to pay a fixed sum of money on a definite determinable date (with the right to enforce payment by some appropriate legal remedy) plus interest even when not earned. ("Not earned" by the debtor, I presume.) George S. Hills, *The Law of Accounting and Financial Statements* (Boston, 1957) pages 119–20.

The "restricted" definition of *Corpus Juris Secundum* and the "debt" of Hills are close in tenor to Kohler. Apparently most accountants have used "debt" as a synonym for "liability" and have therefore been constrained by the legal tests necessary to establish a debt. Not all accountants, obviously; among the examples cited at the outset, liability under leasehold contracts is clearly a "debt" in the legal sense. And yet this is the one case where most accountants will ordinarily not reflect the item at all in a balance sheet.

Vatter's definition is clearly an "accounting" definition and far from the legal concept of "debt."

As distinct from the notions of obligation or legal liability, equities are restrictions upon, or reservations that apply to the assets of the fund; they may arise from legal, equitable, economic, or even managerial considerations. Although some equities are removed by the process of disbursement, they may be discharged or they may disappear for a considerable number of reasons. . . . (Vatter, *Fund Theory of Accounting,* page 95.)

This excursion into the world of definition leaves us with a tentative conclusion—as a minimum, all items which meet the legal tests for "debt" qualify without further ado also as "liabilities." But the legal test does not establish the outer limits of the concept for accountants, either in theory or in practice. We need agreement on the area we do wish to include in the notion of liability. Ideally a definition of "liabilities" should enable us to do several things. For one thing, we should be able, by its use, to tell (a) whether all items labeled as "liabilities" in financial statements really deserve that label, (b) which of two or more alternative practices with respect to a liability is the correct one, and (c) whether financial events described in footnotes or elsewhere really should be reflected in the balance sheet itself. Of equal importance, a definition should enable us to analyze new situations as they arise in the future to determine if a liability element is present. We need this predictive feature to give continuity to what we do, and to reduce our need for and reliance on authoritative pronouncements issued after two or more alternative treatments have already been adopted.

CHARACTERISTICS OF A LIABILITY

The following four characteristics will serve as a starter to establish an accounting definition of liabilities:

1. A liability involves a future outlay of money, or an equivalent acceptable to the recipient.
2. A liability is the result of a transaction of the past, not of the future. "Transaction" is used here in its primary sense of an event involving at least two accounting entities—an "external transaction."

"Transactions" encompass the following types of financial events: (a) The receipt of money from someone outside the enterprise; (b) the payment of money to someone outside the enterprise; (c) the acquisition of goods or services—materials, supplies, power, services of human beings of all types and grades, equipment, land, mineral deposits, leaseholds, etc.; (d) sales of goods or services of all types; (e) lending and borrowing of money on a short- or long-term basis; (f) the imposition and collection of taxes.

Accruals of all sorts are omitted from this list; so are the amortization of costs, as well as all "internal transactions" such as the transfer of work in process to finished goods. These accruals, amortizations, and transfers, however, are all consequences of the transactions listed above, and hence fit into the picture neatly as arising from past events. What do not fit in so neatly are events that have not yet occurred, e.g., next month's payroll, next year's purchase of fixed assets, next quarter's borrowings against a bond issue, etc. Therefore, none of these future events will qualify as a liability under this second characteristic.

3. The amount of the liability must be the subject of calculation or of close estimation. This condition is true generally of all accounting entries and is not restricted to liabilities. Accounting Research Bulletin No. 47,[a] issued in September, 1956, presents excellent material in this connection. After some intro-

---

[a] ARB No. 47 has been superseded by APB Opinion No. 8, "Accounting for the Cost of Pension Plans" (November, 1966). The objective of APB No. 8 is to "clarify the accounting principles and to narrow the practices applicable to accounting for the cost of pension plans." (para. 6) [Eds.]

ductory remarks, the committee states in paragraph 4 that "because of these factors, the total cost of the pensions that will be paid ultimately to the present participants in a plan cannot be determined precisely in advance, but, by the use of actuarial techniques, reasonably accurate estimates can be made. There are other business costs for which it is necessary to make periodic provisions in the accounts based upon assumptions and estimates. The committee believes that the uncertainties relating to the determination of pension costs are not so pronounced as to preclude similar treatment."

And in paragraph 5: "In the view of many, the accrual of costs under a pension plan should not necessarily be dependent on the funding arrangements provided for in the plan or governed by a strict legal interpretation of the obligations under the plan." In other words, let the pension costs be a function of the operating factors to which they relate. Use of the legal definition of debt, however, is relied on in one recommendation of the committee (paragraph 7): ". . . for the present, the committee believes that, as a minimum, the accounts and financial statements should reflect accruals which equal the present worth, actuarially calculated, of pension commitments to employees to the extent that pension rights have vested in the employees, reduced, in the case of the balance sheet, by any accumulated trusteed funds or annuity contracts purchased."

4. Double-entry is taken for granted. If, for example, we do wish to consider the presence and influence of *future* purchases of depreciable assets, for any reason, we should consider the obligation to pay for the blamed things.

RELIANCE ON INCOME EFFECT

One feature both of accounting practice and of accounting theory at the present time is the heavy reliance on the "income effect" to decide whether an item is admissible to the liability section or not. Items which apparently clearly qualify as *debts* are often omitted because their presence or absence will not affect current profits or retained earnings. The leading example here is the case of executory contracts, e.g., leaseholds. Ray Dein comments approvingly on this practice of making the balance sheet dance to the tune of the income statement in the July, 1958 issue of the *Accounting Review* ("The Future Development of Accounting Theory"). Dein quotes Pixley's 1908 book on this point (see page 391 of the *Accounting Review*).

FRAGMENTATION IN STATEMENTS

One interesting manifestation in present-day accounting of this reliance on the "income effect" is the presence of fragments in the statements. Take, for example, the "reserve for estimated loss on purchase commitments." The "loss" is not the debt—presumably we owe the full amount contracted for. Literally the "loss" is the estimated amount of damages to be paid if we breach the contract. But we don't need this type of fragmentation. If we introduce into our double-entry system both the asset (goods on order) and the liability (accounts payable for goods on order), we have no problem with respect to the liability. The asset problem then becomes a problem in inventory valuation and might be solved, for example, by application of the cost-or-market rule. Under this type of analysis, the exceptional nature of the purchase commitment case disappears.

Profit calculation is certainly an important function of present-day accounting, perhaps even the most important single function it can perform. But we shouldn't concentrate exclusively on that aspect to the detriment of everything we do or could do.

Remaining examples. Let us now discuss the specific examples listed at the beginning of this article. We will use the four characteristics previously set up to test each example. These four characteristics are as follows: (1) future outlay of money or its equivalent; (2) result of a transaction of the past; (3) subject to reliable estimation; and (4) part of a double-entry system.

All of the cases involving an outlay of cash in the near future qualify as liabilities under the tests laid down. Estimates of collection costs, of additional costs on completed contracts, and of costs under various types of guarantees involve future outlays of money, clearly result from past transactions, are the subject of close estimation, and are parts of a double-entry system. The case of the estimated loss on purchase commitments has been discussed already, under the heading of "reliance on income effect."

The case of estimated sales returns and allowances is an interesting one. If a refund is to be made, the item is clearly a liability of the sort we are talking about. If instead the allowance merely reduces the amount to be collected from the customer, it is analogous to the allowance for bad debts, and should be so classified in a balance sheet.

The outlays under leasehold contracts clearly qualify as a liability not only under the definition developed in this article, but also under the legal definitions. As a matter of fact, an old case (1903) in Kentucky states the legal principle quite well. A tenant leased a storehouse for a term of five years at a fixed rental per month. After eighteen months, the tenant failed. The court was asked to decide if the rent for the remaining forty-two months was a debt of the tenant at the date it failed. The court held that the contract was a liability. (*Hyatt* v. *Anderson's Trustee*, Ct. of Appeals of Ky., 1903. 74 S.W. 1094.) In recent years warnings have been sounded from many quarters concerning the omission of a substantial debt from the balance sheets of companies leasing properties. But accountants blithely move on, with no trace of the leasehold in the statement of financial position itself.

DEFERRED TAXES

The wisdom of reflecting "deferred taxes" in our financial statements has been widely debated recently in *The Journal of Accountancy* and the *Accounting Review*, among other journals, although the practice itself is becoming more firmly imbedded in published statements as time moves on. Based on our own criteria, we arrive at the conclusion that if they exist at all, these deferred taxes involve a future outlay of money. They also definitely arise out of transactions of the past engaged in by a going concern; they fit into the framework of double-entry. On the basis of reliability of estimate, however, we must walk circumspectly. The strongest case for the allocation of taxes is made in situations such as the ones discussed in ARB 43, page 92,[b] on "disclosure of certain differences between taxable and ordinary income."

[b] ARB No. 43 has been superseded by APB Opinion No. 11, "Accounting for Income Taxes" (December, 1967).

If, because of differences between accounting for tax and accounting for financial purposes, no income tax has been paid or provided as to certain significant amounts credited to surplus or to income, disclosure should be made. However, if a tax is likely to be paid thereon, provision should be made on the basis of an estimate of the amount of such tax. This rule applies, for instance, to profits on installment sales or long-term contracts which are deferred for tax purposes, and to cases where unrealized appreciation of securities is taken into the accounts by certain types of investment companies.

These cases are strong because the probability is high that revenues already realized or recognized in the accounts will be taxed in some year or years. If they have not been declared for tax purposes, but deferred, then the tax on that amount of revenue is almost certain to be paid. The probabilities are somewhat less where we have taken a deduction for tax purposes greater than that shown on our financial statements. We have thereby received the benefit under the law; whether we ever will suffer a corresponding burden later on depends, among other things, on the generation of revenues in the future. To forecast future revenues is riskier than to forecast a tax payment on revenues already in hand.

"Billings on uncompleted contracts" meets the tests laid down for a liability if we interpret these billings as advances by the customer to finance the contract. In such a case, the liability will be worked off by refund of cash, or, more usually, by delivery of the completed product to the customer. Furthermore, under this interpretation, the liability consists of the total amount billed or billable; any costs incurred to date are analogous to work in process, and belong among the assets of the enterprise. If, however, this amount of billings is an excess of billings over related costs, it is an "unrealized profit" less applicable income taxes and hence belongs with the proprietary elements, not with the liabilities. Traditionally, with the possible exception of appraisal surplus, we have put only "realized" gains in proprietorship; this has forced us to put the "unrealized" elements somewhere else. But they don't fit anywhere else in the statement of financial position. Observe that this analysis indicated that the net amount of the excess of billings over related costs does not belong among liabilities, whatever the interpretation of the credit balance may be. If the customer has advanced funds, the gross amount is the liability; if the customer has made partial payment against work which has been completed, the net amount is a proprietary element.

We now come to the group which will not meet the tests for a liability. A "reserve for self-insurance" represents a possible future transaction which may never take place; it is not the result of a past one. The fact that I own a building does not doom me to suffer a loss by fire in whole or in part in any year or succession of years. My failure to make an outlay last year for insurance premiums does not create an obligation to pay out anything to anyone this year or next or the year after that. If a "reserve for self-insurance" has to exist in the statements, it should not be booked through income at all, but only through an earmarking of retained earnings.

The minority interest in a consolidated balance sheet reflects the interest of a group of proprietors, the owners of a piece of one of the constituent elements of the consolidated group. No one is obligated to pay anything to anyone at any time for this alleged liability. To whom are the checks to be issued? By whom will the money be paid? Who sues whom if the payments are not forthcoming?

This minority interest is clearly a proprietary element and should not be forced into the liability category.

Reserves for furnace rebuilding and relining, or for repairs of any type do not qualify either. True, they represent outlays in the future which can be estimated with a high degree of accuracy, but they represent a future transaction, not one of the past. When we rebuild or reline a furnace, we have incurred a cost to be amortized against the subsequent periods of use; we have not paid off an obligation accumulating from past periods. The real problem here is the proper classification of the asset involved, not the determination of a liability. If, for example, we set up the lining of the furnace as a separate asset, amortize it over its useful life, then retire it and show its replacement as a new asset, we have no problem with respect to liabilities. This procedure will probably give us the same effect on income as the "liability reserve" technique, but a better balance sheet will emerge if we treat these cases as involving assets. Instead of fighting to get the "reserve for repairs" recognized as a liability item, which it is not, we should fight for better classification on the asset side and better amortization procedure with respect to the related costs.

CONCLUSION

Relatively speaking, the problems relating to liabilities are simpler than those relating to assets. But the growth of situations in which future obligations loom more and more important in financial position and the underlying acceptance of accrual accounting have increased the importance and the difficulty of the liability section of the balance sheet. By a more rigorous use of double-entry reasoning, and by less reliance on short-term expediency, we can make progress to improve the balance sheet and move it away from its technical function as a post-closing trial balance to its more significant function as a statement of financial position.

B. LONG-TERM LEASES

GORDON SHILLINGLAW

GORDON SHILLINGLAW (1925–), B.A. 45 Brown; M.S. 48 Rochester; Ph.D. 52 Harvard. Currently professor of accounting, Columbia University. Major publications: *Cost Accounting: Analysis and Control* (1961, 1967); *Accounting: A Management Approach* (with Gordon, 1964, 1969). Contributor to handbooks, *The Accounting Review, Journal of Accounting Research*, and other publications.

Was on the faculties of the University of Rochester, 1947–48; Harvard University, 1949–51; Hamilton College, 1951–52; and Massachusetts Institute of Technology, 1955–61, prior to joining the Columbia faculty. Was professor at the IMEDE management development institute, Lausanne, Switzerland, 1964–65 and 1967–69. Served as vice-president of the American Accounting Association, 1966–67.

Principal research interest: developing a standard set of basic principles underlying cost accounting and internal financial reporting systems.

LEASING AND FINANCIAL STATEMENTS*

GORDON SHILLINGLAW

The growth of leasing as a means of financing corporate requirements for plant and equipment has imposed on the accounting staff the task of studying the profitability of lease and sale-leaseback proposals. In applying the techniques of differential cost analysis and time discounting of future cash flows the analyst has had to abandon the idea that annual rentals are simply another kind of annual operating cost. He has had to recognize the fact that the alternative to leasing is ownership, the necessary funds for purchase of ownership rights to be provided from sources generally available to the company.

For purposes of a simple lease-or-buy analysis, ownership costs can be divided

---

* Thomas M. Hill, Myron J. Gordon and Tsvi Ophir of the School of Industrial Management, M.I.T., made many helpful comments on earlier drafts of this paper.

SOURCE: From *The Accounting Review*, Vol. XXXIII, No. 4 (October, 1958), pp. 581–592. Reprinted by permission of the American Accounting Association.

436   NATURE OF LIABILITIES

into two categories, one representing depreciation of the facilities and the other reflecting the cost of funds used to acquire and support continued ownership of the property. Viewed in this light, it is clear that part of the annual rental is actually a financial expense and not a cost of the facilities as such. The remainder of the rental may be regarded as a partial repayment of the "loan" represented by the lessor's advance of the purchase price of the property, roughly similar in concept to depreciation of acquisition costs.

This has raised two questions for the accountant in preparing financial statements for public reporting and possibly for internal reporting as well. First, should the financial expense component of the rental payment be segregated from the repayment-amortization portion? Second, should some recognition be made on the balance sheet of the company's contractual liability for future payments under the lease? The purpose of this paper is to examine these questions and to propose a method for bringing accounting reports into line with the economic facts of the lease.

ANALYZING THE LEASE–OR–BUY PROBLEM

A decision to lease a building or piece of equipment is a decision to forego a current cash outlay for the purchase of rights to use the property and instead to substitute a series of future cash payments during the period of the lease. If the property is purchased, the cash payment gives the purchaser an infinite series of user rights. If the property is leased, on the other hand, the rights cease at the termination of the lease contract. In analyzing the lease proposition, therefore, any value attached to user rights after the end of the lease term must be treated as a cost of the lease.

To illustrate, assume that a building can be purchased for $1,000,000 or leased for 30 years at an annual rental of $85,295. All costs of operating, maintaining and insuring the building will be paid by the user whether he leases or buys. The estimated resale value of the building at the end of 30 years is $400,000. To simplify the presentation, all calculations will be performed without provision for income tax effects, although in practice the effect of differential tax payments must be considered. The time table of differential cash flows is as follows (minus signs indicate cash outlays):

Period	Buy	Lease	Buy—Lease
0	−$1,000,000		−$1,000,000
1		−$ 85,295	+ 85,295
2		− 85,295	+ 85,295
.		.	.
.		.	.
.		.	.
30		− 85,295	+ 85,295
Salvage	+ 400,000		+ 400,000
Total	−$ 600,000	−$2,558,850	+$1,958,850

This time table dramatizes the nature of the lease. By agreeing to a series of future payments and relinquishing rights to any end-of-lease residual values, the lessee can avoid a current expenditure of $1,000,000. Or, to put it the other way around, by purchasing now the buyer can avoid the payment of $85,295 a year for 30 years and can retain the rights to any residual value at the end of that time.

The cost of leasing (or, alternatively, the rate of return resulting from ownership) can be computed by finding the interest rate that will discount the total of the future outlays to a present value equal to $1,000,000. The rate that will do this in the example above is 8%. This can then be compared with the cost of funds from other sources, one of which may be to forego certain internal investment projects in order to provide the funds for purchase of the building.

Once the lease is negotiated, the lessee assumes a responsibility for future payments. This responsibility gives rise to a liability of the lessee, a liability that is not now reflected on the balance sheet under currently-accepted accounting practice. At best, annual rentals and the number of leased properties are indicated in a footnote to published financial statements. Many companies do not report the existence of leases at all. The remainder of this paper is concerned with finding a way of incorporating the facts of outstanding leases into financial statements, following principles now in use for other liabilities of the firm.

LEASE CAPITALIZATION FOR BETTER REPORTING

Accounting for Long-term Debt

Because leasing may be regarded as a method of debt financing, we should look at methods of accounting for long-term debt for indications of how leases might be handled on the financial statements. When rights to the use of property are obtained through purchase with funds provided by borrowing, the asset is capitalized at cost and the liability is valued at the net proceeds of the sale of the issue. (For purposes of this discussion we can assume that the net proceeds from the borrowing are equal to the purchase price of the property.)

In many cases bond discount is shown on the asset side of the balance sheet, either as a separate item or included with deferred charges, and the face value of the bonds outstanding is shown on the liability side of the balance sheet. Most accounting textbooks recommend, however, that bond discount be shown as a contra account to face value on the balance sheet. Under this treatment the balance sheet liability at the date of borrowing is equal, by definition, to the present worth of the future payments under the bond indenture, discounted at the effective yield rate of the specific bond issue. For example, if a $10,000,000 issue of 5%, 20 year bonds is sold for net proceeds of $9,398,000, the cost or yield rate is the rate that will discount future payments of interest and repayment of principal to a present value of $9,398,000, or 5.5% in this example. Turned another way around, the effective liability of $9,398,000 can be found by discounting future interest payments of $250,000 every six months for 20 years and $10,000,000 20 years from now, at a discount rate of 5.5%.

In the case of the self-amortizing loan, similar to the ordinary home mortgage loan in common use today, a fixed sum is paid each period during the term of the loan, this sum to pay interest and a partial repayment of the principal of the loan. For example, if $10,000,000 is borrowed at an interest rate of 5%, annual payments of approximately $802,427 for 20 years will be sufficient to repay the loan and pay 5% interest on the unpaid balance each year. During the first year $500,000 of this payment is interest and the remaining $302,427 is repayment of principal. During the second year, the unpaid balance is only $9,697,573 ($10,000,000 less $302,427) and the interest component of the annual payment is thus only $484,879, leaving $317,548 for reduction of the liability. The effective interest rate is 5% through the period of the loan and the effective liability is gradually reduced. The final payment of $802,427 at the end of 20 years will consist of $764,216 liquidation of the debt and $38,211 interest on the debt outstanding during the final year.

Looking at this transaction from the other end, the present effective liability can be computed by discounting the 20 future payments of $802,427 each at an interest rate of 5%. The present worth of this annuity is $10,000,000, which is the amount borrowed.

The Liability Value of Lease Debt

Borrowing by means of a lease is quite similar to the self-amortizing loan. At the beginning of the lease the lessee has the right to use facilities equivalent to a given sum of money. He agrees to pay a fixed sum to the lessor each year during the term of the lease. When the lease expires he no longer has any debt and he no longer has any right to use any of the money originally borrowed. The difference between the two situations, of course, is that the lease instrument does not specify a rate of interest, nor does it state the amount of funds initially provided by the lessor. These amounts must be computed from the facts of the transaction.

As in the case of the self-amortizing loan, the amount of the liability is the present worth of the future payments under the contract, discounted at the effective rate of interest in that specific liability.[1] The effective interest rate in a lease is equal to the cost rate or rate of return that we found by analyzing the relationship among alternative purchase price, annual lease payments and end-of-lease residual value. This is the cost of the funds borrowed and this is the rate at which future lease payments should be discounted to determine effective liability at the inception of the lease. In our example, the rate was 8% and the liability for 30 future payments of $85,295 each is $960,240.

Of the items that enter into the calculation of the effective rate, current purchase price and end-of-lease salvage value are not specific elements in the formal contract and must be estimated. In a sale-leaseback transaction, of course, the sale price of the property is an integral part of the lease transaction and can be audited. In other instances, the lessor may be willing either to lease or to sell, at the customer's choice, in which case the alternative purchase price is easily obtainable. But no matter what the circumstances, leasing is almost always an alternative to owning and the appraisal of the lease proposal will require an estimate of the price the lessee would have to pay to purchase the same or comparable facilities. The difficulties in the way of obtaining an estimate of alternative

---

[1] Balance sheet capitalization of the lease has been suggested by John H. Myers, "Presentation of Long-term Lease Liabilities in the Balance Sheet," *The Accounting Review*, July, 1948, pp. 289–295; also Albert H. Cohen, *Long Term Leases: Problems of Taxation, Finance and Accounting* (Ann Arbor: University of Michigan Press, 1954), pp. 108–140. Cohen also supports the method presented in this paper.

purchase price are not great and the resulting estimates will generally be auditable.

The other unknown in the calculation of the effective lease cost rate is the value of ownership rights in the leased facilities at the end of the lease term. An estimate of this amount must also be incorporated into the profitability evaluation, but this estimate generally cannot be audited. Although it is true that estimates of end-of-lease ownership values are subject to error, fortunately these estimates do not exert any material effect on lease cost rates for leases that extend 20 or 30 years into the future.

The Asset Value of the Lease

If the lessee's liability under a lease is to be shown on his balance sheet, an offsetting amount must be included among the firm's assets. Does the signing of a lease give the lessee an asset and, if so, at what value should this asset be capitalized?

In order to answer these questions we must examine the nature of balance sheet assets. When a firm acquires ownership of a specific property, what it really acquires is the right to use and dispose of this property. It is not as important that we acquire goods or services as it is that we acquire the right to use them for various lawful purposes. A drill press accompanied by a requirement that it not be used by the purchaser would have little value. Thus it is the rights inherent in ownership for which we purchase property and incur costs.

By entering into a lease the lessee acquires the right to use the leased property for a specified period of time. In many cases the lessee is empowered to sell a part or all of this right by subleasing or assigning the lease. The only significant right that the lessee does not acquire is the right to any residual value the user rights may possess at the end of the lease term.

From this it can be seen that the valuation problem is one of determining the portion of the total current value of the property that is represented by user rights during the term of the lease. To be more specific, what is the cost to the lessee of the rights that he acquires with the lease? This cost can be computed by subtracting from the alternative purchase price of the property the present value equivalent of ownership rights at the end of the lease. In our earlier example, estimated end-of-lease market value of the property was $400,000. The present worth of this sum, discounted at 8%, is $39,760. Subtracting this from the $1,000,000 current market value of the property indicates that the lessee is paying $960,240 for the right to use the property for 30 years. It should come as no surprise to note that this is just equal to the effective liability that we have calculated for the lessee. If the lessee is willing to promise to pay future sums in order to obtain user rights for a specified period of time, and if the lessor is willing to sell these rights in exchange for the lessee's promise, then the liability assumed by the lessee is the best possible approximation to a cost value of the user rights acquired. The accounting entry to record this transaction on the lessee's books is:

Rights to leased property	$960,240	
Liability under lease contracts		$960,240

Thus the essence of the method of accounting for leased property that is supported in this article is to enter the capitalized value of future rental payments in the lessee's balance sheet, both as a liability and as an asset. The liability represents the requirement to make future payments under the lease; the asset represents the cost of the rights to use the property during the period of the lease.

The reader may at this point object to the use of the word "cost" to describe the value that is being assigned to the asset. He will probably say that there is no cost in the accounting sense of the term because no ownership transaction has occurred to give rise to a cost. There is another side to this argument, however. Although it is true that what we ordinarily mean by "cost" is the sum of cash outlays made in order to acquire goods or services, a more fundamental definition is that cost represents the sum of values given in order to obtain certain rights. Sometimes we acquire ownership rights to property without an exchange of cash. The most common instance of this is the acquisition of assets in exchange for capital stock of the acquiring company. In this case outlay cost has to be approximated, either by appraisal of the physical assets or by estimates of market value of the stock issued.

In the case of a lease, the consideration given for the right to use property is the assumption of an obligation to make periodic payments to the lessor in the future. This is essentially the same as borrowing the same amount and using the funds to purchase user rights for a specified period of time. The only difference between the cost of the user rights, thus defined, and the cost of the ownership rights to the property is the present worth of end-of-lease salvage value. This is the only significant right that is not acquired in the signing of a lease and it is only proper that the present value of this right should be deducted from acquisition cost. Thus, although the valuation basis suggested here is not outlay cost it is an approximation to cost. And although this approximation to cost is based in part on estimates that cannot in most instances be audited, the estimates are subject to no greater range of error than when property is acquired in exchange for capital stock and in fact may be considerably less. In our illustration, the present value of residual ownership rights is only $39,760. At an 8% interest rate, an error of $100,000 in the estimate of end-of-lease salvage value would produce an error of only $9,940 in the value of the user rights. Furthermore, to exclude from the balance sheet the property rights accompanying the lease is a far greater error than the relatively slight error that will result from estimating the cost-equivalent value of those rights by the methods described above.

AMORTIZING THE LEASE

The second problem connected with the capitalization of lease rights and obligations is to provide a mechanism for breaking out the interest expense portion of the annual rentals and for amortizing initial asset and liability values over the term of the lease.

The overwhelming majority of corporations now amortize the cost of depreciable property either by the straight-line method or by some declining balance method. Bond discount or premium can be amortized either on a straight-line basis or on a constant percentage yield basis. Self-amortizing loans are handled generally on the banker's basis, which is the constant percentage yield method. Under this method, the effective rate of interest is constant throughout the life of the bond issue. In single-maturity debt sold initially at a discount, the indicated net book liability rises gradually through amortization of the discount as the maturity date comes closer and closer. If the debt is of the self-amortizing type, each periodic payment is divided explicitly into two components, for interest and repayment of principal, respectively. Each period's interest expense is computed as a fixed percentage of the unpaid balance at the beginning of the period. Amortization of principal is greater in the later periods than in the early periods.

Amortization of a capitalized lease liability could proceed along similar lines. For example, if the initial liability of the lease is capitalized at $960,240, representing an 8% lease with end-of-year payments of $85,295 a year for 30 years, the first year's interest expense is 8% of $960,240, or approximately $76,819. The remaining $8,476 of the first year's payment is applied toward a reduction in the outstanding liability, which then becomes $951,764. The second year's interest expense is 8% of this amount, or approximately $76,141, and the remaining $9,154 is debt amortization.

The result of this amortization procedure is to produce, at any balance sheet date, an indicated book value of the liability equal to the present worth of the remaining future lease payments, discounted at a rate equal to the initial capitalization rate, 8% in this illustration.

The constant yield method can also be used to amortize the capitalized value of the lessee's rights to use the leased facilities. Because the initial capitalized amount and the amortization period are the same for the asset as for the liability, the amortization in each period under this method is equal to the debt amortization component of the annual lease payment. There are various ways of computing this, but probably the simplest way of presenting it here is to say that the annual amortization charge represents the difference between the year-beginning and year-ending present values of the remaining future payments for user rights. For example, we found the approximate cost of the 30-year user rights to be $960,240. This is the present worth of 30 future annual payments of $85,295. The approximate cost of user rights for 29 years is obtained by finding the present worth of 29 future annual payments of $85,295, or $951,764. The portion of the original cost approximation that expires during the first year of the lease is thus $8,476, and the accounting entry is:

Expiration of rights to leased property $8,476
Rights to leased property $8,476

The debit is an operating cost of the period and the credit represents a reduction in capitalized net asset value. The credit might be made to a contra account, as in the case of company-owned facilities, but little would be gained by this procedure.

The alternative to this method of amortization is to compute the annual write-off of the asset by the straight-line or declining balance methods in use for the depreciable assets owned by the lessee. The effect of this would be to increase the amount of the amortization in the early years of the lease and decrease it in later years. For example, the first year's write-off under the straight-line method would be one thirtieth of $960,240, or $32,008, and under the double-rate, declining-balance method, $64,016.

There are two arguments that might be advanced in support of the straight-line or declining balance method. First, it is consistent with the methods used to amortize other long-life assets. As we pointed out above, the capitalized value of fixed property is the cost of acquiring the right to use and dispose of that property. As the value of this right expires with the passage of time, a portion of the initial cost is written off as depreciation, generally by a straight-line or declining-balance method. To be fully consistent with this we should use the same method in amortizing the approximate cost of user rights under lease contracts. But consistency has two sides. Straight-line or declining-balance amortization is completely inconsistent with the method used to determine asset value in the first place, and this argues for amortization by the constant yield method.

Second, faster amortization during the early years of life is in accord with the pattern of economic values. Although proof of this proposition is spotty, it is generally believed that economic value, as represented by market exchange value, declines more rapidly in the early years than in the later years of an asset's life. This argument is irrelevant here, however, because what we are amortizing is not the market value of a bundle of ownership rights but instead the approximate cost of user rights. The actual value of these rights to the user may be far in excess of their cost at the time of acquisition and indeed must be if the use of facilities is to be profitable. The cost of the rights is represented at any point in time by the capitalized value of the payments that must be made to secure them. Imperfections in the market for used capital facilities which result in a market undervaluation of future user rights should not be permitted to influence the rate of amortization of the approximate cost of those rights.

In any event, asset and liability should be amortized by the same method so as not to alter reported income and reduce net worth in comparison with present methods of accounting for the lease. In our example, annual rental payments of $85,295 are now charged to expense each year (rentals on manufacturing facilities may pass through inventory accounts before reaching the income statement but the inventorying effect generally will be slight). If the constant yield method of amortization is used on both the asset and the liability, the same total will be charged annually to expense, whereas if the straight-line method is followed for the asset alone, the total income charge will differ from $85,295. If, on the other hand, the lease liability is also amortized on a straight-line basis, the total income charge would be unaffected by the capitalization of the lease. These points are borne out in the following table:

First-year expense	Constant yield amortization of asset and debt	Straight-line amortization of asset only	Straight-line amortization of asset and debt
Asset amortization	$ 8,476	$ 32,008	$32,008
Interest expense	76,819	76,819	53,287
Total	$85,295	$108,827	$85,295

If different methods of amortization are used for the asset and the liability, the book liability for the lease will always exceed the book value of the asset. This is illogical inasmuch as both values relate to the same contract and both arise initially from the same underlying data. Furthermore, such a treatment can be regarded as distorting reported income, as illustrated in the table above, and the dual amortization rates can therefore be rejected.

The main question, however, is whether the amortization of both the asset and the liability should be scheduled on the basis of the constant yield method or the straight-line or other method used by the lessee in calculating depreciation charges. The constant yield method is the only one that is fully consistent with the basis on which lease rights and lease obligations must be capitalized and thus is logically superior to any alternative. Furthermore, no other method will provide a meaningful balance sheet valuation of the lease liability. Therefore, the constant yield method is recommended in this paper for the amortization of the approximate cost of the user rights as well as for amortization of the lease liability.

LEASE RENEWAL AND CANCELLATION

Many lease contracts contain provisions for modifying the duration of the lease by exercising either a renewal or a cancellation option. Should options of these kinds influence the methods used to amortize the asset and liability associated with the lease?

If the lease is capitalized on the basis of the initial term of the lease, both the asset and the liability will be completely amortized as of the date of renewal no matter whether straight-line or constant yield amortization is used. At this point the lessee has the option of renewing this lease, leasing alternative facilities, buying this or alternative facilities or reducing the total amount of facilities used. If the lease is renewed it can be assumed that management has examined the profitability of leasing the property and has found it to be adequate. In making this evaluation, it will have to consider the purchase alternative explicitly just as it did when the initial lease was signed. There is no difference in principle between an initial lease and a renewal, although the estimates of alternative purchase price may be more difficult to make. Therefore, the lease renewal is not sufficiently different to justify a change in method.

Lease cancellation prior to the expiration of the lease term, however, is a different matter. The suggested amortization methods are designed to amortize the initial capitalized amounts over the term of the lease. Prior cancellation will leave unamortized balances on both the asset and the liability sides of the balance sheet, balances which should then be removed from the balance sheet. If the same amortization method has been used for the asset and the liability these balances will be equal and cancellation will merely result in an offsetting entry to clear the accounts. No reported capital gain or loss will result from lease capitalization. If different methods of amortization are used, however, the balances will not offset each other and there will be a capital gain or loss.

It will probably be objected that no capital gain or loss can be realized because there is no capital asset in an ownership sense of the term. Actually, the situation is not entirely dissimilar to an ownership capital loss or gain in that both arise as a result of incorrect estimates as to the appropriate rate of cost amortization. If depreciation is too rapid, a capital gain will result, whether or not the facilities are owned or leased. This capital gain or loss, however, is purely a product of the methods of amortization. This is true for capital gains or losses on many kinds of owned property, of course, but in the case of leased facilities the means of eliminating any such effect are readily available—identical amortization schedules for asset and amortization—and this constitutes one more argument in support of using the same method for amortization of both aspects of the lease.

PROBLEMS OF LEASE CAPITALIZATION

The primary purpose of lease capitalization is to provide a more complete indication of the debt position of the lessee. It also serves to include among the assets an approximation to the amortized cost of user rights to leased facilities. By segregating the interest component in the annual rental a greater degree of income statement comparability among firms with different ownership-leasing structures can be achieved. But the main advantage of the proposed method is that it presents a more meaningful statement of the liabilities of the firm.

The method is not without its difficulties, however. One group of problems centers around the data required to compute the capitalized value of the lease. Some of these have already been discussed, but two that we have not yet touched upon have to do with the length of the capitalization period and the treatment of fluctuating rentals under participating leases. The second group of problems consists of a numebr of arguments made in opposition to the entire concept of lease capitalization. Brief discussion of these problems is desirable at this point.

Participating Leases

Many leases, particularly in food and variety chains, provide for a participating feature in which the lessee guarantees a certain minimum rental plus a given percentage of gross revenues or gross profit. Leases of this kind pose a particularly difficult problem to the accountant who wishes to capitalize lease values on the balance sheet. For a solution of this problem we must refer to the purposes which lease capitalization is designed to fulfill. If, as was stated above, the purpose is to provide a meaningful indication of liabilities, then capitalization should be on the basis of minimum rentals only. For any period in which the participation clause results in rental payments in excess of the minimum, this excess should be reported as a financial expense of the period.

The use of the minimum rental basis will almost undoubtedly understate the approximate cost of the user rights to the property. Some leases are said to be drawn on the assumption that the minimum rental will cover total construction costs, leaving the participation percentages to take care of the risk and capital cost components of the interest charge. But the fact remains that the long-term contractual liability of the firm is represented by the contractual minimum. Furthermore, the inclusion of percentage rentals in the capitalization base introduces an additional estimation requirement into the calculation, and errors in this estimate will ordinarily have a far greater effect on capitalized value than errors in estimated end-of-lease ownership value. For these reasons it seems safer to use minimum rental values rather than expected actual rentals, recognizing that this will make the resulting asset values somewhat less useful for capital return purposes.

Length of the Capitalization Period

In the exposition of the method we have assumed that the duration of the lease should be used as the time period for capitalization of future lease payments. This might be called into question if the period of estimated profitable use is shorter than the term of the lease or if the lease has no set terminal date but rather is cancellable on specified notice by either party. In the former case the capitalization period might be shorter than lease life and in the latter it might be longer. In neither case, however, will the primary purpose of lease capitalization be satisfied if the capitalization period is different from the length of the lease.

Take the case of shorter useful life, for example. It may be decided to enter into a lease for a longer period than the expected useful value of the user rights because the profitability of the facilities in the early years will be more than adequate to offset rental payments for underutilized facilities in the later years of the lease. When the facilities are no longer useful (for example, when a baseball team moves its franchise to another city before its stadium lease expires) the lessee still has a liability for future lease payments. This liability is a significant fact that must be recognized on the balance sheet, which it will not be if the shorter capitalization period is used.

Probably the difficulty in seeing this position stems from a confusion of lease capitalization with estimation of the *value* of user rights. As indicated above, the value of user rights should always be in excess of their cost, value being defined as the capitalization of the earnings that can be produced with the aid of the user rights. If this value is not greater than the cost of the rights the lease should not be negotiated. But as with any other asset, the value of user rights to leased property will change. If this value falls materially it may be desirable to write off the unamortized cost of the rights faster than the amortization of the liability. This suggests one circumstance in which the amortization of the asset might proceed at a different and faster rate than the amortization of the liability. After all, facilities purchased with borrowed money may be written off prior to the maturity of the debt if their useful life is found to be shorter than originally anticipated. These circumstances would probably justify an exception to the conclusion reached earlier that both the liability and the asset should be amortized by the same method and at the same rate. Fortunately, the exception is probably necessary only in rare cases, but it is a possibility that should be kept in mind.

In the case of the lease indefinite as to term, on the other hand, the lessee's liability is extremely limited. If he decides that the user rights no longer have adequate value to him he can terminate his liability quickly, subject only to any termination settlement imposed by the lease. In this case probably the only capitalized liability should be the estimated termination settlement plus rentals for the interval between notification and withdrawal from the property.

Possible Effect on Financial Position

Lease capitalization has three effects on the presentation of the firm's financial position. First, by increasing total reported liabilities it increases the debt/equity ratio. Second, by increasing total reported assets it decreases the profit/asset ratio. Finally, by shifting a portion of annual rentals into the financial expense section of the income statement, it increases reported operating profit and the operating profit/net worth ratio.

The result of the first two of these changes may influence the willingness of outside investors to lend additional sums or purchase additional shares of stock. Capitalization of lease liabilities may come as an eye opener to some investors although most of the large institutional lenders and financial intermediaries are sufficiently aware of the nature of lease liabilities to take them into consideration even without lease capitalization. Even here, however, existing financial reports do not provide the investor with an adequate basis for calculating effective lease liabilities.

If the ability of the lessee to attract funds is lessened at all it will probably be because institutional lenders are frequently under a certain amount of pressure to defend their lending policies before stockholder groups or government supervisory agencies. It is probably easier to defend a loan to a borrower whose apparent debt ratio is well within conventional rule-of-thumb limits than a loan to a borrower who is exceeding these limits. Some companies, particularly in the food chain group, would show some phenomenal changes in apparent debt ratios if lease liabilities were capitalized.

Nevertheless, this argument against lease capitalization cannot be permitted to stand. The same arguments could be made for not reporting any other kind of liability. The question is one of disclosure or partial concealment. Lease capitalization does not create liabilities where none have existed before; it merely adds them up and places them in a prominent place. And liabilities should be kept out in the open for inspection, not ignored or buried in footnotes.

The effect of lease capitalization on the operating profit/assets ratio will depend on the relationship between the cost rate of the lease debt and the operating profit/asset ratio before reflecting the lease capitalization. As with other types of debt financing there is a trading-on-the-equity aspect of the lease. Lease capitalization reflects this in part by adding back to operating income an amount equal to the effective cost of the lease debt times the amount added to assets. In our earlier example, an 8% lease adds $76,819 back to operating income during the first year by shifting this portion of the rental to financial expense. The amount added to assets is $960,240 at the beginning of the year and $951,764 at the end of the year. If the ratio between operating income and operating assets was greater than 8% before capitalizing the lease, then lease capitalization will reduce the indicated operating profit ratio, and vice versa.

This may have some bearing on such matters as rate regulation, excess profits tax computations and so forth, although this is by no means certain. The ratio of net profit to net worth will not be affected, of course, and the ratio of operating profit to total assets will be decreased by lease capitalization. If these ratios are used in regulatory proceedings, the standard ratios might be altered to allow for the effects of lease capitalization. On the other hand, if the standard ratios have some definite meaning either in logic or in law, then there is even more reason for lease capitalization in order to bring reported ratios more closely into accord with actual facts. We must return once more to the fact that a liability exists and financial statements that fail to disclose this liability are incomplete and may be misleading.

Lease capitalization might possibly have one other effect on the financial position of the lessee. One of the factors that reduces the effective cost of the lease is that the full amount of the rental is deductible for income tax purposes, and anything that might defer tax deductibility for a portion of the annual rental would increase the cost of the lease and impair the firm's current cash position. Lease capitalization, however, does not change the nature of the transaction; it merely reports it more fully. The amount capitalized is not the full purchase price of the property (which is the amount that should be capitalized under time purchase arrangements) but rather the approximate cost of the user rights. There is no reason to assume that the Internal Revenue Service would take any different view of the lease than it does now if it were clearly capitalized on the basis described above.

SUMMARY

In recent years the lease has grown in popularity as a device for financing the acquisition of productive property. The lease is a form of debt that does not appear on the balance sheet under current accounting practices. The omission from the balance sheet of the lessee's liability under long-term leases results in an understatement of the debt position of the firm and makes it more difficult to compare the financial position of firms that choose different means of asset financing.

There is, fortunately, a sound basis for capitalizing the lease on the balance sheet. When the lessee enters into a lease, he obtains an asset and assumes a liability. The amount of the liability is the present worth of the lessee's future payments under the lease, discounted at a rate of interest equal to the effective percentage yield-to-maturity cost of the lease financing device. The full value of the asset depends on how effectively the lessee puts the property to work during the period of the lease, but its cost is the sum that is given up in exchange for user rights. This cost can be approximated by subtracting from the alternative purchase price of the property the present worth of the end-of-lease ownership value. This net amount is also equal to the capitalized amount of the lessee's liability under the lease, so that the accounting entry to record the negotiation of a lease fits logically and neatly into the double entry bookkeeping system. These asset and liability values can then be amortized over the term of the lease in such a way as to leave net reported profit unchanged, but with a portion of the annual rental payment diverted to interest expense from the operating cost section of the income statement.

It is maintained in this paper that this method of lease capitalization and amortization is entirely consistent with existing accounting principles for the valuation of assets and liabilities. The major point in dispute is whether the proposed method is in accord with the principle of valuation at cost, and it is maintained here that it is. The problem in deriving cost is to separate from the purchase price of a piece of property that portion of the price that is paid for end-of-lease ownership rights. In the case of most leased property this portion will be relatively small and in long-term leases of 20 years or longer will be virtually negligible. But in any event it is better to accept a small range of error in approximating cost than it is to ignore the value of the user rights by omitting them from the balance sheet.

ALVIN ZISES (1914–   ), B.C.S. 34 New York University. Currently chairman of CNA Nuclear Leasing, Inc., a subsidiary of CNA Financial Corporation. Contributor to the *Financial Executive, Management Accounting* (U.S.), *The Bankers Magazine,* and other journals.

Previously, he was president of Bankers Discount Trust, Inc., and later was founder and president of Bankers Leasing Corporation.

ALVIN ZISES

DISCLOSURE OF LONG-TERM LEASES

ALVIN ZISES

The full disclosure of all contractual commitments, including long-term leases which are material, is in the interest of the public, industry, and the financial community. A few critics of business have hinted darkly at evasion. From this consideration alone full disclosure will benefit management.

With complete agreement on the principle of full disclosure of continuing commitments and long-term leases material in nature, we seek accord only on the method adopted to provide full disclosure. I submit that present rules for the disclosure of long-term leases are completely adequate. The job is to implement present rules rather than to change them.

RULES OF DISCLOSURE

Basic rules for disclosure of long-term leases and commitments may be found both in the American Institute's Accounting Research Bulletin No. 43 [a] and in the S-X Regulations issued by the Securities and Exchange Commission.

---

[a] ARB No. 43 Chap. 14 has been superseded by APB Opinion No. 5, "Reporting of Leases in Financial Statements of Lessee," (Sept. 1964). The recommendations of Chap. 14, as evaluated by the APB, have resulted in relatively more information being "disclosed in financial statements of lessees in recent years, no consistent pattern has emerged, and the extent of disclosure of pertinent information has often been inadequate.... There have been relatively few instances of capitalization of leased property and recognition of the related obligation, which suggests that the criteria for determining when a lease is in substance a purchase require clarification." (para. 3) [Eds.]

Research Bulletin No. 43 states that where the rentals or other obligations under long-term leases are material in the circumstances:

(a) Disclosure should be made in financial statements or in notes thereto of:
(1) The amounts of annual rentals to be paid under such leases with some indication of the periods for which they are payable and
(2) Any other important obligation assumed or guarantee made in connection therewith;
(b) The above information should be given not only in the year in which the transaction originates but also as long thereafter as the amounts involved are material; and
(c) In addition, in the year in which the transaction originates, there should be disclosure of the principal details of any important sale-and-lease transaction.

S-X Rule 3.18 regarding commitments reads as follows:

(a) If material in amount the pertinent facts relative to firm commitments for the acquisition of permanent investments and fixed assets and for the purchase, re-purchase, construction or rental of assets under long-term leases shall be stated briefly in the balance sheet or in footnotes referred to therein.
(b) Where the rentals or obligations under long-term leases are material there shall be shown the amounts of annual rentals under such leases with some indication of the periods for which they are payable, together with any important obligation assumed or guarantee made in connection therewith. If the rentals are conditional, state the minimum annual amounts.

S-X Rule 3.19 states in part:

If present in regard to the person for which the statement is filed the following shall be set forth in the balance sheets or in notes thereto . . .
(e) Pension and retirement plans.
(1) A brief description of the essential provisions of any employee pension or retirement plan shall be given.
(2) The estimated annual cost of this plan shall be stated.
(3) If a plan has not been funded or otherwise provided for, the estimated amount that would be necessary to fund or otherwise provide for the past cost of the plan shall be disclosed.
(g) Contingent Liabilities. A brief statement as to contingent liabilities not reflected in the balance sheet shall be made. In the case of guarantees of securities of other issuers a reference to the appropriate schedule shall be included.

Part V of Rule 5.04 of the S-X Regulations regarding "Property, Plant and Equipment" seems to define materiality in regard to fixed assets and leaseholds as a factor exceeding "5 per cent of total assets (exclusive of intangible assets) as shown by the related balance sheet at both the beginning and end of the period."

Rule 12.16 of Article 12 of the S-X Regulations in regard to Schedule XVI states in note 5: "If the aggregate amount of rents and royalties is not material, a statement to that effect will suffice. State rents and royalties separately if either amount is material."

A footnote in Bulletin No. 43 indicates that a long-term lease is one which has a noncancelable term of three years or more. Short-term leases are excluded from consideration within this commentary.

If all accountants had followed the above-noted rules in published annual reports, full disclosure would have been accorded all such commitments.

CAPITALIZATION OF RENTALS IMPRACTICAL

Some accountants have suggested capitalizing payments to be made under long-term leases and other commitments which perform a financial function, and setting forth on the balance sheet a figure indicating, for example, the value of the right to use the assets and a concurrent liability figure. Such technique, some claim, will eliminate the need for footnotes. Capitalizing long-term commitments on the balance sheet does not conform to the principles outlined above. Such arbitrary figure may have little or no relation to the actual liability. Furthermore, almost all commitments have financing among their motives or effects. The only "leases" which we would now capitalize are those which, as outlined later, are, in fact and in law, debt.[b]

The capitalization technique in its present status endeavors to equate leasing with debt, tries to provide a figure which is assumed to be the amount of liability. An officer of one of the nation's largest banks wrote to me, "I have not yet decided what is the correct method of accounting for long-term leases but it is clear, at least in my mind that leasing and debt are two different things. Anything which is done to make these two types of financing appear one and the same is misleading and this applies to accounting treatment, legal treatment, tax, etc."

Leasing always differs from debt in its economic effect upon the lessee in one or more of the following considerations and such considerations are related to any possible changes in accounting treatment:

    1. Inherently, because of the flexibility inherent in contractual and lease relationships

    2. Legally, because of the difference in impact in event of the lessee being in financial difficulty

    3. Financially, because leasing may make an extra contribution to earnings as a result of special considerations

    4. Tax-wise, because under certain circumstances leasing may reduce the tax burden

    5. Operationally, because of economies in operations performed for the lessee by the lessor

WIDE DIVERSITY IN LEASE RELATIONSHIPS

Lease arrangements lend themselves to a wide and diversified relationship between lessee and lessor. The financial impact of a lease transaction upon termination by the lessee may be nothing or may be substantial. The call upon the lessee may be almost absolute, qualified only by the laws relating to bankruptcy and reorganization as applicable to leases. On the other hand, the transaction may be a percentage lease terminable by the lessee with no penalty or premium. Some leases provide operating, administrative and physical services in varying

[b] APB No. 5 requires recording of lease obligations and related assets "if the terms of the lease result in the creation of a material equity in the property" (para. 10). [Eds.]

degrees. Rents may include charges for these services as well as for local and state taxes and the like.

The "Liabilities and Capital" side of the balance sheet lists various types of securities issued by the company. For the same reason we show various types of securities on the balance sheet, each lease contract would require analysis by the accountant in order to weigh, and to adjust figures for, the economic effect.

LEGAL DISTINCTIONS

"Another consideration," states Ralph L. Gustin, Jr., Second Vice President and Counsel of the John Hancock Mutual Life Insurance Company in *Financing by Lease and Contract* is "the difference in the creditor position of the lender in [lease] financings from that of the lender in ordinary loan transactions in the event of bankruptcy or Chapter X reorganization."

Because of this important distinction between debt and leasing, even in regard to the long-term noncancelable leases Gustin describes in which the lessee incurs all risks of ownership, any arbitrary figure placed on the balance sheet may have little relation to reality as an enforceable claim in event of difficulty. No matter how good the credit of the issuer of securities, whether they be debt or equity— or the credit of the lessee—in back of every investor's mind in varying degree lurks the possibility of financial difficulty. Gustin says:

> In the usual loan transaction the lender would have a liquidated claim (whether secured or unsecured) for the unpaid principal and accrued interest against the one party to whom the loan was made. In [lease] financings, assuming that both the [lessor] borrower and the [lessee] are both in bankruptcy or in Chapter X reorganization, the lender would have such a claim only against the borrower whose credit was not the basis for the loan. Assuming that the lease . . . is breached by the [lessee] either under the terms of the instrument or by rejection by its trustee in bankruptcy or reorganization, the lender, as assignee of the borrower [lessor], would have an unliquidated claim for damages for anticipatory breach of executory contract. As to the [lessee] the lender would be an unsecured creditor whose claim for damages would have to be liquidated as determined by the court. Thus the lender, to the extent that it must obtain satisfaction in the proceedings against the [lessee], is subject to all the problems that proof of damages involves. The amount of provable damages for anticipatory breach of executory contract has always been considered as governed by the state law . . .
>
> In assessing the claim on the . . . lease involved the court will be determining not only what is fair between the contracting parties but also what is fair between competing creditors. . . .
>
> Also damages for breach of an unexpired lease of real estate are not allowed in an amount exceeding the rent reserved for one year in bankruptcy and for three years in reorganization.

Lester E. Dennon, Esq., author of *Secured Transactions* published by the Practicing Law Institute, cites court decisions in support of his statement regarding chattel leases, "There is doubt as to the enforceability of a provision that the lessee upon default would be obligated for all accrued rentals and for the entire unpaid rental. . . . The lessor would be relegated to proving his actual damages."

On the other hand, the corporate purchaser in default under a conditional sales contract is ordinarily responsible for the full time balance.

JUNIOR POSITION OF LEASE OBLIGATIONS

Evaluation of items within the assets side of the balance sheet has been inherent in accounting practice for years. However, the principal amounts reported for debt obligations within the liabilities side of the balance sheet have never been subject to evaluation—but have always been fixed and predetermined. The obligation under lease is never fixed but subject to contractual and statutory limitations which make the legal liability indeterminate and unpredictable.

Because of these statutory limitations reducing the legal liability of the lessee in financial difficulty as to future rental payments, many investors describe long-term "noncancelable" leases as "contingent" obligations.

Furthermore, assuming the lessee is in financial difficulty, the trustee (because of his power to disaffirm the leases) may, and often does, place pressure upon the lessor to alter the terms to conform to what he considers "reasonable." If the trustee deems the lease unfavorable or the leased assets not essential, or if the business is not to continue, the trustee may void the executory commitment or lease.

In event of bankruptcy and the discontinuance of the business, a "noncancelable" lease obligation (and consider all the other varied kinds of leases) has the effect of being junior to that of the bond or debenture holder. Such occurrences, in effect, provide the senior debt with the superior position it enjoys if junior obligations were in the capitalization structure.

If the credit of the lessee is excellent and the possibility of financial difficulty remote, the relative position of any type of financing, whether it be leasing, preferred stock, subordinated debentures or mortgage bonds, is evidenced by the different rates for each type of financing.

Given a choice, commercial bankers and institutional investors who have studied leasing would rather lend to a company that has a moderate amount of lease obligations than to the same company with the equivalent amount of senior debt. This is the reason why a company may generally obtain somewhat more financing through leasing—just as it would through subordinated securities—than through senior debt alone.

FINANCIAL DIFFERENCES

As an example of a financial difference, the Department of Defense specifically refuses to recognize the cost of debt (or equity) as a component of expenses in pricing equipment produced by manufacturers of military hardware. On the other hand, under Armed Services Procurement Regulations 15-205.34 (a) "Rental costs of land, building and equipment and other personal property are allowable if the rates are reasonable. . . ."

Discounting rent at an arbitrary interest factor invites the Defense Department to disallow such factor.

DIFFERENCES IN TAX CONSEQUENCES

Tax economies unavailable under a debt transaction may be produced for the lessee through a long-term lease arrangement. Some may be relatively permanent, others transitory. Rent of land is tax deductible but under ownership land is nondepreciable. Differences between the rental deductions under leasing and the depreciation and capital costs under ownership may sometimes produce favorably timed cash flows for the lessee.

A major tax benefit of leasing is the possible reduction in capital costs. Under ownership, the interest cost of debt is tax-deductible whereas the return on equity, usually considered one measure of equity's cost, incurs a tax requirement. The entire rent in a lease, where the lessee builds no equity in the property, is fully tax-deductible. Furthermore, the shareholder expects growth in earnings and dividends in the future. Original holders forego some or all of such growth when equity is diluted by new issues. Leasing has been used to obtain low-cost, tax-deductible capital as well as to reduce dilution for present equity holders.

A study of equity's cost is cited. On June 16, 1948, General Telephone issued common under rights at $24.75 per share. Ten years later, in 1958, the company announced earnings (before merger with Sylvania) of $3.18 per share. This figure, adjusted for two stock dividends and for estimated cost of issuance and sale, produced an aftertax rate of return on the book value of these shares of 29.8 per cent. The pretax rate of return was 62.1 per cent.

Because law follows the mores and customs of a people, treatment of the leases as debt may eventually cause the taxing authorities to similarly treat all leases as debt. For example, capitalizing rental of land might provide the incentive for various legislatures to remove the deductibility of rental of land.

Capitalizing commitments on the balance sheet may precipitate local tax problems for the taxpayer. Where a governmental entity levies taxes on total capital rather than on capital stock or net income the lessee may be taxed on the leased assets. The Texas Corporate Franchise Tax, according to Commerce Clearing House, consists of:

> the taxes based upon that proportion of the stated capital, surplus and undivided profits, plus the amount of outstanding bonds, notes and debentures (outstanding bonds, notes and debentures shall include all written evidences of indebtedness which bear a maturity date of one year or more from date of issue). . . .

In view of the clamor for taxes, the imagination need not be stretched to foresee how the state of Texas may view the capitalization of long-term commitments if they were reported as "evidences of indebtedness." Other states have laws with similar effect.

WEIGHING ECONOMIC DIFFERENCES

The vice president of a corporation capitalized at $500 million stated, "If we could borrow money and pay no interest whatsoever, our economic analysis disclosed that it was less expensive to lease certain facilities than to own." His reasons were based upon the various advantages outlined above.

I suggest that the figure placed on the balance sheet be adjusted for the operating, financial, and tax effects of leasing. All such adjustments produce questions and problems in reflecting the weight accorded these considerations.

Wide disagreement exists, even among proponents of balance sheet capitalization, in determining the method of computation. This disagreement was deplored in a *Harvard Business Review* study by faculty members Anthony and Vancil. Replies to their questionnaire testing capitalization procedures for a hypothetical manufacturer which leased assets having a minimum annual rental of $1,250,000 produced a wide range of capitalization figures from seventeen respondents. The figures, other than zero, ranged from $2 million to over $20 million—an indication of the indeterminate liability.

With human discretion broadening the area of uncertainty, I cannot see how one figure on the balance sheet can provide the reader of financial statements with more valid information than complete and adequate footnotes. The capitalized figure may offer little relation to reality. Such technique substitutes arbitrary formulas for the considered judgment of analysts. On the other hand, footnotes may accord full information regarding the amount of rents, the lease term, the type of property, and any other obligations or commitments attendant to the leasing transaction.

VALUATION PROBLEMS

Albert H. Cohen who supports the principle of capitalization in his study, *Long-term Leases*, published by the University of Michigan Press, points to "valuation problems" in capitalizing leases. He states that assumptions must be made as to "an appropriate rate of interest and the frequency of discounting." He further states that the capitalization "problem" produces questions because of renewal options and differences in effect between tax and accounting interpretation of a lease transaction.

Where losses and gains are involved under sale-and-lease-backs, additional assumptions and evaluations complicate objective reporting. A "revaluation" of the capitalized figures may be considered, and it is suggested that the gain (or loss) in a sale-and-lease-back may be treated similarly to a "surplus from reappraisal" of the asset, with capitalization of the appreciation or declination. Again, further personal evaluation by the accountant is required.

To avoid distortion, a "tax equalization" account is suggested—assuming no changes in tax rates during the future years of a long-term lease. Interpretation of the balance in the "tax equalization" account presents an additional "problem," states Cohen. A "prepaid" item may be reported in one circumstance. In the other, if "the balance in the tax equalization account were a credit, it would follow that the account represented a liability for taxes not yet paid on income which has already been reported for accounting purposes. . . . The facts that the final result is unpredictable," concludes Cohen, "and that trends may appear and be reversed all within the initial term of the lease make it unfeasible to plan any orderly accounting treatment. . . ."

EXAMPLE OF CAPITALIZATION TECHNIQUE

A case to examine is the balance sheet in the 1959 annual report of a corporation whose stock is listed on a national exchange. Among the assets under the caption, Property, plant and equipment, the last item was (figures changed):

Rights to use of leased facilities at discounted amount
   of related long-term rental obligations—see contra $8,500,000

Among the liabilities, following and separated from the long-term debt, there appeared:

> Rental obligations under long-term leases, discounted over period of leases (including $631,000 due within one year)—see contra $8,500,000

Obviously the company strove to report fairly and objectively the lease obligations which were capitalized within this balance sheet.

The captions distinguish between leased and owned assets and, also, between the lease and other forms of obligations. The capitalized rental figures have a double line underneath, segregating the capitalized lease figures from the other figures within the report. The capitalized lease figures were not added into the totals.

On the other hand, the capitalization technique indicates the obvious shortcomings resulting from evaluation problems and presently used techniques. Both the asset and liabilities figures are identical. The figures seem to be rounded to the nearest one-half million dollars, a result which would undoubtedly raise questions. In order to avoid footnotes (concerning presently outstanding lease obligations) less disclosure is accorded the reader by capitalization.

Some auditors who initially felt that capitalization would eliminate the need for footnotes now recognize the inadequacies of capitalization, and suggest the need for footnotes to describe the capitalized figure. If capitalization results in figures unrealistic and inadequate, why place the figures on the balance sheet in the first instance?

I can state with little qualification that the capitalized figure on the liabilities side of this balance sheet is not the amount of legal liability—which may be more, but would probably be only a fraction of the stated amount in event of difficulty. I am equally certain that the figures recorded for the funded debt and for loans and accounts payable were the exact amounts of the legal liability.

Carman G. Blough, Director of Research for the American Institute of Certified Public Accountants, wrote in the March-April 1959, *Harvard Business Review:* ". . . as the position of the lessor is not quite the same as that of a bondholder it is doubtful if the sum or even the discounted value of the lease rentals would ever be a measure of an enforceable claim in case of financial difficulty."

FINDING ADEQUATE PROCEDURES

For a figure on the balance sheet to be meaningful, obviously standards and techniques need to be developed. The percentage used for discounting future rental payments should be established (and disclosed) after weighing the economic effect. If tax, financial and operating consequences arise, some acceptable technique should be developed which realistically takes such effects into consideration.

Secondly, some leases are considered assets because of the value of the contract. Some long-term leases have been sold at considerable profit. Others may be drags on the company's earnings. Should not the valuable and detrimental leases be measured in accordance with their effect?

When assets are owned, the base is readily determinable at cost. When assets are leased, the lessee has a piece of paper, a lease, which evidences ownership of limited rights to the use of specific assets. The lease, although not a security, has implications of other types of pieces of paper—shares of stocks or bonds. Such stocks or bonds are often recorded on the assets side of the balance sheet of an investing company at market value. The business owning these shares of stock or bonds will have recorded on the liabilities side of its balance sheet its issued securities recorded at book value, and not at market. Where the lease has a market value greater or less than the amount of rent booked for it, why should not the balance sheet reflect this truth?

Accountants who advocate capitalization claim that they may eliminate from the rent any portion comprising operating, tax and other costs. If this elimination may be accomplished, why should not accountants be able to add a factor for economic advantages (or disadvantages) accruing from tax, operating and other effects?

Just as each debt issue or preferred stock issue may have a different rate, each lease may have a different financing rate also—*but in addition the lease relationship may have some highly significant economic benefits unavailable under a debt transaction.*

One accountant wrote to my firm that, "Discounting the actual lease obligations takes into account any advantages that may be present in the negotiated terms. . . ." This would be an endeavor to accord fair disclosure. *But look at the problems that are produced!* If simple discounting were to be suspect by many analysts and investors, how may they consider varying techniques of appraisal to reflect gains, losses, taxes and other considerations?

Another accountant wrote, "Granted some differences as to method of computation . . . but there are differences of opinion when it comes to depreciation and other items." However, the depreciation reserve, like other reserves, is not a commitment or obligation to outside parties. I know of no debt obligation recorded on the balance sheet where the amount of legal liability is subject to assumptions and personal evaluations.

ACCOUNTANT'S EVALUATION REJECTED

I quote below a letter, written by a senior officer of one of the country's largest banks:

> The increasing use of various leasing techniques has made this matter one of real concern to creditors, and the very fullest kind of disclosure should appear in audit reports. New standards for a uniform approach to this problem are needed.
>
> However, there is, I understand, a movement afoot to try to develop a standard treatment of leases by which some asset and liability value could be assigned to them and the balance sheet itself actually adjusted. As a creditor I would object vigorously to such a treatment on the ground that it would be more likely to distort the balance sheet than to present a true picture. Leases are of all kinds: long-term, short-term, cancelable and noncancelable. How could anyone maintain that the same or even similar treatment should be given to a fifty-year real estate lease and a lease on motor vehicles with no termination date but a one-year cancellation clause? How would one treat a ninety-nine year ground rent? Some leases have been so fortunately negotiated as to be a really valuable asset, others may be so burdensome as to be an almost total liability and yet both, under the proposals I have seen, would

receive similar treatment. How about leases which are based on a percentage of gross sales or a percentage of gross profit? There seems to be no possible way of capitalizing these, with the result that the balance sheet of a company whose leases were on this basis would benefit as compared with that of a company leasing in a more conventional manner. What about a lease involving service without a separation of the rental charge and the charge for service?

Following up a step further . . . a long-term purchase commitment for raw materials is a very definite liability, so also is a commitment for pension plan or employment contracts. One of the most certain future liabilities imaginable is taxes: income, payroll, real estate and others. I can see no real reason logically why an attempt should not also be made to assign asset and liability values to these items.

It seems to me that this whole approach leads to a situation where every balance sheet would contain assets and liabilities that were either arbitrarily assigned by formula without consideration of the individual facts of the case, or else were dependent entirely upon the subjective evaluation of the individual auditor. The standard wording of the auditor's certificate could become a mockery, and the task of the financial analyst almost impossible. Balance sheet ratios of the kind used in credit analysis for decades would become valueless and comparative figures would have no meaning. Reconciliation of operating statements and surplus would become unmanageably complex because of year-to-year adjustments in lease treatment.

I believe that the answer lies in a new form of standard exhibit to be attached to the balance sheet, in which full details of lease obligations and leased assets could be provided. This would be more prominent than a mere footnote and would make possible more detailed disclosure. It would also give to the creditor an opportunity to analyze the actual facts and give them the weight he felt they deserved.

EXTENSION OF CAPITALIZATION

At least one writer has declared that purchase contracts and "take or pay" agreements should be capitalized. Some auditors are now capitalizing "Guarantees" and "Contingent Obligations" on balance sheets in annual reports. If the same reasoning is to hold, capitalization should extend to construction, subcontracting, pension and retirement, repurchase and all other off-balance-sheet commitments.

Many of these activities have far greater implication than those of long-term leases. In fact, the Anthony-Vancil survey disclosed in its Exhibit VIII that the "Extent of Long-Term Leasing Reported by [386] Corporations" responding to questionnaires was just 1.0 per cent of total sales of such corporations.

On the other hand, an outstanding phenomenon of the last few decades has been the growth of pension funds and their call upon corporate revenue. These commitments are assuming astronomical proportion.

In the case of large mail order and merchandising companies which subcontract for the manufacture and purchase of merchandise, the effect of capitalizing such commitments would be astounding.

Where utilities contract for purchase of power, the effect would be equally amazing. A common, and I believe astute, practice of investor-owned utilities in the Pacific Northwest is to execute long-term purchase agreements to buy power generated by publicly owned power districts. Public utility districts finance 100 per cent of their requirements through debt alone, do not resort to the higher-cost equity required by investor-owned utilities. Because the interest paid by such public utility districts bears no income tax to the recipient, such interest rates are lower than those borne by investor-owned companies. The low cost of financing enjoyed by the public utility district is shared by the investor-owned companies, is reflected in the price which the companies pay for purchased power. To arbitrarily capitalize such purchase commitments would do an injustice to the investor-owned company and its economically minded management. I see little difference in disclosure principles and requirements between a firm twenty-five year power-purchase agreement and a firm twenty-five year lease on the generating station which produces the power.

A most important reason why capitalization of long-term rentals and other commitments should be approached with extreme caution is that many legal, financial, tax and regulatory problems may be precipitated.

All institutional investors use a common definition of indebtedness which in substance includes all items, except capital stock and undistributed earnings, which appear on the liabilities side of the balance sheet.

DEFAULTS UNDER INDENTURES

We would guess that tens of billions of dollars of long-term indebtedness have been borrowed under indentures which have within them the substance of this widely used and common definition. All term debt indentures have restrictions on the incurring of additional debt by the borrower. We would estimate that about 80 per cent of indentures under private placements have a flat restriction on the borrower, preventing the incurrence of any additional term debt. Counsel has informed me that such accounting treatment, capitalizing lease and other commitments on the balance sheet, would precipitate a default under indentures where "indebtedness" is so defined.

If a borrower has issued long-term debt at rates substantially lower than the present going rates, there is the likelihood in many cases that some institutional investors will use the default under the indenture to effect refunding of the outstanding indebtedness at higher prevailing rates. Literally, thousands of corporations owing billions of dollars in long-term debt would be affected, with repercussions on shareholders, creditors and investors.

I have been asked whether or not the principle of "ex post facto" would apply to such a default. The constitutional guarantee against "ex post facto" does not extend, unfortunately, to balance sheets. This principle is a limitation only on the powers of the federal and state governments. Because restrictive covenants in indentures apply during the term of the indenture, such covenant regarding the incurring of additional debt, as defined in accordance with accounting treatment, would undoubtedly become effective if commitments were capitalized on the balance sheet.

CONSEQUENCES FOR REGULATED INDUSTRIES

Because "indebtedness" is widely accepted as all items, except capital stock and undistributed earnings, which would appear on the liabilities side of the balance sheet, a questionable situation may occur in the public utility industry primarily because of long-term fuel purchase contracts.

The Securities and Exchange Commission regulates those public utilities subject to its jurisdiction under the Public Utility Holding Company Act of 1935. The provisions of this act are very broad. Utilities subject to the act are regulated as to issuance of securities, evidences of indebtedness and capitalization ratios. What may flow from capitalizing long-term fuel purchase contracts, even though the commitments legally and economically differ from debt, may have broad implications. Similar problems face gas pipe line companies, subject to regulations by the Federal Power Commission, in regard to capitalization of long-term gas purchase contracts which some accountants now feel is required treatment.

Practically all, if not all, states have statutes requiring authorization for the issuance of stocks, bonds, notes "or other evidences of indebtedness payable at periods of more than twelve months after the date thereof." In some states the consequences of failure to comply with this requirement are not clear. In other states the statute provides that an unauthorized issue is void.

If "unauthorized" purchase contracts would be capitalized as a financing medium on the liabilities side of the balance sheet, in many jurisdictions such contracts would seem to be void and the investor or seller would appear to have no rights under law.

LEGAL CONSEQUENCES FOR ACCOUNTANTS

Ironically, those accountants who are promoting capitalization may be rushing headlong into that pitfall which they believe capitalization of commitments may enable them to avoid. These accountants claim that capitalization will reduce their exposure to lawsuits traceable to professional incompetence.

The general counsel of a major institutional investor offers the following opinion on this subject: "I agree . . . that footnote treatment seems correct . . . in fact, would question if the capitalization method would not be so misleading as almost to be misrepresentation."

Fortunately a sound technique of disclosure is available to the accounting profession, a technique based on present and growing practice—the use of the schedule. Article 12 of the S-X Regulations has brought the use of the schedule into prominence. The schedule might apply to all contractual commitments of material nature coming within the scope of S-X Rules 3.18 and 3.19 (see Exhibit I on page 283).

Therefore, one schedule, "Schedule of Material Contractual Commitments," may be the report to provide full and adequate disclosure of those activities which do not logically belong on the balance sheet.

ADVANTAGES OF SCHEDULE

The use of the schedule has these advantages:

1. There is no need to define or draw any lines as to the type of commitments to be disclosed. All material commitments may be included.

2. The schedule highlights and gives emphasis to the disclosure of such commitments.

3. By the use of a schedule we need not strain the balance sheet by portraying a picture out of line with reality.

4. More complete and more accurate disclosure is available through the use of the schedule than can be obtained through one figure placed on the balance sheet.

5. Evasion by omission is corrected. The schedule requires all types of contingent and executory commitments to be disclosed. Omission is not a passive but a purposeful act.

6. If the discounted value of the future commitments may properly be applied, the schedule offers space for such application.

The form of schedule may have the following columnar construction:

1. Type of commitment.
2. Amount paid this year (by type of commitment).
3. Estimated balance to be paid during each of the next five years (by type of commitment).
4. Minimum balance to be paid if determinable (by type of commitment). This amount for each type of commitment may, if proper, be discounted over the remaining period by a stated and disclosed per annum percentage.
5. Remaining period (from date of report) over which each major commitment extends.

The dollar amounts in each column may be totaled. Statements are included as to materiality and footnoting other pertinent information.

Investors, financial analysts, creditmen are concerned with all continuing charges against revenue. The suggested schedule will impartially record all such commitments. These may be purchase or repurchase commitments as to inventories, fixed assets, investments, and receivables, pension and retirement plans, labor and management contracts, long-term leases, royalties payable, contracts for construction, guarantees and sureties, warranties under merchandise sold, and other contingent obligations. No material, continuing and contingent charge against revenue need be excluded.

Some accountants claim that only "financing arrangements" should be capitalized. The schedule offers disclosure of all commitments. Every commitment, lease or otherwise, has a present or potential call upon revenue which call may influence a company's earnings or its ability to meet its debt service. Some have claimed that pension commitments should not be disclosed because they may be cancelled with cessation of employment. If, however, a company cannot exist without its personnel, how impermanent, in fact, is the pension commitment?

Some accountants have suggested that a continuing commitment need not be disclosed if it has not been contracted for. Under S-X Rule 3.19, the "*estimated annual cost of the [pension] plan shall be given.*" It appears, therefore, that where a commitment may be a continuing one, the future charges should be estimated.

WHEN COMMITMENTS SHOULD BE CAPITALIZED

There is one type of commitment which should be capitalized on the balance sheet. This is the type of transaction which may, for example, use lease terminology but is, in fact and in law, a debt transaction. It would be so construed by

Exhibit I SCHEDULE OF MATERIAL CONTRACTUAL COMMITMENTS (S-X Rules 3.18 and 3.19)

Type of commitment	Amount paid this year	Amounts contracted or estimated for each of next 5 years and for each of three 5-year periods beyond								Minimum amount of commitment if determinable*	Remaining period (yrs.) from date of report
		Year 1	Year 2	Year 3	Year 4	Year 5	Years 6-10	Years 11-15	Years 16-20		
Purchase and Repurchase for:											
(a) Investments											
(b) Fixed Assets											
(c) Inventory and Supplies											
(d) Other											
Construction											
Long-Term Leases											
Royalties											
Pension and Retirement											
Employee Contracts											
Guarantees											
Contingent Liabilities											
Other (Explain)											
Totals											

* The minimum balance payable, in each type of commitment, may be discounted over the remaining period by a stated per annum percentage. Where such minimum balance is discounted, state the percentage used in each case.

Where amounts both paid and payable for any type of commitment are not material, a statement to that effect for any such type of commitment will suffice. Show amounts separately for each type of commitment if amounts paid or payable are material.

Any pertinent information of a material nature regarding any commitment should be furnished within footnotes to the schedule.

the courts in event of bankruptcy or Chapter X reorganization. Consequently, the economic effect in case of financial difficulty would be identical with that of a debt transaction. Because the economic result would be dependent upon the legal determination, if any question arises in the accountant's mind as to the nature of the transaction, the matter should be settled by counsel. Therefore, that type of transaction, which counsel determines is indeed debt, should be treated as debt —and on the balance sheet.

Paragraph 6 of Chapter 14 of Accounting Research Bulletin No. 43 [c] describes those "lease" arrangements which are, in substance, no more than an installment purchase of the property. Those "lease" arrangements described would under state

[c] The guidelines for determining which lease agreements constitute in substance purchases are discussed in paras. 9–12 of APB Opinion No. 5. [Eds.]

law and the Internal Revenue Code be considered conditional sales. Such "leases" are described as those:

1. Subject to purchase of the property for a nominal sum or for an amount obviously much less than prospective fair value of the property.
2. When the agreement stipulates that the rental payments may be applied in part as installments on the purchase price.
3. When the rentals obviously are so out of line with rentals for similar properties as to negative the representation that the rental payments are for current use of the property and to create the presumption that portions of such rentals are partial payments under a purchase plan.

Paragraph 7 of the same bulletin immediately following states:

. . . where it is clearly evident that the transaction involved is in substance a purchase, the "leased" property should be included among the assets of the lessee with suitable accounting for the corresponding liabilities and for the related charges in the income statement.

As stated such "leases" described in paragraph 6 would be considered, in fact and in law, conditional sales or debt transactions.

GUIDEPOSTS TO CAPITALIZATION

An essential difference between leasing and debt (ownership) is that the lessor assumes some or all of the risks of ownership. In event of the debtor's financial difficulty, the obligation is always fixed and predeterminable. If the borrower's assets are adequate, the debt obligation will be paid in full.

On the other hand, the obligation under an executory commitment including that of a long-term lease is never predeterminable. The lessor's claim is, at most, limited to proof of damages. There, further, may be statutory limitations upon a claim.

In most lease arrangements the lessor as owner assumes the risk of tax depreciation. A tax advantage which may accrue to the lessee will often be to the disadvantage of the lessor. In a paper read before The Association of Life Insurance Counsel on Tuesday, December 10, 1957, Ralph L. Gustin, Jr., warned investors of the import of this risk in lending to lessors:

The potential of changes in depreciation allowances as a source of revenue is indicated by the fact that in some years the total depreciation deductions have exceeded the total of taxable net income of all corporations. Congress has broad powers under the Sixteenth Amendment to make changes: the Supreme Court has referred to this power as follows:

Unquestionably, Congress has power to petition, limit or deny deductions from gross income in order to arrive at the net that it chooses to tax.

Elementary caution, therefore, suggests that the long-term lender [financing a lessor] should not rely exclusively on the allowance for depreciation as determined at the time of the making of the loan for the many years to come.

If the "lessee" hurdles his relationship with the "lessor" and guarantees directly to the "lessor's" lender all the obligations of the "lessor," including payment of the "lessor's" interest, principal and taxes, especially taxes imposed on net income, with no right of set-off whether or not the lessor is in default, then the obligation of the "lessee" is determinable and fixed, the transaction is in fact debt, and the "lease" should be capitalized.

EVOLUTION VS. REVOLUTION

Although very real problems face business today in capitalizing leases and other commitments, evolution over a period of time may eventually enable all the information within the suggested schedule to be placed bodily within the balance sheet as "Commitments."

The accounting profession should recognize, first, that such inclusion of commitments within the balance sheet changes the original and basic concept of the balance sheet. Instead of portraying merely what is owned or owed, it will portray all material, contingent and continuing charges against revenue. The profession, secondly, should determine if that is the direction which the balance sheet should take. Finally, time is required to resolve certain problems. With time, perhaps a few decades, the indenture problem may pass away. Statutory problems regarding taxes and regulation may take longer. The concepts of capitalization and of the discounted value of money may be more widely understood and, if possible, refined to reflect not only the economic effect but a more realistic figure approximating the actual value of the limited right and the actual liability. There is an overwhelming amount of work to be done in the development of techniques that will be acceptable to analysts and investment officers.

Planning evolution and formulating a new concept of the balance sheet inevitably develops one question, "Where do we draw the line?"

The answer seems obvious if we discard the concept of disclosing merely what is owned and owed. The answer is, I believe, to disclose *all material, contingent and continuing calls upon revenue.*

All material and continuing calls upon revenue, as reported in the operating statement, may be reflected within both the present balance sheet and the proposed schedule—later, with evolution, perhaps within or directly below the future balance sheet as it may be conceived and developed. An asset may be recorded which would be the limited rights (rather than the absolute rights inherent under ownership of assets) to acquire the service of things or people. The Capital and Liabilities side may have a separate classification, neither debt nor equity, which may be "Commitments." The location of such classifications I suggest as just under the totals.

The accounting profession must make a decision as to the very basic concept underlying the balance sheet. Unless a fundamental and unified concept is determined, every well-intentioned or ill-intentioned member may construct the balance sheet as he so desires.

CONCLUSIONS

Full disclosure of long-term leases and other commitments would be in the interest of the public and industry. Present rules of disclosure are fully adequate to give the reader of financial statements the facts regarding commitments and long-term leases. It is necessary merely for the rules to be implemented.

Capitalizing long-term rentals and other commitments and placing them on the balance sheet today would incorrectly equate these commitments with debt, would not provide full and objective disclosure but would produce a devastating situation because of:

1. Fundamental problems in determining objectively and fairly the figures to be placed on the balance sheet and in adjusting the figures for operational, tax and other considerations.

2. Possible catastrophic effect upon management, stockholders and creditors under outstanding indentures, current and changing tax laws, and regulation of industry.

3. The legal liability of accountants in public practice if such technique were adjudicated as "misrepresentation."

The proposed schedule may be adopted either as an additional report disclosing all material and continuing calls upon revenue, which calls historically and in accordance with present logic do not belong within the currently constituted balance sheet, or the schedule may be that planned and purposeful evolutionary development which will, with time, link the present balance sheet with a concept which may be accepted sometime in the future.

KENNETH S. AXELSON (1922-   ),
A.B. 44 Chicago; CPA. Currently
vice-president and director of finance
and administration, J.C. Penney Company, Inc., New York. Contributor to
several journals.
   Was partner in Peat, Marwick, Mitchell & Co., 1952–63, prior to joining J.C. Penney Company, Inc. Served on the AICPA Accounting Principles Board, 1968–70.

KENNETH S. AXELSON

NEEDED: A GENERALLY ACCEPTED METHOD FOR MEASURING LEASE COMMITMENTS

KENNETH S. AXELSON

The year 1970 will long be remembered for dramatic downturns in two vital areas: stock prices and hemlines. It will also be remembered by financial analysts as the year when the balance sheet made a comeback.

For a while the balance sheet had been almost forgotten. Earnings growth was the name of the game, and borrowing was considered the smart thing to do. Then all those earnings curves, floating ever upwards, came to an abrupt halt and went into reverse. The money crunch was on and companies began to fail for lack of funds.

Perhaps the single most dramatic business event of 1970 was, of course, the failure of Penn Central. That a business of this size and national importance could become insolvent was a reminder that capital structure and liquidity bear watching just as much as the price/earnings ratio. Suddenly, interest shifted to the bal-

SOURCE: From *Financial Executive*, Vol. XXXIX, No. 7 (July, 1971), pp. 40–42, 44, 46, 48, 50, and 52. Reprinted by permission of the Financial Executives Institute.

ance sheet and there emerged, once again, some of the classical problems that have plagued analysts trying to evaluate the financial condition of companies.

Measuring the extent and financial effect of commitments such as leases, contracts (purchase, service, and employment) and guarantees of third-party loans is one of the perennial problems. This article aims at providing some constructive suggestions about the measurement of lease commitments and the importance of such measurements in financial planning.

ACCOUNTING FOR LEASES TODAY

Leasing has grown very rapidly since World War II. It has been estimated that well over $10 billion of equipment is under lease, about half of which is computers. Much larger yet is the value of real estate, ships, airplanes, or other major facilities under lease.

There are many reasons for leasing. Often it may be the only way to obtain the use of an asset. It also helps the lessee avoid the heavy initial outlays required for purchase; in effect, the lessee shifts to the lessor the problem of financing the investment. Some lessees may actually lack the credit standing to make their own financing arrangements.

Where a company enters into lease commitments to a significant degree as an alternative to financing, such commitments are clearly an important aspect of the company's liquidity. In recognition of this fact, both the Securities and Exchange Commission and the Accounting Principles Board require disclosure of certain pertinent data in the financial statements. Rule 3-18 (b) of Securities and Exchange Commission Regulation S-X states, "Where the rentals or obligations under long-term leases are material, there shall be shown the amounts for annual rentals under such leases with some indication of the periods for which they are payable, together with any important obligation assumed or guarantee made in connection therewith. If the rentals are conditional, state the minimum annual amounts."

APB Opinion No. 5 calls for disclosure by the lessee of the amount of minimum annual rentals and the period over which the outlays will be made. It also requires that current year rentals be disclosed if they differ significantly from the minimum rentals under the leases.

The APB has worked for several years to develop better guidelines for the disclosure of lease commitments. In 1964, the Accounting Principles Board issued Opinion No. 5, which dealt with reporting of leases in financial statements of lessees. And the Board's Opinion No. 7, entitled "Accounting for Leases in Financial Statements of Lessors," was published in 1966. Interpretations of the Opinions have varied and, as a result, the reporting of leases in financial statements has not been consistent from company to company.

The APB is currently studying the various questions which have been raised and expects to issue a new Opinion dealing with the following matters:

What Leases Should Be Capitalized

In defining leases which should be capitalized, Opinion No. 5 uses terms such as "material equity," "equivalent to installment purchases of property," and "significant degree," which have not been interpreted uniformly. The APB intends to clarify these terms and definitions, specify the method of amortizing leased assets, and determine whether capitalization rules apply to short-term as well as long-term leases.

Inconsistencies between Opinion No. 5 and Opinion No. 7

Opinion No. 7 provided that, under certain circumstances, a lessor must treat a lease as a sale, whereas Opinion No. 5 would permit the lessee to treat the same lease as other than a purchase. Therefore, the lessee would not be required to capitalize the leased property on its balance sheet. Some believe that this inconsistency should not be permitted and that the accounting treatment of a given situation should be similar for the parties on both sides of the transaction.

Additional Information Concerning Lease Agreements

It has been proposed that additional information regarding lease agreements would make financial statements more meaningful to the readers of such statements. The APB is seeking to ascertain what type of information might be required to do this and how the data should be presented in the statements.

Calculation of lease commitments

Divergent views have been expressed as to what elements should be used in the calculation of lease commitments. Some of the controversial points are (1) present value of rental payments vs. sum of rental payments, (2) primary term of the lease vs. primary term plus all renewal terms, (3) gross amount of rental payments vs. net amount (after deducting real estate taxes, operating expenses, and other executory expenses), (4) what interest rate should be used in the calculation.

Although the disclosures currently required are helpful, they leave much room for doubt regarding the value of lease obligations. The result is confusion.

FINANCIAL ANALYSTS VIEW LEASES

In dealing with lease commitments, financial analysts tend to take one of the following three positions: one, astonishingly common in this day and age, is to ignore leases altogether; another, much less frequent, is to underestimate the lease obligation; and the third position, the one encountered most often, is overstatement of lease obligations.

To illustrate the effect of the different positions, it will be useful to outline the approach which financial analysts use when they wish to estimate lease obligations.

The first step is to gather as much information on leases as may be available. Here the analyst will most likely turn to the annual reports or SEC filings where references to lease obligations can be found in the financial statements. He will probably find out what the minimum annual rentals amount to and the actual rentals paid. He will also find some indication of the remaining terms of leases. For example, the Penney Company's 1969 Annual Report disclosed that minimum annual rentals at January 31, 1970 (the end of fiscal year 1969) amounted to $61.5 million; that rent expense, including rent based on sales, was $104.5 million in 1969; and that substantially all leases will expire during the next 30 years. With this information, the analyst now proceeds to estimate the extent of the lease commitments.

The most commonly used approach is to multiply or divide the minimum annual rentals by some factor which reflects, in the analyst's judgment, the average remaining term of the leases and the average interest rate built into the leases. This treatment assumes that a lease is the equivalent of a loan repayable in equal annual installments—the annual lease payments—which include both interest on the balance outstanding and a portion of the principal. If one knows the period of the "loan" (lease) and the interest rate, one can derive the principal. For example, a 7 per cent loan payable over 15 years requires a level annual payment of about 11 per cent of the principal. If the annual payment is known, then dividing it by 11 per cent (or multiplying it by 9.1, the reciprocal of 11 per cent) will yield the principal. Thus, if minimum annual rentals are $1 million and the analyst assumes that the remaining terms of the leases average 15 years and the underlying interest is 7 per cent, he will calculate the principal at $9.1 million ($1 million divided by 11 per cent or multiplied by 9.1).

This method is a fast, simple, and quite reasonable rule of thumb given the information available. However, the analyst is forced to substitute judgment for some of the key data needed in this calculation and is therefore subject to various kinds of errors: he may be incorrect in his estimate of the imputed average interest; he may be wrong about the average remaining terms of the leases; the minimum annual rentals may include not only principal and interest on the leases, but also taxes and other executory factors not related to the lease commitments. Even assuming that the analyst guesses correctly for one company, there is no assurance that the same assumptions hold for another company, which means that comparisons may be misleading.

DISAGREEMENT ON MEASURING LEASES

What has been described is one approach to estimating lease commitments. There are others, and results tend to vary widely. For example, we found in 1969 that reports on the Penney Company included estimates of the value of Penney's lease commitments ranging from a low of $500 million (eight times the minimum annual rentals) to a high of $1.3 billion (12.5 times total rents paid in 1969). Moreover, our own calculations, which will be explained below, show that Penney's actual lease commitments at the end of fiscal 1969 fell outside the range of estimates—far below the bottom of the range.

How different methods of calculating lease obligations can affect the evaluation of a company's capital structure is illustrated in Exhibit 1. Here we see Penney's capital structure as of January 31, 1970, under three different assumptions regarding the extent of lease commitments. If leases are ignored, long-term debt amounts to 19 per cent of stockholders' equity—a fairly conservative debt ratio. If leases are valued at eight times minimum annual rentals, long-term obligations, including leases, are nearly equal to equity. If lease commitments are estimated at 12.5 times actual 1969 rental expense, long-term obligations, including leases, are more than twice the amount of equity. Depending on his assumption about the value of lease commitments, an analyst could have rated Penney at year-end 1969 as a company with a large amount of unused debt capacity or one using a considerable amount of leverage.

Further confusion results when one tries to compare different companies, as in Exhibit 2.

Retailer A is a major discount chain that has been expanding rapidly. All its new stores are leased. Retailer B is a leading chain of department stores. It owns a substantial proportion of its stores. If we ignore leases, both chains appear to have strong balance sheets, with A's debt 37 per cent of equity and B's debt 11 per cent of equity. If we value lease obligations, B's debt rises but remains less than half of equity. By contrast, A's debt, including leases, jumps to over 2½ times equity.

Analysis of a company's financial strength should, of course, go beyond formulas and statistical comparisons. There are significant differences between the nature of lease commitments and other forms of debt, so that it can be highly misleading to equate capitalized leases and direct debt. Proper evaluation also requires an understanding of the amount of future cash generation, the degree to which it may be influenced by circumstances both external and internal to the company, potential sources of funds, etc. The good analyst will want to ascertain the nature of each major obligation and make his assessment of its risk characteristics. Nevertheless, when all is said and done, analysts will continue to seek ways to quantify lease commitments to the extent possible. The lack of generally accepted methods of estimation and lack of detailed information on leases opens the way for substantial errors in judgment.

Some analysts, aware of the uncertainties, try to minimize their risk through conservatism by estimating lease commitments too high. This fairly widespread practice has resulted in bias against companies that lease extensively to obtain the use of assets. Such companies need to be and are concerned with the proper reporting of lease obligations. Since retailers, by and large, tend to lease a high proportion of their facilities, they are particularly affected by the confusion over lease obligations.

Exhibit 1 J. C. PENNEY COMPANY, INC.
CAPITAL STRUCTURE AT JANUARY 31, 1970 ($ millions)

	Method of estimating lease commitments		
	No value	Minimal annual rentals × 8	1969 total rents paid × 12.5
Long-term debt—direct	125	125	125
Lease commitments	—	492	1,306
Total long-term obligations	125	617	1,431
Stockholders' equity	656	656	656
Total invested capital	781	1,273	2,087
Long-term debt/equity	.19	.94	2.18

Exhibit 2 COMPARISON OF CAPITAL STRUCTURE AT JANUARY 31, 1970: RETAILER A VS. RETAILER B ($ millions)

	Method of estimating lease commitments			
	No value		12.5 × minimum annual rents	
	A	B	A	B
Long-term debt—direct	27	10	10	8
Lease commitments	—	—	62	21
Total long-term obligations	27	10	72	29
Stockholders' equity	73	90	28	71
Total invested capital	100	100	100	100
Long-term debt/equity	.37	.11	2.57	.41

PENNEY'S APPROACH

In an effort to reduce the uncertainties governing lease valuation, we developed, in 1969, what we believe to be a consistent, rational method of measurement. Our motives in this undertaking were not unselfish; Penney's has substantial lease commitments which we had felt for some time were being over-estimated by analysts. Using our newly developed measurement, we stated the value of our lease commitments in our 1969 annual report. To our knowledge it is the first such statement by any company.

Our 1969 annual report contains the following comment in the information accompanying its financial statements:

> "... Penney's commitments under long-term leases were approximately $285 million at year end. Long-term leases are those which have a noncancellable term of more than three years. These commitments are stated at the present value of all future minimum payments under such leases, after excluding property taxes as well as maintenance, insurance and other amounts which do not constitute payments for property rights...."

OBJECTIVE

The objective of this statement is to present the equivalent amount of unamortized mortgage debt represented by the leases. In developing our method of calculation, we started with an analysis of our sale-and-leaseback transactions where all of the economic factors affecting the lessor and lessee (such as financing arrangements, property taxes, and insurance) were clearly evident. From these analyses, we developed a set of principles for calculating the debt equivalent of these lease commitments. These same principles were then applied to the balance of our leases where the calculations had to be made from lease documents which do not clearly reflect all the economic factors affecting lessor and lessee. We then abstracted the required information from all company leases, developed a computer program for making the extensive computations involved, and individually measured the lease commitment on each of our company's 2,300 leases.

WHICH LEASES?

It seems as though Penney has every conceivable kind of lease that we and a couple of thousand ingenious lessors could design over a span of several decades covering land, stores, warehouses, office buildings, equipment, computers, etc.

Our first step was to determine which leases should be considered in computing the equivalent long-term debt represented by our lease commitments. We reasoned that inasmuch as our objective was to express long-term debt equivalents, we should base our calculations on long-term leases. We have, therefore, included all leases which cover a period of three years or more, which is consistent with general practices followed in the financial community for many years.

Leases with remaining terms of less than three years but an original period exceeding that length have been included. Leases with cancellation clauses have been regarded as commitments up to the earliest cancellation date where such date is three years or more from the beginning of the lease. Renewal option periods which are exercisable at the discretion of the lessee have been excluded because they do not represent commitments until exercised. However, when these options have been exercised, renewal periods have been included if such periods are three years or longer. Straight percentage leases (those in which an obligation arises as sales are consummated rather than by the passage of time) have been excluded.

WHAT AMOUNTS?

In calculating lease commitments, it is necessary to compute the present value of the future stream of payments (Exhibit 3). All minimum annual payments under long-term leases as defined above are included in this calculation, not just those payments occurring beyond three years.

In many leases, the landlord assumes the responsibility for expenses such as real estate taxes, maintenance, insurance, and similar items, and the rental payments are designed to cover these items as well as amortization of the investment and interest. These leases are often referred to as gross leases. Commitments for expenses of this type are considered "executory" in nature because they require the future performance of a service. Under present accounting conventions, executory expenses of this type (which also include employment contracts, raw material purchase contracts, guarantees, etc.) are not reflected in financial statements. Thus, if Penney owned rather than gross-leased such properties, these executory expenses would not be reflected in our balance sheet as liabilities. Accordingly, it is necessary to deduct these executory expenses from the stream of lease payments in order to arrive at the net amounts representing amortization of investment and interest.

We made internal studies to determine the average cost of real estate taxes and other executory expenses for different types of properties. We also determined the average annual rates by which such expenses had increased over the past 10 years. These rates of increase were applied in projecting the amounts to be deducted for executory expenses over the remaining terms of the leases.

Exhibit 3 CALCULATION OF THE PRESENT VALUE OF A LEASE COMMITMENT

1	2	3	4 (2 − 3)	5	6 (4 × 5)
Year	Minimum rent	Executory expenses*	Net commitment	Present value factor†	Present value of commitment†
1	$100,000	$20,000	$80,000	.935	$ 74,800
2	"	20,600	79,400	.873	69,315
3	"	21,220	78,780	.816	64,285
4	"	21,885	78,145	.763	59,625
5	"	22,510	77,490	.713	55,250
6	"	23,185	76,815	.666	51,160
7	"	23,880	76,120	.623	47,420
8	"	24,595	75,405	.582	43,885
Value of lease commitment					$465,740

* Includes real estate taxes, maintenance, insurance, etc. These items are assumed to increase in cost at 3 per cent per year.

† Present value at 7 per cent which was determined to be the approximate rate of interest for the year this lease was signed.

WHAT INTEREST RATES?

After deducting executory expenses, where appropriate, the remaining amounts payable under a lease approximate the sums required for amortization of the investment and interest. In order to determine the amounts attributable to amortization of investment, it is necessary to remove interest from the stream of payments. This requires determination of an appropriate rate of interest.

The effective rate of interest paid by a lessee is the interest cost to the lessor. This is clearly evident in a financing type of sale-and-leaseback transaction in which the lessee's rentals are based on the amounts required to amortize the investment plus interest on the declining amounts of unamortized investment. Therefore, in order to calculate the equivalent amounts financed by leases, it is necessary to determine the lessor's interest rate at the time the lease agreement was executed.

We undertook a study of interest rates in different years used by our lessors to arrive at rentals specified in representative lease agreements. We then made correlation studies of these amounts to various published interest rate indices and from these established a rate for each year which we believed to be representative of the cost of money to our lessors. These amounts ranged from a low of 4.0 per cent to a high of 8.8 per cent.

In the case of renewal periods, the appropriate rate is that which is applicable to the original lease if the renewal payments are fixed in the original lease agreement. If the renewal rentals were renegotiated, then the applicable rate was that in effect at the time of renewal.

An explanation of Penney's method for calculating lease commitments was sent to many security analysts and other interested parties in April 1970. Comments received since that time have been favorable, and it is hoped that our approach will stimulate interest and discussion which, in turn, will hasten the development of generally accepted, specific measurements of lease obligations.

FINANCIAL PLANNING

In the meantime, we have found the measurement of lease obligations an essential tool in our internal financial planning. To provide some perspective, it will be useful to start with a brief description of the Penney Company.

Penney is the second largest general merchandise retailer in the world. We operate over 1,900 retail units and more than 90 per cent of these facilities are leased. Our sales were $3.7 billion in 1969 and have grown, in the last five years, at a compound annual rate of 12 per cent. Net income was $111 million in 1969. Additions to retail space have averaged more than 8 per cent annually in the same period.

The company's rapid growth has required more capital than could be generated internally. As a result, we have obtained additional funds through a combination of methods. Penney sells its customer accounts receivable to J. C. Penney Financial Corporation, a wholly owned unconsolidated subsidiary which finances the receivables through the sale of commercial paper and long-term debt. Cash generated internally provides the parent company's other working capital needs and funds for store fixtures. The balance of capital requirements—mainly land and buildings—is financed through a combination of leases and direct debt. For an idea of Penney's capital structure, see Exhibit 4.

It is management's continuing concern to assure that the financial commitments for expansion are kept in balance with financial resources. The basic objective is to maintain a capital structure and degree of liquidity that will provide access to additional capital, as required, at acceptable costs.

To help us in planning, we undertook two basic studies. First, we looked into the future and projected the external funds that would be required by our expansion plans. We further tried to visualize the effect that adverse economic or money market conditions might have on the need for external funds. We concluded that, for a company such as Penney, it is desirable to maintain the kind of reserve borrowing capacity and liquidity that would be characterized by a prime credit rating from the two major bond rating agencies—Standard & Poor's and Moody's.

Second, with the help of our investment bankers, we made a study of the capital structures of other major retailers and other companies whose debt issues were rated equal to or higher than that which we considered desirable for Penney. We endeavored to consider all significant aspects of each company's performance, including its profits in recent years, growth prospects, capital structure, type of debt obligations or lease commitments, and earnings coverage of fixed charges.

We also took a close look at companies whose ratings have been revised downward in recent years and tried to identify factors which might have caused the change.

These studies confirmed that lease commitments are considered an important factor by the rating agencies. Accordingly, we looked at the capital structure of each company both before and after estimating its lease commitments. In this we had the same problem that has faced all other analysts: in the absence of complete and consistent information it was necessary to use arbitrary rules of thumb.

Our studies also confirmed the opinion of experts that a company can increase its over-all debt capacity with the right mix of direct and indirect debt such as leases.

All this work has given us some feel for what might be a "safe" range of direct and indirect debt, how much additional borrowing capacity might be available to us, and what constitutes a good mix of direct and indirect debt. It should be emphasized that this is an area that does not lend itself to precise measurement. One can expect to deal only in ranges.

To ensure that our expansion plans stay in line with our ability to raise the required funds, we modified our capital budgeting and long-range investment control procedures. Originally they are designed to keep track of expenditures to acquire ownership of fixed assets, which are an important component of the com-

Exhibit 4 J. C. PENNEY COMPANY, INC. AND CONSOLIDATED SUBSIDIARIES, BALANCE SHEET AS OF 1/31/70 ($ millions)

Current assets	851	Current liabilities	565
Investment in subsidiaries	140	Long-term debt	125
Properties, net	369	Deferred credits	15
Other assets	1	Stockholders' equity	656
Total assets	1,361	Total liabilities and stockholders' equity	1,361

pany's capital requirements. But an even more important component to many retailers, including Penney, are leases. Most new stores are leased. Here the indirect debt of the company increases to the extent of the lease commitment. Even if a store is constructed by the company, it may be sold and leased back with a resulting increase of indirect debt.

Our procedure is to maintain a current roster of all capital expenditures and lease commitments. Periodically we prepare five-year projections, by year, of the company's balance sheets, including estimates of lease commitments. By reference to our studies, we can decide whether our projected capital structure has the proper balance. We can determine how much additional direct and indirect debt the company can afford each year. Our expansion program is paced so that additional commitments remain within prudent limits.

INVESTMENT CONTROL SYSTEM

To make sure that Penney's expansion plans stay in line, we use an investment control system that tracks commitments for capital expenditures and leases.

The commitments of each division are controlled within an annual appropriation. The concept of our control system is illustrated in Exhibit 5.

As has been mentioned, periodic forecasts show how the expansion program affects the company's balance sheet. These forecasts also show how changes in the company's cash flow affect its borrowing capacity and ability to grow—a strong incentive for expansion-minded managers to improve current results. At the same time, we do not allow the system to box us in. As changes occur in the financial markets and as new business opportunities arise or old ones fade, the financing program is revised.

Thus, our control over capital commitments now covers leases the same way it covers capital expenditures.

The approach to financial planning and control described above works for the

Exhibit 5 CAPITAL INVESTMENT CONTROL REPORT

	Appropriation	Authorizations		Uncommitted Balances
		Expenditures	Leases	
1971				
Division A	50	20	30	—
Division B	20	10	5	5
Division C	30	—	20	10
Division D	60	—	45	15
Total	160	30	100	30
1972				
Division A	60	25	35	—
Division B	25	5	—	20
Division C	35	—	—	35
Division D	60	—	20	40
Total	180	30	55	95
1973 etc.				

Penney Company, but it is not our purpose to sell it to anyone else. We described it only to illustrate the important role which measurement of lease commitments plays in maintaining the proper balance of growth, liquidity, and sound capital structure for a business such as ours, which acquires the use of fixed assets largely through leasing.

DISCLOSE, DON'T CAPITALIZE NOW

The accounting profession is currently considering whether leases should be capitalized and recorded on balance sheets as liabilities—a matter which touches on many fundamental objectives and complex principles of accounting. However, our experience suggests that the first step must be the establishment of acceptable measurement techniques and disclosure of the resulting lease obligations. When these have been adequately tested in practice and understood by the financial community, the best method of presentation will probably resolve itself.

It is our hope that the approaches discussed in this article will stimulate interest and expedite remedies to the problem of measuring lease commitments.

C. INCOME TAX ALLOCATION

SIDNEY DAVIDSON

SIDNEY DAVIDSON (1919–   ), B.A. 41, M.B.A. 41, Ph.D. 50 Michigan; CPA. Currently Arthur Young Professor of Accounting and Dean of the Graduate School of Business, University of Chicago: Major publications: *The Plant Accounting Regulations of the Federal Power Commission: A Critical Analysis* (1952), *Fundamentals of Accounting* (with Mason and Schindler, 1959), *Studies in Accounting Theory* (edited readings, with Baxter, 1962), *An Income Approach to Accounting Theory* (edited readings, with Green, Horngren, and Sorter, 1964), *Handbook of Modern Accounting* (editor, 1970). Frequent contributor to *The Accounting Review*, *The Journal of Accountancy*, and other journals.

Was on the accounting faculty at Johns Hopkins University, 1949–58, prior to joining the Chicago faculty. Became Arthur Young Professor in 1962 and dean in 1969. Was research director (1956) and president (1968–69) of the American Accounting Association. Served on the AICPA Accounting Principles Board, 1965–70.

ACCELERATED DEPRECIATION AND THE ALLOCATION OF INCOME TAXES

SIDNEY DAVIDSON

In the April, 1957 issue of this Journal Maurice Moonitz presented an analysis of "Income Taxes in Financial Statements" [1] which urged the allocation of income taxes among statement items in a variety of cases. In the July, 1957 issue, Thomas M. Hill [2] indicated the reasons for his oppostion to the suggested inter-period allocation of income taxes. Both articles agree that the most important of the areas of controversy over inter-period allocation arises from the use of an ac-

---

source: From *The Accounting Review*, Vol. XXXIII, No. 2 (April, 1958), pp. 173–180. Reprinted by permission of the American Accounting Association.

[1] *The Accounting Review*, April, 1957, pp. 175–183.

[2] *The Accounting Review*, July, 1957, pp. 357–361.

celerated-depreciation method for tax purposes and straight-line depreciation for financial reporting purposes. These comments will be confined to a consideration of that question only.

In his analysis of this accelerated depreciation case Professor Moonitz seeks to associate the amount of income tax charges with income produced by individual assets. This is a well-nigh impossible task for almost all firms. Income typically results from a successful blending of a variety of economic resources, all of which are necessary to achieve the desired final result. Efforts to allocate the income total to specific assets are likely to be fruitless or misleading. In the usual case income can only be associated with the firm as a whole or with distinct operating divisions which are virtually separate firms. If attention is focused on the income of the entity, the liability for future taxes is likely to be entirely non-existent in most cases.

In deciding whether or not inter-period allocation is appropriate and whether a liability exists, Moonitz points out two controlling questions:

a. Are tax rates expected to remain at substantially their current levels? and
b. Is taxable income expected to emerge each year in the foreseeable future?

If these two criteria were indeed controlling, then recognition of a liability for future taxes might be appropriate. Most firms can answer both questions affirmatively with at least as much confidence as they place, for example, in the service life estimates that control the amount of their depreciation charges. However, two other criteria precede those listed by Moonitz. They are:

1. Are tax rules for depreciation methods expected to remain as generous as they now are? and
2. Will a policy of regular investment in assets subject to depreciation be maintained?

If the answer to these two questions is affirmative, then there will be no future tax liability and questions (a) and (b) need not be raised. Only if questions (1) and (2) cannot be answered favorably is there any need to consider the other criteria.

If we focus attention on the total collection of depreciating assets of the taxable entity rather than on one, or a small group, of its depreciating assets, the question is seen in proper perspective. In the next section the depreciation charges of an artificially simple static firm and of a steadily growing one will be considered. Subsequent sections will deal with the standards for expense and liability recognition and the probability of the non-allocation criteria being realized.

Throughout the discussion that follows the only type of allocation considered is inter-period allocation of income taxes where an accelerated-depreciation method is used for tax purposes and the straight-line method is used for financial reporting purposes. This problem would lose a good bit of its significance, as Moonitz correctly points out, if income taxes were treated as a distribution, rather than a partial determinant, of income. However, he accepts the premise that income taxes are an expense. This analysis will be couched in the same terms, although, for reasons set forth elsewhere, I feel treatment of income taxes as an income distribution results in a more meaningful presentation of income.[3]

---

[3] See Mason and Davidson, *Fundamentals of Accounting*, 3rd Edition, p. 168.

STATIC AND STEADILY GROWING FIRMS

Although a completely static firm is unlikely to be encountered in the real world, its artificial simplicity is useful as an expository device. Let us consider such a firm which owns 5 depreciating assets, each costing $1,500. The assets were acquired at the rate of one each year on successive New Year's Days and all have service lives of five years with zero salvage value. Since this is a static firm, replacement of one machine each year has been made. In company with almost all other American firms, our firm has used the straight-line depreciation method for financial accounting and tax accounting for many years. Thus the depreciation deduction in its tax return and income statement in year 0 (1953) and preceding years was $1,500.

Table 1 DEPRECIATION CHARGES OF A STATIC FIRM

Assets acquired in year	Cost of assets	Depreciation charge in year:						
		0	1	2	3	4	5	6
A. Tax Return Depreciation								
−4	1,500	300	Retired					
−3	1,500	300	300	Retired				
−2	1,500	300	300	300	Retired			
−1	1,500	300	300	300	300	Retired		
0	1,500	300	300	300	300	300	Retired	
1	1,500		500	400	300	200	100	Retired
2	1,500			500	400	300	200	100
3	1,500				500	400	300	200
4	1,500					500	400	300
5	1,500						500	400
6	1,500							500
Total Depreciation Charge on Tax Return		1,500	1,700	1,800	1,800	1,700	1,500	1,500
B. Straight-Line Depreciation in Financial Reports		1,500	1,500	1,500	1,500	1,500	1,500	1,500
C. "Extra" Depreciation ...		0	200	300	300	200	0	0

N.B. All assets have a five-year service life and zero salvage value.

In year 1 (1954) the firm decided to avail itself of the opportunity to use the sum-of-the-years-digits method [4] of depreciation for newly acquired assets for tax purposes but it decided to continue to use straight-line depreciation for financial-reporting purposes. The depreciation charges from year 0 onward are indicated

---

[4] If the double-declining-balance method were used, substantially similar results would be achieved. The sum-of-the-years-digits method is used in this and future illustrations because it gives a somewhat greater degree of acceleration and seems to be used somewhat more widely. Cf. *Accounting Trends and Techniques*, Tenth Edition (1956), p. 156.

in Table 1. During the four year period of transition [5] to the new arrangement, depreciation deductions for tax purposes exceed those for financial-reporting purposes; in years 5 and 6 and in *all years thereafter* depreciation deductions for tax and financial accounting are identical, if our two conditions of no change in the depreciation provisions of the tax law and continued replacement of retired assets are met.

Under these conditions, should an entry charging income and recognizing a liability for "income taxes payable in the future" be made in years 1 through 4? Assuming a 50% tax rate, the entry in year 1 would be:

     Income tax charges 100
     Income tax payable in the future 100
     50% of the "extra" depreciation of $200. This assumes a previous
     entry recognizing the tax currently payable has been made.

In years 2, 3 and 4 similar entries in the amounts of $150, $150, and $100, respectively, would be made if tax rates are not altered. Since tax and book depreciation deductions are the same in *every year after year 4*, the liability would remain on the books in perpetuity unchanged from its $500 amount.

Table 2   DEPRECIATION CHARGES OF A FIRM GROWING AT A 5% RATE

Assets acquired in year	Cost of assets	Depreciation charge in year:							
		0	1	2	3	4	5	6	7
A. Tax Return Depreciation									
−4	1,400	300 Retired							
−3	1,575	315	315 Retired						
−2	1,654	331	331	331 Retired					
−1	1,736	347	347	347	347 Retired				
0	1,823	365	365	365	365	365 Retired			
1	1,914		638	510	383	255	128 Retired		
2	2,010			670	536	402	268	134 Retired	
3	2,110				703	563	422	281	141
4	2,216					739	591	443	295
5	2,327						776	621	465
6	2,443							814	651
7	2,565								855
Total Depreciation Charge on Tax Return		1,658	1,996	2,223	2,334	2,324	2,185	2,293	2,407
B. Straight-Line Depreciation in Financial Reports		1,658	1,740	1,827	1,919	2,015	2,115	2,221	2,332
C. "Extra" Depreciation		0	256	396	415	309	70	72	75

N.B. All assets have a five-year service life and zero salvage value.

A somewhat more realistic model is introduced if we consider a firm which grows at a constant rate. In the first year of the period under consideration

---

[5] The transition to accelerated depreciation will be accomplished in $n-1$ years, where n is equal to estimated service life of the asset. In a more realistic case of a firm with a heterogeneous group of assets, the great bulk of the transition will be completed in $n-1$ years, where n is equal to weighted average service life.

(year −4) it acquires $1,500 of depreciating assets. Investment in depreciating assets grows at a 5% rate each year thereafter. The case is further simplified by again assuming that all assets have a five-year service life and zero salvage value. This firm also changes to the sum-of-the-years-digits method for tax purposes in year 1 and continues to use straight-line depreciation for financial accounting.

Table 2 indicates the results for the steadily growing firm. During the transition period, tax depreciation exceeds book depreciation by substantial amounts. At the end of the transition period this "extra" depreciation declines to a much smaller figure, but grows in *every year thereafter*. If the firm's rate of growth is maintained, the "extra" depreciation not only grows each year but grows by an increasing amount. If Table 2 were extended, it would show that in year 20 "extra" depreciation was $144 and by year 30 it would amount to $233.[6]

If a liability for future taxes were recognized under these conditions, the balance in the liability account would grow each year. After a sufficiently long period, this "liability" might well become one of the major balance-sheet items.

CRITERIA FOR RECOGNITION OF EXPENSES AND LIABILITIES

Does a difference in the deduction for depreciation on the tax return as compared with the books require an accrual entry in all cases, including of course the two examples of the previous section? If our accounting criteria for expense and liability recognition were sufficiently precise and complete, we could measure this situation against the rules and reach an easy answer. Unfortunately the criteria in this area do not permit so easy an approach.

The 1957 Revision of Accounting and Reporting Standards for Corporate Financial Statements may serve as a guide. It says with regard to expenses: Recognition of cost expiration [expense] is based either on complete or partial decline in the usefulness of assets or the appearance of a liability without a corresponding increase in assets. . . . The issuance of product guarantees, notice of adverse court rulings, and similar events establishing the existence of liabilities call for the recognition of cost expiration."[7]

The crux of the matter then is whether the events in these cases have established the existence of a liability.

Concerning liabilities the statement says: "The interests or equities of creditors (liabilities) are claims against the entity arising from past activities or events which, in the usual case, require for their satisfaction the expenditure of corporate resources. . . . The discharge of a liability at a determinable date is normally required by contract or intent of parties."[8]

Any future tax item arising from the cases of the previous section fails com-

---

[6] The general formula for the calculation of the "extra" depreciation assuming a uniform service life (n), a constant rate of growth (r), and an initial investment of X is:
Extra depreciation in year y
$$= \sum \left(X(1+r)^y \left(\frac{n}{\frac{1}{2}n(n+1)} - \frac{1}{n} \right) \right) + \left(X(1+r)^{y-1} \left(\frac{n-1}{\frac{1}{2}n(n+1)} - \frac{1}{n} \right) \right) + \cdots + \left(X(1+r)^{y-(n-1)} \left(\frac{n-(n-1)}{\frac{1}{2}n(n+1)} - \frac{1}{n} \right) \right)$$

[7] *The Accounting Review*, October, 1957, p. 541.
[8] *Ibid.*, p. 542.

pletely to meet these usual tests of a liability. The Federal government recognizes no "claim against the entity" in its record-keeping; "the expenditure of corporate resources" will not be required, neither at a "determinable date" nor at any other time.

Professor Moonitz, in a sense, assumes the existence of a liability by saying that the tax effect produced in one year by differences in depreciation timing has "an unavoidable offsetting tax effect in some other year." If the tax were based on income generated by individual assets, this assumption might be justified. Since the tax is based on taxable income of the entity however, there need not be a future effect for the going concern, as we have seen, if the two basic criteria are met.

The comparison with bond liabilities made by Moonitz seems entirely beside the point. The liability that is recognized in most bond issues is made up largely of the discounted present value of required future interest payments. In fact, in the example cited of a bond issue that is always refunded (a perpetuity, in other words) the present value of the future interest payments is the measure of the entire liability. If it were possible to issue bonds on a perpetual basis at a zero interest rate, would a liability exist? The answer clearly would seem to be no, that such a transaction is in the nature of a gift. That is precisely the effect produced for the going concern by accelerated tax depreciation. So long as the firm follows a regular investment policy, it will receive a "gift" of having its income tax payments permanently reduced. It may well be argued that a gift should not be permitted to distort comparative operating results by reducing an expense, but the solution is to treat income taxes as an income distribution rather than to recognize an expense that simply does not exist.

THE PROBABILITY OF THE NECESSARY CONDITIONS BEING REALIZED

The preceding sections indicate that there will be no liability for future taxes for static or growing firms if depreciation provisions of the tax laws remain unchanged (or become more generous) and a regular policy of investment in depreciating assets is maintained. How likely is it that these necessary conditions will be realized?

Depreciation Provisions of the Tax Law Unaltered

The depreciation provisions of the tax code are a part of the law of the land and the law may, of course, be altered by Congress at any time. However, no substantial indication that Congress feels that the present provisions are too generous and should therefore be altered has come to my attention. In fact, there has been some contention that present provisions are not generous enough and that the amount of acceleration permitted should be increased. All of the history of tax legislation indicates that once special rights [9] are granted, it is very difficult and unusual for Congress to withdraw them, especially if the return to the former rules would result in a doubling-up of tax burdens during the years of return. Current discussions of impending tax legislation all make mention of possible alterations in tax rates (the Moonitz criterion a), but do not hint at less generous depreciation methods.

[9] If tax depreciation exceeds book depreciation, this is an indication that the firm is enjoying a special right.

It is this feature of permanence of the depreciation provisions of the tax law and their general applicability that distinguishes cases of the sort under consideration from those arising under the 60-month amortization provisions of the Revenue Acts of 1940 and 1950. Under those acts, rapid amortization was permitted only for facilities for which certificates of necessity were issued. Even though continuous investment was planned by the firm, there could be no assurance that the new facilities would qualify for certificates of necessity. Consequently when depreciation charges on the tax return exceeded those shown on the financial statements, an offsetting tax effect in a future year or years was possible if the criteria cited by Moonitz were likely to be met.[10] Where accelerated depreciation is available for all assets and is likely to remain so, this problem does not arise.

Regular Investment Policy

The second criterion of a regular investment policy is more difficult to define and to realize. Since an infinite number of asset acquisition and service life combinations is possible, generalization as to what policy of investment would insure that future years' taxes would not be increased by current differences between tax and book depreciation is probably impossible. In almost all cases a pattern of capital asset acquisitions in which each year's purchases are equal to or greater than those of the previous year would suffice.[11] Relatively small declines in purchases punctuating periods of moderate growth would under normal circumstances be accommodated within the assumption as well.

Since conventional accounting procedures and tax regulations both operate in historical cost terms, the series of investments is measured in monetary, not real, terms. During a period of rising prices, fulfillment of the necessary criterion is more likely since it does not require a firm to maintain a constant rate of acquisition of productive capacity but merely of dollar investment.

In recent years our economy has, of course, been characterized by substantial growth rather than merely a maintenance of investment. Aggregate investment in producers' durable goods has grown at an average rate of over 6% per annum in the post war decade from 1947 through 1956.[12] In only two years in that interval, 1949 and 1954, did investment in assets subject to depreciation fall below that of the preceding year. In both cases the decline was less than 5% and was quickly recovered. It would appear that firms in the aggregate have met this criterion of regular or growing investment in capital assets rather satisfactorily over the last decade.

[10] Measurement of the effective present liability, though, would be a substantial task as the next section suggests. Anticipating the analysis there, consider the case of an asset costing $100,000 with a twenty year life depreciated over a sixty month period. Assume a 50% tax rate and that a 6% discount rate is appropriate. In the first year, depreciation on the tax return is $20,000 and on the financial records is $5,000, producing a tax "loan" of $7,500. The loan will be repaid at the rate of $500 a year starting at the end of year 6. The present value of such a stream of payments is only $3,846.

[11] Even with this pattern, sufficient divergence in service lives of different years' acquisitions could produce small adverse effects in subsequent years.

[12] Data drawn from *National Income* (1954 Edition), a supplement to the *Survey of Current Business* (Washington, 1954), pp. 162–165 and *Survey of Current Business* (Feb., 1957), p. 14.

Growth of investment in the economy as a whole does not necessarily indicate growth, or even maintenance, of investment by all firms in the economy. Although the vast majority of income-tax-paying firms are probably at least maintaining their level of monetary investment, two classes of exceptions to this general tendency may be noted. They are firms with a single, or preponderant, indivisible asset and new firms.

Firms owning a single office building or apartment house or operating a single mine are examples of the first class of exceptions. A constant stream of capital-goods investment by such firms is unlikely, and funds made available annually by the earning of depreciation charges are frequently used to reduce bonded indebtedness or are invested in securities. For such firms, income of the entity and income from a single asset are virtually the same. If they employ an accelerated depreciation method in their tax accounting and straight-line depreciation in their financial recordkeeping, recognition of a liability for future taxes might be appropriate if satisfactory assumptions could be made about future profitability and future tax rates. The nature of their individual assets, however, would reduce the significance of the income-tax deferral for these firms. Office buildings and apartment houses are long-lived assets and the "additional" taxes would begin to be paid only in the second half of their lives and would be spread over that entire second-half period. At any reasonable discount rate, the present value of the taxes deferred in any one year would be relatively small. For example, if we assume a $1,000,000 building with a 40-year life, a 50% tax rate persisting 40 years into the future, profitable operations, and a 6% discount rate, the tax saving in year 1 is $11,890 but the present value of the future liability is less than $2,000. In succeeding years the deferred tax liability would grow every year by the present value of that year's deferral plus accrued interest at the assumed rate on the balance in the deferred liability account at the start of the year. From year 13 on the interest accruals exceed the annual tax deferrals and it is well into the final third of the asset's life before the "future tax liability" begins to be reduced. Calculation of the amounts in individual cases is a long and tedious job, but the only other alternative if deferred taxes are to be recognized is to ignore the imputed interest factor implicit in the situation. A failure to recognize interest on liabilities that do not become payable for two decades or more simply ignores the economic reality of the situation. There are too many cases already in existence where accounting fails to recognize economic reality for us to add another to the list.

Newly organized firms will normally make substantial investments in capital assets in their first year of existence. Unless expansion is exceptionally rapid in the following years, that first-year level of expenditure will not be maintained. If the firm's profits make it worthwhile to claim accelerated depreciation on its tax return, but it shows only straight-line depreciation in its accounting records, inter-period allocation of income taxes during this early transitional period to regular investment may be warranted. It seems unlikely that there are many cases of this type where the adjustments would be material after the discount factor is recognized.

When investment expenditures fluctuate erratically, a special problem is likely to arise. One possibility for dealing with such a situation would be to divide the expenditures for depreciable assets into continuing and extraordinary portions, and to attempt inter-period allocation only with respect to the extraordinary portion. The 1955 annual report of National Dairy Products Corporation is an example of a division of plant expenditures for this purpose. In the notes to the financial statements the following paragraph appears:

> The Company, for income tax reporting only, has adopted the declining balance method of computing depreciation. . . . For all other purposes, including the financial statements, the straight-line method is being continued. The reduction in Federal and Canadian income taxes for the year 1955 arising from the additional deduction for depreciation so allowable for income tax reporting is estimated to be $2,850,000. Of this amount, $2,500,000, representing the tax reduction applicable to regularly-recurring additions and replacements of machinery and equipment, as estimated by the management, is reflected as an addition to 1955 earnings through a reduction in the provision for 1955 Federal and Canadian taxes on income. The balance of $350,000 of such tax reduction, which is attributable to additional depreciation for tax reporting on machinery and equipment additions in excess of regularly-recurring replacements, and on buildings, has been deferred and is included in the "Provision for Federal and Canadian taxes on income" in the accompanying balance sheet.

Firms with fluctuating annual expenditures are likely to be the major problem for the auditor. For a seasoned firm, replacement and adaptation to changing technology in a world of rising prices promise a reasonably high level of continuing investment. Occasional peaks of capital asset purchases, especially if their depreciation charges are spread over a long period, are unlikely in most cases to affect adversely income tax charges of future years in amounts sufficient to justify current accruals.

Financial statements are prepared for individual firms, not statistical averages, though, and the auditor must decide whether the firm he is considering falls into what is likely to be a relatively small group of exceptions. In deciding he will have to rely on evidence of past investment policy, indications of long term plans and expressions of managerial intent rather than the more familiar types of objective verification. Assessment of future investment plans is somewhat more complex than deciding whether profits will be earned regularly in the future, but both require the same type of subjective decision. Distasteful though it be, accountants are likely to be faced by this type of problem more often as efforts are made to make income reporting more realistic.

On balance, it appears that the likelihood of the two primary criteria being realized, or of the secondary criterion of continuing profits not being met in those cases where a constant level of investment is not anticipated, is substantial; so substantial that it would seem that inter-period allocation of income taxes from this source should require explanation in the notes to the financial statements.

CONCLUSIONS

Many firms use an accelerated depreciation method for calculating the depreciation deduction to be made on the income tax return, but employ the straight-line depreciation method for calculating the depreciation expense figure for financial statements. In considering the effect of this action on income tax expense and income tax liability, attention must be centered on the taxpaying entity, the firm as a whole. For a static or growing firm, current tax savings from this source will not adversely affect income tax charges of future years. In fact, the growing firm can look forward to an ever-increasing annual tax saving continuing year after year. Only a moribund firm with declining investment in capital assets is likely to be faced by a substantial deferred tax liability, and then only if its dying years are profitable ones.

Although the analysis indicates that a liability for future taxes from this source should be recognized only in rare cases, disclosure of any difference between the amount of depreciation claimed on the tax return and that shown in the income statement is a desirable reporting practice and should be employed regularly.

THE ANNUAL INCOME TAX ACCRUAL*

THOMAS F. KELLER

Biography on page 184.

The periodic determination of an enterprise's operating results is of primary importance to the accountant. He is concerned with a useful and meaningful presentation of these results whether the focus of his work is on financial position or a recap of the activity for the period. In either case he is measuring the net change in assets and the resulting impact on the owner's equity.

The annual tax charge must be measured and recorded in a manner which is consistent with this basic objective. The idea of smoothing or normalizing net income, which has been identified with the phrase "interperiod allocation of corporate income taxes," does not conform with this concept. Instead, the periodic tax charge must be that which can logically and properly be identified with the operations of a specific period.

---

* This article is based on research by the author, the findings of which have been published as a monograph, *Accounting for Corporate Income Taxes*, by the Bureau of Business Research, The University of Michigan, Ann Arbor, Michigan.

SOURCE: From *The Journal of Accountancy*, Vol. CXIV, No. 4 (October, 1962), pp. 59–65. Reprinted by permission of the American Institute of Certified Public Accountants.

ALLOCATION OF THE CHARGE

Historically accountants have considered the tax charge to be incurred at the time taxable income, as defined in the statutes, is realized. The charge has been considered to be a period cost since no direct future benefit is deemed to accrue to the corporation as a result of the tax payment. With the enactment of the Internal Revenue Code of 1954 this traditional procedure became suspect. Accountants, security analysts and many users of financial statements noticed a marked increase in the reported net income. The increase was in many cases traced directly to the reduction in the current tax charge. Naturally the question was raised as to the nature of this reduction in the annual income tax charge.

The problem which existed is illustrated in the following case of the Fixed Asset Company. In accordance with the provisions of Section 167 of the Internal Revenue Code of 1954 the Fixed Asset Company decided to depreciate its recent acquisitions in accordance with the double-the-straight-line method of depreciation for tax purposes. The straight-line method was considered appropriate for reporting purposes, however. The assets cost $100,000, had an estimated salvage-value of $3,700, and the life of the assets was estimated to be three years. The tax rate was 30 per cent on the first $25,000 of taxable income in any one year and 52 per cent on all taxable income in excess of $25,000. The income before depreciation charges, on the new assets, and income taxes was $150,000 for each of the three years. The reported results of operations without giving effect to tax allocation were as shown in the following table:

The Fixed Asset Company
Statements of Income
for the Years I, II, and III

	Year I	Year II	Year III
Income before depreciation and taxes	$150,000	$150,000	$150,000
Depreciation charges	$ 32,100	$ 32,100	$ 32,100
Income tax charges	37,833	60,945	68,646
Total charges	$ 69,933	$ 93,045	$100,746
Net income	$ 80,067	$ 56,955	$ 49,254

The results in this case are fairly obvious. Net income has been reduced each year because the income tax has increased; yet, the tax rate has remained constant as has income before taxes. Do these statements provide a meaningful presentation of the results of operations? There are many accountants who have concluded that this is not a realistic presentation and therefore it is not an extremely meaningful presentation. If the Fixed Asset Company had used the straight-line method of depreciation for tax purposes, then the annual tax charge would have been $55,808 and the reported income would have been constant at $62,092. The total tax charge over the three-year period is thus the same; the adoption of the accelerated depreciation method has merely served to delay the payment of a portion of the tax for a period of time. Certainly management should have the prerogative of deferring the payment of the tax where permitted by law. There is some question, however, as to whether or not the management group should be empowered with the right to manipulate the reported results of operations by the arbitrary timing of the tax charge.

In response to this practice of arbitrarily shifting net income between accounting periods the "neonormalizing school" arose. These accountants have as their objective the allocation of the income tax charge between accounting periods. They argue that the allocation should be effected so that reported net income is normalized or, stated more positively, so that the deferral of the tax payment at the discretion of management should not be reflected in the report of periodic net income. This group has the support of the American Institute of Certified Public Accountants in Accounting Research Bulletin No. 43 where one reads that "income taxes are an expense that should be allocated, when necessary and practicable, to income and other accounts, as other expenses are allocated. What the income statement should reflect under this head, as under any other head, is the expense properly allocable to the income included in the income statement for the year." [1]

Accounting Research Bulletin No. 44 (Revised) states, however, that "where it may reasonably be presumed that the accumulative difference between taxable income and financial income will continue for a long or indefinite period, it is alternatively appropriate . . . to recognize the related tax effect as additional amortization or depreciation applicable to such assets in recognition of the loss of future tax deductibility for income tax purposes."

The bulletin continues by making an exception in the case of some regulated companies. "The committee believes that they [regulatory authorities] should permit the recognition of deferred income taxes. . . . However, where charges for deferred income taxes are not allowed for rate-making purposes, accounting recognition need not be given to the deferment of taxes if it may reasonably be expected that increased future income taxes, resulting from the earlier deduction of declining-balance depreciation for income tax purposes only, will be allowed in future rate determinations." [2, a]

On the basis of these statements one is led to question the *real* motive of this allocation process. Is the proposal for the interperiod allocation of the tax charge merely an attempt to normalize income or does it have a logical theoretical basis? The alternative procedures sanctioned by the AICPA certainly suggest that there is more concern with the effect than with the underlying cause.

Undoubtedly the use of the term "allocation" has caused much of the confusion which surrounds the presently accepted methods of measuring the tax charge. If one accepts the thesis that the tax charge is a period cost, then what

---

[1] American Institute of Certified Public Accountants, *Restatement and Revision of Accounting Research Bulletins,* Accounting Research Bulletin No. 43, a report issued by the committee on accounting procedure (New York: American Institute of Certified Public Accountants, 1953), p. 88.

[2] American Institute of Certified Public Accountants, *Declining-balance Depreciation,* Accounting Research Bulletin No. 44 (Revised), a report issued by the committee on accounting procedure (New York: American Institute of Certified Public Accountants, 1958), p. 2-A.

[a] The relevant sections of ARB No. 43 and 44 (rev.) have been superseded by APB Opinion No. 11 "Accounting for Income Taxes" (Dec. 1967) [Eds.].

does the term "to allocate" mean when used in reference to income taxes? To what is the tax being allocated? Actually the annual charge is not being apportioned at all. Instead the lifetime tax bill is being divided into annual segments, a necessary activity for a realistic measure of an enterprise's operating activity. Basically, the problem of measuring and recording the periodic tax charge is no different from that associated with accounting for other costs. Specifically the problem is threefold: (1) when is the cost incurred? (2) how is it to be recorded? and (3) in what period should it be considered a revenue deduction?

YEAR OF INCIDENCE

The determination of the year of incidence of revenue and of related cost is peculiarly an accounting function. The accrual method of accounting for business transactions has been adopted as the most realistic method of timing the recognition of revenue and cost. This method has also been adopted in principle by the tax statutes, Section 446, and court decisions [3] as an acceptable means of determining taxable income. In spite of this apparent agreement between accepted accounting procedures and the tax statutes, differences do exist in the measurement of business and taxable income. These differences have arisen out of basically different objectives for the determination of income. The objective of determining business income is to measure the results of operations of an enterprise; whereas the objective of income taxation, and, therefore, of the determination of taxable income, is to raise revenue for the support of the Government. Admittedly the basic objective of revenue raising is often made subservient to other less well-recognized objectives. For example, the Congress of the United States has used the tax law as a means of directing corporate activity along certain desired economic, social and political lines. In addition, any revenue-raising tax may occasionally need to be modified because of considerations, such as: (1) equity among the subjects taxed, (2) economic consequences of the law, and (3) administrative feasibility. In spite of these differences both measures of income are striving to measure the same quantity over time.

Thus, in spite of the avowed intention to accept the accrual basis of accounting for tax purposes, there have been several considerations of tax policy which have forced departures from the strict accrual basis in several respects. These have taken two routes. In several instances the tax laws have allowed the exclusion or required the inclusion of items in the determination of taxable income which are not treated in the same manner in the determination of business income. These differences have the effect of changing the total tax bill of the enterprise.[4] In other cases the timing of the determinants of taxable income has been changed from that which is employed in the determination of business income. In these latter cases the total tax bill of an enterprise is unaffected, but the timing of the payments of the tax bill may be materially changed. These timing differences do not, however, destroy the basic intent of the law—to tax the total profits of the

---

[3] See *Woolford Realty Co., Inc.* v. *Rose*, 286 U.S. 319, *New Colonial Ice Co., Inc.* v. *Helvering*, 292 U.S. 435, and *Pacific Grape Products Co.* v. *Commissioner*, 17 T.C. 1097.

[4] For example, the percentage depletion allowance reduces taxable income for the life of the enterprise. In this case the total tax bill is reduced.

corporation. Instead, the time for the payment of the tax bill is merely accelerated or deferred in relation to the time when it would have been paid otherwise.[5]

CAUSE AND EFFECT

As a result of these changes in the timing of the tax payments the traditional method of accounting for corporate income taxes has been subjected to rather careful scrutiny. If the traditional approach of accounting for income taxes is followed, this means that the tax charge is accounted for when the legal liability to the Government arises rather than when the income is earned. The legal liability is said to arise when taxable income is realized and, as has been discussed, this event may or may not coincide with the earning of income.

In general, the accountant is concerned with business transactions which conform to a standard pattern of cause and effect. First, there is the cause, which establishes the proper time for accounting for the transaction. Secondly, there is the effect of the transaction on the business, which is the basis for the recording procedure. The questions accountants must answer in this connection are the following: When does the tax charge accrue, and how can it most effectively be measured?

At what point in the course of business activity does the cause for accruing the tax charge arise? At least two occurrences in the affairs of an enterprise may be considered controlling in this situation. The first, the realization of taxable income, is related to the legal liability of the Government. At the time the liability for the payment of the tax is established, a definite event has occurred that may be considered the cause underlying the incurrence of the tax charge. This criterion is similar to that applied to many other transactions which occur in business operations. For example, the cost of all goods and services is recorded when the legal liability for the payment of the cost is recognized. The other party to the contract has generally performed his agreement; this is the cause for recognizing the transaction in the accounts of the vendee. Admittedly there is no contract with the Government, and neither has the Government by its action created a liability. According to the law of the land, however, a liability has arisen in favor of the Government because of some act or action of the taxpayer; specifically, the corporation has earned income as determined by the tax regulations. The cause has occurred and the effect must be duly recorded.

The second occurrence which might be considered the cause for recognizing the tax charge is the earning of income as measured by accounting conventions for business purposes. It has been established that, in general, the concept of business and taxable income is one and the same. Simply stated, income is the excess of revenue earned during the period over the cost of producing that revenue and any other cost incident to the operation of the enterprise. The major difference between the two measures is one of timing the recognition of the determinants of income. The apparent intent of the tax law was to subject all

[5] There are certain situations which may cause the total tax bill to be changed (see footnote 7); however, the law intends merely to defer the tax rather than to change the total amount to be paid. Some of the areas of possible tax reduction may be eliminated in future amendments to the law; for example, the capital gains tax on assets used in the business, where one of the accelerated depreciation methods is used for tax purposes, may be deleted. In this event gains on the sale of fixed assets would be considered ordinary income and taxed at the statutory rates.

income, with certain minor exceptions, to the tax.[6] Various regulations have been enacted, however, to time the flow of cash into the Government in accordance with several considerations; among them are administrative feasibility and economic, political, and social influences. If the intent of the law is to subject all income to the tax, then it is reasonable to conclude that the earning of income is the cause which gives rise to the tax charge. Theoretically, the total tax payments over the life of a corporation are the same whether the assessment is based on taxable or business income. The only differences which arise between the two methods are those related to the timing of the cash flow to the Government.[7] The accountant is unable to confine himself to the aggregate tax charge; instead he must consider the periodic assignment of the charge. The need for a periodic appraisal of business operations has forced accountants to adopt procedures which associate the cost of producing revenue for a period with the revenue emerging during that period, rather than procedures which associate total cost and total revenue over the life of the enterprise. This same need requires a periodic measure of the tax charge.

If the accountant is to produce the most realistic and meaningful reports, he must account for taxes, as for other costs, in accordance with the principles underlying the accrual basis of accounting. The tax charge which should be included in a report of operations is that which will have to be paid on the basis of the year's operations. Deviations from this charge are likely to render the report less realistic and reduce the utility which might otherwise be derived from it.

CREDIT BALANCE

The accrual of the tax charge should be accompanied by the recognition of a liability to the Government. This accrual is no different from any other accrued liability, for example, the accrual of interest charges on borrowed money or the accrual of wages earned by employees.[8] The cause of the event is different; how-

---

[6] For the court's interpretation of the intent of the law, see *Woolford Realty Co., Inc.* v. *Rose,* 286 U.S. 319; and *Burnet* v. *Sanford and Brooks Company,* 282 U.S. 359.

[7] In fact the total tax bill may be affected by the enactment of a tax law that departs from the measure of business income in levying the tax on corporations. The tax rates may change between the time income is earned and the tax payment is made. Management may take action on certain transactions which will subject some income to lower rates than would have otherwise been in effect; for example, gains on the sale of capital assets are taxed at 25 per cent whereas the depreciation deduction was allowed against revenue subject to a tax rate of 52 per cent. Operating losses which cannot be offset by profits under the operating loss carry-back, carry-forward provision may cause the total tax bill to be changed. In the absence of such special situations—and these are only a sample—the total tax charge is the same regardless of the base used for its computation.

[8] There are accountants who argue that one must assume that the tax rate will remain unchanged and the enterprise will remain profitable if the tax is to be accrued. In all accrual accounting one of the basic assumptions is that the business is a going concern with indefinite life, which assumes profitable operations. The possibility of a change in the tax rate does not negate the advantages to be derived from accrual accounting in this area. The original accrual may be in error if the rates change. If there is a change in rates, a correction may be necessary; however, corrections of accruals are not an uncommon occurrence.

ever, the principles of recognizing the effect should be the same. The accounting profession, through the organ of the American Institute of Certified Public Accountants, spoke out in Accounting Research Bulletin No. 43, Chapter 8, against procedures which decrease income and at the same time increase some portion of stock equity. Certainly such a procedure could not be condoned in the situation under consideration. Accounting Research Bulletin No. 44 (Revised), Paragraph 8, does sanction such activity in the case of public utilities, however. The inclusion of the credit balance as a part of common stock equity has all the earmarks of an attempt to manipulate the reported results of operations. One can see very clearly the public utilities' interest in avoiding the inclusion of the credit balance as a liability because of the impact on its stock equity ratio. On the other hand, one must wonder occasionally about the propriety of financial transactions which are carried out without considering the classification of large credit balances. No one would suggest including a forty-year subordinated debenture bond as a part of retained earnings. Then why should the lending institutions accept as the basis for granting loans financial statements which include a substantial liability to the Federal Government in the stock equity section of the balance sheet? Of course the argument is that this liability will never be paid as long as the utility maintains its current level of investment. It might be pointed out that the bonds payable will in all likelihood never be paid off either. There is no rational basis for the different treatment which the utility has been permitted to employ.

DEFERRED CREDIT

The term "deferred credit" has never been adequately explained; however, in common usage it appears to carry the connotation that the corporation has been the beneficiary of some unearned revenue. In reality, items of this kind are in no sense revenue, either earned or unearned. Rather, they are advance payments to the corporation for services to be rendered; the revenue arises with the performance of the service. Further confusion has been added to this subject with the suggestion that the credit arising from the "interperiod allocation of corporate taxes" is a deferred credit to future expenses.[9] Just what is a deferred credit to future expenses? Such a category is not included in the ordinary discussion of accounting principles. This might be considered to represent an advance payment from some source to aid in the payment of future expenses. Certainly this is not the case at all: there has been no advance payment to the corporation from any source. Instead, the corporation has an obligation to pay a certain sum to the Government based on the reported earnings of the current period and the tax laws in effect during this period. The credit side of the entry is a liability to be sure, nothing more and nothing less, even though in aggregate a portion of it may be deferred indefinitely.

In most cases the amount of deferred taxes will not be paid within the next fiscal period, the ordinary dividing line between current and long-term liabilities. Consequently, the deferred portion of the total accrual should be included as a

[9] The Canadian Institute of Chartered Accountants, *Accounting and Auditing Practices, Bulletin No. 10,* Statements issued by the Committee on Accounting and Auditing Research (Toronto: The Canadian Chartered Accountants, 1954).

long-term liability like other installment payables. When portions of the liability become payable within the following year, those portions should be included in the current liability section of the position statement.

INCOME TAX ALLOCATION

Hill [10] has argued that if tax allocation is to be employed, then the accountant must use the present value of the liability. Since in many cases the period of deferral may be rather long, he asserts that the present value is nominal and, hence, need not be recognized. He argues that the assumption of a zero rate of interest is untenable since it necessarily implies that there is no advantage to the firm in deferring the tax payment. To argue that the accountant should adopt some interest rate which represents the sacrifice cost of yielding liquid funds in evaluating the present value of this liability is to insist on a procedure which is entirely foreign to all other accounting transactions. In no other situation are asset or liability balances derived by applying such a technique. Certainly in the case of interest-bearing obligations the present value of the obligations is indicated on the position statement. In these cases, however, the interest rate used in the determination of the present value is the market rate for comparable grade securities. In no case is the sacrifice cost to the firm of yielding liquid funds used in determining this present value. In the case of the tax deferral there is no explicit interest rate, and in addition there is no evidence that there is an implicit interest rate as in the case of many other "noninterest"-bearing obligations. There has been no evidence to indicate that tax rates will be increased because businesses have been permitted to defer a portion of the tax payment. To the contrary, there is substantial evidence which indicates that, if the incentive which the Government is attempting to provide is successful in stimulating business activity, the tax rate may be reduced without loss of revenue to the Government.

The argument has been presented by some accountants that the credit arising from accounting for deferred taxes should be added to the allowance for depreciation of plant assets. The basis for this position is that the asset which is subject to one of the accelerated methods of depreciation for tax purposes may lose its economic usefulness faster than an asset which is not treated in a similar manner. The argument continues, stating that this is especially true if one accepts the idea that an item of plant has two uses—the production of revenue and the reduction of taxes. In the opinion of the author, the expiration of economic usefulness is a matter to be considered in the establishment of depreciation policy—and it is quite possible that the present methods of depreciation are inadequate. The problems of accounting for the annual tax charge and the annual expiration of plant assets are distinctly different, however. The accountant should not attempt to correct deficiencies in depreciation with his accounting for the annual tax charge. The credit arising from the accrual of deferred taxes is a liability and should not be used as an offset to any asset or group of assets. By delaying the time when the tax must be paid, the Government is providing funds to the corporation to be used in its operations. In this very limited sense the Government

---

[10] Thomas M. Hill, "Some Arguments against the Inter-period Allocation of Income Taxes," *The Accounting Review*, XXXII (July 1957), pp. 357–361.

becomes an investor in the enterprise; a unique kind of investor, to be sure, in that there is no expectation of interest or dividend payments.

DEBIT BALANCE

In the event that a payment, in lieu of taxes, is made to the Government before the liability is accrued, an asset exists. There has been an advance payment to the Government which has economic value. The asset can be used to satisfy a future claim, by the Government, against the resources of the corporation. For example, if a corporation receives rent in advance no income has been earned; therefore, no related tax charge exists. The Internal Revenue Code of 1954 requires that this receipt of rent be taxed in the year received even though there is no earned income. When the tax is paid the corporation is making a payment on a future tax bill. No revenue deduction should be recognized at the time of the payment. Instead an asset should be recognized. Admittedly, the usefulness of the asset is rather restricted in that it has value only in so far as it can satisfy a particular type of claim against the corporation; nevertheless, value is present and the asset should be recognized.

Some accountants have argued that the asset should not be recognized because there is no assurance of profitable operations in the future. This is certainly a valid argument; however, if one adopts this attitude he can hardly support accrual accounting in any form. One of the postulates which is basic to accrual accounting is the going-concern postulate, which has as one of its basic tenets the assumption of continued *profitable* operations.

ADVANCE PAYMENT AS AN ASSET

In accordance with the concept of accrual accounting, therefore, the advance payment does have value and thus qualifies as an asset. Certainly the owners of a business which has received a substantial amount of advanced rental payments and which has paid the tax applicable to these receipts would not seriously entertain a bid to buy the business if this advance payment of the tax were not considered in the offer to buy. If the owners should sell the business without consideration of this fact, the accountant who advised them would certainly be remiss in his duties.

The classification of the asset on the statement of financial position raises some questions. The advance, like other advance payments, should be considered to be a receivable. In this case the corporation may not be able to demand payment of the Government; however, the corporation does have the right to some tax-free income. That is, when the rental income is earned no additional tax will have to be paid. And, in the event that the business should suffer a net operating loss, the receivable under certain circumstances might well represent a claim for cash from the Government. The recommendation that the asset be classified as a deferred charge is rather nebulous, in that the term "deferred charge" has never been clearly defined. Instead the asset might well be labeled "advance payment on Federal income taxes" and be included in the receivables category. If this asset was not to be utilized in the near future, placement in the noncurrent section of the statement might be justified. Such a situation is rather hard to conceive since sound business practice would hardly permit the payment of rent for more than one year in advance; however, if there is a continual advance receipt of rent, there will be a continuing advance to the Government. This situation does not justify the classificaion of the tax advance as a noncurrent asset, however. There are few, if any, accountants who would insist that the minimum balance of trade receivables be classified as a noncurrent asset and that a continuing advance tax payment is in the same category. Individual segments of the advance expire as the rent received in advance is earned. Additions are constantly being made to the advance as additional rental advances are received. The asset balance is thus a revolving balance, quite similar to the balance of trade accounts receivable.

The problem of the interperiod allocation of the corporate income tax can best be solved by adopting the well-known procedures of accrual accounting. The term "allocation" has led to a great deal of confusion in this particular situation. The problem is not technically one of allocation, but rather one of accruing the tax charge in a manner which is consistent with current accounting practice. The problem is not one of normalizing income, but rather one of presenting a realistic and meaningful statement of income. To defer expense recognition to the time of the cash outlay is to provide a major loophole by which the results of operations can be manipulated. It is a task of management to determine when an outlay of cash should be made, but it is the responsibility of the accountant to ascertain that any charge which had its incidence in a given accounting period is included in reckoning the affairs of that period. The cause for the incurrence of the corporate income tax is the earning of income. When the income is earned the tax should be accrued. The tax charge has no economic usefulness for future accounting periods; therefore, there is no problem of apportionment between deferred and expired costs. It is a deduction from the revenue of the period in which accrued. The credit balance which arises as a result of the accrual is a liability. It is not a restriction of the retained earnings or any other part of stock equity, nor is it a contra-asset. It is an interest-free liability to pay a sum of money to the Federal Government in the future. In the event that the tax is paid before the liability is accrued, either an asset account, prepaid taxes or advances to the Government exists, which is properly included in the position statement. The value of the asset stems from the fact that it may be used to satisfy a future claim against the resources of the enterprise. It is not a portion of the tax charge which will contribute to the production of future revenues.

The accountant, therefore, does not have as his objective the smoothing or normalization of income. He is applying the well-known and widely adopted techniques of accrual accounting.

RELATED READINGS

A. PROBLEM OF DEFINITION

Leopold A. Bernstein, "Reserves for Future Costs and Losses," *Financial Analysts Journal*, January–February, 1970, pp. 45–48; reprinted in *The New York Certified Public Accountant*, July, 1970, pp. 541–546. A critical review of reserve practices.

Robert W. Clarke, "Accounting for Self-insurance," *The New York Certified Public Accountant*, August, 1968, pp. 567–571.

B. LONG-TERM LEASES

Another controversy which evolved in the 1960s is whether to capitalize the economic effects of financial leases on the books of lessees. In recent years, at least in the United States, much has been written on the alleged incongruity between two Opinions of the Accounting Principles Board—one which deals with lessees, and the other with lessors. Several of the following articles address this question.

Gerald Alvin, "Resolving the Inconsistency in Accounting for Leases," *The New York Certified Public Accountant*, March, 1970, pp. 223–230. Comparison of APB Opinions 5 and 7.

Charles G. Carpenter and Joseph F. Wojdak, "Capitalizing Executory Contracts: A Perspective," *The New York Certified Public Accountant*, January, 1971, pp. 40–47.

Eileen T. Corcoran, "Reporting of Leases," *Financial Analysts Journal*, January–February, 1968, pp. 29–35. Practical aspects of APB Opinion 5.

William L. Ferrara and Joseph F. Wojdak, "Valuation of Long-term Leases," *Financial Analysts Journal*, November–December, 1969, pp. 29–32. Authors argue that financial leases should be capitalized at the cost of equivalent assets, not at the discounted value of the lease liability.

Donald M. Gilling, "Accounting for Leases: The Fundamental Question," *Accountants' Journal*, March, 1970, pp. 283–286, and B. H. M. Wharton, "Capitalization of Leases: The Case against," pp. 286–287.

David F. Hawkins, "Objectives, Not Rules, for Lease Accounting," *Financial Executive*, November, 1970, pp. 30–38. Review of the controversy in the context of the proposed revision of APB Opinion 5.

Ronald J. Huefner, "A Debt Approach to Lease Accounting," *Financial Executive*, March, 1970, pp. 30–36.

Louis E. Levy, "Off Balance Sheet Reporting," *World* (PMM), Summer, 1968, pp. 3–7; and Alvin Zises, "Capitalizing Commitments," *World* (PMM), Spring, 1970, pp. 29–33. Pro and con on whether lessees should capitalize financial leases.

Alvin Zises, "Law and Order in Lease Accounting," *Financial Executive*, July, 1970, p. 46 *et seq*. In the controversy over the alleged incongruity between APB Opinions 5 and 7, Zises, long a foe of lease capitalization, favors revision of No. 7.

C. INCOME TAX ALLOCATION

Income-tax allocation, or tax-effect accounting, continues to fill the journals. Pronouncements issued by the American and Canadian Institutes in 1967, and by the Australian Institute in 1970, seem not to have diminished the interest of accounting academics and practitioners in either the conceptual or the practical issues.

G. C. Baxter, "A Case for Income Tax Allocation in New Zealand," *Accountants' Journal*, February, 1969, pp. 242–245. See also, Paul A. Griffin, "Income Tax Allocation," *Accountants' Journal*, September, 1969, pp. 66–68.

William H. Beaver and Roland E. Dukes, "Interperiod Tax Allocation, Earnings Expectations, and the Behavior of Security Prices," *The Accounting Review*, April, 1972, pp. 320–332.

R. J. Chambers, "Tax Allocation and Financial Reporting," *Abacus*, December, 1968, pp. 99–123. See also A. D. Barton, "Company Income Tax and Interperiod Allocation," *Abacus*, September, 1970, pp. 3–24, and A. W. Baylis, "Income Tax Allocation—A Defense," *Abacus*, December, 1971, pp. 161–172. Barton replies in the same number, pp. 173–175.

David F. Hawkins, "Controversial Accounting Changes," *Harvard Business Review*, March–April, 1968, p. 20 *et seq.* Discusses APB Opinion No. 11 on income-tax allocation. Also see David F. Hawkins, "Deferred Taxes: Source of Non-operating Funds," *Financial Executive*, February, 1969, pp. 35–44.

Arnold W. Johnson, "The Interpretation of Financial Statements," *Financial Analysts Journal*, November–December, 1968, pp. 75–83, 89. Aspects of deferred-tax accounting.

David F. Linowes, "Comments on Proposed APB Opinion 'Accounting for Income Taxes,'" *LKHH Accountant*, Summer, 1968, pp. 8–12. A review of the debate surrounding the controversial exposure draft.

Carl L. Moore, "Deferred Income Tax—Is It a Liability?," *The New York Certified Public Accountant*, February, 1970, pp. 130–138.

Corine T. Norgaard, "Financial Implications of Comprehensive Income Tax Allocation," *Financial Analysts Journal*, January–February, 1969, pp. 81–85.

Hugo Nurnberg, "Present Value Depreciation and Income Tax Allocation," *The Accounting Review*, October, 1968, pp. 719–729.

———, "A Note on the Financial Reporting of Depreciation and Income Taxes," *Journal of Accounting Research*, Autumn, 1969, pp. 257–261.

———, "Tax Allocation for Differences in Original Bases," *Journal of Accounting Research*, Autumn, 1970, pp. 217–231.

———, *Cash Movements Analysis of the Accounting for Corporate Taxes* (East Lansing: Michigan State University, 1971), 182 pp.

———, "Observations on the Financial Reporting of Depreciation and Income Taxes," *Financial Executive*, December, 1971, p. 32 *et seq.* Survey of companies on the use of income-tax allocation.

William L. Raby, "Tax Allocation and Non-historical Financial Statements," *The Accounting Review*, January, 1969, pp. 1–11. "Tax allocation can and should be rationally applied to historical cost statements, current cost statements, or price-level adjusted statements."

Leonard Spacek, "The Case for Income-Tax Deferral," *The New York Certified Public Accountant*, April, 1968, pp. 271–276.

Wendell P. Trumbull, "Differences between Financial and Tax Depreciation," *The Accounting Review*, July, 1968, pp. 459–468.

William M. Voss, "Accelerated Depreciation and Deferred Tax Allocation," *Journal of Accounting Research*, Autumn, 1968, pp. 262–269.

James B. Waugh, "The Interperiod Allocation of Corporate Income Taxes: A Proposal," *The Accounting Review*, July, 1968, pp. 535–539.

PART 8

PROBLEMS CONFRONTING THE ACCOUNTING PROFESSION: PROPOSED NEEDS

An inference, if not an implication, which recurs in many of the selections in this volume is that a resolution of particular controversies depends, in the first instance, on a fresh review and analysis of the credos and tenets that make up the core of accounting thought and practice. Better solutions to the problems of accounting for inventory, depreciable assets, intangibles, and liabilities, together with the interrelated problem of determining periodic income, will be found only when accountants reexamine their assumptions and beliefs concerning the nature and objectives of the accounting function.

Most of the articles in this part address the broader questions which accountants must seek to answer. They are not confined to problems of particular balance-sheet or income-statement categories, but reflect the authors' concern that accounting, as a discipline concerned with measuring and communicating information for use by economic decision makers, is not achieving its full potential. These are not the views of skeptics or cynics, but of writers who are genuinely troubled about the more basic questions which accountants seldom ask.

Henry Rand Hatfield opens this part by suggesting that the accounting profession, at least in the United States, seems to have distinguished itself more by advances in technique than by advances in theory. Accountants persist in fashioning a terminology after their own idiosyncracies, rather than sublimating personal likes for the good of a standard vocabulary and common meanings. Theory, he adds, should not be confused with doctrine. It does not consist of a collection of maxims and slogans that happen to have survived over the years. Although Hatfield was writing in 1927, and a few of his examples are a bit dated, it is perhaps a confirmation of his argument that the need for a coherent accounting theory is no less imperative today than it was nearly a half century ago.

George H. Sorter, extending a view first espoused by Vatter in 1947, argues that modern-day accounting and modern-day critics are on the side of too much aggregation. The manifold informational needs of the diverse population of users can never be comprehended sufficiently well to allow us to identify and measure the variables to be reported. Accounting can best satisfy users' needs, writes Sorter, by enabling them to predict future events which may serve as a basis for computing whatever aggregated variables may be pertinent to the decisions they are about to take. A prediction of future events is facilitated, in turn, by relating financial information to identifiable events which have occurred, rather than by aggregating data across many such events.

In the next article, Robert R. Sterling sets out to find the force that has had the greatest impact on conventional accounting, and concludes that the dominant factor has been conservatism. It explains the cost rule, the emphasis on realization, and the tendency to resort to subjective estimates only when they would have the effect of lowering reported income. Other arguments for the cost rule, such as the going-concern hypothesis and objectivity, are less potent and convincing. Sterling therefore concludes that historical cost can be justified only on the grounds of conservatism. His message is that the debate over the propriety of historical cost should focus on the role of conservatism in accounting, rather than on arguments that appear, on close analysis, to be specious.

John E. Kane draws our attention to the impact on the accounts of changing prices. He carefully distinguishes between those price movements that may be described as inflation or deflation, and those that mirror structural changes. An adjustment for general price movements, he suggests, would not entail a departure from historical cost, while an explicit reflection of structural changes would constitute a recognition of real gains and losses as they accrue.

Edward Stamp carries Kane's dichotomy into the arena of accounting policy. In a paper which was originally prepared for the 1971 Summer School of The Institute of Chartered Accountants of Scotland, Stamp reviews the arguments for traditional historical cost, and concludes that, as the sole method of measuring financial information, historical cost is deficient. He proposes a solution that goes beyond the mere adjustment of historical cost by general price indices, and opts for a value to the firm analysis like that expounded by Wright and Solomons.[1] Although he concludes that the most serviceable notion of profit should preferably exclude unrealized holding gains, he would nonetheless report a series of profit figures computed on different bases. While Stamp is sensitive to the practical problems of implementation, he believes that these can be solved—and, indeed, that they *have* been solved by certain companies.

In 1969, the United States Accounting Principles Board issued Statement No. 3, which endorsed the findings of its Accounting Research Study on the use of general price-level adjustments. Only one company, to our knowledge, has adopted in its published financial statements virtually all the recommendations contained in Statement No. 3. The company is the Indiana Telephone Corporation, which has been a champion of general price-level accounting since the middle 1950s. An extract from its April 1972 letter to shareholders, together with

---

[1] F. K. Wright's article, "A Theory of Inventory Measurement," is included in Part 4 of this volume. David Solomons' essay, "Economic and Accounting Concepts of Cost and Value," may be found in Morton Backer (ed.), *Modern Accounting Theory* (Englewood Cliffs, N.J.: Prentice-Hall, Inc., 1966), pp. 117–139.

its 1971 financial statements and the auditors' report, is reproduced in this part. Of particular interest is the auditors' opinion. While the auditors are obliged to aver that the conventionally prepared statements (i.e., Column A) "present fairly [the financial position and results of operations] in accordance with generally accepted accounting principles," they add that, in their opinion, the adjusted statements (i.e., Column B) "more fairly present" the company's position and operations.

W. T. Baxter is concerned that the pronouncements issued by professional accountancy bodies may be so conceived and written as to retard the growth and development of accounting thought and practice. Authoritative statements should be confined to an expression of reporting and disclosure standards, without attempting to pronounce upon the theory on which the recommendations are based. Baxter fears that professional bodies' recommendations may discourage their members from thinking through the questions themselves. Authority can, and should, communicate a professional consensus on matters of judgment, but it should not fulfill this role in a way which would foreclose all debate and experimentation with alternatives.

In the final selection, Edward Stamp proposes that independent auditors be relieved of the judicial function they now perform largely behind closed doors. He would expect the auditor to conduct his usual examination, but that he submit his findings of fact and recommendations concerning the form and presentation of the financial statements to a judge for approval. Where the client and the auditor disagree, the client may present his case to the judge. Not only would this procedure assign the investigative and judicial roles to separate and distinct parties, but it would, according to Stamp, make available to shareholders, professional colleagues, and researchers much more information than is now available on the problems faced by auditors in their professional engagements.

A. NEED FOR A COHESIVE THEORY

HENRY RAND HATFIELD

HENRY RAND HATFIELD (1866–1945), B.A. 1892, LL.D.(h.c.) 1923 Northwestern; Ph.D. 1897 Chicago; LL.D.(h.c.) 1940 University of California (Berkeley). Major publications: *Modern Accounting: Its Principles and Some of Its Problems* (1909), *Accounting: Its Principles and Problems* (1927), *A Statement of Accounting Principles* (with Sanders and Moore, 1938), *Accounting Principles and Practices* (with Sanders and Burton, 1940), *Surplus and Dividends* (1943). Contributor to *The Journal of Accountancy*, *The Accounting Review*, and other journals.

Engaged in the bond business, 1885–90, prior to becoming a member of the Washington University political economy faculty in 1894. Joined Chicago political economy faculty in 1898 and was instrumental in establishing the College of Commerce and Administration. After two years (1902–04) as dean of the College, joined the accounting faculty of the University of California (Berkeley). Served as dean of the College of Commerce, 1909–20 and 1927–28, and dean of faculties, 1916, 1917–18, and 1920–23. Formally retired from the active faculty in 1937, although continuing to offer courses until his death.

Was president, 1919, and vice-president, 1917 and 1918, of the American Accounting Association. Was vice-president of the American Economic Association in 1919. He delivered the Dickinson Lecture for 1941–42 "Surplus and Dividends." Was a founder and first grand vice-president, 1913–22, of national Beta Gamma Sigma. Was elected to Ohio State University's Accounting Hall of Fame in 1951.

Perhaps the best known of his writings is "An Historical Defense of Bookkeeping," *The Journal of Accountancy*, April 1924 (reprinted in many places). Hatfield was an accomplished student of accounting history, an astute man of letters, and an entertaining and incisive commentator on financial accounting theory.

WHAT IS THE MATTER WITH ACCOUNTING?*

HENRY RAND HATFIELD

Some there are who have made bold to exalt accounting because of its antiquity and to draw invidious comparisons with the natural sciences. These boast that the essentials of accounting had already been developed at a time when medicine, and biology, and chemistry were still a mass of fantastic superstitions.

Writers who dwell on the long existence of correct accounting methods are prone to exalt the science as representing the old nobility among a horde of upstarts, and to assume that its age is a testimonial of its dignity and worth. But may not these very facts bear a different interpretation? Accounting was well established while other sciences were undeveloped. Is that to say that in four hundred years the natural sciences have made tremendous advances, that alchemy has changed into chemistry, astrology into astronomy, and the medicine man has become a bacteriologist, but that accounting alone boasts of its past, and with more than British conservatism refuses to budge? Antiquity in this case may mean petrifaction; early maturity may mean senile decrepitude; the symbol of the accountant may perhaps be an Egyptian mummy, which was the same four thousand years ago as it is today.

The introduction of bookkeeping was not an isolated phenomenon, but part of a general awakening, when men's minds, after centuries of stagnation and slumber, in a measure broke from the traditions of the past and began to think along new lines. But in other sciences this awakening, or this renaissance, was only a beginning. Is it conceivable that accounting alone came forth in a nearly finished form that needed no improvement?

But perhaps accounting has in reality progressed despite the assertions of its protagonists. It was indeed claimed, more than two hundred years ago, that accounting had reached a state of perfection, and that "without a fault nothing can be rescinded from or added to it." Yet, strangely enough, almost every subsequent textbook has claimed to be a new or improved system and that what went before was practically worthless.

Let us turn from such vague claims of advance and ask for details and specifications. Have substantial discoveries been made in the science of accounting as in other fields of human knowledge?

Yes, says Holland, speaking for the seventeenth century, for my great scholar Stevin, who advanced mathematics through his invention of the decimal system, did also introduce—the compound journal entry.

Yes, says England, for I place beside the name of James Watt, who in the

---

* Address delivered at the annual meeting of the American Institute of Accountants, Del Monte, California, September 21, 1927.

SOURCE: This essay originally apppeared in *The Journal of Accountancy*, Vol. XLIV, No. 4 (October, 1927), pp. 267–79. Reprinted by permission of the American Institute of Certified Public Accountants.

next century invented the steam engine, that of Edward Thomas Jones, whose work was protected by patent and lauded by the governor of the Bank of England as an entirely new system of accounting.

Yes, says Italy, for the nineteenth century saw not merely the dazzling discoveries of Marconi, but the introduction by Cerboni of a really new system superior to double entry and adopted by the Italian government.

Yes, says America, in this latest era, I place on the scroll of fame, alongside the achievement of aviation, the introduction of—loose-leaf ledgers.

A rather sorry list of achievements. Compound entries are but poor rivals to so momentous an invention as the decimal system. Jones' heralded invention is one which those of you who know of it at all remember only as a curiosity. Logismography, despite certain merits, has in fifty years declined rather than expanded. And the loose-leaf system, while a more generally accepted improvement, is, forsooth, at best but a somewhat petty technical device which in no way affects the general principles of accounting.

It would, however, be unfair not to recognize evidences of progress. Three of these are prominent. The unprecedented outflow of serious scientific literature is a hopeful sign. This is so recent that some of you remember its beginning. In England one may take Dicksee and Pixley as the pioneers in this field, and these are both still active accountants; in this country the beginnings were with Sprague, whom many of you knew, and Cole, whom all delight to honor. It were invidious to mention other names. Most of you see a prominent author of accounting literature every time you look in your mirror.

Another bit of evidence exists in the fact that again, after some centuries of neglect, practically all universities in America, and some abroad, are giving serious attention to instruction in accounting. I should hesitate, being an academically inclined person, to mention this before a group of professional accountants. The man who does often contemns him who teaches. But I am emboldened by the fact that my fellow speaker, the sometime president of this organization, is at the same time one of those academic guys, and that many others of your members are in the same boat.

A third evidence of progress is the undeniable improvement in the standing and dignity of the profession which you so honorably represent. Your opinion is sought not only in the ordinary course of business but by the government when it frames new laws, when it needs to wage a war, when it has the vastly more difficult task of arranging for the payment for a war already lost and won. You would not now be represented in the councils of the nation and of the world, if the science had not materially progressed.

It may even be possible to list some specific points in which present-day accounting excels that of former times. The most striking, though to me by no means the most interesting, has been the general improvement in technique, to which America has contributed so much. The problem of modern accounting is to deal with the myriad transactions of big business. Volta's first generation of an electric current was, indeed, the really significant step in advance in the study of electricity; but today the problem is not how to make a laboratory spark, but how to conduct, and control, and utilize, the power of a million horses over a tenuous copper wire. So with bookkeeping, the handling of transactions in enormous numbers is a real problem, not faced in past centuries, but wonderfully achieved today.

In addition I would mention three achievements, one of practical, one of pedagogical, one of theoretical interest. The first is the development of cost accounting (due to engineers rather than to professional accountants, but still an achievement in the science). This I consider the typical contribution of the present generation.

The second is the substitution, for the idea that bookkeeping is in essence a mere matching of debits and credits, of the view that its significant aspect is its striving to present the equation: assets = liabilities + proprietorship. The name of the honored and lamented Sprague stands prominent in this movement. But it was formulated long before his day, and can be traced back to German, American and English writers—for more than a hundred years. But the general adoption of the so-called balance-sheet approach in place of the purely journal method is a recent matter. Paciolo and his immediate successors give no hint of it.

The third point is the effort to introduce some unity into accounting theory instead of regarding its phenomena as diverse. For long it was generally considered that the investment of capital was in marked opposition to the payment of an expense. This view was crystallized in the phrase "capital expenditure or charge against revenue." It assumed that these two were radically different in nature, and one must never be confounded with the other. Today one sees a continuous gradation, land, building, machinery, raw material, expense of labor— each one of a series, each differing only as to length of the service which it renders, each paid for with the view of getting all possible use out of it in the productive process. The development of this point of view is, I believe, a real achievement in accounting theory—one not dreamt of in earlier centuries.

I find real cause for congratulation (I can not say pride, for, alas, I am not one of you) in these indisputable evidences of life, vigor and hence of progress in the profession. It may be ungracious, but perhaps for your souls' good, if my congratulations are tempered by raising the question as to what the science, or profession, lacks. In what is it weak? Where has it failed?

To do this, it is first necessary to ask what is, in fine, the purpose or nature of accounting. It is one of the technical languages wherein the facts of business are expressed. In this it is a twin sister to statistics, which expresses a different set of business facts through a different medium. It is, as it were, the distinction between the French of diplomacy and law Latin, languages at one time indispensable to government functions, each used in a restricted field, each with a separate vocabulary. Accounting is something other than a set of clever devices for beating the income tax with the least damage to one's conscience, something more than a specious way of window-dressing whereby the best possible appearance is given to a somewhat undesirable stock of goods. It is a universal language of business.

The prime requisite of a language is that it be understandable. There is a suspicion abroad that accounting as it exists today is not impeccable in this respect. Hartley Withers has said that "to most of the shareholders, [the balance-sheet] is about as comprehensible as a passage from Browning, translated into an unknown language" and speaks of it as an "impossible cryptogram with an esoteric meaning that is only revealed to an initiated caste, after much fasting and mortification."

Perhaps this criticism is somewhat unfair. The fluent lucidity of Xenophon, of Cicero and of Goldsmith is wasted on one who does not know the languages in which these wrote. Mr. Withers' inability to grasp all the beauties of the annual report of the Steel Corporation may possibly betray his own illiteracy rather than any lack of lucidity on the part of the Steel Corporation or the distinguished accountants who act as its auditors.

In order to be understandable a language must possess a clearly defined terminology, and the lack of this is the chief defect of accounting. As in economics, no new vocabulary has been adopted (I trust I do no injustice to my colleagues who have adopted "equities" in place of "proprietorship and liabilities" or have devised the really picturesque term, "where-got-gone statement"), but the ordinary language of the market place has been used in senses the market place knew not of, and in senses varying with different accountants.

Accounting is almost the only science (with the exception of economics, if that be a science) which is deficient in this respect. Physics may not know the ultimate nature of electricity, but progress has been made in describing its manifestations. When one speaks quantitatively of its various aspects there is no lack of definiteness, and ohms, volts and amperes are standard around the world. The nature of matter may be unknown to the chemist, but the formulas H_2O and C_2H_6O can never be confused, even though, before Volstead, the substances may have been mixed. But it is different with accounting terms, even with those of greatest significance.

This is manifest in respect of the more interesting and important of the two phases of accounting—that relating to the increase of wealth taking place during a fiscal period. Income subject to the federal income tax is indeed a fairly definite term, although, in many cases, a more appropriate rubric would be "the amount which we expect to get away with at the revenue office." But other aspects of the increment during the year are more significant than the amount taxable. Business is not run for the purpose of paying taxes, but for the purpose of making profits (call this by some other term if you wish), and there should be no uncertainty in defining the term, no unavoidable vagueness in expressing the best possible guess at the amount.

But one finds a state of actual confusion in this fundamental matter. Net earnings, net income, gross profits, profits, net profits? I have tried for years to find the proper term to be used and the exact connotation of each of the terms just quoted. I have appealed to academic writers, both economists and accountants, and I find only confusion. I have turned to the courts, and found in their decisions a confusion overwhelmingly ludicrous. If one sees the word "profits" in a textbook he has no idea of its content until he carefully studies the context. Even then he he may still be left in doubt. It is as if one picked up a book and read a single word spelled "d-a-m-i-t." Until he learned whether the book were German or English he could neither pronounce the word, nor know whether it was an inoffensive conjunction or a mildly profane expletive.

So I turn to you, the recognized organization of the ablest group of professional accountants in the world. I turn to you who use the terms every day of your lives. I turn to you, as I would turn to the chemists for the meaning of ethyl alcohol, or as I would turn to engineers to learn what is the meaning of horsepower. I look through formal published statements, and I find that what one of you calls "net income" another calls "profits." I find that by some "income" is a comprehensive term including profits and also other items; by others "profits" is the more inclusive term, from which, certain deductions having been made, "income" remains. I find that a perfectly respectable, nay, an outstanding, accountant approves of a statement in which "net income" represents a remainder after subtracting interest on bonds, while another outstanding, nay, even perfectly respectable, accountant sanctions the use of the same term where interest is not deducted. Does one chemist describe water as a combination of one atom of oxygen with two of hydrogen, while another thinks it legitimate to use the same term for a combination from which one of the atoms of hydrogen is omitted? Does one engineer use a formula in which π is multiplied by the square of R, while another using the same formula omits the exponent of R?

Accounting, however, needs something more than a definite nomenclature. It needs above all else the formulation of sound theories, which can be crystallized into clear terminology. Progress in the other sciences has for its milestones a series of formulated theories, comprehensive and significant. Astronomy was not content with calling the stars by name, but has developed a law of gravity which, starting with a falling apple, gives a rule applicable to suns and spheres remote beyond human comprehension, and which made it possible to posit a still invisible planet. Chemistry has developed theories which, permeating all matter, solve the mysteries of the infinitesimal. Like astronomy, it too was able to predict the existence of missing elements, as yet undiscovered in the laboratory. Biology found the theory of evolution, which embraces the immeasurable expanses of time and makes a continuum of all life in all ages.

But accounting is a laggard. Its great problems (I refer to matters even more significant than that bone of contention, whether in certain places the ink used should be black or red) are not only unsettled but their surface has scarcely been scratched. Some of these may be mentioned in sequence.

Accounting primarily deals with imputed values and records the changes therein. Can progress be made without formulating some theory as to what value is proper for accounting purposes?

There is, indeed, rather general agreement that in the first instance a newly acquired asset is valued at cost. But as to any theory, underlying and supporting this rule, there is general silence. A statement found in a thesis which your own association has crowned with your noblest laurels asserts, "We deny that a given object can have a value to its owner in excess of cost." I am in doubt as to just what the author meant, but surely you and the author alike must agree that what he says evidently is not true.

There are undoubtedly some practical advantages in preferring costs to guesses, but I have still to find any adequate theory or scientific hypothesis which supports the opinion just quoted. Accountants in this respect rely on reiteration in lieu of argument.

In the more difficult problem as to the basis for revaluing assets at the close of a fiscal period, the lack of sound theory is as great, the divergence in practice appalling. On this matter accountants (and for purposes of criticism only, I make bold to include myself among accountants), on this matter we accountants have been—or, more correctly, are—illogical, inconsistent and vacillating. We have arbitrarily laid down different rules for different classes of assets; we have promulgated the phrase "cost or market, whichever is lower," supporting it by a ludicrously inappropriate argument; we have for years strenuously advocated a given rule, only to make a complete *volte face*, when the effects of the great war made a continuance of such a policy unpleasing to one's clients.

The arguments adduced in favor of valuing at cost or market, whichever is lower, are so brilliant an instance of flabby thinking as to deserve some further attention. The stock argument is that such a procedure is justified on the ground that it is conservative. But if conservative treatment is desirable, if, as Neymarck says, accounting is good to the extent that values are underestimated, the rule of cost or market, whichever is lower, is illogical and unsatisfactory. It permits a commodity, which was purchased at the top of the market for $2.00, to be valued at the full present market quotation, say $1.95, but forbids that an article purchased for $1.00 and now risen to $2.00 be valued at even $1.20, although that is 40 per cent. below the actual market. Surely, if conservatism is the goal, it would be more effectively secured by saying that merchandise should always be valued at market less a margin for safety, even though in some cases that represented a marking-up. It is this sort of slipshod theoretical discussion of accounting problems which does little justice to the intelligence of the profession and raises doubts as to the distance which it has traveled since its mediæval beginnings.

Somewhat similar is the problem of the balance-sheet. Accountants agree with Sprague's felicitous statement that the balance-sheet is the starting point and the goal of all accounting procedure. If the balance-sheet is so important, should there be any uncertainty as to its nature and purpose? I speak not now of divergencies of opinion and practice as to insignificant matters of technique, such as the sequence and subdivisions of assets, or whether an item should appear as an addition or as a subtraction from the *contra* side. There should be agreement as to its essential character. But some hold that a balance-sheet is an exhibit of conditions at a given moment—when the clock strikes twelve at the end of a fiscal year. Others assert that the balance-sheet is a history of past events, showing what has been contributed to the concern and how the funds so received have been employed. In one conception, capital funds unwisely invested, "sunk and gone" to use a famous phrase, are no longer existent and hence have no place in a "cross section" of the concern of today. From the other viewpoint, the investment in an unproductive plant is a historical fact, and adequately explains the use made of contributed capital. Do you all know which view is correct? Do any of you consistently adhere to it? Will some one of you explain the proper view to the rest of us?

Depreciation is another matter on which your science has been laggard, although by no means absolutely paralyzed. Substantial progress has been made, but there are still those who speak of depreciation in unscientific terms. Not infrequently statements are prepared in which a given sum is stated as "amount available for depreciation and dividends." Such a confusion of unlike things should not be tolerated by a profession of the standing of yours. It is as though wages and overhead were subtracted from sales and the remainder labeled "amount available for replacement of raw materials and dividends."

Again, there are still those who, both in their practice and in their writings, not infrequently speak of depreciation as a reserve, something held back, or as a deduction from profits. But depreciation is something gone, not something kept; it is, as Cole so cleverly said, a "hole in the assets," and a hole is a difficult thing to hold in any position. Ever to speak of depreciation as a deduction from profits is a glaring error. It is not merely the survival of a form of expression, as when even an astronomer speaks of the sun rising, for even if you accountants know better, the average business man still thinks of depreciation as something other than it is. Or, at least, he did until the internal-revenue bureau allowed a deduction for depreciation. It is of only indirect credit to the profession that it could not put over the right view on a scientific matter until it became financially expedient so to do. If the average business man has wrong conceptions of accounting principles, the profession can not be considered efficient. Even the medical profession did not rest easy until it convinced mankind that the proper treatment of epilepsy was not by means designed to exorcise a devil, and that a horse chestnut in the pocket is unreliable as a prophylactic against rheumatism.

Accountants do indeed agree that if a machine wears out in ten years its cost must somehow be distributed as a charge during those years. But there is no agreement whatever as to the proportion of the amount to be allotted to each particular year. I need not recall the interminable debate over the relative merits of straight-line and curved-line depreciation. Accountants, with rare impartiality, apply one system to one class of assets, another to other classes. It is somewhat as if one applied the Ptolemaic system to the motion of Mars, but regarded Jupiter as operating according to the Copernican system.

More distressful and more pertinent to the present discussion is the nature of the arguments adduced in support of one or the other basis. These are often barren of any vestige of accounting theory. It may be said that the charge should be relatively low in the early years, not because depreciation is less, but because it "is inconvenient to burden the early years" with a heavy charge, or because such a charge would show an initial deficit. Is accounting a device to secure what is convenient, or to show what is real? Should accounting be twisted so as to conceal an initial deficit if one really exists, or should it show the facts? Even the physician does not always alter his diagnosis because it would be inconvenient for the patient just then to have an attack of smallpox. His duty as a scientist is to determine whether that disease is present. The accountant, if a scientist, should be concerned solely in what charges may properly be assigned to the current year as the effect of depreciation.

Sometimes a specious theoretical basis is indeed brought forth, namely, that the straight-line method is preferable to a curved-line method, because the former alone charges the actual cost. Here I argue neither for nor against a particular procedure, but merely assert that accounting in this case shows a crudely unscientific attitude. Whether a straight-line method is preferable or not is subject to discussion. But whatever merits it may have—and these may consist in the virtues of simplicity, ease of application, and understandability—the one thing that is certain and should be unquestioned is that the straight-line method does not charge off each year the amount actually paid for that year's service rendered.

This may be established by assuming that A rents property for two years at an annual rental of $104.76 to be paid in advance on January first each year. The contract is made in December, 1927, but the lease does not begin until January 1, 1928. Just before that date the owner suggests to the prospective tenant that he pay rental for both years on January 1, 1928, instead of paying it in two equal annual instalments. The tenant is perfectly willing to do so, provided proper adjustment can be made. Obviously, unless interest for him is at the rate of 0 per cent., he will not pay $209.52. Assuming a rate of 10 per cent., he would be justified in paying just $200. This is made up of the $104.76 in any case due and payable January 1, 1928, and $95.24, the value as of that date of $104.76 payable a year later. If then he pays $200 for two years' rental, the actual amount paid for the first year is not, as is assumed in the argument under criticism, one-half of the amount paid for two years, but a larger sum. When the interest rate is unknown, the only statement that can be made with confidence is that the amount actually paid for the first year is not the total price divided by the number of years of service.

Even in its progress, accounting has been hampered by careless reasoning. Two instances are in point. The first relates to municipal accounts. The increasing use of a municipal balance-sheet, due to the campaign inaugurated some twenty years ago, has everywhere been hailed as a real improvement. But, unfortunately, it was apparently assumed that the customary form of double-entry balance-sheet, invaluable to a corporation, should be used by a municipality. A spur being a good thing for quickening the speed of a horse, therefore let us use spurs to accelerate our automobiles, forgetful that a pneumatic tire is a quite different thing from a horse's flanks. Only after some years was it recognized that the characteristic of a corporation balance-sheet—the easy comparison of liabilities with the assets protecting them—does not at all apply to a municipality. With little exaggeration it may be said that municipal debt is, in reality, secured by the value of all the assets within the city walls save those which belong to the city and are listed in the municipal balance-sheet.

While modifications of the balance-sheet are now made, municipal accountants generally continue to employ the forms of double-entry bookkeeping. Is it an impossible hope that there is among you some genius who will invent a new form of accounting, particularly suited to governmental accounts? One can not foretell its nature, any more than those whose plodding backs built the pyramids could foretell the exact nature of Watt's invention which was to lift man's burdens, nor than the runner from Marathon, who exhausted himself in hastening the news to Athens, could tell how in future ages news would be brought without runner, without even a road, through the pathless ether. Cerboni attempted a new system, in logiscography, but without notable success. But I long for the appearance of the genius who shall transcend tradition and devise a system of municipal accounting as superior, for that purpose, to double entry, as the latter excels the accounting procedure of Menher and Grammateus. Will not the candidate for this honor kindly raise his hand?

The second instance of imperfect progress is found in the consolidated balance-sheet. This anomalous document is a balance-sheet of a non-existent entity; it combines the debts of one corporation with the assets of another legally distinct corporation; it lists indiscriminately assets which belong to a given corporation with those which do not. It is something new, distinctly American in origin. But the consolidated balance-sheet serves a purpose. The task before you accountants is to agree on the rules for playing this new game. If in this country we play American football instead of Rugby we at least agree on the rules for Americans to follow. But eminent accountants still disagree on such significant matters as the treatment in the consolidated balance-sheet of a pre-existing surplus of a subsidiary company and the value to be attached to the shares of non-consenting stockholders. It is not strange, therefore, that in England there has been much recent discussion as to the legitimacy of this American device. One would similarly question football if umpires were uncertain whether the game consisted in forcing the ball over the opponents' goal or in seeing how long the fullback could maintain his balance while sitting on the ball. You have devised a new and valuable form. It is your task to perfect it.

My argument has been that notwithstanding the excessive claims of its admirers, accounting really is not a mummy, but is alive and growing. Progress it has indeed made, but nevertheless deficiencies appear, several of which have been mentioned. If I am to sum these matters up, it would be by saying that in the busy strife of professional life, in the problem of how to meet the task of serving the innumerable clients flocking to your office and each demanding immediate attention, you have somewhat neglected the higher task of developing a sound set of accounting theories. With the necessary attention to the anise and cummin you have, perforce, neglected the weightier matters of the law. After all, advancement in any service comes most often from the consideration of abstract problems. Pupin made long-distance telephony possible because of research which he carried on in regard to the amplification of waves before there ever was a telephone; the greatest improvements in medicine were brought about by studies of test tubes rather than by diagnosing individuals; the great dye industries are the outgrowth of experiments in chemical laboratories rather than in factories.

American accountants lead the world in technique. They probably also lead the world in the formulation of accounting doctrine. But the present need of the profession is a further development of sound theory rather than improved practice.

B. **NEED FOR REEXAMINATION OF DOCTRINE**

GEORGE H. SORTER

GEORGE H. SORTER (1927–   ), Ph.B. 53, M.B.A. 55, Ph.D. 63 Chicago; CPA. Currently professor of accounting, University of Chicago. Major publications: *An Income Approach to Accounting Theory* (edited readings, with Davidson, Green, and Horngren, 1964), *A Statement of Basic Accounting Theory* (with eight other authors, 1966), *William W. Werntz: His Accounting Thought* (editor, with Trueblood, 1968). Contributor to *The Accounting Review* and other journals.

He joined the University of Chicago accounting faculty in 1955. In 1968–69, he visited the University of Kansas faculty as Arthur Young Professor of Accounting.

Since 1971, he has been research director of the Study Group on Objectives, sponsored by the American Institute of Certified Accountants.

Principal research interests: basic accounting theory and the objectives of accounting.

AN "EVENTS" APPROACH TO BASIC ACCOUNTING THEORY

GEORGE H. SORTER

In 1966, after two years' work, a committee of the American Accounting Association issued *A Statement of Basic Accounting Theory*.[1] Undoubtedly, the most startling recommendations were the sanctioning of current costs and the advocacy of two column (historical and current) reports. To this member of the committee, however, even more startling was that the near unanimous agreement on the recommendations was arrived at by following two very divergent paths originating from two very dissimilar basic concepts about accounting. This split is not confined to committee members but rather seems representative of a more widespread and pervasive difference in the world outside. The majority view of the

SOURCE: From *The Accounting Review*, Vol. XLIV, No. 1 (January, 1969), pp. 12–19. Reprinted by permission of the American Accounting Association.

[1] American Accounting Association, *A Statement of Basic Accounting Theory*, A Report Prepared by the Committee on Basic Accounting Theory (American Accounting Association, 1966).

committee and the predominant faction outside believes in what I here define as the "value" approach to accounting. The minority view, of which I am sometimes the only member, I describe as the "events" approach. This view although implied by some in the past[2] has never to my knowledge been explicitly stated but might have far-reaching implications. This paper seeks to describe and contrast the two schools, present arguments for and illustrate the consequences of an "events" approach to accounting theory; and examine the logic leading to the conclusions embodied in the *Statement of Basic Accounting Theory*. Hopefully, this will provide not only insights and help for the analysis and evaluation of the committee's monograph but perhaps also stimulate discussion and criticism of a new approach and suggest new avenues of research and experimentation to make accounting more responsive to present day conditions.

TWO VIEWS—VALUE AND EVENTS

The Value Theory

The "Value" school within the committee, or as they would probably prefer to be termed the "User need" school, assumed that users' needs are known and sufficiently well specified so that accounting theory can deductively arrive at and produce optimal input values for used and useful decision models. Most of the value theorists visualize accounting's purpose as producing optimum income and capital value or values.[3] This leads to the popular sport of proper matching of costs and revenue. The assumption is that "proper matching" associates costs and revenue to produce the right income figure or figures—the figure or figures optimal for users' decision models.

Several criticisms may be leveled at this value approach.

1. There are many and varied uses of accounting data and it is therefore impossible to specify input values that are optimal for the wide range of possible uses.

2. For each specified use different users utilize a wide range of different decision models, that they have so far been unable to describe, define, or specify. Further, neither economists nor accountants have been able to advance the theoretically correct decision models.

3. The value theory is unnecessarily restrictive. Thus, events such as leases or commitments have, until recently, tended to be excluded from the accounting universe, partially at least, because they did not affect income or net asset values.

The orientation of accounting toward producing income and asset values which are nothing but simple attempts to adjust for the lag between cash outflows and cash inflows has impeded the development of more sophisticated lag models made possible by more sophisticated techniques.

4. The value theory is not useful in explaining many current developments in accounting. Income theory, for instance, does not provide a basis for the current sub-aggregates that are utilized in the income statement such as sales,

---

[2] This idea, like so many others had its origin primarily in the writings and thought of Professor William J. Vatter whom I hasten to absolve from any of its shortcomings.

[3] Not all value theorists are income oriented. Chambers for example can be considered a "value" but certainly not an "income" theorist.

cost of sales, etc. It has also not been helpful in explaining the advocacy of the Funds Statement or in helping the conglomerate and a host of other current problems.

The Events Theory

Proponents of the "Events" theory suggest that the purpose of accounting is to provide information about relevant economic events that might be useful in a variety of possible decision models. They see the function of accounting at one level removed in the decision-making process. Instead of producing input values for unknown and perhaps unknowable decision models directly, accounting provides information about relevant economic events that allows individual users to generate their own input values for their own individual decision models. In other words, given the state of the arts, less rather than more aggregation is appropriate and the user, rather than the accountant, must aggregate, assign weights and values to the data consistent with his forecasts and utility functions. "Events" proponents suggest that the loss of information generated by aggregation and valuation by the accountant is greater than the associated benefit. While they would agree that the accountants' suggested weights and values deserve to be communicated, they would insist that these weights be communicated in disaggregated form so that users always had the nonweighted raw data available as well.

This viewpoint seems particularly appropriate today when little is known about how accounting data is used but may even be preferred when more knowledge about decision models becomes available. It is possible to visualize reasonable decision models that are consistent with an "events" approach rather than a "value" approach. An investor, for instance, attempting to forecast the value of a firm at some future point may utilize two methods: (1) He may base his estimate of future values on the trend, size, and variability of current income or other aggregated values. (2) Alternatively, he may wish to use current accounting data to predict specific future events and then base his estimate of future values on these predicted events. In other words, he may wish to predict income or he may wish to predict sales, cost of sales, taxes, etc. The first model is more consistent with a value approach, the second with an events approach.

The criticism must be met that the "events" approach relies just as heavily upon knowledge of users' models as does the "value" approach. The argument goes as follows. Decisions as to what events are relevant (surely not all events can be recorded) must be made and can only be made with users' needs in mind. Thus, the users' needs must still be known. This is correct. But it seems clear that less need be known about decision models to decide whether or not an event might be relevant for a model than to have to decide how the data fits a specific decision model and what specific weights should be assigned.[4] In the lease example, under an "events" approach, it is only necessary to decide that information about leases, commitments or orders are relevant to a host of decision models for such information to be included in accounting reports. It is unnecessary to

---

[4] "... a goal which by itself may not be so capable of definition as to determine a single perfect solution may nevertheless be clear enough and important enough to rule out some solutions...." from Guido Calabresi, "Fault, Accidents, and the Wonderful World of Blum and Kalven," *Yale Law Journal* (December 1965), p. 222.

justify how, if at all, this information should be weighted in an income valuation model.

To Aggregate or Not to Aggregate

As has been indicated, the real difference between the two schools lies in what level of aggregation and valuation is appropriate in accounting reports and who is to be the aggregator and evaluator. The question as to who is to aggregate or value is not unique to accounting. As Ijiri points out "... any aggregation generally involves loss of information in that the resulting total 'value' may be composed of many—possibly infinitely many—different *components*."[5] It is interesting to note that in two widely different areas there have recently been thrusts toward presenting less aggregated data. In modern statistics it is no longer considered good form to merely report confidence intervals. Instead the plea is for full presentation of the underlying data or distributions.[6] Only the user can decide what is or is not significant, given his loss function. In weather forecasts, we are no longer told that it will or will not rain or snow. Instead we are given probability estimates and must ourselves decide whether or not to carry umbrellas or to send out work crews. We are given the underlying raw data and must assign values consistent with our individual utility functions.

Accounting income has variously been thought of as a measure of how much can be spent and still be as well off as before, as a measure of managerial efficiency or as a basis for forecasting future values. But each of these depends on individual expectations, individual preference functions and individual decision models not on some never clearly defined concept of "proper matching of costs and revenues." Unfortunately this attempt to match, the assigning of weights to generate values, the attempt to aggregate into an income figure, destroys potentially useful information about important underlying events and increases possible measurement errors and biases. Every item on an income statement is the result of at least two processes—the underlying event and the accountants' allocation of the event to a particular time period. This allocation has the purpose of matching in order to derive a "true" income figure or figures. Lifo and Fifo for example are used in an attempt to produce better income figures. Both, however, destroy information about the consumption event. If either Lifo or Fifo is used consumption of two identical units bought at different prices will necessarily be described differently. A user interested in comparing consumption activity for two periods is unable to distinguish between variations caused by the measurement process, be it Lifo or Fifo, and real differences in the consumption levels.

Deferred taxes attempts to secure proper matching of costs and revenues and thereby destroys information about current tax payments. Conventional absorption costing in an attempt to secure proper matching destroys information about production inputs and outputs since cost of goods sold and inventory become dependent on both the level of production and of sales.

The loss of information due to aggregation also holds for the balance sheet. Necessarily, every balance sheet account is an aggregation of two or more types

---

[5] Yuji Ijiri. *The Foundations of Accounting Measurement* (Prentice-Hall, Inc., 1967), p. 120.

[6] See Howard Raiffa and Robert Schlaifer, *Applied Statistical Decision Theory* (Harvard University, Division of Research, Graduate School of Business, 1961), p. 68.

of events (the events recorded on the debit and credit sides of the account). Very often the events so aggregated vary greatly in type, measurability and variability and therefore destroy much information about specific events. For instance, if current costs or values are used, acquisition and consumption activities as well as environmental changes are combined and the reconstructibility of each specific event is impaired. Acquisitions and amortizations or acquisitions and dispositions are events differing widely in possible measurement error. By combining them in asset and liability accounts information about each is destroyed.

As already indicated, income and capital valuations are attempts to deal with lags between cash outflows and cash inflows. These appear to be unnecessarily crude and primitive given current advances in methodology and measurement technique. The presentation of less aggregated data suggested by the "events" approach might stimulate investigation of more complicated but more useful lag and forecast models that could vary for different industries, firms, time periods, or individuals.

SOME CONSEQUENCES OF AN EVENTS APPROACH

This is not the proper medium in which to describe some possible long-range consequences of the "events" approach. In a subsequent manuscript, I intend to speculate on the type of accounting reports appropriate to this approach. Even under the existing accounting framework there are several implications of "events" theory which might help to explain this point of view.

The Balance Sheet

It is currently the fashion to say that the balance sheet or position statement has lost most, if not all, of its significance. But not for event theorists. We view the balance sheet not as a value statement nor as a statement of financial position but rather as an indirect communication of all accounting events that have occurred since the inception of the accounting unit. This indirect communication is provided by summing the effect of all events on the names used in describing these events and then recording the subsequent balances. Inventory, thus, does not report either value or costs but rather describes the acquisition and consumption activities that have occurred. This view has several advantages. It does not purport to report something that is not achieved (i.e., value) and it does facilitate the understanding and analysis of what is described. If the inventory figure, for instance, is visualized as a representation of the inventory, under value theory the accountant must somehow rationalize the particular costs or value figure that he uses. If historical cost is used, the validity of a representation of inventory that ignores value inevitably crops up. If value is used the argument centers about the justification of this rather than some other value. It is certainly difficult to justify either historical costs or any one representation of value. This difficulty does not create so grave a problem for the "event" theorist. Suppose original cost is used. Under an events notion this means simply that acquisition and consumption events, but not environmental changes, are recorded. Original costs need not be justified. One may certainly deplore the absence of information about environmental events (i.e., value changes) but one accepts information about the events that are described (i.e., acquisition and consumption) and uses them in whatever fashion is appropriate.

An "events" approach to the balance sheet could lead to operational rules about balance sheet construction and presentation. The following represents a possible rule. *A balance sheet should be so constructed as to maximize the reconstructability of the events being aggregated.* Various users may thus generate information about particular events they are interested in. One purpose of the balance sheet is to facilitate the preparation of Funds Statements and like reports that provide information about important events.

The Income Statement

For value theorists the purpose of an income statement quite simply is to report income value or values. Under an "events" approach the purpose of the income statement is to provide direct communication concerning the operating events or activities of the firm. Accounting utilizes two forms of communication: an indirect or effect communication of all events (the Balance Sheet) and direct, specific or event communication of certain critical events (Income Statement, Cash Statement, Production Statement, Funds Statement, etc.). The concern of event theorists is not primarily with the final income figure but rather with describing critical operating activities of a firm. The preferred title would be "Statement of Operating Events." Events theory can suggest an operational rule for income statements. For instance, *each event should be described in a manner facilitating the forecasting of that same event in a future time period given exogenous changes*. The deferred tax question would then be resolved by investigating which quantification more reliably forecasts future tax payments. Both Lifo and Fifo would be rejected because they impede the ability to forecast acquisitions and consumptions of inventory in the future.

The "events" school can justify the present organization of the income statement which reports several sub-aggregates such as sales, cost of sales, etc., because these are considered critical operating events. Perhaps this is one instance when an events orientation has already affected the accounting structure.

The Funds Statement

Value theorists, rigidly faithful to their doctrine, have the most difficulty in justifying this statement. They state rather feebly that "... the basic purpose of the Funds Statement is to account for the change in working capital during the period covered by the statement."[7] Such a concept certainly underrates the utility of this statement and leads to trivial discussions as to the proper definition of working capital. The "events" school thinks of this statement as "A Statement of Financial and Investment Events." The Working Capital account merely represents a useful technique to organize the events and prepare the statement. The important consideration is whether a financing or investment event is relevant and should be reported, not whether working capital is affected by a given event. This again demonstrates the flexibility of an "events" approach. Different financing or investment events may or may not be relevant for specific firms or at specific times. The content of the Funds Statement thus need not remain invariate for all times or for all firms.

[7] Perry Mason, " 'Cash Flow' Analysis and The Funds Statement," *Accounting Research Study No. 2* (American Institute of Certified Public Accountants, 1961).

"A STATEMENT OF BASIC ACCOUNTING THEORY" AND THE EVENTS THEORY

Most of the recommendations contained in *A Statement of Basic Accounting Theory* flow more logically from an "events" rather than from a "value" orientation. Why are standards or guidelines necessary at all if a "value" approach is adopted? If users' needs are in fact well specified then accounting should provide the values that made the decision models operate optimally. The only relevant standard then would be the ability of the data to perform in the model. There would be no need for values to be verifiable or free from bias if they work well in a specified model. If, however, users' needs are not well specified suggesting an "events" approach, then it is necessary to employ standards that limit the range and define the description of relevant events.

The need for two-column reporting under a "value" approach is not clear. Presumably, the need arises because different columns are useful for different users; that is, historical cost data is useful for the stewardship function and current cost data for the investment function. This rather inadequate rationale has led to the assumption that the historical costs column was only advocated as a stop-gap measure until current value could sweep the day. This was not the intent of the committee.

Multi-column reporting seems eminently compatible with an "events" view of accounting. The two column report advocated by *ASOBAT* is a step in that direction. As the monograph states, "The historical information reflects market transactions, the current cost information reflects market transactions plus 'unrealized' market influences, and the difference shows the effect of unrealized environmental influences."[8] Since the historical cost column includes descriptions of events other than market transactions (i.e., depreciation, amortization, and other significant accruals) and because market transactions and environmental changes are not the only events that have relevance to the firm, the two columns advocated do not go far enough, but they represent a start.

Separate events should be reported in separate columns because (1) they vary in measurability, (2) they vary in controllability, and (3) they vary in importance from period to period. There is no question that market transactions and environmental changes, for instance, vary in measurability. Market transactions can be relatively satisfactorily described by single numbered quantifications (with relatively little measurement error). There is apt to be little variance around that single number. The same, however, cannot be said about environmental changes or forecasts where description by ranges or distributions could be more appropriate and where measurement errors could be material. As long as a single column is used there will be a tendency to continue to measure events by a single measurement process which is inappropriate for certain types of events and we shall continue to be faced with troubles in assessing measurement biases or errors.

These events also vary in controllability by the managers of a firm. Clearly, market transactions are more controllable than environmental changes but less controllable than conversions. If accounting reports are to be useful in evaluating management then a separation of events by controllability should help in fulfilling this objective.

[8] American Accounting Association, *op. cit.*, p. 31.

Finally, the importance of the different classes of events may vary from period to period. An investor may predict a period of stability where certain environmental changes are expected to be minimal and in order to forecast adequately from accounting data he must then be able to separate the effect of environmental changes from market transactions. This he can do in multi-column reporting. As the importance of different types of events vary, users, according to their estimate of the future, can attach different weights to the different types of events.

At first blush multi-column reporting seems a drastic departure from current practices—but is it really? Presently we use multi-row reporting. We break down the income statement into many sub-aggregates such as sales, cost of sales, S&A expenses, taxes, etc. We break down the balance sheet into many rows by classes of equities and assets. Very little research has been done as to what explains the current level of sub-aggregation and extreme proponents of the "value" school would have a hard time rationalizing the present format of the income statement. Presently the income statement is organized around a functional event structure, and the balance sheet around a functional effect structure. Multi-column reporting would add a "source of events" classification to both reports and instead of accounting reports consisting of a 7 by 1 matrix they would consist of a 7 by 5 matrix. This move from one matrix to another does not seem that revolutionary, and would be facilitated by an events approach.

CONCLUSION

Admittedly, the above represents only a rough and underdeveloped first approach toward a new orientation for accounting theory. Why, then, is it presented here and now? Only in the hope of encouraging the research activities suggested by this approach and also in the further hope that it might stimulate a reexamination of some essential if rarely expressed implicit tenets of present accounting thought. The areas of possible research opportunities indicated by an events approach are many. The following represent a few:

(1) Test whether line by line predictions of events, i.e., the prediction of sales, cost of sales, etc., are more efficient in explaining the future value of a firm than the use of more aggregated figures such as income.

(2) Investigate the present format of accounting reports to see how useful these formats could be, i.e., to what extent do the various subcategories of the income statement and balance sheet covary? To what extent do they provide additional information?

(3) Attempt to develop more sophisticated models to explain the lag between cash outflows and cash inflows, i.e., utilizing funds statements, production statements, and others in an attempt to predict cash flows.

(4) Investigate the information loss due to the aggregations presently used by accountants. How much information is lost by aggregating and combining events to produce one income figure or to produce the different balance sheet amounts? A subsequent extension of this would be an investigation of the information loss due to expressing all economic activities in dollar terms.

(5) Construct useful accounting reports based on an events approach.

Ultimately this paper will find its justification if what is presented here as the conclusion will serve as an introduction to the research activities and the reexamination advocated.

ROBERT R. STERLING

ROBERT R. STERLING (1931–), B.S. 56, M.B.A. 58 Denver; Ph.D. 64 Florida. Currently Arthur Young Distinguished Professor of Accounting, University of Kansas. Major publications: *The Theory of the Measurement of Enterprise Income* (1970), *Accounting in Perspective* (editor, with Bentz, 1971), *Asset Valuation and Income Determination: A Consideration of the Alternatives* (editor, 1971). Frequent contributor to *Abacus* and *The Accounting Review*. Book review editor, *The Accounting Review*, 1969–71.

Joined the faculty of the University of Kansas in 1967 and became Arthur Young Distinguished Professor three years later.

In 1972, he became director of research of the American Accounting Association.

Principal research interest: accounting theory.

CONSERVATISM: THE FUNDAMENTAL PRINCIPLE OF VALUATION IN TRADITIONAL ACCOUNTING*

ROBERT R. STERLING

I CONSERVATISM

Accounting has always been a highly practical discipline. Accountants have been faced with the problem of making immediate decisions in order to meet the exigencies of practice. They have not had the luxury of unlimited reflection before taking a position. In addition, they were not much more than specialized craftsmen when an almost overwhelming responsibility was thrust upon them. They were asked to become stewards of a community's wealth in a period of financial piracy. They were required to have integrity when deceit was not uncommon.

SOURCE: From *Abacus*, Vol. 3, No. 2 (December, 1967), pp. 109–132. Reprinted by permission of *Abacus* and the author.

* The author gratefully acknowledges the criticism of Ralph Blodgett and the support of Dean Joseph McGuire of the University of Kansas.

As a consequence of these factors, there were twin developments: problems were solved in isolation; and the solutions became accepted and rather rigid. Accountants met problems and solved them on the basis of their best judgments about the particulars of those specific problems. Very likely the cognition of a particular problem was completely insulated from a similar problem that they had previously solved. The resulting cognitive dissonance probably did not bother any single accountant because his main concern was with the ethical effects of his decision. Meanwhile, another practitioner in another firm was solving a problem that was only slightly different and often coming up with a vastly different solution. Thus, there developed intra- and inter-practitioner inconsistencies. At the same time, the accountant needed a strong defence against sometimes simply optimistic, occasionally dishonest, financiers. He was placed in the precarious position of being subject to the pecuniary discretion of the person he was obliged to keep honest. In the absence of a cohesive theory, in the absence of police power, in the presence of ignorance and apathy of the community, his only defence was precedent and persuasion. Precedent soon became rule and the rigid application of rules was his only weapon in the face of a powerful adversary.

The accountant passed through the era of swashbuckling manipulation; the era of watered stock and financial bubbles; in short, the era of chicanery by financial overstatement. In addition, he has always been faced with the effervescent optimism of the entrepreneur. The entrepreneur is naturally optimistic about his project. If he were not, he would not be engaged in it. This optimism is exhibited by a tendency to overvalue the enterprise. Faced with the universal tendency to overstate, the accountant conceived his role to be one of temperance. As a steward, he needed to be the ultimate in solidarity and stability. He wanted to insure that the value was *at least* the amount he reported. Often, to combat overstatement, he proposed understatement, perhaps with the hope of striking a balance.[1]

Thus, the most ancient and probably the most pervasive principle of accounting valuation is conservatism. Recently this rule has come under attack. The Finney and Miller texts, which mirror the mainstream of accounting thought, referred to conservatism as a "principle of accounting" through four editions. In the fifth edition, however, they complain about the "fetish of conservatism".

We recognize that conservatism has lost favour in accounting circles, that it is not applied in practice as much as it once was, and that the academics challenge it. Nevertheless, the author considers conservatism to be the most influential principle of valuation in traditional accounting. Other principles, e.g. cost, consistency, realization, going concern, etc., are often given higher (always no less than equal) status. We regard such lists as erroneous and consider conservatism to be a much more fundamental and pervasive principle of practice or behaviour than the others usually listed.

Evidence for this assertion comes more from the accountant's deeds than his words. Accountants violate the historical cost principle when they value at the *lower* of cost or market. The realization convention is violated in the case of instalment sales and the writing *down* of obsolete inventory. The going concern assumption is abrogated when it results in a value *greater* than market. If the

---

[1] It is interesting that one of the consequences of the U.S. Federal Income Tax has been a tendency to reverse the roles. The accountant has had to resist the entrepreneur's desire to avoid taxes by financial understatement.

consistent application of a valuation rule becomes unconservative, accountants usually become inconsistent. The basic "benefit theory" is violated in favour of conservatism in several instances, e.g. advertising and research expenditures.

In addition to these examples, evidence comes from justifications presented in the literature. Many authors take a moderately conservative or even anti-conservative position when they are writing under the head of "Principles". However, when they are discussing the valuation of a specific asset, the recurrent phrase that something "is or is not conservative" is almost inevitable.

For example, Johnson and Kriegman take an "anti-ultraconservative" view in their chapter on accounting theory:

> Misrepresentation was often injected in the balance sheets of businesses by policies involving the deliberate understatement of asset values in order to achieve so-called "conservative" values for these assets.... By these practices, "conservative" values became "ultra-conservative" values *not* fairly presenting the net income and financial position of a given business.[2]

The tone is clearly anti-ultraconservative. Perhaps it is anti-conservative when we juxtapose a statement from an earlier discussion of principles. "The statement of income and the balance sheet, therefore, must be built upon the cornerstone of *truth*." (p. 5.) Yet when they discuss the valuation of stocks, they write:

> The valuation at current market of stocks and bonds held for short-term investment purposes, when market is higher than cost, is a practice not generally approved by accountants. This disapproval rests on the fact that the practice not only involves a departure from original cost as the time-honored yardstick of accounting valuation but also involves accounting recognition of appreciated values. *The practice is obviously not conservative;* and accountants generally have been loth to place an unrealized surplus account on the balance sheet. What support has been given the practice has been defended on the grounds of showing the financial position of the business on a realistic basis. (p. 129. Emphasis supplied.)

It is not clear whether these are the authors' arguments or whether they are reporting the predominant view of the profession. Either case supports our point.

The above quotation sets out two conflicting concepts, conservatism versus realism. Without further argument—the above quotation is the *entire* discussion of the pros and cons of market valuation of securities—they draw a conclusion. They point out that valuation at market "is not generally approved" by the accounting profession and then they support a cost valuation:

> The authors believe that profits and losses on marketable securities should be recognized *only* at the date of their sale. On the balance sheet, marketable securities should be valued at cost. (p. 129.)

Obviously, conservatism takes precedence over realism for both the profession at large and these authors. We suspect that the authors would abandon their strict cost position in a period of deflation.

[2] A. W. Johnson and O. M. Kriegman, *Intermediate Accounting*, 3rd ed, New York, Holt, Rinehart and Winston, 1964, p. 740.

Moreover, they state explicitly the connection of the realization convention to conservatism:

> Today, the doctrine of conservatism is essentially a policy of caution. Revenue, for example, will receive accounting recognition only after it has been realized.... (p. 740.)

That is, the realization convention has its roots in the principle of conservatism. Another widely used text supports this thesis:

> The doctrine of conservatism is illustrated in the application of practices such as the following: increases in the values of assets and anticipated gains are normally ignored until realized by means of sale; declines in asset values and anticipated losses, however, are normally recognized.... certain expenditures are charged in full against current revenue despite the possibility of future benefits.[3]

This text then takes a moderately conservative position: "A conservative approach in the measurement process is desirable." (p. 49.)

Later, the arguments for valuation at market are briefly surveyed and then rejected. The reasons for the rejection in their *entirety* follow:

> Little tendency to accept valuation at market has been shown by the accounting profession. Such procedure has been challenged chiefly on the grounds that it represents a departure from the cost concept and would *violate accounting conservatism.* (p. 248. Emphasis supplied.)

In view of the authors' previous statement, which justifies departure from the cost concept in favour of conservatism, we could infer that the violation of accounting conservatism is the fundamental argument against valuation at market.

One additional reason for our thesis—that conservatism is the fundamental principle—is the odd character of the attacks on it. Much of the literature opposes conservatism because it is not conservative! A common argument against conservatism in one period is that it produces unconservative values in another period. Paton argues that "cost or market is not truly conservative" because:

> A low inventory at the end of one year is reflected in the cost of sales of the ensuing period, and as a result the income of the second period is increased (or the loss reduced) by precisely the amount by which the opening inventory was reduced through the operation of the "conservative" rule.[4]

That is, intertemporally, an apparently conservative procedure is not truly conservative.

A slight variation of this argument is presented in an official pronouncement of the AICPA:

> The argument advanced in favor of immediately writing off discount was that it extinguished an asset that was only nominal in character and that it re-

---

[3] W. E. Karrenbrock and H. Simons, *Intermediate Accounting*, 4th ed, Cincinnati, South-Western Publishing Co, 1964, p 49.

[4] W. A. Paton and W. A. Paton, Jr., *Asset Accounting*, New York, The Macmillan Company, 1952, p. 84.

sulted in a conservative balance sheet. The weight attached to this argument has steadily diminished, and increasing weight has been given to the arguments that all such charges should be reflected under the proper head in the income account, *and that conservatism in the balance sheet is of dubious value if attained at the expense of a lack of conservatism in the income account, which is far more significant.*[5]

That is, the fundamental principle is conservatism, and, therefore, a conservative value on the more important statement is more desirable than a conservative value on a less important statement.

In sum, our primary hypothesis is: *Conservatism is the fundamental principle of valuation in accounting.*

Our secondary hypothesis is: *Conservatism is the premise, often tacit, from which the historical cost-realization rule is derived.*

There is some support for our secondary hypothesis in the accounting literature. We gave some examples above. Some authors freely admit that certain valuation rules are applications of the conservative principle. These are usually authors with a "liberal" bent. Other authors, the most conservative, in fact, if not in statement, strain to justify valuation rules on grounds other than conservatism.

We should not leave this discussion without indicating that we think there are principles of valuation other than conservatism, viz., causality and convenience. Briefly, the notion of convenience is that throughout the history of accounting there has been an unyielding pressure to get *some* statistic out in the shortest possible time, at a low cost, with the least chance of being challenged. This has resulted in valuation rules which are convenient. For example, "cost" (purchase price) is a readily available statistic; "realization at point of sale" is a fairly clean-cut, easy-to-apply rule; "materiality" is a justification for breaking the rules if it is much more convenient to do so. Standard costs are an aberration and, without the notion of convenience, it is difficult to explain their acceptance.

The third principle—causality—is a relatively recent addition, coming from academics who attempted to apply causal reasoning to existing accounting practices. Cost accountants were in the forefront of this process, arguing that cost should be attached to the unit that "caused" the cost to be incurred. They became involved in long arguments over the allocation of overhead, culminating in the recent controversy over direct costing. Another example is "cost-benefit theory" which charges costs to the periods which they benefit, i.e., periods in which those costs "cause" revenue. The "matching" and "attaching" concepts spring directly from causality arguments.

We think that these three principles, singularly or in mixed-weight combinations, are sufficient to explain virtually all accounting valuations. However, the last two principles are not as germane to this paper as the first.

II HISTORICAL COST

As many people have previously pointed out, "cost" has many variations in application and thus it is difficult to analyse the rule in the abstract. We think that the explanation for the variations is contained in our hypothesis. Cost is not

---

[5] American Institute of Certified Public Accountants, *Accounting Research and Terminology Bulletins*, Final edition, New York, AICPA, 1961, p. 129. Emphasis supplied.

a fundamental tenet of accounting; instead it is a derivative of the conservatism principle of valuation. First, and most importantly, the rule almost always yields a conservative value. Cost, particularly of assets which have been amortized, i.e. valued *below* cost, is virtually certain to be below market. If not, it is written down, i.e., when the cost rule is not conservative, it is violated. Second, cost figures are usually far more convenient to obtain than any other value. Ordinarily there is easy access to documents, invoices, cheques which yield a cost of an item.[6] Occasionally, there is some difficulty in obtaining the cost figures and the accountant reverts to conservatism by making a rather low estimate or, if the amount is "immaterial", by assigning a zero value. Third, costs are attached to products or periods by some causally derived rules. Some costs "benefit future periods"—cause revenue in the future—and some value is maintained on the books. Other costs have "benefited past periods"—caused past revenue—and are valued at zero. If a cost produces a product which is "expected to benefit future periods", the cost attaches to the product until it is sold (causes revenue). If the product "loses utility" (loses part of its capability to cause revenue) there is a reversion to conservatism as it is written down. Of course, values other than cost could "attach" so that causality is not a necessary principle for the cost rule. Instead it seems that cost came first and there was a need for some rationale for making the allocations. Causality provided the rationale.

In short, cost is both conservative and convenient, and thus it fits our general hypothesis. Our secondary hypothesis—that cost is a derivative of the general principle of conservatism—is supported by the fact that when cost and conservatism conflict, conservatism prevails. Additional evidence, albeit indirect, for both hypotheses is the manifestly specious character of the arguments for the cost rule. We think that the explanation for this is that the arguments are essentially apologetics for accounting practice. The practice is governed by conservatism, but the authors deny the principle of conservatism and thus are left in the untenable position of defending what they deny. As a consequence, the arguments become strained in attempting to defend the rule.

III ARGUMENTS FOR THE COST RULE

For our purposes it will be convenient to distinguish two broad categories of arguments for the cost rule. The distinguishing factor is the temporal location of the valuation; valuations are made at

1. the time of acquisition (initial valuation)
2. times subsequent to acquisition (subsequent valuation).

Initial valuation is accomplished by setting the acquired asset equal to the cash (or cash equivalent) sacrificed and with this we have no quarrel. We usually find ourselves in disagreement with the arguments but, since the conclusions are identical, we omit the criticism.[7]

---

[6] We say "a" cost instead of "the" cost because, as several people have pointed out, ten different accountants are likely to get twelve different costs. Cf Charles T. Horngren, *Cost Accounting: A Managerial Emphasis*, Englewood Cliffs, Prentice-Hall, Inc., 1963, p. 315.

[7] For a striking exception, cf. Russell Bowers, "Tests of Income Realization", *The Accounting Review*, June 1941, p. 142.

PROBLEMS CONFRONTING THE ACCOUNTING PROFESSION

Our quarrel is with subsequent valuation. Subsequent valuation at historical cost is a measure of past sacrifice which we think is irrelevant to the present valuation. We will analyse only those arguments which are most pertinent to this quarrel.

Finney's Argument

Finney begins his argument with reference to marketable securities and specifically raises the question of subsequent valuation in terms of "revenue realization". Essentially the question is, "Should securities be valued at original cost or at present market price?" There are some accountants who would value at present market price but would not allow the value increment to affect income. Finney does not make the distinction. He is concerned with both valuation and income at the same time.

His argument has appeared in texts and learned journals. For ease of reference, we present it in its entirety with marginal indications of the progress of the argument.

(Question)	Is unrealized appreciation revenue? Let us consider this question first with respect to marketable securities, as to which it is possible to make the strongest case for an affirmative answer.
(Example)	If marketable securities were purchased for $50,000, were worth $60,000 at the end of the year of purchase, and were sold for $70,000 in the following year, was there a $20,000 profit in the second year or a $10,000 profit each year? While it possibly may be said that $10,000 of the profit accrued each year, and while it certainly can be said that a $10,000 profit could have been realized the first year, it nevertheless is true that realization did not occur until the second year.
(Principle, Premise)	The requirements of the accounting principle relative to revenue realization were not met during the first year because, when the management elected not to sell at the end of the first year but preferred to take the hazards of market fluctuation,
(Conclusion)	there was no realization of profit nor any reasonable assurance that a profit would be realized.
(Generalization)	If readily marketable securities cannot properly be valued at a price in excess of cost, although a profit could be immediately realized by a sale at the market price, the valuation of inventories at market prices in excess of cost is under ordinary conditions, even less proper.[8]

In order to understand the argument we must reproduce the principle:

The governing accounting principle is: *Revenue* should not be regarded as *earned* until an asset increment has been *realized* or until its realization is reasonably assured. (p. 364. Emphasis supplied.)

---

[8] H. A. Finney, "Principles and Conventions", *The Accounting Review*, October 1944, pp. 365–366. The argument has also been reprinted with minor changes in the texts. See H. A. Finney and H. Miller, *Principles of Accounting, Intermediate*, 5th ed, Englewood Cliffs, Prentice-Hall, Inc., 1963, p. 176.

Before we can utilize the principle, we need definitions for revenue, earned and realized.

Revenue consists of an *inflow of assets*, in the form of cash, receivables, or other property, *from customers and clients*, and as related to the *disposal of product* in the form of goods or to the *rendering of services*. (p. 363. Emphasis supplied.)

"Consists" and "related to" are not sharp words, but the meaning is clear:

Definition 1. Revenue is the receipt of cash or near-cash from sales.

"Realized", in the Fisher tradition, is unequivocally the receipt of cash. However, when the cash basis of accounting was modified, the terms were retained; some confusion resulted. Finney says:

Realization of revenue does not necessarily require a collection in cash, since a valid receivable from a solvent debtor is an asset in as good standing as cash. The point of sale, therefore, is the step in the series of activities at which the revenue generally is regarded as realized. This point has been generally adopted because (1) it is the point at which a conversion takes place—an exchange of one asset for another—and conversion is regarded as evidence of realization; and (2) it is the point at which the amount of the revenue is objectively determinable from the sale price acceptable to both parties. (p. 363.)

Realization is concerned with the occurrence of an act—a sale—and with the form of assets—cash or near-cash—that can be included as "realized". It is a trifle obscure in light of the phrase about "conversion *being evidence* of realization", because realization is defined as occurring at conversion. Nevertheless, in view of the rest of the literature and Finney's other works,[9] we can define it explicitly:

Definition 2. Realization occurs when cash or near-cash is received from sales.

Earned is simply a synonym. "As used in accounting, however, 'earned' and 'realized' are generally regarded as synonymous."[10] Again "generally regarded" prohibits sharpness, but in light of the above quotation the definition is clear:

Definition 3. Earned equals realized.

Since one cannot have receipts from sales without the occurrence of a sale, it appears that revenue is the more general term. Substitution of "revenue" for "realization" in Definition 2 does not distort the meaning:

---

[9] The latest edition of the Finney and Miller introductory book answers the question in slightly more direct fashion.

When is revenue earned? Revenue is earned when goods are disposed of or when services are rendered. A transfer or exchange occurs. The business gives up goods or renders services and acquires other assets in exchange. There is a performance accompanied by a concurrent acquisition of an asset.

H. A. Finney and H. Miller, *Principles of Accounting, Introductory*, 6th ed, Englewood Cliffs, Prentice-Hall, Inc., 1963, p. 241. As we note in the text, Finney equates earnings with realization.

[10] H. A. Finney, "Principles and Conventions", p. 363.

528   PROBLEMS CONFRONTING THE ACCOUNTING PROFESSION

Definition 4. [Revenue] occurs when cash or near-cash is received from sales.

Revenue is defined as receipts-from-sales; therefore, revenue occurs when the sale is made. There can be no lapse of time as there might be on a cash basis because receivables are included in the "realization". Thus, "revenue" and "realization" are synonyms and "realized revenue" is redundant. Receipts-from-sales is the basic concept. At the very most, the distinction is that realization refers to the *timing* of the receipt while revenue refers to the receipt (inflow) per se. With very little, if any, distortion the general definition may be stated as:

Receipts-from-sales = revenue
= realization
= earnings
= realized revenue
= earned revenue

We can now restate and understand the governing principle:

[Receipts-from-sales] should not be regarded as [receipts-from-sales] until an asset increment has been [received-from-sales] or until its [receipt-from-sales] is reasonably assured.

A "principle" of this kind needs no commentary.

We can now restate Finney's argument.

Is [not-receipts-from-sales] [receipts-from-sales]? While it possibly may be said that $10,000 of the profit accrued each year, and while it certainly can be said that a $10,000 profit could have been [received-from-sales] the first year, it nevertheless is true that [receipts-from-sales] *did not occur* until the second year.

The requirements of the accounting principle relative to [receipts-from-sales] were not met during the first year because, when the management *elected not to sell* at the end of the first year but preferred to take the hazards of market fluctuation, there was no [receipts-from-sales] nor any reasonable assurance that a profit would be [received-from-sales].

No one would deny that "realization did not occur". By assumption, no sale was made and by definition, realization occurs at sale. His conclusion is of the same order. In effect he says "when management elected not to sell there was no sale", i.e., "when there was no sale there was no sale". A more exquisite example of *petitio principii* is impossible to imagine.

Two minor points remain. First, the tense of the last statement is important. It is said there was no "reasonable assurance that a profit *would be* realized". Finney is concerned with the future, with the ultimate profit to be realized from sale, not with the measurement of past events. He says "it certainly can be said that a $10,000 profit *could have been* realized". He does not deny that he could measure the amount that could have been realized, but he refuses to do so because that may not be the amount that will ultimately be realized. That is, the fact that the future price is unknown leads him to reject a known present price. We do not follow this reasoning and in addition we do not understand how it leads to the acceptance of a past price.

Second, the word "certainly" implies *sureness of the amount* that "could have been realized". Could this be interpreted as admission of an objective measurement prior to sale? His second justification of realization is that the sale "is the point at which the amount ... *is* objectively determinable ...", not is *more* objective; yet he seems to imply that there may be other points where the amount is objective. Both of these points will come up again in the sequel.

Finney's argument must be rejected as circular, repetitious and ambiguous. Many explanations for this circularity could be advanced, but in light of the report that he has sold over a million copies to a rather conservative audience, we prefer the hypothesis of a tacit assumption of conservatism.

May's Assumption and Argument

May's argument is presented in an AICPA research study because it is "pertinent for the light it throws on the reasoning behind this guide [realization convention]".[11] We consider it for the same reason.

> Manifestly, when a laborious process of manufacture and sale culminates in the delivery of the product at a profit, that profit is not attributable, except conventionally, to the moment when the sale or delivery occurred. The accounting convention which makes such an attribution is justified only by its demonstrated practical utility.
>
> It is instructive to consider how it happens that a rule which is violative of fact produces results that are practically useful and reliable. The explanation is that in the normal business there are at any one moment transactions at every stage of the production of profit, from beginning to end. *If the distribution were exactly uniform,* an allocation of income according to the proportion of completion of each unit would *produce the same result* as the attribution of the entire profit to a single stage.[12]

The general thesis is correct under the assumption given. If a firm engages in a repetitive process of purchasing and selling at constant prices in constant quantities with constant time lapses, the recognition of income at sale will yield a valid figure. More precisely, it will yield a constant income figure for all temporal instants except the first and the last.

If we take May's assumption of exact uniformity and assign t_0 to the instant of the first purchase (at the inception of the business), which is to be sold at t_1, and another purchase at t_1 to be sold at t_2, etc., and the last sale (at the cessation of the business) at t_n, we can represent the transactions in full as in Figure 1. At t_0 a product is acquired costing, say, $100 and is sold for, say, $125 at t_1. Another purchase for $100 is made at t_1 and sold at t_2 for $125 and so forth until the firm makes its final sale at t_n and closes down.

The accounting rules require that the cost of the merchandise be deferred until sold, at which time the cost expires and is matched against the revenue. There is an asset of $100 from t_0 to t_n. The first revenue occurs at t_1 and the

---

[11] Robert T. Sprouse and Maurice Moonitz, *A Tentative Set of Broad Accounting Principles for Business Enterprises, Accounting Research Study*, No. 3, New York, American Institute of Certified Public Accountants, 1962, p. 13.

[12] George O. May, *Financial Accounting*, New York, The Macmillan Company, 1943, p. 30. Emphasis supplied.

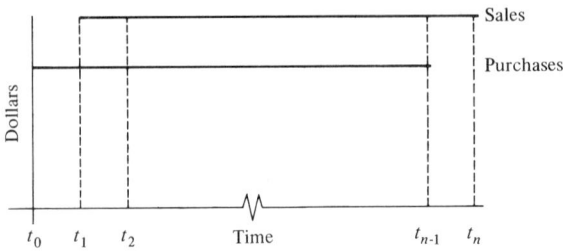

FIGURE 1

asset acquired at t_0 then becomes an expense. Revenue remains constant from t_1 to t_n at \$125 and expenses remain constant at \$100 and thus a profit of \$25 per instant. In short, the accountant shifts the purchase curve one instant to the right and changes its name.

Under these assumptions, the virtues ascribed to the rule are perfectly correct. As May pointed out, the rule would produce the same result as an allocation according to the "proportion of completion". We agree. Our criticism is that he did not go far enough. *Precisely the same result would be achieved by recognizing income* on the cash basis, the sale basis, the purchase basis, or more simply by recognizing it on Tuesdays, equinoxes, or phases of the moon. Except for the first and last instants, *any* temporally uniform basis would produce the same result if the distribution were exactly uniform. Thus, we could ask what is special about the sale basis that would cause us to select it as the only point for revaluations. Unfortunately, May does not address this question. His argument for a sale basis of recognition is equally applicable to all other temporally uniform bases.

May goes on to say that the realization convention should be violated when the stable-firm assumptions are not met and gives construction contracts as an example. With this we can agree, but note that the assumption requires constant prices and constant quantities at all instants in time. Since these requirements are seldom, if ever, met we could conclude that the realization convention should be violated in almost all valuation situations.

May's argument is enlightening because the assumptions are made explicit. As far as we know this is the only place where an accountant has explicitly stated these assumptions in defence of the convention, although others have claimed that the stationary state is a necessary condition for validity. It is tempting to speculate about the relationship of the notions of the stable firm and the stationary state to the notion of the going concern. Some of the arguments for going concern values seem implicitly to assume the stable firm and it may be that the two assumptions are identical. In addition, the argument is enlightening because it requires a future. The purchased good has a value because it *will be sold* in the succeeding time period. However, the fact that the good has a value does not necessarily lead to a cost valuation. Instead the argument seems to turn on convenience and conservatism. It is likely that the convenient-conservative practice existed and May hit upon the stable-firm assumption as a means of justifying the practice. Other observations of May lend some credence to this view; for example, "To me, conservatism is still the first virtue of accounting...." (Ibid., p. 44.)

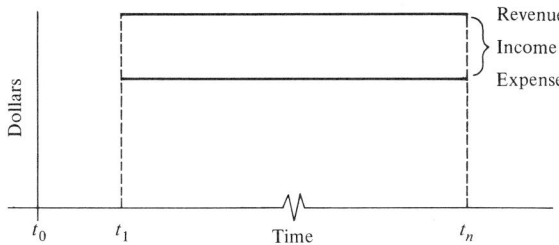

FIGURE 2

Paton and Littleton

About thirty years ago the American Accounting Association became increasingly disturbed about the lack of theory in accounting. It formed committees and study groups in order to remedy the deficiency and "to bring order out of this chaos of conflicting ideas and practices".[13] The result of this concern was the publication of *An Introduction to Corporate Accounting Standards* which, it was hoped, would "be one of the really significant contributions to accounting literature" (p. vi). If acceptance, use, and citation are the criteria, their hopes were realized. *Standards* has had a tremendous influence on accounting thought and has since become a classic. It has been accurately described as the "accountants' theoretical bible". For this reason, we feel obliged to analyse the authors' argument for the cost rule.

Our consideration of *Standards* is much more difficult than that of either Finney or May because we are unable to locate a concise valuation argument that we could analyse. The discussion is somewhat diffuse and the reader will have to depend upon our outline of the argument instead of a complete direct quotation. That is the source of our first criticism. One would hope that such a basic treatise would present a rather full argument for the endorsed valuation method. Unfortunately this is not the case; its lack is a major defect in an otherwise noble effort.

Paton and Littleton's approach is to derive "standards" (norms for behaviour)[14] from "concepts".

> The circumstances surrounding the use of accounting clearly indicate the need for accounting standards. But such standards cannot be determined by an appeal to authority or to common opinion. The doctrines supported by writers and the practices accepted by professional accountants need to be subjected to analysis and coordination, with a consequent sifting out of inconsistencies and unessentials and an integration of essentials. The approach to standards should be by way of the broad function of accounting so that the standards formulated may be relevant thereto, and by way of the *basic concepts or assumptions* underlying accounting so that the standards formulated may be well grounded. To be relevant, a standard needs to be clearly related to the essen-

---

[13] W. A. Paton and A. C. Littleton, *An Introduction to Corporate Accounting Standards*, Chicago, American Accounting Association, 1940, p. vi.

[14] "Accounting standards therefore become responsible for furnishing guideposts to fair dealing in the midst of flexible rules and techniques." Ibid., p. 2.

tial purposes of accounting; to be well grounded, a standard needs to be recognized as resting upon known and accepted assumptions.

The *basic concepts, or assumptions,* here summarized constitute a suitable foundation for the discussion of accounting standards which follows. (p. 7. Emphasis supplied.)

Thus, the behavioural norms (standards) spring directly from the *assumptions.* There are several headings in this chapter, which presumably are a list of these basic assumptions. Under each of the headings there is some statement about *cost,* with no consideration of any competing method of valuation.

Under the caption "The Business Entity", they write:

> With the entity concept as a basis, there is no difficulty in accepting the proposition that all costs legitimately incurred by the enterprise are properly included, in the first instance, in the total of assets. Thus organization expenditures, costs of raising capital, and related charges are elements of enterprise assets and capital. (p. 9.)

Their analysis is concerned with the segregation of business from personal affairs and with the *items* which can be properly included as assets. After they justify the inclusion of certain items, the term "cost" is used as a general description. They do not give reasons for their selection of cost as opposed to another value.

Under the caption "Continuity of Activity", they write:

> To the courts, concerned with the problem of determining immediate equities and restoring rights if damage has been suffered, assumptions with respect to future activity seem largely irrelevant. Hence the stress on "values" and "valuations" rather than on costs and the processes of accounting for costs. *The accountant,* on the other hand, deals primarily with the administration of the affairs of the continuing business institution and *accordingly emphasizes* the flow of costs and the interpretation of assets as balances of unamortized costs. (pp. 10–11. Emphasis supplied.)

They never say *why* he "accordingly emphasizes the flow of *costs*", simply that he does emphasize it. In fact, they say that "earning power—not price . . . is the significant basis of enterprise value." But they then switch to a discussion of income statements, and they define income as the resultant of the proper matching of *costs* and revenues.

Under the caption "Measured Consideration", they introduce the term "price-aggregate"; and then in the summary they conclude that "price-aggregates involved in the exchanges . . . constitute the basic subject matter of accounting". The word "consideration" is being used here in the same way as it is used in the law of contracts, i.e., it means the amount given in exchange. Thus "consideration" appears to be both one of the basic assumptions of accounting and "the basic subject matter of accounting". The next assumption is that "*costs* attach". Then, "*costs are considered* as measuring effort" under the caption "Efforts and Accomplishments". Under the caption "Verifiable, Objective Evidence", they *never mention* price-aggregates or cost (except the cost of obtaining evidence); yet in the summary, the reason given for costs being the basic data is that they are "objective".

The full statement in the summary is:

In general, the only definite facts available to represent exchange transactions objectively and to express them homogeneously are the price-aggregates involved in the exchanges; hence such data constitute the basic subject matter of accounting. (p. 7.)

Their concern is only with exchange transactions; purchase prices are proper for the valuation at time of exchange. But they do not say why they are proper for *subsequent* valuations. One could speculate about the reasons for their conclusions but it would be preferable if they had stated them.

Perhaps the explanation for the use of cost without justification lies under the last heading. Under the caption "Assumptions", they write:

The fundamental concepts or propositions of accounting, like those of other fields, are in themselves assumptions in considerable measure or are predicated upon assumptions which are not subject to conclusive demonstration or proof. (p. 21.)

It appears that cost is one of the basic assumptions which is not subject to proof. Upon this basic assumption they build their superstructure of concepts.

Stout evidence that they assume the cost rule comes from the peculiar character of their methodology. Their approach is tersely stated in the preface. "We have attempted to *weave together* the fundamental ideas of accounting rather than to state standards as such." (p. ix. Emphasis supplied.) That is, they have taken the fundamental ideas that they have found in practice and woven them together.[15] One idea that they found was cost. "The assumption that recorded dollar cost continues to represent actual cost permeates accounting thought and practice, as it does the law". (p. 23.) Upon finding this permeation, and without explicit critical analysis of the effects of using cost, they wove cost in as a basic assumption. It is hardly surprising, therefore, that the final chapter of *Standards* concludes that cost is the proper value for use in accounting.

It would be unkind to accuse them of circular reasoning. Their arguments turn out to be circular but this is because of their methodology. They conceive their role to be one of rationalizing (making rational) the extant practice of accounting. Thus, they are not guilty of circular reasoning because they do not attempt to reason from premise *to* conclusion. They take the existing ideas and try to connect them; they are apologists in the strict sense of the term. As it turns out, they are apologists for a practice that is conservative.

The Liquidity Argument

A number of authors have argued that income should not be recognized until the asset that it represents is in liquid form, a form that is distributable, available to pay dividends. The most readily available (liquid) asset is cash and this may be one of the reasons underlying the preoccupation with exchanges and money.

We do not know exactly why this position is taken. There has been little analysis in the literature since the *Eisner v. Macomber* case. The profession seems to have believed that the court settled the "separation" issue and nothing was left

---

[15] In a later work Littleton makes the process more explicit. He devotes an entire chapter to "Inductively Derived Principles", i.e., principles derived from observing the practices of accountants. A. C. Littleton, *Structure of Accounting Theory*, Menasha, Wisconsin, George Banta Publishing Company, 1953.

to be said. Bowers has pointed out that this is based upon a misunderstanding of the court's decision.

This decision seems to have been misunderstood by many practitioners and textbook writers. The court did not hold, as is often supposed, that a stock dividend in the same class of stock is not income. The earlier Macomber decision had merely denied that the receipt of common stock constituted effective realization if received as a dividend on common stock, that is, if it were merely capitalized surplus which was already a common stock equity.[16]

The court held that the receipt of stock did not effectively change the position of the recipient since it was simply a different form of the equity which he had previously owned. Thus, it could be interpreted to mean that the "income" arose *before* the issuance of the stock dividend.

Because of this misunderstanding, the separation notion seems to be an *assumption* of accountants. This hypothesis is strengthened by the absence of analysis and the occasional explicit statement that it is an assumption. For example, Bowers discards the economic power theory on measurement grounds and then *assumes* availability.

If the economic-power theory has any conceptual superiority the possibility of applying new measuring devices should be studied more carefully. In the remainder of this article it will be *assumed* that the efficacy of any realization criterion lies in two essential attributes, first, measurability, and second, *availability*. (pp. 91–92. Emphasis supplied.)

The reason behind the assumption is that income is not available to pay dividends until it is in liquid form. Accountants "help" management by restricting income (receipts) to assets that are in distributable form. From this they assume that income cannot arise until the availability criterion is met. The argument is confused and unsound.

First, there is the possibility of paying dividends in kind. This has been done, particularly during the Great Depression, but it is cumbersome. It is more convenient to pay cash dividends and, of course, this requires possession of cash before they can be paid. Usually a corporation has several sources of cash. It could, for example, pledge a non-liquid asset on a loan and obtain sufficient cash to pay a dividend.

More important, however, is the confusion of two separate concepts. The possession of cash is a question of fact about the *form* of the assets at a given *moment in time*. The income question is concerned with *changes* in wealth *over time*. If the ability to pay cash dividends is the sole criterion, the income question becomes the ultimate in simplicity. Either the company has cash or it does not, and that is the end of the problem.

In their writings on earned surplus and retained income, accountants not only recognize, they emphasize, the difference between the two questions. They lament the confusion resulting from the equation of retained income to "ability to pay dividends". In an effort to prevent this confusion, they carefully point out that the final determinant of dividend payments is the *availability of cash*, not income.

[16] Russell Bowers, "Tests of Income Realization", in S. Davidson, D. Green, C. Horngren, G. Sorter (eds.), *An Income Approach to Accounting Theory*, Englewood Cliffs, Prentice-Hall, Inc., 1964, pp. 90–91.

Hill and Gordon present a fairly typical statement.

> This order gives recognition to the fact that dividends are legally paid out of accumulated, rather than current, earnings. In this connection, it should be noted that while dividends are declared "out of earnings", they are paid "out of cash". Consequently, insofar as past retained earnings have been invested in productive assets, they are not available for distribution.[17]

That is, dividends are distributions of income, but a *separate requirement* is that the assets must be in distributable form.

When the increment in assets which represents income is reinvested in productive facilities, it is no longer in distributable form, and this is exactly what has happened in the majority of corporations in America. It is very common to find the retained earnings figure to be several times the amount of cash and it is not uncommon for it to be larger than total current assets. It is clear that such a situation prohibits the immediate payment of cash dividends equal to the retained income, and it is clear that accountants recognize this. Their cognizance somehow leads them to the conclusion that liquidity should be the deciding factor in the recognition of current income.

A consistent application of the liquidity argument would require that income could never be more than cash on hand. Thus, even if income were realized upon receipt, it would have to be "dis-realized" upon the transformation of cash to a non-liquid asset. Since most corporations have an aversion to holding idle cash, income would be realized only momentarily.

For example, suppose that a trader started with $100 cash at t_1 and had $150 cash at t_2. This meets the distribution requirement and the unequivocal amount of income is $50. If one instant later he makes a purchase, the distribution requirement is not met. Should we dis-realize the income? If so, has he suffered a loss? Of course the accountant would not dis-realize the income. He would value the purchased asset at $150 (cost) and the difference ($50) would remain in the retained income account.

If the price of this latter asset rose between the date of purchase and a balancing date t_3, a report at t_3 will show a current income of zero regardless of how high the price has gone because the amount of the rise in price is not in distributable form. However, the t_3 report will show $50 of retained income which also is not in distributable form. The only difference between current and retained income is the period of time that is covered. Retained income includes all income from t_1 to t_3 and current income is only that income from t_2 to t_3. Thus, the inclusive income concept, the longer period income, does not meet the distribution requirement, but the requirement must be met before the shorter period income can be realized. Something is not quite right here.

If Devine's notion of administering working capital is taken literally, we can be more insistent that income be dis-realized. He writes:

> For our present purposes the important aspect of income realization is that accountants usually *insist on helping* management administer its working capi-

---

[17] T. Hill and M. Gordon, *Accounting: A Management Approach*, rev. ed., Homewood, Richard D. Irwin, Inc., 1959, p. 51.

tal by *recognizing income only when working capital is available to permit withdrawal* (if desired) without impairing the current position of the firm.[18]

The accountant restricts the amount of legally payable dividends by not recognizing income until it is liquid. Leaving aside the ethical question of the accountant taking it upon himself to do this, it is clear that the accountant could be of even more "help" if he dis-realized income when there was no cash available. If he thinks that management needs help on financial matters, it would be eminently reasonable to reduce income at least to the cash on hand, and perhaps he should even deduct planned disbursements.

We are not seriously suggesting such a procedure. Instead we are trying to emphasize that the problems should be separated by showing that the connection leads to absurdity. We think that the liquidity argument is nothing more than conservatism—Devine's article is an attack on the notion that *losses* need to be "realized"—in evidence again.

The Going-Concern Concept

The going-concern assumption is common to almost all accountants. Textbooks seldom fail to list it as a "standard", "convention", etc. The following is fairly representative:

> When the future is unpredictable, one can only assume a continuity of existence and a business environment to follow that is similar to that in which the enterprise finds itself currently. The business unit, thus, is viewed as a "going concern" in the absence of evidence to the contrary. The continuity assumption is support for the preparation of a balance sheet that reports costs that are assignable to future activities rather than realizable values that would attach to properties in the event of voluntary liquidation or forced sale.[19]

The assertion that one "can *only* assume a continuity of existence" is absurd. One *can* assume anything he pleases about the future. There is a continuing philosophical debate about what one *should* (logically) assume, but we have found no philosopher who prescribes one assumption. Even the most future-minded of the philosophers insist on an evidentially (historically) based *projection*, not an assumption. The high rate of business failures would make it difficult to build an evidential case for a projection of continuity. No business has ever continued "indefinitely" into the future. All businesses, except those presently in existence, have ceased operations. Thus, it would seem more reasonable to assume cessation instead of continuity.

A case could be built for a mean life-expectancy of businesses and this, like other statistical generalizations, would have some conceptual use. However, the generalization is about a universe and to apply it blindly to any particular element in that universe would be a gross misuse of statistical projection. Surely no one would *assume* that a leukemia patient is expected to reach the mean life expectancy of the population.

It is difficult to come to grips with this assumption. There seems to be little

---

[18] C. T. Devine, "Loss Recognition", in *An Income Approach to Accounting Theory*, op cit., p. 163.

[19] Karrenbrock and Simons, op cit.

reasoning behind it and even less evidence. Another investigator had similar difficulties:

> *The continuity (or permanence) of the business enterprise.* Relatively little can be found explaining this concept other than (a) the postulate itself—that in the absence of actual evidence to the contrary, the prospective life of the enterprise may be deemed to be indefinitely long, and (2) [sic] the statement that it is an accepted postulate because continuity is typical of all entities.[20]

Our reading leads us to the same conclusion. We think that the reason why relatively little is said about it is because there is relatively little that can be said about it. We have a propensity to be suspicious of bald assertions and, therefore, we reject (a). A perusal of *Dun's Review of Business Failures* leads us to deny that "continuity is typical".

For purposes of discussion, however, let us make the continuity assumption and examine the valuation consequences.

Futurity is an overriding concern of the accountants. For example, we found it in both Finney and May supra. This is apparently contradictory because accounting is generally thought to be purely historical. Further, most accountants think of themselves as recorders of past facts. Yet benefit theory, the matching process, attaching notions, etc., are clearly futurity concepts. A typical statement of the criterion for distinguishing between a positive and a zero carrying value follows.

> (1) ... any acquisition cost or portion thereof which is productive of *current period* revenue is an expense [zero value], and
>
> (2) ... any acquisition cost or portion thereof which is to be productive of *future* revenue is an asset [positive value].[21]

Thus, to follow these rules, the accountant assumes the continuity of the firm and then *projects* the benefits from each individual expenditure.

From this, he reasons that the proper value of these projected benefits is always equal to the historical cost. This reasoning normally takes the form of concentrating on the intended use and disallowing alternatives and/or sacrifices. The following is typical:

> Even when a disparity exists between old costs shown in the balance sheet and current values, the usefulness of the balance sheet is not destroyed, because in most cases the assets in question will have been acquired to be used and not to be resold. In such cases current values often are of slight significance to a "going concern" (an established business which is being conducted with the expectation of continuing indefinitely), because in most cases, assets with current values differing materially from cost would be such things as buildings, machinery, and equipment that were acquired to be used and not to be resold.[22]

We fail to follow the reasoning that connects intended use and value. We can understand how the expected net revenue from an intended use affects the valua-

---

[20] Arthur Andersen & Co, *The Postulate of Accounting*, Chicago, September 1960, p. 18.
[21] Hill and Gordon, op cit., p. 168.
[22] Finney and Miller, *Introductory*, p. 10.

tion decision of a given entrepreneur, but since those expectations are certain to change over time,[23] the value would also change. Only if one assumed that the expectations remained constant could the intended use have a one-to-one relationship with value. If one takes this view, the intended use notion is additional evidence for the existence of the "stable-firm stable-economy" assumption.

Moonitz and Jordan explicitly deny the stable economy assumption by introducing uncertainty, and defend the use of cost as an initial value. "The choice of cost as the basis of *initial* valuation is, in most cases, reasonable."[24] However, in a refreshingly candid statement, they point out that cost is a conservative value, initially, and further that the subsequent valuation at cost is solely on the basis of conservatism.

> In terms of the basic accounting problem, the cost rule is apparently conservative. Initial entry at cost results in no change in the difference between assets and liabilities; the acquisition of merchandise or of a fixed asset is treated as a "dead-level" transaction without effect on profits or proprietorship. . . . At dates subsequent to purchase, the reasons for adherence to cost differ. Here the *rationale is frankly on conservative grounds*. (pp. 168–9. Emphasis supplied.)

We are in complete agreement with this assessment. Note, however, that their justifications of the cost rule are based on futurity considerations. The theoretical framework is very close to that of Irving Fisher, although the conclusions vary.

Moonitz and Jordan's notion of value is grounded firmly in expected future receipts of *cash*. They make this explicit in several places.

> . . . for only through a carefully prepared projection of *estimated* cash receipts and cash disbursements, based on past experience corrected for anticipated variations, can the value amounts assignable to any of the items that become reflected in the financial picture of an enterprise be even approximately determined. (p. 126.)

Moreover, and this is crucial, these cash receipts must come from the intended use of the assets. In neither of the cases—complete certainty and complete uncertainty—do they ever consider any alternative use of the assets; presumably because they think that only the intended use is relevant to valuation problems. But under complete uncertainty the cash receipts from the intended use are unknown and, therefore, no valuation can be made.

> When the future is presumed to be completely unknown, our accounting must deal entirely with the past. We can prepare, for example, a schedule of cash received to date and from whom, and of cash paid out to date and for what. But we cannot prepare a balance sheet, because each asset in a balance sheet *represents something applicable to the future,* and each liability likewise indicates a commitment to do something in the future. (p. 127. Emphasis supplied.)

The underlying assumption must be of the "locked-in" variety, i.e., the firm is

---

[23] Except perhaps in the very limited case of a government perpetuity.
[24] M. Moonitz and L. Jordan, *Accounting: An Analysis of its Problems*, rev. ed., New York, Holt, Rinehart and Winston, Inc., 1963, Vol I, p. 168.

locked in the market with no alternatives. Otherwise the receipts from an immediate *sale* of the asset would yield some recordable value. We can think of no justification for the intended use valuation other than the locked-in assumption. If this be the authors' assumption, we are basically in agreement with the conclusions, i.e., zero value. However, we do not see why the locked-in assumption should be made.

Because of this futurity notion most accountants claim that income cannot be measured until the enterprise ceases operations. Robnett, Hill and Beckett describe this as an "inherent limitation" in accounting.

> *Business earnings are fundamentally indeterminate short of the total life of the business venture.* Any interim calculation of earnings is, therefore, an estimate.... In the first place, potential difficulty stems from the necessity, noted earlier in this chapter, for forecasting the future in order to interpret the past. *Underlying all interim valuation estimates is the general assumption that the business unit will continue as a going concern,* i.e., that it will function in the future in much the same manner as it has in the past.[25]

Note the odd twist in the juxtaposition of the emphasized statements. All valuations, at all instants in time, are made on the basis of the going-concern assumption. This would include the "last" valuation when the business has ceased operations. Thus, the earnings are *always* indeterminate. Of course this is not their intent. They mean that income is indeterminate until all assets are converted into cash. At that time one can take the difference in the cash magnitudes and determine the income finally and unequivocally.

This again points up the accountant's preoccupation with cash. He conceives income almost exclusively in terms of cash receipts and disbursements but, facing uncertainty, he cannot forecast the cash movements and, therefore, denies his ability to measure income. This is an uncomfortable position. He claims to measure income on the accrual basis but conceives of it on the cash basis and then denies that he can measure it. It is patently impossible to *measure* the future and we could sympathize with the accountants' dilemma if it were not for the fact that it is self-imposed.

We do not understand the going-concern assumption. First, we do not know why the assumption is made and second, we do not understand how it leads to the cost rule. The assumption seems to have sprung from Dicksee's[26] consideration of parliamentary companies (public utilities) which were *required* to continue operations. Thus, the intended use of the asset was the only source of receipts and price fluctuations were irrelevant except at replacement. However, Dicksee did not apply it to private enterprises; instead he suggested a net worth accretion measurement. Perhaps the reason why the specific has become general is that in the periods of rising prices, the net worth accretion rule was unconservative.

This is a point of fundamental disagreement among accountants. We believe that income ought to be *measured* and that measurement is the operation of dis-

---

[25] R. H. Robnett, T. Hill and J. Beckett, *Accounting: A Management Approach*, Chicago, Richard D. Irwin, Inc., 1951, pp. 509–10.
[26] Lawrence Robert Dicksee, *Auditing*, London, 1892.

covering the numerosity of units descriptive of an *existing condition,* not a prognostication of the future.

Objectivity

The assertion that cost is objective is probably used more often to defend the cost rule than any other single argument. There are several lines of reply, any one of which is sufficient grounds for rejecting this argument.

First, the construct criticism. What is or is not objective depends to some degree upon the perceiver's preformed theoretical construct.[27] One cannot get intersubjective agreement from those whose constructs vary. Thus, if the question is on ontological reality, we must first have some method of choosing from among the competing constructs. Perception of reality is an epistemological question of vast consequences. Accountants have been extremely cavalier in their treatment of the problem. Usually they do no more than make an unsupported assertion that cost is objective and that other values are not. We consider that assertion unwarranted and have presented some evidence elsewhere.[28]

Second, the defensive criticism. We agree that cash receipts and disbursements are convenient and univocal. However, that is not the question. Every basic text lists widely varying alternatives for the *initial* recording of cash outflows. The problem of determining which cash outlays should be treated as of a "capital" nature and which as expenses is one of the most difficult problems in accounting. The continuing valuation problems are subject to even wider deviations. Lifo and depreciation disputes are well known, but the myriad of lesser "attaching" alternatives are relatively unfamiliar. The author once amazed himself by setting up a game tree which revealed over a thousand valuation alternatives in a very simple enterprise. The degree of divergence is astounding. A glance at the literature discloses that the most discussed and hotly-debated issue is the lack of uniformity in valuation concepts, in theory as well as practice. For the accountant to reject present values because they are "subjective" is the pot calling the kettle black. Like Paton,[29] we "marvel" at accountants who consider cost to be objective. I suspect, but I cannot prove, that present values would vary less as between firms than historical costs, and thus they would be more objective in the inter-observer agreement sense.

Third, the conservative argument. This has been detailed above. The telling point is that accountants are always willing to record a subjective (other than cost) value if it is *lower* than the objective (cash cost) value. No asset on the balance sheet is valued at its cash cost with perhaps the single exception of land, and land is likely to be valued at cost only if the market price is above or equal to the cost. Almost all assets are valued at less than their cost because they have been subjected to amortization, allowances, lower of cost or market, or some other procedure which results in lowering the value. The result is that the assets are

---

[27] Chambers implicitly uses the construct criticism when he writes:

It is no defense to argue that all accountants or auditors would agree that the method of accounting and reporting used is a method acceptable to them. This would be equivalent to asking the flat-earthists whether the earth is flat.

R. J. Chambers, "Measurement and Objectivity in Accounting", *The Accounting Review,* April 1964, p. 270.

[28] Robert R. Sterling, "An Operational Analysis of Traditional Accounting", *Abacus,* December 1966.

[29] Paton and Paton, *Asset Accounting,* p. 54.

valued at something other than their "objective" cost; they are almost all valued subjectively.

The Study Group on Business Income, in understatement more characteristic of the British, has written:

> Those who have favored adherence to present practice have commonly talked in terms of "factual" and "objective" determinations and "uniformity". They perhaps have not given adequate recognition to the extent to which accounting is necessarily characterized by "postulates", "estimates", "subjective choice of method", and "variety in methods".[30]

This may be true. Perhaps accountants, although they work with the materials daily, have not given adequate recognition to their own subjectivity. We think that a more reasonable hypothesis might be that they resist change, which is simply another aspect of conservatism.

Fourth, the information criticism. The final point is the strongest; yet it is most often misunderstood. Many writers outside the field of accounting continually refer to the precision and objectivity of accounting data. They lament the lack of theoretical validity but excuse it on practical grounds. We believe that the cost figures are neither precise nor objective. However, even if they were, they are irrelevant.

There are a number of management decision models in the current literature which specify the relevant data. The marginal analysis also specifies the relevant data. There is a noticeable absence of historical cost data on any of those lists. A guess at a relevant figure is infinitely more valuable than a precise and objective irrelevancy. If one's decision model prescribes that length is relevant and radioactivity is not, then radioactivity is useless regardless of its precision or objectivity. A rough estimate of length is of some use, no matter how imprecise or unobjective.

IV SUMMARY AND CONCLUSIONS

Accounting is a discipline without any cohesive, unified theory of valuation. The extant valuation methods vary widely for a wide variety of reasons. The result is a confusing array of combinational possibilities of valuation.

We submitted the hypothesis that conservatism was the fundamental principle of valuation. Evidence in support of this hypothesis comes from the following:

1. The history of accounting development produces a natural propensity toward conservatism.

2. Conservatism prevails when there is a conflict between it and other principles.

3. Writers in the field ordinarily justify a specific valuation procedure by appealing to conservatism even though they profess to be anti-conservative.

4. Criticism of conservatism often takes the form of using conservatism as the basic criterion.

5. Arguments for the historical cost-realization convention are manifestly specious when removed from the context of conservatism.

Because of the last point, we submitted the secondary hypothesis that the cost

[30] Report of Study Group on Business Income, *Changing Concepts of Business Income*, New York, Macmillan and Co., 1951, p. 50.

rule is, in fact, nothing more than a manifestation of conservatism. We examined several representative arguments for the cost rule and found them to be neither valid nor sound. We think that this supports both the primary and secondary hypotheses.

Criticism of conservatism as a principle tends to take on a moral tone. Conservative accountants consider it a virtue; anti-conservatives consider it unethical. We would like to avoid moral controversies. Perhaps Hill and Gordon hit on the explanation when they described it as an "inborn tendency". We were not born with the tendency and, therefore, find ourselves in sharp disagreement with the principle.

In terms of measurement-information criteria, it is clear that conservative measurements are not veritable. The final result of a deliberate understatement is deception, no matter how laudable the objective may be. It is clear that the *intent* is to deceive. It is also clear that the desired ends of the conservative are commendable, but we disagree with the means they choose to achieve that end. Since verity is a sine qua non of information, we must conclude that conservatism yields, not only zero information, but also, misinformation.

Historical costs, when they are used, are conservative and we think they are justified if and only if conservatism is justified.[31] Thus, we must also conclude that historical costs yield misinformation. Perhaps the most convincing evidence of this comes not from the above considerations but instead from the real world. In the last Presidential election the candidates revealed their wealth to the electorate. *Life* magazine reported President Johnson's wealth at about $14 million. Previously the figure of $3.5 million had been reported. A reader noticed the discrepancy and inquired about it. The editor replied:

> The accounting firm retained by the President said, in explaining how they arrived at their low $3.5 million estimate: "The investments ... are carried at cost, less allowance for depreciation...." *Life* considers it more realistic to give the amounts these properties would bring in a sale today rather than what they originally cost.[32]

We agree that the present exit values were more realistic and further that this is what people generally mean when they speak of wealth. To report historical costs was misleading because the electorate did not want or expect that kind of valuation. In addition, it misled the electorate in another direction because the wealthier (based on present values) candidate had a smaller original cost. This particular incident may or may not have been a factor in the election. What is pertinent here is that the journalist, a confessed novice in matters of valuation, was forced to supply the desired, realistic information because the expert would not or (if we are to believe his protestations) could not.

---

[31] Historical costs are also convenient; it is much easier to check off an invoice than to find a present price. But, since values are the product of a valuation coefficient and a quantity, the invoice price procedure merely shifts the problem to one of determining the quantity of future benefits. Since these benefits lie in the future their magnitude is in principle unmeasurable and hence the convenience of historical cost is an illusion. Of course, we can avoid the problem altogether by accepting management's estimate of the quantity. Under those circumstances historical costs are very convenient: the only thing the accountant has to do is divide and multiply.

[32] *Life*, 18 September 1964, p. 32.

JOHN E. KANE

JOHN E. KANE (1914–   ), B.S. 36, M.S. 39 Arkansas; Ph.D. 50 American University; CPA. Currently professor of economics and finance University of Arkansas. Major publication: *Retail Sales in Arkansas* (1950). Contributor to *The Journal of Accountancy* and other journals.

Served on the faculties of the University of Arkansas, 1939–40, and Southwestern at Memphis, and was an economist with the Department of Commerce, 1942–43. Has held various positions on the faculty of the University of Arkansas, 1946–56 and 1958 to the present, including that of vice-president for business and finance, 1967–68. From 1956 to 1958, was executive vice-president of the McIlroy Bank. Has served as a consultant to numerous corporations, mainly in the public utility field.

Principal research interests: the long-run relationship among money, prices, and interest rates—deductive considerations and empirical evidence; and problems of regulated companies arising from growth and inflation—economic, financial, and accounting aspects.

STRUCTURAL CHANGES AND GENERAL CHANGES IN THE PRICE LEVEL IN RELATION TO FINANCIAL REPORTING

JOHN E. KANE

SECTION I: INTRODUCTION

Within the past several years there has been no lack of discussion of the problem in financial reporting arising from price changes. Articles dealing with various aspects of the problem are too numerous to list. Yet, although many of these discussions have been highly meritorious, it appears now that no important change in financial reporting will develop therefrom, inasmuch as no one suggestion has found favor among a sufficient number of accountants to assure its adoption as standard, or even as acceptable practice.[1] Indeed, by the spring of

SOURCE: From *The Accounting Review*, Vol. XXVI, No. 4 (October, 1951), pp. 496-502. Reprinted by permission of the American Accounting Association.

[1] A possible exception is the use of LIFO for inventory valuation purposes. However, LIFO had received some degree of acceptance prior to World War II.

1950, after two years of relatively stable prices, interest in the problem appeared to be on the decline, and if a condition of fairly stable prices had continued for another year or two, it is quite possible that the problem would have ceased to have much current interest. But with additional fuel now being added to the fires of inflation, it is to be hoped that accountants and other experts in the field of business administration will continue to explore possibilities for improving financial reporting in times of rapidly changing prices. This paper involves some probing of basic theoretical considerations.

Someone has said that a problem which is clearly defined is already half solved. Herein, perhaps, lies a clue to our inability to find acceptable solutions to the problem under discussion. There is reason to believe that the difficulties which we have encountered are due in part to a failure to clearly define the problem. Specifically, there has usually been a failure to distinguish between a change in the structure of prices and a change in the general price level. A change in the structure of prices involves a change in the prices of certain goods and services relative to the prices of other goods and services, with, therefore, a change in the real economic value of both sets of goods and services. A change in the general price level involves only a proportional change in the prices of all goods and services. If there is a change only in the general price level, this does not in itself imply a change in the value of any good or service, but does imply a change in the value of money and of obligations expressed in terms of a certain amount of money.

It is certainly not true that this distinction has been entirely overlooked in recent discussion.[2] At the same time, a greater part of published discussion of the matter appears to have been predicated on the assumption that there is but a single theoretical problem involved in price changes, whereas in reality there are two distinct problems which are essentially quite different, and which may, therefore, require different solutions.

SECTION II: CHANGES IN THE STRUCTURE OF PRICES

If we are dealing with only two commodities, A and B, and if the price of A increases by ten per cent at the same time that the price of B decreases by ten per cent, we have a change in the structure of prices, but (assuming commodities A and B to be of about equal importance) there has been approximately no change in the general level of prices.[3] This is equivalent to saying that there has been no change in the value, i.e., the general purchasing power, of money. What can be said in regard to appropriate accounting procedures in such a situation?

Accounting Considered to Be the Art of Matching Actual Cost Incurred against Revenue

If accounting is to be considered rigidly as the art of matching costs incurred against revenues earned, it is clear that price changes of this sort should not be

[2] For examples, see the following: (1) Samuel J. Broad, "The Impact of Rising Prices upon Accounting Procedure," *The Journal of Accountancy*, July, 1948; (2) Joel Dean, "Measurement of Profits for Executive Decisions," *The Accounting Review*, April, 1951.

[3] Statistical matters such as the upward bias of composite index numbers are outside the scope of this paper.

allowed to affect the accountant's financial statements, except that they may very well be the basis of footnotes or parenthetical items. In other words, under this basic concept of the nature of accounting, changes in the structure of prices should not be allowed to influence the amounts carried in the financial statements, except as just noted above.[4] Incidentally, it follows from this that if changes in prices are purely structural changes (i.e., if no change in the general purchasing power of the dollar is involved) such a device as the LIFO method of inventory costing can be justified only if LIFO more nearly represents the actual flow of goods (or materials) than FIFO. It must be supposed that from this standpoint the FIFO assumption usually is more realistic than the LIFO assumption, and therefore is to be preferred. In any case, however, the average cost assumption can be defended on the grounds that at any moment it is frivolous to "value" different identical items at different amounts, regardless of differences in actual purchase prices.

The concept with which we are dealing in Section II requires, of course, that the original dollar cost of any particular asset must be equal to the total dollar amounts charged as expense or loss on successive operating statements plus the amount at which the asset is carried on the current balance sheet (or plus the amount received thru disposition, in the case of assets no longer held). For assets which have not been disposed of, this can be expressed symbolically as follows:

$$0 = [E_1 + E_2 + \cdots + E_n] + B \qquad (1)$$

where 0 represents the original dollar cost, E_1 represents the dollar amount of expense or loss charged during the first period, E_2 represents the dollar amount of expense or loss charged during the second period, etc., and B represents the net dollar amount at which the asset is carried in the current balance sheet.

For assets which have been disposed of, the symbolic expression is as follows:

$$0 = (E_1 + E_2 + \cdots + E_x) + D \qquad (2)$$

where D represents the net dollar amount of cash or other assets received in connection with the disposition of the asset.

Accounting Considered to Be the Art of Valuation

On the other hand, if one considers accounting to be the art of valuation, equations (1) and (2) above are not necessarily valid. If there have been changes in the structure of prices, which have been recognized in the accounts, the original dollar cost of any particular asset will not necessarily equal the total dollar amounts charged as expense or loss on successive operating statements plus the dollar amount at which the asset is carried in the current balance sheet (or plus the net dollar amount received thru disposition of the asset). In the place of equations (1) and (2), we have the following:

$$0 = [(E_1' + E_2' + \cdots + E_n') - R] + B' \qquad (3)$$

---

[4] The practice of showing inventory at "cost or market whichever is lower" is, of course, not compatible with a rigid concept that accounting is only the art of matching cost against revenue.

where R represents an upward "revaluation" of the asset; and

$$0 = [(E_1' + E_2' + \cdots + E_x') - R] + D \qquad (4)$$

B' in equation (3) and some of the E's in equations (3) and (4) will presumably be different dollar amounts from B in equation (1), and some of the corresponding E's in equations (1) and (2).

As in the case of equations (1) and (2), the symbols within the brackets represent the net charge (or credit) against the net worth accounts (including revaluation surplus or reserve) resulting directly from the ownership and use of the asset.

Now in the case of equations (1) and (3), since B may be different from B', the amounts within the bracket in the two equations may be different, which is to say that during the useful life of the asset the net effect on total surplus may be different if one is accounting for values, as compared with the net effect when one is accounting for costs.

However, in the case of equations (2) and (4), inasmuch as D is presumably equal to D and 0 is equal to 0, it follows that the amounts in the brackets must be equal; i.e., $E_1 + E_2 + \cdots + E_x$ is equal to $(E_1' + E_2' + \cdots + E_x') - R$. It is this which has led Gilman,[5] among others, to point out that in the long run [6] revaluation of assets is meaningless. This proposition is correct, of course, as long as one attaches to the term "revaluation" the meaning which is implied in this Section II.[7] Thus, there is a basic theoretical conflict between the cost concept of accounting and the value concept only as regards the circumstances under which it is proper to recognize income or gain.[8]

In view of the attention which has been given to the LIFO concept during the past five years, it may be appropriate to digress again, and to point out that under a value concept of accounting the LIFO procedure can not be regarded as having much merit.[9] As is well recognized, the LIFO procedure does not result in the use of current values on the balance sheet, but on the contrary will often result in figures which are less indicative of current values than will the FIFO or average cost procedure. Furthermore, if under a value basis of accounting a distinction is being made between realized and unrealized profit, the use of LIFO will distort this division of profit. Thus, when only changes in the structure of prices are involved, under a value basis of accounting as well as under a cost basis, LIFO can be considered as theoretically superior to FIFO, only if LIFO more closely approximates the physical flow of goods (or materials).

[5] Stephen Gilman, *Accounting Concepts of Profit*, New York, The Ronald Press Company, 1939, p. 546.

[6] The term "long run" as applied to any particular asset is defined as being that period long enough to include the complete charge-off or sale of an asset.

[7] However, as will be pointed out in Section III, it does not follow that a restatement of the dollar amount at which assets are carried on the financial statements is, in the same way, meaningless in the long run. See footnote 14.

[8] This statement is not intended to minimize the importance of the practical differences arising from an attempted application of the two concepts.

[9] Except that under a value concept of accounting LIFO might be used, together with revaluation of the balance sheet inventory amount, to some rough advantage if one is attempting to distinguish between "operating" and "speculative" profit or loss. However, this distinction is not usually made.

SECTION III: CHANGES IN THE GENERAL PRICE LEVEL

An entirely different problem is posed if, instead of a change in the relative prices of various goods and services, there is occurring only a change in the general purchasing power of money. Such would be the situation, for example, if all prices were increasing by exactly ten per cent a year. In a *real* sense, there would be no discrepancy between original cost and market value. Various goods and services would always "exchange against each other" at the same rates. Therefore in a real sense, the question as to whether accounting should be the art of "accounting for costs," or the art of "accounting for values" would cease to be of significance and would become a matter of terminological preference, inasmuch as in real terms (depreciated) cost and value would always be equal. This is to say also that the conflict concerning the proper occasion for the recognition of revenue would cease to be of significance.

Under these assumptions, then, the question is not whether we should account for costs or account for values, but whether we should account for nominal, dollar cost (value) or for real, economic cost (value).[10] In order to distinguish between these two concepts, the former might be referred to as the original dollar cost concept, while the latter might be referred to as the original real cost concept. What is being called here the original dollar cost concept is equivalent, of course, to what has often been referred to simply as the original cost, or historical cost concept.

It is outside the scope of this paper to illustrate a process of conversion of original dollar cost figures to an original real cost basis.[11] However, it should be emphasized that if the original real cost concept is adopted, *all* items on the profit and loss statement, the statement of surplus, and the balance sheet (net worth items included) should be converted.[12] In the case of a business entity preparing original real cost statements for the first time one of the following general rules of conversion would usually be applicable to balance sheet items:

1. In the case of non-cash items other than claims and debts expressed in terms of a certain number of dollars, in order to adjust to an original real cost basis, the amount that would appear on an original dollar cost balance sheet

---

[10] In other words, the question is whether we should recognize changes in the common unit of measure of both cost and value.

[11] The most complete description of such a process is found in H. W. Sweeney, *Stabilized Accounting*, New York: Harper and Brothers, 1936. Other less detailed suggestions have appeared from time to time. The author of this paper has devised and experimented with a procedure which differs from Sweeney's procedure in some theoretical and practical aspects. [Also see "Reporting the Effects of Price-Level Changes," *Accounting Research Study No. 6*, (1963) and the subsequent APB *Statement No. 3*, "Financial Statements Restated for General Price-Level Changes" (June 1969). Eds.]

[12] If it were decided that financial statements should be based upon the original real cost concept, it would nevertheless probably be found desirable to maintain the financial records of a business entity on an original dollar cost basis. In fact, it might be found most convenient to prepare financial statements first on an original dollar cost basis, after which the amounts would be converted to an original real cost basis. It might be desirable to exhibit original dollar cost statements along with original real cost statements.

should be increased (decreased) proportionately to the increase (decrease) in the price level between the date of acquisition (or other type of transaction) and the balance sheet date.

2. In the case of cash and of claims and debts expressed in terms of a certain number of dollars, a balance sheet prepared on the original real cost basis will show an amount identical with the amount that would appear on an original dollar cost balance sheet. However, a loss (gain) on the item should be recognized on the Statement of Profit and Loss, such loss (gain) being equal to the amount of the item multiplied by the percentage change in the price level between the date of acquisition of the claim and the date of the statement. The loss (gain) should be divided appropriately between loss (gain) during the current period, and adjustment to beginning surplus.[13]

For example, if a claim of sixty dollars is received when the price level is one hundred per cent of some base level, and if the price level later rises to one hundred ten, the economic loss arising from holding that claim during the intervening period is sixty dollars multiplied by ten per cent, or six dollars. This can be proved by considering that one must have sixty-six dollars when the price level stands at one hundred ten in order to have general purchasing power equivalent to sixty dollars when the price level stands at one hundred.

In the case of nominal accounts, if a general price increase (decrease) occurs between the time of incurring a certain portion of expense, or the time of earning a certain portion of revenue, and the time of preparing the financial statements, the portion of expense or revenue so involved should be increased (decreased) proportionately to the increase (decrease) in the price level occurring during the same interval of time. The same rule applies to the dividends paid account.[14]

SECTION IV: THE ACTUAL PROBLEM

In an actual situation involving considerable changes in prices, it is likely that there will be changes both in relative prices and in the general level of prices. To say the least, one can confidently expect that important changes in the general purchasing power of the dollar will be accompanied by changes also in the real value (relative prices) of many goods and services. If, as a result of these price changes, one wishes to adjust financial statements, one ought first to consider whether he wishes to adjust for the effect of changes in the real value of certain goods and services, or whether he wishes to adjust for changes in the general purchasing power of the dollar, or both.

---

[13] These rules will result in a balance sheet expressed in terms of the price level at the balance sheet date.

[14] It is interesting to note that the change, as described above, in the *dollar* amount at which assets are carried is no longer "meaningless in the long run" in quite the same sense as in Section II. Thus, adapting the equations shown in Section II, if the general price level changes predominately in one direction,

$$0 \neq E_1'' + E_2'' + \cdots + E_n'' - R'' + B'' \qquad (5)$$

$$0 \neq (E_1'' + E_2'' + \cdots + E_x'') - R'' + B'' \qquad (6)$$

where E_1'', E_2'', etc. continue to represent the *dollar* amount of expense or loss charged on successive operating statements.

If it should be decided to adjust only for changes in the real values of assets, it must first be determined to what extent the real values of assets have changed. If the general price level has changed at the same time that the real value of a particular asset has changed, the entire difference between depreciated original dollar cost and current dollar value would not represent change in real value. For example, if an asset which has a depreciated original dollar cost of one hundred dollars, is now found to have a depreciated current dollar value of two hundred dollars, and if the general price level has increased by fifty per cent since acquisition date, fifty dollars of the increase in the *dollar* value of the asset reflects an increase in the *real* value of the asset, while the remaining fifty dollars of the increase reflects only the decline in the value of the dollar. Simply to state the conditions of this assumed case makes it rather obvious that neither accountants nor business executives are likely to be enthusiastic about financial statements which are adjusted *only* for changes in the real value of particular assets, if important changes in the general price level have occurred concurrently with changes in the real value of the particular assets. However, this procedure should be recognized as a theoretical possibility.

More important, however, is the possibility of adjusting for changes in the general purchasing power of the dollar without adjusting for changes in the real value of any particular asset. As implied in Section III, this can be accomplished by the use of a general price index. It is probably true that what is usually more desired by business executives in times of rapidly rising prices are financial statements which are adjusted for changes in the general purchasing power of the dollar, rather than statements which are adjusted for changes in the real value of particular assets. And from the standpoint of accountants, statements which are adjusted *only* for changes in the general purchasing power of the dollar would not in a real sense constitute a departure from a historical cost basis of accounting, and would, therefore, not involve the lack of objectivity which follows from the adoption of a value basis of accounting. Also the commonly employed test of income realization is compatible with the concept of adjusting only for changes in the general purchasing power of the dollar.

In addition to adjusting for *either* changes in the real value of particular assets *or* changes in the general purchasing power of the dollar, it is theoretically quite possible to adjust for *both* types of changes. The use of current dollar market values or dollar replacement cost has the effect of accomplishing this for the particular assets concerned, without, however, recognizing the loss or gain on cash, receivables, and payables. But ignoring for the moment this deficiency, to be fully meaningful, an upward revaluation of a particular fixed asset to the dollar replacement cost figure should be recorded in such a way as to distinguish between that part of the upward revision which reflects an increase in the real value of the asset, and that part of the upward revision which reflects a decrease in the general purchasing power of the dollar. Sight should not be lost of the facts that an increase in the real value of an asset and a decrease in the general purchasing power of money are entirely different economic developments, that they may arise from entirely different and diverse causes, and that they may have different and diverse effects upon a business entity. To fail to distinguish between these two developments may add obscurity rather than clarity. Inasmuch as the replacement cost basis of asset valuation, as it is usually described, does not involve this distinction, it is theoretically defective if changes in both the real value of the asset, and the general purchasing power of money have occurred.

It is not possible in this paper to compare in any detail either the techniques which might be involved, or the results which might be obtained from the various bases of adjustment mentioned in this section. However, the following table shows different possible results in the case of a hypothetical corporation whose only asset is a non-depreciable fixed asset. The assumption is made that the asset originally cost one hundred dollars, and that its current market value (or replacement cost) is two hundred dollars. It is also assumed that the selected index of general prices has risen from one hundred to one hundred fifty between the acquisition date and the current date. The capital stock is considered as having been sold for one hundred dollars on the same day that the asset was purchased. No other transactions have occurred.

Table I

THE HYPOTHETICAL CORPORATION
ALTERNATIVE BALANCE SHEETS *
CURRENT DATE

	(Col. 1)	(Col. 2)	(Col. 3)	(Col. 4)	(Col. 5)
Assets:					
Fixed Assets	$100	$150	$150	$200	$200
Liabilities and Net Worth:					
Revaluation Surplus		$ 50		$ 50	$100
Capital Stock:					
Original Dollar Amount ..	$100	$100	$100	$100	$100
Price Level Fluctuation Adjustment			$50	$50	
Total Capital Stock..				$150	
Total	$100	$150	$150	$200	$200

* Column 1 figures are based upon the original dollar cost concept;

Column 2 figures are adjusted for changes in the real value of physical assets;

Column 3 figures are adjusted for changes in the general purchasing power of the dollar;

Column 4 figures are adjusted both for changes in the real value of physical assets, and for changes in the general purchasing power of the dollar;

Column 5 figures are based on the dollar replacement cost concept as usually described.

Column 1 shows a balance sheet prepared on the original dollar cost basis. Column 2 shows a possible result of adjusting only for changes in the real value of the asset; as explained above, this is hardly to be recommended. Column 3 shows the result of the application of the original real cost concept; or, in other words, shows the result of adjusting for changes in the general purchasing power of the dollar, but not for changes in the real value of the asset. Column 4 shows the result of adjusting both for changes in the real value of the asset and for changes in the purchasing power of the dollar, with a proper distinction being drawn between the two. Column 5 shows a possible result of the use of dollar replacement cost as that procedure is usually described, without a distinction between changes in the real value of the asset and changes in the general purchasing power of the dollar.

Perhaps the question which must be faced is the one raised in the title of a recent article by William Blackie: "What Is Acounting Accounting for—Now?"[15]

[15] William Blackie, "What Is Accounting Accounting for—Now?" *N.A.C.A. Bulletin*, July 1, 1948.

EDWARD STAMP

EDWARD STAMP (1928-   ), B.S. (hons.) 49, M.A. 52 Cambridge; C.A. (Ontario). Currently professor of accounting theory, University of Lancaster, England. Major publications: *Elements of Consolidation Accounting* (1965); *Accounting Principles and the City Code: The Case for Reform* (with Marley, 1970). Contributor to *The Accountant's Magazine, Accountancy* and other journals.

Was in the practice of chartered accountancy with the Canadian firm of Clarkson, Gordon & Co., 1950–62, becoming a partner in 1961. Joined the accounting faculty of the Victoria University of Wellington (New Zealand) in 1962, becoming professor of accountancy in 1965. Was appointed to the chair in accounting and business method in the University of Edinburgh in 1967, and in 1971 assumed the chair in the University of Lancaster.

Principal research interests: theory and practice of income and value determination; price-level accounting; and comparative accounting standards among the United States, the United Kingdom, and other European Common Market countries.

INCOME AND VALUE DETERMINATION AND CHANGING PRICE-LEVELS: AN ESSAY TOWARDS A THEORY*

EDWARD STAMP

It is of the greatest importance that this lesson should be learnt and acted on by us all: it is that for too long much of our apparent prosperity has been based on illusions. We cannot expect to build a sure prosperity until we rid ourselves of these illusions. . . . All of us must rid ourselves of the illusion that we can buy our way out of the problems of today by mortgaging the future. It seems the easy way—but we know now it is the fatal way.

SOURCE: From *The Accountant's Magazine*, Vol. LXXV, No. 780 (June, 1971), pp. 277–292. Reprinted by permission of the Institute of Chartered Accountants of Scotland and the author.

* The author is grateful to Sir Alexander McDonald, Messrs P. N. McMonnies, W. E. Parker, C.B.E. and Prof. R. H. Parker for reading the text of this paper in draft, and for making a number of valuable suggestions.

Prime Minister Edward Heath, speaking to Young Conservatives about the Rolls-Royce fiasco, February 7, 1971. (Report in *The Times,* February 8, 1971.)

The failure to take the effect of inflation into the books is probably the weakest point of current accounting procedure.... it should not take a wave of bankruptcies to convince the accountancy profession that reform is overdue and would, by enabling market forces to work more accurately, greatly improve the efficiency of British industry. There is a tendency to dismiss this as an academic issue. It is a great deal more important than that.

Editorial entitled "Accounting for Inflation" in *The Financial Times,* February 8, 1971.

* * *

THE IMPORTANCE OF PRICE CHANGES TO THE ACCOUNTANT

An old friend and former partner of mine from Montreal visited me last November, and we spent some time discussing the challenges facing the profession in the future. I said that I thought the three most important problems facing the profession in Britain (and in Canada too) were education, research into accounting principles, and accounting for specific and general price changes. He agreed with me about the first two items, but he dismissed the third as a "dead end". He clearly thought that in the words of *The Financial Times,* it was "an academic issue". I might have been more disturbed by his scepticism had I not reflected that if I were still in practice like him I might very well feel exactly the same way. It will be a healthy sign of maturity in our profession when practitioners become accustomed to taking "academic issues" as seriously as do our colleagues in some of our sister professions.

The volume of the literature on accounting for specific and general price changes is probably more extensive than that on any other subject in the whole area of accounting. This in itself is unlikely to be conclusive evidence to the practical man of affairs of the importance of the subject. Before the practitioner or the businessman will take action he wants to be satisfied as to the answer to at least three questions:—

Is action necessary?
Is the proposed solution logical and reasonable?
Is the proposed solution feasible?

... [T]he bulk of this paper will deal with the second of these three questions, although I shall refer at the end to the third. But first of all we must look at an important aspect of the question of the necessity of taking any action at all. In an address on December 1, 1970 to the Ayrshire Association of Chartered Accountants of Scotland, Mr. G. D. H. Dewar, then President of the Scottish Institute, is reported to have made the following comments when dealing with the subject of inflation[1]:—

Critics, including some members of our own profession, sometimes say that the financial statements now submitted to shareholders are misleading because they do not show the earnings and financial position in terms of pounds ster-

---

[1] See *The Accountant's Magazine,* January 1971, page 4.

ling of the same purchasing power. If inflation had continued at a relatively low rate, there might be no great harm in this, but perhaps the situation is changing this year. Our Institute issued a statement on this subject 16 years ago which is still valid. Any company can, if it wants to, issue supplementary accounts based on pounds sterling of the same purchasing power using, of course, various indices which involve a number of estimates and assumptions. But the question is, do the public really want these price level accounts, because it would cost a lot of money and it might even add to confusion at this stage? May I quote Sir John Hicks, Emeritus Professor of Political Economy at Oxford, who said 'the accounting system, the tax system, and even the general legal system assume a stable value of money. These could only be altered at the cost of much wasted time.' I suppose the answer to this question depends on whether the Government and their advisers can arrest the rate of inflation and hold it at about 3½%. If they cannot, it may become necessary to produce price level adjusted accounts, but I for one hope that this will not be necessary, because the implications of a rate of inflation continuing at that of the current year are extremely serious for this country.

I was surprised to learn from this that Mr Dewar, who is a member of the Accounting Standards Steering Committee, apparently feels that an inflation rate of 3½% is not sufficiently high to warrant adjustments of the accounts. Let us look at this matter a little more closely.

In 1956 the American Accounting Association published a useful booklet entitled *Price-level Changes and Financial Statements: Basic Concepts and Methods.*[2] This booklet was written by Professor Mason, of the University of California at Berkeley, in order to demonstrate the technique of applying a general price-level index to accounting data so that the accounts can be stated in terms of a uniform unit of measurement. What is of interest about this study, in the present context, is the fact that the demonstration dealt with the accounts of an entity which had been in existence for twenty years (from 1932 to 1952), during which time the price index had risen from 58.4 to 114.1 (1947–49 = 100). According to my calculations this represents an average compound rate of inflation of "only" 3.4%, and yet as Professor Mason states "if the results of operations (for the year 1952) are expressed in terms of the dollar of constant value the net income for the year is about 70% of the reported amount, the income taxes have taken about 30% instead of 23% of the net earnings, and the dividends have been in excess of the net income for the year instead of only 70%."[3] In addition, retained earnings, which were reported at $29,300.00 surplus as at December 31, 1952 in the unadjusted accounts (issued capital stock amounted to $200,000.00), were completely wiped out and converted into a deficit of $62,300.00 after the price level adjustments had been made.

In 1968 the Research Foundation of the English Institute produced a similar booklet entitled *Accounting for Stewardship in a Period of Inflation.*[4] In the example given in the English Institute booklet the period covered is only ten years,

---

[2] Obtainable from American Accounting Association, 653 South Orange Avenue, Sarasota, Florida 33577, U.S.A.

[3] *Ibid.*, pages 18–19.

[4] Obtainable from The Institute of Chartered Accountants in England and Wales, Chartered Accountants' Hall, Moorgate Place, London, EC2R 6EQ.

during which the price index is assumed to rise from 100 to 140. This is equivalent to an average compound annual rate of inflation of "only" 3.4%. Once again, even though in this case the assets are not as old on average as in Professor Mason's example, the differences between the unadjusted and the adjusted figures are striking. Indeed both booklets were clearly intended not merely to demonstrate the techniques of adjustment but also to establish, to the satisfaction of practical men, that the adjustments required are material even with a rate of inflation of 3.4%. (It is pure coincidence that both booklets, published twelve years apart, happen to be based upon a 3.4% average rate. But it is surely no coincidence that neither felt it necessary to choose a rate any higher than this in order to demonstrate the necessity of making adjustments.)

The issue can be stated another way. At a compound annual rate of inflation of 3½% the general price level will double in twenty years. If inventory prices move up at the same rate this means that even if there is no growth over the twenty-year period in the physical level of inventories the FIFO valuation of inventories at the end of the twenty-year period will be double what it was at the beginning. Putting this another way it means that 50% of the closing inventory valuation represents entirely fictitious earnings upon which taxes have been paid and which have been credited (net of tax) to distributable reserves.

The effect on depreciation is more obvious and I will not spell it out since I think it is generally understood. But it is important to emphasize that fictitious inventory "profits" can be just as serious a problem as the understatement of depreciation provisions.[5]

Moreover, since a doubling in the general price level means a 50% reduction in the general purchasing power of net monetary assets (cash plus receivables less payables) a company with a "good" quick ratio (monetary assets divided by monetary liabilities) is likely to have suffered further substantial unrecorded purchasing power losses as a result of the inflation. Indeed, the only way the company can hedge itself against such purchasing power losses is by borrowing, and the company may in fact be forced into borrowing in order to deal with the liquidity shortage generated by the problems of replacing assets at higher price levels than those at which they were purchased. I need hardly say that such voluntary or involuntary hedging, with the resultant increase in the gearing ratio, can be bought only at a cost, and in some cases the cost is ultimately a bankruptcy.

I hope it is clear that I am not arguing that the accountant is responsible for curing inflation. What I *am* suggesting is that he is responsible for measuring its effects, in order that businessmen, shareholders, and other interested parties can know precisely what it is that is happening. And I am suggesting that these effects begin to make a material, measurable (but to date, by accountants, unmeasured) difference at an inflation rate well below 3½%.

I believe the accounting profession should act with a sense of urgency in this matter. It would be a relatively simple matter to make objective and verifiable adjustments to published accounts to take account of changes in general purchasing power. Anyone who doubts this should read the English Institute booklet

[5] Speed of inventory turnover does not mitigate the effect as is sometimes thought. It is the size of the inventory carried (in monetary terms) and the rate of change in prices that are the determining factors.

Accounting for Stewardship in a Period of Inflation, referred to above. In my opinion it presents a lucid, elegant, and convincing case for presenting information of this kind in published accounts.

Having said that, I must now say that I believe that general purchasing power adjustments represent only one facet of the whole truth about the financial situation and performance of a company. They present a better approximation to the truth than conventional accounts, but it is still only a part of a total picture which I should now like to paint, albeit with a fairly broad brush, in the balance of this paper.

THE CONVENTIONAL WISDOM OF ACCOUNTING

We must begin by considering the nature of the conventional wisdom, that is to say the rules and procedures which accountants normally use as a basis in preparing financial accounts.

The conventional system is best described as the "Historical Cost—Realised Revenue" basis of determining income and value.[6]

This basis of accounting has evolved over a long period of time. Even before the days of Pacioli, and for a long period thereafter, the system of "venture accounting" was used by merchants, whose main interest was in determining the surplus remaining at the conclusion of each of their "ventures" (ship's voyages, etc.). However, the rise of the joint stock company, in Britain and in other countries, resulted in the creation of a growing number of separate legal entities within whose framework capitalists conducted a *series* of ventures continuing over an indefinite period of time. This led to a growing emphasis on the importance of the balance sheet and, as I have explained elsewhere,[7] to a conservative system of asset valuation which was designed to protect the creditors of family-owned enterprises. In the twentieth century the rise of technology has created an enormous demand for capital beyond the resources of virtually any large family company. The consequence has been the divorce of ownership from management, and the creation of sophisticated securities markets to tap the savings of the domestic (and in many cases the international) community of investors. The result of this is familiar to us all: the Balance Sheet has remained an important document, but the dominant statement today is the Statement of Profit and Loss.[8]

The accountant measures income by the process of "matching" costs against revenues. This matching process, though frequently described as a concept, is in fact merely a technique of measurement; the underlying concepts are more correctly identified in the term "Historical Cost—Realised Revenue" basis.

---

[6] It is assumed that the bookkeeping system operates on the accrual basis. In its broadest sense the accrual basis simply attempts to give recognition in the accounts to the existence of assets and liabilities other than cash. Thus it implies the use of books of original entry such as the Sales Journal and the Purchase Journal, as well as a General Journal. Essentially, if one abandons the accrual basis, one is left with a statement of cash flows.

[7] In *Accounting Principles and the City Code: The Case for Reform* (London; Butterworths; 1970).

[8] It may be noted that it was not until the 1929 amendment of the Companies Act that British companies were required to prepare profit and loss accounts for their shareholders. And it was not until 1948 that auditors were required to report on the profit and loss account. *Ibid.* page 78.

For the costs which are matched in the income statements are the historical values at which the transactions were originally recorded in the books of account. In the case of items where the benefit is received and utilised by the enterprise at virtually the same time that the cost is incurred (*e.g.* wages, and many other current expenses) "Historical Cost" is very close to "Current Cost". But wherever there is a time lag between acquisition and utilisation, "Historical Cost" may well differ from "Current Cost" at the point of utilisation. In the case of these latter items the unexpired costs are stored in asset accounts and will appear as such on a balance sheet. All of the various rules which have been developed by the accountant for the valuation of inventories, depreciation of fixed assets, amortisation of prepaid expenses and deferred charges, etc. are measurement rules for reallocating unexpired asset costs into expense accounts as the assets' services are utilised and expiration occurs. Thus the matching process, so far as it relates to the cost side of the equation, involves the direct charging of current items (such as wages) to expense accounts, and the allocation of expired asset costs to expense accounts. It is the second element of this process which gives rise to many of the difficulties when there is a price change between acquisition and utilisation.

On the revenue side of the equation, the accountant has also developed a concept, the Realisation principle, to assist him in the matching process.[9] Only realised revenues are brought into the income statement to be matched against costs. "Realisation" requires the existence of a market transaction in which the entity has supplied the goods and services contracted for, and the vendee has supplied the required consideration in the form of measurable liquid assets. It is generally accepted by most accountants that cash, marketable securities, and accounts receivable constitute liquid assets for purposes of the realisation concept.

The realisation concept has two obvious and important implications.

In the first place, the requirement that there must be a market transaction precludes recognition of upward value changes even when they are readily measurable. Thus, holdings of marketable securities are not valued on a balance sheet at their quoted stock exchange value on the date of the balance sheet, even when the holding represents only a relatively small investment in the shares of a very large public company, because—in the absence of a market transaction, *i.e.* a sale *by the entity*—realisation has not taken place. The fact that a price has been established on the stock exchange through market transactions is immaterial, since the accounting entity is not a party to any of these transactions.[10]

This can lead to the absurd situation described by MacNeal.[11] Two investors, R and U, each begin the year with £1,000 in cash. R invests his cash in shares

---

[9] As I have written elsewhere on a number of occasions there is a confusing overlap in the literature among terms such as "concept", "principle", "convention", etc. It is beyond the scope of the present Paper to clear up such semantic confusion. As far as I can I shall try to use the words in their conventional associations—*e.g.* Realisation *principle*. Note, however, that I prefer to regard "matching" as a technique or process, and not (as it is conventionally regarded) as a "concept".

[10] Conservatism ("concept", "convention", or "principle"?!) usually requires that a fall in market value below historical cost *should* be recognised by a write down, even although it is unrealised (at least in the case of securities carried as current assets).

[11] Kenneth MacNeal, C.P.A.: "What's Wrong with Accounting?" *The Nation* (N.Y.), October 7–14, 1939. Reprinted in Baxter and Davidson (eds.): *Studies in Accounting Theory* (London; Sweet & Maxwell; 1962), pages 56–69.

of A, and U invests his in shares of B. They each hold their investments until the end of the year, by which time their investments each double in value. U holds on to his investment, but R sells out his shares of A and immediately re-invests, just before the end of the year, in shares of B. If we ignore commission expenses, we have a situation where each began the year with £1,000 in cash, and each ends the year with £2,000 worth of shares of B. Yet the accountant, using the realisation principle, will show R as having realised a profit of £1,000 during the year and ending the year with assets worth £2,000, whilst U will show no profit and will end the year with assets valued at £1,000. This seems a strange result, especially when it is observed that the realised profit is just as vulnerable as the unrealised profit to a future fall in the value of the shares of B.

This illustration underlines the fact that the realisation principle really implies a venture approach to income measurement by a corporation; the acquisition of every asset is regarded as a separate venture, and no profit can be shown until the cash-cash cycle has been completed for that asset, *i.e.* until realisation has taken place.[12]

This brings us to the second implication of the realisation principle, namely that all assets are valued at historical cost—until after realisation has taken place. Thus accounts receivable, being post-realisation assets, are valued at net realisable value, whereas inventories, fixed assets, etc. are valued at historical cost.

There are three exceptions to this general rule. The matching rules relating to fixed assets result in fixed assets being valued at historical cost less accumulated provisions for depreciation; and conservatism[13] dictates that unrealised losses on inventories are recognised when market falls below cost. Such unrealised losses are not normally recognised in the case of fixed assets unless there is a "permanent loss of value".

The third exception arises when production rather than sales constitutes the main constraint operating on the enterprise. In such cases the realisation principle is often relaxed, and thus it is customary for gold mines to value their inventories at net realisable value rather than at historical cost.

Apart from these exceptions, we can see that the historical cost principle and the realisation principle are in a sense opposite sides of the same coin.[14]

There is another important aspect of this situation which should not be overlooked. The rigorous disciplines of the double-entry accounting system demonstrate that there is a close, intimate, and articulated relationship between the income statement and the balance sheet. Valuation rules in the balance sheet have their implications for the income account, and the matching process in the income account determines the values and equities shown in the balance sheet. Thus a moment's reflection enables us to see that the historical cost/realised revenue system implies a concept of income which ensures the maintenance intact of the

---

[12] Since the realisation principle accepts rights to cash as well as cash itself, in testing whether realisation has occurred, the venture cycle can be shortened in many cases to cash-accounts receivable.

[13] See also footnote 10. Exposure Draft 2 of the Accounting Standards Steering Committee has relabelled this as the "prudence concept".

[14] This, however, is only true in the rather narrow sense in which the two "principles" are applied in practice. As we shall see later it is desirable that the historical cost constraint should be relaxed, but this does NOT imply concurrent relaxation of the realisation constraint in its entirety.

original money capital invested in the enterprise. It also assumes that there will be no change in general purchasing power, or in the specific prices of individual assets between acquisition and replacement. These two factors will assume greater significance later when we come to consider alternative bases of income determination.

SOME OBJECTIONS TO HISTORICAL COST

Let us now review briefly some of the advantages and disadvantages of the historical cost[15] basis.

As I have already indicated the historical cost system made a good deal of sense in earlier times when ownership and management generally coincided, and when the family owners of an enterprise were more or less irrevocably and permanently committed to the firm as a venture. The historical cost system had the additional advantage that, combined as it is with various other conservative rules, it generally protected the interests of the only main group of outsiders, the creditors.

In today's conditions, where owners typically move in and out of investments fairly rapidly, and where share ownership is widespread and almost entirely divorced from management, the historical cost basis fails to provide information which is entirely relevant to the needs of users.

An advantage claimed for the historical cost basis is that, although it sacrifices relevance, it achieves a much greater objectivity and verifiability than any alternative system. This is thought to be particularly important by auditors. However, as we shall see later, the substitution of alternative bases of income and value determination does not necessarily involve much loss of objectivity, and if such alternative bases are made additional to rather than in replacement of the historical cost method of reporting, it is hard to see how this objection can stand. Moreover, one has only to consider the various alternative methods which are available, even in the historical cost system, for measurement of profit on construction contracts, determination of depreciation, allocation of costs between joint products, allocation of overheads, provision for bad debts, amortisation of deferred charges and other intangible assets, etc. to realise that even the historical cost basis itself is not as objective as we often like to think. It may be necessary to continue to report historical cost figures, if only for legal and stewardship purposes, but we should not conclude that this is the only useful information that is available.

For it is clear to everyone that, when specific and general price levels are changing, historical cost statements tend to become out of date. In particular, when prices are rising the conventional historical cost system of accounting tends to produce conservative asset valuations in the balance sheet, along with unconservative income measurements in the statement of profit and loss. In a sense I am begging the question of what we mean by value, a question which will be dealt with in more detail later. But in passing we can, I think, accept that cost is only a special case of value, and the tendency to overstate income and understate value during inflationary periods has a doubly inflationary effect on return on in-

---

[15] This abbreviation is used for the sake of simplicity, subject to the comment in footnote 14.

vestment calculations, since the numerator is over-stated and the denominator is under-stated.

But the objections to historical cost as a sole method of presenting financial information can be advanced on more fundamental grounds than this.

The pound, or the dollar, or the franc, etc. is a unit of measurement in the same way as the inch or the centimetre, the pint or the litre, etc. So long as prices remain stable it is possible to add together a series of monetary measurements of cost or value, incurred or received at different points in time, and arrive at a total which has a sensible meaning. However, when price levels change we measure with a rubber ruler if we fail to adjust for the changes in the value of the unit when making our measurements. If price levels change, a pound or a dollar spent in 1950 does not measure the same "value" as a pound or a dollar spent in 1960. Adding together such "values" in a balance sheet, or in the process of matching in the income statement, is to produce a total as meaningless as the addition of values expressed in pounds to values expressed in dollars and/or in francs, etc. This principle is well understood in conversion of the figures in the accounts of overseas subsidiaries when they are consolidated with their parents. Yet it is overlooked in the case of domestic enterprises, since, although a 1960 £ is quite different from a 1950 £, the difference is masked because both bear the same title. Moreover, it is clearly not possible to compare balance sheets and income statements over a series of years simply by making index adjustments to the totals in the statements, since the statements for each year are themselves composed of a conglomerate of "apples and oranges" which cannot be index adjusted without a detailed analysis of each year's figures.

Nor is it simply on the grounds of such broad general principles that we must take objection to unadjusted historical cost figures when price levels change. As I have already indicated, the analysis and interpretation of profit trends, return on investments, etc. is rendered virtually meaningless. And, perhaps even more important to the businessman, in a period of rising prices he is taxed on income a substantial part of which may not represent an increase of purchasing power. In jurisdictions where capital gains are also subject to tax, all or a substantial part of the "gain" may be fictitious and not real.

In view of all this it may seem surprising that so little progress has been made in the direction of improving the quality of financial information either by adding or substituting more relevant figures to those produced by the historical cost concept.

The reasons, however, are not far to seek. Many accountants feel safer with historical costs because they believe they are more objective than any alternative. And they also feel reassured by the fact that in times of rising prices historical cost balance sheets are more conservative. (This is to ignore the fact that the income statements are *less* conservative!) [16]

There are other weighty reasons. The accounting profession feels, reasonably, that it cannot abandon historical cost if the abandonment would not be recognised in law. And it is a fact that tax law and practice, legal definitions of capital and amounts available for dividends, trust deeds, contracts, and many other statu-

---

[16] It is salutary to note that inflation produces deficiencies in conventional income reporting which are opposite in effect to those practices for which Lord Kylsant and others were prosecuted in the *Royal Mail* case!

tory and common law instruments are enacted or negotiated on the basis of historical cost, on the assumption that the value of the monetary unit is stable. I think, for these reasons alone, we must accept that any changes made by accountants must be additional to rather than in substitution of historical cost statements, at least for the foreseeable future. At the same time, it is obviously hopeless to expect the taxation authorities to recognise any other basis of income determination if accountants themselves stick so emphatically to historical cost. In a chicken and egg situation of this kind the accountant must be prepared to make the first move.

MODIFICATIONS OF HISTORICAL COST

In fact, accountants have made several attempts to cure some of the more obvious deficiencies of historical cost accounting. One expedient which has gained acceptance in the United States (as a result of its recognition by the American tax authorities on the basis that if it is applied for tax purposes it must be used in the accounts) is the LIFO basis of determination of inventory costs. By matching the most recently incurred inventory costs against revenues in the income statement it adjusts for price rises (or falls) between the date inventory is acquired and the date it is sold. It thus achieves a closer matching of *current* costs against revenues in the income statement, but it does this at the expense of showing, during a period of inflation, a balance sheet valuation of inventory which becomes progressively more and more out of date.

FIFO, on the other hand, produces a balance sheet valuation of inventory which is current, but results in the matching of out-of-date inventory costs against revenues in the income statement. It is sometimes argued, fallaciously, that FIFO is an acceptable method when inventory turnover is rapid, since it produces up-to-date inventory figures in the balance sheet, and (since turnover is rapid) the time lag in the income statement is relatively unimportant. In fact, as a moment's reflection will indicate, the cumulative over-statement of profits as a result of using FIFO is just as great,[17] pound for pound of investment, as the profit overstatement attributable to the shortfall of depreciation provisions on fixed assets through a price rise. Indeed, the total overstatement of retained profits or reserves, attributable to "inventory profits", can be thought of as the difference between the FIFO and LIFO valuations at the end of the inflationary period.[18]

Another expedient, intended to deal with the problem of fixed assets and depreciation provisions, is to revalue the fixed assets periodically. This practice is not acceptable in the United States (where it is disallowed by the SEC), and it is uncommon in Canada. It is employed by some companies in Britain, and it was very popular in Australia and New Zealand because the tax laws permitted tax free stock dividends to be paid out of revaluation surplus. The procedure is a rough and ready one, and it is not altogether acceptable to management since, although depreciation must be provided on written up values, any excess over

[17] It is greater if "backlog" depreciation is not provided.
[18] Provided that the number of physical units of inventory on hand is always higher, throughout the period of measurement, than at the beginning of the period. This technical qualification (relating to the method of LIFO computation) does not affect the essential substance of my argument. LIFO and FIFO values at the beginning are assumed to be equal.

historical cost depreciation is not normally permitted as a deduction for tax purposes.

A third proposal, of much greater generality and importance, is often colloquially described as "price-level accounting". This entails the restatement of all the figures in the balance sheet and income statement in terms of measuring units of equal purchasing power. I shall assume general familiarity with the procedure,[19] but the main principle involved can be stated concisely and simply. A time series of an appropriate general price index,[20] published by the government, is used as the basis for a restatement of all unexpired costs (assets), liabilities, and residual equities in the balance sheet and all costs and revenues in the income statement, in terms not of the "historical" figures attached thereto but expressed as their equivalent in current purchasing power measured in terms of the current general price level.

There is little or no ambiguity about the nature of the adjustments which must be made, and since published government-determined price indices are used there is no ambiguity about the size of each individual adjustment required. Various indices are available, but this is not likely to produce problems since virtually everyone who accepts the merits of the method would, in Britain, be content to use the government Consumer Price Index, with the Index of Retail Prices as a fine adjustment. Indeed the use of such indices is suggested in the English Institute booklet on the subject, where it is also demonstrated that, once some preliminary "set-up" work is done, the adjustments each year can be made simply and quickly.[21]

Thus it should not be difficult to reach quick agreement on the precise nature of the adjustment to be made to any set of financial accounts in Britain. For this reason the important requirements of objectivity and verifiability can readily be met. Auditors would have no more difficulty in forming an opinion on price-level adjusted accounts than they do on the present conventional historical cost accounts.

GENERAL PRICE-LEVEL ADJUSTMENTS NOT ENOUGH

As the booklets referred to earlier make clear, the figures in price-level adjusted accounts can differ materially from those in conventional accounts, even when price levels are not rising very rapidly. The price-level adjusted figures for income and retained profits will usually be lower than the conventional figures, and this is chiefly attributable to losses on holding net monetary assets, and increased figures for depreciation and cost of goods sold. Very little adjustment, of course, is required in revenue figures since, except in rare cases, these are generally expressed in current terms.

The historical cost basis of accounting results in the matching of historical costs

---

[19] If necessary readers should consult the books referred to in footnotes 1 and 3.

[20] The problem of choosing the most appropriate index is by no means as simple as it may appear. See, for example, E. S. Hendriksen: "Purchasing Power and Replacement Cost Concepts—Are They Related?" *Accounting Review*, July 1963, pages 483–491. Nevertheless I suggest that satisfactory, objective and verifiable adjustments can be made in the U.K. using the basis (and the index) illustrated in the English Institute's booklet, *Accounting for Stewardship in a Period of Inflation.*

[21] *Op. cit.*, especially paragraphs 5 and 34.

against current revenues. Price-level accounting, by adjusting for changes in general purchasing power, results in the matching of historical costs, adjusted for changes in purchasing power since they were incurred, against current revenues. It also reflects losses arising through holding monetary assets through inflation of the general price level.

However, it must be recognised that price-level accounting in no way abandons the realisation principle. All of the methods and procedures traditionally associated with historical cost accounting are preserved in price-level accounting; the only difference is that the "values" are all measured in units of equal purchasing power. Price-level accounting, by correcting for the rubberiness of the ruler, thus involves us in a translation from a maintenance of money capital intact concept to a maintenance of general purchasing power intact concept of income determination. Like the historical cost basis it is still a "venture concept", and in the final analysis it is based upon a presumption that preservation of the general purchasing power of the invested capital is the objective (presumably in order that on ultimate liquidation this can be invested outside the enterprise in general consumer goods equivalent to those whose consumption had to be sacrificed in order to make the original investment in the company). Whether this is a realistic assumption as to the objectives of income accounting will be examined later. But it should be noted in passing that it is not a "long-run going concern" approach.

Moreover, a general price index, particularly a general consumers' price index, is a weighted average of the price changes occurring in a very wide variety of goods and services available within the economic system. Only by coincidence will a change in the general price index correspond to the change in a price, over the same period of time, of any given good or service. Thus, if the general price index has increased, many specific price increases will be lower than that of the index, whilst many others will be higher, and there may well be specific price *decreases*. Furthermore, discrepancies between specific price changes and general price changes are likely to be even greater when the general price index is a consumer index and when the specific price change relates to producer goods such as those represented by the assets of a typical commercial or industrial enterprise.

To put the matter another way, general price-level adjustments will not result in balance sheet values being expressed in terms either of current replacement cost, or current net realisable values. Nor will they ensure that the "costs" being matched in the income statement are in any sense a representation of the current cost of obtaining the equivalent inputs of goods or services. To see whether this fact is of any significance in income and value determination, we must take a closer look at what is meant by the terms "income" and "value".

DEFINITION OF INCOME

One of the best-known definitions of income is that enunciated by Professor Hicks[22] which, modified to meet the special peculiarities of a corporate entity, can be expressed as follows: Income is the maximum value which the corporation can distribute during an accounting period, and still expect to be as well off at the end of the period as it was at the beginning. It is of course assumed for purposes

---

[22] J. R. Hicks: *Value and Capital* (second edition) (Oxford; *Clarendon;* 1946), page 172.

of this definition that no further capital is introduced into or withdrawn from the enterprise during the period.

The crux of this definition hinges upon what we mean by the term "well off". It is clearly a concept which is equivalent to the accountant's notion of equity, or net asset value, and it is evidently a future-oriented concept, since all the benefits from being "well off" reside in the future. In economic terms, well-offness can be defined as the present value, using an appropriate rate of discount, of the expected stream of future net cash receipts of the enterprise. This makes it evident that the concept is a purely subjective one since it not only depends upon expectations of future net receipts, but it is also dependent upon one's (subjective) choice of discount rate. Moreover, as Professor Kaldor has pointed out, although it is a concept of income which aims to maintain capital intact, one has to tread warily since "we cannot first define income as what is left after maintaining capital intact and then define the latter as what is required to maintain income intact, without getting involved in circular reasoning".[23]

Hicks was well aware of this difficulty, and he redefined income in *ex post* terms as the amount of net dividends plus the increment in the money value of the entity's prospect which has accrued during the accounting period; it equals distribution plus capital accumulation. (This definition has been modified slightly from that given by Hicks in order to suit the situation of the corporation as distinct from that of the individual.)

Hicks went on to say, "this last very special sort of 'income' has one supremely important property. So long as we confine our attention to income from property, and leave out of account any increment or decrement in the value of prospects due to changes in people's own earning power (accumulation or decumulation of 'human capital'), income *ex post* is not a subjective affair like other kinds of income, it is almost completely objective. The capital value of the [entity's] property at the beginning of the period is an assessable figure; so is the capital value of the property at the end of the period; thus, income *ex post* can be directly calculated."[24]

It should be noted that this concept of income will be objective provided we can find an objective measure of the money value of the entity's capital. And we should observe that if we are successful in our search we will have a concept of income which aims, like historical cost accounting, at the maintenance of money capital intact. However, as we shall see later, it is only in the long run that the two concepts will coincide, and in any given year they are likely to give quite different measures of income.

Thus, if we are to translate the Hicksian concept of income into practical terms, we must define a measurable concept of value which avoids the circularity against which Kaldor warned. It will be noted that the economist's definition links income and value in much the same way that the double-entry system links the income statement with the balance sheet, and this augurs well for the ultimate practicality of the approach we are now following.

What we are looking for is an operational definition of what we mean by the value of an asset to a firm in current terms, that is to say in terms of current prices rather than in historical costs. Whilst we must note the importance of

---

[23] N. Kaldor: *An Expenditure Tax* (London; *Allen & Unwin;* 1955), page 65.
[24] *Op. cit.*, pages 178–179.

"economic value" (*i.e.* the net present value of the expected stream of future net receipts attributable to owning the asset in question), since the measure of this value determines whether it is worth while acquiring or retaining any given asset, we must also recognise that the subjectivity of the concept makes it useless for objective accounting purposes.

The two current objective values which can be attached to an asset are its replacement cost and its net realisable value. What we have to decide is which of these two is the relevant measure of value for use in the determination of income.

THE ESSENTIAL RÔLE OF VALUE IN INCOME DETERMINATION

For a solution to this problem we must turn again to the discipline of economics. It is well known that the economist, in assessing the costs and benefits of a course of action, is accustomed to using the concept of "opportunity cost". The opportunity cost of an action can be defined as the value of the most attractive opportunity which has to be sacrificed in order to take the proposed action. This concept is widely used in economics and in business management. Indeed, one might say that a successful entrepreneur is born with an intuitive grasp of this concept!

In determining the "value" of an asset one can, as it were, turn the opportunity cost concept on its head,[25] and define opportunity value as the least costly sacrifice avoided by owning an asset. This approach to the problem of measuring the value of an asset to a firm has been adopted by a number of economists, and indeed I am sure that it forms the foundation of Professor Limperg's replacement value theory, which is the basis of the Philips system of accounting (although I cannot verify this directly since his works have not been translated into English).

Although this definition of opportunity value is adequate, a much more pregnant definition was framed by Professor Bonbright, in the following terms:—

> The value of a property to its owner is identical in amount with the adverse value of the entire loss, direct and indirect, that the owner might expect to suffer if he were to be deprived of the property.[26]

Let us now consider the significance of replacement cost, net realisable value, and economic value with respect to the concept of value to the owner, or as we shall now call it, Value to the Firm, as defined above.

Economic Value is a subjective quantity and is the net present value of the expected stream of future net receipts attributable to the ownership of the asset. Indivisibilities will frequently make it difficult to form a clear notion of the expected receipts stream and this, combined with the subjective nature of the estimates and of the discount rate to be applied to them, makes this concept quite clearly unacceptable for valuation purposes. However, businessmen must continually attempt the estimates since, if they estimate economic value to be lower

---

[25] A similar approach to opportunity value with different conclusions is used by Professor Wright. See "A Theory of Financial Accounting", *Journal of Business Finance*, Vol. 2, No. 3 (Autumn 1970), pages 57–69.

[26] J. C. Bonbright: *The Valuation of Property* (New York: McGraw-Hill; 1937), page 71.

than net realisable value, it does not make sense to retain the asset and they will dispose of it.

Thus, the real significance of Economic Value and Net Realisable Value, so far as Value to the Firm is concerned, is that if economic value is higher than net realisable value it will pay the firm to retain the asset for use. If, on the other hand, net realisable value exceeds economic value it will pay the firm to dispose of the asset.

Thus we might define a term, to be known as the "Netback Value",[27] representing the highest yield or "netback" which the firm can expect to derive from the asset if it owns it. Netback value will be the higher of economic value and net realisable value. If economic value is the higher, it will pay the firm to retain the asset for use, thus deriving the highest netback. If net realisable value is the higher, it will pay the firm to dispose of the asset.

It is now possible for us to reinterpret Value to the Firm in terms of these other three concepts. If the firm is suddenly deprived of an asset, the maximum loss which it will sustain as a result will be the lower of the replacement cost of the asset and its netback value.

Thus, if netback value is higher than replacement cost, it will pay the firm to replace the asset, and the cost of replacement is the maximum value of the loss the firm sustains since this is the amount required to restore it to its position before it was deprived of the asset.

If, on the other hand, netback value is lower than replacement cost, then it would not pay the firm to replace the asset if it was lost, since it could not hope to recover, in netback, the cost of replacement. **Thus, under these circum**stances the maximum loss which the firm could be said to have sustained as a result of being deprived of the asset is its netback value.

Normally one can assume, in a profitable going concern, that netback value will be equal to economic value. In other words economic value is equal to or greater than net realisable value and it pays the firm to retain assets for use in the ordinary course of business, whether they be fixed assets, or inventories, etc. In these circumstances there are only three possible combinations of the three factors arranged in order of size, as follows:—

EV	EV	RC
NRV	RC	EV
RC	NRV	NRV

In the first two cases the Value to the Firm is replacement cost. In the third case it would not be worth while replacing the asset if it were lost, but so long as the firm owns it it is better off using it than selling it. According to our rule, Value to the Firm would be economic value, but I suggest that since this is a subjective and nonmeasurable quantity we would not go very far wrong in most instances if we treated Value to the Firm as net realisable value in this case.[28]

---

[27] I apologise for adding to an already burdensome list of accounting jargon. But some identification is necessary here, and "netback" is a term which is very widely used in the petroleum industry and seems relevant to our present purpose.

[28] The case of non-vendible durables is a special problem and is dealt with below. But it should be noted that in profitable enterprises they fall into the second column, not the third.

Management would certainly know that net realisable value was lower than replacement cost, or they ought to know this.

In the other situation, where netback value is equal to net realisable value, three other different combinations are possible:—

NRV	NRV	RC
EV	RC	NRV
RC	EV	EV

In the first two cases Value to the Firm is clearly equal to replacement cost. In the last case it is equally clearly equal to net realisable value. The subjective and unmeasurable nature of economic value is no problem in this instance, since it is presumably known to management that the netback will be greater if they dispose of the asset than if they hang on to it.

We can now see the result of this analysis. We obtain a valuation rule which states, quite simply, that the value of an asset to the firm is equal to the lower of its netback value and its replacement cost. And we can feel reasonably sure that in most cases, in profitable enterprises, this will turn out to be replacement cost. And, if net realisable value is used instead, it will not be on the ground of conservatism but on the ground of economic principle.

If we accept the definition of an asset as a storehouse of future service potential[29] we can see that any attempt to measure the value of an asset must, *ipso facto*, be an attempt to measure the value of the future service potentials. As we have seen, this leads us into the problem of subjective valuations. Nevertheless, as we have also seen, it is possible by a process of analysis to derive an operational definition of Value to the Firm which *is measurable*—provided there is a market economy, and provided there is a reasonable market for the assets in question.

I think it is fair to say that the majority of accounting academics and theoreticians who have studied this question are prepared to accept, in general at any rate, the force of the arguments which I have expounded above. In other words, they would accept that the lower of replacement cost and netback value is a close approximation to Value to the Firm. There is a dwindling band of theoreticians, mainly practitioners, I think, rather than academics, who still favour historical cost, but as I have indicated above I accept the necessity of retaining historical cost, at least for legal purposes, for some time to come.

However, there is one other school of thought which must be considered here. Its most distinguished spokesman is Professor R. J. Chambers, who set forth his ideas in a seminal book, *Accounting, Evaluation and Economic Behavior*, published in 1965.[30] Chambers argues that, in principle, the proper basis of valuation is net realisable value, and he rejects replacement cost, as an expedient which should only be used when net realisable value is indeterminate.

As Chambers readily admitted, a great weakness in his argument is that what

---

[29] Thus, "Assets represent expected future economic benefits, rights to which have been acquired by the enterprise as a result of some current or past transaction". R. T. Sprouse and M. Moonitz: *A Tentative Set of Broad Accounting Principles for Business Enterprises*. (New York; AICPA; 1962), page 20.

[30] Although I cannot accept the central thesis of his theoretical analysis I regard Chambers as one of the leading thinkers in the field of financial accounting theory. The book referred to above is published by Prentice-Hall.

he calls a "non-vendible durable" will be written down to zero immediately upon acquisition, according to his theory. Several arrows (in the form of reviews of his book) have been fired into this Achilles heel, but Chambers, though bloody, is yet unbowed.[31] I do not propose to dwell upon this problem at any length, but it is instructive to see how non-vendible durables would be valued according to the principles I have expounded above. A non-vendible durable is a durable tangible asset which is more or less specific to the firm which owns it. It excludes such readily "vendible" assets as office equipment and machinery, automotive equipment, many types of general purpose building, etc. As Chambers recognised, highly specialised non-vendible assets have, by definition, a very low net realisable value—to which they would be written down according to his principles.

However, it is obvious that, although the net realisable value may be low, the economic value is presumably high, otherwise the firm would not have invested in the assets, and the presumption is that economic value is higher than replacement cost. Thus, value to the firm would equal replacement cost, unless there was a clear and unmistakable indication that the asset had lost its economic value and was not merely non-vendible but non-economic.

VALUE, REALISATION, AND HOLDING GAINS

The implication of an acceptance of Value to the Firm as a legitimate basis for financial reporting is clear. It involves relaxation, but not necessarily abandonment, of the realisation principle.[32] If we accept Value to the Firm as a basis, we are accepting the use of current values prior to their realisation through consummation in a market transaction and, to put this another way, it means that we are recognising gains and losses in value in the periods in which they occur rather than in the period in which they are realised.[33]

On the other hand, such unrealised changes clearly have significance both in the balance sheet and in the income statement. It is convenient to distinguish between the possible ways in which such value changes may be recognised and reported in each of these two financial statements.

If all the assets on the balance sheet are stated in current values (*i.e.* at Value to the Firm) the balance sheet will show the net tangible equity at a value which is much closer to the "true" value of the total invested capital than does a balance sheet expressed in historical cost. Other important subjective values will, of course, be omitted (in particular, goodwill) but it is unlikely that accountants will ever be able to develop a satisfactory method of measuring such values and, as Professor Sidney Davidson has said, it is better to be approximately right than to be precisely wrong.

[31] See, for example, his latest article in *Abacus*, Vol. 6, No. 1 (September 1970), entitled "Second Thoughts on Continuously Contemporary Accounting".

[32] See also footnote 14. It means an abandonment of historical cost, but unless value increments are reported as income the realisation principle—insofar as it relates to revenues—will not be violated. In fact, as I explain in detail below, I believe that in most cases such increments (whether realised or not) are not income. However, the debit side of the increment should be charged against income (as depreciation, cost of sales, etc.), so the realisation principle *is* involved.

[33] Indeed, in the period of realisation the value increment may be zero—or even negative!

I suspect that even fairly conservative accountants are prepared to consider the idea of current values in the balance sheet. After all, many of them have already accepted the idea of recording fixed asset appraisals on the books. The real problem arises when we consider the effects on the income statement.

If price levels are rising, the recording of current values in the asset accounts (in the books and on the balance sheet) necessarily implies higher charges for depreciation and cost of goods sold. This is obvious, and the same thing happens under price-level accounting when the general price level increases, although the principle involved is of course entirely different. The difficulty arises in deciding what to do with the "credit side" (to use terminology with which all accountants will be familiar) of the value increment. These credits represent, in origin, unrealised "holding gains" attributable to holding assets through a price rise.[34] What has to be decided is whether these unrealised holding gains constitute a part of income and, if so, whether they constitute income when they are unrealised or only upon realisation (*i.e.* as the inventory is sold or as the fixed assets are used up.) If realised and/or unrealised holding gains are not to be regarded as income we have to decide what is the theoretical justification for treating them otherwise.

We also have to consider the problem that if, for example, specific prices rise faster than the general price level it can be argued (although not necessarily conclusively) that only that portion of the holding gain attributable to the excess of the specific price rise over the general price rise can be regarded as "real", and the balance must be regarded as "fictitious". Clearly, in matters of this kind, a great deal hinges upon our choice of general price index.[35]

THE PROBLEM OF THE TREATMENT OF HOLDING GAINS

If we turn back to our economic definition of income we shall find that it is not of very much help. To say that the income of the firm is the maximum amount that it may distribute while yet remaining as well off at the end of the period as it was at the beginning does not tell us whether holding gains (unrealised and/or realised) are part of income. If we credit them to some form of capital valuation reserve, then they are not income and the definition will tell us so. Alternatively if we credit them to revenue we thereby bring them into capital ("well-offness"), they form part of income, and once again the definition tells us so! We cannot break out of this circle by relying on our definition of income alone, and we shall have to look elsewhere.

Let us first of all consider the situation where an accounting entity holds an asset through a specific price rise without any change in the general price level. That is to say the replacement cost of the asset increases while the entity holds it, but there is no change in the general price level or in the purchasing power of money in this time period. The accounting entity might be a firm holding a stock of inventory or a fixed asset; alternatively it might be an individual who owns a house or other durable asset. The specific price change has given rise to an unrealised holding gain, and since there has been no change in the general price level all of this holding gain is "real" and none of it is "fictitious".

[34] "Holding gain" (or, of course, loss) is here used in a generic sense. A distinction is made later between "inventory holding gains", and holding gains on fixed assets (which will be denoted as "cost savings") being used in the business.

[35] *Vide supra.* Footnote 20.

Suppose the asset is now sold.³⁶ The result is that what was a real unrealised holding gain becomes a real realised holding gain. Suppose the entity now immediately replaces the asset at the current replacement price. This will require financial resources equal to the original (historical) cost of the asset which has been disposed of, plus the whole amount of the realised holding gain. Under these circumstances, where replacement is a necessary and deliberate part of maintaining the enterprise as a going concern, I suggest that few people would regard either the unrealised or the realised holding gains as income or as distributable.

On the other hand, if the holding gain had developed and had been realised on an asset extraneous to the general run of the business, it might well be argued that the unrealised and particularly the realised holding gain *could* be regarded as income. Since there has been no change in the general price level, all of the holding gain is "real", and presumably the accretion of general purchasing power could be used to advantage by the firm, or by its shareholders in a distribution.

This perhaps provides a hint as to where we might look for a solution to the problem. Let us now consider a slightly different example. Let us suppose that our accounting entity buys an irredeemable interest-paying debenture. Immediately after acquisition there is a fall in interest rates and a consequent increase in the replacement value of the debenture. Let us now suppose that interest rates remain constant at the new low level until after the debenture is sold and the proceeds are re-invested. Under these circumstances it would seem inappropriate to credit the unrealised holding gain to income (where it is subject to distribution) since there has been no increase in real resources in relation to maintainable income. If the holding gain were to be credited to income and distributed, then upon disposal of the debenture the firm would suffer, on re-investment, a realised fall in the amount of its income stream (which is equivalent to the quasi rents of real property). And, of course, the present value of the realised fall in the quasi rents will exactly offset the unrealised holding gain.

It is rather easy to understand what is going on in the case of debentures since there is a clear relationship between capital and income in such cases. It is not so easy, in the case of real property, to decide whether changes in replacement cost represent the equivalent of changes in the discount rate or whether they represent improved expectations (which are not possible in the case of fixed interest securities).

I have already referred to Kaldor's warning against the danger of being trapped in a circular reasoning process when thinking about how to define income and value. Yet we cannot escape grappling with this problem, for as Professor Fisher said³⁷—

> It would seem then that income must be derived from capital; and, in a sense, this is true. Income *is* derived from capital *goods* but the *value* of the income is not derived from the *value* of the capital goods. On the contrary, the

---

³⁶ The proceeds are the net realisable value. For present purposes this is assumed to be equal to replacement cost. If it exceeds replacement cost the excess can be regarded as a windfall profit. See below.

³⁷ Quoted in R. H. Parker and G. C. Harcourt (eds.): *Readings in the Concept and Measurement of Income* (Cambridge; C.U.P.; 1969), page 40. Note that Fisher thinks of income as consumption, and excludes saving (in contrast to Hicks). But this does not vitiate the point he is making here.

value of the capital is derived from the value of the income.... Not until we know how much income an item of capital will probably bring us can we set any valuation on that capital at all. It is true that the wheat crop depends on the land which yields it. But the value of the crop does not depend on the value of the land. On the contrary, the value of the land depends on the expected value of its crops.

If we did not live in a market economy, where prices are established by the forces of supply and demand, our accounting problem would be insoluble. But it is the function and purpose of the market to translate expectations into values, and indeed the only reliable and objective test that we have of the value of expectations is the value set in the market place.

The reference to Fisher focuses attention once again upon the intimate connection between the statement of profit and loss and the balance sheet. And I think it suggests that perhaps an answer to the riddle is to be found in a process which blends the matching idea (appropriate to the income statement) with the economist's notions (especially those of Hicks) which effectively define income in terms of balance sheet changes.

Let us first of all consider the matching process in the income statement, and let us confine ourselves to the cost side of the equation, since we shall be considering realisation when we look at the balance sheet.

As we have already seen, the historical cost approach fails to match like against like, since many of the costs (especially those relating to depreciation and cost of sales) are expressed in historical units of measure of widely differing purchasing powers. Price-level adjustments can correct this, but even they do not give an adequate correction since they fail to take into account specific price changes. If the matching process is to be logical it should clearly match current revenues against the current Values to the Firm of the factors of production which have been expended in deriving the revenues. To put it another way, the current value of the output sold should be "matched" against the correct cost of the related inputs. If this is done, the resultant income measure is generally known as "Current Operating Profit."[38]

Turning now to the balance sheet, I have argued earlier that it is more logical and more informative, and therefore presumably more useful to the reader, to have the balance sheet expressed in current values. The appropriate basis of measurement would appear to be Value to the Firm as defined above. If this is done, the valuation of assets such as inventories and fixed assets will normally be substantially different from the historical cost valuation, and the excess represents accumulated unrealised holding gains which have accrued since the dates of purchase of the various assets.[39] Upon realisation the current costs will flow into the

---

[38] This term, and a number of others, follow the usage of E. O. Edwards and P. W. Bell: *The Theory and Measurement of Business Income* (Berkeley; *California University Press;* 1961), *passim*. This pioneering work should be on the bookshelf of every thinking accountant. The conclusions of the analysis in this paper differ considerably from those of Edwards and Bell, particularly in regard to the treatment of holding gains, and some modification of their terminology has therefore been inevitable in order to clarify my argument.

[39] Post-realisation assets, such as receivables and cash, will of course be shown at net realisable value.

income statement, where they will be matched against current revenues in the process of determination of current operating profit.

The essence of the problem now is to decide whether, and if so to what extent and in what period, the unrealised gains should be regarded as income; and, further, to what extent and in what manner realised gains should be treated as a part of income. We also have to determine whether it is necessary to divide unrealised and realised gains into their real and fictitious elements by making adjustments for changes in the general price level. If we decide to make such adjustments we have to decide which price index is the appropriate one to use.

Whatever we decide to do, it is clearly preferable to make a segregation between current operating profit and holding gains, since they are attributable to two entirely different types of activity, and any assessment of performance, or attempt to predict future performance, will be facilitated if the segregation is made. It is also important to segregate realised from unrealised changes, since they clearly constitute quite different classes of gain of different "quality", and once again assessment and prediction is facilitated if the segregation is made.[40]

Finally, it is useful to distinguish between holding gains (both unrealised and realised, fictional and real) attributable to assets such as inventories which are purchased for resale, holding gains (unrealised and realised, real and fictional) attributable to fixed assets which are purchased for use rather than re-sale (and where realisation will occur as the asset is depreciated and amortised rather than as it is sold), and realised holding gains on fixed assets which have been sold by the firm (where the excess of the selling price over net depreciated current cost at the time of disposal represents a real capital profit).[41] It is convenient to distinguish between these three categories by denoting them as inventory holding gains, cost savings, and windfalls, respectively.[42]

It will, of course, be appreciated that the measure of the unrealised or realised inventory holding gains, or the cost savings, which have accrued on any given asset up to any particular point in time will be a cumulative figure made up of the net of the gains and losses which have accrued in each of the several years since the asset was purchased. The amounts accruing in any given year are clearly of considerable significance, whether they remain unrealised at the end of the year or whether they are realised during the year, and it is customary to describe such annual accretion as a "realisable" inventory holding gain, etc.[43]

A SET OF PROFIT CONCEPTS

It will now be evident that we have managed to break down not only accounting profit but also the economist's concept of profit into their essential components. Readers will find it convenient at this stage to refer to the Exhibit.

[40] The importance of the "quality" of the constituents of even conventional accounts was stressed by J. D. Slater in his address to the English Institute Cambridge Summer Course in 1970. See the Proceedings thereof, *What is Profit?* (London; I.C.A.E.W.; 1970), pages 58–73, especially page 64.

[41] Note that the excess of net depreciated current cost over net depreciated historical cost is a *realised* (real and fictional) holding gain. Normal accounting terminology classifies this plus the windfall as a "capital profit" (in one figure).

[42] "Holding gain", as a generic term, applies only to the first two.

[43] "Realisable" is a useful way of describing this important element; the term was coined by Edwards and Bell (*op. cit.*).

Exhibit ANALYSIS OF COMPONENTS OF VARIOUS MEASURES OF PROFIT

Code no.	Components Description	
COP	Current operating profit	
1	Real realisable holding gains	*i.e.* unrealised and realised, accruing in current period
2	Fictitious " " "	
3	Real realisable cost savings	
4	Fictitious " " "	
5	Real realised capital gains	
6	Fictitious " " "	
7	Real realised cost savings	Fixed assets
8	Fictitious " " "	
9	Real unrealised " "	
10	Fictitious " " "	
11	Real realised holding gains	
12	Fictitious " " "	Inventories
13	Real unrealised " "	
14	Fictitious " " "	
15	Loss on holding monetary assets in current period	
16	Holding gain element in $(5+6)$	

Measures of Profit in terms of above components

Profit measure	Components	Balance sheet valuations
Accounting Profit	$(COP + 7 + 8 + 11 + 12) + (5 + 6)$	Historical Cost
Adjusted Accounting Profit	$(COP + 7 + 11) + 5 - 15$	Adjusted (price index) Historical Cost
Money Profit (Realisable Profit)	$COP + (1 + 2) + (3 + 4)$	Current Values
Real Money Profit	$COP + 1 + 3 - 15$	" "
Real Profit*	$COP + (5 - 16) - 15$	" "

Note (1): Terminology ("gain" etc.) assumes rising price levels, with the rise in specific prices greater than rise in general price level. The terminology (and algebraic sign) changes if these conditions are varied, but not the underlying principles.

Note (2): There is, of course, overlap between $(1 + 2)$ and $(3 + 4)$ and the rest (except COP).

Note (3): 9, 10, 13 and 14 are not included in any of the measures *except* Money Profit (all of them) and Real Money Profit (9 and 13) on a *cumulative basis*.

* As I indicate, in the text, I prefer.

Thus, the concept of profit described by Hicks (unadjusted for changes in general purchasing power) is made up of the sum of current operating profit and realisable inventory holding gains and cost savings. This concept of profit is often described in the literature as Realisable Profit, or Money Profit. The first term is self-explanatory, and the significance of the second will be appreciated later.

If we wish to take account of general price-level changes, it is only necessary to eliminate the fictional from the real portion of the realisable inventory holding gains and cost savings. Real money profit (or real realisable profit) consists of current operating profit plus the real realisable gains, less losses on monetary assets.

Similarly, accounting profit is equal to current operating profit plus both the real and fictional portion of realised cost savings and realised inventory holding gains, together with real and fictional realised capital gains.[44] In the traditional accounting statement of profit and loss, the real and fictional realised capital gains are generally reported separately (without distinguishing between the real and fictional elements thereof), but the realised cost savings and inventory holding gains are "buried" in the reported historical cost figures for depreciation and cost of sales respectively. Thus it is impossible for the reader to see to what extent reported profits are attributable to accumulated inventory holding gains and cost savings.

Similarly, adjusted accounting profit (*i.e.* adjusted for changes in the general price level) is composed of current operating profit, together with the real portion of realised cost savings and inventory holding gains, plus real realised capital gains, less any loss arising from holding monetary assets during the current accounting period. Monetary gains and losses arising in previous periods will already have been absorbed in the retained profits account.

It might be thought, from most of what has been said above, that the "best" measure of profit is that of the economist, adjusted for changes in the general price level, *i.e.* real money profit as outlined above. However, it will be recalled that we have not yet settled the question of whether holding gains[45] ought to be included in a measure of income. Before we try to settle this question, we should note that in the long run real money profit and adjusted accounting profit amount to very much the same thing. Real money profit recognises holding gains in the years in which they accrue, whereas adjusted accounting profit recognises holding gains in the years in which they are realised.[46] In the long run, when all gains have been realised, the accumulation of profits on either basis will amount to the same thing. In the short or in the medium run, the accumulated difference between the two will be equal to accumulated unrealised real inventory holding gains and cost savings. In any given year the difference between income for the year measured on the two bases will be the difference between the real portion of inventory holding gains and cost savings realised in the current period but accruing in previous periods (which will be included in accounting profit) and the real portion of inventory holding gains and cost savings accruing in the current period but not realised by the end of that period (which will be included in real money profit).

The reason why, in the long run, adjusted accounting profit and real money profit amount to the same thing is that they are both trying to do the same thing. They are both attempting to maintain intact the general purchasing power originally invested in the enterprise (plus any further net investment since incorporation). The short and medium term differences (which are of course of paramount importance) arise because real money profit recognises unrealised changes,

---

[44] Using "capital gain" in its conventional sense which equals realised holding gains on fixed assets sold (excess of net current cost over net historical cost at time of sale) plus "windfalls" as defined above.

[45] In the generic sense, including cost savings. Since I do not regard holding gains as part of income I would really prefer to give them a new title. But on balance it seems better to use a term which will be familiar to most accountants who are familiar with the literature.

[46] A similar comparison is of course possible between conventional accounting profit and Realisable Profit.

whereas adjusted accounting income does not. In the long run all changes are realised.[47]

Conceptually, the important thing to note is that both ideas of profit involve the same notion of capital maintenance. In a similar way one can draw parallels between historical cost measures of profit and money (or realisable) profit. In the long run they will amount to the same thing because they each are attempting to maintain the original invested money capital intact. As before, the differences in the short and medium term arise because realisable profit recognises unrealised gains, whereas accounting or historical cost profit does not.

Now I think it is clear that, if one regards the firm essentially as a venture which will ultimately be liquidated, with the proceeds being turned over to the shareholders, a concept of profit which aims to maintain original invested money capital intact will be satisfactory provided that there is no change in the general purchasing power. In the real world, of course, we have to live with inflation and so in the real world it is clear that we will have a better measure of profit if we take purchasing power changes into account, and a profit concept which aims to maintain the original invested purchasing power intact will be more satisfactory when general price levels are changing.

THE RELEVANCE OF CONCEPTS OF CAPITAL MAINTENANCE

However, it is highly questionable whether we can in fact regard the modern business corporation as a "venture" in the sense in which I have used that term above. In a modern capitalist economy, one simply does not regard an investment in shares of a corporation as something which will only be liquidated as a result of the liquidation of the corporation. Corporations (*pace* Rolls-Royce) are thought of as having an unlimited life, and shareholdings are normally realised by the shareholder selling the holding to a third party through the medium of the securities market. The investor is thus not really interested in changes in the general purchasing power of the original invested capital, since he does not contemplate receiving his share of it in the form of a distribution. If he wishes to liquidate his interest in the corporation he sells his shares and he will make his own correlation between the price at which he sells them and changes in the index of general purchasing power. Moreover, even if the shareholder *did* receive a liquidating distribution from the corporation, he may very well decide to invest the proceeds in shares of another company rather than spend them in a way to which the index of general purchasing power would be relevant.

Similar conclusions will be reached if one looks at the matter from the point of view of the directors and the management. They are not normally concerned with applying the resources of the corporation to the purchase of assets whose prices correlate with changes in the general purchasing power. On the contrary, they are much more concerned with changes in specific price levels of the assets which the enterprise deals with in its normal course of business, whether they be fixed assets or current assets. Indeed, the only way in which shareholders and directors come together in this area is over the question of dividends, where presumably changes in the purchasing power of money *are* relevant. However, in this respect shareholders are quite capable of making their own calculations as to the change

---

[47] But, as Keynes observed, in the long run we are all dead!

in the real value of the dividends which they receive periodically from their investments.

In fact, the accountant's concept of the going concern implies that it is the wish and intention of both shareholders and management (to say nothing of employees, creditors, etc.) that the corporation should maintain itself. This, of course, by no means implies that it will maintain itself in the same form. Clearly its substance will change as assets are sold and wear out, and in the short run the replacements (inventories, machinery, etc.) will probably be similar in form to that which is being replaced. But over the medium term it is likely that style changes, product changes, technological improvements, changes in demand, etc. will result in changes in the company's marketing and production planning, and as a result the corporation will slowly evolve into an organism which is materially different in form, substance, and lifestyle from what it used to be.

What all this adds up to is that, whilst a maintenance of capital concept based upon original invested money capital, or upon original invested general purchasing power, is unlikely to be satisfactory, it is difficult to argue that a concept based upon maintenance of real tangible physical assets is superior.

Nevertheless, I believe that it *is* possible for the accountant to select an appropriate maintenance concept which still takes account of the long-term need for the corporation to maintain flexibility and adaptability. I think it can be done (in the absence of very rapid technological change) by taking advantage of the fact that change is an evolutionary process and in the case of corporations it occurs with tolerable slowness. Over a long period of time the corporation may change unrecognisably, but over short periods changes, including changes in the nature of the assets (inventories, fixed assets, etc.) in which the company deals, will be perceptible and readily measurable. Thus I think it is possible to develop a concept of maintenance of real physical tangible capital which will have relevance between the beginning and the end of any given accounting period. Indeed, if this were not possible the process of budgeting would not be possible.

As an analogy I might suggest the process of driving a car through the countryside. There will be considerable differences in surroundings between the beginning of the journey and the destination, but provided the road does not contain major discontinuities, and provided one is not driving at night without lights, it is normally possible to see where one is going and to keep on the road.[48]

If all of this is accepted, then I think we end up with a concept of capital maintenance which aims to preserve the entity's capacity to reproduce itself. If it can do this, then by the slow processes of evolution it will be able to adapt and survive and change its form, as well as, through the process of renewal, its substance.

HOLDING GAINS NOT A PART OF INCOME

If we now direct our attention back to the problem of deciding whether holding gains form a part of income it seems to me that the answer is fairly clear. (For simplicity I will use the generic term "holding gains" to denote inventory holding gains and cost savings.) I think it is clear that the fictional element of

---

[48] In the calculus one uses a similar approach to the one I am describing, in the process of integration.

both realised and unrealised holding gains must be excluded. Moreover, whilst the important distinction between realised and unrealised gains should be preserved, this should be done in the capital reserve section of the balance sheet since neither constitutes a part of income. On the contrary, they represent the amount by which the value[49] of what it is that has to be maintained has increased during the period of the firm's ownership of its assets. Provided the offsetting debits are recovered from realised revenues the firm will be able to maintain itself.[50]

Thus, it seems to me, we come to the conclusion that the "best" measure of profit that we are likely to obtain for the going concern corporation is made up (see the Exhibit on page 573) of current operating profit plus the windfall element of realised capital gains[51] less any loss in the current period attributable to holding monetary assets.[52]

I would also argue that the most informative set of financial statements would include computations of profit according to all of the concepts described in the Exhibit. Furthermore, as I have argued elsewhere,[53] I would like to see, parenthetically or otherwise, a notation of the estimated margins of errors in the various measurements included in the financial statements.

I have not dealt with the location and classification on the balance sheet of the credits arising from the incorporation of replacement costs. The realised and unrealised portions would of course be segregated and shown separately. But should the credits be shown as a part of proprietorship equity, or as a non-proprietorship item (as is often done in the case of "tax-allocation reserves" for example)? This issue can really only be decided after one has settled one's views on the nature of the accounting entity, and this matter is beyond the scope of this paper.[54]

However, one should note that the way the entity is financed will generally not be relevant in deciding the issue. The fact that a company is very highly geared, so that most of the asset financing comes from debt, does not preclude treating unrealised and realised holding gains as increments to equity (without, of course, passing them through the income account). Indeed a public utility financed entirely out of debt capital, might well treat holding gains as a form of equity reserve!

Finally, it is perhaps necessary to emphasize that a decline in replacement cost would be debited to the holding gain "reserve" and would not be charged against

---

[49] *i.e.* Value to the Firm.

[50] In a sense even this is a long-run concept since in the absence of "backlog depreciation" there may be temporary financing problems unless the firm is in a state of dynamic equilibrium.

Note also that unrealised holding gains relate to assets currently owned or in use, whereas realised gains relate to the increase in value of assets consumed and/or replaced.

[51] The "windfall" is not required for capital maintenance. This is why I deem it to be a part of income.

[52] Such losses, if one reverts to a venture approach, can be thought of as unrealised until the cycle has been completed by replacement.

[53] In "Accounting Principles and Management Accountants", an Address to the I.C.W.A. Conference held in the University of Lancaster. Reprinted in *Management Accounting,* May 1971, page 141.

[54] For a good discussion of the various alternatives see E. S. Hendriksen: *Accounting Theory* (second edition) (Homewood; *Irwin;* 1970), Chapter 17.

income. The reasoning behind this is similar, *mutatis mutandis*, to that given above when replacement costs are increasing.

TWO OBJECTIONS TO CHANGE

Let me deal, finally, with a couple of objections which might be advanced against these proposals. The first concerns the objectivity and practicality of the measurement changes which are implied, and the second relates to the supposed damage which might be caused if the suggested changes were to be made.

All objections which rest on the ground of practicality or objectivity are, of course, directed against the recognition in the accounts of unrealised value changes. As I have already pointed out, the historical cost basis (against which unrealised changes are computed) is itself lacking in objectivity, and as Professor Hatfield said many years ago "the objection to recording appreciation because it is a vague estimate applies just as truly to depreciation".[55] It really all boils down to the question of whether the accountant is capable of developing measurement techniques to enable him to compute replacement costs and net realisable values for tangible assets. I have spent a dozen years in practice and I do not have to be told that this is often a difficult problem. It ought to be regarded as soluble in the case of inventories, since if auditors really attempt to determine whether inventories are being properly valued, at the lower of cost and market value, they are supposed to make some effort, now, to determine replacement costs and net realisable values. It can be done, and I think it frequently is done quite successfully in practice. In the case of fixed assets it is possible to use specific and industry-wide price indices in the case of many categories. There will no doubt be a small residuum of assets for which it is impossible to make any kind of objective and reliable estimate of value to the firm. In these cases I would be perfectly happy to see a general price index applied against them, in much the same way as is done in price-level accounting. Such a procedure might not produce the whole truth, but it will certainly be a closer approximation to the truth in most cases than historical cost.[56]

Doubts about the practicalities do exist in powerful quarters, however, and in an interview with Robert Jones (printed in *The Times* on November 11, 1970 on page 27) Sir Henry Benson made the following statement:—

> "The most difficult subject of course is how to deal with proper presentation of accounts in an inflationary society. And unhappily nobody so far has arrived at a practical solution."

This is a very surprising comment since Sir Henry's firm, Cooper Bros., are the auditors of the British affiliates of the Dutch enterprise N.V. Philips' Gloeilampenfabrieken. Philips have not only pioneered a system of replacement value accounting but have demonstrated, quite conclusively, that it is a practical system which can be used effectively by a large multi-national industrial enterprise with affiliates scattered throughout the world. If the Philips system is practical, as it

---

[55] "A Symposium on Appreciation", *Accounting Review*, March 1930, page 33.

[56] Unless there is clear (even if unquantifiable) evidence that the specific price change is manifestly not represented even approximately by the change in the general index. Such cases should be explained in a footnote to the financial statements.

clearly is, how much more practical is the system described in the English Institute's booklet *Accounting for Stewardship in a Period of Inflation,* referred to earlier. Indeed, by comparison with the Philips system, the English Institute proposals are child's play. As I hope this Paper demonstrates, the real problems are the theoretical ones, and it is really not possible to argue any more that a practical solution cannot be found.

The second objection concerns the possible inflationary effect of reporting information such as that which I have described. Thus it is argued that in a time of rising prices, reporting price-level adjusted figures (for example) would have the effect of lowering reported company earnings. Management would then feel impelled to raise prices, with a resultant snowballing inflation.

It is clearly impossible to produce a conclusive refutation of an assertion of this kind without empirical evidence. (It is similarly impossible to *prove* the assertion!) But I suggest that there are other alternatives open to management. They might, for example, try reducing dividends, and they might have a shot at reducing some of their costs, particularly their labour costs, by improving productivity, eliminating feather-bedding, and possibly even compelling the unions to accept wage reductions.

Clearly, in any individual case it will depend upon the forces operating in the market. In some circumstances it might be just as difficult to raise prices as it would be to force down labour costs. Reducing dividends will ultimately raise the cost of capital, and there is no doubt that lower reported earnings will make it more difficult for companies to raise new capital. But surely the point of the whole exercise which I have described in this paper is to reveal the truth as it really is. I can see little merit in living in a fool's paradise, and it is encouraging to see leaders of the business community, like Sir Alexander McDonald, the Chairman of Distillers, beginning to speak out on this subject.[57]

CONCLUSION

In this paper I have been dealing with an area of what academics generally describe as accounting theory. It is an area which is growing in importance, and it is certainly very much more important today than it was even twenty years ago when I started learning about accounting. It is a truism that the more one learns the more one realises how much more there is still to be learnt, but it is a truism which I think applies with especial force to the modern accountant. I would certainly be the last to suggest that we will find all our answers from studying and developing accounting theory. In fact, as I hope I have been able to demonstrate in this paper, the rôle of accounting theory is not so much to provide answers as to make sure that we ask all the right questions. It is only experience that will finally give us the answers.

[57] In a widely reported comment in the company's annual report published in 1970.

INDIANA TELEPHONE CORPORATION: ANNUAL REPORT 1971

[*Extract from the President's Letter.*]

Indiana Telephone Corporation, a "public utility" or "regulated monopoly," must survive in a society which is becoming increasingly regulated by government and in which our medium of exchange is constantly declining in value. Meanwhile, we must attempt to provide a desirable service for a desirable profit.

MONETARY INFLATION IS STILL WITH US

Since Indiana Telephone Corporation was incorporated in 1935 the purchasing power of the dollar has declined from 100¢ in 1935 to 30¢ in 1972. This is a decline of approximately 70%. *In other words, 37 years ago, the dollar commanded 335% of the purchasing power it commands today.* (These figures are based on the Gross National Product Implicit Price Deflator which is published by the United States Department of Commerce. *See chart on page 581.*)

When we refer to changes in the purchasing power of the dollar we are referring to the purchasing power of the dollar as affected by monetary inflation—that is, the direct or indirect printing of money usually related to a deficit in the budget of the government not fully financed by borrowings from real savings. (See Henry Hazlitt's *What You Should Know about Inflation.*)

On August 15, 1971, President Nixon instituted a wage-price freeze (Phase 1) and subsequently he announced Phase 2, with the expressed intention of slowing monetary inflation. We cite you to Dr. Ludwig von Mises' *Human Action* (Henry Regnery Company) and also *Fiat Money Inflation in France* by Andrew Dickson White (The Foundation for Economic Education, Inc., Irvington-on-Hudson, New York), *the first as a theoretical and the latter as an historical indication that these controls will not work.*

AND WE ARE STILL REPORTING THE EFFECTS OF IT

There is an excellent article entitled "Inflation and Current Accounting Practice: An Economist's View" in the December, 1971, *Journal of Accountancy,* written by Dr. Solomon Fabricant (economist of New York University and the National Bureau of Economic Research) in which he sets forth the importance of reporting the effects of price level changes. In another article, "Inflation and the Lag in Accounting Practices," Dr. Fabricant investigates how to report these effects, the cost of such reporting and the degree to which people are misled by unadjusted accounts. He concludes that "It is reasonable to expect that business decisions would be sounder if the accounts were adjusted before reports were released" and that "Improvement in any part of the information would be worth

SOURCE: From *Indiana Telephone Corporation, Annual Report, Year Ended December 31, 1971,* pp. 3–6, 11–27. Reprinted by permission of Indiana Telephone Corporation.

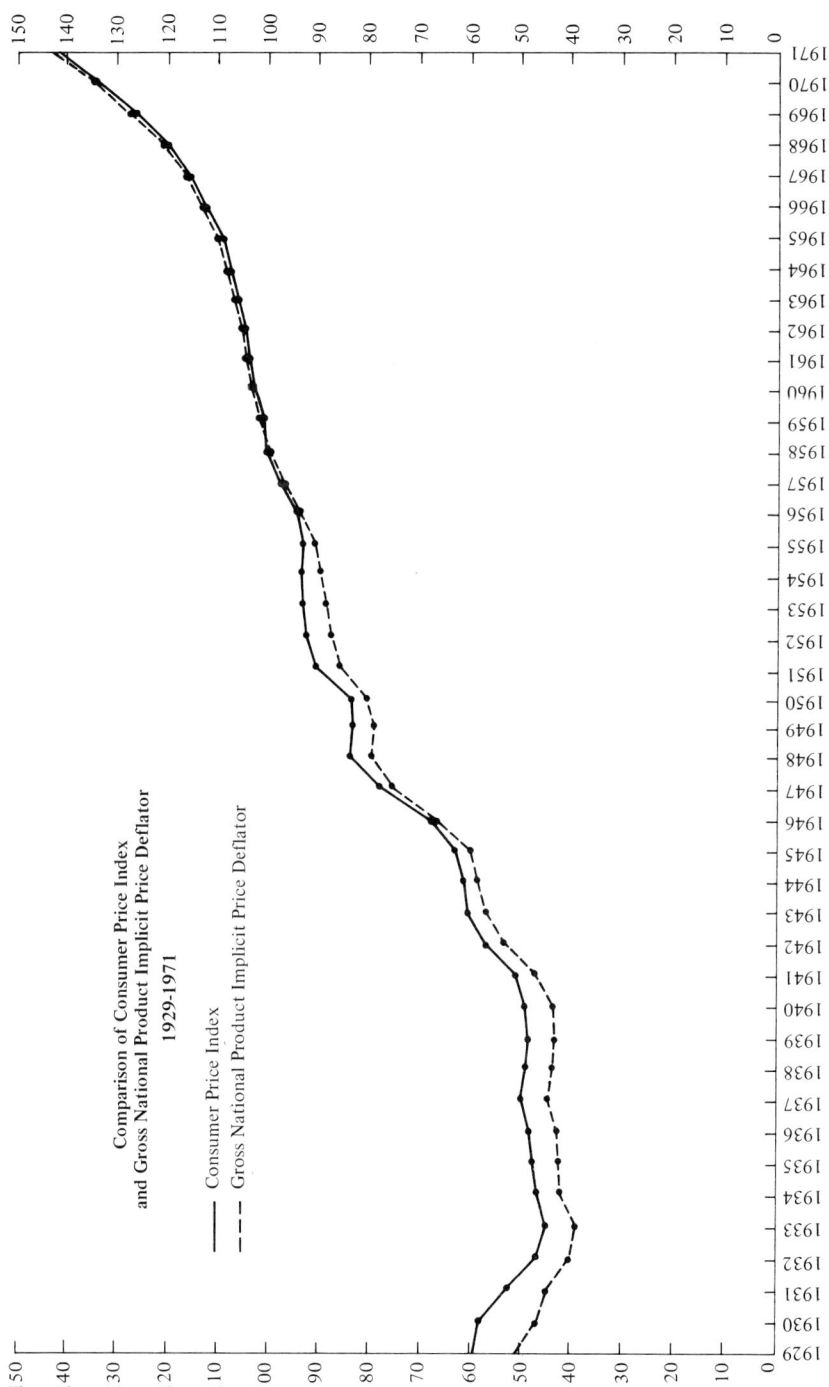

more than its cost." (from *Accounting in Perspective: Contributions to Accounting Thought by Other Disciplines,* South-Western Publishing Company, Cincinnati, Ohio). We concur with Dr. Fabricant.

We fail to understand why businessmen (and their accountants) hesitate to recognize the necessity of reporting the effects of monetary inflation on their businesses. It is important that they know the truth concerning the return of the purchasing power of the dollars their shareholders have invested in the business which they manage for the purpose of providing a product (in the case of utilities, an efficient service to their customers) for a profit.

Some say they do not know how to report these effects. We suspect they have not seriously tried. Others say the results of price levelling are not recognised by the tax laws. *We are dealing primarily with the economics of making our business survive; the tax laws are secondary.*

It is true the tax laws do not recognize the facts of the economic situation and the effects of monetary inflation with the result that capital in the guise of profits is often taxed. It is our opinion that if businessmen would be willing to have the truth about the effects of monetary inflation told, they would more likely succeed in getting these effects reflected in more realistic tax laws. (See Note 2, page 594, for the difference the recognition of price levelling would make in our taxes.)

Perhaps the charts may indicate, where words will not, the importance of more truthful corporate reports for the interests of management, the shareholders and the public.

The chart entitled "Yields on Highest-Grade Corporate Bonds" on page 585, which was based on a Moody's average of 20-year Aaa bonds, is no longer being prepared and therefore we are unable to bring it up to date. However, we believe the story it tells is still current enough to republish the 1962–1970 data.

The Dow-Jones Industrials averages are widely known as an indicator of the market and the economy. The chart on page 583 shows these averages as published in historical form from 1929 through 1971. It also shows what happens to these averages when the Gross National Product Implicit Price Deflator is applied. If it were possible to divide these averages into those companies which have real tangible assets, and those companies which have high earnings based on personal service, the results should be very revealing. On page 583 there is also a similar chart of the Dow-Jones Utilities averages. No telephone companies are included in this group but the chart is indicative of the effect of monetary inflation where there is a long-term investment in plant. Minerals and sources of energy in the United States are fast being consumed and the market should take this into account. *The market should also reflect the fact that our money, although still a medium of exchange, is no longer a satisfactory store of value.*

Banks boast of their growing deposits, but what happens if you apply the GNP Implicit Price Deflator to those dollars? See the chart on page 584 showing the actual deposits in historical dollars and their purchasing power in 1933 dollars of a small county seat bank. Most banks also fail to recognize the necessity of knowing the effects of monetary inflation on their statements because they consider themselves to be dollar-for-dollar institutions. They also fail to give due importance to the necessity of liquidity and sometimes have large amounts of assets not readily convertible into cash. *Also, because they fail to require that their customers report the effects of monetary inflation they do not know the real value of their loans.*

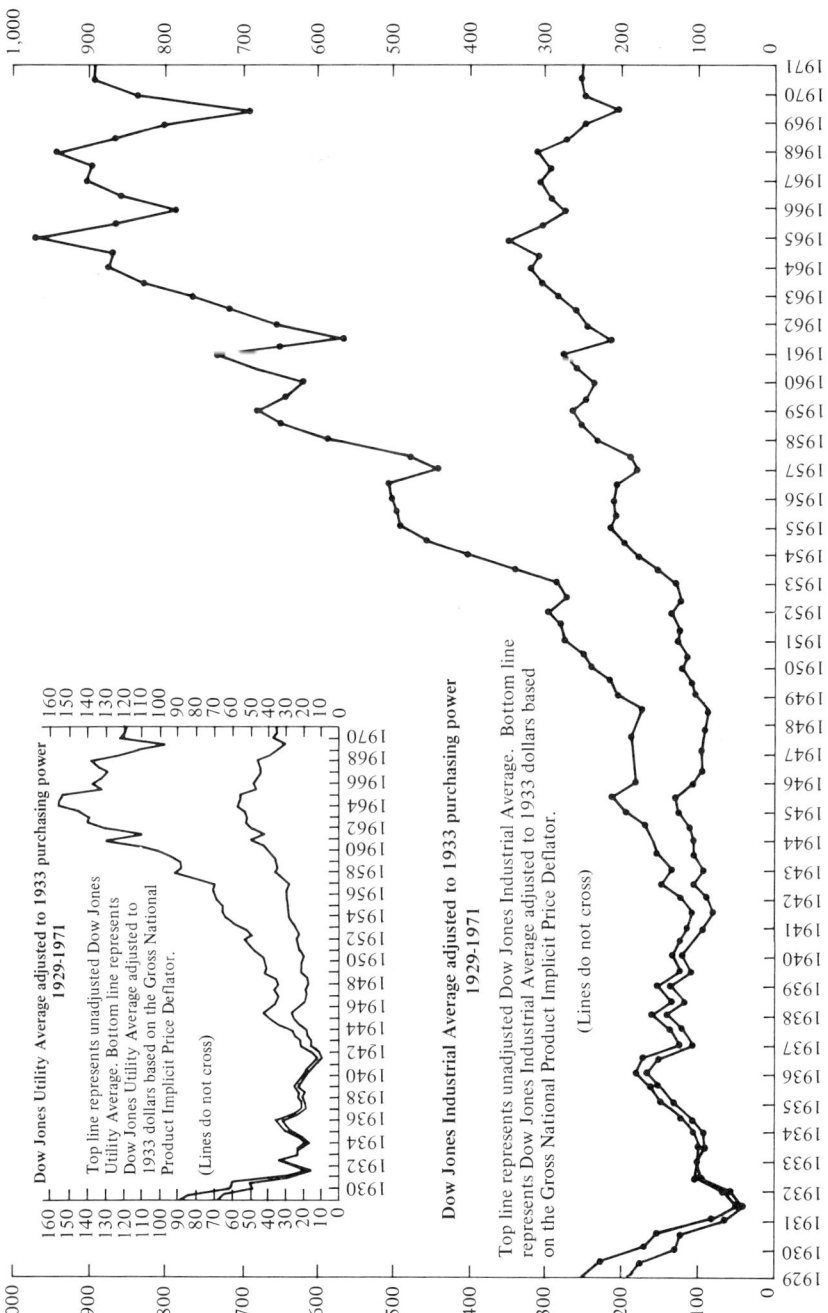

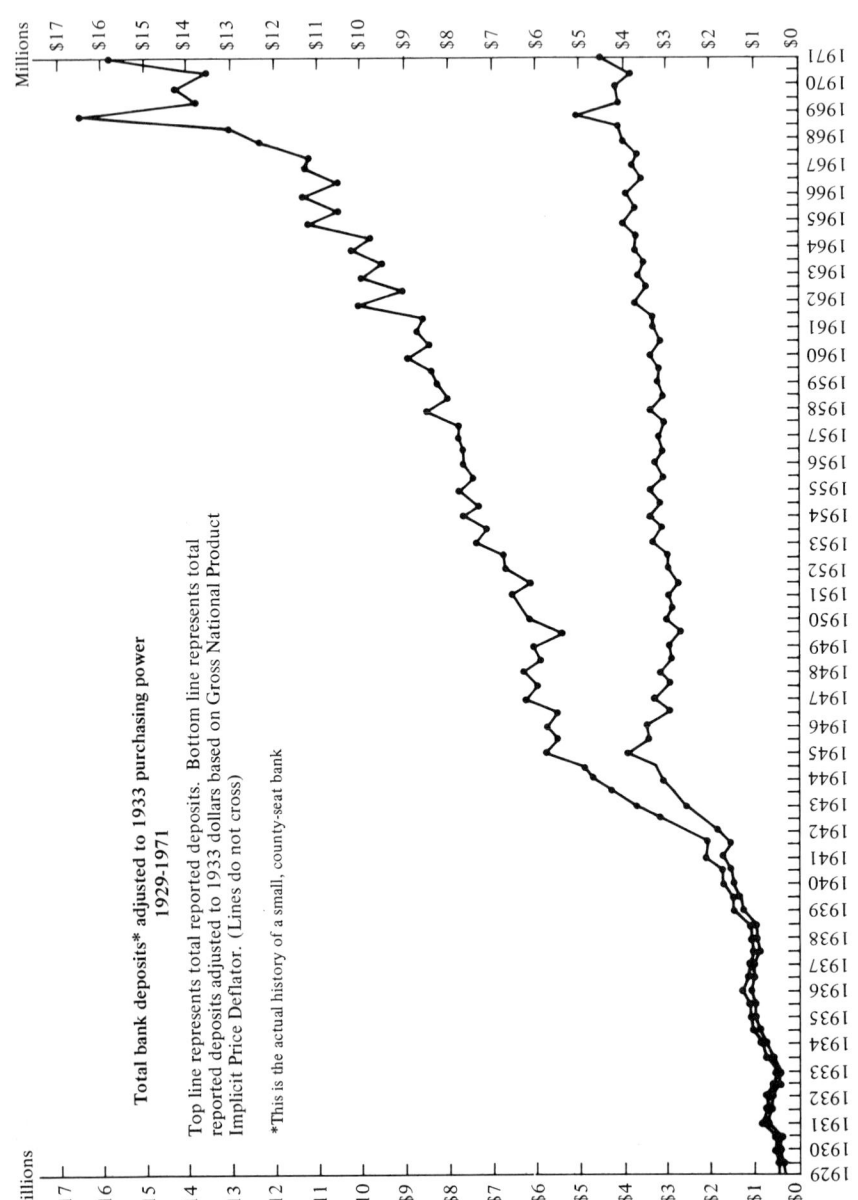

Total bank deposits* adjusted to 1933 purchasing power
1929-1971

Top line represents total reported deposits. Bottom line represents total reported deposits adjusted to 1933 dollars based on Gross National Product Implicit Price Deflator. (Lines do not cross)

*This is the actual history of a small, county-seat bank

Yields on Highest-grade Corporate Bonds (latest data plotted November estimated).

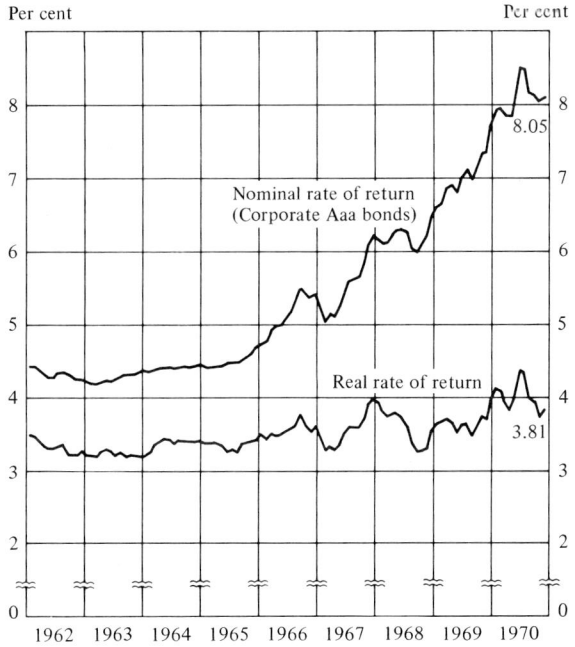

Of course, the only satisfactory solution to monetary inflation is the working of the free market, without interference by government, but in the meantime, since we do not have such a market but have a great deal of interference and the government has tried many panaceas, including wage-price controls, the knowledge of our present problems and an attempt to bring some truth into financial reports (for our management and others who are interested) becomes more and more highly desirable.

PURPOSE OF ACCOUNTING

It seems reasonable to state that the first and basic reason for accounting is to ascertain useful information for the management concerning the business and its operation, and that such information being available for management is then also available for shareholders, other security holders and the regulatory bodies—tax authorities included.

DEBT EXISTS UNTIL PAID

In our financial statements for 1969, 1970 and 1971, we have followed Accounting Principles Board Statement No. 3, "Financial Statements Restated for General Price-Level Changes," with the exception of its recommendations concerning accounting for price level gains or losses on bonds and preferred stock.

We want to inform ourselves but we do not want to fool ourselves.

There are transactions which have occurred in the past, there are transactions currently occurring and there are transactions which will occur in the future. They must each be treated differently when reflecting the effects of monetary inflation.

We can approximate through the use of indices what has happened to the purchasing power of the dollar in the past and currently but we cannot look into a crystal ball and determine what the purchasing power will be when our bonds mature or at the time of future operations of the sinking funds on either our bonds or preferred stock.

In Column A of the financial statements, in accordance with generally accepted accounting principles, past transactions have been reflected in terms of the dollars which were current in the year in which the transaction occurred—historical dollars of the year in which they were expended. *These dollars of 1940, 1960, or whatever year you wish to select, are unlike (regardless of their name) in terms of purchasing power and cannot produce a meaningful result when combined.*

Transactions occurring in 1971 are also stated in terms of historical dollars in Column A but monetary inflation increased even during the year's time. In Column B we have converted these historical dollars of 1971 and all prior years on an annual basis to the purchasing power of the dollar at the end of the year, *thus reaching a common denominator for adding and subtracting likes instead of unlikes.* (If the rate of monetary inflation continues to increase, the time may come when even a weekly conversion is too long or is inaccurate or meaningless.)

As the presently least imperfect and most representative index to describe this variance, we have chosen the Gross National Product Implicit Price Deflator and have used it to convert dollars to a common denominator. Actually, the GNP

Implicit Price Deflator and the Consumer Price Index have not varied greatly over the years (see chart on page 581). For a number of years and until 1964 we used a specific index made for the telephone industry and our Corporation by Earl Carter, a Registered Professional Engineer. However, it became obvious that there was not a sufficient variation between the results of that index and the GNP Implicit Price Deflator to be worth the expense of making a specific index.

Nothing happens to debt until it ceases to exist. It is neither necessary nor meaningful to attempt annually to reflect the effects of changes in purchasing power on the bonds and preferred stock (except for current sinking funds). This is where we part with Accounting Principles Board Statement No. 3 which states that an estimate should be made in the financial statements of what is happening to the debt during its lifetime. Accounting that gets away from current facts and gets into future speculation is not meaningful. *It is not a report of the facts.*

Bonds, i.e., debt, continue until the debt is retired, paid off and ceases to exist. Then, and only then, will we know what the result is in terms of purchasing power gained or lost. In the meantime, even if we change creditors, so long as we owe the same amount of dollars, from the Corporation's point of view nothing has changed in the way of a monetary obligation and the risk is still there.

All of our First Mortgage Bonds, with the exception of a portion of Series 8, have been privately placed with (sold to) institutional investors. Series 1–7 and 9 of the Bonds and the 1967 Series of our Preferred Stock are subject to a sinking fund which retires a fixed amount of securities each year. The first four series of our Preferred Stock and Series 8 of our Bonds are also subject to a fixed dollar sinking fund but the number and value of those bonds or stocks retired is determined by tender offers. *We have reported the effects of money inflation on the bonds and preferred stock which have been retired through the sinking fund because these are changes which have occurred and which can be determined.*

REFUNDING

There seems to be little doubt that monetary inflation will continue. However, we cannot predict its pace and some prominent people differ with us as to the rate of increase. As investors become more aware of the risks of monetary inflation and add an amount for that risk to the return they insist upon receiving for the use of their capital, interest rates (which are made up of originary interest—value for time-preference—credit risk and purchasing power risk) logically will increase.

As we studied our financial condition and the outlook for the future we became convinced that it would be in the best interest of the Corporation and its customers to refund its Series 1–5 First Mortgage Bonds at this time. We thus pay a premium of the difference in interest between now and the maturity dates of those bonds, but we buy for ourselves relief from the necessity of having to go into the market place for refunding purposes in 1977, 1984 and 1986 when interest rates may be much higher than they are now and/or when money may not be available, or may be available only from the government under terms disadvantageous to both the shareholders and customers. It gives us 19 years before any refunding will be necessary. We hope whoever is determining the fiscal policy of the Corporation in the years ahead will, in the interest of survival, apply the maximum allowable amount of earnings to actual reduction of debt.

We have before the Public Service Commission of Indiana a petition to approve the sale of our Series 10 First Mortgage Bonds to John Hancock Mutual Life Insurance Company in the amount of $4,875,000 at 7¾% due in 2008. This issue would refund Series 1–5 plus giving us $1.5 million of new money. There will be a 1% sinking fund starting in 1975 and we have the option of doubling or tripling that sinking fund in any year beginning in 1978.

* * *

INDIANA TELEPHONE CORPORATION
STATEMENT OF INCOME

	Column A historical cost		Column B historical cost restated for changes in purchasing power of dollar	
	1971	1970	1971	1970
OPERATING REVENUES:				
Local service	$ 5,744,356	$5,384,154	$ 5,788,990	$ 5,695,270
Toll service	4,852,156	4,350,496	4,889,858	4,601,883
Miscellaneous	304,522	234,979	306,888	248,557
Total operating revenues	10,901,034	9,969,629	10,985,736	10,545,710
OPERATING EXPENSES:				
Depreciation provision, Note 2	1,943,551	1,541,560	2,497,078	2,026,211
Maintenance	1,486,495	1,427,487	1,505,457	1,523,311
Traffic	1,226,906	1,157,565	1,237,139	1,224,453
Commercial	511,661	449,104	515,637	475,054
General and administrative	1,055,318	1,170,198	1,068,682	1,278,407
State, local and miscellaneous Federal taxes	912,601	648,996	919,692	686,497
Federal income taxes, Note 2				
Currently payable	1,132,500	1,127,087	1,141,300	1,192,215
Deferred until future years	315,800	295,000	318,254	312,047
Deferred investment tax credit (net)	9,708	(14,997)	3,262	(21,018)
Total operating expenses	8,594,540	7,802,000	9,206,501	8,697,177
OPERATING INCOME	2,306,494	2,167,629	1,779,235	1,848,533

Statement of Income (continued)

INCOME DEDUCTIONS:				
Interest on funded debt ..	651,195	659,567	656,255	697,679
Other deductions	36,828	21,355	40,229	24,583
Interest charged to construction (credit) ...	(63,905)	(30,442)	(64,402)	(32,201)
Other income (credit) ...	(95,974)	(98,759)	(96,720)	(104,466)
Gain from retirement of long-term debt through operation of sinking fund (credit)	(15,192)	(15,865)	(15,310)	(16,781)
Price level gain from retirement of long-term debt (credit), Note 1 ..	—	—	(61,137)	(55,175)
Gain from retirement of preferred stock through operation of sinking fund (credit), Note 1	(5,055)	(5,515)	(5,094)	(5,834)
Price level gain from retirement of preferred stock (credit), Note 1 ..	—	—	(12,908)	(12,029)
Price level loss from other monetary items	—	—	87,508	118,125
Total income deductions	507,897	530,341	528,421	613,901
NET INCOME, Note 1	1,798,597	1,637,288	1,250,814	1,234,632
Preferred stock dividends applicable to the period	96,209	97,541	96,957	103,178
EARNINGS APPLICABLE TO COMMON STOCK .. $	1,702,388	$1,539,747	$ 1,153,857	$ 1,131,454
EARNINGS PER COMMON SHARE .... $	3.49	$ 3.16	$ 2.37	$ 2.32
BOOK VALUE PER SHARE .... $	21.45	$ 18.29	$ 20.19	$ 18.14
Stations in service at end of year	75,015	72,569	75,015	72,569

The accompanying notes are an integral part of this statement [only Notes 1 and 2 reproduced].

INDIANA TELEPHONE CORPORATION
STATEMENT OF ASSETS—DECEMBER 31, 1971

	Column A historical cost	Column B historical cost restated for changes in purchasing power of dollar
Telephone plant, at original cost, Note 1:		
In service	$32,681,923	$41,791,787
Less—Accumulated depreciation	10,598,883	14,354,244
	22,083,040	27,437,543
Plant under construction	1,568,243	1,580,428
	23,651,283	29,017,971
Working capital:		
Current assets—		
Cash	679,475	679,475
Temporary cash investments accumulated for construction—at cost, which approximates market	3,074,351	3,074,351
Accounts receivable, less reserve	1,220,555	1,220,555
Materials and supplies	531,855	536,583
Prepayments	71,059	71,611
	5,577,295	5,582,575
Current liabilities—		
Sinking fund obligations	162,000	162,000
Accounts payable	635,552	635,552
Advance billings	315,647	315,647
Dividends payable	23,886	23,886
Federal income taxes, Note 2	242,393	242,393
Other accrued taxes	600,190	600,190
Other current liabilities	713,455	713,455
	2,693,123	2,693,123
Net working capital	2,884,172	2,889,452
Other:		
Debt expense being amortized	201,810	260,266
Other deferred charges	49,616	57,566
Deferred Federal income taxes, Note 2	(1,273,254)	(1,390,176)
Unamortized investment tax credit being amortized over the useful lives of related property	(391,778)	(472,321)
	(1,413,606)	(1,544,665)
Total investment in telephone business	$25,121,849	$30,362,758

The accompanying notes are an integral part of this statement [only Notes 1 and 2 reproduced].

INDIANA TELEPHONE CORPORATION
STATEMENT OF CAPITAL—DECEMBER 31, 1971

	Column A historical cost		Column B historical cost restated for changes in purchasing power of dollar	
	Amount	Ratio	Amount	Ratio
First mortgage sinking fund bonds:				
Series 1, 3% due June 1, 1977 ...... $	770,000		$ 770,000	
Series 2, 3⅜% due June 1, 1977	390,000		390,000	
Series 3, 3⅞% due June 1, 1977	410,000		410,000	
Series 4, 3¾% due June 1, 1984	935,000		935,000	
Series 5, 4¼% due September 1, 1986	870,000		870,000	
Series 6, 5⅜% due September 1, 1991	1,840,000		1,840,000	
Series 7, 4¾% due May 1, 1994	1,995,000		1,995,000	
Series 8, 4¾% due July 1, 2005	2,910,000		2,910,000	
Series 9, 6½% due October 1, 2007 .	2,940,000		2,940,000	
Less—Current sinking funds	(142,000)		(142,000)	
Total first mortgage sinking fund bonds	12,918,000	51%	12,918,000	43%
Preferred stock (no maturity):				
Cumulative, sinking fund, par value $100 per share, 30,000 shares authorized of which 10,000 are unissued:				
1950 Series 4.80%	240,000		240,000	
1951 Series 4.80%	242,900		242,900	
1954 Series 5¼%	333,400		333,400	
1956 Series 5%	256,900		256,900	
1967 Series 6⅛%	686,000		686,000	
Less—Current sinking funds	(20,000)		(20,000)	
Total preferred stock	1,739,200	7%	1,739,200	6%
Common shareholders' interest:				
Common stock, no par value, authorized 500,000 shares, issued 492,086 shares	4,251,785		6,474,592	
Retained earnings	6,295,365		3,500,069	
	10,547,150		9,974,661	
Less—Treasury stock, 4,336 shares, at cost	(5,192)		(7,882)	
Stock discount and expense	(77,309)		(121,103)	
Total common shareholders' interest	10,464,649	42%	9,845,676	32%
Unrealized effects of price level changes, Note 1	—	—	5,859,882	19%
Total investment in telephone business ..	$25,121,849	100%	$30,362,758	100%

The accompanying notes are an integral part of this statement [only Notes 1 and 2 reproduced].

INDIANA TELEPHONE CORPORATION
STATEMENT OF CHANGES IN FINANCIAL POSITION

	1971	1970
Funds were provided by:		
Operations—		
Net income per column A	$1,798,597	$1,637,288
Items which did not require current expenditure of funds—		
Depreciation—Charged to income	1,943,551	1,541,560
Charged to clearing accounts	41,558	52,665
Deferred Federal income taxes	315,800	295,000
Investment tax credit (net)	9,708	(14,997)
Interest charged to construction	(63,905)	(30,442)
Amortization of deferred charges	—	75,849
Net salvage on plant retirements	56,514	139,045
Miscellaneous, net	9,162	(15,505)
	4,110,985	3,680,463
Funds were expended for:		
Gross additions to telephone plant	3,411,941	3,315,190
Cash dividends—Common stock	182,906	182,906
—Preferred stock	72,001	97,197
Redemption of bonds and preferred stock	182,000	182,200
	3,848,848	3,777,493
Increase (decrease) in working capital	$ 262,137	$ (97,030)
Increase (decrease) in working capital represented by changes in:		
Cash and temporary cash investments	$ 938,143	$(706,557)
Accounts receivable, less reserve	(47,043)	32,393
Accounts payable and advance billings	(326,056)	35,043
Dividends payable	85,510	61,647
Accrued taxes	(87,290)	598,058
Other current liabilities	(344,822)	(148,366)
Other	43,695	30,752
Increase (decrease) in working capital	$ 262,137	$ (97,030)

The accompanying notes are an integral part of this statement [only Notes 1 and 2 reproduced].

INDIANA TELEPHONE CORPORATION
STATEMENT OF RETAINED EARNINGS FOR THE YEAR 1971

	Column A historical cost	Column B historical cost restated for changes in purchasing power of dollar
Balance, December 31, 1970	$4,751,675	$2,506,142
Net income	1,798,597	1,250,814
	6,550,272	3,756,956
Deduct:		
Cash dividends declared—		
Common stock, annual rate—$.50 per share ..	182,906	184,327
Preferred stock	72,001	72,560
	254,907	256,887
Balance, December 31, 1971	$6,295,365	$3,500,069

The accompanying notes are an integral part of this statement [only Notes 1 and 2 reproduced].

NOTES TO FINANCIAL STATEMENTS

1. Explanation of Financial Statements

In the accompanying financial statements, costs measured by the dollars disbursed at the time of the expenditure are shown in "Column A—Historical Cost." In "Column B—Historical Cost Restated For Changes in Purchasing Power of Dollar" (where the amounts in A and B differ), these dollars of cost have been restated in terms of the price level at December 31, 1971, as measured by the Gross National Product Implicit Price Deflator. Since 1954, the Corporation has presented supplemental financial information recognizing the effect of the change in the purchasing power of the dollar relating to telephone plant and depreciation expense in the annual report to shareholders.

In computing the amounts set forth in Column B of the accompanying financial statements, the Corporation has followed the methods set forth in Statement No. 3 released in June, 1969, by the Accounting Principles Board of the American Institute of Certified Public Accountants, except that, contrary to Statement No. 3, the effects of price level changes on long-term debt and preferred stock have been reflected *as income in the year in which the debt and preferred stock are retired (as required by the specific instruments under which they were issued) and not refinanced.* The Accounting Principles Board has tentatively taken the position that all such amounts should be taken into income in the year of price level change. *In the opinion of the Corporation's management and of its independent public accountants, such tentative viewpoint of the Accounting Principles Board does not result in a proper determination of income for the period.* "Unrealized Effects of Price Level Changes" recognizes the excess of adjustments on the Statement of Assets over the adjustments of Common Stock and Retained Earnings.

Dollars are a means of expressing purchasing power at the time of their use. *Conversion or restatement of dollars of differing purchasing power to the purchasing power of the dollar at the date of conversion results in all the dollars being treated as mathematical likes for the purpose of significant data.* The resulting financial statements recognize the change in price levels between the periods of expenditure of funds and the periods of use of property. *Accordingly, the earnings, results of operations, assets and other data available for use by management and other readers of financial statements provide important information and comparisons not otherwise available.*

No one would attempt to add, subtract, multiply, or divide marks, dollars and pounds. The failure to change the title of the monetary unit may be partially responsible for this violation of mathematical principle. This conceals the fact that mathematical unlikes are being used and therefore unfortunate results have been produced by generally accepted accounting methods.

2. Recovery of Capital and Return on Capital

Under the law of Indiana, the Corporation is entitled to recover the fair value of its property used and useful in public service by accruing depreciation based on the "fair value" thereof and is entitled to earn a fair return on such "fair value." The amount shown in Column B for telephone plant approximates the fair value of the property as determined based on the principles followed by the Public Service Commission of Indiana in an order dated September 1, 1967, authorizing the Corporation to increase its subscriber rates.

In the accompanying financial statements, Column A includes depreciation expense based on historical cost and Column B includes depreciation expense, as well as other expenses, on the basis of historical cost repriced in current dollars to reflect the changes in the purchasing power of the dollar. Also, the annual reports to the Indiana Commission are in the same basic form shown herein.

It must be kept in mind that this determination of depreciation expense is a year-to-year estimate and there are involved the questions of obsolescence, foresight, and judgment giving due consideration to maintenance but the regulatory process does not adjust even to this accurately.

If use of property, obsolescence and current denominators (in the case of monetary inflation) are used accurately by way of keeping the allowable expense of depreciation current and rates sufficient to return it along with a fair return, and the proceeds are immediately invested in property used and useful in the public service, there more likely will be a real return of capital and a fair return thereon. However, if monetary inflation continues, as it usually does, purchasing power of capital is unlikely ever to be truly returned. *It must be observed there is a substantial lag in the regulatory process. In rate making there is no guarantee of recovery of capital or of an adequate rate of return to the Corporation. This is an added risk which should be considered in estimating a fair return.*

Since the present Internal Revenue Code does not recognize the costs measured in current dollars, they are not deductible for computing Federal income tax payments, and the Corporation in fact pays taxes on alleged earnings which do not exist in true purchasing power. If they were deductible, as they should be, reductions in Federal income taxes as shown in Column B of $266,000 in 1971 and $252,000 in 1970 would result. By requiring the use of the Uniform System of Accounts for utility accounting and by virtue of the Internal Revenue Code, the Government has condemned and confiscated during the last 7 years over $1 million (in terms of the dollars of the years in which they were paid) of the assets of this Corporation through taxation of overstated earnings. This is true to a greater or lesser extent in each case where we have been able to ascertain the facts. We do not understand why this is currently concealed by management and accountants—to their detriment.

For book and financial reporting purposes, the Corporation provides for depreciation on a straight-line basis over the average service lives of the various classes of depreciable plant. In 1971, the overall rate was 6.3%. For Federal income tax purposes, beginning in 1967, an accelerated depreciation method is used and a provision is made in the Statement of Income for the taxes deferred as a result thereof.

AUDITORS' REPORT

To the Shareholders of Indiana Telephone Corporation:

We have examined the statements of assets and capital of INDIANA TELEPHONE CORPORATION (an Indiana corporation) as of December 31, 1971, and the related statements of income, retained earnings, and changes in financial position for the year then ended. Our examination was made in accordance with generally accepted auditing standards and accordingly included such tests of the accounting records and such other auditing procedures as we considered necessary in the circumstances. We have previously examined and reported on the financial statements for the preceding year.

In our opinion, the accompanying financial statements shown under Column A present fairly the financial position of the Corporation as of December 31, 1971, and the results of its operations and changes in financial position for the year then ended, in conformity with generally accepted accounting principles applied on a basis consistent with that of the preceding year.

In our opinion, however, the accompanying financial statements shown under Column B more fairly present the financial position of the Corporation as of December 31, 1971, and the results of its operations for the year then ended, as recognition has been given to changes in the purchasing power of the dollar, as explained in Note 1.

ARTHUR ANDERSEN & CO.
Indianapolis, Indiana,
March 1, 1972.

C. NEED FOR A REEVALUATION OF ACCOUNTING "AUTHORITY"

WILLIAM T. BAXTER

WILLIAM T. BAXTER (1906–   ), B.Com. 29 Edinburgh; CA (Scotland). Currently professor of accounting, London School of Economics and Political Science. Major publications: *The House of Hancock: Business in Boston, 1724–75* (1945), *Studies in Accounting* (edited readings, 1950), *Studies in Accounting Theory* (edited readings, with Davidson, 1962), *Depreciation* (1971). Frequent contributor to *The Accountant*, *The Accountant's Magazine*, *Accountancy*, and other journals.

Was lecturer, 1934–36, in the University of Edinburgh and professor, 1936–47, in the University of Cape Town, prior to occupying the first full-time British chair in accounting, 1947.

RECOMMENDATIONS ON ACCOUNTING THEORY

W. T. BAXTER

I. THE NEED FOR A REVIEW

Various societies of accountants have now for some years been issuing official statements on our profession's problems. What I have mainly in mind are of course the "recommendations" and "bulletins" published by the Institute of Chartered Accountants in England and Wales, and by the American Institute of Certified Public Accountants. These started to come out in quantity soon after

source: From *Studies in Accounting Theory*, edited by W. T. Baxter and Sidney Davidson (London: Sweet & Maxwell Limited [U.S. distributors: Richard D. Irwin, Inc., Homewood, Ill.], 1962). Reprinted here by permission of Sweet & Maxwell Limited, London. The present version, unchanged from the Baxter-Davidson book, is based on an article originally published in *The Accountant* of October 10, 1953, and reproduced by permission.

Hitler's War, and they now add up to a substantial volume covering a long list of subjects. Their influence on accounting and auditing is great, and is likely to become greater. So some review of this development seems not out of place.

Almost every accountant must find the recommendations exceedingly useful in his day-to-day work. They provide him with a code of rules on all sorts of difficult points (notably where the law leaves awkward gaps); and they save time, thought, and worry. They have also served the general public well by raising the quality of published statements.

In view of these benefits, it may seem churlish, and academic in the worst sense, to attack the recommendations. Nevertheless I shall try to argue that at least in one aspect (which could be changed) they are doing a great disservice. And many other accountants—even if they do not share my feeling that the recommendations have already gone too far—may perhaps like to discuss how much further the process of recommending can with propriety go. Where is the limit? Are we to look forward to the day when every detail of our work has been dealt with? Should our goal be—as high authority has hinted apropos the question of price levels—super-recommendations by a massed assembly representing *all* the professional bodies?

Another reason for airing the matter is this. Some accounting societies have so far made few or no recommendations. Their members may well have some feeling that the omission betokens lack of zeal and public spirit. They should recognize that a policy of official silence has in fact much in its favour. However, this most emphatically does *not* mean that inertia should be lightly excused, or that accounting societies need take no part in furthering knowledge. On the contrary, they should do everything in their power to encourage education, debate and research. For instance, they could give great help by setting up much-needed scholarships (perhaps to be awarded on the results of the professional examinations) to enable their brilliant young men to study further.

II. SCOPE OF THE REVIEW

A recommendation tends to contain three types of ingredient:
1. A description of the given problem;
2. A reasoned discussion, often based on fundamentals, on how best to solve the problem; and
3. The recommended solution.

It is mainly (2) that seems objectionable. For here the accounting society weighs intellectual principles, analyses the *pros* and *cons* of the alternative arguments, and decides that one view is better than the others; in short, here authority tells us what is true. Is it wise for any group of men to say what is "true" or "right" in matters of theory?

By "theory" I mean the attempt to explain, in terms of fundamentals, what accounting is and what it tries to do; I thus assume that accounting is a branch of knowledge, like law or physics, with basic principles that are worth exploring. (One might use phrases like "scientific laws" instead of "principles" or "theory," but that would suggest work among test-tubes. Other phrases, employing "abstract knowledge" or "scholarly learning," might sound a bit pompous. On the whole, "theory" seems the neatest word to cover what we have in mind.)

The distinction between (2) and (3) can best be seen by contrasting our recommendations with a set of *working rules*, for instance the Companies Act or the Football Association's rules of play. Such rules are a framework designed to make something run smoothly; unlike the recommendations, they consist only of (3), and do not start off with a discursion into the philosophy of, say, companies or football. The test of a good law is that the institution works well; it is not educational but practical.

Consider, for instance, the problem of how assets should be dealt with in a balance-sheet. When a writer on accounting tries to show us the best method, he probably builds up his case by discussing and judging various theories. But when a law says that company accounts must show the values in such-and-such ways, it does not analyse all the theories and then tell us which satisfies logic. It merely issues orders. It tells us *what*, and perhaps *how*, but not *why*. So we can obey this kind of law without feeling that we are being forced to accept a particular theory, and that our freedom of thought is being lessened. Besides, few citizens of a lively democracy grow up believing that everything in their laws is sensible; we hear much criticism of laws, and we accept that we have the right—indeed the duty—to try to repeal or reform bad laws.

Of course, even the answers to *what* and *how* can be influenced by theory. Normally the makers of a law must have some theory in mind when they draft it. A legislature may even be forced to choose between scientific theories, *e.g.*, public health law assumes that the views of Pasteur and Fleming are right. But the choice is made merely so that hopeful lines of development can be tried without delay, and should not imply that the official seal of approval has been put on any theory; if the experiment fails, it can be promptly scrapped without loss of face. Legislators who went further—to the point of explicity endorsing a theory—would exceed their function, and would indeed be threatening our freedom of thought. Similarly, if an Act of Parliament includes definitions, these are not meant as revelations of final knowledge, but only as tools for making effective the particular set of rules; a judge may even hold that the definitions in one Act do not apply in the context of another Act on a dissimilar subject.

An obvious corollary seems to follow. When rules are prescribed for published accounting statements, they should not only avoid *why*, but should be chary about *how*. The stress should be on *what*. Authority can set minimum standards of disclosure without dragging in much theory; if it prescribes methods—particularly in the context of valuation—it must inevitably choose between theories. A terse list of minimum requirements, such as is given in the British Companies Act, works well and leaves honest men tolerably free to think and experiment. It provides a floor, not a ceiling.

Our views on recommendations may thus depend on whether we look on them as law or research; we may indeed regard a rule in (3) as useful, and yet object to its preamble in (2). In many cases, the tenor of the recommendations suggests that contributions to both theory and law are the aim. Whatever the intentions of their framers, there can be little doubt that they have been accepted by wide audiences as official and definitive pronouncements on theory.

We shall thus restrict the scope of our review to the parts of recommendations that pronounce on theory, or imply adoption of a theory, and shall say little about the other parts that proffer rules for minimum action on technical problems. Likewise we are not concerned with recommendations that adopt a different pattern, or deal with non-technical problems. They may for instance be concerned instead with *public policy*. A professional body sometimes advises its members to follow a common policy on questions that have little to do with the intellectual content of its members' work. For instance, it may make statements on "professional ethics," fees, registration by the state, and so forth. Such types of advice should be judged by standards quite different from those useful in our present review. If, for example, a body of architects or lawyers advises its members to charge a uniform scale of fees, or pay its assistants a standard wage, we judge the issue in the light of our views on the benefits or otherwise of economic monopoly; if it commends integrity to its members, perhaps we merely wonder whether it is not preaching to the converted in most cases, and wasting its breath in the rest.

Again, a recommendation may deal with *definitions* and *uniform practice*. To some extent these can be handled in ways that avoid theory—in which case they too fall outside our discussion. But such matters infringe on theory more often than might be supposed; and so we must give a little space to them.

One other matter should be made clear. Our review will make its point better if it omits all discussion of whether individual recommendations on theory have in fact been right or wrong. What is said here is thus not meant as criticism of any recommendation's content. Indeed, we may for our present purpose agree that every word in every recommendation seems entirely true; and yet we may think that a policy of making recommendations on theory will, in the long run, be disastrous.

III. ORIGINS OF RECOMMENDATIONS

I should like to admit that, when official statements on accounting principles were first published, I was enthusiastic about them. My doubts have arisen since, on seeing how the new venture has developed.

Looking back, one remembers certain features in early statements that have unfortunately not usually been copied since. Consider the *Statement on Accounting Principles* of 1938. It was published by the American Institute, to whose members it was commended in a foreword; but it bore the names of three distinguished authors—Messrs. Sanders, Hatfield and Moore—who had been formed into an independent committee to do this bit of writing (and who were not even members of the Institute). Under such an arrangement, the Institute was plainly doing its duty to foster discussion, and yet was itself not taking sides. That kind of procedure goes far to disarm criticism.

Since this venture, the trend has been for the statements to be drafted by committees much more closely linked with the sponsoring body, and for the latter to back the conclusions in a much firmer way. The American Institute, for instance, set up its own Committee on Accounting Procedure to issue research bulletins. Bulletin No. 1 explained the aims and methods. It stressed the growth of corporate organisation, and therefore the social importance of good accounts; and it noted that there "has been a demand for a larger degree of uniformity in accounting." The committee stated that its rules were not intended to have retroactive effect; also they may be subject to exception, but "the burden of proof is upon the accountant clearly to bring out the exceptional procedure and the circumstances which render it necessary."

This has perhaps a somewhat mandatory ring. But the American bulletins have in fact used two safeguards that make their tenor less authoritarian: the members of the drafting committee are named in recommendations, and any member who disagrees with the majority is entitled to have the fact of his dissent recorded in the document. At least one American committee has had the courage to say bluntly that an earlier pronouncement by itself now seems wrong.[1]

The Institute of Chartered Accountants in England and Wales announced its first recommendation as follows:

> The Council has requested the Taxation and Financial Relations Committee to consider and make recommendations to it on certain aspects of the accounts of companies and it is proposed from time to time to publish approved recommendations for the information of members. It is, of course, a matter for each individual member to consider his responsibility in regard to accounts presented by directors, but it is hoped that the recommendations to be made will be helpful to members in advising directors as to what is regarded as the best practice.[2]

These words are as modest and cautious as anyone could wish. They show how undogmatic the original plan was; and they suggest that the Council did not foresee the eventual scope of the recommendations, or the deference with which they would be treated.

IV. THE CASE FOR RECOMMENDATIONS

It would be ungenerous not to set down at length the good that has been done by the recommendations. Their benefits have obviously been great.

Recommendations have been so widely accepted that they have in fact acted very like a supplement to the law. What we may call extra-parliamentary control can often eke out statutes in a useful manner, particularly at the experimental stage; the rules of a stock exchange are another example of such control. In England, the early recommendations did much to prepare the way for the 1948 Companies Act, and indeed have in fact been absorbed into that Act. In America, the interplay between the Institute's bulletins and the S.E.C. regulations clearly is close; and the absence of a counterpart to the Companies Act enhances the bulletins' value as a code of standards.

The recommendations may thus serve as private forerunners and reinforcements to the law. Their record in this work has on the whole been excellent—notably in procuring full, frank, and consistent accounts.[3] The auditor has special cause to be thankful for them; the task of persuading his clients to comply with

---

[1] *Accounting Problems Arising from Devaluation of Foreign Currencies*, Research Department, American Institute of Accountants (1949).

[2] *The Accountant*, December 12, 1942, p. 354.

[3] Some other writer may like to examine the question of what safeguards (if any) are needed if a private group is to make rules, almost with the force of law, that affect non-members. Already one company has felt impelled to try to stop publication of a statement (alleged to have been prepared without normal opportunities for hearing objectors) that seemed likely to damage the company's borrowing status: *Appalachian Power Company v. A.I.C.P.A.*, 268 Federal 2nd 844 (Court of Appeals for the Second Circuit).

high standards in published accounts is sometimes delicate, and the recommendations have greatly strengthened his hand. They have also aided the analyst by fostering uniformity.

Though the recommendations have been less successful in the realm of theory, they have yielded some benefits. As each recommendation is first suggested, amended, and then adopted, undoubtedly it gives rise for a time to discussion and interest. Again, many of us used to deplore the fact that our profession's leaders never could spare time to write about their work; whatever the faults of the new system, it does prompt these men to tell us a great deal about what they think, and what they regard as usual practice.

We thus have cause to feel grateful to the drafters of recommendations; and this review should on no account be construed as an attack on them. Obviously they have devoted much time and care to their task, and have been prompted by a high sense of public service. If harm should in the end come from their work, the blame should attach more to disciples who have accepted their teaching too eagerly, and have invested it with an *ex cathedra* quality that could not perhaps have been foreseen.

It is not unusual in human affairs for a thing to be started with the best intentions, and yet to develop aspects that threaten harm. My plea is that we should now review the good and bad alike, and see whether we cannot guide future growth in directions that are wholly good.

The recommendations' benefits are clear and present. Their ill results are hypothetical, and will show—if at all—in the future. Moreover these ill results are suggested by experience in other fields of study; and conceivably accounting is unlike these in nature and difficulty. If accounting differs from other subjects in its nature, then the arguments that follow may be weakened. But I see no reason to think that it is different.

V. THE CASE AGAINST RECOMMENDATIONS

The case against official recommendations on theory is threefold. First, men do not always become better at research when they work as a group. Second, if authority takes direct part in the pursuit of truth, it may hinder rather than help. Third—and most important—there are no sure signs by which truth can be recognised.

The first objection need not keep us long; admittedly it is not always a strong factor. To judge from experience in most fields of learning, men tend to do their best research when left to their own devices. There are many exceptions; a large team of chemists may be the quickest means of dealing with a laborious task, and a government committee may be admirable at sifting evidence and assessing opinion. In general, however, thinkers are apt to be hampered by close connection with a team or with a powerful institution. The link may curb initiative, or bring a need for diplomacy and compromise. The welfare of the institution may seem more important than truth; thus the authorities of the Church could not deal fairly with the ideas of Copernicus and Galileo because these ideas clashed with official pronouncements of the past.

The second objection is much weightier. It is an indirect way of saying that freedom is necessary for progress. "Freedom" here means the absence, not merely of crude tyranny, but also of benevolent authority that makes us respectful to some ideas and hostile to others. Man should be able to think freely and without bias, so that the stream of new ideas can flow strongly; and he should be able to discuss and experiment freely and without bias, so that all ideas can be criticised and tested with rigour. If authority intervenes—by joining in the quest itself or by giving its *imprimatur* to some favourite idea, let alone by making attacks on personal liberty—the chances of progress are lessened. Men cease to think so freely—whether from fear, or powerful preconceptions, or belief that others can do the job better; and therefore the stream of new ideas dries up. They cease to discuss and experiment so freely; and therefore criticism loses its edge, and ideas are not put to a stern test.

This train of reasoning leads to the third objection. How can we tell what is true? Even the objective tests of the laboratory are not final (and pronouncements on accounting must surely be based on discussion, and so be far from objective). Under strong criticism, many ideas soon prove false. Others satisfy all immediate tests, yet should be accepted as tentative only, for they, too, are likely to show flaws as the years go by. Even after an idea has survived triumphantly for centuries, some critic may shatter it, or else show it to be capable of improvement. Einstein was able both to generalise Newton's theory and to correct it for conditions that had not previously been considered. No human being —however distinguished—can certainly foretell which idea will become a casualty. As Bacon says: "Truth is the daughter, not of Authority, but of Time."

The root of the matter, surely, is man's fallibility. Only if we believe a statement to have divine inspiration can we treat it as beyond doubt.

It may be helpful to ask why learned bodies do not in general issue official solutions to questions puzzling their members. Why, for instance, does the Royal Society not organise a team of Fellows to solve this or that intractable problem of physics? All three objections suggested above are relevant to the answer. The Fellows may perhaps feel that they work better apart. Their training in science has made them sceptical, and more apt to test and attack than to defend ideas. They have learnt from the experience of centuries that their "laws" can never be regarded as final. If the Society gave official approval to theories, its members would probably soon be rent by a schism between an orthodox and a dissenting party; and sooner or later (the chances are) the Society would be proved wrong, and would be forced to utter an embarrassing recantation.

Similarly, official recommendations by an institute of engineers would have to be framed with some care. Assume, for instance, that it advised its members to build bridges in a uniform way, based on the best current knowledge. For a while, standards might well be raised. But research would in time point to better bridges; nonconformist bodies of engineers would be free to build these, while the orthodox would be denied the fruits of advancing science.

Exactly what do we mean by "authority" in this context? A wide sweep should be given to the word; it here includes all forces that can give weight to some ideas at the expense of others. Privilege is bad for ideas as for men; only if they can jostle one another in a democratic way is the best likely to reach the top.

Authority may thus rest (at one end of the scale) on prestige only, and (at the other) on power. Occasionally the brilliance of a single thinker can cause his views to be treated with deference. A close-knit school of able thinkers may well dominate opinion to an unhealthy point—even if they lack organisation and can impose no sanctions. The harm becomes vastly more formidable when the authority controls education, or can mould adult opinion. It reaches its worst when authority has total power. In its extreme forms, we are all agreed that it is evil—and that the evil persists whether or not the views that it promulgates happen to seem true or false.

Happily, we are here concerned with authority at its mildest and most benevolent. Nevertheless, we may wonder whether, in the realm of mental freedom, even a slight degree of control must not lead to harm.

VI. TRAINING AND INNOVATION

With our recommendations, the basis of authority is of course mainly the prestige of the bodies concerned. But this is of a high order. We all know in what respect such a body is held by the bulk of its members. Moreover, its drafting committee will include many of the profession's best-known men. It gives the recommendations its whole-hearted backing and much publicity. In consequence, the issue of a new recommendation is treated as a matter of great moment by the accounting Press; this attention is fitting, though one could wish that the notices were a shade less passive and fulsome.

The recommendations must therefore have a considerable influence on the thought of the mature accountant. On the immature mind—that of a young man in training—their impact must be deep. They are given conspicuous place in his textbooks and correspondence courses, and so play a large part in moulding his views when he is still impressionable and uncritical. They naturally appeal to the feebler type of teacher, who finds it easier to recite an official creed than to lead a brisk argument. Even before the days of recommendations, accounting textbooks and teachers preferred in general to state facts rather than explore theories. Their main concern was painstaking description of normal practice; scant space was accorded to the reasoning behind the practice, and next to nothing was said of controversy. This dull and sterile approach has now been made far more likely. If an official answer is available to a problem, why should a teacher burden his examination candidates with other views? Further, the body that gives the answers also controls the examination. A young man has thus good cause for minute and respectful study of its statements. And his question paper does not often include such items as: "Discuss Recommendation No. —. Set out the grounds for supposing that its reasoning is (a) correct, and then (b) fallacious; and give your own views on this point."

Thus the recommendations tend to rob our young men's education of its power to enrich and stimulate. On such a spare diet, they may perhaps still train well enough to master the techniques of today. But their minds will be less fit to solve the new problems of tomorrow; and such fitness is no bad test by which to judge an education.

Recommendations must also to some extent cramp the mature accountant's thought. They relieve him of responsibility for intellectual decision—a state that is comfortable, but hardly stimulating. They may hinder him if he wants to try out new ideas or make experiments. In America, one important experiment has already been stopped because it offended "accepted accounting principles" as set forth in a bulletin: the S.E.C. compelled the U.S. Steel Company to amend 1947 depreciation figures based on the current price level, and so prevented all further experiment in this field by companies under S.E.C. control.

Even where there is no legal prohibition, recommendations could endanger a thoughtful auditor if they were used as evidence in lawsuits. Consider for instance a case that hangs on questions of auditing theory—say, the valuation of stocks and wasting assets when price levels change. Suppose that a company follows the advice of an auditor who sincerely believes a recommendation to be wrong; that the company thereafter runs into financial trouble, and that it sues the auditor for negligence. In such a case, the determining test would probably be the standard of behaviour followed by good professional practice. Hostile counsel would treat the recommendations as powerful evidence, and could make the most damaging use of the auditor's deviation. The defence might have some difficulty in proving that many conscientious but inarticulate accountants still regard the issue as open to argument. A judge or jury might well be swayed decisively by the recommendations, and give a verdict against the auditor.

An analogy is tempting. Suppose that the medical profession's first dislike of antiseptic surgery had crystallised in a hostile recommendation; that one of Lister's patients had died; and that the deceased's relatives had brought a suit for negligence. What would have been the effect on surgery?

Such cases must inevitably crop up sooner or later. Where an auditor is faced with this risk, the temptation to play safe—by abandoning his independence of judgment—is very great. Yet a pliant attitude in such matters is scarcely compatible with the dignity of his profession.

VII. OTHER KINDS OF RECOMMENDATIONS

Section II suggested that there are some kinds of recommendations which may seem to avoid theory, but in fact are apt to be entangled with it. Let us consider these briefly:

a. *Definition.* If precise and uniform meanings can be given to our terms and figures, then doubtless we shall be able to exchange ideas with more ease and clarity. Also, accounting data will be more consistent. (The Royal Society *has* set up a standing committee to make recommendations on the symbols, signs and abbreviations used in scientific publications.)

Standard definitions are, however, not without their drawbacks. If speech is made rigid, it cannot evolve to meet new needs. There may be a clash between the ordinary and the technical use of a word. Both the American and the English Institutes have pointed out the ambiguities of "reserve" (which in everyday speech can mean something quite different from its sense in a balance-sheet), and have tried to restrict its meaning helpfully; yet even this restricted use may still bewilder rather than enlighten the public.

Further, words are seldom quite neutral in the battle between ideas. With "goodwill," for instance, the ordinary meaning stands out so strongly that it obtrudes when we are trying to unravel the technical concept, and thus colours our understanding of "goodwill" in accounts. Again, choice of a definition often demands a choice between ideas. For example, any definition of "depreciation" is almost sure to be tendentious.

Thus an official link between a word and an idea is likely to bias our minds. What is almost as bad, some definitions have an air of finality that checks inquiry, and leaves students with no exciting sense of being explorers in a great and unknown territory.

b. *Standard practice.* Uniformity in presentation of published data (minimum content and method of layout) has strong arguments in its favour—provided it neither cramps honest business nor begs ideas. If a choice between words or methods clearly is arbitrary and free from any pretence of research, it is not likely to damage future thinking or to act as a straitjacket; for example, whether traffic keeps to the left or right of the road is an arbitrary matter, and uniformity yields a gain in convenience, so no one regards a standard rule as an attack on freedom. Therefore, when we are attracted by uniformity, a good test is perhaps this: if a decision between possible terms or practices can be reached by tossing a coin or pulling words from a hat, then uniformity is unlikely to do harm.

However, it is one thing to say that such-and-such items must be shown and explained, and quite another to say how their size must be calculated. The size of the figures is a matter of valuation theory; and, as is shown by our hot debates on such matters as depreciation, income measurement, asset valuation, and the effects of changing price levels, this is certainly an area in which we are far from knowing where truth lies. Rules for standard practice should not prescribe valuation methods. Even rules on how items should be grouped in a balance-sheet may impinge on principle; thus, if they say that allowance for deferred tax must be shown in (or out of) the owners' capital group, they are in effect forcing us to swallow a particular view on the valuation of capital.

Perhaps "standard" should here mean "usual," *i.e.*, what is normal but not necessarily right. For convenience, the reader of published accounts should be able to rely on their compliance with standard practice—unless he is given clear warning to the contrary, and (where this would not mislead) a note of what standard practice would have shown. An accountant should always reserve his right to depart from the standard, on giving notice, if he thinks the standard does not fit the particular case, or the reader's current needs, or his own views on theory.

c. *Legal opinions.* Counsel's opinions, given at the request of an accounting society and sent out to its members, are not usually classed as "recommendations." To round off our review, however, we should ask ourselves how such statements fit into our reasoning.

The opinions do not seem so dangerous as recommendations on theory, on two grounds.

First, no wise man tries to be expert in everything; outside his own province, he can to some degree accept ideas from others without sapping his mental independence. *Second,* as we noted in Section II, the law does not pretend to state absolute principles. When a lawyer is trying to find what is "true" or "false," he is mainly concerned with the arbitrary—though no doubt exacting—task of interpreting words (especially those in statutes) according to the intentions of their users and the rules of his craft.

VIII. CONCLUSIONS

If the above arguments are sound, where do they lead us? Perhaps the recommendations that should be made on recommendations are:

a. Official statements on accounting cover a number of very different things, which are often hard to separate. They include:

Working rules, *e.g.*, for company reports.

Guidance on professional policy.
Definitions.
Suggestions for uniform accounting.
Legal opinions.
Abstract theory.

None of these is without its pitfalls. However, given due care and caution, the risks seem worth taking—except in the case of theory. Official quests for the abstract are apt to bear little fruit and to run into great hazards. No human being, however impressive his trappings, knows what the truth is.

b. Recommendations should not only confine themselves to rules for action, as contrasted with principles, but should stress this restriction in their scope. For instance, if a recommendation suggests a definition of "current assets," it might expressly disclaim any attempt to elucidate principles, and describe the rules as being based merely on convenience or custom.

c. The more concerned a statement is with theory, the stronger is the case for not treating it as an official recommendation. A group of distinguished accountants who have debated a subject, and who wish to help us by announcing their conclusions, would not have the least trouble in finding a publisher.

d. A recommended "standard practice" should be explained in terms of normal behaviour—something that the user of published accounts can take for granted if nothing to the contrary is said. The accountant, acting in good faith and with due warnings, should feel free—indeed obliged—to vary the practice when he deems it unsuitable. Final responsibility should still rest on the accountant's own judgment; where possible, the rule should be cast in the form of minimum standards, thus leaving room for improvement.

e. The objections to a recommendation become much less marked if it is described as the work of certain named persons. We all know that individuals can err; we all tend to look on institutions as infallible. Therefore recommendations should—following the American example—be signed by the men who approve the final draft.

f. A dissenting opinion at once adds a valuable extra dimension, making the recommendation far more useful as an aid to the mind. Therefore great pains should be taken to foster and express minority views.

To conclude. Recommendations by authority on matters of accounting theory may in the short run seem unmixed blessings. In the end, however, they will probably do harm. They are likely to yield little fresh knowledge; "the best test of truth is the power of the thought to get itself accepted in the competition of the market." [4] They are likely to weaken the education of accountants; the conversion of the subject into cut-and-dried rules, approved by authority and not to be lightly questioned, threatens to reduce its value as a subject of liberal education almost to *nil*. They are likely to narrow the scope for individual thought and judgment; and a group of men who resign their hard problems to others must eventually give up all claim to be a learned profession.

[4] Dissenting opinion of Judge Oliver Wendell Holmes in *Abrams* v. *United States*.

THE PUBLIC ACCOUNTANT AND THE PUBLIC INTEREST

EDWARD STAMP

Biography appears on page 552.

The recent proposals for the integration of the accountancy profession in the United Kingdom[1] have drawn attention to the fact that numerically, in relation to accountants employed in industry and Government, the importance of the accountant in public practice is diminishing. A similar trend is evident in North America and in Australasia, and elsewhere. Yet no one would deny that the function of the auditor, in lending credibility to financial statements, has been growing in importance, rapidly and steadily, over the last fifty years. With the growth of the large industrial corporation, entrepreneurs have been unable to supply the required finance from their own resources. This has led to the development of highly sophisticated securities markets in which corporations are able to obtain finance from national—and increasingly from international—communities. Ownership has become divorced from management, and one of the links between the two is the periodic reports on financial condition and progress which are made by managers and directors to shareholders. Such financial reports are relied upon heavily by investors, prospective investors, creditors, security analysts, Governments, and others. The role of the auditor, in lending credibility to these financial statements, is vital in establishing and maintaining confidence in the capital markets. Without such confidence the whole basis of our capitalist system, with its divorce of ownership from management in virtually all major enterprises, would be destroyed.

Thus the continuing importance of the auditor's role is not in dispute. It is a matter of public interest that he should discharge his functions in the most effective manner possible. It is not, however, the purpose of this article to examine auditors' techniques, which have, on the whole, kept pace with the growth in sophistication of the accounting information systems whose reliability they are designed to investigate. Rather, its purpose is to examine the relationships which exist between the auditor and his client company, the shareholders and directors thereof, and the public at large, and to suggest modifications which seem desirable if the public is to continue to have faith in the role of the auditor.

Before looking at these relationships, however, it is worth considering for a moment the manner in which the auditor "lends credibility to financial statements" and, in particular, the under-pinnings of financial accounting theory and practice upon which he bases his judgements.

It is generally conceded that it is the responsibility of management to prepare

SOURCE: From *Journal of Business Finance*, Vol. I, No. 1 (Spring, 1969), pp. 32–42. Reprinted by permission of *Journal of Business Finance*, Spring issue, © 1969, Mercury House Business Publications Ltd. and the author.

[1] See, for example, *A Scheme for the Development of the Accountancy Profession in Great Britain and Ireland*, published on 25th July, 1968 by The Institute of Chartered Accountants in England and Wales. The Institute estimates (para. 21) that 60–70% of its members now enter industry and commerce within three to four years of qualifying.

the financial statements which are submitted to shareholders and others.[2] The duty of the auditor is to make such examination of these statements, supporting schedules, and the books and records of the Company, and to obtain whatever other evidence he deems necessary. Having examined and evaluated this evidence, the auditor is then required to express his independent professional and expert opinion as to the truth and fairness of the financial statements. It is this opinion upon which shareholders and other readers of the statements rely when they use the Company's financial statements.

The wording of the standard form of audit report issued in the United States illustrates clearly the frame-work within which the auditor must form his opinion. The usual American report reads as follows[3]:

> We have examined the balance sheet of X Company as of June 30, 19___ and the related statement(s) of income and retained earnings for the year then ended. Our examination was made in accordance with generally accepted auditing standards, and accordingly included such tests of the accounting records and such other auditing procedures as we considered necessary in the circumstances.
>
> In our opinion, the accompanying balance sheet and statement(s) of income and retained earnings present fairly the financial position of X Company at June 30, 19___, and the results of its operations for the year then ended, in conformity with generally accepted accounting principles applied on a basis consistent with that of the preceding year.

The standard form of Canadian report is virtually identical. British, Australian, and New Zealand reports differ in several respects, partly as a result of the specific requirements of the Companies Acts (which govern their wording to some degree). In particular the British report states that the accounts give a "true and fair view of the state of the Company's affairs" and of its profits for the period under review.

Yet despite the differences in wording, the essential point remains. Whether it is made explicit, as in the American report, or whether it is implied, as in the British report, the auditor judges the fairness of his client's financial statements in relation to a corpus of "generally accepted accounting principles".[4]

This phrase is, unfortunately, deceptive. Many of these so-called "principles" are not principles at all but merely descriptions of current or, even worse, past practice; rules which in many cases are drawn up on an *ad hoc* basis to deal with the expediencies of a passing moment. Accounting principles are riddled with inconsistencies and illogicalities, and there are so many alternative "generally ac-

---

[2] In the United States the Securities and Exchange Commission has stated that 'the fundamental and primary responsibility for the accuracy of information filed with the Commission and disseminated among the investors rests upon management' (4 SEC 721 (1939)). The provisions of section 148 of the U.K. Companies Act 1948 cover the same essential point, although (as is usual in the U.K.) it is the directors upon whom the responsibility is explicitly laid.

[3] *Statements on Auditing Procedure No. 33* (New York, American Institute of Certified Public Accountants, 1963), p. 57.

[4] For a closely argued analysis of this proposition, leading to the conclusion that published financial statements do *not* present a 'true and fair view', see W. P. Birkett, 'True and Fair—the Law and Accounting', *The Australian Lawyer*, Vol. 7 (1968), pp. 97–115.

cepted" ways of dealing with most accounting problems that it is almost true to say that practically anything is "true and fair" to some accountant. What masquerades under the title "generally accepted accounting principles" is a state of chaos. Can any other words describe aptly the situation where, as Chambers pointed out in a recent article, there are over a million combinations of mutually exclusive rules each giving a true and fair view of a Company's state of affairs and its profits?[5] Many of these rules defy even common sense. Thus in writing their report[6] on the collapse of the large Australian Reid Murray Group the two Inspectors, B. L. Murray, Q.C. (now Solicitor-General of the State of Victoria), and B. J. Shaw, commented:

> We now say that neither of us is skilled in accountancy and we are aware that much of what we have said will not be accepted by the accounting profession generally. On the other hand we believe that we are accustomed to the use of common sense, and common sense has compelled us to reject a number of the accounting practices used in the Group and, apparently, regarded as acceptable by accountants.[7]

The practices to which the Inspectors referred were used in drawing up financial statements which received an unqualified audit report from a major Australian and internationally affiliated accounting firm.

The criticism of "generally accepted accounting principles" has mounted steadily in recent years, and it has not by any means been confined to Australia. An enormous amount of critical material has been published in the United States over the last ten years, and the situation has received unfavourable comment recently in Britain from such quarters as Sir Frank Kearton,[8] and in comments on the latest G.E.C./A.E.I. accounts (where a substantial portion of the discrepancy between estimated and recorded profits was attributed to "differences of judgement" over the choice of which accounting principles to use).[9]

It is not my intention to dwell on this situation in the present article. The profession is moving to correct matters, although a final resolution of the problems will not be possible until a coherent body of accounting theory has been devel-

---

[5] R. J. Chambers, "Financial Information and the Securities Market", *Abacus*, September 1965, p. 16.

[6] *Interim Report of an Investigation under Division 4 of Part VI of the Companies Act 1961 into the affairs of Reid Murray Holdings Ltd. and certain of its Subsidiaries* ... (Government Printer, Melbourne, 1963).

See also, E. Stamp, "The Reid Murray Affair", *Accountancy*, August 1964, pp. 685–690.

[7] *Ibid.*, p. 107.

[8] Sir Frank, Chairman of Courtaulds, stated in June 1968 that he had written to the President of the Institute of Chartered Accountants to complain about the multiplicity of generally accepted accounting principles, and the problems this generates in reconciling pre- and post-acquisition "principles" in take-overs.

[9] In October 1967, during a 'take-over battle' with G.E.C., A.E.I. forecast profits of £10 million (before tax) for 1967. In July 1968 it became known that in fact A.E.I. suffered a loss of £14½ million in 1967. £5 million of the shortfall was attributed to 'matters substantially of fact'. The remaining £9.5 million was attributed to "adjustments which remain matters substantially of judgement" (adjustments which it is believed related mainly to differences in the "principles" used in accounting for contracts).

oped, and this is many years off at present.[10] The point is that in the meantime an auditor is faced with the fact that in any given company it is possible to "accept" many different methods of measuring the value of assets, of determining liabilities, measuring income, and hence of drawing up the financial statements of the enterprise. In choosing between these various methods the auditor is required to exercise his professional judgement. Let us consider for a moment the problems to which this gives rise.

In the situation described, where principles are so ill-defined, and where such a large element of judgement is required in interpreting and applying them, the multiplicity of principles (over-lapping, contradictory, and alternative to each other as many are) must make the role of the auditor appear to some as a sinecure. Yet, it is not a sinecure to a professional man of conscience. An auditor is under a good deal of pressure to find a satisfactory "compromise" when he finds himself in disagreement with a client on matters of "principle". There are usually some other public accountants around who will take over if he resigns, or if he is prepared to acquiesce in being fired, as the City of London Real Property Case[11] demonstrated only too vividly. Under such circumstances, if the auditor can find some way of rationalising his client's wishes, some way of accepting his client's choice of "principle", who will cast the first stone? Indeed, with the present lamentable proliferation of acceptable alternatives open to management, one of the few bed-rock principles, and it is a highly subjective one, is the moral one of doing what is right. This can lead to the absurd situation where an auditor may find himself taking a stand against what might, in other circumstances, be quite acceptable technically, simply because he questions the probity of the client's motives in deciding to do what has been done. Dr. Johnson said that courage may not be the greatest of the virtues, but it is the one without which all the others are useless. Quite so, but it would be a pity if the courage and integrity of an auditor seemed to be the only defence that shareholders had against the possible depredations of management.

There is another aspect of this situation, and it is one which cannot be lightly disregarded. It is well illustrated by the Reid Murray débâcle, where the auditors were very conscious that the group of companies was in a very precarious financial position. The ultimate catastrophe (which eventually occurred) might well have seemed possible if not probable. The auditor's report was a "clean" one, even though (as the Inspectors suggested) the auditors must have had misgivings. Supposing the misgivings had culminated in a qualified report. The collapse would still have occurred and might indeed have been precipitated, and the argument *post hoc, ergo propter hoc* would then undoubtedly have been raised against the auditors. There can be no doubt that such considerations must weigh heavily in the minds of auditors considering qualifying the accounts of companies in a poor financial situation, since it is impossible subsequently to establish that if their judgement has been less harsh the crash would still have taken place.

---

[10] Apart from private research being done in universities, most of the work in this area is being conducted by or under the sponsorship of the American Institute of Certified Public Accountants. See, for example, their *Accounting Research Studies* of which ten have so far been published. Britain is lagging far behind the Americans in accounting research.

[11] For a brief summary of the facts, and the ultimate conclusion see *The Accountant*, June 29th, 1963, pp. 842–847, and July 13th, 1963, p. 39.

Such pressures are increased by the fact that, unlike the lawyer, the auditor weighs the evidence and draws his conclusions behind a veil of secrecy. Even the fact that he has had a difference of opinion with his client is not revealed unless his report is qualified. As a result, the auditing profession does not have a body of case law to which an auditor can refer for guidance on contentious issues arising with clients. On the other hand, although this is hardly a mitigating factor, the auditor has the assurance of knowing that unless there is a major collapse, or an investigation, the quality of his judgement is not likely to be reviewed by third parties.

Under such conditions it would be surprising if a form of "Gresham's Law" did not come into operation, with bad accounting principles driving out the good. Nor is it surprising that there has been pressure from many parts of the financial community in favour of developing and enforcing a set of rigid rules, backed-up by a statutory enforcing agency along the lines of the American Securities and Exchange Commission.

In my view such a cure is likely to be worse than the original disease. It is true that the S.E.C. puts a great deal of authority behind the accountant who insists that S.E.C. requirements must be met. There is no doubt that the independent public accountant needs all the authority that he can get to back up his position. The trouble with an S.E.C.-type solution is that it diminishes flexibility by introducing a set of written rules. If the rules are couched in general terms, they will be too vague to be of any real value. On the other hand the more precise and specific they become the less scope there is for an evolutionary adaptation to changing circumstances, since the process of changing the rules is likely to be a long and difficult process. Yet it seems likely that the demands for a "British S.E.C." will increase unless something is done to improve the present situation. There is, however, an alternative to the S.E.C., and it is one that is suggested by, and can be evaluated in the light of, a further consideration of the role and purpose of the auditor.

The essence of the auditor's role and function is to make an expert examination of a company's financial statements, and the evidence supporting them, and to formulate and express an independent judgement of the fairness of such financial statements. His work consists essentially of the process of collection and expert assessment of evidence, combined with an independent judgement of the fairness of the representations made by management to the outside shareholders on the strength of such evidence. Thus it is clear that, in a very important sense, the auditor is a judge. He reports his judgement to the shareholders, but his judgement is made on statements prepared by management (whose interests may very frequently conflict with those of the shareholders and of third parties who may read and rely upon the financial statements), and the auditor is himself responsible for seeking and collecting the evidence required to support the management's statements. Thus the professional relationship which now exists between the professional accountant and his client is quite different from that which exists between a professional lawyer and his client. This is well brought out in the comments of Lord Denning, made in his dissenting opinion in the *Candler* v. *Crane, Christmas* case:

> There is a great difference between the lawyer and the accountant. The lawyer is never called on to express his personal belief in the truth of his

client's case; whereas the accountant who certifies [sic] the accounts of his client is always called on to express his personal opinion as to whether the accounts exhibit a true and correct view of his client's affairs; and he is required to do this, not so much for the satisfaction of his own client but more for the guidance of shareholders, investors, revenue authorities, and others who may have to rely on the accounts in serious matters of business.[12]

The strength of our system of justice and of the fabric of our society depends very heavily on the confidence which the general public places in the judicial system. As I have outlined earlier, it appears that in like manner the confidence of the general investing public in the securities markets, and thus the strength of the capitalist system, depends in large measure on the degree of confidence and trust that shareholders, etc., place in the *judgement* of professional auditors *qua* judges. One's faith in a judge, however, is based upon certain attributes of his office, which are not at present possessed by the professional auditor. Let us examine some of these attributes in more detail.

In the first place the evidence and arguments upon which the judge forms his opinion are, except in rare cases, heard in open court. The accountant, by contrast, reaches his decisions behind a cloak of secrecy. In the end he produces a report, but this is a formal document which is seldom qualified so as to give any hint that there might have been any differences of opinion between the auditor and his client's directors on matters of accounting principle. In the accounting profession, which regards "full disclosure" as such an important principle, it seems odd that the work of the auditor has to be performed in this cloak and dagger atmosphere.

This brings me to a second point. Not only shareholders and investors remain ignorant of what has been discussed and decided. Even more important, the rest of the profession is denied the advantage of perusing the evidence and the decisions, and weighing them in their own minds in the future when deciding similar problems of their own. Similarly, research committees are excluded from access to invaluable material which would greatly aid them in their attempts to codify a set of "principles" into some kind of integrated and consistent structure (as is done in the law). Principles should not be mere descriptions of current practice, but, nevertheless, a real and intimate knowledge of the facts and problems of current practice is invaluable, if not essential, in the process of arriving at a logical and consistent theory of accountancy.

In short, the present procedure makes it impossible for accountants to accumulate a body of precedents similar to those available (and so invaluable) to lawyers in their work. Moreover, the absence of any record of evidence and decisions makes it impossible for thoughtful and disinterested critics to analyse what has been done, with the objective of pointing out ways in which improvements can be made. In a word it inhibits progress. And, by placing a veil around what has been decided and done it may put a premium on mediocrity and incompetence.

A third important difference between the auditor and the judge lies in the fact that an auditor is employed and paid by his client. This is not so in the case of a judge, who is not paid by those upon whom he sits in judgement. Is it possible that a judge in a court of law would be regarded as impartial in his judgement if he were? A judge serves the public interest and it is ultimately the public

[12] (1951) 1 All E.R. at page 434.

which gives him his financial independence. It is difficult to accept that the general public would believe its interest was best served by having judges paid by appellants, or by defendants, or even by counsel.[13]

Another important point of difference lies in the method of appointment. Judges are appointed by the Crown in this country. Political appointments to the Bench are not unknown, particularly in the United States (where judges are often elected). But in virtually all instances judicial appointments are made in such a way that the public interest is considered. It would be unthinkable today to suggest that a judge should be appointed by a party to the proceedings, or that he should hold office during such party's pleasure. Auditors, on the other hand, are appointed nominally by one party, the shareholders. In fact, in public companies in particular, it is the other party, the management and directors, to whom the auditor looks for his remuneration and his security of tenure. The public interest is not represented in the process at all.

Several of the above comments reflect somewhat unfavourably on the independence of the position of the auditor, particularly in his relationship to the general public. This situation is made worse when one considers that many auditors are heavily involved in providing services other than that of judging the fairness of the financial statements. Many auditors are also involved as tax advisers, management consultants, etc. Such advisory services may cover a very wide range of accounting and business problems, and the quality of the advice given may in many circumstances be revealed, or otherwise, by the form of accounting presentation and disclosure which the client adopts and on which the auditor must pass judgement. Much has been written elsewhere about the impairment of auditors' independence which results. Yet it is naive to expect that such lucrative management advisory services will be lightly abandoned by the auditing profession. An auditor is in a very favourable strategic position to give such advice. Moreover, there is a great deal of value to clients in having their auditors handle such ancillary consulting assignments. There are reciprocal benefits in the conduct of the audit and the consulting work in having one professional firm to do both jobs since knowledge and experience gained in the one spills over into the other. Yet although the economics of the situation encourage the development of such "ancillary services", it is difficult to dispute the fact that their provision by an auditor appears to diminish his independence.

There is another respect in which an auditor is not even required to assume the appearance of independence, at least in British jurisdictions. Thus there is no requirement in the Companies Acts preventing an auditor from holding shares in a client company. Most people might find it difficult to accept that an auditor owning a perhaps substantial investment in the shares of a client company could legitimately be regarded as "independent". Such an unfortunate possibility is compounded by the fact that a reader of an auditor's report has no way of knowing whether or not the auditor owns shares in the company upon which he is reporting since he is not required to say!

From all that has been said above it seems clear that it is difficult to equate the independence of the auditor *qua* judge with the independence of a judge in

---

[13] An apparent exception is the independent arbitrator who is usually paid by the parties in dispute. Such appointments are, however, of a non-recurring nature and there is no question of the arbitrator's 'security of tenure' being jeopardised by his decision.

a court of law. Not only does the auditor frequently lack the appearance of independence, he sometimes lacks its reality. The traditional answer to such a charge is that it is irrelevant since the really crucial factor is the independence of the auditor's "state of mind". Unfortunately it is impossible to make an objective assessment of a state of mind. It can be judged perhaps by the end result of the mental processes, but since this, in the case of an auditor, is his opinion on the client's accounts, such an assessment is a question begging operation at best.

It seems clear that people would pay little respect to a judgement in our courts of law if the judge did not have the appearance as well as the reality of complete independence of those whom he has judged. It seems equally clear that the judgement of financial statements ought properly to be done by a person or persons clearly independent of the company, its directors, managers, and shareholders.

Consideration of these factors suggests that perhaps the most sensible way of dealing with the problem might be to relieve the auditor of the burden of the judicial function. This would entail the transfer of this function to some other party or parties, and I will deal with this point shortly. For the moment let us examine the auditor's residual role.

I suggest that the auditor should be expected to act the role that is now played by a lawyer representing his client. The auditor would advise his client (the management of the company), and he would represent his client before a judge or board which would be truly independent of the client.[14] The auditor, as a professional accountant, would make an examination of the facts, and collect or cause to be collected all the necessary evidence; he would consider and weigh this evidence and form his opinion on the client's financial statements; he would then advise his client as to the proper course to follow in presenting the financial information to the outside world, including the shareholders. The auditor would be employed by the management of the company, *de jure* as well as *de facto*, and he would be responsible for determining, discovering, evaluating, and documenting all debatable or contentious matters in much the same fashion as he does under the present system. He would express his opinions and advice to the client and recommend the course to be followed; but he would also be responsible for ensuring that all relevant material pertaining to the accounts was brought to the attention of the judges, as I shall describe shortly. Whilst he may feel that a certain course should be followed, may recommend it to the client, and the client may adopt it, the auditor would be responsible for seeing that the judge was fully aware of all aspects of all material contentious or debatable points.

Once the auditor and client had decided their positions the auditor would present to the judge or board all necessary details of matters which had to be judged. The auditor, and the client if necessary, would appear before the judge and give verbal evidence; matters would of course be expedited—as they are now in large accounting firms when two or more partners confer on a client's affairs—by the advance preparation of a detailed memorandum by the auditor explaining the pros and cons of all contentious items for the benefit of the judge. In fact submission of such a report by the auditor would be mandatory in all cases, even in cases where no contentious items existed (in which case that fact would be

---

[14] From an operational point of view the "client" can be defined as "management". In the broadest sense this of course includes the directors (although as noted in footnote (2), the practice in the U.S. is to de-emphasise the directors' role).

stated). The onus would be on the auditor to make sufficient examination so as to disclose all such items, and to bring all aspects of them before the judge. It might perhaps be argued that this duty is *too* onerous and that a "devil's advocate" should be employed by the judge to dig up any facts which ought to be considered and which have not been brought to light, or brought forward, by the auditor. I must reject this, not merely on the grounds of delay and expense; in my view a professional auditor can be relied upon—must be relied upon—to act responsibly and with integrity and to disclose all relevant facts. He must also be relied upon to *discover* all relevant facts.

Nor do I believe that the imposition on him of this responsibility would thereby fail to relieve him of the "judge function". The auditor would be responsible for collecting, appraising, and presenting evidence. He would also be expected by his client to judge the evidence and render opinions and advice (to the client). But the *judge* would only require the auditor to present the evidence, facts, and opinions; as far as the final judgement is concerned, that would be the responsibility of the judge alone. While the legal analogy is obvious, it perhaps becomes more so if one makes the comparison with French legal procedure rather than with that customarily used in Anglo-Saxon courts.

Judges, and there would clearly need to be several to deal with the work involved, although they would not necessarily sit together in deciding all issues, would be appointed from the ranks of the most able and experienced members of the profession. The appointment would be for a long term and would be full time and it would be expected to be regarded as the crowning achievement of a man's career in public accounting. The appointment would be made by the profession, not by the government, and judges' salaries would be paid by the profession out of a fund raised by a levy on all firms audited.[15] The levy would require to be enforced by statute and the basis of the charge would need careful consideration.

The judge would be empowered to review files, examine witnesses and cross-question the auditors and their clients. Judgements would be published in exactly the same way in which legal judgements are now published. Proceedings would normally be public but judges might hold them *in camera* if they saw fit. Precedents would be established in exactly the same way as is now done in legal practice.

Auditors would represent their client's interests, subject to the proviso that they would have a professional responsibility for ensuring that all material evidence was brought before the judge. All contentious matters would be decided by the judge, and if a collapse ensued as a result of disclosures made, no odium would attach to the auditor.

Now I cannot of course attempt to anticipate all of the possible objections which might be raised against my proposal, but one of the potentially most serious is the possibility that implementation of what I have suggested would lead to delays in the submission of accounts to shareholders. Shareholders deserve our sympathy in this matter, and not all of them are especially well served at the present time. The longer the time interval between a company's year end and the

---

[15] Alternatively, the fund could be raised by an annual levy imposed and collected by the State. There seems to be no reason why this should introduce a political flavour into the scheme. Indeed, the Judges could be appointed by the Crown on the advice of the profession.

date a shareholder receives a copy of the Annual Report the more out of date is the Report and the less its value to the shareholder. The auditor is a potential bottleneck since the Annual Report obviously cannot be made available until after the auditor has signed his statement of opinion. Thus the interval between the year end and the date of the auditor's report represents the minimum length of time the shareholder must wait (and they wait several weeks or even months longer in most cases). It is instructive to examine the interval in the case of some major companies. Some illustrations, from different countries, are as follows:

Name of company, and year end	Interval, in days between year end and date of auditor's report
Cable Price Downer (New Zealand), 31st March, 1968	116
Australian Consolidated Industries, 31st March, 1968	87
Colonial Sugar Refining (Australia), 31st March, 1968	82
Distillers Corporation (U.K.), 31st March, 1968	109
Unilever, 31st December, 1967	82
English Electric, 30 December, 1967	60

Yet there are other examples which serve to illustrate how much of a "cushion" there is in present practice. Thus I.B.M., an international corporation with assets in excess of $5.5 billion, has its auditors report signed 23 days after its year end. Marks and Spencers' latest report took only 17 days (and in the previous year, 1967, it took only 14 days). This points up how much slack there is which, if taken up by intelligent use of modern accounting and auditing methods, would provide more time—if this is needed—for implementation of my proposals.

I am not, however, by any means convinced that what I propose need necessarily involve any further delays in the publication of results. Anyone with experience of the administration of an audit practice knows that a great deal of time is generally and necessarily spent by the senior staff, the managers, and the partners of a firm in discussing tricky and contentious issues and attempting to resolve them. Many of these discussions take place with members of the client's staff. In a well-run practice discussion also takes place between partners seeking second, and maybe even third or fourth opinions on the really difficult matters. In the better auditing firms partners' judgements are collective, not individual, and much time is spent in arriving at these judgements, because, as I have indicated, it is one of the most onerous responsibilities of an auditor to sit in judgement on his client's statements. If the final judgement had to be made by a third party, I can see no reason why the time involved need be any greater. The auditing firm's partners would present the judge with a memorandum which they would later discuss with him. This would be a discussion between experts and there would be few wasted words. The only really difficult problem might be the scheduling of the judges' time so as to avoid bottle-necks. This is a relatively simple problem in logistics and need not be regarded as critical.

If necessary, provision in the governing rules of procedure could be made to permit auditors to issue opinions off their own bat subject to later review by the judge. This would take care of urgent problems where the issues of principle were cut-and-dried and where clear precedents existed. Severe penalties would of course be imposed on anyone who took improper advantage of this procedure. Judges would be armed with powers, similar to those vested in the S.E.C. in the United States, to deal with offenders.

Indeed, one can even contemplate an alternative form of procedure which would certainly avoid delay in all but the most exceptional cases. The profession might establish a judicial procedure similar to that outlined above, arming the judges with the powers I have described, but with the proviso that judges would not exercise these powers unless approached voluntarily by a public accountant and asked to act.[16] The onus would then always be on the auditor, in cases where he did not so approach a judge and where difficulties later appeared, to justify his failure to avail himself of the judicial machinery. Such a scheme would preserve the advantages of the judicial approach while at the same time providing a short-circuit in cases where it was self-evident that it was unnecessary.

Another possible objection is that my proposal will destroy the auditor's independence. But, as I have already pointed out, his independence is eroded beyond repair already in many cases. Nor is it clear that it is necessary for him to be independent unless he is required to deliver an independent judgement. If the judging function is passed on to a judge, the auditor no longer needs independence. He will of course require competence in his work, and honesty and integrity in his presentation of his client's case and position to the judge—but he needs these qualities now, as does the practising lawyer. It is surely not impossible to conceive of a non-independent auditor retaining his professional honesty and integrity. It might indeed be less difficult for some of the weaker brethren to demonstrate these qualities if my proposals were to be adopted.

Let us now look at the other side of the question, and examine some of the advantages which might be expected to flow from the adoption of the proposals.

In the first place it would liberate the auditor from his present dichotomous role of professional adviser and judge. It will in no way diminish the importance of judgement, however; the auditor will still have to exercise all the qualities of professional judgement that he does now, in the examination and assessment of evidence and in the formulation of an expert opinion, and he will be called upon to argue the case for his and his client's opinions and judgements before the judge. He will also have the heavy responsibility, moral as well as intellectual, of ensuring that all the relevant points, pro and con his own opinion, are brought to the attention of the judge.[17] But he will no longer be placed in the invidious and in many ways ridiculous position of having to judge, publicly, his fee-paying client.

This will, I believe, increase his stature, and that of the profession, in the community, and will silence many of the critics, particularly those who come forward when a crash takes place and when there is an opportunity of shifting some of the blame on to the heads of the auditors.

Secondly, I believe that my system would provide a very effective focus to which ideas and proposals for the reform and development of accounting prin-

---

[16] This is reminiscent of the proposals made by Leonard Spacek, senior partner of the major U.S. firm of Arthur Andersen & Co., in his article "The Need for an Accounting Court", *The Accounting Review*, July 1958, pp. 368–379.

[17] Such a moral obligation is not unknown in legal practice.

ciples could be directed. There are already bodies and groups which are responsible, within the present organisation of the professional accounting bodies, for work in this area—research committees and foundations, etc., to say nothing of the work being done in universities by academics, and their importance would not diminish. But the work of the judges would not merely help in defining and codifying and giving authority to accounting principles, it would implement them. The judges would not be merely advisors, they would execute decisions. Moreover, they would have the responsibility of ensuring that their decisions on accounting principles were not just good decisions in themselves; they would be required to see that they were *consistent* with those being made in other companies and in other parts of the country. Any particular auditing firm may be able to do this now, to some extent and with some of its clients, but there is little co-ordination and consistency between auditing firms on many matters—the fracas in the U.S. recently over the investment credit demonstrated this to those who had not realised it long ago.[18]

There may be some tendency on the part of the judges—and it will have to be controlled—towards conservation and even ossification. It is a tendency to which many older men are prone. But judges' decisions will be open to criticism, and critics will at least have a central and conspicuous target to fire at rather than the present moving and largely invisible one.

In this way I believe there is reason to hope that my proposal would lead to a rapid increase in the rate at which progress is made in the solution of the dilemmas of principle which now face us.

Thirdly, because the judge's decision would be published, as legal decisions are now, along with all the evidence (except obviously confidential material) relevant to the decisions, the veils of secrecy which now conceal so much of the sacred cows and rules of thumb of so-called accounting theory, *as it is applied in practice,* would be stripped away. Moreover, the publication of the judgements would promote the making of sound and consistent decisions by auditors and management before bringing them before judges, since the managers and auditors would have the precedents available. Most important of all, publication of the judgements would make it possible for academics and other thoughtful people to extend the range of their criticism of accounting theory and practice. In fact the scope for analysis and criticism would be increased by an enormous factor. This would have results whose benefits are incalculably great. All of the intellectual resources and analytical abilities of the academic world could be brought to bear on the analysis and criticism of the developing body of decisions and precedents. At the moment all that is available to the academic—in the absence of failure and the consequent Inspector's Report (and even these are seldom produced outside Australia)—are company Annual Reports which, it is no exaggeration to say, conceal more than they disclose in most cases. Even the best Annual Reports tell nothing of the pros and cons that were considered in producing the final product, and many give little clue at all to the accounting "principles", conventions and rules, actually used in preparing the financial statements, let alone any discussion of the reasons for rejecting alternative courses of action. I am quite sure that an important reason for the slow and uncertain development of accounting theory,

---

[18] For a brief summary of the issues involved see opinion No. 4 of the Accounting Principles Board (New York, A.I.C.P.A., 1964).

compared for example with Medicine and Law, is the fact that whereas there is ample documentation of the facts and the problems of Law and Medicine the practice of accountancy is, by contrast, very poorly documented, and accountants have developed a tradition of secrecy. Under such circumstances it is hardly surprising that the sacred cows and the rules of thumb are reigning supreme throughout much of present day practice.

The implementation of these proposals should be left to the profession. But I do not rule out the possibility that it might be necessary for the Government to act instead, if the profession were unwilling to do so. This could well lead to the establishment of the equivalent of a Securities and Exchange Commission, armed, however, with more extensive powers than are now exercised by that body. Either way, one could expect a rapid increase in the quality of accounting information presented to shareholders and there is no doubt that such a development is in the public interest. The very high degree of public interest in the quality of the performance of the audit function was emphasised right at the beginning of this article.

If one is realistic, however, one must accept that neither the solution which I have outlined above nor the introduction of an S.E.C. is likely to be acceptable to the accounting profession. Let me close by outlining briefly a third possible solution to the problems.

All companies would be required to publish a complete and detailed description of the accounting principles they use in preparing their accounts. Whenever any of these principles or procedures were changed the Company would be required to publish full details of the changes made and the reasons for making them. Either the accounting profession or a specially constituted government agency would maintain a complete record of all of the principles and procedures currently in use, the justification for their use, and the reasons for changes which have been made. This record would become the equivalent of the case law and statute law available to lawyers, and it could be readily maintained and kept up to date on a computer.

Instead of judges, the profession would establish an advisory board whose function would be to advise, and if necessary give rulings to auditors on any problems relating to accounting principles which might arise in an auditor's practice and which he thought fit to bring to the board. The onus in all cases would be upon the auditor to decide whether it was necessary for him to approach the board with a problem, or, having approached the board, whether he should accept its ruling.

In this way the accounting principles being used by companies would be brought to light and fully disclosed, and there would be the maximum opportunity for the evolution of accounting principles. On the other hand, the increase in the disclosure of what is actually going on behind the scenes in the preparation of company accounts would increase the likelihood of actions being brought against a company, its directors, or its auditors by members of the general public, including shareholders, former shareholders, creditors, etc. However, an auditor faced with such an action need have little to fear provided he had availed himself of the advisory services of the board. Thus, although auditors would be exposed to greater risk of action, they would be better protected in dealing with an action, provided they could clearly demonstrate that their judgement had had the prior endorsement of the profession.

This solution will not do much to remedy the visible factors which appear to diminish the auditor's independence. But it would do a great deal to speed up the development of accounting principles, and by giving the auditor authoritative support in his interpretation of these principles in contentious areas it should greatly strengthen his independence of mind and outlook. In a sense this solution is a compromise; but a workable compromise is well worth having if it will result in much fuller disclosure of the present state of "generally accepted accounting principles" and hence in a much more rapid improvement in the quality of such "principles".

RELATED READINGS

The 1960s and 1970s have been decades for questioning accounting doctrines. Such traditional notions as conservatism, going concern, and consistency have been subjected to intensive, critical examination. The cry for some kind of current value has become more general and unrelenting. As more scholars have agreed that traditional historical cost must be supplanted by current value, they have disagreed on the *kind* of current value which is most apt. The following articles reflect these trends. Readers should also consult the Related Readings at the close of Parts 2 and 3.

John J. Anderson, "Accounting for Equity Securities Held by Fire and Casualty Insurance Companies," *The New York Certified Public Accountant*, November, 1971, pp. 813–819. Discusses the impact on the industry most vitally affected of a possible requirement that unrealized holding gains be recognized in income.

Anon., "Growth, Historic Cost and Profit," *The Accountant*, October 19, 1968, pp. 518–521.

Norton M. Bedford and Toshio Iino, "Consistency Reexamined," *The Accounting Review*, July, 1968, pp. 453–458.

────── and James C. McKeown, "Comparative Analysis of Net Realizable Value and Replacement Costing," *The Accounting Review*, April, 1972, pp. 333–338.

Leopold A. Bernstein, "General Price Level Financial Statements—A Review of APB Statement No. 3," *The New York Certified Public Accountant*, January, 1970, pp. 39–42.

Harold Bierman, Jr., "Discounted Cash Flows, Price Level Adjustments and Expectations," *The Accounting Review*, October, 1971, pp. 693–699.

C. E. Caldwell, "Application of Current Value Accounting—The Philips Model," *The Australian Accountant*, October, 1968, pp. 555–561.

R. J. Chambers, "Methods of Accounting," *The Accountant:* "Elements of Price Variation Accounting," February 26, 1970, pp. 299–303; "Historical Cost Accounting and Its Variants," March 5, 1970, pp. 341–345; "Price-level Adjusted Accounting," Mar. 19, 1970, pp. 408–412; "Replacement Price Accounting," Apr. 2, 1970, pp. 483–486; "Present Value Accounting," Apr. 16, 1970, pp. 551–555; "Continuously Contemporary Accounting," Apr. 30, 1970, pp. 643–647.

──────, "Second Thoughts on Continuously Contemporary Accounting," *Abacus*, September, 1970, pp. 39–55. For a dialogue on the meaning of "value to the owner," see the ensuing articles by F. K. Wright and Chambers, *Abacus*, June, 1971, pp. 58–72.

Tom K. Cowan, "Progress through Dilemma: A Compromise Solution to the Problem of Accounting for Changing Prices and Values," *Accounting and Business Research*, Winter, 1971, pp. 38–45.

Ralph W. Estes, "An Assessment of the Usefulness of Current Cost and Price-level Information by Financial Statement Users," *Journal of Accounting Research*, Autumn, 1968, pp. 200–207, and Vincent C. Brenner, "Financial Statement Users' Views of the Desirability of Reporting Current Cost Information," *Journal of Accounting Research*, Autumn, 1970, pp. 159–166.

Two questionnaire surveys which conclude that traditional historical-cost information should be supplemented, but not replaced, by price-level or current-cost measures.

James M. Fremgen, "The Going Concern Assumption: A Critical Appraisal," *The Accounting Review*, October, 1968, pp. 649–656.

Reg. S. Gynther, "Accounting for Price Changes—Theory and Practice," *Society Bulletin No. 5* (Australian Society of Accountants), October, 1968, 26 pp.

———, "Capital Maintenance, Price Changes, and Profit Determination," *The Accounting Review*, October, 1970, pp. 712–730.

Nils H. Hakansson, "On the Relevance of Price-level Accounting," *Journal of Accounting Research*, Spring, 1969, pp. 22–31.

William H. Hannum and W. Wasserman, "General Adjustments and Price Level Measurement," *The Accounting Review*, April, 1968, pp. 295–302.

Loyd C. Heath, "Distinguishing between Monetary and Nonmonetary Assets and Liabilities in General Price-level Accounting," *The Accounting Review*, July, 1972, pp. 458–468.

Orace Johnson, "Toward an 'Events' Theory of Accounting," *The Accounting Review*, October, 1970, pp. 641–653. An extension of Sorter's thesis.

Herbert C. Knortz, "Economic Realism as a Reporting Essential," *Financial Executive*, March, 1969, pp. 21–30; reprinted in *The New York Certified Public Accountant*, December, 1969, pp. 929–937. "Economic Realism" is defined as "current economic value."

James C. McKeown, "An Empirical Test of a Model Proposed by Chambers," *The Accounting Review*, January, 1971, pp. 12–29.

R. L. Mathews, "Income, Price Changes and the Valuation Controversy in Accounting," *The Accounting Review*, July, 1968, pp. 509–516.

Richard Mattessich, "On the Perennial Misunderstanding of Asset Measurement by Means of 'Present Values,'" *Cost and Management*, March–April, 1970. See the ensuing dialogue between R. J. Chambers and Mattessich on valuation and measurement: March–April, 1971, pp. 30–42, and July–August, 1971, pp. 12–23.

Abram Mey, *On the Application of Business Economics and Replacement Value Accounting in the Netherlands* (Seattle: International Accounting Studies Institute, University of Washington, 1970), 31 pp. See also George M. Scott, "A Business Economics Foundation for Accounting: The Dutch Experience," *Accounting and Business Research*, Autumn, 1971, pp. 309–316.

Maurice Moonitz, "Price-level Accounting and Scales of Measurement," *The Accounting Review*, July, 1970, pp. 465–475.

R. H. Parker and G. C. Harcourt (eds.), *Readings in the Concept and Measurement of Income* (London: Cambridge University Press, 1969), 402 pp. Twenty-four reprinted essays and an introductory paper by the editors on various concepts of income, value, and capital.

Morris R. Perlow, "Accounting Recognition of Holding Gains and Losses on Marketable Securities," *The New York Certified Public Accountant*, February, 1969, pp. 95–100.

G. Edward Philips, "An Entity-Value for Assets and Equities," *Abacus*, December, 1968, pp. 142–152.

Boris Popoff, "The Price Level Adjustment and Accounting Realism: A Case Study of a New Zealand Company," *The International Journal of Accounting*, Spring, 1971, pp. 15–35.

Lawrence Revsine, "On the Correspondence between Replacement Cost Income and Economic Income," *The Accounting Review*, July, 1970, pp. 513–523.

Paul Rosenfield, "Reporting Subjunctive Gains and Losses," *The Accounting Review*, October, 1969, pp. 788–797. A critical analysis of the place of replacement prices in financial accounting.

Howard Ross, *Financial Statements: A Crusade for Current Values* [Sir Isaac Pitman (Canada) Ltd., 1969], 177 pp.

———, "Is It Better to Be Precisely Wrong than Vaguely Correct?," *Financial Executive*, June, 1971, pp. 8–12. Argument for the use of current values in the balance sheet

Keith Shwayder, "Expected and Unexpected Price Level Changes," *The Accounting Review*, April, 1971, pp. 306–319. Criticism of an aspect of APB Statement No. 3.

Robert R. Sterling, "The Going Concern: An Examination," *The Accounting Review*, July, 1968, pp. 481–502. A critical analysis of the meaning and use of "going concern" in accounting.

*———, *Theory of the Measurement of Enterprise Income* (Lawrence: The University Press of Kansas, 1970), 384 pp.

——— (ed.), *Asset Valuation and Income Determination: A Consideration of the Alternatives* (Lawrence, Kans.: Scholars Books Co., 1971), 152 pp. Papers by Ijiri, Bell, Staubus, Chambers, Solomons, Vatter, Bedford, and others.

Edward L. Summers and James Wesley Deskins, "A Classification Scheme of Methods for Reporting Effects of Resource Price Changes" (with Technical Appendix), *The International Journal of Accounting*, Fall, 1970, pp. 101–120.

Charles A. Tritschler, "Statistical Criteria for Asset Valuation by Specific Price Index," *The Accounting Review*, January, 1969, pp. 99–123.

A. van Seventer, "The Continuity Postulate in the Dutch Theory of Business Income," *The International Journal of Accounting*, Spring, 1969, pp. 1–19.

J. Vos, "Replacement Value Accounting," *Abacus*, December, 1970, pp. 132–143. A view from the Deputy Manager of Accounting, of N. V. Philips' Gloeilampenfabrieken.

S. C. Yu, "A Reexamination of the Going Concern Postulate," *The International Journal of Accounting*, Spring, 1971, pp. 37–58.